Fragmented Societies

*A Sociology of Economic Life beyond the
Market Paradigm*

ENZO MINGIONE

Translated by Paul Goodrick

Basil Blackwell

Copyright © Enzo Mingione 1991

First published 1991

Basil Blackwell Ltd
108 Cowley Road, Oxford, OX4 1JF, UK

Basil Blackwell, Inc.
3 Cambridge Center
Cambridge, Massachusetts 02142, USA

British Library Cataloguing in Publication Data

A CIP catalogue record for this book is available from the British Library.

Library of Congress Cataloging in Publication Data

Mingione, Enzo.
    Fragmented societies: a sociology of economic life beyond the market
paradigm/Enzo Mingione.
        p.   cm.
    Includes bibliographical references (p.) and index.
    ISBN 0–631–16399–9 (hardback)
    1. Economics—Sociological aspects. 2. Economic history—20th century.
3. Social history—20th century. I. Title.
HM35.M54   1991   90–653
306.3—dc20   CIP

Typeset in 10 on 12 pt Baskerville
by Photo·graphics, Honiton, Devon
Printed in Great Britain by T.J. Press Ltd, Padstow, Cornwall

Fragmented Societies

Fragmented Societies is the first volume in a new series, *Studies in Urban and Social Change*, published by Blackwell in association with the *International Journal of Urban and Regional Research*.

Contents

Figures

Tables

Foreword

There is undoubted force in the criticism that the concepts and theories of social science work better in understanding the past than in helping us to come to terms with contemporary events. Thus, issues such as the way the globalization of economic life meshes uneasily with the politics of the nation-state are described more often than theorized. The political upheavals and economic restructuring of Eastern and Central Europe seem to have caught the specialists in these areas by surprise. Words such as welfare, planning, party, state and bureaucracy have all acquired negative connotations, whereas market, enterprise, movement, citizenship and freedom are seen to be unproblematically good. Things fall apart: our benchmarks are all in the past. Adjectives like industrial, modern or Fordist are increasingly used to describe a world left behind.

With great courage, sound scholarship and an enviable breadth of experience and understanding Enzo Mingione has attempted to make sense of the confusing kaleidoscope of *Fragmented Societies*. Basing his analysis on the classical works of Marx, Durkheim and Weber, Mingione provides his own theoretical perspective, bringing together micro-analyses of household work strategies with macro-analyses of world systems. Few scholars have dared to undertake such a task. More often we are presented with over-general banalities or over-detailed 'case-studies'. I applaud Mingione for taking risks and for attempting an exceptionally ambitious task. In leading us away from the increasingly barren conventional wisdom of the past decades Mingione has made a substantial contribution to the renewal of social science in the 1990s. Firmly asserting the centrality of sociological analysis, Mingione nevertheless engages with the sister disciplines of economics and politics. His sustained critique of over-simple notions of the social functions of markets should stimulate many generations of students. This serious, thoughtful and refreshingly cosmopolitan book should make an impact well beyond the academic community. It has significance for serious students of society throughout the world.

R. E. Pahl
University of Kent at Canterbury

Preface

This book is the result of research which began at the end of the 1970s
and lasted for ten years. At that time I had just concluded an investigation
into the life strategies of the rural population in the province of Messina.
From this investigation emerged the predominant importance of extra-
agricultural resources, in particular state pension payments and remittances from emigrated relatives, compared both to the declining role of
self-provisioning in agriculture and the persistent weakness of agricultural
strategies aimed at the market and rationalization of production
(Mingione, 1981). The results of this research suggested how it might
be possible through qualitative investigation to debunk two opposite
stereotypes: that of southern peasants fossilized within subsistence strategies based on a large amount of traditional self-provisioning; and that
of the inevitable rapid spread, also in the South, of modern forms of family
farming oriented towards commercial and professional specialization and
increasingly complemented by outside activities that are compatible and
often cohesive with the modernization of agriculture. Starting from my
previous research into the urban question and the labour market, and
encouraged by the growing international interest in informal activities –
at the time it was becoming a real vogue in advanced capitalist countries
– I launched head first into an investigation of survival strategies among
the poorer urban strata in Messina and other nearby towns. The need
to interpret the phenomena identified during the course of this investigation and to give them a comparative, historical and geographical
meaning led me almost immediately to move into a much more controversial area than merely verifying that these strata, characterized by
persistently low monetary income from work and often by precarious and
irregular conditions of work, engaged in complex subsistence strategies
in which informal activities, self-provisioning and forms of exhausting
domestic labour by females were essential elements. Even the empirical
confirmation that these strategies vary markedly between different social

groups or areas in the city, are subject to considerable change through time and therefore cannot be explained away by the opposition between 'traditional' and 'modern', poses serious problems of interpretation to anyone who desires to go further than simply describing the phenomenon. In this sense, a short piece of local research has provided the opportunity for a long comparative look at the problems involved in contemporary transformations in life strategies and forms of work in different social contexts.

The idea of writing *Fragmented Societies* matured during the course of 1987, after I had written a paper on the comparative interpretation of informal activities for the Annual Meeting of the American Sociological Association, to which I had been invited as a foreign guest speaker. This paper was so full of ideas and so like the plan for a book that many friends who had already read several of my articles on the subject suggested that I should undertake the venture. The immediate and positive response of the publisher, Basil Blackwell, to my proposed project was the decisive factor. Although I realized the difficulties involved, the need to rewrite many of the pieces I intended to include in the book, and, further, the necessity of writing entirely new sections, I could not have imagined that it would grow to such proportions, take up so much time and compel me to modify, even radically, so many of my original working hypotheses.

The articles and papers, written between 1983 and 1989, that have been partly incorporated into this work are listed at the end of the Preface. Some of them are only stages in an intellectual development that has taken me far from the views I previously held; others, above all the more recent, have been for the most part reproduced here, though the need to insert them within the overall explanatory logic of the work has imposed important changes. The construction of the book is clearly based on my personal development and selection of ideas. In the process it is likely that some interesting notions have not been developed, while others existing from the outset have been kept and have strongly influenced the final result.

Chapter 1 is entirely dedicated to the theoretical framework. In particular, it deals with the question of the 'market paradigm', which, though being central to the study of informal activities, did not emerge sufficiently in shorter works or those focusing on strictly analytical or comparative problems. In my opinion, a rigorous and convincing criticism of the market paradigm forms the key element in giving a meaning to the growing heterogeneity of work and the complexity of the mixes of social inputs found in the life strategies of different social strata in various contemporary social settings. So long as the market paradigm, in its

several versions, remains implicitly or explicitly dominant, it is impossible
to understand fully the complex organizational systems of contemporary
societies in which competitive individualism exists but is subject to the
highly diversified control of different sociality mixes, and in which the
associative references to interest groups and to bureaucratic institutional
apparatuses are intertwined with the play of diverse kinds of reciprocity
networks.

Chapter 2 is dedicated to the question of work, the significance of its
heterogeneity and the systems for regulating it. In chapter 3, I tackle
the tricky problem of theorizing and analysing modes of social reproduction. This had already seemed highly important to me in previous
works (1985; 1987b), partly incorporated here, but in the present work
I have gone into it more thoroughly in an attempt to overturn the
classical approaches which assume that activities directed at producing
monetary income are the sole central factor in structuring and explaining
the social order in different types of industrial societies. I have moved
towards an approach that starts from the realistic observation that monetary incomes, however important, are persistently inadequate for
explaining life strategies and living standards. Hence the hypothesis that
contemporary social systems cannot be fully understood by starting from
an analysis of occupational structure and its changes, and that an attempt
to overturn the procedures for attributing meaning is equally indispensable for explaining the heterogeneity of forms of work, not to mention
the significance of unpaid domestic labour, kinship, friendship and community solidarity and many other phenomena. This operation, however,
bristles with difficulties, if only because it cannot count on a solid
tradition of previous theoretical and analytical work.

In chapter 4, the meanings of recent trends and changes both in
advanced capitalist countries in the post-Fordist age and in other contemporary societies are discussed. In the first case, I consider it important
to deal with the problems that spring from the rise in rates of unemployment, the restructuring of welfare systems, the ways in which tertiarization is occurring and the social significance behind contemporary societies' inability to find just and acceptable solutions for increasing strata
among the labour supply. In the second, the socio-economic origins of
the profound changes in countries under state socialism are discussed,
at least in a preliminary form, as well as the pattern being assumed by
social life in underdeveloped countries in the age of hyperinflation, urban
gigantism, accentuated forms of social polarization and the spread of the
informal sector – the only means to survive for vast masses of people.

In chapter 5, I have constructed five general models based on the
diverse historical interactions of the three main fields of social structuring

of economic life: market competition, as in itself a force destructive of systems of social organization; organizational systems of the associative kind, based on common interests and on increasingly institutionalized conflicts over the redistribution of industrial resources; and adapted or new reciprocal networks, based on the priority of long-term group interests over the immediate interests of single individuals. Recent paths involving intensified transformation of the five models have highlighted a whole series of problems and are helping to give different meanings to the spread of informal activities in various social settings; none the less, they also point to a common outcome in the spread of a social fragmentation that is not expressed in the classical forms of conflict and integration but represents a new challenge to the contemporary social order.

Chapter 6 is entirely devoted to the case of Italy and includes both a large part of my report on irregular work in Italy to the European Community (1988b) and the results of research into the survival strategies of low-income groups in southern cities (1985). Despite the fact that the inclusion of this chapter entailed greatly extending the length of the book, I felt it necessary to provide an analytical context in order to verify the validity and significance of my theoretical assumptions.

Lastly, chapter 7 is an extended version of three papers I presented at international conferences in 1988 and 1989. In this chapter I put forward a socio-political interpretation of the consequences of social fragmentation, starting from considerations of the transformation of systems of social stratification and of the impact that these same transformations may have on systems of political representation and the running of contemporary societies. These are more than anything else initial observations that need to be developed further as the syndromes of fragmented societies unfold, and as the ability of social scientists to study and understand them improves.

Enzo Mingione

Articles and papers by Enzo Mingione on topics developed in Fragmented Societies

1983a, *Urbanizzazione, classi sociali e lavoro informale*, Milan, Angeli, ch. 4, pp. 197–275.
1983b, 'Informalization, restructuring and the survival strategies of the working class', *International Journal of Urban and Regional Research*, 7, no. 3, pp. 311–39.

1984a, 'La "scoperta" dell'informale e i suoi problemi', *Politica ed Economia*, 9, pp. 9–10.

1984b, 'The informal sector and the development of Third World cities: preliminary answers to some basic questions', in *Regional Development Dialogue*, UN Centre for Regional Development, Tokyo, 5, no. 2, pp. 63–74.

1985, 'Social reproduction of the surplus labour force: the case of Southern Italy', in N. Redclift and E. Mingione (eds), *Beyond Employment*, Oxford and New York, Basil Blackwell, pp. 14–54.

1986a, 'Ciclo dei servizi e complessità sociale', *Economia e Lavoro*, 20, no. 1, pp. 111–22.

1986b, 'L'approccio sociologico e le economie urbane di sussistenza', *Argomenti*, no. 19, pp. 46–64.

1986c, 'Settore informale e strategie di sopravvivenza. Ipotesi per lo sviluppo di un campo di indagine', in F. Bimbi and V. Capecchi (eds), *Strutture e strategie della vita quotidiana*, Milano, Angeli, pp. 289–302.

1986d, 'Attività informali e stili di vita dei ceti urbani a basso reddito nel Mezzogiorno', in *Sud, Sud*, nos. 10–11, Reggio Calabria, Centro Regionale d'Intervento per la Cooperazione, pp. 2–20.

1986e, (ed.), *Inchiesta, Economia informale, strategie familiari e Mezzogiorno*, 16, no. 74, Bari, Dedalo, 1986; 'Introduzione', ibid. pp. 1–3; 'Il caso del Mezzogiorno in una prospettiva di interpretazione comparativa', ibid. pp. 97–103.

1987a, 'Lavoro informale e stili di vita nel Mezzogiorno', *Politica ed Economia*, no. 5, pp. 67–72.

1987b, 'Urban survival strategies, family structure and informal practices', in M. Smith and J. R. Feagin (eds), *The Capitalist City: Global Restructuring and Community Politics*, Oxford, Basil Blackwell, pp. 297–322.

1987c, 'Economic development, social factors and social context', paper for the ASA Annual Convention, Chicago, 17–21 August.

1988a, Underground Economy and Irregular Forms of Employment (*travail au noir*): chapters 1 (The History and Recent Sources of Irregular Forms of Employment) and 2 (Old and New Areas of 'Travail au Noir') of the Final Synthesis Report, European Community, Division V, 'Politique de l'emploi et du marché du travail'.

1988b, Underground Economy and Irregular Forms of Employment (*travail au noir*): The Case of Italy, Final Report, European Community, Division V, 'Politique de l'emploi et du marché du travail'.

1988c, Underground Economy and Irregular Forms of Employment (*travail au noir*): The Case of Greece, Final Report, European Community, Division V, 'Politique de l'emploi et du marché du travail'.

1988d, 'Work and informal activities in urban Southern Italy', in R. Pahl (ed.), *On Work: Historical, Comparative and Theoretical Approaches*, Oxford and New York, Basil Blackwell, pp. 548–78.

1988e, 'Social factors and social stratification in industrialized cities: the new forms of polarization and social marginalization', paper presented at the International Conference on Trends and Challenges of Urban Restructuring, Rio de Janeiro, 26–30 September.

1989a, 'Social polarization and fragmentation in different industrial urban contexts', paper presented at the International Conference on Urban Sociology and Urban Life, Barcelona, 3–5 May.

1989b, 'Social classes and power in contemporary fragmented societies', paper presented at the International Conference on Self-government and Social Protection in the Urban Settlement and at the Enterprise, Moscow, 26–30 September.

Acknowledgements

During the long period that has ended with the writing of *Fragmented Societies*, I have accumulated debts to many people who have helped and advised me, as well as to institutions that have supported my work. I would like to mention here at least the most important and most recent.

The *Facoltà di Scienze Politiche* at Messina University made a decisive contribution to my work by providing me with a very fertile environment for intellectual discussion with students and colleagues. Furthermore, I was frequently allowed time off to participate in international conferences and granted a two-year sabbatical that was invaluable in giving me the opportunity to travel abroad, to visit up-to-date libraries to consult texts in English and French, and to write articles and, finally, this present work. The Fondazione Bignaschi put a well-equipped office at my disposal. The International Sociological Association's Research Committee on Regional and Urban Development has been a resource of enormous value as a setting for a very keen exchange of ideas taking place in a long series of conferences in which I have been able to discuss and verify my ideas as they gradually developed. If the global outlook of this book is a virtue, then it should be put down to the solid network of intellectual debate that grew up around the Committee. In the last few years, I have been invited to the Universities of California at Santa Cruz and at Los Angeles, the Fernand Braudel Center at the SUNY (State University of New York) at Binghamton and the University of New England at Armidale, all of which have afforded me further opportunities for discussion and the use of efficient libraries.

If the quality of the English is an improvement on previous works, then this is due to the laborious work of translating and editing carried out by Paul Goodrick, who never wavered in the two years of practically weekly meetings required to finish the book. The secretary of the Fondazione Bignaschi, Nicoletta Carmi, devoted two years of hard toil to putting the numerous versions of the manuscript into the computer and correcting, printing and photocopying them while, at the same time, managing to carry out many other tasks. Domenico Guglielmo has been very generous in helping me whenever I was in difficulty with the electronically produced tables in chapter 6 and with the computerization of the bibliography.

Several friends read the preliminary drafts of many of the chapters, considerably longer than the final versions, and were forthcoming with valuable suggestions and advice. Among many others, I would like to thank especially Raymond Pahl, Michael Harloe, Edmond Preteceille, Mauro Magatti, Adele Pesce, Alessandro Bonanno, Enrico Pugliese, Giovanni Arrighi, Ivan Szelenyi, Antonio Tosi, Nico Leotta and, in particular, Mark Beittel, who enabled me to correct many errors thanks to his very careful and critical reading. It goes without saying that the limitations of the ideas expressed in this work are all my own responsibility, and in some cases they are due to my obstinacy in the face of the generous advice offered by friends. In conclusion, I should like to express my gratitude to two scholars who have recently died and who played a very important role in my intellectual development. Vincenzo Tomeo introduced me to the discipline of sociology when, as a law student, I was desperately seeking a way to avoid embarking on a legal career. I hope I have learned from this excellent teacher the importance of tireless dedication to study and students. Frequent meetings and long discussions with Ruth Glass paved the way for an intellectual approach that is always sharply honed, lucid and intent on identifying the weak and the oppressed in society and on giving priority to thinking about their interests, without being distracted by the allure of ambition and power. It is impossible for me to match Ruth's intelligence and dedication, but I hope I have used to the best of my ability the privilege of having been one of her most devoted friends in the last years of her life.

Introduction

The radical changes taking place in Eastern Europe are putting back on the agenda the question of the market as a more efficient means of stimulating economic growth than centralized planning. The failure of the systems of centralized control adopted in countries under real socialism is now beyond any doubt. However, recent events in Eastern Europe make it urgently necessary to understand how different types of industrial society actually function. This involves, to begin with, both accurate criticism of the paradigm of the self-regulating market and analysis of the complicated processes of social organization.

Although an interest in informal working activities provided the initial stimulus to writing *Fragmented Societies*, I now believe that the most important result has been the above-mentioned criticism of the market paradigm. In this introduction I want to consider this question but also broaden the discussion. I intend to give free rein to my thoughts without any attempt to be systematic, passing from the simple reporting of events to wide-ranging interpretation. This is indispensable if we are to use imagination when interpreting social reality. Nowadays, our imaginative thinking has become clouded by both the complexity of reality and narrow academic specialization. It is further hindered by the established rules of interpretation and the vast and widely dispersed number of works which must be read in order to understand even limited areas of contemporary societies. We are now, however, only just beginning to piece together a mosaic from millions of pebbles, some of which fit and some of which do not. The general pattern of this enormous mosaic already exists and all we can do is add or replace a few pieces in order to provide what we believe to be a more valid or up-to-date interpretation of some areas in the overall picture. It is also true, though, that the pattern changes while we are at work and that the details depend on the sense of the overall design; moreover, it is difficult to be certain about which previously laid trails to follow and which to abandon, and how to modify the ones we decide to follow. This is a very difficult task and one that it is impossible for a single academic or even for a small homogeneous group to undertake. Only a closely knit network of researchers engaged in critical co-operation has any chance of continuing with the mosaic and, in this respect, both the provocative use of one's imagination and a thorough study of the details play an important role. Here, I shall try to limit myself to a few of the imaginatively provocative ideas that served as a basis for working out the details of this book.

The question of the market has many aspects, and these are difficult to disentangle. What seems to me important above all is to distinguish between the problems posed by the market as a political concept and as an interpretational category. In other words, the starting-point consists of two interconnected questions: in what sense and with what limitations does more market freedom bring about politically and socially desirable efficiency in production; and, what meaning does the criticism of the market paradigm assume with regard to the first question and to the enormous problems created by transformation in contemporary societies. The criticism of the market paradigm is a crucial question of interpretation, even apart from the political debate over how much market freedom and what kinds of regulations are desirable in order to guarantee an increasing production of resources and their redistribution in ways that do not undermine the levels of solidarity and integration indispensable for reproducing social and economic life. Beyond the criticism of the paradigm of the self-regulating market, all societies in the industrial age are held to be subjected to market tensions, and so the discussion focuses on the various combinations of factors of social organization, which depend on the historical period and the social forces and resources existing in different settings. Free trade and neo-liberalism do not form the predominant characteristics of the market but are rather socio-organizational combinations, forms of social control over competition that differ from the typical forms adopted by social democracy or in centrally planned economies. This difference is not only institutional and thus apparent in the political programmes of governments; it is also articulated over the entire wide-ranging organization of social and economic life in forms of cohesion and tension, in the structuring of individual identity, and in the strategies of families, firms, kinship and friendship networks, and of communities and interest groups. Even if the experiences of the Thatcher government and the Reagan administration alone are taken into consideration, it is difficult to conclude that they have been characterized by genuine de-regulation and not by a transformation of existing regulatory systems which benefits particular social groups and promotes certain forms of behaviour to the detriment of others. The apparatuses for social regulation in the United States and Great Britain are today more extensive and complicated than at any time in the past. But the problem goes far beyond the evaluation of systems of institutional regulation, because human behaviour is conditioned by rules and factors that have been generated by socio-historical processes in no way connected with the outcomes of economic competition. In this sense, the criticism of the paradigm of the self-regulating market is an essential element in grounding both the sociological and economic interpretations of socioeconomic relations. It is also indispensable for shifting the focus of explanation onto socio-regulatory systems and their complex interaction with economic competition and increased efficiency in the production of resources within socially feasible contexts, that is, where efficiency does not involve unacceptable costs in terms of social disgregation.

At the origins of the social sciences we find the concept of *homo oeconomicus*. Underlying it is the idea that the advent of industrial society has freed acquisitive economic activity from a more or less strict subordination to ethical-religious principles and from the control exercised by a form of social organization which is rigidly structured into closed hierarchical groups lacking in mobility and independence for the individual. This conception of *homo oeconomicus* acts as a foundation for economic and sociological interpretations of industrial societies and for the division of labour between the two disciplines. The fundamental problem lies in the fact that recognition of a high degree of autonomy in economic activity forms the basis on which the social sciences are constructed; but autonomous competitive-acquisitive behaviour not only does not exist in reality – this is traditionally widely acknowledged in the social sciences – but neither can it be defended as a scientific concept. Competitive-acquisitive action has meaning in terms of sociality only in so far as it is conditioned by processes of socialization and by 'rules' that differ from those typical of pre-industrial societies, but which are exogenous to the pure concept of free market competition. The continuity between the economic and the social spheres cannot even be interrupted at the cognitive level, as sociologists and economists have done in forming their different disciplines. Too strong an emphasis on the autonomy of economic-acquisitive action variously codified in the paradigm of the market has led to an unjustifiably stereotyped picture of industrial man. This picture is schizophrenically divided between an abstract, socially shapeless individuality and a sociality that is the miraculous effect of generalized competition. From this an economic science that is well established and politically acceptable, and a weaker, critical and controversial sociology (Giddens, 1982), have developed along their own lines, often polemicizing against and trying to hegemonize one another, with the result that a whole series of important phenomena and processes typical of contemporary societies have been neglected.

An intense criticism of the paradigm of the self-regulating market does not necessarily imply a radical denial of the importance of the division of labour between economists and sociologists nor, even less so, a plea for the supremacy of sociology. This present work might generate a different impression, not only because my own sociologist's point of view comes across more emphatically but also because of my conviction that a re-evaluation of this point of view is crucial in order to compensate for the diverse forms of economistic influence that have prevented a deeper understanding of important processes of social transformation. I am also convinced that besides criticism of the market paradigm, greater attention must be paid by all those who specialize in particular fields to redefining the sense of the continuity between the economic, political and social spheres. This began some time ago and has been intensifying in recent decades through the work of Hirschman (1970, 1977, 1982), aimed at redefining the continuity between the economic and the political spheres, and through many contributions in which economists themselves have brought about a crisis in their own interpretational models (see, for example, Marsden, 1986). Moreover, the dividing line between sociology and economics is also shifing. I shall not go into details here so as not to repeat what is said later on. However, I want to raise several general issues that have been overshadowed in this work.

I think that it is particularly important to tackle the question raised by Abrams's *Historical Sociology* (1982) concerning the fact that the bimillenarian tradition of Western rational thought has established a dualism between individual and society which became a founding element in the social sciences, even against the explicit conviction of several thinkers. The idea that the self, the individual personality, constitutes an abstract entity that can be separated from socio-historical processes has contributed to implanting the paradigm of the market deep into the various approaches adopted in the social sciences. Individual competitive-acquisitive behaviour is then reconstituted in terms of sociality on the basis of the contents and results of competitive action. In classical sociology, Marx gives priority to the aggregation of collective interests in terms of social classes; for Durkheim and the structural functionalists it is the link of functional complementarity that cements industrial society together; while according to Weber it is the rational content of socially significant action that acts as the bond. The individual-society dualism in sociology has also led to the deep-rooted incompatibility between structuralist and behaviourist approaches. If Abrams is right, this is no small problem, and it is not enough to be aware of its distorting effect in order to eliminate it. It is impossible to imagine the extent of the collective effort in multidisciplinary research that would be required to reconstruct in context and without a break in continuity the socio-historical processes underlying individual identities and their active interplay in producing these same processes. Abrams, Giddens (1984) and Habermas (1984; 1987) have opened up a path in this direction by insisting on the importance of historical processes in structuring action contexts and individual personalities; it is clear, however, that there is still a long way to go before a better understanding can be reached of societies that are becoming every day more complicated and heterogeneous. In trying to achieve this better understanding, I believe that an interesting approach is the critical and cautious use of the concept of 'strategy' as an instrument for giving priority to reversing the artificial separation between individual and social group. Indeed, a correct use of the concept of strategy cannot ignore the conceptual unity between individual action and the specific social context in which an individual is located. The former is the essential constitutive element of strategies, while the latter is indispensable for attributing sense to a concatenation of successive actions, in the case of individual strategies, or to a set of actions carried out by more than one individual, in the case of family, trade union and group strategies in general.

The student who wants to understand contemporary societies in terms of processes of structuration, social formation of identities and strategies of behaviour cannot avoid the vast question of social classes. This is especially the case if his critical awareness allows him to perceive inequality, discrimination and the serious lack of resources as injustices that the commitment to research must help to eliminate. Self-criticism and criticism of dogmatic or too flexible uses of the concept of social class constitute a necessary starting-point for reflection (Pahl, 1989b), but they do not lead very far in the understanding of contemporary societies. In particular, the rigid concatenation in Marxism linking socio-occupational position, development of a social consciousness, and political organization and mobilization leading to precise outcomes in terms of collective action and political strategy, has always presented problems as regards the logical rigour of this interpretation (Lockwood, 1988). Today, this concatenation risks becoming a cage immobilizing the Marxist contribution in the sterile attempt to redraw a profile of the working class that fits in with the decline of blue-collar workers and the increase in heterogeneous white-collar employment and service jobs in general, retired workers and family nuclei that pool several incomes from different sources. Despite the importance of this critical starting-point, it is none the less important to recognize that classes, in as much as aggregates of socio-economic interests that play a primary role in structuring social identities and various kinds of behaviour and forms of political alignment, have not yet become extinct or been replaced by feminist, ecological, ethnic, cultural, nationalist, local and other movements. The interweaving of interests is undoubtedly a complicated one and the increasing heterogeneity of the structure of tertiary employment imposes a radical revision of existing interpretations of society. However, no contemporary society has reached such high levels of social equality in terms of socio-economic opportunities and the redistribution of abundant resources that it is in a position to master the difficulties now posed by the concept of social class. It is probably true that class is of less significance in explaining different typologies of political and electoral behaviour, but it is also true that the understanding of contemporary societies involves more mature ways of incorporating the concept of class (Miliband, 1989) and not the abandoning *tout court* of this fundamental instrument of interpretation.

Taking for granted that the criticism of the paradigm of the market is correct, the crisis of the centrally planned economies and the profound changes in Eastern European countries represent the most acute symptoms of the growing inadequacy of all institutional systems for controlling societies that are increasingly heterogeneous. This characteristic is apparent both in economic organization, where service activities are extending their influence, and in the complex individuality and identity promoted by various historical processes of socialization, the spread of mass education and audio-visual media systems, and by the growing receptiveness to feminist and ecological issues. In different ways, these problems are creating mounting difficulties for all institutional regulatory and governmental systems, as shown by the recent experience in Sweden, the basic failure of the neo-conservative and neo-liberal projects of Thatcher and Reagan, the uncertainty over the Japanese political system after forty years of stability and the dramatic situation of governments in underdeveloped countries.

What has been said above gives rise to many difficult questions concerning the political prospects for contemporary societies. Today, there is a serious risk of seeing the extraordinary changes taking place in Eastern Europe as a reassuring confirmation of the stability of representative democracies and the system of nation-states as they have developed in Western Europe, and of their adequacy to respond to the challenge of the most important contemporary changes. I have encapsulated this process in the term 'social fragmentation', perhaps neglecting an in-depth analytical definition in favour of a provocative and generic terminology. It seems to me that the above-mentioned and other phenomena have paved the way for great instability on a global scale and, consequently, also for social tension and change which may find expression in long and painful conflicts.

By way of concluding this introduction, I would like to mention two disputed issues that seem to me to be extremely important politically: that relating to the system of nation-states and that to the connection between political systems and forms of participation. Those national communities that were formed and consolidated in dramatic processes during recent centuries (Tilly, 1975) are passing through a particularly critical phase. It is not just a question of the relationship between the nation-state with its sovereignty over a limited territory and economic operations at the multinational or global level (Giddens, 1982), nor solely of the separatist movements existing in many countries with a multinational makeup, like the Soviet Union, Yugoslavia or India. There is also the problem of different races living together, following the failure of the American melting pot experiment, at a time when the great majority of nations are or are becoming strongly multi-ethnic. At an even more general level, there is then the difficulty of combining a local sense of belonging that has always been strong or has more recently grown strong, with the wide potential opened up nowadays by freedom of movement. The question is whether and how the present reality of national citizenship can be rendered more elastic to accommodate all these tensions. An obvious example is the political unification of Europe, where the plan to redraw the boundaries of national citizenship – one possibility would be a Europe composed of large regions – is for the time being a vague dream opposed by rooted national interests. However, what is more and more apparent each day is that the pace at which tensions mature is quicker than the time required for far-reaching changes in institutions. It is important to understand that this does not only apply to the Soviet Union under Mikhail Gorbachev, but also to all those countries in which the processes of social fragmentation are strongly eroding the bases of national citizenship, laboriously constructed in other times to meet very different needs of cohabitation from those existing today.

A similar argument can be stated with regard to political institutions and forms of participation in the management of power, Participational democracy has not progressed very far and has often failed miserably in a demagogic frenzy of meetings, committees and referenda. In the meantime, representative democracy is showing clear signs of old age that not even the most daring institutional engineering is able to eliminate. All electoral systems, all forms of political party, all attempts at political decentralization are revealing defects that are growing worse as societies become more fragmented. To this must be added the ambiguous political impact of the spread of television on populations whose average level of education is rising but which are also increasingly made up of heterogeneous and self-aware individuals. The fact that the content of power relationships has become progressively weakened, descending to more generic and empty sloganizing, and leading as a consequence to the undermining of the delegation of power and the representation of interests and, therefore, of the capacity to govern, seems to me a very serious problem. It is a problem that places worrying question marks over the prospects for all contemporary societies.

1

The theoretical basis for a critical
sociology of economic life

1 THE LIMITATIONS OF COMPETITIVE MARKET
PARADIGMS

Informal activity as a starting-point for the dismantling of the market paradigm

In recent years, sociologists studying economic change have felt an increasing sense of unease which, despite its different manifestations, seems to have a common origin, namely, a growing dissatisfaction with the concept of 'development' and the various theoretical paradigms which express it. The failure of the various paradigms of 'development' is, however, a complex problem. It is a question both of changing social reality and of inadequate instruments of interpretation. An important point which needs to be clarified is whether the conceptual instruments have been rendered inadequate by changing reality or whether they have always been so. I hold that the second of these two theses is correct and I shall devote most of this chapter to discussing it.

There are two main reasons for the sense of unease increasingly felt by social scientists. On the one hand, the growing interest in previously ignored or undervalued socio-economic phenomena such as informal activities, self-provisioning, the economic role of family and ethnic relationships and the variety of household work strategies, cannot easily be accommodated within a theoretical framework of analysis predominantly built around the patterns of official employment and of rational economic behaviour by single individuals. On the other hand, recent patterns of tertiarization and industrial restructuring have rendered more and more complicated and heterogeneous even the official employment structure of advanced capitalist countries, which have remained the main focus of attention for Western social scientists. Sociologists in particular are facing enormous difficulties in explaining different life-styles, changing patterns of social inequality and household arrangements at a time when rising numbers of married women are going out to work and young people are experiencing lengthening periods of unemployment. These are just two of the crucial trends in contemporary advanced capitalist societies which also emerge from conventional quantitative analysis. The impact of these trends on social stratification is difficult to interpret when dealing with a specific situation in a single region or relatively homogeneous country; it is even more difficult when two or more situations within the same type of society are compared, and becomes intractable when a wide-ranging international comparative perspective is adopted. But, at the same time, social scientists have a growing awareness of the importance of global links, of the fact that local economies and societies are not isolated and cannot be fully understood outside of a global theoretical framework. At the root of these difficulties lie problems of immense theoretical importance involving the entire tradition of the social sciences.

I shall begin the discussion with the question of informal economic activity for two reasons: first, it has been empirical research into this problem which led me to write this book; second, among various important issues, it is the one that presents the clearest challenge to conventional economistic approaches to interpreting social reality. For this second reason in particular, it is also likely to be the most complicated and difficult to solve of all the questions facing scholars today, as will be seen in the course of this book.

In their introduction to a collection of essays on informal activity, Ferman and others argue that:

> Until the 1970s the silence on informal activity was part of the historical development of formal, rational, industrial economies, whether these were captialist or socialist. In the early 1970s in the United States and Europe, scholars began to rediscover a long-ignored phenomenon. Goods and services did not have to be produced and consumed in officially recognized and registered enterprises. Instead they could be made, traded, swapped, and bartered among members of informal networks. (Ferman et al., 1987, p. 12)

Informal activities have always existed throughout the industrial age: they are not only a pre-industrial phenomenon or a post-industrial alternative (Gaughan and Ferman, 1987, p. 24); they are not typical of primitive social organizations or characteristic of isolated groups, ethnic minorities, exotic or 'culturally different' communities; they do not consti-

tute a separate economy or optionally alternative forms of economic
behaviour to the official rationally-based formal economy.[1]
The silence on informal activity has been a constitutive element of the
approaches used to interpret economic behaviour in the industrial age.
This means that the silence has not stemmed from a relatively minor
lack of attention to an area of social relations that during the periods of
industrial development has become less and less important, but rather
that it has been a necessary element in constructing consistent interpretative paradigms centred on rational and atomized market-competitive
behaviour. As I shall try to show, these paradigms are incompatible
with any consideration of informal activity.[2] At this point, my critical
discussion of the scientific paradigm used to interpret industrial societies
has moved far beyond the single question of informal activity and now
directly addresses the most important problem: the paradigm of the self-
regulating atomized market as the main pattern of social organization in
the industrial age.

Beyond the market paradigm: the problem of embeddedness

According to Karl Polanyi (1944/1975; 1977) and many other anthropologists, market-competitive behaviour is one of three basic forms of social
relations of exchange, the other two being reciprocity and redistribution.[3]
There is a crucial difference between the pure concept of market exchange
on one side and that of reciprocity and redistribution on the other. The
first makes sense as a concept only if it is assumed to operate free of
any socio-organizational constraints, while the second and third are
meaningful only within forms of social organization. The various systems
of reciprocity and redistribution determine not only patterns of social
relations of exchange but also patterns of social organization. Reciprocity
is a form of exchange based either on delayed or on eventual restitution,
or on restitution to somebody different from the actual donor. For these
reasons, actions of reciprocal exchange depend on a set of established
socio-organizational networks which fix the rules as to who gives and
who receives, what is given and at what time. Similarly, redistributive
exchange does not make sense beyond the existence of established
relations and rules that determine what resources are taken from the
direct producers for redistribution, to who they are allocated and in what
ratios, and also who does the taking and for what reasons. Market
exchange, on the contrary, makes sense as an abstract concept only if it
is perceived as a finished transaction taking place between as many
actors as possible who are unaffected by other kinds of established social
relations. Market competition, for instance, would be highly ineffective

in fixing prices if buyers regularly preferred to deal only with particular sellers, or if only a few potential sellers were authorized to do busines with a particular category of buyers, and so on. The idea that the market is an organizational system confuses the possible results of a set of atomized interactions – defined under abstract conditions which cannot exist in *social* reality – with the operational conditions for this very set of interactions. As Albert Hirschman has noted,

> large numbers of price-taking anonymous buyers and sellers supplied with perfect information . . . function without any prolonged human or social contact between the parties. Under perfect competition there is no room for bargaining, negotiation, remonstration or mutual adjustment and the various operators that contract together need not enter into a recurrent or continuing relationship as a result of which they will get to know each other well. (Hirschman, 1982a, p. 1473)

The fact that market relations do not constitute *per se* a socio-organizational system does not affect the usefulness of the abstract model of the market or of the idea put forward by Max Weber, and later by Fernand Braudel, that the diffusion of market social relations has functioned like a powerful economic computing device in standardizing price-cost ratios and allowing rational economic accounting; but accounting is not synonymous with organizing. Market interaction does not take place within the abstract model of an atomized society or in a self-organized system involving a set of necessarily unrepeatable competitive social relations because occurring by chance; such a system is in fact an absurdity. On the contrary, it occurs within historically established conditions of social organization, shaped by complex mixes of reciprocity and redistribution. These mixes undergo change in order to accommodate the increasingly faulty working of diffused market interaction, but they have not been replaced by a socio-organizational system brought about by market interaction itself, which is conceptually impossible. At this point we come to the crucial problem of the social embeddedness of the market.

In this regard, the important points are these:

1 The chief reasons for the formulation of the question of embeddedness and the main lines of interpretation;
2 the consequences of having persistently ignored this question;
3 the way in which embeddedness can be theoretically conceptualized and applied within action-based and structural approaches and

within present alluring post-functionalist attempts to combine these two approaches.

The majority of social scientists consider the market as separate from and autonomous of social conditioning; it is even considered by many to be the dominant form of social behaviour or the dominant structuring force in social life.[4] Consequently we have approaches that, independently of any specific discipline or method, have their roots in individual atomized competitive behaviour. This is clearly the case with classical and neo-classical economists for whom a social context exists only as a sub-product of market interaction.[5] But it also applies to a large part of the sociological tradition, as I shall try to demonstrate in the following section.[6]

In broad outline, I argue that these characteristics of the dominant interpretations have systematically led to three related analytical errors. They may be defined as overestimating the importance of the *industrializing trend*, insufficient attention being paid to phenomena which exhibit *continuity within change* and an underestimation of the *social conditions and resources* underlying economic change, particularly those deriving from socio-organizational patterns based on reciprocity.

As will be seen in the following sections, different variations of the assumption that there exists a 'fundamental industrializing trend' are built into the main sociological theories. What I mean by this is that socio-economic change moves in a single direction which underlies all the different variants, giving them a more or less standardized form; as a result, the changing social picture is composed of features typically found in all industrial societies. In the first place, it is not entirely a platitude to observe that sociological paradigms have developed in parallel with Western industrial societies and have always exhibited a greater capacity to explain these rather than other kinds of societies. The other side of the coin is that sociologists have incorporated the assumption of a 'fundamental industrializing trend' into their theories because, in some cases and for a long historical period, it has constituted an effective way to simplify social complexity.[7]

So far, I have been arguing from a purely hypothetical perspective. To prove that the market paradigm and its three analytical errors are built into all of the most important sociological approaches requires a more detailed analysis. In evolutionary or functionalist interpretations of social change (for example, Emile Durkheim and Talcott Parsons) the process is explicit and relatively easy to locate. It is more difficult to reconstruct in interpretations which reject evolutionary-functionalist explanations, as is the case with Marx and Weber.

A preliminary outline of the theoretical approach

If it is assumed that the market is not one of the organizers of social life in the industrial age but – as will be seen shortly, following Polanyi – a disorganizer, the problem changes. Now it is a question of seeing how different kinds of market-competitive tensions are accommodated within socio-organizational patterns formed by other systems of social organization.[8]

A correct social analysis and interpretation of economic life in the industrial age consists in combining three complex sets of interdependent variables: factors and behavior of the communal or reciprocal type; factors and behaviour of the associative/redistributive type; and competitive market tensions and behaviour. A proper discussion of this interpretational strategy has to be postponed to section 3 of this chapter. It is, however, necessary to introduce here some points in order to facilitate the understanding of my approach. This is based on the assumption that there are only two pure types of socio-organizational factors: reciprocity and association. Both can be expressed in different subcategories and contribute to varying extents to the shaping of different social organizations, also referred to herein as socialization mixes. Associative factors are based on common interests deriving from similiar conditions relating to employment and/or property. They are assumed to become increasingly important with the emergence of the industrial mode of production and to be crucial in fixing the rules of redistribution typical of the industrial age.

The question of 'embeddedness' is typical of all industrial societies in as much as they are characterized by a considerable intensity in social relations based on market exchange. More precisely, in all those societies in which a large and increasing part of production is not for direct consumption by the producers, and distribution takes place within exchange relations, the question arises as to how the latter are to be regulated by a specific socialization mix, a combination of associative and reciprocal factors. This comprehensive and contradictory regulation defines the very terms of the question of 'embeddedness' in different industrial societies. In this sense, the question applies also to socialist societies, which are characterized not so much by the absence of market relations but rather by a form of embeddedness different from that found in capitalism. Furthermore, it is important to emphasize that the complex interplay of the three sets of variables operates on two levels. These two levels can be logically distinguished but, in so far as they are integrated into a unitary process, they rarely assume the appearance of distinct stages, which makes analysis difficult. The first level is that of the origin of different kinds of market tensions in a given socio-organizational context, structured into subsystems of association and reciprocity characterized by a certain degree of instability. The second level arises from the fact that the spread of these tensions leads in turn to an unstable rearranging of the entire socio-organizational system, and so on.

The simplest example that comes to mind is that of the enclosures, because this system developed throughout a long historical period and was, in part, characterized by the exceptional fact that the two levels were separated into two distinct phases. The intervention of the authorities and the landowners (associative system) in order to limit feudal community rights (reciprocal system) was not determined by immediate market requirements. Instead, it was caused by the internal socio-organizational relations, which were also power relations, only in those contexts where the socialization mix was characterized by a high degree of instability.[9] In the long run, the enclosures favoured the spread of competitive market behaviour within the entire socialization mix by modifying both associative and reciprocal relations.

Tensions are produced by the different forms in which competitive behaviour spreads. The differences depend on the diverse social contexts in which the forms develop. It is important to insist both on the question of the indirect impact and on that of the complex contextual nature of the changes in the two socio-organizational systems. Such emphasis serves to avoid unfeasible functionalist or determinist approaches and it places the accent on the persistence within change of a deep and unresolvable lack of cohesion at the socio-organizational level. Exaggerating for the sake of clarity, we may say that, on the one hand, socio-organizational reaction more easily accommodates competitive behaviour within the social context and, on the other, it stifles its capacity to spread further. The experience of the socio-institutional control of markets provides an obvious confirmation of this process.[10] In parallel, the adaptation of associative and of reciprocal systems magnifies the possible extent of non-cohesion, because the two systems are organizationally separate and the greater strength of modern associative/redistributive systems is incapable of either eliminating systems based on reciprocity or subjecting them to total control. In my view, the clearest example in this respect is that of socialist societies, since in them the redistributive system takes on a dominant role which does not prevent families, kinship groups, ethnic communities and solidarity networks of operators/consumers in the second economy from acting in a way that does not cohere with the way the institutional associative/redistributive system functions.

When taking a critical look in the next section at Weber's contribution,

I return to the question of embeddedness from a methodological perspective based on the analysis of the motives behind individual action. The reason for mentioning this now is the fact that this different approach leads to the same conclusions. Economic action based on market exchange is founded on divergent interests and therefore on competition. For example, a buyer wishes to purchase at the lowest and a seller to sell at the highest price possible. It cannot reasonably be supposed that atomized social actors will come to a 'market' compromise for reasons of natural 'morality' or because they already foresee that the outcome will be a compromise acceptable to both parties. This is widely proven by the fact that no sooner does the opportunity arise than exchange becomes characterized by swindling. The weaker the socio-organizational contexts of both kinds, the more this is likely to occur. The shopkeeper may as a rule demand too high a price if he is not compelled to display fixed prices, or he may do so to the occasional customer. In contrast, it is unlikely that a customer will steal something from a large store equipped with advanced security systems or from the corner shop. Atomized market behaviour is an abstract model without rules. In reality, *market behaviour occurs according to rules that are set not by the market itself but by the socio-regulatory contexts*. Concrete action is not, therefore, individualistic/atomized but conditioned by these contexts.

To conclude, I should explain what I mean by 'industrial organized' tendencies. What has been interpreted as organized capitalism is in part the fruit of short-sighted ethnocentrism and the predominance of the market paradigm and in part a real phenomenon of which I give a summarized description that differs from the usual one. A prolonged phase of economic expansion has been fuelled by the market penetration of the entire world and unfolded under conditions increasingly favourable to the advanced countries. It has allowed the latter to minimize the lack of cohesion between the diffusion of market relations and the systems of socialization, as well as within such systems, the balance of which is tilting more and more towards the associative side; hence the strong role assumed by the state and the widespread existence of institutional industrial organizations and conflicts. As a result, for many years markets subjected to increasing control have remained competitive and efficient. A further result has been the apparently unlimited growth of forms of industrialization that are conflictual, divided, inequitable and still afflicted by old or new problems, but at the same time organized.

If attention is shifted to the last twenty years and the methodological approach is modified in favour of a less ethnocentric one that also focuses on reciprocal contexts, the immediate impression is that lack of cohesion is a much more widespread phenomenon. This is so both within the two sets of socio-organizational processes, where one of the most important indicators is the informal economy, and between these and market tensions, where a *prima facie* indicator is the emergence of neo-conservative and neo-liberal political forces and policies. Even considering only the advanced capitalist countries, contemporary societies are neither disorganized nor less organized than those in the 1950s and 1960s. Socioorganizational balances are now more complicated because the interplay of contexts based on reciprocity has become important and visible. At times this interplay astonishes the observer and some would even say that it is superior or more organized than in the preceding phase. But, as will be seen during the course of this book, it is also necessary to look at the lack of cohesion in the various processes of reorganization in contemporary societies. One of the principal aspects here is the fact that societies in which the associative contexts are less strong are also less prone to conflict, but also less open to being governed by a central authority.

2 SOCIAL FACTORS AND THE INFLUENCE OF THE MARKET PARADIGM IN CLASSICAL SOCIOLOGY

The Marxist approach

Marxist focusing on *social* as opposed to economic relations of production is consistent with the approach already mentioned. Often, it is only a question of translating some terms and concepts into a more accentuated socio-anthropological explanatory method, and of finding ways to resolve the problem of the dichotomy between structure and action along different lines from Marx's ambiguous approach. This ambiguity is not so much due to the interest in collective action as to the explicit influence of classical economics. It is this very influence that leads Marx to include a version of the market paradigm in his approach. For Marx, industrial societies are founded on the interrelationship between market competition and social factors of the associative kind, first of all social classes and the state. Market competition constitutes the privileged field of analysis for individual action, but it does not by itself possess the direct capacity to structure society, whereas social factors predominate in structuring society as well as generating collective action. Marx's incorporation into his approach of the dichotomy between structure and action is achieved without resolving the problem of how to make the two lines methodologically compatible. The sphere of individual action is dealt with mainly within the market paradigm in terms that exclude intrinsic conditioning by systems of social control. Hence the rigid and economistic form that the laws of capitalist development finally assume, but also the fact that these very laws often stand in a logical-analytical contradiction with other essential elements in Marxist thought. Typical in this regard is the conflict between the abstract theorization of social classes and their socio-historical analysis.

Organizational factors of reciprocity are underestimated, at least as regards their interplay in industrial societies: such interplay is confined within the analysis of material social reproduction, which is never developed further, though not entirely forgotten. Marx would have agreed with the idea of a changing interconnection of associative and reciprocal systems as fundamental structural elements in the social relations of production. The theory of primitive accumulation confirms this interpretation.[11] Moreover, socio-economic processes within specific social formations cannot be explained solely or chiefly by recourse to abstract laws of change in the mode of production. On the contrary, they have to be explained through analysis of the complex interplay of specific transformations, which takes into account the particular combination of associative and reciprocal factors, including processes of preservation, change and adaptation. Marx himself puts forward an example of this variation in analysis in his historical-political writings on social classes and the class struggle in France in the middle of the nineteenth century (Marx, 1973).

The crucial point is that within the Marxist approach a greater explanatory value is attached to the laws of the accumulation of capital than to socio-organizational processes and relations. In particular, this results in a lack of attention to the interplay of the different spheres of reciprocity, with both individual competitive action and the organizational parameters set by associative contexts. Examples of the first kind of interplay are ethnic or family entrepreneurship and variations in the communal form adopted by corporate structures; examples of the second are the discrepancies between, on one side, class interests and loyalties and, on the other, the requirements, needs and traditional customs binding individuals to families and kinship systems. For this last reason, Marxist class analysis is always a limited interpretative instrument, but particularly in cases where the attraction of reciprocal loyalties is strong or increasing. Another of the most manifest symptoms of oversimplification is the scant attention paid to processes of *preservation/change*, for example the persistence of small entrepreneurs, artisans, peasants and shopkeepers in the face of proletarianization and the interplay of kinship, friendship, community or ethnic relations also as original and recurrent factors in all forms of capital origination and accumulation.

In Marx's approach, many questions are left unresolved for which it is possible to follow a line of interpretation different from that developed by the orthodox Marxist tradition. For example, the socio-organizational patterns of reciprocity are generally underestimated, but at several crucial points in Marx's intellectual development they assume a decisive import-ance, on which neither Marx himself nor the Marxist tradition has dwelt.

In the first place, Marx often insists that the relationship between capital and labour is one of complementarity. Capitalists and workers are two sides to the same context of work and of conflict: they need one another in order to exist as such, and the exploiting of one class by the other produces a clash of interests. Marx does no more than develop the macro-social significance of the question. What needs to be done is to translate this very approach into a consistent micro-social version: the capitalist enterprise is at one and the same time a socio-organizational context of reciprocity (complementarity) and an associative context (exploitation, conflicting interests, class struggle). This version provides a springboard for considerations of great importance for both analysis and a political perspective; these considerations, in turn, give rise to important consequences at the level of macro-social relations. Take the interest of the trade union movement in economic expansion and, nat-urally, increasing employment as a way to defend jobs, even when this entails giving taxpayers' money to 'exploiting' capitalists, and so on.

Then there is the question of the transition from pre-capitalist to captialist modes of production. Marx was convinced that pre-capitalist social organizations, in general characterized by the supremacy of recipro-cal factors, cannot by definition be penetrated by capitalist relations of production. This is one of the few cases in which social scientists, excepting anthropologists, have given priority to the economic role of reciprocal contexts. This question is looked at again in chapter 2 in relation to proletarianization. Here it is interesting to note that Marx sketched out a theory of the interference between associative factors, as with the violent intervention of the enclosures system or of colonialism, and reciprocal factors, as with pre-capitalist communities, where the market is not the direct 'instigator' but only the possible final beneficiary.

Other important contributions of Marxist thought to the understanding of current societies are discussed in the course of this book with reference to specific problems. It is worth mentioning here that two issues of theory appear particularly important to me: the problem of 'material social reproduction', to be dealt with in chapter 3; and the problem of class and politics, which will be discussed in chapter 7.

The Weberian approach

Weber's contribution to the theoretical understanding of contemporary society may be succinctly expressed in a twofold message: the automony/-pre-eminence of 'homo oeconomicus' and the spread of behaviour which uses a rational strategy to achieve ends.[12] The complex causes, rhythms and phases of industrial transformation cannot be explained in full because they are conditioned by the effects of 'historical charisma'; nevertheless the industrializing trend is a cornerstone of Weberian thought. In Weber as in Marx, we have an interpretative paradigm of socio-economic change which is capable of accounting for diversity and discontinuity. None the less, Weber's contribution is also critically discussed in order to eliminate the negative influence of the market paradigm.

The ideal type of rational behaviour is fundamentally a methodological parameter (see Weber, 1947, p. 92). As such it has a *logical* priority, which cannot automatically be transformed into a *real* one. In other words, since the interpreter is able to reconstruct the conformity between means and ends, he uses this priority reconstruction in a positive (real rational actions) or in a negative (real irrational actions) way in order to make sense of social actions. At this methodological level the terms rational or irrational are totally free of substantive evaluation: they do not indicate good or bad, modern or traditional, or what leads to more or less social efficiency. Neither do they evoke different forms of social order. In this sense, Weber explicitly adopts a methodological strategy that is an alternative to functionalism (1947, p. 107).

The other side to the Weberian methodological approach is the fact that the motives for social action are interpreted from the point of view of the, at least in principle, socialized individual actor, as will be seen shortly. This consideration tells us two things. The first is that Weber rejects assumptions which are impossible or absurd from the point of view of the individual socialized actor. For example, he does not assume immediate motivation-based links between goal-oriented individual rational economic action and economic efficiency. The rational motives behind individual social action have nothing to do with the final overall outcome which is far from the actor's own specific interests. This may form a different level of analysis focusing on the results of a system of rational actions. In other words, when I buy a car at the cheapest price possible, I am not interested in the fact that this behaviour could produce an efficient economy. This may not be the case with rational economic actions oriented to an absolute value (*wertrational*) when this value itself is some form of economic efficiency. We could take as an example the impact of propaganda by governments aimed at convincing people to buy home-produced rather than foreign products in order to boost the national economy. The second is that individual actions cannot be properly considered as atomized. On the one hand, as Parsons puts it: 'Weber, with his strong emphasis on institutional variability, was almost completely free of the grosser biases involved in the received economic doctrine of "rational self-interest"' (in Weber, 1947, p. 52). On the other, Weber is as controversial as Marx on the specific issue of market competitive behaviour, but for different reasons.[13]

Weber's programme for interpreting societies of the industrial age is torn between the need to give priority and an autonomous sociological significance to increasingly important goal-oriented economic action and a recurrent intuition that this kind of action is always subject to various kinds of social conditioning. I shall look briefly at this theoretical dilemma in relation to three questions treated by Weber: the typology of 'Solidary Social Relationships'; the 'Regulation of the Market'; and the tension between 'The Formal and Substantive Rationality of Economic Action'.

As the quotations below show, Weber's typology of solidarity-based social relationships has much in common with my brief outline in the previous section of the approach adopted in this book.

> A social relationship will be called 'communal' if and so far as the orientation of social action – whether in the individual case, on the average, or in the pure type – is based on a subjective feeling of the parties, whether affectual or traditional, that they belong together. A social relationship will, on the other hand, be called 'associative' if and in so far as the orientation of social action within it rests on a rationally motivated adjustment of interest or a similarly motivated agreement, whether the basis of rational judgement be absolute values or reasons of expediency. (Weber, 1947, p. 136)

It is clear that Weber's typology depends directly on rational/irrational ideal types of economic action and, as a consequence, differs from the anthropological classification of social relationships of exchange despite certain similarities. It is also clear that his typology is not responsive to the possibility that some actions also define socio-organizational systems while others do not. This difference emerges with great clarity in his list of 'purest cases of associative relations' and of examples of communal relationships.

1 The purest cases of associative relationships are: (a) rational free
market exchange, which constitutes a compromise of opposed but
complementary interests; (b) the pure voluntary association based
on self-interest, a case of agreement as to a long-run course of
action oriented purely to the promotion of specific ulterior interest,
economic or other, of its members; (c) the voluntary association of
individuals motivated by an adherence to a set of common absolute
values, for example, the rational sect, in so far as it does not
cultivate emotional and affective interests, but seeks only to serve
a 'cause'. This last case, to be sure, seldom occurs in anything
approaching the pure type.
2 Communal relationships may rest on various types of affectual,
emotional, or traditional bases. Examples are a religious brother-
hood, an erotic relationship, a relation of personal loyalty, a national
community, the *esprit de corps* of a military family. The type case is
most conveniently illustated by the family. But the great majority
of social relationships has this characteristic to some degree, while
it is at the same time to some degree determined by associative
factors. No matter how calculating and hard-headed the ruling
considerations in such a social relationship – as that of a merchant
to his customers – may be, it is quite possible for it to involve
emotional values which transcend its utilitarian significance.
(Weber, 1947, pp. 136–7)

The major debatable point here is the classification of 'rational free
market exchange' among the purest cases of associative relationships.[14]
This is perfectly consistent with Weber's methodology, for which the
dichotomy of ideal types of actions is the starting-point, but it raises
controversial questions that Weber is unable to solve. On the one hand,
Weber is compelled to perceive social modes of regulating the market as
exceptions rather than rules.[15] On the other, he is conscious of how
deeply market competition is socially and institutionally regulated by a
number of socio-political factors and this shows up when he deals with
the 'regulation of the market'; here he mentions a number of factors
which I would define as of both the associative and the reciprocal kind
(Weber, 1947, p. 181–4). Also, a further field of tensions which Weber
defines in terms of a divergence between 'formal and substantive rationality' (Weber, 1947, pp. 184–6 and 211–18) is opened up by the discrepancies between the system of goal-oriented rational economic action and
that aiming to achieve the absolute value of providing '. . . a given group
of persons . . . adequately . . . with goods by means of an economically
oriented course of social action' (Weber, 1947, p. 185). I would define

the latter as the most deeply associative regulated form of economic behaviour, economic planning being one example. Here Weber takes the opportunity to discuss the controversial relation between free-market rationality and economic planning and analyse the case of socialism in terms which are consistent with what I argue in this book.

Weber, too, seems to be entrapped within the classical paradigm of the self-regulating market. This is not so much a matter of the methodological typology of rational economic action towards an end since in as far as it is a tool of analysis, this typology is still entirely valid. Rather, it relates to Weber's assumption that the mutuality or complementarity of interests is so much stronger than competition that it defines an associative relation, apart from other factors of social regulation. Despite a great distance in terms of method, Weber is here near to Durkheim's solution – discussed below – according to which in the division of labour the complementarity of interests prevails over their diversity as the origin of 'organic solidarity'. Weber is, however, especially responsive to the fields of tension opened up by his solution to the question of market behaviour, and he explicitly deals with a series of disputes centred on the problem of the social conditioning of market action. On the other hand, the difficulty and depth of Weber's methodology lies not so much in individualism/universalism as in the fact that his approach, as a crucial operation of interpretation, imposes the need to trace the complex ideal combinations among a plurality of actions. In this sense, Granovetter (1985, pp. 507–8) is right to assert that the problem of 'embeddedness', counterposed to the paradigm of atomized individual action, is compatible with Weber's programme.

Beyond the Durkheimian notion of organic solidarity

As a result of the market paradigm's influence on sociologists, the main way in which they have dealt with economic behaviour and economic development has been to treat them as independent variables and examine their social consequences. At best, social factors and contexts have been taken as secondary conditions or constraints. For this reason, the main empirical inputs into the analysis of society are usually historical macro-economic and demographic data on income, productivity, the distribution of occupations, demographic movements and so on. It is only as derived variables that the various contexts of social relations have been included and sometimes 'measured'.

At this point, it is worth mentioning Durkheim's scientific project since it is based on the autonomy and priority of social variables.[16] Giving priority to his own discipline (sociology as a superior science), Durkheim erected his entire analysis on an independent variable which is sociological *par excellence*, that is 'social solidarity'. His project ran into trouble because the conceptualization of organic solidarity proved methodologically debatable, as I shall try to show presently.

Durkheim offers a rather convincing explanation of the social nexus, mechanical solidarity or solidarity by similiarities, which holds together and organizes pre-industrial societies. His concept of social units linked by mechanical solidarity is similar to the idea of a social formation organized through predominant links of reciprocity. Durkheim presents a powerful vision of a 'rarefied' society made up of segments – local communities – with rare opportunities for communication or social interaction between individuals belonging to the different segments. A relatively weak nation-state, but one that applied criminal law forcefully, is sufficient to maintain social order.

Modern industrial societies are more and more 'densely' based on high rates of geographical mobility, urbanization, intensive interaction among strangers and the growing division of labour. Consequently, Durkheim writes:

The question that has been the starting point for our study has been that of the connection between the individual personality and social solidarity. How does it come about that the individual, whilst becoming more autonomous, depends ever more closely upon society? . . . It has seemed to us that what resolved this apparent antinomy was the transformation of social solidarity which arises from the ever-increasing division of labour. (1984, p. xxx)

According to Durkheim, the form of social solidarity typical of modern industrial societies is the organic one, which arises among people who are different but see the complementarity existing between them. In order to evaluate this solution critically, it is necessary to step back and briefly discuss Durkheim's method. In fact, the question of complementarity here arises in a completely different methodological setting to that of Weber, where complementarity is assumed to be important within competitive economic behaviour.

Durkheim assumes the methodological priority of society over individual behaviour: society exists as a changing structure in which human life is regulated beyond the orientation or motives of individual action. At this level Durkheim's thought is largely free from the influence of the market paradigm, not because he does not believe in atomized behaviour but because he separates the question of society from the question of individual behaviour. Social organization is studied by sociologists not only in terms of what it is but also what it *should* be. Imperfect social organization produces anomie, non-regulated atomistic behaviour, lack of order and absence of society. Let us see how he poses the problem in the preface to the second edition of *The Division of Labour in Society*.

> Liberty . . . is itself the product of a set of rules. I can be free only in so far as the other person is prevented from turning to his own benefit that superiority, whether physical, economic or of any other kind, which he possesses, in order to fetter my liberty. (1984, p. xxxiii)

> If anomie is an evil it is above all because society suffers through it, since it cannot exist without cohesion and regulation . . . Competition with one another engenders mutual relationships. (1984, p. xxxv)[17]

According to Durkheim, modern societies increasingly find themselves in difficulty and are characterized by high levels of anomie (lack of social regulation) because industrial activity, and the accompanying highly developed division of labour 'has acquired such a position in the overall life of society [that it] can clearly not remain unregulated without very profound disturbances ensuing' (1984, p. xxxiii). Organic solidarity is not a self-regulatory attribute of divided but complementary individual functions. In other words, the Weberian emphasis on complementarity in individual competitive action is not important for Durkheim. The crucial form of regulation/organic solidarity evolves as a collective process. Within this process the role of the state and of the political system is important in fostering and enforcing a social order based on contractual law, but it is insufficient and depends on the development of the really crucial collective sphere producing organic solidarity and the structure of social regulation. In his own words, 'this mode of adaptation only becomes a rule of behaviour if a group bestows its authority upon it' (1984, p. xxxiv). This group is what Durkheim calls a 'corporative institution', that is, a form of social organization in which individuals with the same socio-occupational interests associate with one another not only to defend such interests *but mainly* to regulate co-operation with other complementary corporative institutions. Durkheim expresses the vision of an industrial society where behaviour is atomized but controlled by associative organization. Within this vision mechanical solidarity, or socio-organizational systems based on reciprocity, is fated to disappear completely because the role it plays cannot be accommodated in the socio-organizational patterns of an industrial society. The functions of the family, the domestic society and the inheritance system will be transferred to the corporative institution.[18]

The Durkheimian approach is structuralist and normative to such a high degree because it is founded on positivist and evolutionary foundations, which were fashionable at the time Durkheim was writing but which became discredited a few decades later. However, Durkheim's obsession with the fact that industrial society would become socially regulated, that it cannot be regulated by a segmented pre-industrial order, and his powerful analysis of the social consequences of anomie in various areas of social life have to be recognized as important contributions that are still relevant to contemporary sociology.

It is my belief that the sociological tradition has neglected Durkheim's two most important ideas: first, that interpretation of social life in the increasingly 'individualizing' industrial age must, above all, be founded on social variables, that is to say, different forms of solidarity; second, that relationships governed by horizontal solidarity between people in the same social condition or people with common interests are particularly important variables in industrial societies.

The economistic temptations of Parsons

Despite his oversocialized system of interpretation (Wrong, 1961), Parsons none the less adopts the paradigm of the atomized individual actor (Granovetter, 1985). The methodological synthesis he carries out leaves no room for Weber's plurality of and tension between different types of action and, at the same time, it suppresses Durkheim's emphasis on collective structures of social regulation. It is the content itself of atomized individual action in terms of social function that builds up institutions or regulative structures. This solution, however, does not free Parsons's approach from the influence of the market paradigm because the predominant function of an atomized system of individual actions in an industrial society remains economic competition. We end up in a closed circle in which economic action is regulated by social institutions, the ultimate meaning of which is determined by their being functional to atomized competition. The result is strong economic determinism, which is not what Parsons intended.

The only example I look at here is Parsons's well-known theory of the trend towards the nuclear family. He underlines the progressively diminishing probability within industrial transformation that work resources will be directly handed down from one generation to the next. This change leads to a rapid decline in multi-generational adult households and their replacement by nuclear ones consisting of a couple with dependent children. Even though Parsons's formulation of the theory is less crude than as presented here, the functional interpretation of the family in the industrial age[19] neglects many social and economic relationships involving the family, confines the latter to the autonomous but limited sphere of affection and consumption, and, what is even more important, completely subordinates the transformation of family structures to their supposed function in industrial development. The point may be expressed as follows: once nuclearization has taken place, following the pace of industrial development, adult family relations are almost irrelevant to the economy and society.

What happens in reality, however, is that with the process of nuclearization kinship relations become modified and in many occupational strata the role of handing down entire work resources is also lost; yet they are still decisively important both as social and economic resources which are passed from generation to generation and as a way of regulating socio-economic life. Rather than being eliminated by industrialization, networks based on reciprocity may lose in importance and certainly interact differently with the economy and with associative socio-organizational patterns. Parents' sacrifices to enable their children to study, wedding presents or help in starting a working career, grandparents helping out with the children, support given to old parents by their children – not to mention the even more important fact, economically speaking, that new entrepreneurship originates in and relies heavily on family and other reciprocal networks – are all part and parcel of social life even in the most advanced industrial societies. It is precisely for this reason that the presence or absence, and the extent and quality, of such networks within different strata, groups and social contexts, plays an important role. If the presence or otherwise and the extent of kin resources also constitute a significant difference within a socio-demographic structure based on nuclear households, there is no reason for sociologists to focus their attention on the decline in the complete handing-down of socio-occuptional roles from one generation to the next to the neglect of the emergence of new and close relationships between family members living apart. The fact that in some social contexts there is a marked propensity for socio-occupational roles to be passed on (self-employed workers, artisans, small businessmen, peasants, entrepreneurs, etc.), often where adults of different generations do not cohabit, is an additional reason for also investigating this sociological variable as an independent one also in relation to economic behaviour and the processes of industrial development.

A similar line of reasoning can be advanced for the various theoretical versions of the decline in forms of community solidarity and their replacement by more individualistic and competitive social relationships.

Geiger and his precursory emphasis on small businesses

Lastly, I would like to mention briefly the almost forgotten contribution of Theodor Geiger. In 1949, the very year in which C. Wright Mills's book *White Collar* appeared, with its interpretation of the decline of the old and rise of the new middle classes, Geiger published an analysis of the transformation of social stratification in which, in contrast to Wright Mills, he insists on the persistence and the prospects for the growth of small businesses, above all those of modern and technologically up-to-date artisans. He polemically contests Marx's interpretation, which he sees as wholly centred on centrifugal processes (increasing social polarization) that modify the social structure and paying very little attention to centripetal processes (the growth of intermediary strata). Even when, a few decades later, some writers discovered that 'small is beautiful' or that it is 'bountiful' or that, at all events, the persistence of the microfirm and of self-employed workers is a significant phenomenon, worthy of the attention of economists and sociologists, no reference was made to Geiger's contribution.[20]

The point on which I wish to insist is that neither Geiger nor the writers anticipated by him identified the sociological question of the small business as a form in which the market and associative and reciprocal factors of social regulation intersect that is 'different' from that of the large enterprise. Geiger's hypothesis is that 'restratification' to the benefit of small businesses and artisans using advanced methods is furthered by both electrification and light electrical technology. This is very much like the almost exclusive emphasis which, with the revolution in electronics and in informatics in mind, many contemporary writers place on the technological factor or on a combination of the latter and economic conditions. In this sense, what we have is a different, and equally questionable, version of determinism. Geiger's technology-bound reasoning is plausible and backed by documentary evidence, but it does not allow for the complex reality of the intersecting of socio-organizational factors with economic behaviour. Thus, Geiger's modern 'electric' artisan did not take root, at least in the way he expected, not so much because the technical conditions were lacking but because he was squeezed out by the further development of the socio-organizational forms typical of the Fordist phase. During the same period, the mass white-collar worker indicated by Wright Mills asserted himself precisely as the typical social figure of those same socio-organizational forms. The failure of Geiger's interpretation should be a sufficient lesson to ensure that the main focus of attention lies on factors of social organization.

3 A REFORMULATION OF POLANYI'S INTERPRETATIVE MODEL

Polanyi's controversial criticism of the market paradigm

Durkheim's obsession with the social regulation of industrial societies resurfaced years later in the work of the economic historian and anthropologist Karl Polanyi (1944/1975; 1957; 1977). His contribution was based on very different methodology, analysis and fields of research. According to Polanyi, industrialization does not generate a new social relationship governed by solidarity and based on differentiation/complementarity, as is the case with collective corporative institutions. The consequence of this is that Polanyi is more radical than Durkheim. A system based solely on individualism and competition, on a self-regulating market, would not be a society characterized by high levels of anomie but would in fact be incompatible with any possible form of social relationships and ultimately mean the end of society. It is the very radicalism of Polanyi's criticism of the self-regulating market paradigm and his elaboration of the devastating historical evidence against it that make this author fashionable today when the market paradigm is in crisis, after he had been almost forgotten during the decades of the Fordist golden age. However, there exists a risk in drawing inspiration from Polanyi without critically discussing the methodological ambiguities of his approach.

In *The Great Transformation* (1944/1975) Polanyi combines specific 'micro' tools from anthropological analysis with a historical look at socio-economic change in Western societies from the end of the eighteenth to the beginning of the twentieth century. Polanyi uses anthropological concepts to argue for the 'natural' incompatibility between economic competition based on a unconditionally dominant market and any kind of social organization. Historical analysis at a 'macro' level enables him to bring to the fore various kinds of transformation which can be found in social contexts undergoing industrialization. In the first place, there is the change-adaptation of traditional social contexts due not only to the onslaught of individualism arising out of market competition but also to a reaction against this type of aggressive behaviour. Then, there is the formation of new social relationships which are specifically oriented towards repairing the damage which may be inflicted on society by the uncontrolled spread of competition between individuals; they include trade unions, trusts, cartel agreements, laws and regulations controlling economic and professional activity, the direct intervention of government in the economy and so on. We are no longer just dealing with an inert combination of the weakening of traditional forms of solidarity and the advent of new social contexts which are more equipped to prevent disgregation induced by rampant individualism, but rather with a transformation of social context as an independent factor in the process of industrialization. For Polanyi, the ways in which the social context is changed are both the results and at the same time the conditions of industrial transformation.

The typology which Polany has pinpointed historically may be taken as a starting-point, but the methodological foundations to his economic anthropology are in general relatively weak and not suitable for comparative sociological analysis. A discussion of the main reasons for this weakness will make it possible to adapt the micro-analytical concepts of reciprocity and redistribution to a macro-analytical style of research.

Unlike the classical sociologists, the merit of Polanyi is that he directly attacks the paradigm of the self-regulating market. If it is true that industrial societies are founded on the freeing of economic behaviour from strong political and religious conditioning, then the question must also be put as to how far this autonomy from factors of sociality can extend. Polanyi underlines the fact that the full independence of a marketregulated economy means the subordination of society to market laws and that such subordination is incompatible with the very survival of society.

A self-regulating market demands nothing less than the institutional separation of society into an economic and political sphere. Such a dichotomy is, in effect, merely the restatement, from the point of view of society as a whole, of the existence of a self-regulating market . . . Such an institutional pattern could not function unless society was somehow subordinated to its requirements. A market economy can exist only in a market society . . . A market economy must comprise all elements of industry, including labour, land and money . . . To include them in the market mechanism means to subordinate the substance of society itself to the laws of the market. (1944/1975, p. 71)

Labour, land and money are not true commodities, he notes, but in order to function the market has to commodify these elements; thus it is based on three essential 'fictitious commodities'. To carry out this operation the market needs, precisely, socio-regulative institutions, though this applies only in industrial societies where exchange becomes the predominant form of economic behaviour. This fictitious commodification is, however, incompatible with the working of the other two institutional forms of complex social regulation, reciprocity and redistribution. The historical evidence produced in *The Great Transformation* is aimed at demonstrating that the history of industrialization is based, on the one hand, on the spread of the market into the area of true commodities and, on the other, on the reaction of socio-regulative contexts to prevent the complete commodification of fictitious commodities, in other words, to save society from certain death. In his own words, 'social history in the nineteenth century was thus the result of a double movement: the extension of the market organization in respect to genuine commodities was accompanied by its restriction in respect to fictitious ones' (1944/1975, p. 76). For Polanyi too, therefore, the problem of embeddedness presents itself in terms of the market's direct need for institutions of social organization and not in terms of interaction with the systems of redistribution and reciprocity. He holds this view despite the fact that the historical evidence he puts forwards is not particularly convincing.

The motivation for Polanyi's choice of method can be found in his posthumously published work, *The Livelihood of Man* (1977). In it, he tries to apply conceptual tools from structuralist anthropology within a method of economic analysis based on the model of atomized individual action. In my opinion, Polanyi's methodological weakness lies precisely in the failure of the way in which he undertakes this application; this does not mean, however, that the adapting of anthropological concepts to the different perspective of macro-social research is not viable. Using a medical analogy, what he does is to transplant an organ without worrying about how to prevent rejection.

Polanyi's approach is based on two concepts: 'forms of integration' and 'supporting structures'. The first comprise reciprocity, redistribution and exchange and are defined as follows: 'forms of integration thus designate the institutionalized movements through which the elements of the economic process – from material resources and labour to the transportation, storage, and distribution of goods – are connected' (1977, p. 35). The supporting structures are the equivalent of what I have defined as the socio-organizational factors underlying the relations of reciprocity and redistribution. According to Polanyi, 'the supporting structures, their basic organization, and their validation spring from the societal sphere' (1977, p. 37). The question is why exchange, defined as a movement 'between any two dispersed or random points in the system' (p. 36), is in need of a supporting structure. Polanyi's answer is that 'exchange, as a form of integration, is dependent on the presence of a market system, an institutional pattern which, contrary to common assumptions, does not originate in random actions of exchange' (p. 37). This answer is unconvincing, and not only because it breaks up the analogy with the other two concepts in as much as the socio-organizational form is included in the definition of reciprocity and redistribution but not in that of exchange. No symmetry or hierarchy can exist without an organizational system, while chance is the contrary of such a system. The answer is also unconvincing because it ends by reducing a conceptual tool to an existing reality which it is supposed to explain. The fact that a diffused system of exchange does not exist outside of social regulations cannot be introduced into an abstract model that is by definition incompatible with them. On the other hand, it is precisely the historical analysis carried out by Polanyi, and others, that demonstrates that there is no need to invent an impossible independent social structure supporting the market to explain its forms of embeddedness. It is enough to combine changes in the other two forms of sociality. If families, different community systems, associations, the state and trade unions, all typical of industrial societies, did not exist, exchange would not be regulated but neither would a market society exist. What Polanyi considers as the market's social institutions can be traced back to several important socio-organizational factors of the associative type. Polanyi's mistake lies in the fact that he transplants the micro-anthropological concept of redistribution into a macro-social analysis and, as a consequence, overlooks the continuity between socio-organizational factors, especially of the associative kind, and redistributive processes. This continuity is, on the contrary, fundamental for all macro-social approaches.

All the solutions which accept the idea of market self-regulation cannot avoid the need also to conceptualize regulation by exogenous factors. Consequently, the very concept of market ends up by playing the dual role of 'organizer' and 'organized'. To put it a different way, this is not simply a play on words, it is a matter of defining one of the organizing factors of contemporary society, often considered the most important in societies called 'free market' societies, as subject in turn to being organized by external factors.

The concept of reciprocity and its applicability to the industrial age

The abstract concept of market exchange is as such incompatible with forms of social organization while in reality systems of market exchange, understood both as structures and as series of actions, are highly social-ized. As we saw, this question has given rise to a set of solutions that are all conceptually inadequate because they attribute sociality to elements inherent in the concept of market. Whether in the structural versions of Marx, Durkheim and Polanyi or in the Weberian-style methodology of action or in the structural-functionalist synthesis, the concept of market becomes a monstrosity, in part an abstract construction and in part a realistic description where the latter negates the former. The starting-point for overcoming this impasse is the interplay of the three sets of variables which I began to illustrate in section 1. In order to continue, it is necessary to clarify how the concepts of reciprocity and redistribution function as research tools for not only a micro-social but also a macro-social analysis.[21]

An anthropological approach is useful as a starting-point because it allows us to identify a typology of social relations that is significant both in terms of content and in terms of organizational logic or its absence. It is a question of adapting the concepts formulated to serve micro-analysis to make them compatible with an approach oriented to the macro-analysis of social organization. Market exchange has already been discussed sufficiently. Before moving on to reciprocity, I want to discard explicitly the possibility that passing from a micro- to a macro-approach entails, on the one hand, losing the social-organizational significance of the concept and, on the other, neglecting other possible pure typologies of social relations that refer to different organizational systems.[22]

The question of the loss of socio-organizational significance lies at the heart of the translation of the two concepts into sociological terms. That of neglecting other pure typologies is, in my view, resolved by the discussion below in which the concept of redistribution is homologized in principle with that of associative relationship. I agree with Weber that on a purely conceptual level there are no other relationships than associative or communal ones.[23]

Reciprocity is a type of social relation that only has meaning within an organizational system, because exchange is not concluded in a single act, transactions are potentially inequitable and the commitment to reciprocity is vague or, at most, implicit.[24] For this reason, reciprocity refers to forms of social organization involving a varying but always limited number of individuals who, at the very least, know specifically of each other's existence and engage in more or less frequent personal contact. Both in the case of reciprocity and in that of association the sense of the social relationship is given by different types of common interests, and this is reflected in the underlying form of social organization. To take this distinction to its extreme limit, one could say that whereas in reciprocity the defence of a group interest requires some members to make individual sacrifices, which may be compensated for by other members in different ways and at different times, associative relations advance the interests of all the members of an association and defend them against those who are not members. The difference becomes evident, that is to say, less prone to assuming a mixed meaning, if two examples from opposite ends of the spectrum are considered. The common interest of the family assumes a meaning independently of its members' individual interests and involves unequal sacrifices and exchanges. The common interest of the trade union is not separate from that of its members and whenever some of them systematically benefit more than others from trade union action, this weakens the organization and can in the long run lead to its break-up. It is precisely for this motive that Weber holds associative relationships to be founded upon rational actions: an actor directly defends his individual interest in an action whose means can be measured against its ends or an absolute value. On the other hand, communal relationships are founded upon irrational actions: an actor does not defend his own direct interests but those of the community.[25]

The question of the group interest having priority over the immediate interests of individuals constitutes the core of the concept of reciprocity as a factor of social organization. Also derived from this is the fact that the interaction between reciprocal and market tensions is substantially different from that between association and market tensions. We are here moving on to a level of analysis where pure concepts no longer exist but are transformed into instruments for interpreting a complex and thus mixed reality. An important example will clarify this point. Consider the difference between the socio-economic logic of a family business, in which the factor of reciprocity is predominant, and that of a large enterprise, mainly organized according to associative factors, such as obtaining maximum profit and the institutionalized conflict between the interests of the enterprise and those of the workers. Studies of family farming have highlighted many elements in this difference.[26] Unfortunately, during the period when the market paradigm prevailed unconditionally, what emerged from these studies was more often put down to the exceptional nature of agriculture than taken up as a suitable starting-point from which to build a different model of the interaction between industrial growth and socio-organizational factors. More recently, light has begun to be shed on elements of this hidden interaction through the attention paid to ethnic entrepreneurship, self-provisioning and the success achieved by more community-based variants of capitalism such as that of Japan or the 'Third Italy', as the centre and north-east of the country is called.

Lastly, it is worth referring to the question of the multiplicity and variety of reciprocal systems and to the power relations within them. It is evident that each individual is involved in many different and changing systems of reciprocity, from the cohabiting family to the kinship network, from one or more circles of friends to the neighbourhood or village system, from the firm where one works or the school where one studies to companions at work or school. These systems may be more or less strong and more or less rich in resources, in the sense of being able to subordinate immediate individual interests to those of the system itself. Systems rich in resources are also stronger for reasons based on an indirect application of Weberian rationality in that the possibility of more substantial compensation is evident. But the reverse is not true: a poor and socially isolated family is still a strong system with few resources. Reciprocal systems may be voluntary (friends) or partly involuntary (the family). This variety is important and differs in different times and societies and under different conditions. As far as regards historical processes, I take the opportunity in chapter 3 to discuss the weakening of the local community and the parallel strengthening of family solidarity during the course of industrialization in several countries in Western Europe. It is clear that a high degree of geographical mobility tends to lessen involvement in reciprocal networks. Emigration, on the other hand, can be a source of new, potentially rich, networks, as is the case with ethnic entrepreneurship.

In as much as they are socio-organizational contexts, reciprocal systems are by definition systems of power. The family and the question of patriarchy are the themes relating to industrial societies that have been studied most. It is, though, important to point out that even in terms of power reciprocal contexts are markedly different from associative ones. Not only is a father-boss different from a foreman, but his power tends to change, also in different directions, with the growth of technologically advanced modern family businesses or with the urbanization of the poor rural strata in underdeveloped countries and the development of the informal sector. In the same way, managers and foremen have a different kind of power, exercised in different ways, in more community-oriented enterprises than in those characterized more by associative divisions, as shown by Dore's recent comparative studies of Japan and other advanced capitalist countries (1986; 1987).

The diversity and the changes in the power structure of reciprocal systems is both connected to the meaning and importance of their common goals and to some general social conditions. In theory, it is true that reciprocal patterns of social organization are further removed from individual autonomy or self-interest than associative ones, as pointed out in Weber's classification of social relationships, where the communal type are seen as irrational because they do not relate directly to the interests of the individual, or in Durkheim's political project of transferring the domestic domain to the corporations. For this reason, the power structure of organizations based on reciprocity can be extremely authoritarian. Take the example of the original legal structure of the Roman family where the *pater familias* had the right of life and death over all the members, including adult children. Conversely, the power structure can be extremely loose and democratically distributed among members; this occurs in voluntary networks that are relatively less binding in socio-economic terms. The best example is that of a present-day network of friends. But, in this case too, where the objective is more significant, it is also likely that the power structure will change and become more authoritarian. An instance is that of a group of friends who decide to go on a long holiday together involving difficult conditions, such as sailing or a wildlife adventure. A much more unequal power structure will probably emerge. One of the friends will act naturally as a leader and those least able to cope with the difficult conditions will to some extent be denigrated and dominated by the others. This may eventually lead to a partial or total discontinuation of the friendship. Take a second, even more striking, example: The power structure of a group of teenage friends changes completely when the group becomes transformed into a street gang. Not only does the structure become authoritarian and hierarchical with a leader and deputy leaders set above the rest, but it may possibly lose its voluntary character. When this happens members who try to leave the gang are threatened.

Following these considerations, it is clearly a good rule not to idealize reciprocal social organizations as generally less authoritarian or more balanced structures of power than large associative ones.[27] However, reciprocal patterns of social organization are more open, though only in the industrial age, to changing their internal power structure in order to accommodate an increasing need for individual autonomy and self-fulfilment than large associative ones, at least under certain social conditions. This is a point that the classical tradition in sociology has entirely overlooked. The best example are the transformations, not yet complete but none the less radical, that have occurred in the family power structure in the advanced capitalist countries, particularly of social groups with average or above-average incomes. Age and gender asymmetry has substantially decreased and the scope of the organization is more often negotiated than dictated by a single member; individual aspirations and vocations are taken into consideration even when they appear to be in conflict with previous assumptions about the perspective and scope of the family.

The greater flexibility of reciprocal networks in accommodating individual autonomy compared to large associative organizations is not a paradox, considering their more manageable size or, in other words, the fact that individuals are closer to the decision-making apparatus and can better negotiate with and influence it. Correspondingly, the decision-making apparatus may be more receptive to individual needs and aspirations. This flexibility and receptivity is found only in societies in the industrial age when the diffusion of competitive behaviour and the parallel emergence of individual self-consciousness in a comprehensively changing social context, dominated by associative socio-organizational patterns, leads to the dismantling of the social order based on a strict subordination of individual interests to those of groups based on reciprocity. Furthermore, this process is conditioned by the fact that the opportunities and options available to such groups for attaining their goals must not be too constraining or limiting. This is particularly visible in the case of the family. Renegotiation of the power structure is much more likely in the case of families with a full range of opportunities than in that of families condemned to struggle for bare survival.[28]

Associative socialities and processes of redistribution in the industrial age

The homologizing of the anthropological concept of redistribution and the sociological one of associative factors cannot be fully accomplished. From the viewpoint of macro-social analysis, processes of redistribution do not constitute a system of social organization independent of associative and reciprocal factors. The redistributive process is, like the market, regulated by the complex and changing interaction between the two socio-organizational systems. In this sense, to reduce redistribution conceptually to the associative system is to adopt a flawed approach, because it excludes the role played by the system of reciprocity in orienting the logic of redistributive processes. On the other hand, making these processes into an independent factor of social organization is a serious error, made by Polanyi in his transplanting of the concept of redistribution. Although this conceptual operation is not entirely successful, I shall try to give it plausibility by showing that the logic of association takes on a meaning only if related to the processes of redistribution and that in all types of industrial society the latter are mainly inspired by organizational principles of the associative kind.

Within an anthropological approach, redistribution takes place in a closed and limited organizational context. In the typical phenomena which anthropologists study – primitive economies and societies, tribes and isolated villages – the dominant socio-organizational factor is reciprocity. A varying share of resources is regularly withdrawn from the consumption taking place within the narrow contexts of reciprocity in which these resources are produced and redistributed by the community's political chiefs. The latter are selected according to different systems of power, which are however always consistent with those that originate in reciprocal systems, often involving an interweaving of patriarchy and gerontocracy. The redistribution is carried out following rules laid down by tradition but which, in general, reflect three requirements: to put off consumption of excess resources in anticipation of periods of scarcity; to privilege and underscore the power structure; and to assist community members who are not sufficiently protected by the narrow system of reciprocity, such as widowers, childless old people, invalids, orphans and so on. In the micro-perspective of the anthropological approach, this form of exchange takes on a significance different from that of reciprocity. For scholars interested in macro-social analysis, it concerns only a broader sphere of reciprocity compared to a more restricted one.

The question of processes of redistribution has a radically different significance in industrial society. The latter is a dense society characterized by increasingly complex forms of the division of labour and by the spread of different kinds of exchange relations and, therefore, of the casual interaction between strangers. The final goals of a part of the redistributive process are not different, just wider and more complex; it is the underlying socio-organizational context that is substantially different, just as the ways of producing the resources are different. In fact, it is the industrial methods of producing resources that pave the way for a new redistribution of the product between the different social actors involved in its creation; these are not only capital and labour but also different types of workers and of representatives of capital. Both redistribution by the state, the one that still resembles the anthropological process in some of its goals, and private redistribution, can be controlled by socio-organizational factors of reciprocity only to a limited degree. Hence the expansion and growing importance of associative factors.

Associative sociality takes on a socio-economic meaning only under two conditions: first, that there are horizontal common interests to defend and, second, that the defence of these interests has some effect on processes of redistribution, whether public or private.[29]

The social sciences have accumulated a considerable store of knowledge on the parallel growth of associative sociality and the industrial economy and on the meaning of these socio-organizational factors relative to processes of redistribution. I do not have in mind only the Marxist line of class struggle and the struggle for power, but also the Durkheimian vision of organic solidarity and Weber's theory of rationalization. It is important for the persistent role of reciprocal factors within distributive processes no longer to be overshadowed by other factors; this also applies to the non-cohesion and socio-organizational mixes that the different associative and reciprocal systems continue to produce in response to the different social tensions created by the presence and spread of market-competitive behaviour. For all these reasons, I hold that the conceptual coupling of associative factors and redistribution is plausible as a simplification and as a way to overcome the error of Polanyi, but only on condition that the analysis focuses sufficiently on reciprocal factors also with regard to processes of redistribution.

In concluding this section, an observation must be made on the question of power inside associative contexts and on that of their presumed or real monopoly of the representation of political interests and, therefore, of power in society as a whole. Generally speaking, my position is close to the Weberian line of interpretation with regard to both the first and the second questions, partly because on these questions Weber does not privilege rationality at all. The idea that associative contexts always express a power structure founded on the best possible defence of the interests at stake is decidedly simplistic and does not take into account the fact that reciprocal relations develop within associative contexts. Hence the sundry forms of nepotism, not only or principally within the family, and a whole series of complications which are usually hardly considered.

The question of the representative nature of associative contexts with respect to power in general is even more complicated. I will confine myself to two questions. In the first place, it is evident that some interests, and so the associative contexts that represent them, are privileged compared to others in different historical types of industrial society. The question is so important as to play a significant role in classifying societies. Capitalist societies are held to be such because they privilege business interests, socialists are held to be such because they privilege the interests of the working class. This first level is still a superficial one: in order to understand the political system, it is necessary to examine how the imbalance in the representation of interests works in practice.[30] At this point there emerges once again a complex interweaving between associative factors and those of reciprocity.

Lastly, it seems to me that in reality almost all the political systems of the industrial age have equipped themselves to represent and therefore to govern associative interests, which are divided and competing for the redistribution of resources. Reciprocal systems come into play as elements inside the associative organizational context: nepotism and networks of influence in the political class or in the bureaucracy. Fragmented societies are characterized by the growing importance of reciprocal contexts that interfere with associative loyalties. The question of the future of socio-political systems concerns precisely the kinds of reaction to this transform-ation. It is not only a matter of the outcomes of the experiments in democracy in Eastern European countries, but also of the transformation of politics in advanced capitalist countries and in underdeveloped ones. I shall return to this idea in chapter 7.

4 A CRITICAL CONFRONTATION WITH CURRENT INTERPRETATIONS OF INDUSTRIAL CHANGE

Introduction

There are many interpretations of the nature of industrial societies and what lies in store for them in the future. During the analysis of related problems in the following chapters, several contributions are considered that have dealt specifically with the labour market, occupational struc-ture, life strategies and various practices of social reproduction, the different processes of informalization and explanations of changes in social stratification. At the same time, I believe it is important to discuss briefly some interpretations of society from a theoretical angle so as to enrich and clarify my approach.

The making of general observations on such wide-ranging problems is a hazardous affair. They are worth putting forward only in order to clarify the sense of the contemporary debate surrounding the prospects of industrial societies. Many of the interpretations of current societies are different variations of a common vision: the growing complexity of homogeneous social aggregations, whether structures or behavioural systems, which are divided but organized along clearly associative lines such as social classes, mass political parties, nation-states, big industrial undertakings and so on. This vision is in part a reflection of real changes taking place in advanced industrial societies, both capitalist and socialist, and in part it is the result of errors induced by the influence of the market paradigm. The latter has underrated both the role played by several social factors and the crucial importance of the socio-economic interdependence of the processes that characterize change in different societies. The first of these errors has been to concentrate attention on associative factors to the neglect of reciprocal factors. Furthermore, associative factors are frequently misinterpreted as being a product or function of industrial growth. Thus, a decisively important phenomenon has been overlooked: the area of tension between the spread of competitive behaviour and increasingly accentuated forms of individualism and the development of more and more structured contexts of sociality, which, in theory, increasingly suffocate and work against the unrestricted engaging in competition by individuals. The real situation in this area cannot be understood without taking into account interrelationships at a global level, and this leads us to the second error of vision. To put it plainly, if only the experience of societies defined as developed are analysed in terms of autonomous worlds, then growing individualism and competition and expanding socialization appear to be compatible to a large degree. Persistent inequality or poverty or conflict, which are more and more taking on institutional forms, appear as functions of an inexorable process of industrial growth. In reality, the theoretically diverging impulses of individualism and sociality reproduce a strong area of contradiction which in the developed countries is mitigated, but only in part, by the resources drawn from underdeveloped countries. For this reason, the big crises and transformations in social orders never occur within a national framework but rather on a worldwide scale.

Many current interpretations have difficulty in giving a convincing explanation for the new features as against those of immediately preceding societies, taken for granted as well-known. My doubts concerning these interpretations are not about terminology but are essentially centred on two limitations of the term 'post', or 'after', which is the most frequent attribute used to label contemporary societies – for example, post-industrial, post-Fordist, post-modern and so on. First, it places an excessive and parodistic emphasis on the difference between 'before' and 'after', which undervalues both the existence in preceding societies of a whole series of features also typical of present societies and the significance of continuity within change. Second, the use of this term often masks the inability to understand in what way contemporary societies are different from previous ones. The point is that, to a certain degree, the passing of time always brings about change in the nature of social formations. Such change is not linear or evolutionary and cannot often be defined as revolutionary. Social change in the industrial age is intense, that is to say, significant social transformation takes place within a shorter time-span than in pre-industrial societies. Re-stated provocatively, the 'post' societies or 'service' societies or 'disorganized capitalism' can be said to be unconvincing as explanatory terms because they describe real changes which are not, however, particularly significant relative to the dominant characteristics of contemporary societies. Marx would say that capitalism has not been overcome; Durkheim that we have not achieved or gone beyond the need for organic solidarity; and Weber would not see a new age characterized by diverse tensions within the processes of rationaliz-ation. In my opinion, the limits of current interpretations still lie to a large extent in the fact that they have not freed themselves from the paradigm of the self-regulating market by criticizing it; as a consequence, they do not concentrate on socio-organizational factors and on their discontinuous and varied transformation throughout the entire industrial age and in those societies affected, to varying extents and in diverse ways, by the tensions deriving from the spread of competitive market behaviour. Having said this, I shall attempt to develop my brief dis-cussions of current literature on the subject along positively critical theoretical lines, limited to outlining the approach adopted in this book.

The world economy and the critique of the development paradigm

The first area of current literature I want to discuss is of the group based around the Fernand Braudel Center and the journal *Review*. The criticisms mentioned above do not apply to the contributions of this group. They have concentrated on the history of industrialization as a process, emphasizing in particular the complex and changing forms of socio-economic interdependence at the level of the world economy. The specific problems that make discussion of their contributions worthwhile concern the critique of the development paradigm.

In its more radical versions, for example Rostow (1960), the develop-ment paradigm rejects the idea of interdependence between development and underdevelopment and attributes to all countries the same possibility of development and attributes to all countries the same possibility of development passing through more or less identical phases. By focusing on historical and changing interdependence in different periods, the World Economy Group has traced a historical map of regions and countries which, unlike that of dependence theory, is not structured according to a twofold division between development and underdevelop-ment but a threefold one instead: core, semi-periphery and periphery. This structure is important because it allows the passage of several countries from one condition to another during the discontinuous history of the industrial age, an explanation that is difficult to ground in the development/underdevelopment dichotomy. This difficulty arises when one has to explain how a dependent country, that is one whose market resources are being siphoned off, can free itself from this subordinate condition and establish the relations of dominance necessary for starting a belated process of development.

Despite my substantial agreement with the World Economy version of global socio-economic interdependence, I almost always use the development/underdevelopment dichotomy for reasons of simplicity; the only exceptions are those cases in which the concept of semi-periphery is indispensable for explaining the structure of socio-organizational processes and the way they change. Within the analytical framework of my approach, it is important to point out that it may be possible to hypothesize for some historical periods a situation in which the semi-periphery is characterized by significant combinations of market tensions regulated by reciprocal factors: small businesses, stable and protective industrial networks, family entrepreneurship, etc.[31]

The research carried out by the World Economy Group has led to a devasting critique of the development paradigm. Exemplary in this respect is the particularly radical contribution of Wallerstein (1983). He maintains that the historical process of industrialization has failed completely to bring about that progress and those forms of emancipation from material needs and poverty that even Marx held to be a positive achievement of capitalism. On the contrary, the standard of living enjoyed by the vast majority of the world's population has taken a decisive turn for the worse. Wallerstein's thesis is not motivated by a romantic longing for the lost world of the past but is, rather, the inevitable outcome of a line of thinking that I share. This is that the violent destruction, above all in the periphery, of various social systems of subsistence for the purpose of integrating them into the global market economy leads to a worsening of living standards for most of the population, a situation which industrial society has shown a historical incapacity to compensate for or even reverse. Those involved are, first of all, the huge masses of the world's population in the periphery, but extensive social strata in the advanced capitalist countries also continue to be affected. This contribution can also be incorporated usefully into my particular approach because it works precisely on the two interconnected levels, the national or local and the global, of the typical contradiction in the process of industrialization between competition and individualism, on one side, and forms of socialization or factors of social organization on the other.

The world economy and industrial history in terms of long waves

The theme of the phases of industrial history, understood as a discontinuous process of change, is an indispensable instrument for my analysis. The theory of long waves formulated by the World Economy Group is especially convincing for three reasons: it is structured on a worldwide scale; it is not economistic, that is to say, it allows the transformation of contexts of sociality to be taken into account; and it is largely compatible with partial and sectoral periodizations specifically referred to herein, in particular that related to the forms of segmentation of the labour market (Edwards et al, 1982) and that connected with the development and crisis of Fordist societies (Lash and Urry, 1987).

To make discussion of this question brief, I refer exclusively to one of Arrighi's (1986) specific contributions rather than to the full debate. Furthermore, where convenient, I have changed Arrighi's terminology in order to accommodate the concepts of social factors introduced above.

In the words of the author:

> Long waves are primarily a reflection of the temporal unevenness of competitive processes in the capitalist world economy . . . unlike all previous social systems, capitalism tends to generate innovations that break up whatever customary order has been, or is being, established at any given time. This tendency heightens competitive pressures which, in turn, call forth new customary orders. (Arrighi, 1986, p. 1)

One of the main inputs to this interpretation of industrial history are the economic data on the capitalist business cycle viewed in terms of Kondratieff waves. These data form the quantitative indicator of the cyclical process of transformation of what Arrighi calls the interenterprise system (IES). The quantitative figures on the business cycle then need to be filled out with qualitative historical explanations not only of the changing features of the IES but also of the role of the other two interlinked systems: the interstate system (ISS), reflecting the balance of political power and the degree of political protection and competition at a global level, and the household system, reflecting the various and changing ways of reproducing different kinds of wage-labour on a worldwide scale. Not including transformations in the household system, a simplified diagram of the periodization of industrial history is shown in table 1.1. I also leave out any specific discussion of the historical transformations of the household system, as this will form the argument of chapter 3.

The waves of the business cycle as defined by Kondratieff are made up of three stages:

> A phases are characterized by the prevalence of specifically developed 'customary arrangements that buttress relations of co-operation and complementarity . . .'; B phases are characterized by high levels of '. . . struggles that bring into the open relations of competition and substitution'; and 'Transitions from B to A phases can be accounted for by the fact that "excessive" competition sooner or later calls forth countervailing tendencies which, over time,

crystallize in a new set of to-become customary arrangements. Transitions from A to B phases, in turn, can be accounted for by the fact that customary arrangements reflect truces in the competitive struggle but do not eliminate the tendency for surpluses to accumulate unevenly among enterprises. Sooner or later, this uneven accumulation generates a new round of competition that progressively destroys the existing pattern of input-output relations and brings into existence new ones.' (Ibid., p. 4)

The historico-economic data on business cycles confirm the trends for the four Kondratieff cycles shown in table 1.1; but by themselves they are not sufficient to explain the qualitative meaning and the discontinuities of the cyclical trend. The historical process of industrialization can only be understood by starting from a more detailed qualitative analysis of the balances and imbalances that develop within the complex interweaving of the three systems on a global scale.

In stage A, economic competition takes place within a context of socialization that has become relatively stablized on the two fronts of the typical modes of reproducing the labour force and of the political power relations at a world level. The latter guarantee that 'core' enterprises will have access to additional resources so that they can continue operating, even though the stability of productive networks and growing social regulation reduce the level of free competition. In this sense, Arrighi draws attention to an important and often underrated question, which coincides with what I have indicated about the changing importance of systems of reciprocity both inside enterprises and in the relations between them: 'As commodity producers, capitalist enterprises are just as keen as states and households in establishing customary arrangements that ensure stability of operations' (ibid., p. 3). A phase of unbalanced growth occurs, but one guaranteed by relatively high cohesion between competition and socialization and within the different forms of associative and reciprocal socialization. The process of unbalanced growth leads to the build-up of tensions, if only because it has to be continually fed with resources from outside, which are obtained by market relations penetrating into areas of economic subsistence on an increasingly global scale in order to keep the relationship between competition and sociality under control in the core areas.

When the compensatory effects in the specific historical order within each stage A die out, the imbalance between competition and historical forms of sociality explodes into an economic, political and social crisis. The result is that stage B is characterized by heightened economic competition due to the instability of economic relations, excessive forms

Table 1.1 *Kondratieff cycles in industrial history*

Period	A 1787 1790	B 1810 1817	A 1844 1851	B 1870 1875	A 1890 1896	B 1914 1920	A 1939 1945	B 1967 1973
Kondratieff	(K1	) (K2	) (	K3	) (	K4	)	
Political leadership	British --------------------------> None > USA -------------------------->							
Economic leadership	British --------------------------> Mult-> USA --------------------------> Mult-iple							
Economic revolution primary:	Industrial --------------------------> Organizational -------------------------->							
secondary:	Transport --> Information -------->							

Source: Arrighi, 1986, p. 13 (reproduced by permission of the Fernand Braudel Center, State University of New York at Binghamton)

of rationalization and the struggle to find new ways to mitigate and control the tensions existing between higher levels of economic competition and more adequate forms of socialization.

The process of cyclical transformation, but with marked qualitative discontinuities, takes place more and more on a worldwide scale in the sense that market relations are imposed even on the remotest subsistence economies. Further, it involves a whole series of questions, ranging from the politico-military relations between states to modes of survival and the different standards of living and life-styles of the various strata of the population, to the technical conditions of production. None of these aspects can be fully understood if taken in isolation.

There is no point in looking here at the historical analysis suggested by the theory of long waves since this is discussed in later chapters. Of interest, however, are Arrighi's conclusions on the prospects for contemporary societies, given the impasse that characterizes stage B of the fourth Kondratieff cycle. According to him, the crucial question for which it is difficult to find an answer is: 'What prevents a new breed of capitalist enterprises from exploiting the reserves of unemployed, non-wage, and part-life-time wage labor that the Organizational Revolution created or left untapped in the peripheral and semiperipheral zones of the world-economy?' (Ibid., pp. 31–2). The question is a difficult one because the historical process of industrialization has reached a high level of non-cohesion between socialization and individual competitive behaviour. At present, this is increasingly reflected in the fact that systems of reciprocity attach more importance to the individual and his self-expression than associative systems. What is required, in theory, to deal with this impasse is a volume of resources which it is difficult to imagine peripheral and semi-peripheral areas being able to supply. The primary reason for this is that, in those areas too, survival is guaranteed to a rising extent only by re-forming systems of defensive reciprocity, like the informal urban sector. On the one hand, these systems help to preserve a certain portion of the labour supply at very low wages but, on the other, they hinder the further expansion of the system of exploitation and incrementing the value of capital. This seems to be a closed circle from which not even the limitless rise in the external debt of underdeveloped countries is able to provide an escape, at least under present conditions. Or, as Arrighi concludes,

> capitalism in the age of the Organizational Revolution has produced in the peripheral and semiperipheral zones of the world-economy an environment hostile to further capitalist penetration. Caught between rising job rents in the core zone and a hostile environment

in the peripheral zone, capitalist accumulation may be approaching
its historical limits. The next Kondratieff might well be the last.
(ibid. p. 32).

The conflict-ridden impact of individualism and 'consumerism'

The question of the mounting tension in advanced capitalist countries
between the automony of the individual on the one hand, and capitalist
growth and forms of socialization on the other, has recently been examined in works by two neo-Marxists, O'Connor and Gorz. Before looking
at what they say, something must be noted on the question of alienation
in Marx.

For Marx, alienation is a phenomenon typical of capitalist relations of
production in so far as the worker is separated from control over the
means of production and, as a consequence, 'alienated' from the content
and product of labour. Alienation is the typical form of socialization of
labour in the capitalist era, but it is also founded on the principle of
freedom and individual autonomy in that its precondition is the opportunity represented by the free sale of an individual's labour power in the
capitalist market. In other words, the separation of the workers from the
means of production is reflected both in the alienation of the conditions
of socialization and in the freeing of individuals from a social order which
did not permit the emergence of individual identities. Thus, for Marx,
alienation is a highly contradictory condition and the principal expression
of the permanent tension between the autonomy of the individual and
forms of socialization. As Marx sees it, alternative forms of socialization
built through class consciousness and the collective praxis of the working
class are indispensable for overcoming this tension in socialism. In this
sense, Marx's solution is not radically different from that of Durkheim,
who sees in the development of associative structures of co-operation a
way to further the individual's independence and freedom. On this
question, both O'Connor and Gorz put forward solutions that differ to
a large extent from Marx's.

The question of the contradiction between individualism and socialization in advanced capitalist societies is at the centre of two important
contributions by O'Connor (1984; 1987). He focuses on the USA and
on the problem of the crisis in capitalist accumulation, intended in a
broader sense than the mere theorization of economic crisis. The tensions
that build up between individualism and consumerism, and the extensive
and overbureaucratized associative patterns of social organization, are
singled out as the key factors in the crisis.

In this respect, the USA provides an especially interesting example because these tensions are particularly strong for two reasons. First, the long period of economic and political hegemony exerted by the USA over the world economy during the last fifty years has supplied it with enough external resources to compensate for the widening gap between an accentuated individualism and marked patterns of associative organization. Second, the persistent importance of a diversified range of ethnic minorities has meant a dualistic organization of survival that is not supported by a wide-ranging welfare state. The white majority increasingly involved in the associative forms of socialization has been able to rely on private services offered on the market because they receive relatively high wages, which leads to the high cost of labour, while the diverse minorities have relied on various kinds of reciprocal arrangements. Some of them have been more successful and in a position to provide resources to support the reproduction patterns of their particular group, like some Asian minorities involved in ethnic entrepreneurship, and others less so – for example, the black community (see Stack, 1944). From this perspective, the USA has always been a relatively fragmented society with a strong emphasis on individualism counterbalanced by the utilization of abundant external resources and by extremely diversified socialization mixes.

According to O'Connor,[32] the promotion of individualism and consumerism is one of the essential conditions for the development of advanced capitalism, but it is also increasingly contradictory in at least two ways. On the one hand, individualism means high wages and decreasingly flexible conditions in the utilization of the labour force or, at least, a large section of it. On the other, a maturing individual identity becomes increasingly intolerant of the large bureaucratized forms of associative socialization, equally essential for the development of advanced capitalism and, in fact, the other side of the same coin.[33]

With regard to prospects for the future, O'Connor puts forward a solution which is different from the orthodox Marxist one described above. He argues that, in advanced capitalist societies,

> struggles against material and social reification and for 'social individuality' are the most useful weapons at hand to combat the attempt by capital and the state to ideologically construct and politically use the current crisis to restructure economic, political, and social life with the sole purpose of renewed capitalist accumulation, including a new 'long wave' of ideological innovation. (O'Connor, 1984, p. 23)

The problem is to clarify what 'social individuality' is, and why and how it develops, within a framework of compatibility with the concepts of socio-organizational factors introduced in the first sections of this chapter. O'Connor does not give sufficient consideration to interconnections at the level of the world economy. In this sense, the deepening of the contradiction between individualism and forms of socialization and the potential ripening of struggles to assert alternative forms of socialization should be placed in relation to the crisis in the compensatory mechanism financed by external resources transferred from underdeveloped to developed countries. In other words, the resistance of the first to contemporary forms of uneven capitalist penetration is an essential condition for the development and success of struggles and movements in favour of alternative socialization in the second.[34]

Apart from specifying the importance of the conditions of interdependence at the level of the world economy, O'Connor's vision of the emerging trends towards social individuality are compatible with the approach of this book, even though it must be underlined that we are dealing with a preliminary intuition rather than a fully worked-out theory. The emergent alternative forms of socialization are based on parameters of reciprocity that reveal a growing receptivity towards the individual's need for independence and self-fulfilment.[35] According to O'Connor, the current phase in the USA, but also in the other advanced capitalist countries, is characterized by the clash between two alternative models of society/socialization.

> The first was statism and/or corporatism, a kind of 'capitalist collectivism' which emphasized 'reindustrialization'. The second was localism and populism, a kind of 'workers' collectivism' which stressed the theme of 'democracy'. Both were based on new and revived cultural concepts (distorted and real) of the individual as a social entity. (O'Connor 1984, p. 241)

This clash involves also a state of interdependence such that O'Connor points to the fact that

> the ability of 'social individuality' to legitimately compete with 'individualism' in the ideological market-place perversely depended on the development of the vicarious democracy characteristic of corporatism and/or authoritarian versions of social individuality manifest in monopoly state capitalist regimes. (O'Connor, 1984, p. 247)

Gorz's interpretation is similar to the concluding suggestions put forward by O'Connor, at least with regard to the problem of the contradiction between individualism and socialization. The differences are due to Gorz's accentuated dualism which, in my opinion, is an error not only because it overemphasizes some changes in the occupational structure, but even more because it artificially separates situations that are inextricably interdependent.

Gorz (1982; 1988) interprets advanced capitalist societies as divided on two fronts: that of alienated labour and the associative forms of socialization, increasingly bureaucratized and repressive towards individual self-fulfilment, and that of self-valorization activities including non-work, casual work, self-provision and the production of direct use-values. Despite his insistence on the fact that this latter front is local, communal or family-based in nature, he fails to consider the complex interweaving of socialization that also involves this front in forms of reciprocity, and, furthermore, sees the growing importance of this front as leading to the establishment of a non-society, that is, of ways of living freed from the constraints of socialization.

The fundamental steps in the development of Gorz's argument are as follows. He starts from the idea that the contradiction between individual autonomy and forms of socialization is not typical of capitalist societies but rather of all social forms based on industrial production.[36] Within this perspective, Gorz points out that socialist industrialization based on the control exercised by large bureaucratic apparatuses cannot eliminate the tension between individual autonomy and forms of socialization. As a consequence, he raises reasonable doubts about the orthodox Marxist solution of the emancipation from alienation through the associative praxis of the working class.

According to Gorz, advanced capitalist societies bring about a social realignment in as much as they are decreasingly able to promote social integration through stable forms of socialized and alienated labour. The result is the growing number of individuals who are excluded from having long-term employment as the main reference point in their lives. These individuals form a non-class in the sense that they do not undergo social integration by means of strengthened priority interests created by their common work situation.[37] Gorz specifies that 'the term "non-class" should not, of course, be taken to imply the absence of social relations and social organisation. It is used to designate the process of subtraction from the social sphere of an area of individual sovereignity beyond economic rationality and external constraint' (Gorz, 1982, p. 75). He seems conscious of the existence of a complex interwoven mix of socialization, which gets lost, however, in his conceptualization of a 'dual society' (ibid., pp. 90–104). Thus the sphere of alienation and associative bureaucratized socialization is seen to persist even while the sphere of non-

alienation and the number of people who privilege individual self-fulfilment beyond the control of associative forms of socialization are increasing.[38]

Although Gorz is apparently aware of the dialectical interconnection
between the two processes, his dualistic approach does not allow him to
work out a realistic analysis of the field of tension in terms of the
cohesion/non-cohesion between different forms of socialization that are,
in part, alternatives and, in part, complementary. He does not see that
there is no clear division between individuals predisposed to autonomy,
the neo-proletarians, and those subjected to the socialization/alienation
of work or between different spheres of social life. His thesis is incompatible with the evidence which shows that in some social settings the
maximum opportunity for self-provisioning is typical of those who are
integrated best into the associative system: the ones who have a stable
permanent job which remains a reference point and fundamental interest
in their lives (see Pahl, 1984).

Lastly, it is worth looking briefly at Gorz's interpretation of the modifications in the occupational structure. He is convinced that the numerical
decrease in workers employed for life in the large manufacturing and
tertiary systems also fosters a decline in associative loyalty and in the
alienated identification of an individual with his work.

The question is anything but simple. First of all, it must be stressed
that stable waged employment in the large manufacturing and tertiary
systems has always been less important numerically than in terms of the
structuring of industrial society. As a consequence, the evidence of a
reduction in numbers should be seen in the light of the significance that
such a decline may assume for the structuring of late industrial societies.
The increase in casual jobs, occupational instability, forms of self-employment and jobs in small businesses is not in itself sufficient to explain the
decreasing importance of work in structuring the identity of individuals.
It is a matter of seeing which are the subjects who do not identify with
their work and what this signifies in terms of the processes of socialization.

Not all present transformations confirm the hypothesis about the
decreasing importance of work in structuring social identity. In particular, the rise in the percentage of female workers can be interpreted as
leading in the opposite direction. Even where jobs are part-time, de-
skilled and provide a supplementary income, they play a more important
role in defining female identity than the complete absence of a direct
identification with paid work found in full-time housewives. Another
example is that of the prolonging of job instability for young people,
where the difficulty of finding a job does not necessarily demotivate all
of them. Finally, this question is even more problematical in the case of

the self-employed, the semi-self-employed or those working in small firms or in the new vertically disintegrated industrial systems. All these forms of work are strictly complementary to the restructuring of the overall occupational system and, in this sense, they cannot be considered as unrelated to the drop in employment in the large enterprises. At the same time, it is possible that the significance of work in terms of identifying with it is strong, at least for some of these workers. The question should therefore be formulated in terms of change in the socialization mix, and consequently, also of transformation in the tension between individuality and socialization, but along more complex lines than Gorz's dual vision of society.

Considerations on the 'after' societies

The same question crops up with regard to the many interpretations that put the emphasis on the 'after industrial' or 'post-Fordist' societies. It is important to understand to what extent these transitions modify the system of structuring society in terms of socialization mix and of the tensions between societies and individual competitive behaviour. Here I would like to dwell on two points: the passing beyond a stage defined as modern or Fordist and characterized by the predominant spread of associative socio-organizational factors, and the impact of the growing dominance of service employment. The two points are interconnected in the sense that the ways in which associative organization develops under-lie the growth in services. The latter, in turn, forms one of the elements in the crisis affecting the associative system of organization.

The latest writings have stressed in various ways two important changes in the history of advanced capitalist societies during this century:[39] the development of a more and more organized capitalism despite divisions reflecting mainly conflicts of interests within the associative system; and the fact that from the end of the 1960s this long-term trend has been interrupted and partially reversed, giving way to a more heterogeneous social order. If judged solely from the standpoint of the internal cohesion of its associative factors, such an order comes across as a form of disorganization. For the sake of brevity, I refer directly only to the important contribution by Lash and Urry (1987).

These authors document extensively the way in which organized capitalism matured along different but convergent paths in five countries (Britain, France, Germany, the United States and Sweden). They concentrate almost exclusively on the development of the associative system of organizing society. In this respect, their comparative analysis is useful but not fully satisfactory. Since, for them, social organization coincides with associative patterns, little attention is devoted to the transformation of reciprocal factors and to their persistent and changing organizational role within different complex mixed systems. Consequently, the increasing importance of new and old instances of reciprocity is not viewed in terms of a changing organizational form but rather of a disorganized system. A different historical model of organizing capitalism where patterns of reciprocity maintain a relatively greater relevance, such as in Japan, is not at all considered as a possible variant of industrial development both during the organizational age and beyond. Lash and Urry argue that

> it is necessary to distinguish between organization 'at the top' and organization 'at the bottom'. Organization at the top here includes, for example, the concentration of industry, increasing inter-articulation of banks, industry and the state, and cartel formation; organization 'at the bottom' includes, for example, the development of national trade union bodies, working-class political parties, and the welfare state. (Ibid., p. 4)[40]

An important limit to the contribution by Lash and Urry lies in the underestimation of the international conditions which allowed the expansion of organizational patterns in different ways in the five countries. As already stated above, economic growth accompanied by progressively reinforced regulation is inexplicable within isolated economies. The two processes are rendered compatible only through the appropriation of external resources. Also, the conditions under which external resources are appropriated differ in different countries and vary greatly during the different periods of industrial history. Moreover, as argued by Arrighi above, the difficulty in recreating viable conditions of international appropriation must be considered as one of the main elements on which to base an understanding of the present situation. It is not only a question of increasing competition with a small number of so-called newly industrializing countries (NICS) or the supranational interests of a growing number of capitalist corporations, both included by Lash and Urry among the factors promoting disorganizational tendencies. It is also, and mainly, a question of the difficulty in attaining new levels of capitalist penetration due to the resistance encountered in the underdeveloped areas. These new levels are needed in order to maintain cohesion in the advanced capitalist countries between, on the one hand, increasing individual consciousness and diversity and, on the other, the forms of associative socialization capable of keeping this transformation under control.[41]

Lash and Urry document the rise and subsequent decline of associative patterns of social organization on various different fronts, ranging from diverse aspects of economic and financial organization to the development of trade unionism and of class alignment in politics, the organization of the labour market, urbanization, the emergence of the welfare state and of the cultural configuration of modernism. Their idea that we are moving into the age of disorganized capitalism appears to me to be compatible with what I would call the fragmented nature of modern societies, which are not actually disorganized but exhibit a less cohesive mix of associative and reciprocal patterns. They raise various points which are discussed during the course of this book. There are two, however, that are worth looking at here. The first concerns current changes in the structure of politics. The second regards the role of the growing and increasingly heterogeneous service class.

As far as the transformation of politics is concerned, I tend to agree with Lash and Urry that the crux of this question lies in the slow and conflict-ridden decline of the role of the nation-state. This is especially visible today in relation to the restructuring of the welfare state in advanced capitalist societies. They correctly point out that

> because of the salient division between the people and the state much potential support will be diverted into generating less bureau- cratized, more decentralized and in cases more privatized forms as the welfare state of organized capitalism makes way for a much more varied and less centrally organized form of welfare provision in disorganized capitalism. (Ibid., p. 230)

More generally, I agree with their analysis of the destructuring of national politics through three processes: internationalization; decentral- ization and dislocation; and the increasing importance of the service class and of the transformation in the very structure of society (ibid., pp. 300–13). The second and third processes are discussed extensively elsewhere. The first is worth a few words here. For Lash and Urry, internationalization takes place 'from above' in three main ways:

1 The widespread appearance of 'global corporations with an inter- national division of labour and high levels of vertical disintegration' and the parallel 'declining distinctiveness of companies producing fixed products for a given (generally) national market (whether financial or industrial)';

2 'the growth of new circuits of money and banking separate from those of industry which are literally out of control of individual national economic policies'; and

3 'the development of new international state structures, and of modes

of entertainment and culture which transcend individual national societies'. (Ibid., p. 300)

What should also be included is the increasing importance of international interdependence accomplished from below in terms of human existence on a global scale, international public opinion, audio-visual information and multiple contacts between diverse cultures. It is also for this reason that it is difficult to accept the term 'disorganized' as used by Lash and Urry. If we look at the operations of the financial markets or of the new conglomerates, but also at the internationalization of culture, habits, information and human interaction, societies appear to be much more organized today than they have ever been in the past.

I shall now look at the services both in term of employment, that is the appearance of an extensive and heterogeneous service class, and of patterns of consumption that are crucial in determining the quality of life. The importance of this point is undeniable on both fronts, even though I would not define current societies as post-industrial or service societies.

Worldwide job figures confirm the growing importance of employment in the service sector. In advanced capitalist countries, service jobs are now the most numerous and are still increasing, while the decline in manufacturing employment is showing no signs of coming to a halt. In the overwhelming majority of the less-developed countries, where agriculture is relatively or absolutely the main source of work, service employment outstrips that of manufacturing. Not even the experience of the newly industrializing countries, in which manufacturing jobs have expanded considerably, has been sufficient to reverse this trend.

The two important questions that relate service employment to the processes of social structuring, and which recur frequently, are the heterogeneous nature of work in the service sector and the scale of the economic organization of services following the fiscal crisis of the welfare state (O'Connor, 1973). The reality behind both these questions helps in various complex ways to weaken associative factors and to make reciprocal networks increasingly important. As will be seen more clearly below, the heterogeneity of service work goes much further than the lines of division noted by those who have studied segmentation of the labour market.[42] There are in fact not just two or three main segments but a myriad of different areas, ranging from the new highly skilled professions, passing through a series of different, more or less stable, self-employed activities and a series of jobs in large enterprises, to temporary employment and informal fragments of work.

Both the question of the heterogeneity of working activities and that concerning their range and the size of tertiary enterprises connect up with an important problem to which I shall return briefly when discussing the consumption of services: the problem of the diverse modes of providing services. Regarding the size of service activities, this sector shows very diversified features which prevent it being subjected in a uniform manner to the processes of concentration and centralization typical of the organization of production in manufacturing. It is true that state welfare bureaucracies have the potential to reach extremely high levels of centralization and standardization and that some private services, like banks and insurance companies, informational services and in some cases even trade, may be subject to concentration drives. But in all these cases, the necessarily privileged relationship with the customer/consumer imposes on the organization of services a certain receptiveness towards reciprocal networks and, consequently, a relatively high degree of autonomy for the local unit from the centralized bureaucracy. The importance of these relationships helps to explain why some services exhibit considerable resistance to concentration and why the local branches retain a substantial degree of independence and variety.

Finally, the question of the consumption of services must be considered in connection with the quality of life and with different ways to provide them. The importance of services in shaping the quality of life is beyond argument. Access to higher qualitative levels of education, health, information, culture and so on is a necessary condition for establishing a high standard of living, much more so than material wealth with no access to such qualitatively advanced services. Such access is only partially regulated by the market in the usual sense that the more money you have the better the service you can buy. For this reason, a quick look at the different modes of provision and their changing mixes becomes essential.

There are three basic modes of providing services, which are internally differentiated and contribute to forming the specific mixes for different social groups at different times. The first is self-provisioning: it ranges from traditional domestic or communal arrangements to innovative modern forms of self-service based on the use of technologically advanced equipment (Gershuny, 1978; 1983; Gershuny and Miles, 1983). The second is state provision of welfare services. It varies greatly in terms of quality, universality, distribution of costs between users and taxpayers, and the degree of centralization and citizens' control of the bureaucratized apparatus. The third mode of provision is through the private market. In this case, too, there are a variety of models but, for the sake of simplicity, I will mention only three possibilities:

1 A dispersed model based essentially on small local providers and typical of the retail trade but which no longer exists in some countries, following the spread of supermarkets and large chain stores;

2 a concentrated model with its basis in large corporations that either have direct control over most of a standardized business or financial control over the operations of marginally autonomous local units;

3 a polarized dualistic model based on a sort of qualitative division between a section of market provision controlled by large standardized chains or units and another section of dispersed provision controlled by small operators – for instance, the current situation of restaurants, with fast-food and restaurant chains on one side and small quality-based restaurants on the other.

During the Fordist age the tertiarization model was mainly based on the complementary expansion of state and concentrated market provision of services. This is the reason why for a long time tertiarization did not appear to run counter to the predominance of associative patterns of social organization. Differences exist between current models, and they are even more evident if considered on a global scale; but in general they are based on the continuing importance of traditional self-provisioning, on the growing impact of innovative self-provisioning, on a more limited, less universalistic and standardized, and more decentralized and locally controlled mode of welfare state provision, and, lastly, often on a polarized model of market provision. Each one of these trends suggests the weakening of associative and the increasing importance of reciprocal patterns of social organization.

Finally, a question which needs addressing is why, given these conditions, it is not appropriate to define present societies as post-industrial or service societies. My preliminary answer is that current trends in the transformation of service employment, consumption and provision cannot be fully understood outside of the uneven process of industrial development. It is not the services as such which determine the tendencies towards fragmentation, or more precisely the newly arising importance of reciprocal networks in combination with a weakening of associative ones and with the growing complexity and potential lack of cohesion between different social-organizational patterns. Rather, they are indicators of global tensions between market competition and individuality and the modes of socialization. Such tensions and their various different forms are typical of the whole industrial age.

5 REINTRODUCING SOCIAL FACTORS AND SOCIAL CONTEXT

The transformation of social factors: further clarification of concepts and method

The way in which socio-organizational factors of reciprocity have been transformed and their varying role both in the structuring of present-day societies and as basic inputs in industrial development have been inadequately investigated. The fact that macro-social analysis has systematically neglected this fundamental area of social life makes it difficult to understand phenomena that are particularly extensive nowadays, such as the informal economy and the more strongly community-based instances of industrial growth seen in Japan, the Third Italy, ethnic entrepreneurship or, more generally, in the persistence of family and small enterprises.

I shall now outline the crucial problem posed by the industrial transformation of reciprocal factors. The various socio-organizational arrangements based on reciprocity typical of pre-industrial societies were incompatible with the increasing independence and self-awareness of the individual promoted by industrial production and the division of labour. Interrelationships of the reciprocal kind were based on the subordination of individuals to the group to which they belonged. Hence the widespread idea in the classical tradition that the establishment of industrial society would eliminate reciprocal forms of social organization or, at least, radically limit the range of their influence. This process, however, has not occurred. Instead, a complex and discontinuous transformation has been taking place, which is still highly contradictory both in the relationship between individuality and reciprocal socialization and in terms of lack of cohesion within the socialization mixes. The significant aspect in this transformation is that reciprocal networks and the individuality promoted by industrial growth have not been incompatible. Socio-organizational factors of reciprocity show a considerable capacity to adapt and become more receptive towards individual awareness, though still remaining forms of social organization that in the immediate term put the interest of a group before those of its various members. In terms of a general theory, all that can be done is to put forward an hypothesis about the effects of more and more heightened forms of individualism. Reciprocal contexts are forced to take into account diverse individual characteristics and interests when formulating group goals and strategies and, at the same time, individuals are led to interpret opportunities for self-fulfilment in relation not only to immediate individual interests but also to diverse reciprocal networks that impose limits and sacrifices, but offer appreciable rewards in the foreseeable future as well.

Patriarchy and its consequent gender and age bias forms a particularly fertile ground on which to discuss the transformation of socio-organizational contexts based on reciprocity. I shall, however, confine myself to a few schematic observations which may serve to clarify further what I mean by transformation of forms of socialization where the identity of the individual is in the process of emerging.

Generally speaking, patriarchy represented the rule for the organization of pre-industrial systems of reciprocity. If considered from this angle, what we have is a way of organizing society and distributing power that only has meaning in its collective dimension as an attribute of the reciprocal network and a negation of all individuality, including that of the patriarchs. The broad assumption can be made that the advent of the industrial age led to three complex trends within the transformation of this collective form of organization which appeared, wrongly, to be inherent in reciprocal systems and, correctly, incompatible with the full development of individualism. The first trend regards the relationship of adaptation between patriarchy and individualism, which ends by changing the former from an attribute of collective organization into an unstable and incongruous hierarchy of dominant and subordinate individualities, the first adult males and the second primarily women but also children, young people, minorities and so on. The instability and incongruity are due to the fact that patriarchy and individualism are both distorted by being fused together, given that patriarchy is a form of collective negation of individuality and that the development of individualism, even in the strictly economistic sense of freedom to compete on the market, is highly intolerant of alien forms of hierarchy. Hence the second trend: a permanent and mounting tension between the growth of individuality and the persistence of patriarchal principles as they have been incorporated into industrial society. It is also essential to stress that the transformation of patriarchy into an anomalous hierarchy of individuals is triggered by the increasing importance of associative factors and at the same time becomes a fundamental way of organizing them. The third trend consists in the fact that, transformed into a hierarchy of individuals, patriarchy becomes an attribute of the socialization mix as a whole and not only of the reciprocal networks. The gender bias found in trade unions, political parties, broader political movements and professional bodies confirms this trend.

This schematic picture does not deal adequately with the wide-ranging debate opened up by the feminist movement,[43] but it does serve to clarify some of the questions underlying the logic of this book. First, it illustrates the fact that the conflictual relationship between individuality and forms of coercive and discriminatory socialization runs through the entire socialization mix. In this sense, patriarchy is uniquely significant in that it has been transformed from a dominant way of organizing collective identity in contexts of reciprocity into a system of extremely diverse socio-organizational elements, compatible with individualism, though in highly contradictory ways, and spread throughout the entire socialization system. Thus one of the most important phenomena of our times, the emergence of female individuality with its awareness of being different but not subordinate, is anything but typical of the family and the community and comes into conflict with patriarchy also, and in my view above all, in associative contexts.

Secondly, the picture outlined above eliminates a persistent misunderstanding: it is not necessarily the case that the tension between individuality and patriarchy is more pronounced and resistant in reciprocal than in associative systems. On this matter, I confine myself to putting forward the hypothesis that, contrary to expectations, patriarchy may turn out to be more pronounced and deep-rooted precisely in the associative system. In theory, this hypothesis might appear to be a weak one because the defence of common interests is not easy to reconcile with the principles of division and discrimination between those with identical interests on a basis that has nothing to do with the interests themselves, as is the case with gender or age. This theoretical assumption is, however, nullified by the historical process that has gradually shaped the associative factors, making them receptive to forms of hierarchy and discrimination. The way associative contexts function, as well as their historical articulation, makes it necessary to look at another question related to efficacy and dispersion in the defence of common individual interests. In this case too, I shall limit myself to a few observations.

Even though associative contexts establish themselves as organizational forms that defend common individual interests, their nature as forms of socialization is reflected in the limitation imposed on individual freedom. This limitation is the result of two processes: compromise in reconciling differing and divergent interests, and the dispersion resulting from the bureaucrarization of the defence of interests. Studies on neo-corporatism from the viewpoint of workers' interests have made a notable contribution to the understanding of the first process (see, for example, Goldthorpe, 1984; Lange and Regini, 1987). The benefits obtained from a corporate arrangement may be greater than from generalized competition, but they are less than what a limited number of individual and collective actors can achieve by not falling into line with the arrangement accepted by the vast majority. This limited consideration is merely aimed at underlining the existence of a systematic gap between individual interests and the benefits of association. The gap grows wider when the interests at stake are more numerous and it is more arduous and complicated to reach a compromise. Organizational dispersion has been highlighted by the studies carried out into bureaucratization and forms of leadership.[44] The more extensive and complex the organizations for defending certain interests, the more this defence is supported by and interwoven with the particular interests of the organizational apparatus and the leadership. It is true that the apparatus and leadership are legitimized by their providing the most effective defence possible, but it is also true that these same defended interests are treated as instruments for consolidating the privileges of the apparatus and the leadership, which inevitably gives rise to marked forms of dispersion.[45]

I now return to the question of the tension between individuality, in particular the emergence of women's awareness of being different and not subordinate, and forms of socialization still characterized by patriarchy. Contrary to expectations, it is likely that in the advanced capitalist societies[46] exactly the opposite is the case, for two interconnected reasons. In such societies, reciprocal contexts are characterized by a wider range of social opportunities than is found in less developed societies; therefore, female emancipation can be demanded and negotiated as a strategy that is also in the interest of the reciprocal network. One of the many examples is the fact that discrimination in the family against girls going into higher education has almost completely disappeared. Furthermore, associative apparatuses are more numerous, deep-rooted and bureaucratized and, consequently, less flexible than the growth in demands by individuals. It is likely that this aspect is also reflected in an increasing lack of cohesion between the diverse subsystems of socialization. What causes a certain degree of confusion here, too, is the fact that, hypothetically, reciprocal contexts have become receptive to individual needs, whereas throughout the entire first stage of industrial history they constituted the most serious obstacle to the development of these needs. Thus, the tension within the overall system of socialization appears today to have been reversed, given that the associative system which has freed individualism from the collective constraints of the pre-industrial system of reciprocity ends up by consolidating the values of dispersion and restraint that block individual initiative, as well as the impulses towards emancipation of those individuals on whom industrial history has imposed subordinate forms of existence.

From the theoretical picture that has been outlined so far at least two other conceptual problems emerge which need to be looked at briefly. The first regards the conceptualization of 'society' and 'social context' as homogeneous units of analysis. Traditionally, 'society' has been taken to mean a social organization that coincides with the nation-state. Nowadays, this correspondence poses serious problems both on the front of global interdependence and on that of an increasing heterogeneity at the local and sectoral levels, as was seen in the preceding section. These problems cannot be given a satisfactory definition in the sense that there are no new parameters within which it is possible to locate, in general, a precise unit of analysis sufficiently homogeneous and stable through time. For this reason, the term 'society' is used in this book in the traditional sense of being identical to the nation-state, while keeping in mind the caveats imposed by the problems just mentioned.[47] The term 'social context' has been used to define more homogeneous, local, historical and sectoral subunits. In this case, the need to use the same term often and with many different nuances might be confusing; none the less, I have not been able to come up with a more satisfactory solution.

The second problem concerns how my analysis relates to economic concepts, data and theory. One of my aims in writing this book has been to make a contribution to economics, but it has not been written by an economist; therefore, the input at the level of economic analysis is necessarily indirect. This limitation is felt above all in the fact that when the theoretical and analytical instruments typical of economics are turned into generic terms, they are not sufficiently precise. Thus, the concepts of economic cycles, accumulation, growth and so on still function more like approximate indicators than precise scientific instruments of interpretation. However, this approach is justified in its intent to shift attention on to social factors and their varying interplay in conditioning economic behaviour, expectations and opportunities. The shift is, in my opinion, of such importance today that it is worth undertaking an experiment in analysis notwithstanding the great limitations imposed by the heightened specialization of the social sciences. We are at the start of a long and difficult journey on which there must be more than just one traveller; otherwise his solitary contribution will be almost totally futile. It is therefore the task of many to criticize, complete and even radically alter the present contribution so that it may effectively attain the goal of a better understanding of societies that are moving towards the third millennium.

Putting social factors back in: examples and their theoretical significance

It is only recently that a whole series of studies on socio-economic change have rediscovered the possibility of taking social factors as a starting-point. It is no accident that this has taken place after the impact of the 'industrializing trend' has grown weaker. The studies to which I am referring deal, among other matters, with the labour supply, ethnic entrepreneurship, industrialization based on small and medium-sized enterprises, informal activity and self-provisioning in advanced capitalist countries, the second economy in socialist countries and the informal sector in the cities of underdeveloped countries. Women's studies and feminist literature have also been important in shifting the focus of attention on to the historically structured tensions between discriminatory forms of socialization and the emergence of female individuality, when dealing with major economic issues. Within certain limits, the way sociologists view economic processes is undergoing a radical change as regards not only their social consequences but also the independent influence of social context and social relations, considered as important factors in shaping the various different outcomes of these same processes.

At this point it is worth while to caution against any attempt to carry out a too radical revision. Such an approach does not in fact eliminate the significance of macro-economic trends involving the standardization of consumption and work patterns, the strategies of big business, industrial and financial concentration and restructuring, rationalized forms of behaviour and so on. Instead, the significance of these phenomena should be interpreted within different social contexts which interact and, therefore, do not simply form an indifferent background. One of the postulates which emerges here is that sociological approaches may be rearranged without losing the benefits deriving from accumulated scientific knowledge.

Recent research into ethnic entrepreneurship in the USA (Light 1972; 1979; 1983; 1984; Bonacich, 1973; 1975; Bonacich and Modell, 1981; Light and Bonacich, 1988; Cummings, 1980) insists on the possibility that where they exist to a sufficient extent, ethnic resources may be used to compensate for a lack of 'standard capital resources'. This is true of at least some ethnic groups and of the initial phase in attempts to become established. In the long run, such resources may remain unchanged or be transformed into normal capital resources. In the latter case, the buffer of ethnic origin grows progressively less effective in the face of market competition. Arguments in favour of the possible diversity of a model of industrial development characterized by the marked influence of reciprocal social patterns have arisen out of studies on family farming (for recent contributions see H. Friedmann, 1979; 1980). These studies, however, stress the particular specificity of agriculture and of community solidarity in rural contexts. The contributions on ethnic entrepreneurship, together with studies on the community-based industrial model in Japan (Dore 1986 and 1987) and on the industrial growth promoted by a system of small-scale enterprises in the Third Italy (Bagnasco, 1977), have helped to widen our range of vision so that we now perceive the persistent and changing importance of economic activities based on reciprocal patterns of social organization that extend well beyond the agricultural sector.

The expression 'diffused industrialization' is used to refer to industrial growth based mainly on persistent systems of small and medium-sized enterprises. Research into this kind of industrialization in the Third Italy, in the 1960s and 1970s, insisted on the fact that under certain general conditions some patterns of social relations – a large presence of family farming favouring the persistence of reciprocal networks and their trans-formation into a basis for every kind of economic venture, a social context which is not especially subject to migration, the presence of community solidarity and urbanization at the level of small and medium-sized towns – constituted useful resources for achieving substantial economic growth when following particular strategies. Reciprocal networks both in terms of family entrepreneurship in every economic sector and of co-operatives, consortia and other collaborative organizations among small operators in the same or different branches of activity have been the essential elements in this model of industrial development as an alternative to concentration and centralization of production, as can be seen in detail in chapters 5 and 6.

In his examination of a sample of inhabitants on the Isle of Sheppey in Britain, Pahl (1984) notes how in a context of industrial decline households which manage to hold on to one main income from a full-time job do not in the end passively succumb to a worsening of the general economic climate, since they suceed in supplementing their income through innovative self-provisioning and complementary formal and informal activities undertaken by every adult member of the family. In particular, they are able to dedicate time and resources to self-provisioning, made easier by technological innovation. It is important to note that in the explanation of phenomena subject to economic change all three examples mentioned above include macro-economic processes but do not treat them as the only independent inputs in the sociological analysis.

Another example emerges from the recent work of Szelenyi (1988) on the origin of contemporary peasant entrepreneurs in Hungary. The example is important because it embodies a variation on the theme of the adaptation of social networks based on reciprocity. This interpretation assumes that there may be socio-cultural characteristics and contexts with a strong 'regressive' potential in the biological sense: that is, they remain latent for a period and reappear at a later stage. In answering the question as to who the protagonists are in the recent wave of family enterprises in agriculture, permitted and encouraged by the latest reforms, the authors support the hypothesis that they are individuals or families which were middle-ranking peasant entrepreneurs in the immediate post-war period. They subsequently escaped being fully proletarianized or transformed into cadres and remained in a kind of 'parking orbit'. If this hypothesis turns out to be correct, then a reading of the social consequences of socialist industrial development exclusively in terms of proletarianization or transformation into cadres is clearly inadequate.

If it were extended to all the socio-economic spheres in which family or small-scale economic initiatives still operate, this discussion would have even wider implications. Such initiatives do still exist or may start up again or come into being as a result of innovation. Szelenyi's hypothesis suggests that the predisposition to become a small entrepreneur may be preserved through adaptative strategies over a relatively long time in a hostile political climate and re-emerge later on when it becomes less hostile.

The structure/agency dichotomy within the scope of this book

Before briefly outlining the approach and typological scheme that has been adopted in this book, it is important to take up again the discussion of some of the methodological points that have already emerged in the first section of this chapter in relation to the lines of interpretation used by the classical thinkers. The first concerns the way to read the interpretation based on a critique of the market paradigm in relation to the current methodological debate that is centred on the 'structure-consciousness-action' controversy. The arguments that I adopt and the manner in which they are presented are to a large degree neutral in respect of this dispute. On several occasions, I have indicated that my approach can be formulated in two versions: by following either a structuralist line or that of the sociology of individual action. It cannot be denied, however, that I lean towards a solution that is more structured than the method based purely on individual action. In my opinion, to lean in the opposite direction – as Boudon (1986) suggests – is perhaps more rigorous from a methodological point of view, but it has the drawback of being less effective in interpreting processes of change. Also, by following this line, it is difficult to attain the preferred methodological objective of a comparative sociological analysis of economic change: the identification of significant typologies of interaction between individuality and competitive behaviour, on the one hand, and different kinds of sociality mixes on the other.

The method followed in this book, however, is an imperfect compromise between the two different approaches. Without going too far into this methodological debate it is worth recalling its essential stages. The starting-point is, on the whole, the repudiation of the systematic structural-functionalist synthesis carried out by Talcott Parsons. The weak point in his synthesis, which is also the element that allows him to construct a comprehensive system of interpretation, lies in the fact that the structural meaning of behaviour is given by its 'function' and it is this which introduces an unacceptable deterministic slant into sociological analysis. Tensions, unforeseen outcomes, undesirable side-effects and complex phenomena of interdependence, all matters of great relevance in the life of society, are obscured by the functionalist emphasis. Repudiation of Parsons's functionalism brings with it, however, a corresponding loss in the capacity of interpretation to be systematic. The clearest example is that of R. K. Merton's version of structural functionalism. For Merton, the systematic synthesis of sociological interpretation is not given *a priori* by an overall picture that singles out the principal functional links; rather, it is constructed in steps by accumulating limited or middle-range theories that are compatible with one another. But whereas the approach of middle-range theories is still relevant today, the construction of a general coherent system of intermediate theories must be considered a failure.

To occupy the methodological ground lying between the two approaches with their pronounced elements of convergence is justified in relation to two opposed requirements. On the structural approach side, what is needed is to verify working hypotheses in such a way that they are constantly related to the final unit in social analysis, that is the meaning of individual action. On the sociology of action side, the necessity arises to construct compatible subsystems of the meanings of individual action in order to overcome the impasse of its infinite variety and unpredictability and to move beyond the narrow limits of a multiplicity of sectoral and specific interpretations.[48]

My attempt to raise the question of interpretation in terms of both the possible methodological approaches has been dictated by the reasons given above. A further reason, however, is my belief that the laborious procedure of restructuring the approaches applied in sociology in order to free them from the influence of the self-regulating market paradigm and restore an independent function to the variables of sociality can contribute effectively towards facilitating a non-eclectic process of convergence. Having said this, however, I do not think that the thesis upheld above, and which I apply herein, is indifferent towards the methodological debate on structure-consciousness/identity-action. The most important conceptual instruments originating from this debate have not yet been sufficiently tested and systematized; nevertheless, they are placed within a methodological approach receptive to the convergence between the identification of social contexts and that of typologies of sociologically relevant action. What we are dealing with are two concepts of independent social inputs: first, that of social factors, which are, in general, all the different kinds of solidarity as they have been adapted throughout the changes affecting traditional life and as they are renewed in their interaction with different forms of economic change; second, that of social context, that is a specific mix of these same factors as they originate in various historical forms in different geographical areas or social groups.

As Crow (1989) rightly points out, one of the most significant methodological instruments used today in order 'to go beyond the classic structure/agency dichotomy' (ibid., p. 1) is the concept of strategy. I also agree with his repeated caveats about the inadequate methodological grounding of this instrument. The term is applied indiscriminately to both individual and collective forms of behaviour and, in the latter case, both in contexts of associative sociality such as trade union strategies, and of reciprocal networks such as family strategies. The meaning of the concept of individual strategies is quite clear. These are a series of actions which are interlinked because they all aim at achieving an objective; so what we have is a mode of connecting at the interpretational level numerous actions that are inexplicable when taken singly. The use of the concept of strategy for collective entities is more complex since it imposes a dual process of reconstruction, involving not only the way in which single collective actions are related to the final objective but also the way in which, and the reason why, single individual actions are related, in different terms and to different extents, to collective strategy. Given that here the term strategy is widely used in association with the household, it is important to clarify the terms of this specific use.

The concept of household strategies is useful if strictly subordinated to two limiting conditions. First of all, a household strategy is never independent of the actions, needs, expectations and individual natures of its members, even though it is never just a simple aggregate of these factors. Consequently, a household strategy makes sense if we have the instruments to understand in what specific and changing ways individuals negotiate and participate in its formulation and implementation. As Pahl defines it, a strategy is the household's 'particular mix of practices' (Pahl, 1984, p. 20, n. 7). Second, we need to ascertain the embeddedness of different households in different socialization mixes, as constituted by associative and reciprocal relations, which make strategical options more or less viable (Morris, 1987; Harris and Morris, 1986). In other words, the meaning of household strategies is not unconnected with the broader social context, and the analysis of strategies makes no sense outside of an interpretative framework in which it is possible to reconstruct the interrelationship between the strategies and the social context.

Towards a complex hypothesis about the transformation of contemporary societies

Before concluding this chapter, I will summarize in outline the main features of the interpretational model I have adopted. This model is defined in terms of typologies characterized by different forms of interaction between the economic competition fostered by industrial growth and the parallel development of individual identity and the socialization mixes. The construction of these typologies is undertaken in detail in chapter 5, following a wide-ranging discussion of themes that are fundamental for such an operation. In chapter 2 in particular, I dwell on the concept of work, on current changes in occupational structure and on the meaning that may be attributed to these phenomena. Chapter 3 looks at the subject of social reproduction practices both from a theoretical angle and through a comparative analysis of different social spheres. Some important current trends are treated in chapter 4, which are more or less connected with what are defined as informalization or the diffusion of informal activities and the unofficial economy, in the broad sense of the term.

The interpretational typologies on which this work is based rest on the following presuppositions.

1 Processes of industrialization should be understood in terms of the transformation of socialization mixes, always made up of associative and reciprocal factors. This transformation occurs in the presence of the growing requirement for individual market competition or of opportunities to engage therein.

2 The impact of industrialization in terms of generating conditions of

individual competition and stimulating the emergence of individuality is diversified in time and space and for different social groups or types of individuals. The most marked division is that between development and underdevelopment. This division is so clear-cut that it must be adopted as one of the cornerstones in the construction of typologies.

3 In all cases, industrialization brings with it very important tensions between the spread of individualism and forms of socialization and within socialization mixes between associative and reciprocal factors. Not only do the latter not die out, they are also transformed in varying and non-linear processes so as to accommodate and absorb emerging individualism. At all events, neither industrialization accompanied by the emergence of increasingly important associative factors nor that accompanied by a stronger adaptation of reciprocal contexts resolve the tension between individualism and socialization. It resurfaces in critical forms whenever unstable global balances based on the flow of resources from underdeveloped to developed countries are upset by the consequences of the contradictions that have gradually built up and by the new needs that have emerged along with the development of individual self-awareness.

4 It is, therefore, possible to point to a further typological division when the emergence of associative sociality prevails over the adaptation of reciprocal systems. This division characterizes both 'developed' and 'underdeveloped' countries in different ways. So what we eventually have is four types of interaction matching development/underdevelopment with associativity/reciprocity. This general typology makes sense only if referred to concrete societies in precise historical periods. This is neither easy nor evident, above all because the first division has been sufficiently explored even though it is not always clear-cut;[49] whereas the second has only recently been explored to a small extent.

5 Within this approach, the experience of socialist societies may be considered a radical variant of the industrial growth model accompanied by associative sociality. In fact, socialist countries are characterized by the pre-arrangement of forms of associative/redistributive socialization in order to keep a tight rein on the impact of market competitivity and the development of individualism. In this case too, however, the tension between individual needs and associative forms of socialization is not eliminated, nor is the non-cohesive interplay of reciprocal networks completely stifled. The extension of the second economy is the most visible sign of the transgressive interaction, relative to official forms of sociality, between market behaviour and reciprocal systems.

These five models provide no more than a basic picture, that is, a necessarily generic synthesis of the main operations of simplification that are applied in interpreting diverse concrete social realities. In chapter 5,

I move on to a preliminary discussion of the models, examining them in the light of documentary evidence on contemporary societies. In chapter 6, three of the five models are re-examined in the light of the specific and more widely documented research into the characteristics of the Three Italies that has been undertaken during the last few decades.

NOTES

1 To put it differently, and focusing only on one important area of informal activities, that based on kinship, 'it would appear that some form of kin-based informal economy is necessary to any type of social formation. However eroded and attacked in modern industrial society, a familial infrastructure still serves as a support for all other sorts of economic activity' (Gaughan and Ferman, 1987, p. 21).

2 'Bringing the informal economy into the wider picture of economic activity thus challenges our accepted categories of economic behaviour' (ibid., p. 24).

3 The characteristic of the anthropological method is that it studies relatively limited, closed and isolated systems of social organization that are not particularly affected by frequent outside interference, social mobility and intense social relationships between strangers. As will be seen below, this characteristic makes it necessary to adapt anthropological concepts if they are to be used to interpret open macro-social systems, which all industrial societies are. On the whole, however, the classification of pure forms of exchange constitutes a useful starting-point for an interpretation of socio-organizational factors despite the fact that other classifications of relations based on exchange are possible (see, for instance, Davis, 1972; Cheal, 1988). This is because the latter can all be traced back to the logic of the pure forms or of a combination thereof; for example, a gift is different from maternal care but the underlying logic of both is that found in a reciprocal network.

4 In a recent article Mark Granovetter argues that 'the majority view among sociologists, anthropologists, political scientists, and historians . . . sees the economy as an increasingly separate, differentiated sphere in modern society, with economic transactions defined no longer by the social or kinship obligations of those transacting but by rational calculation of individual gain. It is sometimes further argued that the traditional situation is reversed: instead of economic life being submerged in social relations, these relations become an epiphenomenon of the market' (1985, p. 428).

5 Classical and neo-classical economic approaches have been very effectively criticized by Hirschmann (1980; 1977) for their incapacity to take into consideration the 'independent' impact of political power. In my opinion, an equally devastating critique could be founded on the 'independent' impact of socio-organizational factors.

6 As Granovetter puts it: 'despite the apparent contrast between under- and oversocialized views, we should note an irony of great theoretical importance:

both have in common a conception of action and decision carried out by atomized actors' (1985, p. 485). This common conception can be traced back to the acceptance of the paradigm of the market as an independent system of social organization. In the case of undersocialized theories, the way this paradigm works is explicit, since society is considered a subproduct of individual atomized market-competitive behaviour. For oversocialized theories, two variants can be indicated. The functionalist one is based on the presupposition that there exist systems of social control that develop as a function of the market, which establishes the requirements of efficiency and functionality. These systems are interiorized by individuals through forms of socialization that steer atomized social agents towards competitive behaviour 'according to the rules'. The second variant is differentiated internally through the adoption of different structuralist approaches. It assumes that competitive behaviour operates in different ways in divergent social spheres, whether social classes, ethnic minorities or segments of the labour market. In this case, too, the structuring of social behaviour is in the last analysis 'determined' by the independent play of market forces. The forms of social organization are 'determined' by the push of economic forces.

7   As Granovetter correctly argues, 'the idealized markets of perfect competition have survived intellectual attack in part because self-regulating economic structures are politically attractive to many. Another reason for this survival . . . is that the elimination of social relations from economic analysis removes the problem of order from the intellectual agenda, at least in the economic sphere' (1985, p. 484). These arguments are more convincing if supplemented by that of the strong ethnocentrism of the modern social sciences.

8   The question is equally relevant within the Weberian social action approach. Rational economic action is only one among many abstract ideal types of social actions. In this sense, it is a theoretical tool which takes on an interpretational meaning only when it is applied to social reality. Like other ideal types, it possesses an explanatory force only under given conditions. As Granovetter argues (1985, pp. 507–8), not only is the question of embeddedness consistent with the Weberian programme but it also provides an important opportunity to go beyond the traditional division in methodology between structure and agency.

9   This was the case, for example, in England but not in Holland, where the socio-organizational system of late feudalism was on the whole different. In England, this transformation led to a commercial rationalization of extensive agriculture and the formation of an urbanized surplus population available for wage-labour, but which in reality was left with no choice but vagrancy and the *cour des miracles* for a long period.

10   In chapter 2, I look more closely at different forms of socio-institutional regulation of the market in the industrial age.

11   In my terms, the Marxian theory of primitive accumulation constitutes an important example of social change based on the passage from socio-organizational systems dominated by reciprocal arrangements to others dominated by associative social relations. It is important to underline again

the fact that Marx interprets this process as a radical transformation of the *social* relations of production.

12 As Boudon maintains (1986, p. 43), 'the Weberian model could be considered as being universally valid'. But this is only true at the methodological level. If it were possible to confine Weber's contribution to a universal antinomological method excluding any interpretation which goes beyond its specific field of enquiry, there would be no problem. At the same time, however, this would deny any theoretical relevance to the vast contribution made by Weber to the study of contemporary society. In the last analysis, any radical application of Weber's methodological universalism sacrifices the capacity to interpret industrial society with strict methodological rigour. On the other hand, the procedure for selecting 'sociologically significant' action and constructing 'ideal types' entails certain necessary steps which in turn are acts of interpretation. This inevitably means that the universal purity of the methodological paradigm is 'tainted'. See, for example, Poggi (1983).

As Parsons notes in his Preface to the English edition of Part 1 of *Wirtschaft und Gesellschaft*, to lay the emphasis on methodology would overshadow what was Weber's 'dominant interest'. 'Throughout Weber's scientific career run two major threads of interest, in the methodology and theoretical formulation of social science, and in the understanding of the social structure and dynamics of modern Western civilization. Undoubtedly the latter was his dominant interest, the former being regarded as instrumental to it' (in Weber, 1947, p. 78).

13 Curiously enough, Parsons tends to attribute Weber's idea of the priority of *homo oeconomicus* and the relative autonomy of rational economic action to the supposed influence of Marx: 'Weber tended to take the Marxian form of statement of the problems implicitly for granted and treated the "economic system" as a more autonomous entity, functioning according to laws of its own, than it really is' (in Weber, 1947, p. 55).

14 A minor point of disagreement is the fact that, even from within the Weberian approach, I find it difficult to accept the concept of 'national community' as a communal relationship rather than as an associative one based on shared interests.

15 This contradiction immediately comes to the surface when Weber explains what he means by 'participation in a market'.

> Participation in a 'market' is still of another kind. It encourages association between the individual parties to specific acts of exchange and a social relationship, above all that of competition, between the individual participants who must mutually orient their action to each other. But no further modes of association develop except in cases where certain participants enter into agreements in order to better their competitive situations, or where they all agree on rules for the purpose of regulating transactions and of securing favourable general conditions for all. It may further be remarked that the market and the competitive economy resting on it form the most important type of the reciprocal determi-

nation of action in terms of pure self-interest, a type which is characteristic of modern economic life. (Weber, 1947, p. 139)

16   It is only fair to note that in this respect Durkheim drew much inspiration
     from the work of Auguste Comte (the first English edition appeared in
     1853). I have not considered Comte here merely to avoid making the
     discussion too lengthy.

17   In this sense, it is Durkheim that inspired Parsons and the structuralist-
     functionalist school in terms of a methodological approach that oversocializes
     and, at the same time, is based on the atomized behaviour of the social
     actor (Granovetter, 1985).

18   In this connection, see the final remarks of the 'Preface to the Second
     Edition' of *The Division of Labour*, where Durkheim explicitly states that 'if
     domestic society is no longer to play this role (the management of continuity
     in economic life), another social organ must indeed replace it in order to
     exercize this most necessary function'. It is worth suggesting that, all things
     considered, the socialist societies of the Brezhnev age resembled much more
     the model of social order idealized by Durkheim in his early works than the
     ideas on socialism expressed by Marx in his study of the Commune of Paris.

19   Even if the hard functionalist approach of Parsons towards the family has
     been generally abandoned, some of its crucial elements can be found in one
     of the most important recent works on the subject in the USA (see Berger
     and Berger, 1983).

20   See, among others, Granovetter (1984) and Steinmetz and Wright (1989),
     which are both dedicated to the case of the USA and stress the fact that
     self-employment and small activities have remained important even within
     the most highly concentrated economy in the world.

21   The significance of coupling the anthropological concepts of reciprocity and
     redistribution with the sociological ones of community and association must
     be briefly explained. In this context, it is also necessary to explain the
     selection of terms that characterizes my approach: from the pair reciproci-
     ty/community I prefer to use the anthropological term whereas I opt for the
     sociological term in the second pair.

     The methodological compatibility between reciprocity and community is
     easier to explain and resolve because the distance between sociology and
     anthropology in terms of the methods used to study the relevant phenomena
     is not great. Anthropology studies socio-organizational contexts at the micro-
     level while in sociology they are often defined by the concept of community.
     If the nation as community is excluded from the Weberian list of communal
     social relationships, what we have are systems of interrelation in which the
     organizational logic consists fundamentally of reciprocity. None the less,
     neither the closeness of the terms nor the greater precision of the concept
     of reciprocity in evoking the specific socio-organizational logic of the struc-
     ture or system of actions are, in themselves, enough to explain my preference
     for the anthropological term. The decisive factor is that the term 'community'
     is used with dissimilar meanings both in everyday language and in sociology
     and also within the latter. In common language 'community' frequently

NOTES 67

and also within the latter. In common language 'community' frequently defines not only micro-organizations but also a nation, a large town, a political party, a social class, an interest group, a profession and so on. As a technical term in sociology, the family is not a community, but tens of thousands of sociologists and economists scattered throughout the world and without any contact between them are often referred to as a community. In this sense, the use that I make of the concept of community is sharply delineated by the socio-organizational form that characterizes social inter-relationships, namely reciprocity. Finally, it is worth mentioning the fact that there exists a further reason for preferring the term 'reciprocity' to that of 'community'. At several points in this work I use the term 'community' to define a particular kind of reciprocal relation, that is, the community understood in the spatial sense of village or neighbourhood network.

22 The existence of an area of reality involving a mixture of reciprocity and association has no effect on the significance of the concepts, but rather on how they are used to interpret different real forms of social organization.

23 This is an established line in all classical sociology, whether in terms of the duality of *gemeinschaft/gesellschaft* formulated by F. Tönnies (1887) or that of Durkheim's organic and mechanical solidarity.

24 I would mention, among various others, the following definitions of 'reciproc-ity' and 'redistribution' by the American anthropologist Marshall Sahlins (1988), explicitly inspired by Polanyi.

On a very general view, the array of economic transactions in the ethnographic record may be resolved into two types. First, those 'vice-versa' movements between two parties known familiarly as 'reciprocity'. The second, centralized movements: collection from members of a group, often under one hand, and redivision within this group, this is 'pooling' or 'redistribution' ... Their social organizations are very different. True, pooling and reciprocity may occur in the same social contexts – the same close kinsmen that pool their resources in household commensality, for instance, also as individuals share things with one another – but the precise social relations of pooling and reciprocity are not the same. Pooling is socially a *within* relation, the collective action of a group. Reciprocity is a *between* relation, the action and reaction of two parties. (pp. 188–9)

25 This is also the reason why sociologists define associative relation-ships as horizontal, since they directly involve all those who share the same interest, and communal ones as vertical, as they involve only the specific community in the narrow sense. It is useful to recall that this definition in abstract spatial terms diverges from the spatial models of anthropologists, who insist instead on the symmetry within reciprocity and on the vertical hierarchy in redistribution (see Polanyi, 1977, p. 36).

26 In the course of this book, I return at various points to the question of the persistence and transformation of family farming. Among others, see Friedmann (1979; 1980); Shanin (1987); Mottura (1988).

27   This is not an uncommon error among students of the urban informal sector in the underdeveloped world, the most influential among them being Ivan Illich (1981).

28   I would like to mention one example which also acts as a warning against frequent value-laden considerations on family strategies and morality. In a recent interview with a mother and head of the family in one of the large informal-sector communities found in underdeveloped countries, the woman explained the reason why she sent her children to school outside the community, which entailed a considerable sacrifice. She had noted that the local schools devoted most of their resources to providing the pupils with reasonable lunches and paid too little attention to the quality of education. She had gone to speak with the headmaster to complain and insist that the main duty of a school is to provide a good education, while it should be the responsibility of the family to feed its children. The headmaster had replied that the large majority of the parents in the community were not interested in the quality of education but very keen that their children should get at least one good meal a day, which they themselves were unable to provide at home. So the school devoted more resources to providing meals than to hiring good teachers. The way the mother herself presented the case immediately made clear something that social scientists often forget. It is not a question of good parents devoted to maximizing their childrens' achievements versus bad selfish parents who sacrifice them to the family's immediate interests, but rather one of unequal opportunities and resources.

29   For this reason, it makes no sense to distinguish state from private redistribution at the conceptual level; if anything, the problem exists at the analytical level since associative realites can have a differing influence on the two processes or because a different mix of association/reciprocity may assume a different significance. Take, for instance, the role of the trade union within the more community-based economic system in Japan or the complex mix of associative and reciprocal sociality when there is a Labour government in Britain, the Labour Party being, at least in part, the expression of the trade union movement, which leads one to suppose also the existence of an integrated network of reciprocity involving union and party leaders. At the analytical level too, however, the distinction should be made with caution because in reality the process producing the resources that are redistributed is the same and, also for this reason, social organizations centered on associative or reciprocal interests are rarely confined to only one of the two sides of redistribution. This hypothesis is confirmed by the historical experience of organizations that in theory limit the scope of their activity to the private-economic side, like trade unions, associations of industrialists, professionals and farmers, and even cartels, trusts and co-operatives. It is also confirmed by the opposite experience of political associations such as parties, environmental groups and so on.

30   In the course of this book, I shall deal further and in different ways with the question of representation of interests. Among others, see the contributions included in the collection edited by Suzanne Berger (1981)

focused on the organization of interests in Western Europe.

31 The sociological interpretation of the specificities of the so-called Third Italy (comprising the north-eastern and central regions) (Bagnasco, 1977; Paci, 1980) suggests a possible overlapping in the Fordist age of the semi-periphery and socio-economic systems persistently characterized by a high presence of small economic operators and, consequently, based on intensive reciprocal economic relations. See Arrighi (1985) for a discussion of the concepts of core, semi-periphery and periphery and an extensive documentation on the characteristics of semi-peripheral societies.

32 O'Connor describes the fundamental conception underlying his work thus:

the recomposition of capital, the working class (and salariat), and the state through historical economic crises and traditional class struggles revolutionized the conditions of social and economic reproduction not only within society and the state generally. The thesis is that these new conditions of reproduction and conditions of capitalist accumulation became increasingly incompatible. The basic reason, which we have made the focus of this work, was the development of ideologies of individualism and their practices, which flourished in the USA in proportion that the expansion of the division of social and industrial labor abolished traditional 'individuality'. It is argued that although these ideologies appeared to be indispensable for economic and social domination and integration, they increasingly subverted both. (1984, p. 8)

33 This is how O'Connor describes the latest developments in the contradiction between individuality and advanced forms of capitalist socialization:

In place of privacy or freedom from interference, there developed centralized state and large-scale capitalist intrusion into private life; in place of autonomy and self-direction grew dependence, passivity, and individual wills colonized by capital and the state; instead of self-development grew standardization, apathy, and self-stultification. In place of political individualism and a society based on voluntary groups established to defend the interests of free individuals, there developed a kind of 'corporatism' in which individuals exist to legitimate the interests of 'intermediary associations'. In place of economic individualism, there developed the forced collectivization of the capitalist division of industrial labor. (ibid., p. 18)

34 In other words, the failure of Reagan's plan to reorganize the forms of socialization, lucidly pointed out by O'Connor a few years beforehand in terms of the irremediable contradiction between a neo-conservatism that lays emphasis on rigid forms of socialization and a neo-liberal ideology that by its very nature cannot tolerate them (ibid., pp. 236–7), must be viewed in the context of the persistent crisis of the compensatory factors existing in the world economy, as outlined above in the quotation from Arrighi on p. 39 above.

35   'A new and less expensive way of life based on new living and working conditions free of omnipotent fantasies of American individualism presupposes a shift of hegemonic cultural values in more co-operative or communitarian directions' (O'Connor, 1984, p. 240). 'One catalogue of the cultural elements making up these struggles included communitarian values and close attention to community needs; participatory democracy and the right of members of organizations; holistic approaches to environmental, health, educational and other issues; and support for democratic government planning and co-ordination' (ibid., p. 241).

36   'What is at issue, then, is a form of alienation inherent not only in capitalist relations of production, but in the socialisation of the process of production itself: in the workings of a complex, machine-like society. The effects of this alienation can be attenuated, but never entirely eliminated' (Gorz, 1982, p. 9).

37   'Whether they work in a bank, the civil service, a cleaning agency or a factory, neo-proletarians are basically non-workers temporarily doing something that means nothing to them' (ibid., pp. 70–1).

38   'It is possible to enlarge the non-market field of autonomous, self-managed and self-motivated activity, encouraging auto-centred production and training, and replacing some of the services currently supplied by commercial organizations or bureaucractic administrations with mutual aid, co-operation and sharing'; 'The extension of the sphere of autonomy is thus predicated upon a sphere of heteronomous production which, though industrialized, is restricted to socially necessary goods and services that cannot be supplied in an autonomous manner with the same efficacy' (ibid., pp. 98, 101).

39   Besides Lash and Urry (1987) the great majority of the literature on the decline of Fordist societies also assumes that Western capitalism has passed through a phase of relatively accentuated social organization and is subsequently entering into a phase where heterogeneity and flexibility (Tarling, 1987) reduce the capacity for organization/standardization.

40   The different lines along which organizational experiences and tendencies develop can be explained by taking into consideration three factors:

First, is the point in history at which it begins to industrialize. The earlier a country enters into its 'take-off', the less organized *mutatis mutandis* its capitalism will be. This is because countries which are later industrializers need to begin at higher levels of concentration and centralization of capital to compete with those which have already been industrializing for some time. Second, there is the extent to which pre-capitalist organizations survive into the capitalist period . . . And the third factor is size of country. For the industry of small countries to compete internationally, resources were channelled into relatively few firms and sectors. Co-ordination between the state and industry was then greatly facilitated, if not necessitated. At the same time there would tend to be higher union densities, more 'organization' of labour, where there were relatively few firms and sectors. (Lash and Urry, 1987, pp. 4–5)

41 Another limit concerns the critical standpoint the two writers adopt towards the Marxist and Weberian traditions (ibid., pp. 2–3). They believe that both traditions see capitalist development as characterized by discontinuous and varying trends towards increasing associative organization and would not accept the idea of disorganized capitalism. As seen in section 2, they are right only in part in the sense that both traditions underrate the persistence and non-cohesive interplay of reciprocal factors. But, as already noted, Lash and Urry forget this point themselves and, consequently, do not criticize Marxists and Weberians on this more justifiable ground. Thus, their criticism does not rest on a sound basis. The Marxist tradition has been mostly critical of Hilferding's idea that capitalism would become increasingly organized. Marxists have argued that the persistence of contradictions and struggles would ensure high instability and continuously changing situations. It is on this ground that they can be reproached with having *undervalued* the organizational potential of capitalism in the advanced capitalist countries, as fed by resources deriving from the uneven global expansion of market relations. Weberians, too, can be accused of having underestimated the potential for organization under the given conditions of the Fordist age. The starting-point for this critique is the emphasis laid on the non-cohesion between the different levels of rationality, for instance bureaucratization versus the diffusion of economic rationality, on the persistence of irrational actions and on the tensions between social control and individual freedom of action.

42 I shall return to this point in chapter 2 when considering the question of the segmentation of labour markets.

43 I shal come back to the important contribution of feminist literature and of recent women's studies in chapter 3, in discussing the theorization of social reproduction.

44 Starting with the classic contributions of Weber on bureaucratization in general and of Robert Michels (1915/1962) on the bureaucratization and formation of autonomous leadership interests within the mass political parties, there is now an extensive literature and documentation on the subject. A wide-ranging discussion of the subject is included in Alford and Friedland (1985). A different theme concerning the role of interpersonal relations in society and within political organizations is discussed in depth by Eisenstadt and Roniger (1984).

45 Gorz's criticism of the huge apparatuses involved in socialization, mentioned in the preceding section, drew its inspiration precisely from this problem.

46 The particular features of the Japanese case are taken up again in chapter 5. See mainly Dore (1986; 1987); Fukutake (1989); Nishikawa (1980); van Wolferen (1989).

47 The sole important exception in this book is that of Italy, where the internal

heterogeneity is very marked and structured along lines of division that are so far from 'normal' regional imbalances – this is explained at the beginning of chapter 6 – as to suggest that the term 'society' be adopted for two or three (depending on the historical period considered) large regional aggregates.

48 The most important recent attempt to work out theoretically an intermediary method is that of Giddens (1984). I do not dwell here on what this author says because his proposal has not yet been tested by research, and, in my view, is vague and difficult to verify.

49 A still open question is that of the semi-peripheries and historical change in the international division of labour: for example, the contemporary emergence of the newly industrializing countries.

2

Informalization and the variety of working activities

1 THE MEANINGS OF A PERSISTENT VARIETY OF WORKING ACTIVITIES

A brief introductory discussion of the term 'work'

Before examining the issues dealt with in this chapter – mainly the evidence of and reasons for the growing heterogeneity of working activities – it is important to discuss briefly the term 'work'. My motive in doing this is not philosophical or of a general theoretical nature, but merely to clarify what kind of activities are to be included. Also, my use of the term differs from that which has become common in the industrial age. The term 'work' is generally associated with employment, usually with official employment, to such an extent that the two concepts almost entirely overlap; thus work has become a relatively narrow and precise concept. This is an obvious consequence of the typical distinction in industrial society between the economic and social spheres of human life. Furthermore, the assumption of an increasing predominance of the economic over the social sphere has lead to the 'work-centred' social analysis which was the object of criticism in chapter 1.[1]

In pre-industrial societies work had a much broader and less precise meaning. Working activities were associated with fatigue and unavoidable tasks as opposed to leisure, eating and resting. The fact that the workplace was very often in the home or in close proximity to it contributed to the lack of precision in the use of the term. In other words, the impossibility of clearly distinguishing between these two spheres of human experience meant that the definition of the term was loose and uncertain. There was no clear separation between work time and non-work time; nor did the division of labour follow precisely demarcated lines, at least for the ovewhelming majority of the population. It is not surprising that the definition, made in an industrial context, of pre-industrial peasants as 'agricultural workers' is highly problematic. These workers were mainly but never exclusively agricultural producers. Moreover, although all individuals, including children as early as possible, had to work very hard during certain periods, there was nothing like the time/work pressures which have become typical of industrial societies. However imprecise it may appear now, a loose concept of this kind was, broadly speaking, reasonable for those times. In line with local traditions and customs, people knew what had to be done, when, and who was best fitted for each task among the members of the community.

In order to go beyond formal employment and work-centred paradigms, we need a concept of work which is widely based and comprehensive but also appropriate to different kinds of contemporary societies. It should also make clear what is included and what excluded, and possibly what the main reasons are for the uneven allocation of different kinds of work and how they relate to one another. Within this perspective, work should include all types of formal employment, but also a variety of irregular, temporary or occasional activities undertaken to raise cash and various activities that produce use values, goods and services for direct consumption either by the individual and his/her household or by other individuals and households, which are more or less necessary for the survival of individuals as distributed in different household structures. As we shall see later on, it is necessary to take into consideration a wide spectrum of different activities which take on different meanings in terms of both conventional macro-economic analysis and the sociological analysis of life-styles and socialization mixes. Obviously, the crucial issue is how to use the concept of work as a bridge between the two fields of social analysis without slipping back into a work-centred paradigm. I will discuss this problem from different angles throughout this work, but chiefly in this and in the following chapter.

An attempt to define the concept of 'work'

It is worth underlining the central and most controversial part of the above definition: the criterion for inclusion of an activity as 'work' is whether it contributes to material survival. This criterion is not as materialistic and self-evident as it may first appear. It is a historical, cultural and social construct in the sense that it varies with time, different local cultures and different social groups, which means that it has to be verified against these three lines of variation, at least in an approximate manner. This is both the strength and the weakness of the definition: the more convincing it is, the greater its analytical role; but since the checking operation is particularly difficult and uncertain, some confusion will inevitably arise.

Apart from this crucial question, other factors leading to imprecision are not particularly relevant or can be dealt with using common sense. Two trivial examples of the uncertain dividing line between work and non-work will serve to explain this. First, playing cards and betting are activities that may indeed raise a monetary income, although more frequently people lose money. A relatively small number of individuals engage in this kind of activity professionally as a way of making a living. Some of them may be as respectable and officially recognized as professional sportsmen, as in the case of professional bridge players. For the latter, and also for less respectable professional gamblers, playing cards or betting are a real form of work. But occasional gamblers do not engage in this type of activity as work but for personal pleasure, even when they are addicted to it.

The second example concerns shopping. In industrial commodified societies, shopping is normally considered a necessary working activity. A certain number of upper- and middle-class women, and increasingly men too, will also go shopping for fun and pleasure. They examine the latest fashions on display along Park Avenue or in Harrods and use the occasion to have tea and pleasant conversation with friends. Is this a form of work or not? The upper-class wife of a successful professional man or of a top manager would have no difficulty in arguing that this kind of shopping is necessary in order to maintain the 'status' of her household. This may be so, but the point is that discussion of such a case is not really relevant within the perspective of this book. It would be different in the case of a research project focusing on the life-style of and the sexual division in the upper classes.

Let us briefly return to the question of considering work as an important link between economic and sociological analysis. The apparently obvious assertion that work has served to bridge the gap between the two spheres of human life as it has opened up in the industrial age conceals a crucial methodological difficulty. Without a comprehensive theory of social reproduction, the bridging works in one direction only: the historical distribution of different kinds of work among different social groups explains their different life-styles. This is to remain entrapped within an economistic approach in which social factors are dependent variables. The logic of industrial capitalist development ends up by explaining more or less mechanically every important aspect of social life. The range of working activities has been studied within this frame-work, paying excessive attention to the diversity of official employment mostly from the standpoint of political economy. Too little attention has been paid to social organizations, life-styles and survival strategies, which should be viewed as original co-determining factors in the heterogeneity of working activities, rather than as mere consequences of it. I am thinking, among others, of the studies on labour market segmentation and on the impact of the tertiarization of employment structure.[2] Even informalization or the presence of informal activities has often been interpreted, as we shall see shortly, from different points of view which are almost exclusively concerned with its macro-economic origins and impact. This lends further support to my argument about the predominant role of economistic interpretations in the social sciences. In order to avoid falling back into this approach, it is important to understand that the heterogeneity of work is in fact a result of the simultaneous effect of both economic and social factors. This is the main reason why, having anticipated the range of types of work in this chapter, and prior to discussing some important macro-economic trends, I will devote the next chapter to constructing a theory of social reproduction.

Analytical evidence for the growing heterogeneity of work can be obtained by looking at three different areas: diversification of official employment; the persistence or diffusion of informal activities in different kinds of societies (industrialized, socialist, underdeveloped) with distinct but parallel patterns; and contemporary changes and persistence in the patterns of both domestic labour and self-provisioning activities. As the second and third areas will be extensively discussed throughout the book, it will be sufficient here briefly to touch on some crucial aspects in the first. These relate to labour market segmentation, industrial restructuring and the tertiarization process.

Labour market segmentation

The theory of labour market segmentation, and the version formulated by Edwards (1979) in particular, underlines the fact that in advanced capitalist countries labour markets operate by being structured into three large non-competing areas. The two primary segments of the market are increasingly characterized by internal competition, a relatively high degree of inner stability, and growing insensitivity towards competition from the labour supply with secondary segment characteristics. Consequently, the social conditions of workers in the lower primary segment tend to differ more and more from those of workers condemned to the fierce competition for jobs in the secondary segment. Contrary to orthodox market theories, in this approach growing competition on the labour supply side leads to an increasing differentiation of the conditions of workers in each of the different segments. Primary workers will remain unaffected while secondary workers will suffer worsening conditions in terms of relative income, work stability and security. I will return to this point later when discussing labour markets and the social origins of the regulatory process, which is the cause of the division between these different segments.

It may be worth while to mention that labour market segmentation also occurs under different conditions in socialist and underdeveloped countries. In socialist countries, an important and persistent differentiation has been noted between the conditions of workers in top-priority sectors, for example the military-industrial complex, and those of workers in the rest of the planned economy. Although the latter do not face competition from surplus labour, they are persistently disadvantaged by having lower priority in the access to official resources, a situation which is aggravated when economic growth is low or negative. In underdeveloped countries, multinationals or firms crucial for the state establish a primary segment, with limited protection, where working conditions – however bad they may be compared to those of primary workers in advanced capitalist countries – are incomparably better than those enjoyed by local workers in the competitive and informal sectors.

Industrial restructuring and employment in services

The analysis of industrial restructuring can be linked to the theory of labour market segmentation as a further historical development in the following way.[3] Segmentation produces an increasing rigidity in the industries which mainly operate with labour in the primary market. Increasing international competition forces these industries to find ways of creating a cheaper and more flexible labour force. This cannot be done by straightforward dismantling of the segmenting mechanism as this would have devastating social consequences and might be met by strong political opposition, and not only from the workers' political and trade union organizations. Therefore, the paths followed in order to achieve more flexibility have involved vertical disintegration, relocation of labour processes and the re-emergence of various old and new forms of subcontracting. Such conditions further heighten the heterogeneity of work. Both the primary and the secondary segments survive and, often, the new workers cannot be classified as belonging to either. The social and geographical impact of de-industrialization, relocation and new ways of organizing industry leads to a striking and expanding range of working activities.

Both labour market segmentation and industrial restructuring are considered almost exclusively in terms of the manufacturing sector. But the great employment transformation of our age is the emergence of a vast tertiary sector, which now forms the major part of the economy. Employment in services has overtaken that in manufacturing as the main source of jobs in every advanced capitalist country. It is also increasing so quickly in underdeveloped countries as to induce many analysts to speak of 'over-tertiarization', by which they mean that where directly productive activities have not been strengthened, this process will only further weaken the economic fabric of these countries. I shall return to the tertiarization process in chapter 4. Here it is important to underline the impressive contribution made by tertiarization to the increasing diversification of the official employment structure, as well as to the diffusion of informal activities, which are increasingly concentrated in the service sector in different societies worldwide. The employment structure in services is different and much more heterogenous than in manufacturing. It does not only include a vast diversified group of office and service workers, a persistently larger quota of self-employed and small-scale independent workers (some of them high-income professionals or entrepreneurs, others on relatively low incomes, such as street-vendors and shopkeepers, independent taxi-drivers and repair men), but also an increasing number of unskilled workers with very low incomes and no job tenure or security. The diversity within the sector is such that the theory of labour market segmentation cannot deal with it. Also, in many cases the different working processes cannot be measured according to the quantitive criteria of productivity for a number of reasons, including the fact that workers deal directly with customers, that the work has a higher qualitative content and is difficult to define, and that the productive unit is very small and cannot be Taylorized. A substantial proportion of service workers are, moreover, employed by the state. In this case, both recruiting and the organization of work depend to some extent on a political rationale which has little to do with economic efficiency. This rationale is expressed in two different but complementary ways. The state as employer gives a much higher priority to maintaining consensus than to the immediate efficiency of the workers. For their part, the workers build up a position of power within the state organization from which to defend their conditions of work and living standards.[4] Unlike workers in the primary segment of the labour market, state employees develop an increasing interest in the expansion of employment because, rather than leading to internal competition, newcomers often push the older workers further up the career ladder, thus reinforcing their independent status and power.

The analysis grounded in political economy gives us an impressive picture of this great and increasing diversification of work but tells us little about how this heterogeneity is rooted in social contexts: whether or not social factors play a determinant role in the creation and uneven allocation of various forms of employment, and how the latter match with and are complemented by different survival strategies in the social sphere of life. This is the theme I will deal with in the following sections and chapters.

2 THE ANALYTICAL FRAMEWORK FOR EXAMINING CURRENT TRANSFORMATIONS IN WORKING ACTIVITIES

A preliminary hypothesis for breaking down the concept of work

I should now like to propose a preliminary and hypothetical breakdown of the concept of work, as it was broadly defined in the previous section to include every 'human activity contributing to material survival', where survival is viewed as socially organized within a household structure which varies according to time, place and social group.[5] The classification in table 2.1 takes as its starting-point the tripartite division of activities into formal, informal and domestic or household used by Gershuny and Pahl (1979). I have broken this division down further in order to distinguish more clearly between activities whose significance differs either in terms of the monetary economy and the accumulation process or of family organization and the reproduction process.

The difference between the first five categories and the last three is immediately evident. Different mixes of activities from the two groups entail varying costs of reproduction and levels of commodification. The differences between the five categories of paid work are more difficult to specify. Formal work is entirely transparent in both its employment and income structures. In a highly regulated society, it reflects within the reproduction process the basic cost of labour, possibly complemented by various kinds of state contributions, and the capacity for monetary consumption. It also contributes fully to the state fiscal system. Mixed work does not fully reveal the income/cost of labour and the consumption capacity and partially defrauds the fiscal system. Pure informal work remains undetected and unrecorded and defrauds the fiscal system to a large extent. I will assume that it provides a lower rate of income per hour of work than formal work; this has important consequences for reproduction patterns and the capacity for consumption. Criminal activities are distinct from the other forms in that they are very heterogeneous, difficult to detect and differ from other informal activities in terms of who engages in them, the levels and stratification of income involved

Table 2.1 *A spectrum of informal activities*

Formal	Informal						
Legal		Illegal		Not provided for by law			
						Non-monetary	
Monetary							Private
Public							
I	II	III	IV	V	VI	VII	VIII
Pure formal activities	Mixed formal/ informal activities	Activities that elude fiscal, social security or labour legislation	Criminal activities	Paid activities or transactions not provided for by law	Reciprocal or voluntary unpaid activities	Self-provision-ing (within the household)	'Normal' domestic work
Examples							
Every productive activity that is wholly performed according to existing regulations	Formal activities that contain informal elements: e.g. partial 'black' payment	Second (black) jobs; employment without contract; informal self-employment	Theft; drug trafficking; fraud	Barter; car-washing by young children	Reciprocal work; helping neighbours; various kinds of voluntary and social work	Vegetable gardens for self-consumption; do-it-yourself activities	Cleaning; child care; preparing meals

Source: Adapted from Mingione, 1985, p. 20, as modified by Boer, forthcoming.

and the disruptive effects for the state. Paid activities or transactions not provided for by law is a category of work which is indeed unrecorded, informal and monetary but which, unlike all other informal categories, is not illicit because it lies outside the scope of legal regulations. Where no provision is made in law for the declaring of income for tax purposes in the case of temporary casual activities with earnings below a certain level, this category will inevitably be fairly extensive, including occasional baby-sitting, small temporary jobs done by housewives, students and pensioners, and so on. Where, on the contrary, legal provisions are very strict and require an income tax return even for occasional low-income employment, this category is bound to be very small. It overlaps with strictly informal activities, with the obvious exception that it does not evade paying tax.

Reciprocal and supportive activities involve one household spending some of its time to ensure the survival of another; they therefore belong to the reproduction pattern of the receiver rather than the provider. Finally, the distinction between normal and exceptional work for self-consumption is not clear enough because it changes over time and from place to place. However, it is important to distinguish the small tasks of everyday domestic life from those maintenance, improvement or agricultural activities which require specific skills or long periods of training and/or practice; consequently, exceptional activities are either optional or a necessity depending on whether a household has an adequate or inadequate income. The broad area of self-provisioning may be divided into traditional activities and new/innovative ones – that is, activities made possible by the use of modern do-it-yourself tools or other technologically advanced devices. But this distinction should be made with great care, because in many advanced capitalist areas traditional self-provisioning is being revitalized through new light technology equipment, such as sewing and knitting machines for home-produced garments or mini-tractors for vegetable growing. As for the other categories, it is important to take into consideration the local social and cultural context. The presence and the extent of the last three categories even in advanced capitalist societies constitutes an initial confirmation of the limits to the commodification process.

The meanings of different combinations of work

Different combinations from the range of activities mentioned above affect levels of subsistence and social reproduction, and consequently the costs and productivity of labour, as well as the structure and potential for expansion of a society's capacity to consume. Further, such different combinations condition and are conditioned by social organization and, above all, by the real prospects for development of different types of social context.

The range of activities identified acts as an analytical instrument which introduces the dual significance borne by the different categories of work with respect to both economic development and diversified patterns of survival. It can also be used as the basis for an abstract discussion on the interconnections between different kinds of work. In theory, it may be true that insufficient monetary resources will force people to turn increasingly to self-provisioning as a way to survive. However, as Pahl (1984) notes, in present-day reality households with insufficient monetary resources in an urban advanced capitalist society are unlikely to be involved in a high degree of self-provisioning because they do not have the time, instruments, capital, professional skills and social relations which favour the diffusion of innovative self-provisioning in such a social context. As we shall see, the picture is rather different in southern Italian cities (Mingione, 1985 and chapter 6, below; Serpieri and Spanò, 1986) and in Third World cities (Bromley and Gerry, 1979). In fact, the only correct response to the question as to how low-income groups manage to survive is: 'it depends on the specific historical social context they find themselves in.' So, in order to use the defined range of activities as more than just a means of listing a set of different categories with different meanings, it is necessary to supplement it in two directions.

First, we need to add to this range another similar analytical device which breaks down the different kinds of survival resources entering the reproduction mix of households. It is obvious at first glance that households survive not only by means of the resources obtained through the work of their members but also through those received from external sources. The latter may make survival possible even where the resources raised by work for income and work for direct provision are insufficient. Conversely, where such external resources are substantial they may explain the case of households with a high standard of living but a relatively low capacity or willingness to produce a large amount of resources internally. Second, the two ranges have to be reconsidered in the light of a socio-historical analysis with the aim of making them less descriptive and more interpretative. This will be done in chapter 3, where patterns of social reproduction are discussed extensively from a historical and comparative socio-geographical perspective.

The range of resources used for material survival

I want now to illustrate the second kind of analytical range. The starting-point from which it is constructed is a consideration of the different meanings assumed by the wide variety of resources which contribute to household survival, that is the reproduction mixes. A distinction is made between 'internal' resources, deriving directly from the households them-selves, and 'external' resources, which are contributed by the state, the community, charities, friends and kinship networks. This distinction is not always sufficiently clear but it is useful in order to introduce the importance of social factors and socialization mixes. Although they are important in shaping different opportunities for income-providing or self-provisioning activities, this aspect is easily underestimated. By contrast, it is immediately evident that 'external resources' depend directly on the socialization mixes in which the households are embedded. In other words, if we do not take into account the historical transformation of social factors and socialization mixes, it is impossible to say what and how many 'external resources' of various kinds, originating from kinship or community systems or from the welfare state or associative solidarity, are available at different times to different social groups. In both cases we can distinguish between monetary resources obtained in the formal market, monetary resources provided from outside that market (informal in the strict sense or traditional monetary economies) and non-monetary resources for direct consumption (see table 2.2).

The main assumptions underlying my interpretational approach are these:

1 Although level 1 is the principal source of survival resources in an industrialized context, which is how it is seen in conventional economic or employment analysis, the other sources should also be taken into consideration since they play a complementary role; moreover, there are various cases where level 1 has a very minor impact on the reproduction mix.

2 Level 1 contributes substantially to the formation of the direct monetary cost of subsistence at formal market prices, that is the historical cost of labour, and at the same time to the spending capacity of house-holds (aggregate demand), after savings have been deducted and con-sumption credit on future working income added.[6] This means that the greater the extent of level 1, the higher the cost of labour and the greater the aggregate demand. This may also be considered a restraint on any potential for further expansion: the higher the level, the less able it is to expand further under given historical conditions. However, such an

Table 2.2 *Classification of survival resources entering the reproduction mix of households*

	'Internal': produced by the households themselves	'External': contributed by the state, kin, friends and self-help networks
Formal market monetary resources	Income deriving from various forms of formal employment (1)	State-subsidized incomes Inheritances Formal donations and gifts Other formal subsidies (2)
Monetary resources originating outside the formal market	Income deriving from various forms of informal or traditional work (3)	Informal donations, loans, subsidies, gifts (4)
Non-monetary resources	Domestic work Self-provisioning (5)	State services Donations in work or in kind Free community assistance (6)

indicator is controversial and needs to be discussed further in terms of the limits to commodification and shifts in the regulatory system; this is done in the last section of this chapter.

3 Level 2 directly complements level 1 in terms of formal market monetary resources: it indirectly increases the cost of labour, for example through state expenditure, and directly increases aggregate demand.

4 Levels 3 and 4 contribute monetary resources and are thereby both involved in the formation of the cost of labour (level 3 directly and level 4 indirectly) and of aggregate demand. However, they avoid control by the formal market and by the state with the result that prices, costs and taxation rates are different, leading to a fundamental problem arising from the fact that a process of informalization is now under way.

5 Levels 5 and 6 are the areas of unpaid work. Both, but mainly 5,

are fundamental survival resources and have been mistakenly overlooked in traditional analysis. Level 5 principally, complemented by level 6, is to a certain extent related to levels 1 and 2 in the sense that insufficient income may be complemented by long hours of self-provisioning and domestic work or by contributions from the community, family, friends and the state. But this complementary relation varies a great deal in time and place and among different income groups. In fact, the modes of providing domestic and self-consumption goods and services can also vary widely according to the technologies available, their cost, the possibility of investment in durables which increase productivity, the quantity and quality of the output, and the organization and division of labour within this sector (see chapters 3 and 4, below; Pahl, 1984; Gershuny and Miles, 1983; Burns, 1977).

6 I have also assumed that the distinction between formal and informal is possible only when and where the economy is subjected to a relatively high degree of regulation by the state, business corporations and trade unions, defined broadly as the associative institutional regulatory system. This has come about through a historical process of recording, standardizing and laying down professional standards and rules for an increasing number of economic activities; the system has gradually come to encompass every kind of monetary transaction and is tending to impose control also over an increasing number of non-monetary transactions, as instanced in contemporary trends in family legislation. The historical process is not a linear one, in which the more 'advanced' a country is the more it is subject to regulation; in many underdeveloped countries the level of regulation is relatively high. Nevertheless, we can distinguish clearly between the early industrialization of developed countries, when the level of regulation was very low, and the later stages of industrial development on a world scale, when the level is higher (see section 6 of this chapter). The term 'formalization', it should be noted here, has been avoided in order to emphasize the fact that the regulatory process is not the reverse of informalization. The two are closely connected and may easily develop along the same lines; that is, the more an economy is highly regulated the more informal patterns of work become convenient, while on the other hand a deregulating pattern usually leads to a situation in which some informal practices return to formal conditions. In this respect, deregulation policies may not automatically lead to the revitalized market expansion expected by neo-conservative policymakers, but only to the surfacing of previously hidden parts of the economy. Whether or not they flourish depends on conditions independent of the regulatory system, of which, as I have already argued, the social context is the most important. I will come back to the interrelation between social factors

and context and the regulatory process at the end of this chapter.

7 The history of industrial development has been interpreted as a continuous movement towards the expansion of level 1 (which initially also incorporated level 3). But this shift has been far from simple and linear, as various examples cited in the course of this book will show. Adopting an approach in which the historical aspect of the problem assumes only minor importance, Gershuny (1983, p. 38) describes twelve possible transformations in the mode of providing goods or services, that is, changing from one to another of the four most important productive networks: formal, household, communal and underground. if the state is included as a fifth productive pole, the number of possible transformations increases to twenty; however, I think it is preferable in the context of a historical approach, also inspired by Polanyi's ideas, to consider the twelve transformations here (see figure 2.1).

The above-mentioned shift has involved massive social changes in terms of economic growth, patterns and rates of employment, distribution and levels of income and the quality of life, all of which have been unevenly distributed among the different social groups at different times. At this stage, I will not deal specifically with the historical transformations since such a discussion presupposes at least a preliminary knowledge of how different regulatory processes and different survival strategies have developed historically. Here it is sufficient to bear in mind that industrial development has also been based on fundamental changes in modes of survival and the quality of life which have exerted tremendous feedback effects on industrial development itself, even though this reciprocal relationship has often been underestimated and relatively ignored.

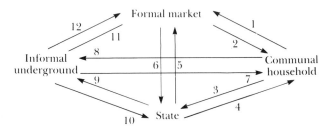

Figure 2.1 Twelve possible historical transformations (reproduced from Gershuny, 1983, p. 38, by permission of the Oxford University Press)

3 RESTRUCTURING AND INFORMALIZATION: FROM ANALYSIS TO INTERPRETATION

Problems in interpreting the diffusion of informal activities on a global scale

Contemporary social changes in the direction of more direct self-consumption, and of more communal and informal work, cover a wide range of activities undertaken in different settings and, even more important, they have been interpreted in a variety of ways. The origins of contemporary interest in non-monetary or informal activities are particularly difficult to trace because they are complex and diverse. The emergence of this problem has been accompanied by a renewed interest in the work of Karl Polanyi (1944/1975; 1977). As I have already underlined in chapter 1, Polanyi insisted on the evidence that market/monetary transactions have only in part taken the place of pre-industrial relations and have done so in a variety of ways at different times. The 'great transformation' has not negated the 'social economy' and a large number of relationships lying outside the mainstream market are still important for understanding the everyday economy and people's daily existence. The recent attention given to 'the social economy' (see Lowenthal, 1975; 1981) has been directly inspired by Polanyi's seminal work.

The term 'informal sector' was first used (Hart, 1973) in socio-economic anthropological studies of Third World cities.[7] Increasing interest has been shown in the fact that the impressively persistent wave of urbanization and urban growth has been accompanied by the development of a variegated 'popular economy'. This appears as a combination of multifarious activities undertaken for direct subsistence and for a low monetary income. The most important activities include animal rearing in overcrowded slums, street-vendors and food stalls, hawkers, rickshaw operators, garbage collection, rudimentary self-help building and repairs, traditional handicraft workshops, industrial homeworking in subcontracting chains, domestic services and laundering for the middle classes, as well as illegal activities. Family, ethnic, regional and neighbourhood networks have always made it possible for these various activities to coagulate into a poor but socially protected way of life. In the 1980s many international agencies (mainly the International Labour Organization, the World Bank and the United Nations) noticed the economic 'miracle' of the informal sector in Third World cities and began to consider the idea of promoting industrial development on the basis of this sector instead of through conventional 'development policies'. I will return to this question in chapter 4 (pp. 250–6).

In the late 1970s increasing attention, anticipated by an important work written by Ferman and Ferman (1973), was devoted to the presence of 'informal' activities in advancd capitalist countries.[8] At the same time, more and more attention was also being paid to the expansion of the 'underground' or 'subterranean' economy.[9] Still in the same period, the important role played by the so-called 'second economy' in the socialist countries came under greater scrutiny by both Western and local scholars.[10] It includes a variety of different activities, which are grouped together only through the common negative factor of being outside the official state-controlled economy.

The origins of the contemporary wave of studies and their critical background are very diverse. They include the vast feminist literature on the historically changing role of women's domestic work; the sexual division of labour and female employment;[11] the work inspired by Schumacher's (1973) idea that 'small is beautiful'; the various studies on the 'household economy';[12] and the extensive literature on labour market segmentation.[13] This wave of studies is reflected in a number of recent international conferences[14] and collective publications.[15] Lastly, it is important to underline the fact that these wide-ranging interests are connected with and lead to new interpretations of post-industrial society in general,[16] and of class stratification, political policies and work/survival strategies. The attention paid to phenomena which on a global scale at first appeared to be common to different kinds of societies gave rise to an important comparative debate. The fact that these phenomena have had an accentuated local character has led to a variety of interpretations.

The most important distinction to be made is whether trends towards informalization are interpreted as long-lasting transformations or as temporary consequences of economic and social crisis. I find the former more plausible. It is true that long and deep-seated economic crises typically produce an increase in self-employment and in irregular or seasonal work and a return to traditional, local market or extra-market activities as a consequence of high unemployment. But the present problems of employment are not only a result of the economic downturn and slow growth. In the long run, automation and industrial restructuring and relocation reduce to an increasing extent the levels, in terms of either duration or numbers, of formal employment in industrialized areas; this reduction is even greater when the rate of investment in technological change and restructuring rises (see Jallade, 1981; O'Connor, 1984). Also, the diffusion of informal activities is substantially generated by the pace of tertiarization, as will be seen many times in the course of this book, and the mode of expansion of services cannot be interpreted at all as a 'contingent' event. Furthermore, the studies of local informal activities in advanced capitalist countries have accumulated evidence against interpretations which see the spread of such activities as only a temporary effect of the crisis, especially the fact that the unemployed only engage in them to a relatively small degree (Foudi et al. 1982; Pahl, 1984) and that the regional and time distribution of highly diffused informal activities does not at all coincide with the pattern and periods of economic difficulties. Explanations based on contingent factors are even less convincing when the informal sector in Third World cities and the 'second economy' in socialist countries are also taken into consideration. These phenomena have been growing stronger over a relatively long period and largely independently of limited growth or stagnation. In fact, if any connection with the economic cycle can be established it is rather the reverse, that is, a correlation between economic growth and the diffusion of informal activities. For example, the second economy appears to be more extensive in regions and countries which are doing economically better than others, such as Georgia, Armenia and Hungary; and the 'informal sector' mushroomed in Brazil, Singapore and Taiwan during their recent economic miracles. But the fact that in the last-named countries the subsequent economic slowdown has not significantly affected the trends of the informal sector tends to confirm that the correlation between the informalization process and the ups and downs of the official economy is a weak one.

Structural interpretations of change in advanced capitalist societies

There exist a number of structural interpretations of the diffusion of informal working activities which focus mainly on advanced capitalist countries. The differences between them lie in the extent to which they emphasize certain themes and how they treat particular or local aspects of a very complex phenomenon. Five lines of interpretation are worth discussing here.

First, the placing of the greatest emphasis on technological change in industrialized societies as the most important factor in a new wave of socio-economic development can be seen in Gershuny's social innovation thesis. He argues that technological change affects ways of providing services for mass consumption (Gershuny, 1978; 1983; Gershuny and Miles, 1983), and that new technologies supply the means for achieving an increase in the informal provision or self-provision of services. An example from the field of education is the use of videos or computers with/by either individuals or informal community groups. While it is in general true that light technologies and changes in the mode of providing services contribute to a certain extent to an increase in the vitality of small-scale activities and to the spread of some informal practices, it is also true that this interpretation underestimates various aspects of present social change. These are: (1) the consequences of the uneven spread of advanced technologies among classes and over different geographical areas; (2) the exploitative use of informalization and technological change through corporate restructuring; and (3) the critical feedback from this transformation in terms of underconsumption resulting from increased unemployment, underemployment or job transfer and restructuring. The same emphasis on technological change may also lead to opposite conclusions, as is the case in the work of Castells (1983; 1984; 1985; 1989), who underlines the exploitative consequences, the isolation experienced by individuals and the further diminishing of their potential that arises out of technological transformation.

Second, a line of interpretation has been developed from Schumacher's thesis that 'small is beautiful' (1973). Informalization is seen as an alternative way of producing and surviving against the suffocating and alienating control exercised by big corporations and the state (Heinze and Olk, 1982; Szelenyi, 1981). The potential innovative political character of some forms of informalization is underlined, but the possible relations of 'exploitation' and indirect control embodied in the expansion of the informal sector wherever it is found are underestimated.

A third interpretation concentrates principally on the possibility of neo-dualistic superexploitative connections between informalization and new developments in the concentration of capitalism on a world scale in terms of new forms of reproducing cheap labour, of direct exploitation, either through the appropriation of unpaid work through self-service or through various forms of subcontracting, or of indirect exploitation, expansion of some privileged markets for do-it-yourself tools, electronic and information-processing equipment, financial control, dismantling of state intervention, etc. (Bromley and Gerry, 1979; Portes and Walton, 1981). This interpretation overemphasizes the importance of informalization in manufacturing, given that evidence from both advanced capitalist and underdeveloped countries shows an increasing concentration of informal activities in services.

A different version of this approach can be found in authors who have studied the combination of high rates of exploitation in family work and extensive irregular employment (part-time, moonlighting, outwork, etc.) in industrializing areas where small concerns are still predominant (as in North-Eastern and Central Italy; see Bagnasco, 1977; Paci, 1980). In this interpretation, too, the manufacturing side is overstressed. Moreover, follow-up studies of cases of diffused industrialization in North-Eastern and Central Italy (the so-called 'NEC model' – Bagnasco, 1988) show that informal activities in manufacturing have sharply decreased with the consolidation of an export-oriented industrial system, which in order to function more effectively needs to operate within the framework of the regular economy, as is demonstrated in chapter 5 and 6.

Finally, some authors have interpreted the informal sector as a new option among the survival strategies available to households in industrialized countries. Informalization is held to be one of the possible responses to inflation, the jobs crisis and the rigidity of formal work and consumption (Ferman et al, 1978; Pahl, 1980; Gershuny and Pahl, 1981). This interpretation underlines the fact that, under certain conditions, do-it-yourself or informal activities become not only advantageous from the economic point of view but are also the best way of obtaining certain goods or services quickly or of the quality required. This is true to a certain extent, but it does not fully explain the complex phenomena involved and is of no use for a comparative study, such as the one undertaken here.

Implications and possible development of structural interpretations

None of these five ways of interpreting such informalization is in itself erroneous. The fact is that they are partial explanations, because they take into account only some of the phenomena that go to make up the informalization process. As Gallino points out, the diffusion of informal activities is simultaneously: '(a) an inescapable outcome of the development of the late capitalist economy; (b) a free and creative choice of social innovation; (c) a set of small recipes for survival; (d) a return to pre-modern social relations with the support of modern technologies' (1983, p. 7). It is also true, however, that these and other structural interpretations of the present change in social patterns have a very important point in common. They express a radical change in the understanding of the industrialization process as a long-term tendency. It is no longer possible to accept the assumption that, in general, industrial development can be explained in terms of the ever-increasing importance of: (a) wage work, variously graded and segmented at different times; (b) organizational patterns in large manufacturing and tertiary concerns; (c) bureaucratic apparatuses, foremost among which is the nation-state. Informalization, peripheral or diffused industrialization based on small and/or subcontracting firms, increases in new forms of chronic unemployment and underemployment and the fiscal crisis of the state have undermined the premises of practically every important approach towards interpreting industrial development, with the exception of the one adopted by Polanyi (see Polanyi, 1944/1975).

The collapse of the old assumption has given rise to certain difficulties but has also led to the discovery or rediscovery of important characteristics of contemporary societies, particularly the impact of different social factors and socialization mixes, as already argued in chapter 1. It is also worth mentioning that while the line of interpretation based on industrialism was totally inadequate to explain the social trends in underdeveloped and socialist countries, the new common attention towards phenomena broadly labelled informal is giving rise to a comparative debate, which could turn out to be very fruitful for understanding the prospects for society on a world scale.

Apart from the question of the variety of working and survival strategies, among which the problem of the spread of informal activities is crucial, this revision of previous interpretations has other important consequences. For instance, two positions are of interest. Pahl (1984; 1985; 1986; 1988b), for one, insists that the sociological analysis of stratification, political and social behaviour, marginalization and the structuring of diversified life-styles should be based on household strategies rather than on the occupation and income of the breadwinner. Bagnasco (1985; 1986b), for another, stresses that the recent processes of diffused industrialization and economic restructuring have entailed an important readjustment to the balance between the various criteria for resource distribution. He identifies the four most important of these as reciprocity, the invisible hand of the market, the organization of large concerns and political exchange. The tendency of the last two to prevail over the first two has been weakened by a rigidity crisis and, consequently, reciprocity and the hidden hand of the market have gained renewed importance, although under very different conditions from those which existed in the past when they were the predominant criteria. Informalization in a broad sense can be seen as an important symptom of this redefinition of the criteria for the redistribution of resources both on a local and general scale. I will come back to these and other interpretations of current patterns in social change in the final chapter.

4 TOWARDS A COMPLEX ALTERNATIVE LINE OF INTERPRETATION

An ideal map to explain informalization in relation to different social networks

It is now clearer that the problem we are dealing with has two sides to it: the real processes of current social change, and the capacity of social scientists to understand and make sense of these changes in complex societies for which it is both extremely difficult and very necessary to work out a general explanation for highly complicated phenomena.

As to the first theme, it is evident that various kinds of informalization processes constitute only partial aspects of the global picture of social change. Consequently, they can only be explained by starting from an understanding of the more general logic behind the new international division of labour, of the processes through which work and the economy are being restructured and of the new forms of marginalization or social promotion of different social strata. This connection explains both the variety of informalization processes and the possibility of interpreting them from different angles. It also explains why the debate on the informal sector and activities has become so topical and important: they form a crucial aspect of the different ways in which societies are being restructured.

The second theme can be summed up as follows: social scientists are having great difficulty in interpreting current social change, since they have had to abandon the theoretical paradigm used with some success for the last 200 years. As well as other phenomena, trends in informalization do not fit the interpretative models traditionally used to explain industrial development. To help visualize this difficulty of interpretation, I have constructed figure 2.2 (see p. 94), which shows both the complexity and variety of the social networks in which broadly informal activities take place, and that the binary concepts (commodification/decommodification; public/private; production/reproduction) used to explain and simplify social reality cannot be applied in the attempt to understand processes of informalization.

Figure 2.2 is based on three assumptions: (1) there are four areas of social relationships which are involved in the informal sector in the broad sense: kinship, friendship and neighbourhood networks, community, the household and the strictly informal sector involving irregular or illegal activities carried out for a monetary income or other advantages, of which only the last is totally included within the broad concept of informality; (2) there are large areas in which the different networks overlap; (3) the broad informal area is divided into two parts by the three most important binary concepts used for interpreting societies in the industrial age: monetary/non-monetary (commodification versus decommodification); public/private; production/reproduction. The first two assumptions reflect the multifaceted and complex diffusion of informal activities. The third expresses the difficulty involved in giving a clear-cut meaning to a generically understood informalization process, at least when applying these three dual divisions. The point I wish to make is that the expansion of informal activities cannot be interpreted

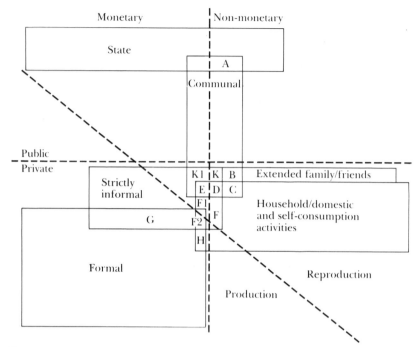

Figure 2.2 Subsistence resources networks: overlapping areas, dualist interpretation intersections and broad informal areas (shown by broken lines)

Explanations and examples of the overlapping areas in Figure 2.2:

A = The state provides resources to promote communal activities, i.e. money, seats, capital to organize cultural or voluntary local welfare activities.

B = The basis for communal activities is provided by extended families or groups of friends.

C = Example: communally organized child care where parents volunteer on a rota basis.

D = As C, but some parents do not contribute their time and are replaced by others whom they compensate in kind.

E = As C, but parents pay cash to employ childminders informally.

F = Example: part of the produce from an allotment is sold for cash to neighbours (F1) or to a shop (F2) or it is exchanged for other goods or services (F).

G = Moonlighting or irregular work in a formal economic unit; unregistered income deriving from formal activities; subcontracting between a formal unit and an informal one, etc.

H = As F, but the produce is sold officially (registered sale).

K = Communal activities utilizing informal work which is paid for either in cash (K1) or in kind (K).

directly as a process of decommodification (transformation from monetary to less monetary or non-monetary), or one of privatization (shift from public to private concerns), or as an expansion of the area of reproduction as opposed to that of production.

Given that it is practically impossible to understand informalization processes with the help of conventional binary concepts, it is helpful to deal with the problem by using an alternative approach in which limited sub-problems are isolated one by one, making it relatively easy to put forward a hypothesis about current social transformations. Of immediate interest are two aspects which appear in figure 2.2. The first concerns the importance of the social network in which informal activities are located or, possibly, a combination of different networks. This is a crucial factor in understanding the nature and impact of the presence or spread of informal activities. The second aspect concerns the possibility of using figure 2.2 together with figure 2.1 (which lists the twelve most important socio-historical transformations) in order to verify whether or not some informalization transformations cut across the lines established by the explanations based on a binary pattern and thereby assume a clear-cut meaning relative to the latter.

Networks and informalization

The question of networks requires a brief anticipation of the discussion in the final section of this chapter, in particular with regard to the structure of social regulation. The state and the formal sector of the economy are by definition the loci of an associative institutional form of social organization. Other networks are more likely to express reciprocal forms of social organization. This is obvious for household, kinship, friendship and community networks. We still do not have a clearly defined picture of what have been called strictly informal activities. Recent studies of different kinds of societies support the conclusion that although such activities differ greatly in diverse social contexts, they are usually accompanied by some sort of network with reciprocal features.

The informational aspect is the most evident and recurrent of these features. By definition, informal activities are not officially recorded and publicized even when they are not illegal and are tolerated by the authorities. Economic operators and customers are involved in a network of information which is based on a certain degree of reciprocal trust. The network opens up or remains closed depending partly on the extent to which the informal activity is able to expand, and partly on how many people it can involve before becoming too risky or economically inconvenient. The more informal activities are illegal, the tighter the protective reciprocity of the informational network has to be, which in these cases tends to coincide with its operational range. The 'underground' part of the second economy in state socialist countries constitutes a good example of this point, as will be shown more clearly in chapter 5. Economic operators, managers and to some extent workers in official manufacturing or commercial concerns need a large strong network if they are both to obtain the required input and distribute the unofficial output. The network should be large enough in both directions to allow such informal operations to be sufficiently complete. At the same time, it has to be limited enough and characterized by high levels of reciprocal advantage in order to avoid the control of the authorities.

The obtaining of reciprocal benefits is also a frequent characteristic of strictly informal activities in different societies, both in provider/customer and employer/employee relationships. For instance, when an irregular plumber does a repair job for a cash payment, even when he charges the same as an officially registered worker or firm – which is seldom the case, unless he offers other advantages to the customers such as immediate service – he pockets the amount due in tax and the customer pays no tax either. The same occurs when an employer hires a moonlighting worker for additional hours of work. In these two cases the network of information and trust is very important. Finally, there are cases in which particular combinations of different reciprocal networks assume great importance, the informal sector in Third World cities being the most complicated. Family, community, sometimes regional and ethnic solidarity, a wide informational/-trust network are all involved to a certain extent in making possible the diverse livelihood arrangements found in the informal sector.

The diffusion of informal activities and its impact in terms of commodification or decommodification

As will be seen in the final section of this chapter, such an insistence on the importance of networks and on the difference between associative and reciprocal arrangements is crucial in order to understand not only processes of informalization but also current trends in social change. Let us discuss briefly the various possible meanings of informalization as a social transformation. With the help of figures 2.1 and 2.2, it is possible to formulate many different but real examples which show that informalization entails decommodification in one context and commodification in another. It is worth mentioning a few examples which appear significant within the present debate. Comparative studies of informalization in the First and Third Worlds have at times been difficult to carry out, because in the industrialized countries informal activities express an overall trend towards decommodification whereas the growth of the informal sector in Third World cities has been often accompanied by increased commodification. However, the question of transformation can be posed only if we know or if we can assume not only in what area of our figure the informal activity is now located but also in what area it originated. A subsistence peasant who migrates to the informal sector of a large city moves (with regard to the level of commodification) in the opposite direction to a blue-collar worker in an industrialized country who asks a friend to repair his car instead of going to the usual expensive service station. Commodification tendencies in underdeveloped countries within the urbanization process and the decline of subsistence agriculture are in general quite easy to point to. What is more difficult to discover is the significance that should be attributed to the degree of protection which the reciprocal network in the informal sector offers against the potentially greater threats posed by dependent industrialization. It is clear, however, that the existence and growth of the informal sector provide the only explanation as to how the millions of inhabitants in large Third World cities can manage to survive.

The informalization process in advanced capitalist countries cannot be interpreted as decommodification. Examples can be given in which almost every social and economic transformation may have consequences in any part of the area which is defined as broadly informal; then there are additional patterns to be taken into consideration in terms of commodification/decommodification. To what extent can the move from employing a formal or informal worker for household repairs to do-it-yourself be considered a decommodification transformation, if expensive tools have to be bought which will not be widely used? But the real problem is that informal activities cannot be understood unless they are seen in relation to the question of social regulation. I will argue that different mixes of social regulations are essential in order to explain the existence and the social structure of industrial societies. The existence and diffusion of informal activities of various kinds in different contemporary societies do not *per se* imply social crisis or a new pattern of development.

If we understand what informalization signifies within a complex diversified pattern of social regulation which is the key to how contemporary
societies work, we will be able to use evidence of informalization to
understand better the prospects for present-day societies. But before
tackling this problem, it is necessary to return to the question of the
origins of an increasing heterogeneity in working activities and examine
it from a more theoretical point of view.

5 PROLETARIANIZATION AND THE SETTING-UP OF INSTITUTIONALIZED LABOUR MARKETS

A critical examination of the Marxist theory of proletarianization

Both Marx's theory of proletarianization and conventional labour market
analysis have been used to formulate a theory of the progressive homogenization of industrial societies, as found in interpretations based on work-
centred models. A closer examination of these interpretations in the
light of historical and current evidence of the controlled and distorted
functioning of markets, however, shows a different and more complex
picture. Marx's theory of proletarianization is twofold. First, the existence
of a group of potential workers compelled to sell their labour power in
order to survive, because they have been freed from legal restrictions and
excluded from other options, is one of the important preconditions for
capitalist accumulation. Second, capitalist accumulation itself activates
a process of proletarianization in order to obtain a sufficient supply of
labour and one which is independent of unmanageable demographic
factors. The first aspect is an essential part of the theory of primitive
accumulation and the second is fundamental to the theory of capital
accumulation.

Marx insisted that historically the creation of a large group of free
workers had occurred prior to capitalist take-off. In shaping his interpretation of how free labour was formed, Marx is, unusually, particularly
receptive to social factors and puts forward the idea that some aspects
of primitive proletarianization may not only represent a historically
earlier phenomenon but also a persisting *de facto* precondition for such a
process to happen. The case for granting historical precedence to this
process is clear. Where capital accumulation is not well established and
still weak and uncertain, it cannot compete with social habits that are
deeply rooted in different traditions. These modes of survival – alternatives to the free sale of labour – are eradicated through the use of force.
The main evidence on which Marx constructs this part of his theory is
based on the enclosure laws introduced in Britain. They represented an

act of violence on the part of landlords in evicting peasants in order to deprive them of the customary right to farm a part of the common land. However, this evidence has an odd side to it: the final beneficiaries of this forced eviction, whom Marx considered to be the first modern capitalists, the industrial merchants and small handicraft employers, do not appear at all in this dramatic episode and the landlords' motives have nothing whatever to do with the creation of a free labour force. Yet, the enclosures were indisputably acts of violence which broke the back of a pre-industrial communal mode of survival, thus compelling at least some of the members of a community to migrate to cities and in the long run to become, among others, the forerunners of the modern proletariat.

Colonization worked according to the same logic. In this case, too, one notes a certain degree of involuntary interaction and the absence of proper capitalist forces from the process, at least as far as the early, violent phase is concerned. The Spanish colonial conquest of Central and South America was undertaken mainly by an army of aristocratic soldiers for the purpose of forcing the more or less enslaved indigenous population to work in the gold and silver mines, and at a later date on the large plantations. Whichever part of the world is considered, the fundamental idea is that in order to obtain free wage workers you literally have to drive them out of or away from the social contexts and conditions which permit forms of survival other than offering one's labour on a free market. These social contexts resist the weak pressure from capitalist competition that exists in the initial phase of capital accumulation. Furthermore, there is enough evidence that they are not even easily penetrated by an established and mature form of accumulation based exclusively on market competition. It is on this ground that it is possible to argue that the patterns of 'primitive' proletarianization not only historically but also logically pre-date the free supply of labour on the market. However primitive, backward and miserable the traditional communal and socially protected ways of survival may appear to 'modernizers', they will create difficult obstacles to the creation of a free proletariat for as long as they are allowed to exist. This is so not only in the case of remote Amazonian tribes or African villagers but also in that of peasants or artisans in advanced capitalist countries.

If the violent breaking-up of social arrangements is not only a historical but also a logical precondition for a free labour supply, it should be incorporated into any Marxist theory of capitalist proletarianization. Marx further argues that through capital concentration and uneven increases in productivity, petty commodity producers are ruined and expropriated and inefficient capitalists are pushed down into the proletariat. At the same time this process gives rise to surplus population, the so-called 'industrial reserve army'.

Marx devotes a chapter of *Das Kapital* (vol. I, chap. XXIII) to explaining the logic of this process and documents the historical forms assumed by the surplus population. His arguments on this point are supported not only by his own research but also by an impressive set of evidence relating to later developments on a world scale and up to the present period. However, this question raises two important and controversial points. First, although the persistent formation of a surplus population became an essential part of his theory of capitalist accumulation, Marx did not progress much further in integrating it into his interpretation of the capitalist system as a whole. I will come back to this shortly and again in chapters 3, 4 and 7. Second, Marx and, to an even greater extent, the orthodox line in the Marxist tradition have used this side of the theory of proletarianization to defend the idea of a generalized impoverishment of the working class. If a totally free labour market is assumed, this conclusion is unavoidable. But historical evidence does not support this conclusion, nor show the persistent existence of an unregulated labour market. The idea that capitalist development creates surplus population can be defended even if it does not also lead to generalized impoverishment, provided it is complemented by a theory of social regulation on two fronts: the protection of employed workers from the devastating effects of excessive competition, and the provision of means for survival to different groups within the surplus population. Such a complementary theory would assume that many competitive pressures inside the proletarianization process are relocated and exert their effects elsewhere. This process thus becomes simultaneously one of marginalization of the working class in the broad sense (actual and potential) and of the progressive diversification of their conditions of existence.

I will now piece together the various elements in this discussion in order to see if a clear picture can be obtained. In Marx's view, capitalist accumulation both presupposes and produces an extensive supply of labour freed from any alternative form of control over or dependence on the means of subsistence. For this to happen, barriers of custom and forms of social protection have to be destroyed, not only through economic competition but also and mainly through the politically motivated use of force, which in a first phase has no connection with the specific goal of capitalist accumulation but later forms an essential and inherent part of capitalist strategy. At the same time, capitalist accumulation creates a relatively large social group whose control over the means of subsistence, though not ended, is seriously weakened. In order to survive and avoid direct competition with free labour, this group requires new as well as old forms of social sheltering. Consequently, the concept of social protection, in its various different forms, is extended from the 'not yet proletarianized' to the different types of surplus population and eventually to other groups which resist proletarianization, such as petty commodity producers and the so-called 'old middle class'. If this were not the case, we could not explain why these social groups do not become immediately proletarianized or just stop surviving in an economic system dominated by a level of market competitiveness which they are unable to match. The connection between broad social shelters, or protective socialization mixes predominantly based on reciprocal networks and arrangements, and capitalist development is now seen to be much more complex: the shelters are simultaneously undermined and recreated. It is not yet the two-way relationship formulated by Polanyi, but neither is it as simplistic as the form it used to take in most orthodox Marxist interpretations.

Critical observations on the Marxist approach towards the 'old middle class'

A reinterpretation of the Marxist theory of proletarianization along the above-mentioned lines also gives rise to some useful considerations on the problem of the 'old middle class'. As I have already remarked, the proletarianization theory assumes that they exist, are progressively expropriated and consequently incorporated into the supply of free market labour. It is not clear which groups, and under what socio-historical conditions, are going to be directly proletarianized and which ones will remain for a temporary period in the 'parking orbit' of the surplus population. Marx is explicit only in the case of the peasants who, he says, often follow the indirect route via the latent component of the industrial reserve army. But the really important point here is that both Marxists and non-Marxists have assumed that these strata are remnants of a pre-industrial order condemned to die out gradually. The definition 'old middle class' or 'classes' itself suggests such an assumption. The historical evidence on their decline is controversial (Granovetter, 1984; Steinmetz and Wright, 1989). In the nineteenth century, there was a long-term trend towards a substantial decrease in the number of self-employed workers in the advanced capitalist countries; but this took place mostly in agriculture and as a side-effect of the general decline in agricultural employment. In some countries and during periods of economic crisis, however, their numbers have risen. Lately, tertiarization, much more than industrial restructuring, has brought about a considerable increase in their ranks. As I have already argued, the service sector is in general much less concentrated and much more difficult to concentrate than manufacturing. Although it cannot be denied that until now a historical tendency for the old middle class to decline has been at work, the whole question needs to be rediscussed and particular attention paid to the patterns, structures and socio-organizational trends of the service sector.

On the other hand, the idea that the old middle classes are a remnant from a pre-industrial economic order is in fact mistaken. There is little doubt that shopkeepers, self-employed craftworkers and even peasants have not only been transformed but largely generated and multiplied by industrial growth itself. It would be paradoxical to see in the growing army of self-employed service workers a remnant from a pre-industrial mode of production. Here, too, industrial development generates social niches and economic opportunities where self-employed and small-scale activities can operate and which for various different reasons cannot be immediately or directly invaded by concentrated corporate enterprises. The case of petty trade in what are now advanced capitalist countries is a clear example. There was a long period in which a substantial increase in the number of shopkeepers and petty traders occurred before concentrated capital discovered a way to penetrate the sector and proletarianize a large part of the workers. This process was not linear, did not happen everywhere, was partially reversible and never involved all forms of trading. The relatively high degree of variation in different national and local contexts cannot be reasonably explained without referring to the crucial role of social factors.

Proletarianization, historically, has taken different forms. In many late-developing countries in Europe, the process was never completed and most of those employed in the expanding sectors of industry were peasant-workers.[17] This pattern had repercussions on the trend towards urbanization and projected the crucial role played by adapted socio-organizational factors based on reciprocity into the industrial age. A persistent but changing combination of traditional rural activities and life-styles, together with limited consumption on the one hand and manufacturing employment in modern industry, wage-labour and modern forms of association on the other is, for instance, typical of many Italian regions (see chapter 6). Once again, what we have here is a specific combination of social factors and patterns of industrial development.

To summarize: if the results of industrial development and proletarianization as discussed above and schematized in figure 2.3 are taken as given and also the fact that social conditions, regulations and protection have prevented a general homogenization of working and living patterns, the inescapable conclusion is that Marx's theory leads to a very complex picture. The range and distribution of working and living conditions show a wide variety of different types. They may sometimes become simplified and standardized when market competition is at a high and rewarding level and/or when a rather high rate of political violence is effective in breaking down the defences of protective social networks. But most of the time the combination of pressures works in the opposite direction, at least on a world scale where a certain degree of standardization at the core is compensated for by a massive shift of social contradictions towards the periphery and widespread marginaliz-ation.

Critical considerations on labour market analysis and theories

Labour market analysis often takes a different starting-point from that adopted in Marx's theory of capitalist accumulation. Whereas Marx formulated the theory of the formation of the industrial reserve army in order to underpin the idea of a *sufficient* labour supply, labour market theories have to deal with the difficulty of explaining how the market would work in the likely possibility of *excess* labour supply. 'The repro-duction of the capacity for work would be prevented if the labour market were a "cover-all" institution; it would consequently destroy itself' (Offe, 1985, p. 26). This is true even if we disregard Polanyi's highly significant observation that labour is a 'fictive' commodity and that 'no society could stand the effects of such a system of crude fictions even for the shortest stretch of time unless its human and natural substance as well as its business organization was protected against the ravages of this satanic mill' (Polanyi, 1944/1975, p. 73). Labour market analysis is forced to come to terms with the fact that the labour market is quite unusual compared to the market for genuine commodities. The most important differences concern the supply of labour and also the nature of the employment contract (Offe, 1985). Let us look briefly at the specific aspects of the labour supply which make it very different from other commodities and in the final analysis a 'fictive' one.

First, unlike real commodities, labour is not supplied or produced by market-controlled mechanisms, with the result that its quantity and quality cannot be regulated by the market and are highly inelastic. They depend on historical demographic trends as well as on the historical patterns characterizing the removal of barriers or protective social div-isions, mentioned in the first part of this section. Second, in a totally unregulated market situation labour is time-inelastic as its supply depends 'upon the *continuous* flow of *adequate* means of subsistence' (ibid., p. 17; italics in original). And the fact that we are not dealing with

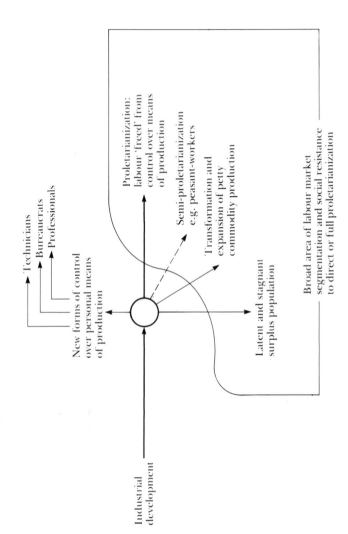

Figure 2.3 Proletarianization and other social changes

common perishable commodities but with the life or death of human beings assumes, most of the time, great importance in the organization of societies. Third, labour is also relatively price-inelastic in the sense that its supply cannot be kept up if the means of subsistence decreases and falls below a minimum survival level. Or to put it in Offe's words: 'through the use of technological change, production can very well be maintained even with a fall in labour input per unit of output, while reproduction of labour power cannot be maintained with a fall of income per household' (ibid., p. 18). If these three aspects are considered together, it is obvious that a highly competitive unregulated labour market is either a conceptual absurdity or a historically devastating event. The British parliamentary reports on the conditions of the urban working class in the first half of the nineteenth century, the Blue Books on which Marx and Engels drew extensively, more or less illustrate the devastation caused, even in a limited situation where the labour market was highly competitive and only regulated to a very small extent, but still at an early undeveloped stage.

If it is assumed that the market cannot regulate the supply of labour according to its expected saleability, as happens with real commodities, but that partially independent historical processes proletarianize a number of potential workers and systematically destroy social bonds and shelters, the conclusion must be that the operating of an unregulated market will inevitably lead to the persistent destruction of labour power because of its time and income rigidities. Such a bizarre outcome is not only unacceptable from a moral point of view and incompatible with historical social formations which react in defence of society, but it is also untenable in terms of the internal logic of the labour market itself. This is the reason why I would use the expression 'conceptual absurdity'. The excessive supply of labour at a given moment of time in a situation governed by pure market logic would mean that a part of the supply, the unemployed, dies of starvation because of time-rigidity and also that the employed workers are obliged to accept a relatively long period of decreasing income below the minimal historical level of subsistence. As a consequence of the price-rigidity of labour, its quality would deteriorate irreversibly and its demographic renewal would be seriously jeopardized by an increase in the child mortality rate. If capitalism is still not fully developed it can rely on a continuous fresh supply of 'not yet proletarianized' workers, but this solution cannot work in the long term. Thus, an unregulated labour market is not historically feasible and in social terms it is a nightmare.

Without a dense and complex set of social regulations the 'labour market' would not exist. These regulations have succeeded in excluding from the market a large number of potential workers and controlling the influx of labour onto the market in various ways, which differ in time and space. In other words, the labour market operates only on the necessary condition that social institutions and factors prevent a considerable number of potentially active workers from offering their labour on the market. Logically speaking, this is a valid point because the same argument is used for real commodities to explain how market mechanisms are overridden, but not their very possibility of existence. For instance, the price of some agricultural commodities is raised artifically, in opposition to market competition, when the state buys up huge quantities for the purpose of rigging the market. In this case, it is said that these commodities are outside the market or non-market goods. By analogy, and paradoxically, the labour market should be considered by economic analysts as a non-market. 'As new as the labour market is as a social institution, the self-protection of society from its consequences commences almost simultaneously with the institutionalization of labour markets' (ibid., 1985 p. 59).

It is not by chance that the impact of labour market tensions has seldom produced the same degree of social devastation as that recorded among the English urban working class in the first half of the nineteenth century: the undermining of the family, a high degree of work mobility, instability and individual competitive behaviour, the absence of solidarity among workers, low and decreasing wages, extremely low standards of living and higher rates of mortality and morbidity in the city compared to the countryside. As soon as extensive social reaction began to set in, it became transformed into a set of social shelters and shifts which generated an increasingly complex and heterogeneous social order. In general, the negative effects from the formation of an institutionalized labour market have been increasingly transferred to and cumulated within the underdeveloped countries, especially in the countryside. Here, poverty, famine and malnutrition made their appearance more rapidly.

The institutionalization of labour markets, the protective strategies of trade union movements, the substantial impact from large groups being excluded from the possibility of supplying their labour, have totally underminded the potential for social homogenization, attributed in theory to a market interaction which in reality cannot exist. The role of social factors and context has been as crucial as that of state intervention or of associative pressures. The heterogeneity of social conditions has not only been produced by labour market segmentation or by the division of the population into an active and an inactive part, but also by the extensive presence of self-employed and small-scale activities and of various kinds of subsistence arrangements based on reciprocal networks and solidarity.

Moreover, this last consideration means that serious doubt must be thrown on the operational impact of competitive tensions in the real commodity markets and confirms once more what I argued in chapter 1: that the market should be viewed as a set of tensions which produce social reactions and not in itself as a social regulator.

As already stated, the argument formulated here does not mean that the complex operation of developed institutionalized and regulated markets and that of labour markets in particular is fair and equalizing. On the contrary, regulations and limitations shift all kinds of negative consequences towards specifically penalized social groups and geographic regions. This process also sets in motion a counter-reaction from defensive social factors, whereas powerful interest groups act politically in an attempt to disactivate and destroy these defences in order to implement the shift of negative conditions towards the margins of the social system. Consequently, the highly complex nature of contemporary societies is not only a result of the diversified impact of an increasingly regulated and institutionalized labour market but also of the different potentials for reaction and successful resistance.

6 THE CONDITIONS AND CONSEQUENCES OF REGULATORY PROCESSES

Social factors of the associative and reciprocal kind and the regulatory process

An increasing number of economic interpretations of contemporary capitalism accept the idea that capitalism is not a simple free-market society but an organized one:[18] they insist on the crucial importance of different ways of regulating industrial societies. It is only worth mentioning in passing the obvious fact that socialist societies cannot be understood at all if their mode of regulation is not taken into consideration.

These interpretations are useful and a step in the right direction compared to traditional orthodox economics based on the assumption that an unrestricted market and its 'laws' are the main source of social organization. However, the way they conceive the regulatory process differs substantially from the one adopted here. They are, at best, typically concerned with only one of the two main social sources of regulatory options: the one which I have broadly defined as 'associative'. Interest groups, trade unions, cartels, etc., directly or through the state, and even the state itself, bring into being the institutional regulations needed to prevent, at different times and in different social contexts, competitive market tensions from undermining the social order and, thereby, also the very possibility for capitalism to survive as a form of society. In my view, this is only a part of the picture and by itself cannot fully explain the various regulatory processes.

At the roots of social regulation in general during the industrial age there are both associative and reciprocal kinds of human relationships. As already stated in chapter 1, the structuring of industrial societies is the result of the complex interactions between three orders of factors: competitive tensions, associative relations and reciprocal relations. Although it may be true that the importance of the last decreases with the development of industry, as suggested by classical approaches in sociology from Durkheim to Tönnies and Weber, it is also true that they do not die out and thus continue to play a crucial and diverse role in contemporary societies. It is not easy to simplify the complex chain of interactions and reactions which characterize the regulatory process in general, but this exercise is vital in order to understand contemporary societies and in particular the different trends in informalization, which are nothing but aspects of this process. The aim of this section is to identify some crucial moments in the general regulatory process during the industrial age so that they can be traced in specific social phenomena through time and space.

These crucial moments broadly concern two important aspects of the regulatory process. The first is based on the assumption that reciprocal arrangements, since they do not disappear, have different ways of responding to competitive pressures and to the emergence of increasingly important associative systems. We saw in chapter 1 that the pattern of industrial development may differ to a considerable degree when recipro-cal arrangements are incorporated more systematically and substantially into the social organization of the industrial age (what could be called the Japanese model). This variant is also important because it continues to recur in different versions and at various times, such as diffused industrialization in North-Eastern and Central Italy, or the ethnic entrepreneurship of Japanese, Chinese, Korean and Cuban minorities in the USA, or the return of 'parked' rural workers to running family farms in Hungary. More generally, it is important to understand what the regulatory potential of transformed and adapted reciprocal networks is along two lines: the limiting of market tensions beyond the confines established by the associative regulatory structure and the absorption of market tensions in ways which are either prohibited or not properly taken into account by the associative regulatory system.

The second crucial moment concerns the associative regulatory process and involves some issues that have been discussed with regard to prolet-arianization and to the priority attributed by the logic of capitalist development to the violent undermining of defensive community networks so that industrialization can be extended further. From this perspective, the associative regulatory process assumes two aspects: the setting of limits to the devastating penetration of destructive market tensions into community networks and, at the same time, the reshaping of social organization based on reciprocity in order to make it compatible with industrial development. As will be seen below, this apparent contradiction is made possible by the twofold result of the industrial regulatory process on a world scale: the creation of strong associative limits against competitive tensions and the compatible defensive adaptation of reciprocal networks in advanced capitalist and socialist countries is accompanied by devastating attacks on the defensive reciprocal networks in the underdeveloped world.

The distinction between associative and reciprocal systems, beyond a strictly localized anthropological analysis, is bound to be a difficult one to make in the industrial age. In fact, regulations and limitations rooted in the community are likely to remain hidden; this applies both to those oriented against the market and even more to those which absorb market tensions in violation of associative regulations. When they become explicit and institutionalized, this is often due to a process of incorporation originating in the pressures of associative interest groups. As a consequence, the regulatory process appears to be the result of associative relations. What follows is a signficant example to clarify this and other points.

An example: the social regulation of child labour

Child *labour* is continually regulated by the family within a changing local tradition. The legal regulation by the state of the *employment* of minors emerged as a major obstacle to the extension of a free industrial labour market in every industrialized country in the second half of the nineteenth century. As mentioned in the previous section, this and other limitations prevent the possibility of an excessive labour supply wrecking the labour market and the industrialization process. At the same time, it also stops the corrosive effect on the reciprocal system or on the family nucleus itself brought about by the spread of market competition; consider the devastating picture of the English urban working class given by the parliamentary reports which led Engels to believe that the working-class family would shortly disappear.

There is little doubt that families held to a customary diversified mode of regulating and limiting child labour even after the introduction of laws against the employment of minors. The laws may have affected patterns of change in family regulation but, possibly, less than the previously existing competitive pressures and less than the persistent impact of diverse local conditions. For instance, it can be readily assumed that the internal division of labour in rural families did not change at all as a consequence of the new laws. Through the creation of a modern institutional social shelter around the family, which from then on developed in various directions, the regulatory process helped to transform family structure; but it did not end the, more or less hidden, direct social control of the family over child labour.

This example also serves to shed light on one of the most important original factors in different kinds of informal activities: the *de facto* incompatibility between reciprocal and associative regulations. It may be used to underline the impact of at least three different types of incompatibility. The first concerns activities which institutional regulations do not take into account, for example, domestic or self-provisioning work. In this case, the involvement of children is entirely regulated by the family's customary organization of its labour; it is informal in a wide sense but in no way illegal. The second relates to child labour in various kinds of family businesses. It borders on the limits laid down by law and is informal in a much stricter sense. It may overstep these limits as it becomes more extensive, permanent and full-time and when used by a family business which is not that of the child's own family. The third is informal and illegal and regards the possibility that a family's need for cash may force the children into various forms of illegal employment. This last type also takes the extreme form, not uncommon today in cases of extremely deprived social groups in large cities both in underdeveloped and advanced capitalist countries, of families pushing minors into illegal activities, like prostitution or dealing in drugs, or making no attempt to stop them engaging therein. Examples of such extreme cases can be found nowadays in the Philippines, Brazil, Thailand and even in southern Italy or among the black minority in the United States. In general, the third type may be interpreted as resulting from the reduced effectiveness of the regulatory protection provided by both reciprocal and associative social relations in the face of market pressures. On the other hand, the second type constitutes a good example of divergent regulatory structures which in their different ways are a defence against both an extensive labour supply and business competition. There is little doubt that the family business is a form of economic enterprise that is to a high degree socially regulated and protected by a reciprocal network, as will be argued more extensively below and in chapter 5. Within this framework, a certain level of family-protected child labour is one of the possible organizational options for remaining competitive with conventional and more productive concerns. A further element that can be deduced from the example is that reciprocal regulations are more likely to be implicit rather than explicit and institutionalized, but this is not always the case.

I shall now go on to discuss some of the possible areas of reciprocal regulations and their interrelation with the pressures from market competition and with social systems based on associative organization.

The reciprocal regulatory impact on the family business

Within the organizational patterns of the family business, the rationale of reciprocity assumes great importance and is often an obstacle to the extension of competitive behaviour and an alternative economic strategy. The maximization of a family's work potential, the saving in transport and housing costs and through self-provisioning, and the consolidation and extension of the reciprocal network, maintain a high priority in the strategies of family businesses. By adopting such priorities, these kinds of economic ventures are shielded from exposure to full competition and directed towards goals, chiefly family welfare, that are in part alternatives to the pure accumulation of capital. Research into petty commodity production in agriculture, handicrafts and more recently family businesses in the service sector confirm this picture.[19] Generally, the family business holds a large potential supply of labour back from competing on the market and fixes a limit to the extension of commodified consumption patterns.

The family business is also a potential source of social regulations which are incompatible with associative ones and, as such, an area in which various kinds of informal activities may arise. We have already seen some examples with regard to child labour, but there are many others in various areas of employment. Family helpers, for instance, are very seldom employed on a regular basis. Small family enterprises are likely to adopt recruiting and employment strategies which diverge from official ones and are mainly based on kinship, friendship and local or ethnic networks. They may not register their workers or keep proper books and records as laid down by legal regulations and often evade paying taxes. Conversely, and in tandem with the above, in some social contexts the limits imposed by the family business network may become institutionally recognized and granted a high degree of enforcement by the state. The forms that such institutionalization assumes are usually a special tax system, favourable social security and financial arrangements, obstacles to capital concentration and penetration in certain areas reserved for family businesses and, possibly, even the setting-up of public co-operative networks providing free consultancy and services (marketing, accountancy, advanced technology, etc.) only to small entrepreneurs.

The impact of reciprocity on social regulation: the limits to full commodification

The second interesting area of reciprocal regulations concerns the persistence of limits to the full commodification of social life. Unpaid domestic work is the most important visible example of such a limit. Traditional and innovative forms of self-provisioning must also be placed in this category; there is little doubt that they are organized and regulated within a reciprocal network and that they constitute an impediment to the full extension of market relations. It is also evident that they escape the control and logic of associative regulations. Worth mentioning is an important apparent paradox with regard to vegetable gardening. This is a consistently widespread practice in advanced capitalist countries and even more so in socialist ones. The apparent paradox – I will show presently why it is not a real one – lies in the fact that one of the major battlefields of industrialization and 'modernization' has been subsistence agriculture. Millions of peasants, mainly in underdeveloped countries, have been evicted from the land they used to cultivate for survival, as landed estates have been transformed into plantations and used for extensive farming. At the same time, the colonizers continue to tolerate persistent subsistence agriculture in their own countries, and in many cases suburban vegetable gardening has expanded and increased productivity through the use of innovative light technology.

There are also other reciprocal networks, less visible and seldom given consideration, which continue to limit the spread of commodification. Kinship, friendship, neighbourhoods and local communities continue to operate, to a certain extent, according to an alternative rationale with respect to competitive tensions and associative regulations. Within these networks, individuals and households are able to obtain resources at conditions that differ from those imposed by the main patterns of commodification. For example, the lending of money, cars and durables to friends and relatives restricts the extent to which the same operation can occur in the fully commodified economy; banks, car and video rental firms and, perhaps, manufacturers suffer to some degree from the persistence of such practices. The impact is even greater when we take into account household repairs, small-scale building work and basic domestic services such as unpaid childminding by relatives. In this area, too, the degree of compatibility versus incompatibility between the limits of opportunities fixed by reciprocal networks and institutionalized associative regulations is important for discovering whether certain practices are more or less informal or illegal. Where, for instance, bank account interest is taxable, the lending of money to friends or relatives at a low interest rate is in reality a minor tax fraud. On the other hand, these limits to commodification become institutionalized when central or local government recognizes, organizes and/or contributes to voluntary local associations for the purpose of providing extra-market resources to certain or all categories of citizens.

Local community solidarity and reaction against market competition

I call the third area community solidarity and resistance to market competition. Several tendencies in this area have become visible in recent times but were probably also at work in the past more or less hidden from sight. Examples of this kind of communal reaction and limitations to the extension of market competition range from resistance to redevelopment, persistence of local community customs or the transplanting of ethnic traditions into immigrant areas, to the recent upsurge of interest in environmental protection, where community-based opposition resists the siting of a polluting factory in their area even though it would bring new jobs. This case also demonstrates both the possibility that community regulations may not be fully compatible with associative ones and that they may become incorporated in the associative regulatory system and consequently institutionalized. Banking 'lotteries' (Light, 1972) and ethnic entrepreneurship are to a certain degree informal since they do not comply with the laws governing such activities. The same happens with the patterns of consumption of local or particular groups outside the main market system, like unauthorized street-vendors welcomed by the community or the persistence of barter, weekend markets and 'garage' or 'car boot' sales. Local environmental protection issues, on the other hand, are adopted by more associative-oriented movements, absorbed by local authority policies and eventually institutionalized.

This typology and set of examples fits well with the idea of a rather complex pattern of triple two-way interaction between market tensions and the two different structures of the regulatory system. The reciprocal regulatory structure is both transformed and an active condition relative to both market tensions and the associative regulatory structure. It reacts in at least two different ways: either by absorbing competitive tensions outside of the rules established by the associative regulatory structure or by resisting competitive tensions beyond it: for the former, see the above-mentioned different cases of illegal employment of children or the use of communal and ethnic resources for modern economic activities, and for the latter the above-mentioned cases of reciprocal limitation of the commodification process. As already stated in a preliminary manner in chapter 1, these complex patterns of interaction have to be taken into consideration when elaborating socio-historical typologies of industrial societies.

The associative regulatory process

It is not strictly necessary to present examples of associative regulatory processes, since social scientists have recently reconstructed their impact, though with different emphases than those adopted here.[20] There are, however, some problems that need to be briefly discussed at this point. Furthermore, the specific relation between institutional regulatory patterns and the outcomes of informalization will be discussed in chapter 5 when introducing a specific comparative analysis of the diffusion of a wide range of informal activities. As I have already argued, wide-ranging regulations of an associative kind have to be considered an essential part of industrial development and are prompted by the very diffusion of competitive market tensions. An unregulated industrial society does not make sense; neither does an industrial society under the dominant control of reciprocal social arrangements, which, first of all, are incompatible with an adequate extension of the commodification process and the supply of free labour.

The associative principle of social organization depends on the fact that a relatively large social group happens to have similar interests even if the individuals of which it is composed do not come into contact, do not know each other and are not likely ever to meet. Both the Weberian concept of interest group and the Marxian concept of social class fit the definition up to this point. The modern concept of nation-state may be considered the prototype of an associative/redistributive social organization, in the sense that common national interests formed the associative framework which cemented together a number of reciprocally regulated segments in pre-industrial societies. In the industrial age, the nation-state is also, but only according to some approaches, the arena in which different social classes or interest groups exert pressure in order to have resources redistributed and regulations introduced that are favourable to them. The modern debate on the nature of the industrial state could be read as encompassing a spectrum of positions that differ in the importance attached to each of these two aspects. At one end, there are the theories of the political class and of elites which deny the importance of the state as a conflictual arena and insist on the complete autonomy of the power process. At the opposite end, one could pick out an uncritical Marxist

interpretation of the state which denies any room whatever for independent political action beyond class structure and struggle. This is not the
place to resume this controversial debate;[21] I will therefore opt for a
middle course according to which the state has interests that are to
some extent autonomous and not influenced by the process of mediation
between different interest groups.[22] At all events, it is difficult to deny the
increasing importance of the political class in the broad sense, including
politicians and bureaucrats, as a separate interest group or groups which
act to defend their own existence, reproduction and welfare.

It is very important to keep in mind that the system of associative
regulation is always the result of multiple pressures and never the unadul-
terated project of a single interest group. In recent years, both ends of
the political spectrum have been too hasty in labelling the regulatory
process a consequence of either a trade union socialist strategy against
the free market or a policy of authoritarian state capitalism against the
workers. Nevertheless, it is quite clear to me that the interests which are
working in favour of regulation are many and diverse: the economic
interest of those who want protection against unfair competition or
even against the dynamism of newcomers ready for any sacrifice; the
expansionist industrial interest of those who desire a better basis for
restructuring and competing on the international market; the interest of
the workers in improving wages and conditions and state welfare provisions; the interest of consumers in protection against unrestricted competition and health-damaging products; the interest of state apparatuses
in controlling greater resources to enable them to run an increasingly
complex and differentiated society; and many other besides.

This plurality of interests in regulation raises an important question
as to which groups are most likely to have their particular interests
recognized and implemented and why. This is not the place to discuss
this crucial issue at length, so I shall confine myself to a few brief
observations. In a given society and political system, different interest
groups do not have equal opportunities, as Charles Lindblom points out
in polemical disagreement with the current literature on interest groups.
'By some unthinking habit, many such works treat all interest groups as
though on the same plane, and in particular, they treat labour, business
and farm groups as though operating at some parity with each other'
(Lindblom, 1977, p.193). It is obvious that in capitalist societies the
asymmetry of power works in favour of business interest groups, and in
each specific context of the ones which have grown more influential. The
outcome in terms of regulation cannot be viewed as resulting exclusively
from their strategy, but it is likely to reflect their predominance in the
balance of power. Conversely, in socialist societies business interest

groups are particularly weak, but this does not automatically mean that the interests of the workers have top priority, as will seen in the conclusion to this chapter. By keeping in mind the asymmetry in the balance of power within each specific social context, it possible to understand the meaning of even regulative outcomes which differ to some extent, not to speak of the crucial difference between capitalism and socialism in this specific area.

The worldwide nature of the regulatory process

As I have already stated, approaches based on regulated capitalism usually forget two essential aspects of institutional regulatory processes in the industrial age: their immediate complex interrelation with reciprocal patterns of regulating social life, and the fact that the regulatory process takes place on a global scale. On the other hand, it was seen in chapter 1 that classical sociological analysis takes up the vital point that the incursion of associative regulations transforms reciprocal arrangements and reduces their importance but fails to devote adequate attention to their persistency and renewed capacity to resist both associative regulations and market tensions. I have discussed this point above, but it is important to underline further that the transformation and persistency of reciprocal social systems, and consequently their potential for reacting, varies widely in different contexts, both geographical and social, and that this fact assumes a great importance for the way in which significant social typologies and models of social interaction are drawn up.

The worldwide nature of the regulatory process is made evident by a simple logical argument. In a closed socio-economic system, the more regulation is effective in limiting the devastation of the social order produced by the diffusion of competitive tensions, the more it weakens the impact of the competitive tensions themselves. Under such conditions, the regulations end by suffocating industrial economic growth. For both regulation and growth to be possible at the same time, the process of industrial development has to find ways of diverting competitive tensions to areas where they can be absorbed, rather than merely setting up barriers to prevent social chaos. This has meant that increasing associative regulation in the 'core' countries and to the benefit of social groups deeply involved in industry, for example the Fordist working class, has been accompanied by an aggressive destruction of community-based social shelters in the periphery, in the sense of both underdeveloped countries and marginalized and deprived groups. This parallel process has to a certain extent permitted the absorption of competitive tensions and prevented the decline of the cumulative benefits from market competition. It is only in this context that the compatibility between increasing regulation and high rates of industrial growth in the advanced capitalist countries can be explained, as well as economic and social crises, uneven development, the changing division of labour, and the emergence and decline of specific regulatory systems and requirements at a local or national level. If inadequate regulation in terms of specific historical requirements leads to a relatively high degree of social fragmentation, but not necessarily social conflict as chapter 7 will show, regulation accompanied by insufficient relocation and final absorption of competitive tensions in the periphery will bring about a critical decline in the very complex world system of industrial development.

The regulatory/industrialization process in general has been possible as a cycle of successive adjustments promoted by the increasing pressure of powerful interests groups in order to eliminate effectively the obstacles of unsatisfactory regulation, insufficient relocation and absorption of competitive tensions, and inadequate transformation of the regulatory structure based on reciprocity. It would be quite possible to analyse the periodic crisis of industrial development as a crisis in the system of social regulation.[23] Also, and more importantly, current trends do not make much sense within a purely macro-economic analysis, while in terms of social regulation and organization they take on great significance. In this context, informalization bears witness, though in as many diverse forms as there are different societies, to the fact that associative regulatory structures are less effective in achieving their goals. From the economic angle, this is reflected in a schizophrenic situation: insufficient commodification (slow growth and stagnation) and the vigorous dynamism of decentralized, innovative and unconventional economic enterprises. The economic analyst falls prey to a state of confusion. One day there is the persistent crisis of capitalism, the next a newly rejuvenated capitalism able to super-exploit the new opportunities provided by subcontracting and industrial restructuring. As we saw in chapter 1, the present situation appears to some as a trend towards disorganization, to others as a trend towards new more complex forms of social organization; in both cases, their failing is that they persistently confine their attention to the associative side of the organizational system.

It will be seen below that to understand what is happening is not an easy task; but it is not as difficult as when one tries to explain everything from the limited perspective of macro-economic analysis. It is not a problem of disorganization or hyper-organization, but rather one of an emerging, distinct combination of the two organizational structures, the asociative and the reciprocal. This is the meaning behind the term 'fragmented societies', which does not stand for 'disorganized' or 'disrupted', but simply for an increasingly intricate and diversified system of social organization. It is no wonder that the degree of non-cohesiveness between contemporary trends materializes decreasingly in conventional social conflicts, which are an expression of tensions within the associative subsystem of regulation, that is, the very component which is becoming less effective in the global regulatory system. The crucially important question is whether the trends towards social fragmentation are compatible with industrial societies, both capitalist and socialist, or not. If not, as is indirectly argued in this section where it is assumed that industrial social systems require an extensive coherent organizational structure in order to reproduce themselves, it becomes important to initiate discussion of where these tendencies may lead. But this discussion cannot be based exclusively on the aspects of economic development and associative regulatory conflicts. It should fully incorporate social factors, context and the role of the regulatory network of reciprocity.

Before concluding this chapter, it will be useful to consider briefly the problem of the nature of the industrial regulatory system in socialist countries from the angle of the balance of power between different interest groups. Ideologically, the socialist political leadership would argue that they have given priority to workers' interests; but whether this is *de facto* the case is debatable. It is true that business interest groups are structurally weakened within this associative regulatory system, which gravitates towards strict social control over the disruptive and socially divisive effects of the diffusion of competitive tensions accompanying industrialization. Both economic growth and the extent of international readjustment required to maintain growth at a sufficient level are sacrificed to this goal. This does not mean that they become irrelevant. On the contrary, socialist societies are also interested in achieving an adequate capacity to increase those resources strictly produced within an industrial structure. And this applies even more so when we consider that the socialist regulatory system is by nature oriented to a radical reshaping and weakening of the reciprocal regulatory structure, specifically the networks which are highly hierarchical and bound to produce as a consequence dangerous asymmetries in the social structure and incompatible absorption of competitive tensions. It is no wonder that in the Soviet Union even the family came under attack in the immediate post-revolutionary period and that socialist countries have been the least tolerant of independent community or family initiatives.

In the following chapters I shall argue that this regulatory system becomes translated into 'underproductive' tendencies and that the incompatibilities accumulate in an unusual way in the so-called 'second economy'. The real problem is that in order to establish a strong system of associative regulation, the role of interest groups has to be strictly codified and subsumed within the workings of the state/party bureaucratic apparatus, which becomes the only legitimized interest group or, more exactly, federation of interest groups. Consequently, the answer to the question about the balance of power between interest groups, and particularly those representing the workers, turns out to be twofold. The balance of power is measured by the mode and the extent to which interests are incorporated in the mechanics of the central bureaucracy. Independent or new interests which are not filtered in this way will inevitably remain weak and be repressed, or pass through a difficult period before being fully accepted and established: an example is the experience of the Solidarnosč trade union movement in Poland. In other words, the interests of the workers are preselected according to the main goal of the regulatory system, that is, the minimization of the disruptive impact on society from the diffusion of competitive tensions. In this perspective, full employment and the basic provision of universal welfare are given a high priority, whereas the level of wages or the quality of sophisticated forms of welfare receives a low priority.

On the other hand, the fact that the regulatory system is set up in order to keep competitive tensions under control structurally limits its capacity to increase productivity in general. Furthermore, its simultaneous exposure to global competition aggravates this limitation by imposing priority redistribution of resources in favour of some crucial social and economic areas, for instance the military apparatus, heavy industry, general basic infrastructures, scientific and bureaucratic strata, etc., and to the detriment of others like housing and local infrastructures, light consumption goods industries, the quality of life of unskilled workers and their families, and so on. It is mainly in the context of these latter penalized areas that the reciprocal networks absorbing market tensions in unauthorized ways give rise to the development of the 'second economy' and that, more recently, alternative associative interest groups have emerged, which support the need for reforms and challenge the *status quo* of the regulatory system. All of this will be subject to verification in terms of specific periods and social contexts within a comparative perspective in the latter part of this book.

NOTES

1   See Godelier (1980) for a critical discussion on the historical origins of the concepts of work and employment in various languages. See also Pahl (1984; 1988a) for recent critical approaches to the patterns of work and employment in pre-industrial and industrial societies.

2   The concept of labour market segmentation was introduced in the USA in the 1950s mainly by Kerr (1950; 1954) and then developed by various authors; important contributions have been made by Doeringer and Piore (1971); Gordon (1972); Edwards et al. (1975); Piore (1979a); Edwards (1979); Wilkinson (1981); Gordon et al. (1982); Sabel (1982); Wood (1982). An accurate introductory discussion of the origins and developments of the literature on this subject is contained in Villa (1986), pp. 5–27.
    Increasing attention to the importance of the service sector is reflected in a vast range of both economic and sociological literature; see, among others, Fuchs (1968), Stanback Jr et al. (1983), Miles (1983) for the first, and Bell (1973), Gershuny (1978) for the second.

3   The literature on this subject is now vast, ranging from the seminal work of Braverman (1974) through important studies on de-industrialization (Blackaby, 1978; Bluestone and Harrison, 1982) to a large number of works dealing with flexible production, the new international division of labour, the transformation of the production process and the division of labour. Among the many authors I will mention only Frobel et al. (1980); Piore and Sabel (1984); Burawoy (1985); Scott and Storper (1986); Tarling (1987); Lash and Urry (1987).

4   See mainly the recent works by Clawson (1980); Abercrombie and Urry (1983); Urry (1986).

5   In this sense, survival is not intended as 'bare survival' but as a socio-historical concept inclusive of diverse standards of living for different social groups at different times.

6   Within the approach I have adopted, the impact of different financial strategies and transactions is ignored for the sake of simplicity. But, in reality, they constitute fairly important resources for shaping different life-styles. Both the opportunity to obtain credit at a relatively low interest rate, and the opportunity to save substantial amounts of money on which interest can be earned at a rate which is appreciably higher than the inflation rate, play a decisive role in changing life-chances and structuring different social groups.

7   An extensive bibliography on studies of the informal sector in Third World cities is contained in Rogerson (1985). See also the more recent critical essay by Gerry (1987). In addition, I should mention three recent books: Sreeramamurty (1986); Menefee Singh and Kelles-Viitanen (1987); Jagannathan (1987). Extensive critical discussions on the use of the concept can be found in Bromley and Gerry (1979) and in Portes and Walton (1981).

8   The debate on informal activities in advanced capitalist countries has now given rise to a large number of works. Specific studies based on local empirical research are, however, still few. See mainly the study on Detroit by Ferman (Ferman et al., 1978; Ferman and Berndt, 1981) and that on the Isle of Sheppey in Kent by Pahl (1984).
    The most important contributions in English on the informal underground economy and the second economy as well as on the informal sector in Third World cities are critically reviewed in a recent volume of the *Annals of the*

American Academy of Political and Social Science edited by Ferman et al. (1987). More recently, the European Community has commissioned a comparative study on informal activities in the twelve countries of the Community; see the single monographs and summary report (EEC, 1989b). See also the more recent discussion on a conceptual level sparked off by the contribution of Portes and Sassen-Koob (1987) criticized by Pahl (1989a).

9   See also, among others, Heertje et al. (1982); Bawly (1982); Simon and Witte, (1982); Tanzi (1982); Archambault and Greffe (1984); Adair (1985); Alessandrini and Dallago (1987); Feige (1989).

The attention paid to the underground economy originated in the USA with the attempts of two leading economists to calculate hidden monetary income and transactions (A. Gutmann, 1977; 1978a and b; 1979a and b; 1980; Feige, 1979). The discovery of a substantial and increasing level of underground monetary activities soon caught the attention of the media (*Business Week*, 1978; 1982) and of the political authorities in various countries.

10 A series of important contributions are included in the works edited by Galasi and Sziraczki (1985), Alessandrini and Dallago (1987) and by Grossmann (1988). See also Mars and Altman (1987); Galasi and Sik (1988); Shlapentokh (1989).

11 Feminist writing has raised two crucial interconnected lines of discussion: the importance of unpaid domestic work in shaping unequal gender relations and the persistence of gender discrimination in the workplace. Among the wide range of contributions, see Balbo (1976); Kuhn and Wolpe (1978); Michel (1978); Saraceno (1980); Fox (1980); Barrett (1980); Amsden (1980); West (1982); Tilly and Scott (1987); Beechey (1987).

12 For a socio-anthropological point of view, see the contribution by Meillassoux (1981, originally published in French in 1975). Among others, see also Burns (1975; 1977); Netting et al (1984); Smith et al. (1984).

13 See the works mentioned above, n. 2.

14 Perhaps the most important conference dedicated exclusively to the informal economy has been that organized by the Italian Council for Social Sciences (CISS) in Frascati, near Rome, in November 1982. Some of the papers were published in Italian (Bagnasco, 1986b). But many other conferences and workshops have taken place since then in Italy, the USA, Holland, Germany and other countries.

15 Apart from those works already mentioned in the preceding footnotes and concentrating only on recent sociologically oriented literature, I should also mention Henry (1981); *Inchiesta* (1983); Redclift and Mingione (1985); Pahl (1988b); Portes, et al. (1989).

16 See the last part of chapter 1 for references to, and a discussion of, the literature on post-industrial societies.

17 Villa (1986), for example, documents the importance and persistence of peasant-workers in the Italian steel industry. Peasant-workers in the North were extremely important in Italian industrialization (Castronovo, 1975) prior to the massive migration from South to North in the 1950s and 1960s, but they have probably played an important role in various other European

countries and in Japan, too.

18 See Hodgson (1988) for an extensive critical discussion of the approach and references to the most important contributions in English.

19 As far as concerns the persistence of family farming and its difference compared to proper capitalist activity, see H. Friedmann (1979; 1980) among others. Family businesses and self-employment in other economic branches have recently been attracting increasing attention even in the United States, a country which is supposedly the most extreme case of advanced capitalism (see, for instance, Granovetter, 1984; Steinmetz and Wright, 1989).

20 The most accurate recent comparative study on this subject is the account of the maturation and crisis of Fordist societies given by Lash and Urry (1987). The main difference between this study and other 'institutionalist' approaches and the approach I have adopted in this book arises from the fact that the former ignore the impact of changing reciprocal social arrangements in regulating different paths to industrialization.

21 Reference to the debate on the nature of the capitalist state and the political conflict between various interest groups is made in chapter 4, in the section devoted to the welfare state.

22 The automony of the political sphere has been defended recently by Luhmann (1979; 1982) within his updated socio-political version of *System Theory*.

23 See, for instance, Lash and Urry (1987).

3

Towards a theory of social reproduction: the meanings of different survival strategies

1 A THEORETICAL APPROACH TO SOCIAL REPRODUCTION

The concept of 'social reproduction' in the tradition of the social sciences

At this point in the text, the importance of rethinking the historical links between reproduction processes and industrial development becomes evident and some challenging difficulties emerge. In the social sciences, the term 'reproduction' has traditionally been attributed four distinct but not unrelated meanings.

From a strictly socio-biological point of view, reproduction refers to the social conditions connected with procreation and the early years and education of children.[1] In this sense, both sociologists and anthropologists have studied the social conditions which form the varied background to the biological process in which a fertile couple achieves conception and a period of pregnancy ends with the birth of a new human being. Later, other social conditions are crucial in various ways in allowing the baby and subsequently the child, a technically non-autonomous living being, to survive through his/her childhood.

A recent French school of sociology (Bourdieau et Passeron, 1964; 1970) has used the term *'reproduction'* to define the phenomenon of educational and cultural transfer from schools, families and societies to children and young people. This phenomenon characterizes the historical process of conservation and change of values, culture, language, habits, hierarchies and differentiations in specific social formations.

The third definition and use of the term 'reproduction' is broader and may be seen, at best, to encompass the other three. It defines the conditions through which a specific social order is preserved, or reproduced, and adapted without losing its main typical features as a result of social change.

The concept of 'social reproduction' used in this book expresses the diverse conditions and organizational relations which allow human beings to survive in various social contexts and groups. In this sense, it is synonymous with 'livelihood' or 'survival strategies'. This particular use of the concept is meaningful only in industrial societies when human reproduction practices become separated from strictly productive ones, and the latter are assumed to be crucially important in structuring social organization (the Durkheimian and structuralist traditions) or in understanding human patterns of behaviour (the Weberian and behaviourist traditions). In pre-industrial societies the problem is radically different. Assuming that the general aim of human organization is survival, when activities that we now call strictly 'productive' take place in the same social organizational context (households as embedded in various community networks) of what may strictly be called 'reproduction', the theoretical explanations of societies, however different, do not tackle the problem of dealing with two separate spheres of human life and the possible elements of compatibility or incompatibility between the two.

The advent of the industrial age has posed a controversial theoretical question concerning reproduction, not only because this sphere of human life has *de facto* become generally separated from the strictly productive socio-organizational context, but also because in tandem modern social theory has been built, along various different lines, on the assumption that the logic of production must be afforded almost complete priority over that of reproduction. Consequently, as soon as reproduction became a separate field for social theory, it was at the same time reduced to a residual problem; one that could be almost entirely explained by the constraints imposed by the development of production in terms of the social division of labour, capital accumulation or the diffusion of rational economic behaviour. In other words, very little attempt has been made to formulate a theory in which this area of human life is an independent variable able to determine patterns of social organization and of human behaviour.

It is only recently that the sociological tradition has begun to construct a theory around the term social reproduction in this sense. Some related problems have been considered from the limited perspective of two subfields of sociology, one specializing in the family and the other in consumption. Both of these specialized approaches seriously restrict the possibility of understanding the complex interrelations between changing patterns of social organization deriving from the reproductive sphere and those deriving from the sphere of production. Until recently, most analyses have come to the conclusion that family life and consumption patterns are exclusively determined by a combination of universal biological needs and the restrictions and options made available by different forms of industrial development.

In broad terms, mainstream sociology of the family has argued that industrialization leads to the development of a nuclear family largely 'freed' from productive goals, tendentially isolated from significant and important social networks, and solely devoted to private life, biological reproduction and organizing monetary consumption. It is true that relatively recent critical sociological analysis has rejected the narrow perspective involved in Parsons's theorization of the isolated nuclear family and has stressed the importance of kinship and community networks.[2] Also, historical studies have discovered that in Western societies the nuclearization of family structure anticipated rather than followed industrial development.[3] Nevertheless, this has not resulted in any attempt to formulate a theory of the independent and interdependent role of social reproduction patterns in relation to different paths of industrial development.

The sociological analysis of consumption has mainly focused on the patterns of monetary consumption and the appearance of mass consumerism, based on homogeneous class or status models, influenced by advertising and marketing and largely dependent on the availability of money and credit. Again, within this framework there is no room for a concept of social reproduction beyond the patterns of standardized consumption by households, generally intended as comprising couples with dependent children. Even more blatant is the fact that the more recent focus on the changing balance between public, market and various forms of privatized or innovative do-it-yourself provisioning has not been immediately translated into attempts to analyse theoretically the connection between different patterns of reproduction and socio-economic development.[4]

Sociological and historical studies of family life and consumption patterns are very important for understanding and theorizing about social reproduction, and here I will make frequent references to this literature. However, it is important to note that the main goal of this work is not a critical review of this literature; thus, references will be limited to areas which appear crucial to a theoretical analysis of changing and diversified patterns of social reproduction. At the same time, it may be useful to underline once again the essential fact that limited specialized analysis of the family or of various patterns of consumption unsupported by a theory of social reproduction are not harmful or wrong *per se*, but rather because indirectly, and nearly always unconsciously, they lend credence to a strictly economistic vision of social life. According to the latter view, the ultimate independent factors structuring any modern form of human organization are exclusively those that derive from industrial development, formal employment and genuinely productive activities.

Marx's use of the concept of social reproduction

Although in Marx's work the term 'reproduction' is largely used in the same sense adopted here and has a potentially strong theoretical status, the tradition of Marxist studies has been unable to make concrete progress beyond the limitations and economicism affecting mainstream sociology in this area of inquiry. Let us briefly see why.

For Marx, the problem of reproduction is one of the crucial aspects of his theory of the capitalist exploitation of wage labour and of labour power as a commodity in market-based societies. His theory of the exploitation of wage-labour is founded on the argument that labour power is the only commodity whose price, fixed within the commodity price system as studied by the classical economists, expresses an exchange value that is much lower than the total value it creates during the labour process. The classical economic theory of commodity prices is based on the combination of the two laws: market competition and production costs. The actual price of a commodity in a market system is fixed by the interaction of supply and demand, apparently in total independence from the costs of production of the commodity. However, in a market system the free circulation and competition of capital in search of the maximum profit possible forces the price system towards a high degree of correspondence with the actual costs of production, which can be accurately calculated beyond market fluctuations and thus constitute the economically realistic accounting basis of the system. The production of commodities that are overpriced with respect to their average production costs is particularly profitable: consequently new capital is attracted until the increased supply of such commodities cancels out the relative advantage within the competitive market system. The same happens in reverse with relatively underpriced commodities: the outflow of capital, bankruptcy and restructuring re-establish a 'normal' balance between prices and production costs.

Also, the price of the commodity labour power, that is its wage, is fixed by market competition through fluctuations in supply and demand. The level at which it settles cannot be accounted for in advance or determined theoretically: all that is possible is to hypothesize a process, similar to the one above, in which the price-setting mechanism for this particular commodity is ultimately reduced to a specific, and clearly different, law of production costs. It is at this point in the formulation of his theory that Marx has to face the question of social reproduction. In order to continue to supply their labour power, workers must be able to survive, generate children and raise them as the next generation of labourers; this is the reason why Marx uses the term 'reproduction' and not 'production' in the case of labour power. Furthermore, so that they do in fact supply their labour power workers must have no viable alternatives for survival other than the sale of all or part of their labour power. In this way, the reproduction patterns of the labour force and – for reasons that we shall see in a moment – of the total population constitute a crucial element in the cycle of capital, and practically the only one that cannot be explained by its own internal logic. The patterns of survival of human beings, their marriage and procreative strategies, are at best subject to only partial and indirect control by capital through monetary wages, commodified consumption and, even more indirectly, through state intervention in the areas of repression, education and health.

At least in *Das Kapital* where the cycle of capital is examined at a basically abstract level, Marx limits his analysis to, on the one hand, a strictly essential and simplified set of assumptions and, on the other, a number of social and historical considerations necessary for demonstrating the plausibility of these assumptions. Marx assumes that in order to elaborate a general theory of capitalism it is sufficient to consider the interaction between the wage system and the patterns of monetary consumption, as if it were the only source of survival. The strict definition of the wage/reproduction cost in terms of which capitalist-produced commodities are historically necessary to support a working-class nuclear family is connected with this interaction. Furthermore, he analyses in depth the historical and logical plausibility of this part of his theory in two ways: first he presents historical evidence to support the actual possiblity that in order to survive, increasing sections of the population are left with no alternative to selling their labour; second, he sets forth evidence and arguments supporting the idea that parallel to the cycle of capital there exists the means for keeping the level of demand for labour under flexible control, through mechanization and increases in labour productivity, and the means for generating a recurrent surplus in the supply of labour – the theory of the industrial reserve army.

The crucial elements in a neo-Marxist critical theorization of social reproduction

I shall now set out the assumptions underlying Marx's approach to the social reproduction of the labour force in a modified version appropriate to the contemporary debate.

1 The patterns of social reproduction of labour power, intended in a broad sense and inclusive of present, future and potential wage-work, affect the capital accumulation process in two different ways; they determine the cost, quantity and quality of the labour supply both for the present and the following generation; and they contribute to setting the limits to the system's capacity to consume capitalist-produced commodities which are essential to the survival of the population.

2 Although these patterns are strongly influenced by the different operations of capital, they are not under the direct control/command of capital. They depend on pre-existing, socio-historical conditions and, to a certain extent, on the availability of different options for the unit of reproduction, as embedded in different socialization mixes.

3 The influence of capital on the social-reproduction patterns of the labour force is not only limited by the interference of other conditions and options; it is also bound to be an extremely conflict-ridden process. The main capital input is the structure of the demand for labour, as articulated in the numbers and quality of jobs (levels of productivity, specialization, ability to command, etc.). The interconnection between the complex specific structure of demand and the complex specific patterns of social reproduction will result in a wage/income structure and in a specific capacity of monetary expenditure on subsistence goods and services produced and sold within the market system (commodification). The imbalance between these two parallel phenomena gives rise to two possible outcomes, which variously characterize the cycles of capital at different times and places. Accumulation accompanied by a high rate of commodification of reproduction patterns and parallel intensive disruption of local subsistence economies leads to a tendential above-average increase in the cost of reproducing labour power (or to put it more simply, it produces high wages), which can limit or impair any further potential for capital to expand. Conversely, accumulation accompanied by a disproportionate growth in excess/surplus population (or in other words, persistent non-commodified patterns of social reproduction or, possibly, the radical emergence and spread of innovative forms of self-provisioning with large monetary savings) results in insufficient commodi-

fication and a strong tendency towards overproduction.

4 The quantity and quality of the labour supply not only depend on demographic trends but, more importantly, on complex processes of commodification, proletarianization, resistance and innovation in non-commodified social contexts, re-formation of surplus population, violent displacement of subsistence economies, and so on. These processes and their contradictory significance in terms of extending or reducing, on the one hand, competition among labour and, on the other, the potential to consume subsistence commodities within the cycle of capital involve nearly the entire population and point to the necessity of going well beyond the strict analysis of the capitalist productive cycle and of examining in depth patterns of social reproduction.

Marx himself, however, went no further than the historical considerations mentioned above, while traditional Marxist studies have in general insisted so strongly on the limitation set by Marx to the equivalence between wage-work and monetary consumption that they have reached conclusions not unlike those already noted in mainstream sociology. In reality, Marx's interpretative framework relative to reproduction encompasses two different methodological lines. The first is particularly restrictive and simplifying. It is based on the assumption that the link between reproduction and the capital cycle is in every case increasingly subject to the simple and easily quantifiable relation between wage-labour and monetary consumption. The historical arguments put forward by Marx aim precisely to show that such an assumption is correct. Marx's reason for adopting this restricted line is not due to a supposed priority of theory but for economy of analysis. Having chosen to interpret the cycle of capital at a high level of abstraction, he considers that this line is the most suitable for defining the basic theoretical significance of reproduction and that there is no need to dwell on the complex socio-historical analysis of specific variations.

In the way he constructs his theoretical framework, and even more in the socio-historical arguments put forward to support his simplifying assumption, Marx suggests a much more complex line of interpretation of social reproduction. This interpretation is useful for analysing the meaning of survival strategies that remain heterogeneous and composite, despite a general move towards commodification, and which, through their very diversity, characterize different specific paths of industrialization. In other words, Marx's theory asserts the importance of examining the conditions of social reproduction and supplies conceptual tools for understanding their significance in relation to the process of industrial growth. It does so in a way which is largely independent of his decision to simplify the analysis, which by no means denies the fundamental importance of specific analyses for understanding the socio-historical picture and its processes of change.

Regarding this second line, several important areas of analysis are immediately pertinent to the following questions:

1 The persistence and innovatory character of forms of self-provisioning understood in a broad sense to include both domestic work, in its changing guise in diverse social contexts throughout the industrial era, and all activities involving self-consumption whether traditional or modern, which means bringing in the debate on the significance of mixed figures such as worker-peasants;

2 the possibility that the survival of cohabitation is based on the common benefit derived from combining several incomes (income-pooling); a question which, in industrialized countries, also became, during the Fordist phase, one of the relationships between the main or family income and complementary or secondary income;

3 the survival strategies of old and new strata of self-employed, as well as of all the conditions for reproduction permitted *in toto* or in part by social relations foreign to wage-labour, and also more generally the variable links that are forged between family enterprises, different contexts not based on wage-labour and capitalist concerns in diverse social systems and historical periods.

Before proceeding further, it is worth clarifying two points with regard to the theoretical framework provided by the second method of treating reproduction. It was explained how Marx found it indispensable to analyse reproduction from a theoretical perspective in order to develop his theory of exploitation and labour value. It must be underlined, however, that Marx's theoretical framework relative to reproduction does not necessarily imply an acceptance of the theory of labour value. Indeed, as we have seen, the concepts on which the framework is based are formed from elements elaborated by the classical economists and largely accepted by the social sciences and historiography of the industrial era: the existence of labour power as a commodity and, therefore, of a labour market; the untypical nature of the renewal of labour power compared to the production of commodities; the coexistence of areas of social life not fully subject to commodification with others entirely commodified and the importance of defining the relation between the two.

The second point requiring clarification is the fact that this second line can be applied in a form more or less consistent with its Marxist underpinnings and, as an analytical tool, produce results largely unforeseen by Marxist predictions. An example of the former is its use to estimate the level of exploitation or the formation of social classes, or within a completely non-Marxist horizon, to evaluate the impact on new industrial investment of diverse social conditions. As we have already anticipated, this second side to Marx's theory of social reproduction has been largely ignored in Marxist studies and, parallel to this, it has not been developed by sociologists as an instrument for analysing the connections between industrial development and survival strategies in macro-social contexts.

It is probably true that through the commodification process industrial development has drawn increasingly wider strata among the population into reproduction patterns largely, but not exclusively, characterized by the relation between wage-work and monetary consumption. This process, however, has been a discontinuous and diversified one depending on both specific models of development and the different impact of local social patterns of reproduction. Also, it is important to take into account the evidence showing 'that a substantial part of labor power in the capitalist world-economy is not generated through exchange in a labor market but through a system of reproduction that at first sight does not seem to be part of the capitalist production system at all' (Smith et al., 1984, p. 8).

Nowadays, advanced capitalist countries are faced with a decrease in manufacturing employment in large industry and the parallel diffusion of informal practices and innovative domestic and self-provisioning activities. We cannot automatically argue that such events contribute to the creation of a social economy accompanied by a decommodification process in which the direct command of capital over the social organization of reproduction is inevitably declining. I believe that the only way to make progress in this area is to undertake a detailed analysis of the complex relations between two factors: the various trends in industrial development and the reproduction patterns of large strata of the population, seen both historically and in their contemporary diversity. Particular attention should be given to the different reproduction patterns that reflect and influence the changing and conflicting requirements of the development process. We are still far from a full understanding of these relations. For instance, although we can assume that industrialization has involved a parallel commodification process, this has been historically varied and often contradictory. Recent research on women has shown that long hours of domestic work have persisted throughout history, unaffected by changing levels of female employment. Studies of under-developed regions, both rural and urban, show the persistence to varying degrees of subsistence 'economies' based on activities the aim of which is direct consumption by members of the household. Detailed research into the life-style of the working class in the West through different historical periods has found that the commodification process has been quite slow and discontinuous in eliminating some self-provisioning activities (home maintenance, food processing, the making of clothes, etc.) and documented the long-lasting importance of crucial mixed social profiles such as, for example, that of peasant-workers.[5]

Unless encompassed within a theory of social reproduction and the interrelation between the latter and industrial development, all these phenomena, including the supposed spread of a wide range of human activities called 'informal' because they do not conform to the profile and requirements of officially regulated employment, have no meaning outside of a historical account or their simple description and listing. This is the reason why the basic concepts and theoretical framework have been introduced in this section. In the course of this chapter I will undertake a preliminary discussion of the unit of reproduction, the household, as embedded in different social contexts, and of the changing structure and patterns of householding. Then I shall proceed from a first simplified model of different patterns of social reproduction to a progressively more complicated analysis and to discussion of a possible systematic typology of reproduction patterns and households in contemporary advanced capitalist countries. Finally, at the end of the chapter, I shall briefly discuss how the theoretical framework can be applied to socialist and underdeveloped countries.

2 THE PROCESS OF HOUSEHOLDING AND THE STRUCTURE OF SATISFYING SUBSISTENCE NEEDS

The concept of household and social reproduction

The basic unit of social reproduction is, for the most part, located in the household.[6] For this term to be of use in the analysis undertaken here, it must first be made into a clearly defined working concept. This is not as unproblematical as it appears. For my purposes, a household cannot be simply viewed as a statistical or physical unit of co-residentiality, but must be seen as a set of changing social relations which establish a set of mutual obligations (basically, a reciprocal form of social organization) aimed at helping its members to survive. Here, survival is not only intended in a strict sense but also includes strategies for promoting welfare and possibly social mobility, both within the same generation and from one to the next. The basic elements in a household are income,

or better resource-pooling, survival as the end of its organizational structure and reciprocity or mutual obligation as the main organizational
form. It should be made clear from the very start that by adopting this
definition there is no intention of isolating the household system from a
more general variable social context in which it is embedded, that is,
community, kinship, friendship and other networks contributing in different ways to the patterns of reproduction. Nor does this definition entail
denying the existence of an internal differentiation of interests or of
conflict between individual strategies.

However, the limitation of using a statistical term within a different
conceptual framework poses serious problems. This is clearly underlined
in the following quotation.

A major problem with the household as concept is the conflation
of several dimensions into a single term: a physical or spatial
dimension referring to a building; a social or demographic dimension which refers to a given population of people who inhabit,
occupy, or somehow use the facilities of a spatial unit collectively
and/or who interact in terms of certain sets of relationships between
and among them, and a conceptual dimension referring to a relative
area of being and action within a total system of ideas that together
'make sense' of the world for a group of people. (P. Woodford-Berger,
quoted in Friedman, 1984, p. 47)

First I shall look briefly at the problem of the discrepancies between
the concept of the basic unit of social reproduction and the use of the
term 'household' in its physical co-residential sense and, secondly, at the
concepts of family and kinship.

Co-residence does not always automatically lead to income-pooling
and mutual obligations for the purpose of survival, nor is it strictly
necessary to be co-resident in order to be involved in household strategies.
There are various possible examples of both possibilities. The first
includes simple and obvious cases, such as people renting out rooms to
paying guests or a group of unrelated persons sharing a large house
with entirely independent 'budgets' apart from the shared rent and/or
occupancy expenses; this has to be taken into consideration when the
statistical household unit is used for analysing reproduction strategies.
The second may give rise to even more complicated cases: separated or
divorced parents live in different households but share mutual obligations
mainly for the survival of children; seasonal or temporary migrant workers are not resident all of the time but are fully part of the household's
reproduction strategy. This last case is particularly widespread in certain

periods in underdeveloped regions, and the survival of such households cannot be explained without accounting for the contribution of non-resident members. (See, for instance, Martin and Beittel, 1987.) On the other hand, there are some individuals who may depend for survival largely or totally on non-resident relatives, for example, students living away from their families. Moreover, although individuals are strictly classified as living within one statistically defined household, in an approach based on social reproduction they may be seen to participate in two or more households, contributing and/or receiving resources and sharing mutual obligations. It is apparent, therefore, that the statistical structure of households is only an approximate indicator of existing reproduction units; analysis will have to look for and take into account possible specific and important discrepancies. Besides this last observation, there is a further even more problematical question concerning the fact that physical co-residence does not tell us anything about the kinds of resources involved and to what extent they are pooled in order to achieve the goal of survival. For instance, socio-historical and ethnographical studies on the survival strategies of working-class families in the West widely document the fact that both the husband-father and young working adults retain a variable part of their wages for personal use, while this is less common in the case of the wife-mother; she usually gives high priority to the family reproduction strategy even when allocating the money from her wage-work.[7] As will be seen shortly, the term household can be used in social reproduction analysis on condition that the substantial divergence of cohabiting households from the purely statistical picture is clearly spelled out and taken into consideration.

Family, kinship systems and social reproduction

It is by now obvious that the question of social reproduction is very closely related to the concept of family and kinship. This is not the place for an extensive discussion of this important question. I shall therefore limit myself to a few points which are essential to increasing our understanding of social reproduction in contemporary societies.

The sociological and anthropological concepts of family and kinship are built on the assumption that societies respond to a specific biological condition by setting up socio-organizational networks based on reciprocity, which vary historically and geographically. This condition is the necessity that two fertile adults of different gender must come together in order to produce a new human being and, more importantly, that in order to survive offspring need a certain amount of care from at least one adult (see Gellner, 1973). This condition requires an additional socio-organizational arrangement to enable adults to survive during the period when they have to devote at least part of their attention to babies and very young children. Almost the only social arrangement used to deal with this biological constraint has been the family and kinship systems. As we have seen, the reproduction approach is ultimately founded on the same basic original biological limitation. It is obvious that the presence of dependent children is not indispensable for entering into or continuing mutual obligations and resource-pooling for survival: there are marriages without children or after grown-up children have left home, or survival agreements other than those aimed at biological reproduction. However, the biological reproduction condition can easily be considered the basic element on which both the kinship systems and social reproduction strategies are founded. This fact is reflected, at least in advanced capitalist countries, in the statistical structure of households with regard to conjugal families and life-cycles (Bryman et al., 1987). The large majority of non-family households comprise single people living alone; they are either young adults who have left their original family and have not yet formed a new one, or surviving widows and widowers in their old age, or divorced/separated persons. The recent sharp increase in the number of single households is also due to a relative growth in the number of people who never marry or live for long periods outside marriage, both late-married and separated/divorced persons who do not remarry; but it is mostly the result of a sudden jump in the number of single elderly persons whose spouse has died (for the most part, women).

The strong connection between family/kinship systems and reproduction strategies is important both in terms of inputs and outputs to the social reproduction approach in a number of ways. In this perspective, reproduction practices are considered in their close relationship with life-cycles, where demographic factors determine biological preconditions and shape the socio-historical institution of marriage, not only legal but also de facto marriage. Moreover, it could be easily argued that the most important social network in which the household, defined as the unit of social reproduction, is strictly embedded is the kinship/sibling system as it has developed historically in different locations.

In recapitulating the discussion of the relation between the reality of households and the social reproduction process, it is important to underline once again the basic elements that specifically characterize an analysis of social reproduction in terms of both its difference from the statistical measurement of households and employment and its interdependence with, rather than subordination to, the strictly defined capitalist accumu-

lation process – or, in socialist countries, the system of planned redistribution.[8] Kathie Friedman lists five main factors in the household analysis
of social reproduction:

1 The boundaries of membership defined by the operation of
income-pooling (in terms of numbers, generations, kin-relatedness;
2 the percentages of kinds of income pooled (wages, profits, subsistence, rent, gifts) by age and gender of household members;
3 the degree to which the household is co-residential;
4 the allocation of tasks and rewards among household members
(by gender and age group); and
5 the structure of internal decision-making within the household
allocation of tasks, allocation of rewards, and collective behaviour
vis-à-vis the outside world (including political action and
investment). (Friedman, 1984, p. 49)

To these five factors I would add the fact that the reproduction process is
not fully encompassed by households but is influenced by other reciprocal
factors in society, in particular the kinship system and the local community. These six factors define a social background in which continuity,
adaptation, and the specific interaction between local historical conditions and industrial development is paramount. In other words, the
twofold contradictory processes of proletarianization/commodification
and of the expanding capitalist use/exploitation of forms of non-commodified subsistence arrangements to reproduce the labour force cheaply,
cannot fully explain the historical diversity and social change found in
patterns of reproduction. However, these last two aspects are important
for defining the significance that different conditions of social reproduction may assume with regard to the industrialization process. In
essence, this means that reproduction arrangements and the process of
householding have to be studied in their interdependence with the cycle
of capital, or state redistribution in socialist countries, taking into account
social factors that they are not able to bring under their complete control.

*Basic observations on transformation in the patterns of social
reproduction in the industrial age*

A full historical analysis of the change in social reproduction patterns on
a global scale in the industrial age is beyond the scope of this book.
Nevertheless, a preliminary discussion in terms of approach and identifying the main social factors affecting household strategies is necessary
in order to explain the significance behind the increasing heterogeneity

of working practices and life-styles and, in particular, what have been called informalization tendencies.

The six factors mentioned above indicate that an analysis of the historical process of social reproduction is a complicated exercise. Apart from the opportunities (in terms of demand for labour) or restrictions (in terms of violent destruction of survival chances) produced directly by capitalist development or state-socialist policies, the main areas involved are demographic features, local social solidarity arrangements, and the diverse solidity and adaptability of socio-economic contexts generating survival resources as alternatives to wage-work, such as household production, direct commodity production and various self-provisioning strategies including domestic work. Also, it is important to discover what is the ultimate effect of these resources on the cycle of capital in terms of the balance between insufficient commodification and the creation of cheap labour.

The importance of demographic factors is shown by the difference in population growth in France and England during the last century, as revealed by Tilly and Scott's comparative analysis (1987, pp. 91–3). In France, the birth rate had been relatively much lower than in England during the period of the Revolution, and this was reflected in the fact that, subsequently, there were fewer fertile women overall among the various age groups making up the female population. Moreover, this factor continued to depress the birth rate in France relative to England for over a century. What makes the relative difference even more significant is that one would expect the reverse to have been the case, given the much greater extent of the peasantry and productive households (also in urban areas) in France. In this respect, when compared to the situation in England, the dynamic of the supply of wage-labour in France, as in other European countries, was limited throughout the entire nineteenth century and beyond on two fronts: the smaller increase in population and the persistence of large numbers of productive households. This aspect has in various ways become an inextricable part of the specific model of industrial growth. It probably helped to contain the effects of extreme urban poverty like those shown in the Parliamentary reports in England in the last century and which resulted from the uncontrolled formation of a labour market, as discussed in chapter 2.

Another element differentiating the experience of industrialization in continental Europe from that in England is the important role played by different types of worker-peasants. Their wages, in spite of being insufficient, helped to keep the peasant economy on its feet, though it was no longer able by itself to guarantee survival, while self-provisioning, subsistence-based savings and the persistence of the reciprocal background supporting the peasant family have continued to complement the inadequate levels of workers' wages.[9]

Furthermore, demographic factors condition the householding process in terms of the elements making up historically established socio-demographic practices, which change relatively slowly in relation to the new opportunities arising from industrial growth. Consider the impact of a social norm preventing all young people from marrying, the varying extent of and grounds for celibacy or the variable extent of customs delaying marriage. In this sense, the regulatory process relative to the life-cycles adopted by both urban and rural productive households in Europe is fairly well documented. These social practices are all the more evident if we take into account the fact that the following two facts are now widely accepted. First, the conjugal family took root in Europe before or at the same time as industrialization and was not a consequence of the latter (Goode, 1963). Second, this type of productive-reproductive household exerts a direct control over the balance between resources and needs. In general, the productive households were created only where there were sufficient means of production in the form of, for example, land inherited or leased for life or an artisanal workshop or small shop. In periods when the wife-mother was at least partially engaged in producing and rearing children, servants or apprentices could be hired for little more than their board and lodging. These periods were complemented by a subsequent phase in which children of a working age in excess were sent to work as servants or apprentices in other families.

Already, from the very outset, less stable than is apparent from the above schematic description, this model has, it is true, been shaken by the spread of opportunities for wage-work; nevertheless it has also demonstrated a varying capacity to persist and adapt. In this perspective, one cannot deduce that there has been a clear historical transition from the model based on the productive household to one predominantly based on the wage family. The latter poses quite serious problems of interpretation in terms of its potential for explaining social reproduction. These problems are reflected historically in the poverty of English workers in the last century, in the diverse forms of social complementarity that have matured in different ways and periods and in present-day issues related to industrialization in underdeveloped countries. The question revolves around the fact that *a single wage has been enough to guarantee the survival of an entire family only as an exception and under special circumstances.* In this regard, when I talk of the historical phase in which the family wage appeared, I am referring not only to a limited number of families in some advanced capitalist countries; I also have in mind those social situations where the so-called family wage is in most cases supported by welfare programmes, without which it too would be inadequate (think of the cost of totally private housing, health, education and transport). In particular, the wage family is unable to get by the critical stage when only the husband-father is officially employed and the wife-mother is partially engaged in producing and raising children and the latter are too young to work. The historical period of working-class poverty in England clearly shows the devastating effects of this critical moment, only compensated for in part by forms of solidarity or complementary social organization that allow the wife-mother to go on working or undertake temporary informal work or that bring in resources to supplement the single wage. Proof of this comes from the fact that where working children make a substantial contribution to income-pooling, the working-class family only manages to survive, but never to grow rich. It is only in this situation that one family member, the housewife-mother to more than one worker, dedicates practically all her energy to domestic chores (see Tilly and Scott, 1987). The social reproduction patterns of the wage family in its various historical forms is the object of more detailed analysis below.

However, what is worth delineating immediately are the fundamental lines along which householding was transformed relative to life-cycles in the experience of advanced capitalist countries. In the space of less than a century and through a succession of radical changes, the pattern of reproduction in which the critical stage was represented by the period of biological reproduction, when the husband-father was the only one earning an (insufficient) wage, has given way to one in which the critical stage comes much later, when teenage children leave school and have difficulty in finding a job while, at the same time, being caught up in forms of conspicuous consumption. Obviously, both these different patterns of social reproduction cannot be explained solely by referring to monetary incomes and without mentioning those social factors that complement them in diverse ways. This is even truer if we also look at different social situations and strata.

Different patterns in satisfying subsistence needs

Before attempting a first abstract analysis of the structure for satisfying subsistence needs, I shall mention briefly the advantages and limits of the main tool available for this type of analysis, household time-budgets. It is useful but raises several difficulties. First, the data is relatively limited and not easy to compare.[10] Second, time is not always the best measure of social reproduction practices, especially where it is important to grasp the qualitative nature of such practices. For example, forty hours of domestic labour involves a series of tasks which may be carried out in completely different ways: to take just one operation, using the washing-machine twice as week as opposed to taking the washing to a launderette once a month. For these reasons, in what is said below reference is made principally to abstract times; only in a few cases, where there is precise information on some advanced capitalist countries over long periods of time, are concrete studies of the variation in family time-budgets utilized. The other analytical tool for documenting the changes in social repro-duction strategies, employment statistics, presents just as many problems of a practically symmetrical kind. Historical series of not perfectly com-parable data exist, but do not tell us much about reproductive practices. These methodological difficulties ultimately explain why, except for direct local research, analysis of reproductive practices must be kept at a high level of hypothesis and abstraction.

The structure for satisfying families' subsistence needs can be con-sidered in terms of different configurations of monetary consumption in relation to needs which are satisfied by unpaid domestic work or activities directed at immediate household consumption or resources contributed from outside the household, such as redistribution from the state and various contributions deriving from different reciprocal networks. One starts from the hypothesis that in order to satisfy a variable part of their subsistence requirements, households have working resources at their disposal which they use in part directly (normal domestic work is the most important example) and in part to obtain a monetary income; with the latter they purchase the goods and services needed for family reproduction.

To these two fundamental resources others should be added, such as services provided by the state free of charge or at a political price, and various forms of private or public assistance and solidarity, like gifts or charity from relatives or friends, unions or associations. A further possible resource for household survival is the use of saved or inherited wealth, either through the income it generates or through its direct expenditure or use (Dale Tussing, 1975). The way in which these different forms of meeting subsistence needs are combined depends on many factors and on the specific, historically determined, social class under consideration.

Industrial development in the advanced capitalist countries has involved a progressive shift from low to higher subsistence levels and from high levels of work for direct consumption to ever higher levels of monetary consumption. Of course, the combination of ways of satisfying subsistence needs also depends on specific factors whose importance varies according to the phase of economic development, and it has a considerable effect on the dynamic and composition of the demand for goods and services (Balbo, 1980). No distinction is made at this point between formal and informal working activities; they will be considered together as working activities that serve to procure a monetary income. Furthermore, I make no distinction between goods and services consumed in formal and informal circumstances, and view both as components of monetary demand. The latter also includes the consumption of welfare services and subsidies provided by the state or by other collective bodies, like private companies or trade unions. At this initial stage, there is no discussion of the important difference between monetary income deriving from waged and salaried work and that produced by various forms of self-employment, both traditional and the newly expanding ones.

The combination of resources utilized in reproduction is connected with, among other factors, labour market conditions and processes; that is to say, with the need to mobilize or freeze specific sections of the labour force at given costs and quality levels. The most important historical example is primitive accumulation. The mobilization of pre-capitalist agricultural workers provides, on one hand, an increasing labour force for developing industry and, on the other, destroys pre-capitalist self-provisioning networks, thereby making possible the consumption of at least part of increased capitalist production.

The other side to the logic of this process is that social reproduction is a key point at which labour supply and labour demand intersect. Within the household as a unit of social reproduction, embedded in different supportive reciprocal networks, decisions are taken according to the varying and changing internal distribution of power on which is the best possible allocation of available resources to meet subsistence needs, given the existing relations between work opportunities and income and the parallel possibilities of saving subsistence expenses through labour for direct self-provisioning, and/or given the existence of other reciprocal or redistributive resources. In this sense, the complex structure of reproduction expresses, among other processes, the formation of the labour supply at given conditions of labour demand and of overall work opportunities.

In figure 3.1 I have tried to illustrate three hypothetical combinations of contemporary family reproduction strategies by including different quotas of work for self-provisioning. Model A illustrates an 'intermediate' combination of domestic work and reproductive requirements satisfied by means of monetary income; model B shows a maximum level of requirements satisfied by means of monetary income and public welfare assistance, which maximizes the availability of family members for external work; and model C shows a prevalence of work for self-provisioning, with consequent very low monetary incomes and limited opportunities

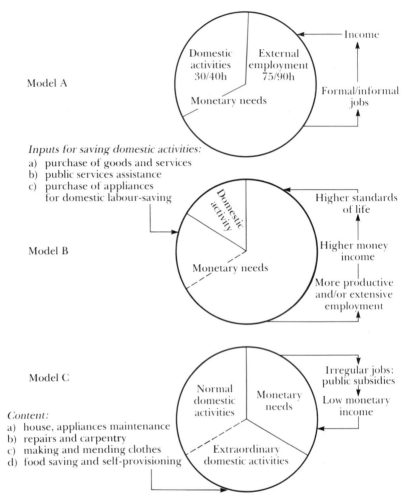

Figure 3.1 Household reproduction models according to different combinations of money income/consumption and domestic and self-provisioning activities

for external work. These models are to be considered as schematic and purely hypothetical even though the data relative to hours of work and of domestic activities are derived from recent longitudinal studies comparing time-budgets (Gershuny, 1988).

In model A, the underlying hypothesis is that domestic work for reproducing a nuclear family of four persons, two adults and two minors, amounts to about thirty-five hours a week distributed between the family members according to cultural models, but usually carried out by women, here assumed to be working full-time or nearly so. In reality, the time dedicated to domestic work in the case of women without outside employment is considerably greater. At this stage, the possible impact of different household structures in terms of number of persons, age groups and family relations is not taken into account. This variable is, however, important and changes considerably over time. The most important change in this respect is the relative increase in small and single-person households. The four-person household (two adult parents and two children) has not been selected because it is typical, but merely as an example to underline what I have to say on the impact of the problems relating to social reproduction in an initial interpretation.

In order to reduce the hours of domestic work, and thus pass from model A to model B, which normally involves a different use of the female labour force (full-time and/or more productive or qualified employment), a clear increase in family income is required. This permits the purchases of labour-saving devices (domestic appliances) the purchase of external labour or its products (servants, babysitters, precooked foods, laundry services, household cleaning services, etc.) and/or the introduction of efficient state or collective welfare services (crèches and nurseries, full-time schools, company and school catering services, etc.). Naturally, the more efficient the public or collective contribution is, the more income and time the household can save and use for other purposes. The economic and cumulative utility of efficient welfare services in a capitalist system is thus immediately evident. Model B illustrates a greater possibility of external employment. This is translated into higher rates of activity according to the income level of the household, the cultural models expressed by the household and, above all, the combination on the labour market of existing demand with the supply effectively freed from domestic and self-provisioning work.

Model C does not illustrate a self-consumption/rural situation preceding capitalist development, where household reproduction has clearly different qualitative features, but rather a capitalist one in which high unemployment or underemployment considerably reduces monetary income and compels the household to provide for its reproduction by means of greater self-provisioning. Some of the necessary consumption of the urban household, for example a part of the food, accommodation, transport and energy requirements, is provided for out of the low monetary income, but a very large part is achieved through domestic work and self-provisioning, such as home-made clothes, maintenance of dwellings and household appliances, economies in food or the direct exchange of work with neighbours, relatives, friends, etc.

Taken together with the list of subsistence requirements in table 3.1 (p. 146), a reading of figure 3.1 (pp. 148–9) suggests some hypothetical considerations, especially with regard to the more important socio-economic effects of current economic processes and policies. In advanced capitalist countries, a combination of increasing unemployment and casual employment and the crisis of the welfare state, with welfare programmes being reshaped in an increasingly privatized or less universalistic direction, may be assumed to produce a large number of shifts from model B to model A and from model A to model C. But these changes have to be discussed in a much less abstract way and with greater attention to accuracy; it is necessary to consider both the specific social factors involved in reproduction strategies and in the life-cycle and the different composition of households relative to the potential impact of the twofold crisis in employment and public welfare provision.

At this stage, it may be useful to anticipate some considerations in this direction in order to clarify the meaning of this preliminary formulation. The contemporary development of mass unemployment in industrialized countries appears to be a persistent structural phenomenon affecting mainly two groups: young people entering the labour market for the first time and, to a variable extent in different areas, adult workers displaced by de-industrialization. Increasing male unemployment goes hand in hand with rising rates of married females in work. On the other hand, it is obvious that privatization of public services and deterioration of welfare programmes will disproportionately affect households that are more highly dependent on welfare, particularly the elderly, families with young children or with handicapped members, single-parent families and so on.

A reasonable hypothesis is that in an urban context it is difficult to find social factors able to compensate for a high number of critical situations; on the opposite front, it may be readily assumed that the lack of even weak compensation is a serious aggravating factor in, for instance, the case of socially isolated households and recent migrants or ethnic groups suffering discrimination. Following on from this hypothesis, it may be assumed that three types of households are currently facing considerable and mounting difficulties. They are:

1 Households with dependent children where the father/husband has been made redundant through de-industrialization, is unable to find a new job and joins the long-term unemployed. He may or may not receive unemployment benefits; in the latter case there is the possibility that he will find casual/informal work, but this provides no real solution to the problems facing his family. The fact that the mother-wife has a part-time or full-time job and is able to maintain the family is obviously

important. However, in general it is not an adequate solution either, since her income is usually insufficient by itself to ensure the family's survival. Given this last observation, it can also be said that single-parent families with dependent children, numbers of which are rising rapidly in advanced capitalist countries, are in the same difficult situation – even more so when the single parent is the mother.

2 Elderly households dependent on low pensions, which are increasingly affected by the deterioration in, or lack of, welfare provisions, particularly when they are socially isolated or when their children or kin are unable to help them.

3 Households with long-term unemployed adult children in the very period of life when they go in for conspicuous consumption. This situation will be coped with more adequately by parents who are both in full-time employment, but may push the father into moonlighting and the mother into extending her part-time to full-time employment, at least where possible. The possibility exists that the critical nature of this type of situation will be aggravated by the fact that in the same period the grandparents of the young unemployed enter into the above-mentioned critical phase and need support from their children to survive. Age calculations show that this is not at all an improbable event, considering that the average age of one generation of children is between twenty-five and thirty, so that grandchildren in long-term unemployment between sixteen and twenty-one will have grandparents aged from sixty-six to eighty-one. It should also be stressed that as time passes and the young adults are persistently unable to find a job, the critical situation worsens both for them and for their ageing grandparents.

3 A TENTATIVE HISTORICAL ANALYSIS OF THE REPRODUCTION PROCESS

The theoretical framework for interpreting the historical change in the patterns of social reproduction

Qualitative changes in the social reproduction patterns are extremely important, and at the same time, they are difficult to acknowledge in an abstract way. Among the factors which contribute to a certain degree of uncertainty, there is the impact of changing and stratified levels of labour productivity. In this respect, it is practically impossible to show the whole range of stratification at different times and to avoid a circular causal explanation. In short, increased productivity of work is reflected in increased income per working hour and, consequently, in the greater monetary cost of reproducing a more productive labour force, as well as

Table 3.1 *Principal subsistence needs according to the mode of satisfaction within different hypothetical models of household reproduction*

Classification of needs into categories		Mode of satisfaction		
Housing	Rent and property	M	M	M/I
	Energy, water, heating and other expenses	M	M	M
	Installations: building	M/I	M	M/D
	maintenance/repairs	M	M	D/I
	Furnishings: construction/purchase	M/I	M	D/I
	maintenance	M/I	M	D/I
	Household appliances: purchase	M	M	(M)
	maintenance/repairing	M/I	M	D/I
	Administrative activities	D	D	D
	Cleaning	D	M	D
Food	Cost of food	M/I	M	M/I/D
	Cleaning/preparation/cooking	D	M/D	D
	Purchasing activities	D	M/D	D
	Cooking and serving instruments	M	M	M/I/D
Clothing	Cost of self-provisioning labour	M	M	D/M
	Purchasing activities	D	D	D
	Ordinary repairs	D	M	D
	Extraordinary repairs	M	M	D
Transportation	Private: costs	M	M	M
	maintenance repairs	M	M	I/D/M
	petrol/taxes	M	M	M
	Public or collective means	M	M	M
Other	Health assistance:			
	medical care and drugs	M	M	M
	non-professional care	D	M	D
	Recreation, culture, information	M	M	M
	Assistance to children and the elderly	D/M	M	D

D   Domestic and self-provisioning activities
M   Monetary consumption
I   Informal consumption

NB: The expression M includes the possibility that the service is provided by public or collective forms of assistance.

in substantial qualitative changes in the labour reproduction process. Alternatively, it could be argued that improvement in the qualitative standards of the social reproduction of the labour force helps a potentially more productive labour force to develop. I would argue that the problem of original causation is not very important as long as we recognize that there is a strong two-way causal link between both processes. A small stimulus from one side may thus be reflected in accelerated changes on both sides, if the historical conditions are ripe and there are no barriers to prevent them from interacting, such as massive state intervention to redistribute the benefits of increased productivity to different areas of social reproduction. Historical evidence shows that state intervention has various possible consequences, which require specific investigation; I will return to this problem below and in chapter 4.

Since the establishment of a widespread – but never universal – system of family wage reproduction, Western societies have generally experienced two crucial historical transitions in their patterns of reproduction and labour productivity. I believe that a further transition may now be in progress.[11] The first transition was connected with the legal abolition of child employment and the decrease in female employment, which led to the modern form of unpaid domestic work in working-class households. The second was connected with a sharp increase in the rate of female employment, in particular of married women, which again was reflected in changes in social reproduction patterns. The present one reflects the problem of employment, that is, the structural increase in the surplus population of industrialized countries and the diffusion of informal activities. Figure 3.2, which illustrates reproduction patterns, does not show the qualitative changes, which must be taken into consideration separately. It is inadequate for picturing the different ratios of productivity/income with sufficient precision.

The unit of reproduction has at its disposal mostly working capacities which, within a limited freedom of choice, are conditioned by the historical phase of development and by the socio-cultural background of the unit. They may be used for working activities that either procure a monetary income with which to purchase subsistence goods and services or directly provide goods and services useful for subsistence (self-provisioning and domestic work). Furthermore, the unit may also be able to count on resources from outside, such as assistance from the state or from public bodies, or on contributions in the form of income or free goods and services provided by private individuals or bodies within reciprocal social networks, such as gifts from relations, neighbourhood solidarity, or solidarity among friends and colleagues.

The combination of work for self-provisioning and for monetary income

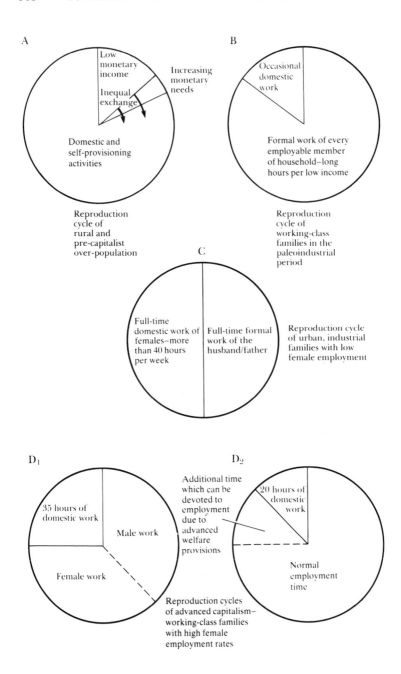

A

Low monetary income

Increasing monetary needs

Inequal exchange

Domestic and self-provisioning activities

Reproduction cycle of rural and pre-capitalist over-population

B

Occasional domestic work

Formal work of every employable member of household–long hours per low income

Reproduction cycle of working-class families in the paleoindustrial period

C

Full-time domestic work of females–more than 40 hours per week

Full-time formal work of the husband/father

Reproduction cycle of urban, industrial families with low female employment

D_1

35 hours of domestic work

Male work

Female work

D_2

Additional time which can be devoted to employment due to advanced welfare provisions

20 hours of domestic work

Normal employment time

Reproduction cycles of advanced capitalism–working-class families with high female employment rates

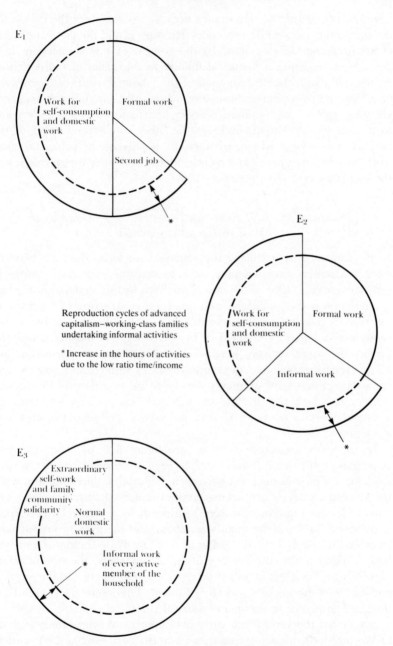

Figure 3.2 Reproduction patterns in different historical periods and social settings

acquires a fundamental importance because it constitutes the reason for the connection between the reproductive process and the general process of accumulation/development. In the context of this connection, it is possible to recognize a historical duality in the cycles of reproduction: on the one hand, the reproduction of the labour force directly involved in the process of capital accumulation where, albeit in different historical and geographical combinations, working activity for income is undertaken to a considerable extent; and, on the other, the reproduction of the surplus labour force where, whether the population be urban or rural, work for self-provisioning and reciprocal arrangements are prevalent and the monetary cost of subsistence is low.

The consolidation of wage-family patterns of reproduction in Western capitalist countries

In the context of reproducing the active labour force, the ratio between work for self-provisioning and work for income can vary greatly in different societies. One of the most important factors in determining this combination is the qualitative and quantitative structure of the demand for labour. There is a considerable historical difference between the reproductive balances attained at the early stage of industrial demand for labour, based on very long working hours and, in particular, low hourly remuneration and the employment of women and minors, and the balances that have gradually developed in the course of the present century in which the demand for labour is increasingly selective and stratified, working hours are shorter and salaries and labour productivity are rising.

In the early industrial context (see figure 3.2, B), once the pre-industrial productive communities had been abandoned, at least in part, work for self-provisioning was necessarily reduced to the minimum, while the subsistence levels of working families remained extremely low. The costs of labour reproduction were kept down by a high relative surplus population, but even the quality of labour and the level of productivity remained relatively limited. Owing to very low living standards and very long working hours, the average life-span was short, the rate of infant mortality declined less in industrial cities than elsewhere and the physical endurance of the workers was fairly limited. This summary is useful but does not do justice to the socio-historical variety of combinations which accompanied the spread and early development of wage-family systems in Western industrializing countries up to the beginning of the twentieth century. I will, therefore, briefly discuss some of the relevant considerations.

Wage-family systems arose out of and developed in parallel with changes in productive household systems. The latter had become predominantly based on the conjugal family and, in general, applied the restrictive householding rules described in the previous section in order to balance internal productive potential with reproductive resources. This balanced circuit, which was not expanding demographically but which involved strong social control, was progressively undermined by the spread of opportunities for wage-work. Young people with, but also those without, the means of household production, in the countryside and cities alike, were able to marry and form a family. In no case did this event suddenly and completely eliminate the existing productive household systems. On the contrary, a persistent and complex complementarity has characterized the specific experiences of such systems. As already mentioned, a wage-family system without external social support is at no time able to survive, especially during the phase of the life-cycle when the wife-mother has to devote a part of her time to biological reproduction. This constraint limits the spread of proper wage-family systems and ensures that the reproduction of wage-labour stays within productive household systems in various ways. I have already mentioned the longlasting importance of the worker-peasant experience in continental Europe. Another form of complementarity is found in the cottage industry system. It was based on the fact that what became a special form of wage labour continued to be reproduced within a productive household organization. This system was very widespread in England during industrial take-off and has remained important throughout other experiences of industrialization up to the present age, although, as we shall see shortly, under changing conditions. A third relevant example of arrangements that limit the spread of a pure wage-family system is the possibility that workers may move from one system to the other at difficult times: in particular, pregnant mothers go back to their home villages during the intensive phase of biological reproduction and return to the industrial city as soon as the youngest child is old enough to work. As I have already stated with regard to peasant-workers, for as long as they last these experiences serve to subsidise the parallel complementarity and persistence of relatively low wages, on the one side, and of productive households on the other. This also contributes to maintaining the commodification process at relatively low levels and, as a consequence, it slows down the accumulation of capital.

These complementary systems become a growing obstacle to the diffusion of big industry, which expands at a very fast rate and needs a fully urbanized stable working class. This last trend and its negative effects on reproduction are particularly visible in the English experience.

Here both rural and urban productive households suffered an early, radical and rapid decline as a result of the establishment and growth of an industrial system whose production was increasingly destined not only for the domestic but principally for the world market.

Migration and urbanization mean that, in general, the reproduction strategies no longer benefit from the resources provided by historically consolidated community support. It is not by chance that this event has been one of the features of industrial transformation most often underlined by sociologists, beginning with Comte and Durkheim. Urbanized families without complementarity arrangements with other not too distant productive households found themselves in desperate need of social support in order to survive during periods of biological reproduction; this period was reduced to a minimum by the general practice of making children work, but still lasted at least four to six years. In the special case of company towns, particularly in mining areas, the company provided a primitive welfare solution to the problem which acted in conjunction with the strong community feeling that developed in settlements where everybody was living and working in close contact. This is one of the earliest examples of the family wage solution (here related not to a single worker but, at least, to a father with children); in this case, the wife-mother was forced out of employment and had to work very hard in the home to support her entire working family. Particularly in mining areas, this reproductive solution reflected the fact that child labour was particularly valuable given the technical conditions of the times. Children could work in much more restricted spaces and both save money and reduce risks.

Elsewhere, there is sufficient documentation to suggest the spread of at least two possible arrangements, often in combination, for supporting the survival of wage families that are relatively isolated from productive households and community solidarity. The most important has certainly been kinship. Industrialization and urbanization have clearly changed the meaning of kinship ties but, overall, these have been reinforced rather than weakened in terms of solidarity.[12] Although this event has been considerably neglected in the sociological tradition, it is a logical consequence of the early phase of industrial transformation. Migration and technical advances in communication weaken community ties but eventually strengthen kinship relations. Brothers and sisters tend to settle in the same area and to help each other. Within the early wage-family organizations, brothers and sisters often worked together and with one or both parents, for rather long periods of time – in some cases more than ten years. Moreover, property is by definition much less important for wage families than for productive households, which certainly means a weaker intergenerational link from the economic point of view but also a potential for reinforcing collateral links freed from any competition and litigation over property. It is important to mention this fact because it will become fully established and highly influential in the organization of working-class life well beyond this initial stage.

The second common solution reflects a mix of neighbourhood solidarity and primitive child care systems. It allows wife-mothers to get round the burdens of biological reproduction and go on working, particularly in informal and part-time jobs (for instance, street-vendors in English cities in the nineteenth century were often married women) but even in full-time industrial employment.

The family wage system

Only various combinations of these social arrangements explain how survival became possible where individual wages were insufficient and the capacity for self-provisioning very limited. However, these diverse kinds of early wage-family systems, whether complemented or not by a high degree of partial or total reproduction of wage-work within persistent productive household systems, turned out to be highly unstable histori-cally. From the angle of capitalist accumulation, they signified a large potential for under-commodification which increasingly acted as a brake on economic growth. Their effect on the workers' conditions of life, on the other hand, was to keep them at persistently low levels at the very time when increasing numbers and concentrated production in factories were favouring the formation of trade unions and working-class political parties. This led to a more or less radical transformation in the repro-duction patterns of the Western working class.

This early situation then gave way to a later one based on a greater selectivity in the demand for labour and on a progressive shortening of working hours with parallel increases in income, which reflected more than proportional increases in productivity. The standard of living of the workers' families rose, and there was a growing need to dedicate a part of the family's working potential to self-provisioning. Domestic work in the modern sense of the term established itself even in the context of working-class families. (For the Italian case, see Ingrosso, 1979.) It is important to note that the 'solution' generally adopted for the repro-duction of the labour force in a manner more suitable to the requirements of industrial development was the allocation of a considerable amount of unpaid female labour to domestic work. This solution tended to keep down the cost of reproducing labour, but it imposed a discriminatory selectivity on labour demand/supply and withdrew from the sphere of direct capitalist accumulation a whole series of activities that remained external to the logic of the market for goods and services and socialized within predominantly reciprocal arrangements.

In general, it is important to note that this transformation has a contradictory side: it is certainly an important step towards an increasing commodification of everyday life, but at the same time it reinforces and diffuses the separation of a sizeable area of persistently non-commodified social relations. Relative to the previous stage of wage-family patterns of reproduction based on extremely low income deriving from long hours of labour by every member of the household able to work, this is only an apparent contradiction, but it inevitably turns into a real one when viewed in a forward-looking historical perspective. At this stage the constitution of working-class domestic units simultaneously reflects and permits very substantial rises in the productivity of wage-work and parallel, but less than proportional, increases in the commodification of reproduction patterns of wage-work. In an age of increasing restrictions on child employment, the working-class housewife becomes a sort of reproduction manager who devotes all her time not only to the welfare and reconstitution of her husband's labour power, producing babies and caring for young children, but also increasingly to a social investment aimed at improving the quality of the labour force from one generation to the next. She is in charge of early education, makes sure that children go to school and that they acquire greater skills and the potential for productive wage-work.

In specific historical experience this transformation has been slow and contradictory, and it is far from complete. Unpaid females devoting all their time to domestic work first became established in middle-income groups, particularly among the emerging urban white-collar class where salaries were sufficient to keep the wife-mother at home but often insufficient to hire a full-time servant. I have also mentioned the conditions that made this solution convenient in mining areas at an earlier date. Among the urbanized working class the practice was first adopted in the case of wives-mothers with working children in the household contributing several wages to the income pool (for France and England see Tilly and Scott, 1987). This was especially the case in localities where employment opportunities for adult females were few or declining: for instance, in English textile cities and factories where the combination of restructuring, relocation and labour-saving technology produced very early on a sharp reduction in jobs mostly held by female workers. This transformation did not have immediate direct effects on the patterns of organizing reproduction in the remaining productive households. And it is important to stress this fact because, with the exception of Britain and to a lesser extent the United States and the Scandinavian countries, the majority of the population in industrializing countries still engaged mainly in agriculture well into the twentieth century. It is no accident that late industrial development has meant very sharp drops in the rate of female employment with the direct transformation through migration and urbanization of female agricultural workers into full-time working-class housewives.

The so-called 'family wage' (intended as the single wage of an adult male breadwinner) has represented a limited historical experience; it was able to take root only at certain times and under specific conditions and probably constituted only an unstable form of transition to a phase characterized by the development of welfare provisions, consumerism and the return of increasing numbers of married women to employment.

Reproduction patterns typical of the Fordist-welfarist model

After the First World War, reproductive patterns tended to change, assuming one of two different forms. The first (figure 3.2, C) is based on very high rates of domestic work, on the assignment of the greater part of the female labour force to unpaid domestic activities, and thus on a supply/demand of female labour which, at least in the non-agricultural sectors, is relatively limited, particularly to adult working women before marriage or the birth of their first child. The second (figure 3.2, D1/D2) is founded on the need to continue supplying the market with large amounts of female labour, and thus on the limitation of domestic activities, which is compensated for by the purchase of substitutive goods or services or by efficient welfare state provisions. Furthermore, a certain proportion of these domestic activities, which it is difficult to reduce, are carried out by members of the family unit (mainly women) in addition to their full or part-time employment. The monetary cost of reproducing the labour force is lower in the first than in the second case, not only in terms of the total wage bill but also of the total social cost. However, the actual valorization of capital is clearly smaller because the reproductive agent's capacity for monetary consumption is less and many reproductive goods and services remain outside the capital accumulation process.

The process of social reproduction based on a growing rate of working wives is conditioned historically by several important factors and changes, in particular by what I would call the 'benign spiral' of the welfare state. Investment in welfare programmes has a twofold effect: first, it reduces the burden of housework through full-time schooling, nurseries, efficient hospitals and health services; and second, it expands the supply of female labour while, at the same time, leading to a gradually rising demand for female labour in these same welfare services.

As will be seen below, and as is immediately apparent from figure 3.2, it is obvious that these reproductive practices and the parallel benign spiral of the welfare state are very costly in economic terms. Much more than in the case of previous social transformations, this latest one is accompanied by necessarily unequal relations on a worldwide scale and by a more radical penetration and domination of capitalism in under-developed countries. In this sense, what we are dealing with is not so much an option of historical change in labour markets where the internal reserves of labour that are easy to mobilize, above all huge masses of peasants and underemployed agricultural labourers, have long since dried up. It is, rather, a complex transformation made possible only by an expanding domination of the world market and, at the same time, by the different but converging interests of industrialists and the relatively powerful workers' organizations; the former are interested in the expan-sion of mass consumption and further increases in labour productivity, the latter in improved conditions of life.

In general, advanced capitalist societies are also characterized and dominated by the coexistence of these three original conditions with the lack of extensive internal reserves of labour that are easy to mobilize. The existence of an important variant or restriction relative to this possible development must, however, be noted. It consists of the possi-bility of mobilizing vast influxes of migrant workers at relatively low cost. The case of the United States shows the most striking impact by this latter condition in two respects: first, an advanced programme of universal state welfare may not fully materialize, and second, the survival strategies of various strata of workers display an increasing diversity. These strategies range from high cost conditions, a high degree of com-modification, the complete absorption of mass consumerist behaviour (where even married women increasingly stay in employment, but rather in the area of semi-privatized welfare), to the diametrically opposite situations of cross-border Mexican agricultural labourers, whose low daily wages serve to support their families back home.

Even though one cannot talk of a generalized historical change from the first (C) to the second (D1/D2) model of reproduction after the Second World War, it can nevertheless be observed that during this period the second model found a more radical expression in the indus-trialized countries lacking large internal reserves of labour, apart from women tied to domestic activities. In these cases, it became convenient to promote the release of a portion of the female labour force and the importation of an immigrant labour force from less developed countries.

Sufficient transfers of resources from underdeveloped countries were indispensable in order to modify radically the local reproduction patterns, both through increases in wages and the implementation of efficient welfare programmes.

The switch from the prevalence of one model to the other, on the other hand, was slower in countries possessing internal labour reserves, for example Southern European countries like Italy. In these cases the social reproduction patterns of the labour force were persistently characterized by, on the one hand, the presence of wage families in an urban context, complemented by weak and delayed welfare programmes, and on the other, the persistence of poorly commodified patterns of reproduction of productive households in the countryside and in small towns. The patterns of economic development rendered the latter decreasingly viable, favouring either their definitive abandonment or various changes in policy to make it possible for them to persist. This involved increasing monetary contributions deriving mainly from state pensions and emigrated members' remittances, but also from productive rationalization and specialization, the development of part-time agricultural employment in combination with other jobs, and later on the redevelopment of industrial homeworking.[13]

The marked and differentiated change-over from cycle C to cycle D1/D2 in many advanced capitalist countries after the Second World War helped to accelerate economic growth, to increase the difference between the development rhythms of different areas, and to render much more complex the stratification of the costs and modalities of reproducing the labour force. These areas ranged from the least developed, where the amount of monetary consumption remained low, to areas where female employment in non-agricultural activities remained low owing to the large proportion of women tied to domestic activities, and to others in which private work for self-provisioning was reduced to the minimum and the service-industry sector, both public and private, underwent a great expansion.

The contemporary diversity of reproduction patterns in advanced capitalist countries

There are considerable differences between the patterns of reproduction of the labour force in advanced capitalist countries even when we limit our observation to those with high rates of female employment. In the extreme case (figure 3.2, D2), high income and efficient welfare services permit a considerable reduction of the time spent on domestic activities (up to twenty hours per week), with an almost optimum use of both male and female working capacity for income earning. As will be seen in chapter 4, various contradictions and conflicts also arise from these arrangements, due in particular to the difficulty of overcoming increasingly unacceptable sexual discrimination. However, there also exist numerous cases of reproduction patterns characterized by different arrangements. In these cases (figure 3.2, D1), the domestic work level is high (between twenty and thirty-five to forty hours per week) and, in view of its unequal distribution between the sexes, women find it very difficult to combine their domestic work with full-time outside employment; the result is more absenteeism, less professionalism and a working career handicapped by additional discrimination.

Before considering the present situation, I want to raise an important problem concerning the role played in reproduction cycles by the different sizes and qualities of households. This is a complicated point because both size and quality change over time and space, so that generalizations are rather hazardous. On the whole, it is thought that industrial development gradually promoted the transformation of large households deeply embedded in close-knit kinship and community reciprocal systems into small and socially isolated nuclear ones.[14] Moreover, this fragmentation of the household structure is now believed to be proceeding further as a consequence of the declining birth rate, the high number of divorces and, above all, the ageing of the population and the extended life-span. I have already mentioned some elements that throw doubt on the accuracy of the first part of this assumption. In particular, I have pointed out that the consolidation of a structure based on the conjugal family in Western European countries has usually proceeded or accompanied industrialization and not been a consequence of it; it has therefore also characterized productive households, at least in the form they assumed at the start of the industrial age.

There have been two main demographic consequences arising from industrial take-off for the reasons already mentioned: the increase in the share of the marrying population and the lowering of the marriage age. Before the practice of birth control became widespread in the period between the end of the nineteenth and the beginning of the twentieth century, a combination of demographic factors led to an increase in population and, to a lesser extent, in the average number of members of households. It is probable that it was the very processes of industrialization and the reproductive combinations of wage families and productive households which favoured among the latter a new increase in extended forms; this is in line with the above-mentioned establishment of collateral family links within wage families. On the whole, reproductive complementarity between productive households, in particular peasant ones, and the wage pooling of household members give rise to the possibility of widening the horizons of households beyond the narrow conjugal family. The increased life-span that enables a growing number of parents to survive well beyond the adulthood and marriage of their children also contributes to this phenomenon. In wage families, on the other hand, it is quite unlikely that different generations of adults will live together beyond the period in which young unmarried children go out to work and contribute at least a part of their salary to the family budget. Thus, the problem becomes one of following the dynamic history of the decline and persistence of productive households. Only in this sense, that is, in the way the process furthers the decline of productive households in the form of large multi-income reproductive units, is the argument acceptable which states that large households are transformed into smaller nuclear ones, particularly during the Fordist age.

This process of transformation has important consequences for the organization of reproduction cycles, and in particular of domestic activities. Large households, particularly when they are embedded within a stable reciprocal system of networks, undertake a high number of hours of domestic and self-provisioning work (which, however, may involve a lower per capita share than in smaller units) and are usually able to produce much more through (extraordinary) self-provisioning than small nuclear households. This transition from larger to smaller units takes place according to different time-scales and at varying rates in diverse regions since it depends on whether productive households persist or decline.

Other demographic trends also exert an important influence and tend to confirm the second part of the initial proposition, although with important local variations. In general, the population in advanced capitalist countries is ageing, while birth and marriage rates are decreasing. This means that there is a steady increase in very small households composed of one or two people, either young or old but predominantly the latter. This process influences the reproduction patterns because, in the main, these households have below-average monetary incomes and are compelled to engage in consumption or production activities classified under III to VI in table 2.1. Welfare state services are required in order to assist the reproduction of these households, help them to meet serious difficulties and prevent both the basis of consensus and the capacity to consume from being seriously weakened. This entails a continuous increase in the demand for state welfare intervention. On the other hand, the absence of state intervention and housing shortages in large cities may block the diffusion of small households. The enforced cohabiting of different adult generations in the same household often leads to other kinds of problems and to conflict.

In addition to these trends, a considerable increase in single-parent households, particularly the number of households headed by women, single persons, divorcees or widows, has been observed in various countries. This tendency, combined with the persistence of job/wage discrimination against women and of the unequal sexual division of domestic work, may also lead to increasing conflict and to strong pressures for costly welfare state provisions.

I am well aware that, while the above abstract illustration of reproduction patterns is mainly based on time-budgets of middle-aged couples with school-age children, the real picture is greatly influenced by the increasing importance of different kinds of households in terms of the number of cohabitants, family relations and age groups. Therefore it is important to follow up the question of survival by examining life-cycles (see, mainly, Bryman et al., 1987).

4 INFORMALIZATION AND SOCIAL REPRODUCTION IN ADVANCED CAPITALIST COUNTRIES

Economic crisis, informalization and changes in patterns of social reproduction

I shall now consider the period starting from 1970, the complex effects of the economic crisis on the reproduction process and, above all, the feedback from reproduction strategies to the economy, with particular emphasis on the impact of informalization. In this section the discussion is very general and abstract, while in the next a more detailed typological analysis of households subject to different kinds of informalization pressures is undertaken. Both sections are almost exclusively devoted to the experience of industrialized capitalist countries; other experiences are touched upon only in the final section of this chapter.

The most important effects of the recent economic crisis on the various reproductive patterns of the labour force derive from the high rate of inflation and from the complex restructuring of employment. Furthermore, the fiscal crisis of the state plays an important part in modifying the circumstances of social reproduction. The combination of inflation, the dismantling of public welfare services and reduced employment in medium to large industrial organizations tends to shift the balance between work for self-provisioning and work for income in favour of the former, thereby leading to a reduction in aggregate demand and in the capacity to accumulate. These very general trends have, however, diversified impacts on households and are counterbalanced by the effects from increased employment of married women and possibly aggravated by the coinciding deterioration, limitation or cancellation of state welfare programmes. In line with this, it is easy to give completely opposite examples of contemporary changes in family life-styles: one is based on their substantial improvement and the other on their critical deterioration.

Take the case of a couple aged thirty with children in a country where public welfare provisions are still relatively good, for example, Sweden. They both have a good full-time job in solid enterprises and are in the very period of life when substantial promotion and increases in income are obtained. They invest their extra income in means of self-provisioning, in the best education for their children, and perhaps in further higher education for themselves to upgrade their positions in the segmented labour market. Their parents, or at least their fathers, are still in employment and in good health and do not need any survival assitance from their children; on the contrary, they may still contribute resources to help improve the life-style of their grandchildren and provide them with better educational opportunities. This picture could just as readily apply to a blue-collar worker at Volvo married to a local council social worker, both of relatively modest working-class origins and average education.

As an opposite example, let us take an older working-class family (aged forty-five to fifty) with children in their late teens, living in a place badly hit by de-industrialization and the deterioration in welfare services, such as Liverpool in Britain. The husband-father is made redundant at the very time in his life when his children cannot find a job and remain among the long-term unemployed, while his ageing pensioner parents and parents-in-law increasingly need the support of their relatives. If the wife-mother has always been a full-time housewife or she also loses her part-time job due to the cuts in local government expenditure imposed by central government (both cases are not improbable), the deteriorating condition in the survival patterns of this household becomes even more dramatic. Even the unlikely combination of unemployment benefit with casual and temporary work would not help to solve their problems. This too may be the picture of a normal working-class household where by 'normal' we mean that it does not necessarily include social or ethnic discrimination against coloured minorities or foreign guest-workers.

The plurality and diversification of possible impacts from current socio-economic transformation have to be taken into account but do not conceal the above-mentioned directions in which the general trends are heading. In abstract, we have to begin working on the prevalent negative consequences of this situation. The starting-point is the circular transmission of the crisis, from the productive to the reproductive system and back to the productive system, considering that under present conditions there is no fall in the cost of labour sufficient to revive the economy as a whole on account of the segmentation of the labour markets, the impact of labour-saving technologies and the saturation of manufacturing production in combination with persistent competition from cheap labour in newly industrializing countries.

If not all reproduction units, then certainly a large proportion of them come up against, to a greater or lesser extent, the problem of a reduction in the income used to purchase subsistence goods and services. This is often accompanied by a drop in the quality and quantity of public reproductive services owing to the fiscal crisis of the welfare state. The tendency for self-provisioning work to increase, rather than generally lowering the cost of reproducing the labour force, widens the gap between the cost of 'guaranteed' labour, which rises with inflation but is offset by the decreasing number of workers, and the cost of the remaining part of the labour force, both employed and employable. Even if one takes for granted a reduction in the standard of living for a large number of households, which in any case is reflected in the reproduction patterns by the increase in work for self-provisioning compared to monetary incomes, the diverse units in varying socio-economic contexts must seek to re-balance reproduction by means of various combinations of three possible solutions: an absolute increase in self-provisioning work, including reciprocal exchanges with neighbours, friends and relations; the diffusion of various forms of informal or occasional activities; and external contributions which make household survival feasible.

The impact of the diffusion of informal activities on social reproduction

The spread of informal activities has a number of common characteristics with regard to the process of reproduction. In as much as they are phenomena connected with the labour supply or the availability of independent labour, informal activities are one of the consequences of the employment crisis, in the context of which unemployment and non-employment increase without a parallel decrease in the cost of reproduction of guaranteed labour. Availability for informal work thus increases and, at the same time, the cost of reproducing this type of labour decreases, for the very reason that the increase in self-provisioning and domestic work resulting from the crisis involves above all informal work. In this sense, both in general and on average, informal working activities reveal a lower ratio between gross income and working times than that found under formal working conditions. There are exceptions, like some second jobs that require professional qualifications. The lower time/income ratio, that is, the lower cost of labour, in the various forms of decentralization and subcontracting, suits the need for economic concerns to limit or reduce the average cost of labour, even though they are unable to do so in the concentrated units of production in which they mainly operate.

The second characteristic common to nearly all informal activities is the complex role that they assume with regard to the functioning of the state and public organizations. The evasion of certain obligations of a fiscal, social or contributory nature, and even the ignoring of laws against, for instance, the employment of minors, the carrying out of dangerous work without taking due safety measures and the use of illegal immigrant labour, is typical of informal activities and continues to make them profitable for the entrepreneur and advantageous for the consumer. Apart from leading to a drop in revenue, thus cutting the spending capacity of public bodies, the spread of informal activities considerably reduces the possibility of reproduction processes being subjected to public control and state intervention as they become progressively more varied. If informal workers avoid paying taxes and other legally required contributions, the state finds itself compelled to neglect certain interventions that are necessary as a result of the social reorganization founded on the spread of informal activities. On the other hand, some governments may be content that the diffusion of informal activities partly reduces the need for government intervention, for example through self-building in place of public housing, babysitting for cash instead of public institutions for child care. Informalization involves, therefore, the development of accentuated and diversified tendencies towards social fragmentation, which derive from the schizophrenic nature of the relationship between the increasingly complex structure of social reproduction, the process of public intervention and capitalist accumulation.

Informalization introduces two types of contradiction that could have radical consequences with regard to the prospects for social conflict. The fact that many households are simultaneously reproducing formal and informal labour creates competing pressures with which the households are unable to cope. A contradiction of this kind is more common in highly industrialized cities, where there is an increase in multiple job-holding and informal work by members in the families of guaranteed workers in order to obtain complementary incomes. These serve to counterbalance the erosion of income due to inflation, unemployment and the deterioration of services and public assistance. Working commitments within the household unit not only tend to increase, thus taking up nearly all available leisure time, but also to be distributed in a discriminatory and inequitable manner.

The unequal distributional effect of different kinds of high work loads occurs in a radical form in cases where the husband-father in formal employment has an informal second job and the wife-mother is confined to domestic work, including extraordinary domestic work and non-domestic subsistence work such as the cultivation of a vegetable garden (figure 3.2, E1). In fact, the need to engage in domestic and self-provisioning work eventually extends in proportion to the difficulty of organizing reproduction in a complex situation. The most recurrent profile of multiple moonlighters, that is workers with irregular/non-registered second, third or more jobs, tends to confirm this picture.[15] Most of the time, such a person is an experienced male worker aged thirty to fifty and married to a full-time housewife; further, with the exception of a number of cases arising out of professional interests or involving a transitional period between jobs, the motive behind multiple employment is that it happens to be the 'easiest' way to raise more cash at times of high family reproduction requirements, nowadays mostly coinciding with periods in the life-cycle when there are non-employed teenagers in the household. Thus, it is important to underline that increasing youth unemployment and increasing rates of moonlighting are two sides of the same coin in societies which are unable to create enough viable opportunities for the new generation of young people but provide a large number of irregular jobs for their fathers on top of their full-time occupations. Extensions in working hours and the unequal distribution of work loads (figure 3.2, E2) also occur when one member of the household has a formal job and another an informal one. The sex, age and ethnic division between informal and formal activities varies, depending on the relative strength and protection that specific groups enjoy in the labour market and formal employment structure. Members in a strong position will be better suited for formal employment and second jobs while those in a weak position will have to rely on sporadic, informal low-paid jobs.

The second contradiction concerns the difficulty of combining the increase in self-provisioning work necessary for reproduction with the low working hours to income ratio usual in the case of informal working activities (figure 3.2, E3). This contradiction is more common where there are systematic concentrations of informal work. Interesting examples are the areas of industrialization mainly based on medium-sized and small concerns using informal labour, such as indirectly remunerated work by members of the household helping out in a family business; non-payment of the legal minimum wage and social security contributions; outwork; and subcontracting. In these cases the whole process of reproduction depends, as far as monetary income is concerned, on informal or mixed employment. The combination of informal employment or, at any rate, of employment with a low working-hours-to-income ratio and the need to dedicate relatively long hours to self-provisioning activities implies the existence of particular organizational forms of the reproduction unit and the presence of stable and strong reciprocal networks at the level of the community, relations or friends. Only a compact kinship and community structure based on solidarity or rigorously organized associations with interests in production and reproduction could maximize the utilization of labour on both fronts. Only where these preconditions already exist is it possible for this type of highly informalized economy to spread.

Although it is impossible to explain simply the influence of informal work on patterns of reproduction, it is possible to point initially to three combinations of particular interest: (1) informal work is carried out as a second job by the sole breadwinner while the housewife spends considerably more time on domestic work in order to permit the sole breadwinner to engage in two activities (figure 3.2, E1); (2) a formal and an informal job are carried out by different persons, with an increase in work for self-provisioning needed to meet the more difficult reproduction requirements (figure 3.2, E2); (3) a prevalence of informal activities and the necessity for long hours of self-provisioning work require, in addition to great sacrifices and a well-organized reproduction unit, forms of solidarity at the family, friendship or community level (figure 3.2, E3).

In all three cases the amount of time spent in working activities is very high, involves discrimination between the sexes and the various age groups, and gives rise to contradictions that are one of the final results, in the reproductive context, of the employment crisis.

The historical background to the transformation of informalized reproduction patterns typical of productive households

Before moving on to an analysis which looks at specific types, it is worth turning to the question of productive households and some forms of self-employment, in so far as such contexts are more suitable for changes in terms of informal work. In this respect, it is necessary to outline the historical process by which these areas of production/reproduction were transformed, since this has not been fully dealt with in the previous section.

Putting it abstractly, the historical transformation of the ways in which productive households are organized, above all those of the peasants who formed the overwhelming majority of the population until very recently, at least in continental Europe, may be considered as the consequence of a growing need for monetary resources. This led to households becoming progressively less self-sufficient and more exposed to the market. In model A in figure 3.2 this trend is shown by an arrow indicating the tendential widening of the monetary sphere.

In the European historical experience this process began at a point where levels of self-sufficiency were high. This was the result of a historical accident: the almost complete halt to intercommunal trade between the eighth and tenth centuries, a period which also coincided with the creation of medieval socio-political institutions. Hence the particular character of European feudalism compared to that of the Asiatic or pre-Columbian social systems. From almost immediately after the renewal of trade, and even more in the sixteenth and seventeenth centuries, and under the pressure of inflation brought about by the establishment of colonial empires, the development of urban economies in conjunction with a reduction in self-sufficiency led to the considerable reorganization of productive households. It was mainly the growing opportunity/necessity to complement strategies of social reproduction with wage income that permanently modified the conditions of existence and organization of such households, beginning with increasingly less rigid controls and limitations on householding; for example, younger sons were now also permitted to set up a family. The complementary nature of wage income allowed peasant families to adapt to increasingly difficult conditions. The latter were due to the decline in sources of monetary income on their farms, brought about by competition and falling agricultural prices, at a time when changes in family structure and in production were producing an ever greater need for monetary income. A result of this was the rising indebtedness of the European peasantry in the last century, above all in countries undergoing rapid industrial growth like France and Germany. This adaptation based on combining a subsistence economy with partial wage supplements took the form of persistent and widespread chronic rural poverty in some parts of Europe, in particular in agricultural regions in the South (see in this connection the case of the Mezzogiorno discussed in chapter 6).

It is important to underline how and why these forms of adaptation are now increasingly creating areas of intense informalization. The phenomenon is not due so much to changes in the organization of this type of household, but rather reflect the impossibility of them adapting to ever more restrictive institutional regulations. The organizational basis on which productive households and some types of self-employment operate can only remain feasible through increasing resistance to state regulation and taxation, brought about by the development of large concerns and the welfare state. And this leads to the spread of informalization. These forms of organizing working activities are able to survive by adopting the following strategy: evasion, at least in part, of taxes; continual recourse to temporary 'black work' in building, hawking and tourism; exchange of non-registered work days in agricultural labouring; the use of all the labour available among family members and acquaintances during harvest time; and many other combinations. Such strategies become more and more complicated and problematical as the need for monetary resources grows; at the same time, they become increasingly informal as the extension of restrictive regulations makes many of these options illegal.

I shall return to the ways in which this complex process unfolds at the beginning of chapter 5. At this point it is worth making two further observations. The subsistence combinations by which productive households adapt to changing circumstances may take on very diverse meanings relative to the processes of industrial development. In chapters 5 and 6, I analyse the case of the so-called Third Italy (the North-East and Centre) where, in particular social and economic conditions, the combination turned into a resource that served as a basis for a particular process of development. At the opposite end of the scale, a strategy based on informal practices and black-market labour continued to be, in most cases, one of poverty, involving the greater difficulty to survive (for the question of resistance to informal work by the poor in Naples, see Pinnarò and Pugliese, 1985). An exception may be that of radical and localized improvement of informal mixes, as in the case of Greek peasant families in zones affected by a massive growth in tourism. This variation too can only be explained by the presence of a large number of productive households that adapt to specific socio-economic developments within not very effective regulatory contexts (EEC, 1989b).

Finally, it must be pointed out that poverty-based strategies do not generally overlap with informal strategies. Such overlapping is only probable where traditional economies still predominate. In urban-industrial contexts from which these economies have long since been eliminated, Pahl (1984) is right to insist that there exist different forms of informalization in which households with unemployed members or other such difficulties have a very limited access even to informal work or consumption strategies. This will be considered in greater detail in the next section.

5 THE IMPACT OF INFORMALIZATION ON FAMILY SURVIVAL STRATEGIES: LOCAL DIFFERENCES AND TYPOLOGICAL VARIANTS

Informalization and changes in the social structure of households

In order better to understand current changes in social reproduction patterns as they are affected by diverse informalization tendencies, I shall briefly summarize the discussion on the socio-demographic and economic-employment background to householding processes and the variety of survival strategies. A first group of factors relates to the quantitative and qualitative changes in the demographic structure of households and, consequently, to differing access to resources and variations in internal divisions of labour. A second group is connected with access to the formal labour market on the basis of sex, age and ethnicity. Finally, the geographical mobility of households in combination with different local mixes of social factors also influences access to certain survival resources. As I shall show in this section, among the most important contemporary social conditions influencing survival strategies is the degree of social stability achieved; it reaches its highest levels where a local community has been relatively little changed by emigration or immigration, but it can also remain at a high level when a homogeneous group migrates and settles together in a new social setting.

Some important changes in the social structure of households and families are taking place in industrialized countries, although at different intensities and at varying rates. The changes indicated below are largely confirmed by recent data.[16] Moreover, these trends are more radical in more advanced countries and regions and in large cities, where do-it-yourself technology and informal activities are probably spreading more rapidly. They are:

1 An increase in households made up of one person or a couple. This trend is occurring at different rates and times in practically every industrialized country as a consequence of various factors, whether demographic (mainly the higher percentage of old people and elderly females surviving their husbands, and the decline in the birth-rate), social (possible rise in the divorce rate and fall in the marriage rate) or economic (increased opportunities for working women; increase in the minimum pension and other welfare provisions). This trend may be partly counterbalanced by 3, below.

2 A decrease in large households due to the decline in intergenerational households and the falling birth-rate. Both these factors, but particularly

the first, are highly dependent on the extent to which productive households and small family businesses have persisted, the manner in which they have been transformed (for instance, into specialized family agricultural enterprises or into state-assisted peasant farms), and lastly, the type of change they are undergoing at present.

3 A rise in the number of households and families headed by a female with, or even more often, without the presence of an adult male for the reasons given in 1, above.

4 The growing inclusion of women in the employment structure, especially married women. This process shows a varied geographical pattern, because it depends on local labour markets and on local culture and traditions.

5 A drop in the employment rate for younger age groups due to high unemployment and to a longer period of education. This trend will have a negligible effect on the household structure, apart from the amount of resources needed, in countries where many students live away from their families, and a major effect where they remain at home.

6 The increasing geographical mobility of households, which creates a number of disadvantages in the areas of both emigration and immigration since it reduces to varying extents some reciprocal resources for survival (mainly communal, kinship and friendship networks) available to unstable groups.

On the basis of these six trends, it can be argued that the process of householding is becoming more differentiated, with the result that it is difficult to grasp clearly the interplay of various advantages and disadvantages. I shall explain this by means of some simple illustrations. While it may be the case that single-person or couple households need fewer total resources to survive, it is also true that they need greater per capita resources and that they are often penalized as regards access to certain resources. If they suffer additional handicaps due to gender, age, physical disability, lack of support from relatives or a community (because, for example, they have recently moved), they may face serious survival difficulties. Since in small households advantages or disadvantages are unlikely to be counterbalanced, these households tend to polarize into the very poor and the very rich, depending mainly on the income level of the wage-earner.

Moreover, I should underline that some relevant changes in the householding structure ought to be considered in combination with the impact of the transformation trends in terms of life-cycles. Both the average age of marriage and the percentage of the population that never marries are increasing, contrary to what happened in the early phase of industrial society. The implication is that between the ages of twenty and forty, and perhaps even beyond, the possibility that people will either live on their own or with their original family instead of within a nuclear family context is on the increase. In conjunction with the declining birth-rate, to which it is also a contributory factor, this tends to reduce progressively the number of close kin relations to whom a person can turn for immediate support and assistance. This factor is rapidly gaining in importance and should be read, together with the increasing life-span, in the following way. As at present the average duration of life is seventy-five years and the retirement age is sixty-five, it can be argued that for about ten years many people may need increasing help from their kin, while a relatively small percentage, say 20 per cent, have no descendants on whom to rely. Both the length of this period and the percentage of those with no descendants are probably rising: a plausible hypothesis would be in the order of fifteen years and 30 per cent for the generation which is now forty years old, and possibly twenty years and 40 per cent for the generation which is now aged twenty. This rapid increase is bound to represent the most radical change in the householding process, together with the impact of persistent long-term youth unemployment, although the latter, instead of being aggravated by demographic trends, will become less dramatic given that a decreasing birth-rate means fewer young people entering the labour market.

The household structure has been modified by the various events described above, by the secular commodification process, involving the dismantling of its internal productive capacities, and by the more recent crisis in the welfare state, leading to the declining quality/quantity of the services. In this modified form, the household structure is particularly affected by the impact of informalization in two directions: the development of self-service/do-it-yourself activities, and the reproductive needs created by the diffusion of different forms of informal and innovative communal activities. Both developments act upon the household structure in two ways: they modify survival strategies, perspectives and potentials, and they affect the internal division of labour (where it exists) between the sexes and age groups.

The first general impression is that in moving in completely the opposite direction to the tendencies mentioned above, the informalization process creates tremendous incongruities and difficulties within the household structure. This impression is often confirmed by more specific considerations and special surveys, as I shall now try to show.

Informalization and survival strategies

Let us first consider the consequences of informalization as it concerns the survival strategies of households. The spread of strictly informal and innovative community activities can be considered under two different headings: the possibility of engaging in informal consumption, and its consequences. Activities of the broadly informal kind generally affect household relations of reproduction for two reasons: problems caused by the ratio of working time to income, and intra-household organizational problems caused by the possible discontinuity or other special character-istics of such activities.

If it is assumed that, in general, the income to working time ratio in the informal sector is lower than average and totally unaffected by legal controls, so that working times may reach very high maximum limits, then it follows that in order to survive either partially or totally at the same historical average level as formal workers' households, survival strategies have to be based either on long hours in informal activities, additional contributions from self-provisioning, complementary extra-household income, either in kind or from work, or – as is often the case – on a mix of these three conditions. For this reason, active involvement in the informal sector is easier for relatively large households and for those which are socially and geographically stable. Stability is also necess-ary given that informal activities are frequently connected with a close-knit network (neighbourhood, networks of friends and relatives) which fails to become established where there is a high turnover and mobility of labour (Foudi et al., 1982).

In such a situation, the survival strategy of the household becomes heterogeneous and complicated and is either based on very long hours of proper informal work or very long hours of self-provisioning and domestic activities; whichever is the case, it is also complemented either by cash transfers from the state or from relatives abroad or by a firmly established and prosperous local network of solidarity.[17] Often the prob-lem becomes more intricate because of the irregular nature of informal activities. Seasonal or other periodical downturns or upturns complicate the organizational patterns of households involved in the informal sector. This possibility creates greater difficulties for households with only one wage-earner engaged in irregular informal work.

Innovative community initiatives create similar problems. They work in favour of stable, medium-sized and standard households to the disad-vantage of outsiders, latecomers and small, unstable or unorthodox house-holds. A very simple example is where a neighbourhood group of parents organizes a communal system of childminding. Single householders and others without children will be excluded and may eventually suffer from not being involved in the network which results from the initiative. Newcomers may find it difficult to gain admittance as the activities have been organized without their contribution. Departing families will suffer if, as is likely, they have to reorganize themselves completely in their new place of residence. Large households without problems, for instance aged or handicapped members, will find it difficult to be involved to the same extent as the other participants and may eventually find themselves isolated.

The same kind of problems are easy to find with regard to informal consumption. Newly arrived, unstable and small households will not have the necessary information and easy access to informed networks (Ferman et al., 1978). If and where informal consumption signifies a considerable saving, ease or difficulty of access can constitute an important source of discrimination. There is some evidence that on the consumption front middle- and high-income groups benefit more than low-income groups; the latter are more unstable and have less time and resources to enable them to become involved in an informal network (Pahl, 1984).

The expansion of self-provisioning, do-it-yourself and other work for self-consumption has even more paradoxical effects on the household structure. This kind of informalization is generally based on the capacity of a household to invest an increasing portion of its income in the purchase of durables which increase marginal productivity and, consequently, decrease the cost and/or increase the quality of some services and goods, which are then produced for the direct consumption of the household. This activity is both time-consuming and costly, although it can lead to savings in the long run. It is evident that this transformation is to the advantage of relatively large and to the disadvantage of smaller households. The latter will be involved much more for symbolic/status reasons than for economic convenience and only when they have sufficient income. The idea that the 'innovation' of self-service based on relatively advanced technological home equipment also helps the poor or long-term unemployed manual workers to survive is mistaken (evidence is contained in various surveys: Foudi et al., 1982; Pahl, 1984; Pahl and Wallace, 1985).

The overall picture is that survival strategies become more varied and complex as a result of changes brought about by informalization, which also discriminate against some social groups and some forms of household. Furthermore, these changes transfer to the households responsibilities which they are not prepared to bear. But the picture becomes even more problematical if we take into account the household's internal division of labour.

Informalization and changes in the internal household division of labour

From this point of view, it is important to understand how informal, neo-communal and self-consumption activities are divided in terms of gender and age, compared with formal employment divisions, in the context of household organization. The general assumption that strictly informal jobs are done mainly by women, the young and the aged is unfounded. On the contrary, there are kinds of informal work which are done almost exclusively by adult males, as in the case of moonlighting, the holding of a second job in addition to a regular one. There are other kinds of informal activities which are carried out almost exclusively by females, such as outwork, others again which are more commonly carried out by the young or the aged, and some which involve every household member including children and old people. On the basis of these differences it is possible to establish only a simplified set of types, as follows:

- Type A Formally employed male 'moonlighters' plus varying numbers of non-employed. Moonlighter households are less likely to include other employed members unless the household is relatively large, for the very reason that the majority of the cases of moonlighting are motivated by the need for additional cash in an employment structure where it is easier for the already full-time employed members than for other members to find a second job.
- Type B Formally employed males plus informally employed females and sometimes children.
- Type C Formally employed males plus informally employed young or old persons and sometimes other members. The presence (C1) or absence of a full-time housewife may constitute an important distinction.
- Type D Informally employed males or females (D1) and other non-employed members where, especially in the case of informally employed males, it may be important to distinguish between the presence (D2) or absence of a full-time housewife.
- Type E Two or more informally employed members involved in the same informal enterprises. The presence of a full-time housewife completely uninvolved in the informal family enterprise is unlikely, except in the cases of sectors where the employment of women is culturally and historically excluded, as it is in building in Mediterranean countries.

– Type F   Two or more informally employed members involved in different non-family informal enterprises; here again the presence (F1) or absence of a full-time housewife makes a difference.

The common types, although with variations according to area, are A, B, C1, D1, D2, E (particularly common in areas of industrialization persistently characterized by small concerns, at least during a variable take-off period) and F. The sexual division of labour ranges from the extremely radical division of A, where the male is subject to long hours of formal and second employment while the housewife is absorbed by long hours of domestic/supportive work, to the relatively pre-modern, possibly not very discriminatory but extremely time-consuming, organization of an informal family business in E.

Two points need to be made to complete the picture:

1 The lower working time to income ratio of informal activities is probably in addition to the discriminatory time to income ratio of women, the young and the aged, so that D1 and D households, where the informal worker is young, or a recent migrant, or a member of a repressed minority, or elderly and without a regular pension, are likely to fall below the poverty line.

2 Domestic work is largely carried out by women, even when they are employed on a part- or full-time basis or have an informal job. As time consumed in household domestic activities does not substantially decrease in line with technical innovation and household capital investment, partly because of the increased qualitative requirements of the household (see also Gershuny, 1983), the time pressure on women tends in some cases to become very great (in my typology B, D and F). It is clear that renegotiating gender divisions in domestic work is a slow, complicated process that is almost never based on simple rational criteria. For instance, there is evidence that unemployed adult males are among the least likely to increase their share of domestic activities, even when their wives are in full-time employment (see Pahl, 1984).

With the possible exception of case E, to which I refer again specifically in chapters 5 and 6 when dealing with social transformations in areas characterized by the persistent presence of family businesses, informalization appears to accentuate the discriminatory patterns of the intra-household division of labour.

Type A households have not been studied from the point of view of the internal division of labour, but it is possible to put forward some hypotheses. The moonlighter is usually male, middle-aged (thirty to fifty) and the sole 'breadwinner' in an above-average-size nuclear family – at least this is the picture obtained from regular surveys in the USA and from empirical research in Italy. He will therefore be totally unable to help with the heavy burden of domestic activities, which are borne by his wife alone. As I have already mentioned, this type reflects one of the present paradoxes of labour market segmentation and of the unequal distribution of employment. It may be easier for a middle-age worker to find an informal second job to complement household income than for his wife or his adult children to find any kind of formal employment. Thus, it is not very unusual today to find a full-time housewife and one or more unemployed young persons in the moon-lighter household.

The situation may be even more difficult and discriminatory in types D and F, as revealed by surveys in Southern Italian cities, extensively discussed in chapter 6. Here the housewife is oppressed by the burden of long hours of domestic work and cannot be helped by the informal worker (or workers) occupied elsewhere, either working or looking for work.

There is also evidence from studies on outworking women[18] that the division of labour and household survival organization are extremely difficult in type B. The working hours of these women are very long (always more than sixty hours per week) and the family organization creates tensions and internal conflicts. Although informal work, in particular outwork, and possibly part-time formal employment for women, are more flexible as regards fitting in with daily domestic requirements, this has not led to a more satisfactory life and has not eliminated gender discrimination.

It is worth making a few observations with regard to case E. The necessary starting-point is the fact that independent family economies differ greatly from one another and the internal organization of work is variously structured according to sex and age group. A strongly hierarchical/paternal structure is typical of relatively backward forms of organization in which women and children are totally subject to the authority of the head of the family, the father-boss. This hierarchical and discriminatory structure puts up partial resistance, at least culturally speaking, to certain social transformations, such as the increase in state assistance and complementary incomes and the growing educational gap between parents and children. In contrast, those cases are more complicated in which forms of industrial growth arise out of this type of family economy. Such forms involve mixes of activities in different sectors (the most important example is the combination of family farming and summer or winter tourism) or specialized modern instances of family-based agricultural production. The possibly high professional level of children, who may be graduates in agriculture, accountants or computer experts, and the particularly important and demanding role played by women help substantially to weaken the hierarchical and authoritarian elements in this type of organized family economy. Looking at the picture as a whole, however, two phenomena need to be indicated which are still connected with these households, at least as long as the rate of irregular organizational forms remains high: first, working hours are very long and fatiguing and directly affect living conditions, since the work is undertaken in the home or nearby; and second, where the traditional hierarchy of family structures coincides with the organization of work, the consequences for women and young persons are more or less negative in the long run.

Lastly, I propose to look at some changes in the internal division of labour presumably produced by the extension of innovative community initiatives and self-provisioning of the do-it-yourself type. Most of the burden of innovative community activities tends to fall on women, especially when they involve caring for children, the disabled and the aged. This creates a difficult situation for households in which women are already saddled with an onerous time-budget because they are the main or the only 'breadwinner', or have the dual responsibility of domestic work and formal or informal employment, or are taken up with exceptionally long hours of domestic work.

The rapid increase in these kinds of households makes the expansion of innovative community initiatives a problematical question. In fact, either these households have to give up access to them or, more likely, the women accept an additional burden which stretches them to the breaking point. The situation may become acute where these initiatives develop as a substitute for previously existing welfare state provisions, as recently suggested by Gershuny (1983). For example, a public nursery is replaced by a communal service where parents take turns to look after children for two half-days per week. In most cases the mothers will have to work eight or more additional hours per week. For the majority of them it will create difficulties, while for others, who are in full-time formal or informal employment, it may be impossible. The latter will have to hire a childminder, if possible, or find a different solution to the babysitting problem. Some mothers may be able to rely on relatives, such as grandmothers, but nevertheless the change discriminates against recent migrants and mobile groups, who are in any case most probably the weakest or worst off.

Self-provisioning and do-it-yourself activities are more difficult to consider under this aspect because they transcend gender and age divisions. If anything, there is a tendency to assume that they are carried out mostly by middle-aged males. This is probably true for some activities, like making household durables or furniture, car repairs, building and carpentry, etc., but not in every case, and not for other services, such as making and repairing clothes, gardening, food preserving etc. In this case, too, there is discrimination against households in which members are overemployed in other activities: moonlighting or working long hours, poor full-time housewives, full-time employed women, etc. This is a further example of a paradox in contemporary societies: those who have the greatest need of access to do-it-yourself and self-provisioning facilities lack the money or time.

Informalization and specific local features

Informalization produces many difficulties in the household structure and does not solve the problem of inadequate levels of income because it is combined with a persistently discriminatory division of labour in both society and in the household. As such, it is likely to increase the probability of family crises and to render the management of the household more complicated. Only if it is combined with radical and progressive changes in the division of labour in society and within the household can it become an acceptable way of solving survival difficulties. In society, this involves a decrease in formal working hours of adult men and an increase of acceptable employment opportunities for the young and for women, while in the household an increase in the contribution of adult men and an improvement in some important welfare state provisions to diminish the domestic burden.

In a sense, nearly everything I have said up to now points to the fact that the informalization process has served to increase the importance of some local characteristics as against universal patterns. Paradoxically, this is happening at the very time when technological progress, one of the most important factors in the informalization process, is becoming less and less hindered by local restrictions. In theory, education, shelter, a computer, a telephone line and an electricity supply are everywhere the requisites for a survival that is perfectly integrated into 'world society'. But what is true in theory, and also in practice for a small group of households, is not true in the reality of everyday life for billions of people. The 'delocalization' potential of advanced technologies combined with broad informalization can work in one direction only: the diminishing role in direct production by the metropolitan cores in advanced capitalist countries. And this specific use of advanced technology for 'delocalization' continues a pattern that was initiated not so much by technological change itself but mainly by the growing disadvantages and high costs of congestion and concentration. In general, informalization becomes more or less widespread and develops different characteristics in different localities.

Perhaps the most important condition is the relative stability of local communities. In fact, innovative community initiatives, strictly informal networks and even some forms of self-provisioning and do-it-yourself find a more congenial ground for expansion in stable and compact communities or even in new communities composed of migrants from one region or belonging to a specific ethnic group. This condition has been only recently rediscovered as one of the factors favouring the recent wave of industrialization in North-Eastern and Central Italy as well as in other areas in the First and Third Worlds (Piore and Sabel, 1982). It may be found in small and medium-sized cities and in regions which have not been too deeply affected by the radical transformations produced in the period of rapid industrial growth; but also in some parts of industrial cities and metropolitan areas where recent or earlier settlers are relatively homogeneous socially and ethnically and in terms of regional origin. The advantages of stability in this respect, involving the possibility of recourse to large and compact kinship networks, the persistence and continuity of neighbourhoods and community solidarity and co-operation, can be defined only by means of careful local sociological studies, which would probably show that they are irregularly distributed. For historical reasons, a town may suffer waves of emigration while another which is not far away may remain stable, or a neighbourhood in a large city may remain untouched by redevelopment and so remain relatively homogeneous while another becomes a strange mix of old and new settlers. In this regard, therefore, local realities may react very differently to informalization process.

Other kinds of informalization may become more or less widespread for different historical reasons, which again can be identified only by studying local characteristics. For example, a single-industry textile and clothing area may have been characterized from its early industrialization to the present period by the persistence of outwork and then revitalized, also with the aid of new technologies, by the impact of informalization and so-called flexible production. Old single-industry areas abandoned by manufacturing concerns may be transformed into service/tourism areas with a very high degree of informal and do-it-yourself activities (Pahl, 1984).

The variety of informal developments is such that many other examples could be given. But two important points have been sufficiently demonstrated: first, that informalization patterns are unequally distributed, and, second, that the degree and character of informal developments are only clearly visible on a local scale. This means that it is extremely difficult to construct a social geography of the expansion of various kinds of informal activities in which account is taken of the size of cities, the specific nature of regional economies and the varying features of different urban areas. It is, however, a task which will have to be undertaken if we are to understand the advantages and disadvantages of these developments for various social groups and, more generally, to assess the socio-economic prospects for survival in what I call 'fragmented societies'.

6 PROBLEMS ARISING FROM THE ANALYSIS OF CHANGING REPRODUCTION PATTERNS IN SOCIALIST AND UNDERDEVELOPED COUNTRIES

The methodological significance of changing reproduction patterns in capitalist and socialist societies

In this last section, I examine the implications for socialist and under-developed countries of changes in the conditions of social reproduction. My analysis is essentially of a methodological kind with few references to actual processes of informalization; these are dealt with further in the chapters that follow. Before proceeding, it is worth reviewing the methodological significance of changes in the patterns of social repro-duction found in capitalist societies.

The fundamental question is the way in which the monetary wage forms a link between patterns of reproduction and the cycle of capital; it does this by expressing at the same time the labour cost and the levels of commodification contained in survival strategies. Monetary income, however, cannot account for survival on its own. Analysis of social reproduction brings out the importance of diverse social conditions and of various other contributions that complement an always inadequate monetary income. The reproductive mix varies historically and in differ-ent social contexts; but even in those cases where it is correct to speak of a 'family wage' earned by a single adult male, other complementary resources are no less important. From this perspective, it is immediately clear that industrialization has been accompanied both by marked changes and developments in associative sociality and by different ways of adapting forms of organization based on reciprocity. Communal ties do still exist, although they have been weakened and largely transformed; but at the same time there has been a change in the several levels of kinship and other contexts of reciprocity (from friendship to workplace communities) and the resources they may provide. It is a fact that the cost of labour and the degree of commodification are significant relative to the cycle of capital; this does not mean, however, that the important

modifications occurring within the patterns of social reproduction, particularly depending on patterns of social organization of the reciprocity
kind, can be ignored. Therefore, I have had to structure my analysis on
two interconnected but distinct levels: first, that of the most important
changes in survival conditions where the extent of monetary income is
one among many factors, and, that of the link with the cycle of capital
where despite its primary importance, the monetary element must be
considered as always insufficient, and consequently analysed in the context of variable and complex mixes of resources. The development of
domestic labour and of welfare programmes or the preservation/adap-
tation of household economies characterized by reciprocity, subsistence
or self-provisioning can only be explained, also in relation to the cycle
of capital, by taking the analysis of reproduction as a starting-point.

The above remarks can help in deciding how to approach the problem
of social reproduction in socialist countries. The first question to ask is
in what sense is it possible to talk of social reproduction in contexts
where, by definition, no labour market or cycle of capital accumulation
aiming at increasing levels of commodification should actually exist. (At
this point I cannot enter into a discussion of the possibility that through
their necessary participation in the world market, the socialist economies
are subject to restraints imposed by capital accumulation and the labour
market; such a discussion would be too long and complicated.)

Recently, when dealing with the question of defining socialism in
connection with a different problem, I formulated an answer in these
terms:

> I would suggest two criteria: first, a relatively high degree of central
> political control of the exposure of the local economy to world-
> market relations; second, a centralized system of redistribution of
> resources – to both production and consumption ends – along lines
> which are not only different (for this is characteristic of any modern
> mixed-welfare economy) but largely divergent from the market
> distribution system. (Mingione, 1987, p. 36).

From this perspective, the precondition for tackling the question of social
reproduction in socialist societies lies in identifying the priorities typical
of centralized systems of redistribution, both as regards productive investment and interventions in reproduction, and the logic behind these
priorities; it also lies in identifying the consequences of this process for
the structuring of society. Implicit in this formulation of the problem is
the assumption that just as in other industrial societies, socialist countries
also experience a separation of productive from reproductive practices.

This assumption is obviously the necessary starting-point for an analysis of the patterns of social reproduction in these contexts. The problem becomes, therefore, one of establishing how the separation comes about; or, in other words, of examining the decline of the unified process of production and reproduction in a system in which the propulsive force is not formed by the cycle of capital with its concomitant requirements of producing wage labour and commodifying social reproduction. This problem, too, requires an answer in terms of socialist strategies for industrial growth.

As we saw in chapter 1, socialist industrial experience is characterized by political strategies that promote the industrial transformation of production through the prior setting up of systems of associative sociality on an institutional basis; these systems keep competitive behaviour under control in order to limit the inequalities and disruptive effects arising from the spread of individual competitive behaviour. To achieve this objective, socialist central planning redistributes resources in three fundamental directions: the sufficient allocation to industrialization; the formation of areas of associative sociality to complement social reproduction (a base of essential welfare services); and the effective undermining of reciprocal relations that may obstruct industrialization or act to preserve or magnify social inequalities.

The final question presents the greatest obstacle to understanding the transformations of social reproduction that have taken place in socialist societies. The process of socialist transformation, above all in the Soviet Union and China, also grew out of situations in which the vast majority of the population lived in the countryside and existed within various kinds of peasant economies and communal village sociality. It is not by accident that the Soviet experience has been accompanied by a debate on the nature of peasant productive households and their future prospects. The contributions to this debate by such historical personalities as Chayanov and Bukharin are still relevant today.[19] I will limit myself to a few schematic considerations.

The socialist transformation of the countryside: a lost war against reciprocal networks

To begin with, in order to promote industrialization socialist regimes are forced to raise the productivity of agriculture and channel increasing amounts of resources into industrial development. A form of social organization based mainly on productive households is hardly compatible with such objectives, at least for the following reasons. Peasant economies have too fragmented a structure to allow both rapid and effective transformations of production and the bureaucratic control indispensable for maximizing the channelling of resources. Furthermore, productive accumulation by households always constitutes a form of market that gives rise to growing and uncontrollable inequalities. Hence, for example, the great Stalinist repression of the kulaks, the wealthy peasants. Socialist transformation in the countryside involves various combinations of large state farms, co-operative and collective farms and more or less limited and controlled individual or family initiatives (Szelenyi, 1988). In capitalist societies, change in social reproduction in the countryside is basically characterized by the growing need for complementary forms of monetary income, as well as by urbanization and immigration. In the socialist experience, too, this change leads to a more or less massive exodus from the countryside, but it also takes place under the strict control of the institutional-associative networks. In theory, such controls should be compensated for by the supply of resources from the centre to help both increase production, through investment in agricultural development, and modernize the very patterns of social reproduction, through the development of education and health systems, public transport, etc. These forms are supposed to make good the loss of the reproductive capacity of relations based on reciprocity and favour a progressive equal-ization of the conditions of social reproduction. This goal was impracti-cable within the traditional social settings, since these were characterized by marked imbalances in the production of resources and in the decision-making process controlled by patriarchical villages and kinship reciprocal networks. The realization, always only partial, of this project of trans-formation depended on the possibility of actually allocating sufficient resources and doing so effectively. This should be verified in specific cases not only with regard to the resources gradually made available, but also relative to the requirements expressed by the other priority objectives within a strategy directed towards industrial growth and the transformation of the patterns of urban reproduction, themes to which I will refer shortly.

What I have said about the transformation of social reproduction in the countryside and the concomitant measures to compensate for the undermining of existing systems of reciprocity gives only an abstract idea of the situation. In reality, this process always comes up against the impossibility of its ever being fully accomplished. This situation allows reciprocal systems to persist and adapt and to react in turn on the process of transformation. What we have here is the fact that socialist regimes do not have sufficient resources to permit them to break up peasant society once and for all and at the same time increase agricultural production, promote industrial transformation and provide adequate infrastructures to support reproductive compensation through redistribution in both the cities and the countryside. The persistent falling short of the socialist plan means that reciprocal systems take on new life as essential elements in survival strategies and, especially in agriculture, also as productive activities.[20]

Urban patterns of social reproduction in socialist countries

The first impression one has of the styles of urban life in socialist countries points to a model based on the close complementary relation between low monetary incomes and an extensive network of public services that are either free, like health, education and welfare assistance, or provided at very low subsidized prices, like transport and council housing. The iron grip that this complementary relation has on a society strongly limits the role of reciprocal systems. However, a closer look reveals that these reciprocal systems still possess plenty of room for manoeuvre, above all because the objective of equitable forms of complementarity is far from being reached. This falling short results not only from planning errors but, to an even greater extent, also from structural distortions in the socialist strategy for organizing society. Whereas in the next chapter I shall discuss this question in general terms, it is worth making some comments here on problems specifically connected with the patterns of reproduction.

These problems are caused by the inadequacy of resources, both in terms of the inability to increase production sufficiently and, in particular, of the ways in which scarce resources are distributed. The most manifest problems are connected with the food question, and even more, with that of housing. There are important similarities between these two sectors. Besides being crucial for the production of primary subsistence goods, they are both based on organizational models that differ from the factory system and they both come up against difficulties when it comes to increasing production. Moreover, it is generally the case that in socialist societies both sectors are penalized in the redistribution of investment and become the least able to satisfy social needs.

We have already seen in general terms the reason why agriculture is sacrificed. It could be added that within a long-term perspective it is more and more difficult to deal with a complex pattern of organization articulated in three different spheres: collective production; small-scale production for the market; and widespread production for self-consumption, often found to a marked extent in urban areas as well.

The question of residential housing is also a complicated one. Simplifying, it can be said that building is the only sector involving very costly urban investment from which socialist regimes can afford in the short term to divert huge sums to other investment projects. By doing this, they also produce the 'positive' side-effect of discouraging accelerated urbanization; the end result, however, is to create a chronic deficit and permanently distorted redistribution in the processes of socialist development.[21]

At the level of the social relations of reproduction in an urban context, the deficits in the food and building sectors have the undesired but inevitable effect of promoting reciprocity, ranging from kinship and family solidarity to the exchange of work in self-building, friendship networks and intergenerational cohabitation. What we are dealing with are not only social relations that have been classified as part of the so-called 'second economy'; more importantly, they are widespread heterogeneous relations of daily life whose sole common feature is that they reflect, as more or less transgressive behaviour inconsistent with the ideals of socialism, the inadequacy for social reproduction of the iron link between wages and state-provided public services.

To all this may be added the parallel effect, which works in the same clearly transgressive direction, of those distortions that have become rooted in the industrial process of producing and distributing consumption goods. The networks that permit direct access to such goods before limited quantities reach the shops are extensive and growing, in proportion to the inadequate increase in the production of consumer durables and the extent to which the latter enter the standard of living of the masses. It is these networks that form the backbone of the second economy.

Clearly, the availability of detailed historical studies of the changes in survival strategies in different socialist societies would allow far more relevant comparisons to be made; further, it would probably also be possible to construct a more sophisticated theoretical framework than the rudimentary one adopted here. As stated above, and also to avoid repeating what is stated in the next two chapters regarding the processes of informalization, I will go no further than these general preliminary remarks. Nevertheless, one last observation is worth making in conclusion, relating to the sexual division of labour and the domestic workload in socialist societies. In theory, the sexual division of labour should be less marked in these societies; and this should be reflected as much in high rates of female employment as in access to jobs at all levels for women and in much smaller numbers of full-time housewives. The data confirm, in general, that female employment is high and full-time housewives are not a large category. The question of access to jobs at all levels is more controversial; such access is partially confirmed by the data for several professions, like doctors and engineers. In contrast, access by women to the top positions in the state and party bureaucracy is still very limited.[22] This last fact should give rise to much thought, in that these are the key positions in the social structure. Within the general terms in which I have posed the question, it is in fact possible to give an initial answer that fits in with what I maintained above. To the extent that the complementary relation between public services and wages is insufficient to sustain social reproduction there enter into play both stronger pressures on women to make good the shortfall in resources, for instance through domestic work or queueing in front of shops, and the recourse to various kinds of traditional reciprocal networks, which are discriminatory in nature; consider, for example, the patriarchal peasant family or, in some parts of the Soviet Union, the traditional Islamic family and community.

Transformations in patterns of social reproduction in underdeveloped countries

It is possible to deal with the question of social reproduction in under-developed countries using the same method adopted for the advanced capitalist ones; nevertheless, considerable difficulties of analysis arise. In underdeveloped countries, too, the course of family strategies is related to the cycle of capital, through the cost of labour and the level at which subsistence consumption is commodified. However, in such cases the industrial transformation of patterns of reproduction is an even more heterogeneous process than that followed in advanced capitalist countries where, at least for many decades, the diffusion of associative relations and the consolidation of 'Fordist' trends have constituted a common background. Contemporary societies in the Third World were once characterized by greatly differing traditions based on various reciprocal systems for organizing social life; these systems have been adapted and integrated into the world market in different ways and at various times. Therefore, what I have to say must remain at a fairly abstract level. A general model for the transformation of patterns of reproduction in these countries must take into account two different processes: the violent destruction of traditional subsistence systems to make integration into the capitalist market possible; and the continual reshaping of systems of sociality that allow social reproduction under conditions of chronically low wages and monetary incomes.

I have already commented on the first process when discussing the question of primitive accumulation. It is worth underlining that this process has continued throughout many centuries; even today the integration into the world market of tribes in Borneo or the Amazon region requires the use of force to make their traditional ways of producing and surviving impracticable. Furthermore, the kinds of societies that stood in the way of primitive accumulation were very different one from the other. They comprised not only tribal or village economies, but also extensive consolidated systems that had been partially open to international trade for many centuries, as in the case of the Chinese Empire. The immediate results of the transformation were manifold. They ranged from the extermination of entire populations to their enslavement and the introduction of commercial slavery on a massive scale, from the relocating of populations to the establishment of diverse systems based on land ownership in which a limited and controlled subsistence agriculture complemented poorly paid wage-labour; it has often been noted that the feudal systems which were dying out in the West were imposed on societies in the East and South.

The second process can be considered as similar, in a certain sense, to those adjustments to social reproduction that were typically carried out in advanced capitalist countries in the nineteenth century, at a time when wages were very low. In this case, however, global social change has not lessened competition at the level of the labour supply in relation to increases in labour productivity; on the contrary, it has led to continual increases in competition among those supplying their labour as capitalist penetration (the first process) draws new populations into the world market.

Up to a few decades ago, the most important transformation in the reproductive patterns of Third World countries took place in the countryside. It generally took the form of diverse combinations of subsistence agriculture complemented by very low monetary incomes from various types of wage-work, but mainly seasonal labouring on plantations and large farms. Numerous social and anthropological studies have shown the specific features found in the multiple variations on the basic model of chronic rural poverty;[23] here it is only possible to refer in general to the principal common features of this model. Its origin lies in the fact that the violent uprooting of the pre-capitalist balance of reproduction has produced, among other things, radical changes in systems of land tenure. In many cases extensive plantations have been set up that are different from the feudal latifundia in Europe and, in particular, seek a continual supply of very cheap wage labour, or alternatively, use slave labour. The diverse ways in which peasant families are able to work a small plot of land are rarely adequate for achieving self-sufficiency at a subsistence level. The growing pressure from extensive colonization of agriculture leads to a progressive worsening of conditions for such families: their need for a complementary monetary income continually increases, while at the same time they find themselves competing with growing numbers of potential wage-labourers, which brings about a fall rather than a rise in the rate of earnings. Furthermore, the role played by an extremely important demographic factor must be underlined. This particular system of social reproduction is characterized by high birth-rates. It is important to understand that what appears to be a paradoxical effect of the poverty cycle, or an irresponsible act on the part of the poor which condemns them to remain in or sink deeper into misery, is instead a rational response to the constraints imposed by industrial development.[24] Subsistence economies are from the very start inadequate, and therefore never form the basis of a householding process as happened in Europe immediately preceding industrialization. In order to cope with the progressively diminishing yield from these economies, poor families need to combine a large number of individual wages, which are always very low. This is the only strategy open to them, given the permanently inadequate level of wage earnings. The way they achieve their objective is to produce numerous offspring; and this is even more the case in societies where females are discriminated against in wage employment, with the result that importance is attached almost exclusively to having male children.

In all its variants, this model is so defective as to be highly unstable in the long run, but also difficult to modify because protected by its own internal logic, its integration into the capitalist world economy and, above all, the crucial role it has assumed in the local systems of social stratification and political domination. Besides revolutionary flare-ups, the instability of the model shows up in the fact that it provokes increasing waves of migration, which grow into an exodus. The migrants also head for the industrialized countries and, as described below, contribute to the growing fragmentation of the social fabric; but most important of all, they are one of the elements feeding the irresistible surge of hyper-urbanization in underdeveloped countries. In the wake of this phenomenon, it is now becoming increasingly important to understand the patterns of social reproduction in Third World cities.

The triangle formed by rural poverty, subsistence economies and low complementary wages is a widespread and typical experience during the different social changes that take place in the industrial age. In underdeveloped countries, the combination of subsistence activities is generally more fragile and vulnerable; there are no positive outlets of any kind, only a spiral of worsening conditions that in some situations may result in large-scale famine and chronic malnutrition. A comparison, even at a superficial level, with similar developments in industrialized countries shows that the origin of these deteriorating situations does not lie only, or even principally, in the agricultural systems. The malign spiral of poverty is engendered much more by the fact that wages remain at a persistently low level and, if anything, tend to fall due to the continual expansion of the labour supply. In this sense, the high birth-rate has an unexpected adverse effect, but one that inevitably results from poor families adopting what for them is the only possible strategy. In other words, the more families have to rely on a growing number of monetary incomes that are always low and tend to fall as a means of complementing decreasingly self-sufficient forms of survival, the more they are compelled to produce more children, which in turn further augments the supply of labour and helps to depress individual monetary incomes, and so on. The increasingly short-term rationale underlying family strategies based on a high birth-rate also explains why birth control policies are so unpopular and difficult to implement in many underdeveloped countries.

This 'malign spiral' did not take root to the same extent in European societies during the last century, for reasons already discussed above. In underdeveloped countries, not only does the survival strategy based on families with many working members remain essential in the countryside, it is also of great importance in the cities, even if probably this importance has been declining in the last decade as documented by a persistent decline in the urban birth-rate. This helps to explain the urban patterns of social reproduction and, in particular, the formation of the so-called informal sector.

At first sight, there are serious reasons for maintaining that the combi-nation of survival predominantly based on subsistence and self-pro-visioning cannot be widely transferred to urban contexts. One reason is that such a strategy is based on a degree of self-provisioning for food that is not fully practicable in the city. The main difficulty, however, is that methods similar to large savings on subsistence items, in particular on the cost of housing and transport, cannot be adopted in cities. Yet the modes of social reproduction of the growing urban masses in under-developed countries have introduced into the cities exactly this triangle of survival, even if here persistently low individual monetary incomes potentially subject to a decline in real terms form the most important part of the arrangement.

The first element of subsistence in an urban context is a mix of monetary incomes, which are generally low if taken one by one and may, as a consequence, be numerous within a single household. All the mem-bers of large households contribute to income-pooling, including children as soon as they are able to. Some of this income may be obtained directly or indirectly through formal employment. Adult males may be wage-workers in manufacturing concerns, both indigenous and those run by multinationals. However, these jobs mostly last for short periods, given the high turnover of labour and the absence of guaranteed employment. It is these workers' conditions of social reproduction that explain the persistence of an economic system based on extremely low wages. Adult females often work as full-time housemaids. On the other hand, some income is obtained directly inside the closed circuit of the informal sector, mainly from work involving self-help building, but also from services, transport, trade and other activities. Another source of income originates in illegal activities, as Hart's pioneering work on Ghana (1973) revealed, and many subsequent studies have confirmed.[25] We also find independent or semi-independent activities such as hawking, handicraft and homeworking. All of this serves the sole purpose of surviving in a state of poverty or, at most, improving standards of living and, sometimes, of enabling some more stable and remunerative activities to be undertaken inside the community such as the renting out of shacks or houses in excess of a family's real need, the running of a restaurant or a shop in a brick edifice and so on.

The other two essential elements to complete the picture of urban subsistence are the savings achieved through subsistence survival and the forms of solidarity/reciprocity, especially those based on family and kinship but also including community, charity, and sometimes even tribal ties. The largest saving is represented by the dwelling; in fact these kinds of reproductive systems are often defined according to the type of shelter: shacks or other dwellings, always built illegally on land that does not belong to the inhabitants or for which they have no legal claim. However, it is not always possible to make a direct link between an illegal shelter and the informal sector. Even when governments manage to supply popular housing at reasonable rents, there is still the problem that poor households have inadequate incomes, and the survival strategies of these strata, which form the overwhelming majority of the urban population, continue to be tied to the informal sector. Wherever possible, food is also included among saving subsistence. The keeping of chickens is common, but it is not unusual to find larger animals as well in the overcrowded slums. Savings on the cost of food and housing are always limited compared to what is possible in subsistence economies in rural areas; this disadvantage generally finds a compensatory factor in the greater opportunities for obtaining monetary income, not through substantially higher wages but rather through a greater number of incomes of a less occasional and seasonal kind.

I have already discussed and will devote further attention to social relations of reciprocity and solidarity in the following chapters. Here it is worth commenting on the models of work organization and its internal division. The close observer is particularly struck by the variety of forms; from among these, however, there emerge two models which though practically the reverse of one another are still able to coexist in some contexts. One model is highly patriarchal with some variations involving patronage. In this system, the position of the young and especially of women is one of total subjugation. Power is held by the elder heads of the most important families on an authoritarian and hierarchical basis. The other model comes close to being matriarchal and takes root particularly in contexts where men are constantly on the move and tend not to assume family responsibilities; these contexts often coincide with labour markets that are especially competitive and unfavourable to adult males. In this system, the mother not only supervises social reproduction but also co-ordinates a highly complex family organization: she takes charge of distributing resources; she controls the destiny of her children, deciding who goes to school and where, who goes to work and what kind of work; she manages and participates directly in self-help building activities; and she may plan investments and formulate the family's strategies and political position.

Before concluding this chapter, I will briefly summarize its main theoretical findings within a global comparative approach. Everywhere, the industrial age has brought about a variable and changing degree of separation of productive human behaviour from an originally unified productive-reproductive collective organization based on reciprocity and, in general, on strong patriarchical principles. In other words, the diffused and increasing potential for procuring individual income, mostly in the form of wages, outside the economic system of the household has enormously changed the organization of industrial societies compared to pre-industrial ones. However, reproductive strategies have remained basically subject to patterns of reciprocity, which in turn have changed in order to accommodate the growing pressures of individualistic behaviour. The emergence of individualistically based interest groups originated by the industrial division of labour and the growing importance of associative organizations has radically changed the reproductive strategies, but nowhere has it been able to cancel diversified forms of reciprocal solidarity. This has also been the case in socialist societies, which in principle are more resolutely engaged in eradicating reciprocal relations from the organization of society. The analysis of change in reproductive strategies in different societies during the industrial age has shown that it has been a dramatic process in which the tensions between associative and reciprocal factors of social organization have persisted. In this analysis, the entire area of reciprocity, its adaptation, its non-cohesiveness with diverse principles of organization, its particular ways of absorbing market tensions has not been neglected. Nevertheless, little knowledge and few analytical tools have been accumulated due to the strong influence of the market paradigm in its various verions. Only a renewed 'tradition' of reproduction studies will be able in the long run to fill in the gaps in our understanding of contemporary societies that have resulted from concentrating solely on diverse forms of association, the division of labour and market competitive behaviour.

NOTES

1   This definition is not intended to refer to the sociobiological approach in anthropological studies (see mainly E. O. Wilson, 1975; 1978; and, among the critical responses to Wilson's *Sociobiology*, Sahlins, 1976, and Rosenberg, 1980), but rather to the possibility that 'reproduction' is used by social scientists to define a set of social relations strictly originating in biological reproduction. See Harris (1981) for a discussion of the different ways in which the concept of reproduction has been used; see also Goody (1976) and Dickinson and Russell (1986).

2   The criticism of the functionalist theorization of the nuclear family is briefly anticipated in chapter 1. The foundations of this theorization were laid in Parsons and Bales (1955). Different approaches, and critical of the functionalist theory, are contained in, among others, Close and Collins (1985); Dickinson and Russell (1986); J. E. Goldthorpe (1987).

    For a comprehensive theoretical discussion and review of the literature on the role of the community in modern social life see Lyon (1987). The question of kinship and other social networks is dealt with by, among others, Farber (1971); Bott (1971); Schneider (1980); Barnard and Good (1984); Gellner (1987); Grieco (1987); Milardo (1988); Wellmann and Berkowitz (1988).

3   The point was first raised and documented by Goode (1963). See also Levine (1977); Goody (1983); Tilly and Scott (1987); Casey (1989).

4   For this point of view see mainly Gershuny (1978; 1983).

5   For the general picture see Hann (1987); for the Italian case see the already mentioned study by Villa (1986) on steel and construction workers.

6   'The unit of analysis employed for the analysis of primary reproduction is usually the household, for statistical purposes, determined as the co-residential unit' (Evers et al., 1984, p. 33).

7   The gender difference in the allocation of personal incomes for family purposes is confirmed and documented by recent studies: see mainly Brannen and Wilson (1987) and Jan Pahl (1989).

8   It is useful to compare what has been stated so far with the concept of household adopted in recent works by the research group on 'Households' of the Fernand Braudel Center at the State University of New York,

Binghamton. Their concept is similar to the one I use here: 'Households make up one of the key institutional structures of the capitalist world-economy . . . the multiple institutional structures of a given historical system (a) are in fundamental ways unique to that system, and (b) are part of an interrelated set of institutions that constitute the operational structures of the system' (Wallerstein, 1984, p. 17). According to this approach, at least in the version put forward by Wallerstein – not completely shared by other members of the group (see for instance Friedman, 1984; J. Smith, 1984) – a multiple set of household arrangements explains the reproduction of wage labour in different locations and periods of the world economy in ways which are highly typical of the capitalist historical setting. Wage-labour and monetary consumption are always only a part of such arrangements, but the meaning of different household strategies is seen mainly with respect to the reproduction of wage-labour. The problem is that this kind of approach imposes an unrealistic determinism on the patterns of social reproduction. They appear to be under the sway of worldwide capital accumulation and the aim of social reproduction strategies is not 'survival' but the reproduction of the labour force in various ways that are compatible with the cycle of capital. This 'real' and not only 'methodological' choice explains Waller-stein's insistence on historical discontinuity. A certain degree of historical discontinuity is undeniable as soon as capitalism becomes the dominant mode of production on a global scale and a large part of the world's population is either forced, or finds it convenient, to accept the logic of wage labour/monetary consumption in order to survive. But the conditions and the goal of social reproduction are not exhausted by this logic. Socio-demographic factors, local historical settings and the presence or absence of certain survival options are inputs to reproduction practices that stand in an interdependent relationship with the cycle of capital.

9   See mainly the extensive collection on peasants and peasant societies edited by Theodor Shanin (2nd edn, 1987).

10 The issue of how much the commodification process and technological innovation modify the nature of and time devoted to domestic activities is still controversial. There has been a long-term reduction in the time spent on housework, which differs according to social class (generally greater among the working class than the middle class), both with regard to full-time housewives and working women (Vanek, 1974; Gershuny, 1983; 1988).

11 This periodization of the transformation in the main patterns of reproduction in advanced capitalist countries is consistent with the one formulated by studies on long-term transformations in systems of labour market segmentation. See mainly Edwards et al. (1982). The 'proletarianization' phase is reflected in the indiscriminate employment of children and women; the 'homogenization' phase in the abolition of child labour, the decrease of female employment and the creation of modern domestic work within working-class households; and the 'segmentation' phase in a marked return to paid employment of married women. If this is true, the present crisis in segmen-

tation patterns coincides with the diffusion of informal activities, which thus assume a fundamental role in the reorganization of the capitalist labour process.

12 See, among others, Goode (1963); Close and Collins (1983); Tilly and Scott (1987).

13 I document and discuss this process when referring to the case of southern Italy in chapter 6.

14 It is probably true that, as Litwak (1960) argues, solidarity relations among different households of relatives form a 'modified extended family'. For this condition to come about, it is nevertheless necessary that different nuclei continue to live relatively close to one another. When high geographical mobility means that related nuclear families live far apart, the modified extended family tends to be less common.

15 Sufficient evidence exists to confirm this point, at least for Italy and the United States. See the results of the following works of research: Gallino (1982); Ragone (1983); Reyneri (1984); Paci (1985); Clutterbuck (1979); Michelotti (1975); Miller (1972).

16 Selective data available on Britain, Italy and the USA confirm the trends towards a more fragmented household structure (see table on p. 195).

The rate of female activity increased in every country of the European Community between 1973 and 1977, with the exception of Ireland (1975–77), as shown by Eurostat data. In Italy, France, Belgium, Britain and Denmark the increase was substantial: more than 4 per cent in only five years. The proportion of married women working increased throughout the 1970s from 49 per cent in 1971 to 52 per cent in 1978 (C. C. Harris, 1983, p. 218).

17 The surveys on Southern (Mingione, 1985 and chapter 6 below) and Central and North-Eastern Italy (Paci, 1980) tend to confirm those points: the informal workers with above-average income work more than 60 hours per week; the others survive with a very low and irregular cash income because domestic work exceeds 60 hours per week in medium-sized households (four persons) and 75 hours in large households (more than five persons).

As chapter 6 also shows, in the South survival strategies are complemented by external monetary resources contributed by the state and emigrated relatives, while in the north-eastern and central regions the picture is completed by a wealthy and stable network of solidarity.

18 See, among others, the recent extremely interesting study on industrial homeworking women in Mexico City by Beneria and Roldan (1987). An up-to-date critical review of the literature is included in this important contribution.

19 The debate on the socialist agrarian question and on the role of the peasantry was particularly heated in the USSR in the 1920s and 1930s. See mainly Chayanov (1925/1987) and Shanin (1972).

20 Concerning recent developments in Hungary, see mainly Szelenyi (1988) on the re-emerging importance of family entrepreneurship in agriculture.

21   See, for example, the debate on the Hungarian case: Konrad and Szelenyi
     (1977); Szelenyi (1978; 1983); Hegedus and Tosics (1983). See also the
     issue of the *International Journal of Urban and Regional Research* (1987, no. 1),
     dedicated to housing inequalities in Poland, Hungary and Czechoslovakia.
22   A recent article by Meier (1989) confirms this kind of 'political' gender
     discrimination in the case of the GDR, a country where the rate of female
     employment is amongst the highest in the world.
23   The processes that lead to the diffusion of poverty, food shortages and
     famines in the countryside of underdeveloped countries are now well docu-
     mented. See in particular Aziz (1975), George (1976), and, particularly,
     the important contribution of Amartya Sen (1981).
24   Raymond Boudon (1986), in his critical discussion of 'The notion of ration-
     ality' (pp. 46–51), stresses the variability of the concept of rationality on
     the basis of important studies of social behaviour in underdeveloped coun-
     tries. In particular, quoting the results of the study by S. Epstein, *Economic
     Development and Social Change in South India* (Manchester, Manchester Univer-
     sity Press, 1962), he underlines how a rather high birth rate is perfectly
     rational from the point of view of family farmers in sugar-cane production,
     as they combine male employment required on the farm and a certain
     amount of off-the-farm employment necessary to complement both survival
     of the family and investments in order to update family farming activities
     (p. 50).
25   See, among others, Hart (1978); Ruiz Perez (1979); Birkbeck (1980; 1982);
     Bromley (1981).

Recent changes in household distribution in Britain, Italy and the USA

Britain (extract taken from C. C. Harris, 1983, pp. 218–19, reproduced by kind permission of Unwin Hyman Ltd)	% 1961	% 1979	
Households with children	54	46	
Households with no children present	26	27	
Two or more families	3	1	
Single persons and non-family households	16	26	

Italy (Population census)	1971	1981	change %
Households with 1–2 members	34.7	41.7	+39
Households with 3–5 members	55.2	53	+11.2
Households with 6 or more members	9.6	5	−39.9

Milan (Demographical reports)	1971	1983	change %
Single households	19.4	36.1	+105.5
Households with two members	27.4	23.8	−3.7
Households with 3–5 members	50.2	38.9	−14.3
Households with 6 or more members	3	1.1	−58.3

USA household change: 1970–82, in thousands (Norton, 1983, p. 20)	1970	1982	change %
Married couple family with own children under 18	40.3	29.3	−4.2
Married couples without own children under 18	30.2	30.1	+31.1
Other family male householder	1.9	2.4	+61.7
Other family female householder	8.7	11.3	+71.0
Total non-family households	18.8	26.9	+88.4
of which single persons	17.1	23.2	+78.3
Total households (in thousands)	63.401	83.527	+31.7

4

Informalization and current
transformation trends

1 INDUSTRIAL RESTRUCTURING, FLEXIBLE
EMPLOYMENT AND MASS UNEMPLOYMENT

The main elements in the crisis of the Fordist-welfarist model

In the previous chapter, I discussed extensively the fact that industrial
development has produced a varying set of interrelated arrangements
based on the one hand on different employment conditions and related
levels of income and on the other on complementary reproduction patterns. Important changes in the employment structure and/or in the
reproduction patterns inevitably destabilize these arrangements and bring
about considerable social transformations. Although diverse types of
contemporary societies are becoming increasingly heterogeneous, up to
the late 1960s the three main types of societies, advanced capitalist,
socialist and underdeveloped, were characterized by the predominance
of a specific employment/social reproduction arrangement. The family
wage system complemented by secondary incomes and welfare provisions,
which from now on will be referred to as the Fordist-welfarist model,
was firmly rooted and extending its reach in advanced capitalist countries. The low wage and high employment system complemented by
extensive but basic welfare provisions, provided through centralized state
redistribution, was the specific model of socialist societies; though based
on an ideology of equality, the implementation of this redistribution was
in practice full of contradictions. A combination of persistently low wages
and incomes earned by a large number of potential workers, and the
complementary factors of urban subsistence, informal activities and community arrangements, had now become the typical situation in underdeveloped societies where massive uncontrolled urbanization was occurring at an increasingly rapid pace. While it was generally considered
that the first and second models were stable, at least at that time, and

would develop further along the same lines as in the past, the third was mainly perceived as a dramatic outcome of the global patterns of industrial development and as a persistent negative constraint on economic growth. Academics and politicians were convinced that the social situation in the underdeveloped part of the world would soon become explosive, but they were unable to come up with any clearcut practical solution. Paradoxically, we now have to admit that while the first two models have been progressively destabilized by subsequent developments, the third still persists and is even spreading.

In this chapter, I briefly discuss the main socio-economic trends which have led to the situation described above, devoting particular attention to the changes which have affected the employment and welfare systems in advanced capitalist countries and to how these changes are reflected in life-styles and survival strategies. Moreover, the significance of the diffusion of informal activities is underlined. In the final section, the main contemporary trends affecting socialist and underdeveloped societies are touched upon, and in particular those that further the expansion of both the second economy and the urban informal sector.

The model of employment reproduction that gradually became established in various forms in advanced capitalist countries up until the late 1960s was based on the family wage of the adult male head of a household, the complementary incomes of other members and on the further, indispensable, complement of state-provided welfare services. It has been seen that this model shows a degree of variability in terms of both space and time. Its geographic variability reflects both economic and occupational differences and diverse social and cultural conditions. Its temporal variability reflects, on the whole, the more or less efficient development of modern welfare systems through what could be called a 'benign spiral' of growth in state services that serve to improve living standards and increase female employment in these same services.

In the 1970s, existing welfare systems were overwhelmed by economic crisis, the restructuring of industry, financial upsets and political difficulties. All these factors helped to throw light on the weakness of the Fordist-welfarist model in all its diverse variants. They also played a role in destabilizing the link between employment and patterns of social reproduction that characterized the model. A further consequence was that the social conditions within which the link is made became more heterogeneous or, in other words, fragmented.

One of the contradictory aspects of this model lies in its high and growing costs, which, in the last analysis, are paid by the less developed countries subject to ever-increasing pressure from an expanding world market. The conditions of expansion and domination on the world market are based on high rates of growth in labour productivity and production in several branches of manufacturing industry. In the long run, these high rates have diverse detrimental effects on the model. In the first place, the equilibrium between economic expansion, growth in labour productivity and levels of employment is fragile and, in some cases, it was already collapsing in the 1960s. Since 1970, employment in manufacturing has tended to decline uninterruptedly and at a growing rate in all advanced capitalist countries, especially in medium to large concerns, which form the backbone of the Fordist-welfarist model. At the same time, the high increases in productivity in manufacturing industry have caused big rises in operating costs in economic sectors where such increases cannot be absorbed; this applies in particular to some kinds of services and above all to state welfare services. The welfare state is everywhere in difficulty and what I have called the 'benign spiral' of this system no longer operates. The combination of these last two phenomena has a further negative effect on the employment crisis: a persistent and increasing lack of opportunities for secure full-time jobs paying a family wage is coinciding with an abundant supply of workers with average levels of education and high job expectations. These workers are the result of the post-war baby booms and grew up in the golden years of the 'benign spiral' of welfare. At this point, two areas providing a growing number of jobs comes into play: flexible industrialization and the expansion of private services. However, they are not able to compensate for the decline in guaranteed jobs in large manufacturing concerns. In this sense, the occupational/reproductive model that was taken as the starting-point of the discussion has been greatly destabilized, resulting in a widening complex diversification of social conditions.

Before moving on to questions relating to flexible industrialization and mass unemployment, it is important to mention two other highly contradictory features that typify the Fordist-welfarist model. The first is the model's indifference towards maintaining a balanced relationship with the environment. The model presupposes high rates of growth and it is evident that the latter can only be achieved if the constraints to which they are subjected in the interests of the whole community are extremely limited. The other side to the process of growth is the diffusion, likewise subject to only limited constraints, of individualism and mass consumerism (O'Connor, 1984). In this way, a mechanism has been created whose destructive effects on the environment are devastating. It has become entrenched because three of the most powerful interest groups in society think along the same lines about economic expansion. The business lobby is in favour for obvious reasons, the state because growth provides the resources for expanding public services, necessary for maintaining and extending political consensus. Lastly, the trade union and political wings of the labour movement see wage levels and, at least until the crisis of the 1970s, growing employment as dependent on economic growth. Undoubtedly, the deterioration of the environment and public awareness of this danger have contributed to undermining the model of growth based on large concerns and on a totally committed state bureaucracy.

Equally serious, and perhaps even more so, are the inconsistencies introduced into the model by the second critical feature: the structural discrimination against women. The occupational/reproductive model in question reserves access to life-long working careers providing a main family wage almost exclusively to male adults and relegates women to jobs viewed as sources of secondary income. At the same time, however, the increase in welfare services not only has the combined effect of freeing some women from domestic chores and offering them employment in these same services; it also leads to equality for women in access to services, in particular education, that socialize people in the world of work, and the universalistic ideals to which it gives rise increasingly conflict with the reality of discrimination. This is especially the case where welfare services have become effective. Seen retrospectively, it is not at all surprising that there has been an upsurge of feminist movements; the 'women's question' forms a glaring structural inconsistency deeply rooted in the model based on the triangle of family income, secondary income and welfare services. The growing destabilization of the dominant model has not produced a solution to the problem of gender discrimination. On the contrary, the outcome has been an increasing diversification of the actual social arrangements linking the occupational structure and strategies of social reproduction.

The myth and reality of flexible industrialization

Before briefly examining flexible industrialization as a breeding ground for irregular working activities and as a setting in which to move beyond the dominant model, it is worth underlining that, however important it may be, this area of change in employment is still small relative to the much greater impact of tertiarization as a whole. Most research into the labour market, changes in occupational structure and also informal activities, has concentrated on manufacturing industry. As a consequence, it has ignored or at least underestimated the context of services; however, it is precisely the latter which, in socialist and underdeveloped countries as well, plays a much more important role in explaining both the transformation and fragmentation of occupational/reproductive models and the diffusion of informal activities.[1]

For at least the last ten years, a wide-ranging debate has been taking place on contemporary changes in the organization and employment structure of industry.[2] Here, I must limit myself to a few critical remarks that are essential for clarifying the way in which industrial transformation helps to destabilize the Fordist-welfarist model.

As Sayer (1989) has recently shown, the simplified radical hypothesis of an extensive transformation from what have been called Fordist organizational patterns to largely different flexible ones is open to doubt. The majority of industrial concerns do not appear to have been organized in line with strictly similar Fordist patterns before the recent changes; neither are they being transformed in the same or similar ways that could be simply defined as more flexible. Moreover, rigidity and flexibility are complex and relative features, which take on quite different meanings in diverse social and economic contexts. The transformation follows various paths in different local contexts and it is increasingly difficult to form an overall picture which makes sense if one also takes into account the growth of manufacturing employment within strictly traditional organizational patterns, for instance the car industry in Brazil or in South Korea and the expansion of small-scale manufacturing in various traditional and modern advanced sectors in the Third Italy, as well as the radical decline of employment in medium-sized and large manufacturing concerns in many industrialized countries, which is often accompanied by increasing financial concentration, company mergers and the formation of conglomerates. Finally, the term 'flexible' has often been attributed to different sets of organizational relations, in particular to the accumulation process (in my view this is highly misleading); to the labour process, where more flexible organizational patterns mean the possibility of increasing the turnover of workers and the creation of a variety of non-standard enterprises either directly or through subcontracting; or to the production process and to the goods produced, where these patterns mean a growing capacity to meet the increasingly diversified requirements of different customers using the same production line.

Despite these caveats with regard to so-called flexible industrialization, it is none the less clear that some substantial transformations are taking place in manufacturing employment on a global scale and that they contribute to the increasing heterogeneity of work and to the diffusion of some forms of irregular employment. In general, manufacturing production is still increasing at a rather high average annual rate (from 3 to 6 per cent) in nearly every advanced capitalist country after a more or less general slow-down in the 1970s; at the same time employment in manufacturing, particularly in medium-sized and large plants, is persistently and substantially declining.[3] On the other hand, while self-employed activities and jobs in small enterprises in the manufacturing sector are either increasing or decreasing to a lesser extent, the average number of workers per unit over the whole of industry is dropping rapidly. This last change is totally independent of trends towards financial concentration where mergers, acquisitions and the formation of conglomerates are on the increase; expanding manufacturing employment in the so-called newly industrializing countries not only pays lower wages, but it is also characterized by organizational patterns differing from those which have become established in plants producing similar goods in advanced capitalist countries, even when two plants are branches of the same multinational corporation.[4]

The least controversial result of these changes is the marked decrease in the number of manufacturing jobs that pay a standard family wage, are fully tenured and characterized by strong internal labour markets.[5] This does not necessarily mean that the conditions of employment or the labour market relations affecting the remaining and declining number of workers are automatically deteriorating in all branches of manufacturing. But, going beyond purely labour-saving technology, the crucial problem in the transformation of employment on a large scale is the reversal of the previous pattern of vertical integration towards different strategies based on vertical disintegration (see Storper and Walker, 1988; Scott, 1988; Sayer 1989). With few exceptions – the most important being Japan (see Dore, 1986 and 1987) – until the beginning of the 1970s the development of mass production in manufacturing was characterized by a high degree of vertical integration; that is, every operation from Research and Development to the marketing and sale of the product was closely tied into the organizational structure of an enterprise. This meant that even low-skill labour-intensive jobs unfavourably situated in the labour market, for instance jobs in maintenance and cleaning, were upgraded to proper tenured occupations, at least within the medium to large manufacturing employment system. The combination of the growing size of productive units leading to an expanding tertiarization in employment structure and the productivity gap (see section 3 below) between manufacturing and service jobs caused vertically integrated organizations to become less and less profitable, and at the same time increased the relative advantages of systems which had developed different forms of 'organized vertical disintegration' (Sayer, 1989), such as Japan or the Third Italy. In this sense, a current important factor in de-industrialization, and also one of the leading aspects of contemporary trends towards vertical disintegration, is the contracting out of operations involving the intensive use of service labour. This change is not only reflected in job statistics in terms of decreasing manufacturing and increasing service employment but also, and substantially, in conditions of work and in wage levels – for, unlike large corporations, small subcontracting firms can easily hire casual, untenured and irregular workers. The same is also happening with directly productive manufacturing operations, particularly in the case of labour-intensive processes which are relatively difficult to incorporate into high-productivity strategies and which can be subcontracted out at advantageous terms to underdeveloped or socialist countries, or to industrial homeworking units (Frobel et al., 1980).

Although the debate is still continuing as to how far the organization of manufacturing industry in Western capitalist countries has become post-Fordist or flexible, it is none the less safe to say that the present transformation is bringing about a sizeable decrease in the number of tenured jobs offering a family wage and a corresponding, but much less substantial, increase in a number of highly diverse working activities, including self-employment, industrial homeworking and casual and irregular forms of labour.

The advent of a new age of mass unemployment

What has been called the age of mass unemployment (Malinvaud, 1984) is partially a consequence of this de-industrialization trend, but it is also connected to recent changes in the service and state employment structure (see the next two sections) and in the main types of potential workers making up the labour supply and their expectations. In the years between the mid-1970s and the early 1980s, unemployment rates rose steeply in practically every advanced capitalist country from low frictional levels of between 2 and 5 per cent to much higher levels, previously believed to be incompatible with socio-political stability. Advanced capitalist countries seem to have entered an age where chronic unemployment can reach relatively high levels without having a particularly destabilizing effect on the socio-political order. This is closely tied up with the transformation of the employment structure and with the changing make-up of the two main types among the mass unemployed: adult male workers made redundant by de-industrializing manufacturing concerns and, to a minor extent, also by the dismantling of the welfare state in some regions; and, even more numerous, young people who find it increasingly difficult to obtain a permanent job which does not fall too short of their expectations and life requirements.[6]

Let us briefly consider some issues concerning unemployment which

appear closely related to the transformation of the employment/repro-
duction model and to the diffusion of irregular working activities. It is
obvious that high levels of adult male unemployment generated by
de-industrialization are to be found particularly in areas which are
characterized to a high extent by this phenomenon, for instance manufacturing regions where factories are closing down and/or moving out. The
problem becomes especially serious where the local economy is unable
to promote counter-tendencies mainly in terms of increasing specialization in services or attracting new high technology industries. But even
when the loss of employment is relatively offset by gains in other sectors,
a marked variation in the quality of jobs penalizes former semi-skilled
manufacturing workers in the 'dependent primary segment' of the labour
market. New occupations are inevitably polarized between highly professional work and jobs with a high skill content in the advanced technology sector, and casual, temporary and part-time employment. As
former manufacturing workers have no possibility of obtaining jobs of
the first kind and do not easily adapt to the downgrading implicit in the
second, particularly if they are the breadwinner in a relatively large
household, they find themselves in great difficulty even in regions characterized by a notable expansion in employment. This is substantially
confirmed by empirical evidence, especially from the United States where
labour markets are less subject to state and trade union control and
redundant workers are not afforded much protection. Perhaps the most
radical case is the metropolitan region of Los Angeles, where the number
of occupations has increased by slightly more than the official number
of inhabitants but the majority of black adult males made redundant by
the disappearance of the car industry have not been able to find a new
job (Soja, 1989). A different kind of confirmation comes from empirical
research on irregular and informal activities (Foudi et al. 1982; Pahl,
1984). The typical unemployed manufacturing worker is rarely involved
in such activities. When receiving unemployment benefit, the risk is too
great relative to the small amount of money obtained. When not on
unemployment benefit or when this is low enough to be legally compatible
with a certain amount of work, a combination of other reasons comes
into play: marginality in respect of the information/opportunity networks
which make these activities possible; the frequently time-consuming nature of such activities, which thus prevent a proper search for a better
job; and the fact that both customers and employers, but particularly
the latter since they might have to pay heavy fines or be obliged to hire
officially unemployed workers taken on irregularly, find it much more
convenient from a legal standpoint for an irregular job to be done by an
already regularly employed worker, or by a student, a pensioner or

a housewife, rather than by an unemployed person seeking full-time employment.

As will be seen in the following chapter, the unlikely combination of unemployment and irregular work does not apply to certain kinds of traditional workers whose type of employment is in decline, particularly agricultural and building labourers in relatively undeveloped areas. Their work profile consists of life-long alternation between periods of regular employment and periods of unemployment complemented by a certain amount of irregular work. But this is a different matter to the one being discussed here, which is the unemployment of workers previously employed in medium-sized or large manufacturing concerns.

Youth unemployment is an even more complicated matter, where once again both the contemporary chronic undersupply of employment opportunities and the mismatch between an increasingly polarized employment structure and the characteristics of the labour supply play a crucial role. It is important to begin by identifying the new entrants into advanced capitalist labour markets. They are the children of the last phase in the post-war baby boom, who were socialized and educated in highly individualist, consumerist and welfare-oriented societies. They had a long education and in their teens were involved in conspicuous consumption. When they come onto the labour market they face a situation in which not only is there a decreasing number of job opportunities in terms of tenured employment, but in which most opportunities for work are highly polarized. This entails, in general, two phenomena which are both reflected in growing rates of unemployment: an increasingly long period throughout which young people are idle, alternate periods of unemployment with temporary jobs or undertake various kinds of casual and irregular work while officially unemployed; and a growing number of young people who eventually settle down for life in a down-graded working career characterized by high job mobility and intermittent unemployment.

Both in the early period of industrialization, when apprentices received no wage and often had to pay to learn a craft, and in more recent times, when we find, for instance, casual part-time or temporary employment of college students, it is not unusual to find young people experiencing periods of instability in their working lives and undertaking casual and experimental forms of employment. Present developments, however, are becoming increasingly problematical from a structural point of view, and they represent a pathological condition of contemporary societies. The major problem derives from the fact that the employment system is more or less oriented towards generating both a large excess of increasingly fragmented, casual, temporary, part-time and irregular secondary jobs relative to the potential number of young workers able to fill them for a limited initial period in their working careers, and an insufficient and further declining number of tenured primary working opportunities relative to a labour supply which is highly educated and in which more and more women demand, need and deserve to embark upon primary working careers. The excess of secondary, fragmented and informal working opportunities is filled by an expanding number of moonlighters and foreign guest-workers (this explains why these types of employment are increasing at the same time as youth unemployment is rising), by young workers condemned to ever longer periods of work instability before entering a stage of relatively greater tenure, and by increasing numbers of former youths (now in their thirties) left behind by developments in the labour market. Females still make up the disproportionate majority of the latter, but probably the success of demands for equal opportunities will result in accelerating the growth of the male component while slowing down, though under present conditions not stopping, the growth of the female component. With regard to this last question, it is worth noticing that existing employment systems are unable to create on a mass scale the semi-family-wage jobs needed to support equal opportunities for male and female workers and a large number of twin-career families, and to prevent the increasing number of female-headed households from falling into poverty.

Finally, increasing youth unemployment has an important impact on the householding process in combination with the life courses of both parents and children. Mention was made in the last chapter of the severe problems that families have to face during periods in which they support the survival of young adult children in long-term unemployment, when they are in addition at an age characterized by conspicuous consumption. At present, it is probably the case that a majority of households enjoying a family wage plus various additional secondary incomes are able to cope with this burden, while a large and increasing minority without a family wage are in serious difficulties (Pahl, 1984). But the situation is on the point of rapidly changing for the worse, even if we take into consideration the fact that the greatly reduced birth rate will alleviate the burden in future decades. In general, working careers are now more unstable and begin later than under the previous family wage system. It is clear from what has been said above why they are more unstable. Further, young people begin working later than in the past in that more and more frequently the majority of them do not enter into relatively tenured jobs until in their late thirties. In these cases, the ones who marry and have children early on, possibly in a period when their original families have enough resources to offer a high degree of support, may run into serious trouble when their children are young unemployed adults and they are still at the start of a tenured working career. On the other hand, workers who postponed marriage and having children to a later date could face a critical situation when they are close to retirement age and their children have not yet found a job.[7]

The increasing differentiation in employment/reproduction patterns described above is one of the most important factors contributing to contemporary social fragmentation.

2 THE IMPACT OF THE PRIVATIZATION AND DE-UNIVERSALIZATION OF THE WELFARE STATE

The various kinds of welfare states

In the preceding chapter I pointed to the importance of welfare programmes in shaping the occupational/reproductive model that has developed in the advanced capitalist countries during this century, especially in the period between the end of the Second World War and the economic difficulties of the 1970s. Though taking on a great variety of forms in different countries, welfare services have been essential in setting up the dominant model, which I have called 'Fordist-welfarist', but they have also been a central contradictory element leading to its instability. In the present period, the difficulties with which all political systems are struggling in the wake of the fiscal crisis of the state have resulted in the restructuring of welfare programmes. This is a crucial factor in the destabilization of the model and in the spread of various kinds of irregular occupations. The question which must be answered is how the welfare system came to be a fundamental contradictory element and play a central destabilizing role. However, before dealing with this problem, two difficult questions need to be tackled: first the wide variety of welfare programmes in different countries and the consequent processes of development and restructuring that have characterized them; second, a wide-ranging theoretical controversy over the nature, limits and contradictions of the welfare state.

The considerable diversity in welfare systems depends on the interaction of numerous factors ranging from the varying composition of and balance between the social classes to differences in economic history and political-institutional set-ups, and to the variety of important sociocultural factors. Much attention has been paid to the British and Scandinavian models and to what has been seen as a counter-model, that of the United States. The first has acted as a reference point for the extent of the state's direct provision of welfare services. In the second, the implementation of welfare policies has involved private enterprise, non-profit institutions, the federal state and individual states, without in general ever reaching the degree of universality and commitment found elsewhere (see Korpi, 1980). In contrast, less notice has been taken of the experience of other countries.[8]

The variety of systems also assumes a great significance in relation to the problems I am directly concerned with, as I shall try to show below. In general, however, it has not substantially affected the trends which have led, at first, to the consolidation of the Fordist-welfarist model and, subsequently, to its progressive break-up. The transformation and extension of the, more or less private, communal or collective ways of benefiting from services such as education, health and public transport have profoundly altered the life-styles of millions of people. Current developments are bringing about further changes of equal importance. In every case, it has not been and is not solely a question of the transformation and extension of the ways in which services crucial to the quality of life are used, but also of a radical transformation in occupational structures. These two questions are inseparable in the sense that it has proved impossible to pass through the phase of welfare services without massively expanding employment in this sector. In some cases, however, a notable rise in employment in welfare services has not had the effect of a substantial improvement in their quantity and quality (see the example of Southern Italy in chapter 6). For this reason, the impact of variety and change should be evaluated separately in terms of the services provided, employment levels and job quality, and the way in which these two interlinked transformations are reflected in reproduction strategies.

Considerations on the theoretical debate on the welfare state

The extensive debate on the welfare state can be dealt with here only in a limited fashion; I shall therefore confine myself to a few aspects that are essential to any treatment of the problem of change in occupational/re-productive patterns. Basically, what I am interested in is clarifying how and why the Fordist-welfarist model emerged in its diverse variants, what its social contradictions are in the area of the welfare state, and where the main contemporary trends in the transformation of the ways of providing welfare services are leading to.

A direct link can be made between the origins of welfare services and two questions that were discussed in the last two chapters: the need to regulate and limit the labour market; and the chronic inadequacy of monetary incomes as the sole guarantee of family survival, above all for wage-earning families in urban contexts, which, by definition, are especially poor in traditional resources based on reciprocity. The problem, therefore, originally involved two different social areas, although in reality they cannot be completely distinguished; for example, children, housewives and pensioners belong simultaneously to both areas. On the one side, survival had to be guaranteed for those who were excluded from the labour market and not able easily or conveniently to find solutions in traditional reciprocal networks, which at the same time were being undermined. On the other side, there was the need to compensate for constantly insufficient monetary resources, decreasingly supplemented by traditional arrangements rooted in reciprocal relations. Moreover, the process of compensation had to suit the differing historical conditions of industrial growth in each country. The existing historical conditions then led to growing problems of a qualitative kind, as industrial societies gradually became characterized by the higher productivity of labour, higher rates of urbanization, the reduction to a minimum of productive households and the greater selectivity and complexity of labour markets.

This way of formulating the problem, however, is too deterministic and evolutionist. In reality, the twofold need of limiting the labour market and complementing chronically inadequate incomes is varyingly expressed in social tensions, political conflicts and limits to industrial growth, the outcomes of which are also markedly diverse. The literature on the origins of welfare systems in various European countries from the second half of the nineteenth century has noted two very different models within which the first social security and health care programmes developed. The first is the preventive or Bismarckian model, which granted from above the first welfare services in the hope of forestalling any further strengthening of working-class organizations; the second is the demand-oriented/conflictual model, in which the appearance of welfare programmes reflected the strengthening of workers' organizations.[9] This consideration gives rise in itself to two aspects that have been widely discussed by the critical literature on the welfare state: first, its complexity is largely due to the plurality of social forces that interact politically in achieving diverse objectives; and second, the big incongruities and contradictions that arise depend on structural limits which emerge out of the specific interplay of social forces. In this perspective, welfare programmes are not automatic responses either to the requirements of capital or its predominant fractions, or to those expressed by the labour movement, or even to the specific aims pursued by the dominant political class.

Generally speaking, there are two possible ways to explain the strategical limits to state intervention. The first explanation is rooted in a neo-Marxist approach and has recently been reformulated by O'Connor (1973), adopted by Gough (1979) and in part, but with a different emphasis, also by Habermas (1975) and Offe (1984). In brief, it points to the fact that state intervention is caught between two areas of involvement that are potentially incompatible: the need to ensure that capital accumulation is maintained and extended, and the need to underpin the very legitimacy of state intervention. A capitalist political system which penalizes average levels of accumulation will be overwhelmed not only by powerful business lobbies but also by the potentially devastating effects of economic crisis. In contrast, a system compelled to neglect consensus and legitimacy by the pressure to provide almost exclusive aid to capital accumulation risks being overwhelmed by the effects of the political crisis brought about by its de-legitimization and loss of popular support. We shall see presently how the contradictory developments of welfare programmes may be read in the light of this theoretical approach.

The second explanation arises out of a neo-functionalist perspective and has been worked out recently by Luhmann (1982). In this approach, state intervention is seen as increasingly overloaded with objectives that by their very nature are not fully compatible with one another. From the standpoint of the internal functioning of the state, the problem is not so much that of the social contradictions resulting from the impossibility of satisfying too many divergent alternative needs as of the growing incapacity to make limited strategic choices. According to Luhmann, the aims of achieving consensus and supporting accumulation are not necessarily incompatible, but it has been verified that state intervention which is overloaded with objectives loses its ability to be selective and becomes paralysed. Remaining within the limited framework of immediate intervention at the political level, the problem is posed in this case in terms of the capacity to set up selective strategies that are adequate to the overloading of requirements. Above all, state intervention needs to be reduced and simplified by giving precedence to a small number of essential programmes that are compatible and consistent with one another.

In my opinion, the two approaches are not incompatible but tackle the question from two different angles, both of which may be of help in understanding the developments in welfare policies. The first puts the emphasis on a long-term process and the interconnections between political action on one side and demands from socio-economic forces on the other. The second, in contrast, concentrates on the internal mechanisms in the political process and its immediate capacity to select feasible and consistent objectives and achieve them. From this point of view, Luhmann is right to insist on the decisive importance of the processes of selection; however, this does not exclude the possibility that a government which is effective in the short run may also allow worsening economic and social problems to accumulate and put off trying to resolve them, since they are due more to basic underlying contradictions than to the government's incapacity to make immediate choices.

The debate on the welfare state has helped to forge some analytical tools that are useful for studying the trends analysed in this book. In particular, it is worth adopting the distinction made by Offe (1984) between 'allocative' and 'productive' state activities, according to which the former include various forms of income redistribution and the latter are directed towards the production of welfare services. The first type of intervention is further divided into clearly visible social assistance and insurance policies (benefits, pensions, monetary and other transfers to strata of the population considered needy) and into a less visible area which is growing in importance and which has been defined as fiscal welfare (Titmuss, 1966). In the second case, the state carries out a substantial redistribution of resources to the advantage of certain social strata, in general middle-income groups, and to the detriment of all other taxpayers. It does so through a complex play of tax exemptions and reductions, selective toleration towards some tax-evaders and the state-subsidized granting of credit on easy terms. The fact that these forms of intervention are less visible is not of secondary importance. Welfare programmes based on direct redistribution often involve social stigma for the users: they are labelled as 'poor', 'unemployed', 'council house tenants' and so on. As Johnson rightly notes, 'stigma is used as a deliberate policy' (Johnson, 1987, p. 12). In direct contrast, the beneficiaries of fiscal welfare, though at times receiving what are very substantial contributions, are neither stigmatized nor marginalized.

Welfare programmes and income redistribution

I shall now examine the contemporary developments and trends in welfare programmes from two different angles: that relative to policies of allocation and transfer, and that relating to systems for producing services in the public interest. They both have to be linked to the diversified historical course of the decline in social organizations based on community life and reciprocity, their transformation or adaptation, which within the processes of urbanization and urban growth have rendered the role of traditional strategies less and less effective both in ensuring the survival of growing strata of the population and in complementing the social reproduction of wage families, whose monetary incomes continue to be inadequate. To a certain extent, the greater or lesser persistence of these social organizations is directly proportional to the urgency with which the need to develop both assistance and service-producing welfare programmes is expressed, in the sense that it is the need to replace traditional reciprocal arrangements, but in a context of large-scale qualitative changes in the requirements of social reproduction, which leads to the appearance and development of welfare programmes. Where this need is not strongly felt, even the qualitative change useful for industrial growth does not occur; and this situation is, of course, reflected in forms of underdevelopment.

Social insurance programmes of the reallocational kind were the first to appear on a systematic basis in the last quarter of the nineteenth century. But, in a certain sense, state welfare programmes and legislation aimed at the poor have a longer, more interesting and complicated history, especially in England. With regard to this country, the question of the Poor Laws takes on a central theoretical role in Polanyi's treatment (1944/1975) of the emergence of the conflict between society and the industrial market; these laws preceded by more than a century the introduction by Bismarck of national insurance schemes in Germany. In order to shorten my treatment of this difficult question, I have confined myself to underlining in general terms the interrelationship between, on the one hand, the development of welfare assistance and, on the other, the progressively increasing delimitation of the labour market and the related changes in terms of surplus population. In this sense, programmes for redistributing income, above all those aimed at reducing poverty, prior to and after the establishment of the welfare state and programmes for dealing with unemployment have always been characterized by a basic inconsistency between the need to provide for the survival of social strata that are unable to work, or only have access to poorly paid activities, and the need not to weaken incentives for too many potential workers, thereby provoking undesirable wage rises. Only in the limited period from the Second World War to the 1970s, and only in a few countries benefiting from the huge resources resulting from the global penetration of capitalism, was the iron grip of this contradiction partially loosened through emphasizing the idea that advanced capitalist societies could only gain from policies in support of incomes, among which social security and unemployment benefits play an important role.[10]

This basic inconsistency has always been and is now increasingly reflected in various forms of 'insufficiency' that characterize welfare programmes of the redistributional type. On top of these inadequacies there are a growing number of processes in which ways of working and consuming are being informalized. Redistributional welfare programmes are aimed at compensating for 'abnormal' inadequacies in monetary incomes involving a limited part of the population. Where they can be applied, their effectiveness is measured by their capacity to bring as many people as possible and as soon as possible back to the state of 'normal' inadequacy. I will look briefly at this question with regard to the most important social insurance programmes that are worth considering here, that is, those relating to poverty and unemployment, old age pensions and pensions for surviving dependents. The area of health will be referred to when dealing with the provision of services, but reasons of space make it impossible to dwell on the question of invalidity and other possible goals of redistribution.[11]

The underlying logic is clear enough in the case of programmes relating to poverty and unemployment, but more problematical with regard to the pension system. Poverty and unemployment are by definition two conditions characterized by the serious inadequacy of monetary incomes. They may coincide, especially where welfare programmes are lacking or deficient. However, this compounding is always only partial, because in many cases a state of poverty reflects the possibility of access solely to jobs with inadequate wages or the impossibility, *tout court*, of working. Further, it tends to decrease as a contextual effect of the development of national insurance schemes and the spread of jobs offering secondary incomes, where unemployment no longer entails immediate destitution because of the support from other income-earners in the household. The idea behind national and social insurance schemes is that they help people to pass through a difficult stage as rapidly as possible; the goal is not only to ensure survival in an urban context where the minimum indispensable level of monetary income is high, but also to avoid cumulating and passing on conditions of acute social disadvantage from one generation to the next, thereby making them chronic. Behind the Keynesian version of programmes for supporting incomes there also lies the conviction that by preventing a dramatic fall in monetary spending capacity, such programmes limit the effects of economic crises and facilitate the renewal of investment, subsequent rises in employment levels and, consequently, a substantial return of the poor and unemployed to normal conditions of employment and reproduction. This strategy worked, even though arguably at the cost of extending underdevelopment in the Third World, as long as industrial investment continued more or less to bring with it increases in employment. It is based on the assumption that high welfare spending in periods of economic crisis make it possible to get through difficult times rapidly, return to a situation of low levels of poverty and unemployment and, as a consequence, to a phase of contained welfare spending. The effectiveness of Keynesian strategies has been seriously compromised by the advent of the era of labour-saving investment, which has contributed to their decreasing popularity at the very time when they are increasingly needed for the immediate purpose of giving large sectors of the population the chance to survive in difficult circumstances.

The inadequacies and inconsistencies of these welfare programmes were, however, already clearly visible in previous periods. The area of poverty has never been reduced below a substantial bottom layer of the population, and the related programmes have almost never prevented a disadvantaged condition from being transmitted to children among the poor. The most interesting case is represented by the ambitious programmes in the war against poverty during Lyndon Johnson's presidency in the USA. As critics belonging to the radical school have pointed out (see above all Dale Tussing, 1975; Cloward and Piven, 1971), despite being adopted in the richest country in the world in a period of great prosperity, these programmes made no impression on the extent of poverty nor on the perverse mechanisms by which it is passed on from one generation to the next; if anything, they served to keep the poor in check politically and bolster the system of consensus, undermined by the decline of the city centres and the waves of black revolt in the large cities.

Similarly, assistance for the unemployed has not in general prevented a more or less constant proportion of long-term unemployed from falling into poverty. Frequently, the inadequacy of unemployment benefit has become a permanent element complementing low-income, occasional, temporary or intermittent jobs, which are becoming increasingly informal as the regulation of working conditions is extended. In several sectors, this complementary role of unemployment benefit has become so extensive as to form real institutional logic underlying welfare programmes, as is seen in the case of Italy in chapter 6. In other words, the goal of these programmes has not so much been to make survival possible until new employment is found, but rather to allow the undertaking of working activities that provide an income so low as to be totally inadequate for survival unless complemented by welfare benefits. The growing fragmentation of the labour market and the structure of employment in the private tertiary sector seems to be pointing in the direction of a further extension of this 'improper' function of welfare programmes. Yet this is nothing new; throughout the entire period of capitalist development, a series of welfare programmes for dealing with poverty and unemployment, as well as for providing old age pensions and pensions for surviving dependents, have in reality served to support a substantial number of extremely low and inadequate incomes from work. In my view, what should be underlined is that these programmes have enabled a two-tier system of employment based on extreme social inequality to persist even in spite of the development of the Fordist-welfarist model. When this dominant model entered into crisis the system broke up, leading to a further diffusion of the most disadvantaged kinds of jobs.

What I have to say about the pension system is of necessity very limited and concentrates on the latest trends. Practically all pension systems are based on the idea that a certain amount of income should be put aside during a person's active life for use when he or she is no longer able to work because of old age or invalidity, or, in the case of pensions for surviving dependents, dies leaving behind a family. Existing pension systems are running into increasing difficulties as a result of three factors: first, the decrease in the number of working years within a life-cycle due to both a delay in starting to work, resulting from long periods of education and nowadays the growing long-term unemployment of young people, and an earlier pensionable age, stemming from early retirement and a reduction in the minimum age, above all to meet the increasingly urgent need to inject new blood into the workforce; second, the extension of the average lifespan which lengthens the pension-drawing period and increasingly involves periods of semi-independence and chronic illness during which the cost of survival is very high; and third, the devaluing by inflation of pensions built up over many years. It is therefore possible to point to three general levels of inadequacy in pension systems. The most general concerns the fact that the calculations on which the systems were originally based now have to be re-done: previously, the amount required to support a household of elderly persons for, at most, ten years was saved during forty to fifty years of work, whereas now the period of saving has dropped to between thirty and forty years and the period of maintenance in old age has risen to between twenty and thirty years. The second and third levels have regard to the great inconsistency in the relationships between needs and resources in the two distinct periods into which the lives of old people are often divided. In the first period, the pension is generally not too inadequate and old people are, moreover, still able to go on working. It is often the case that the institutional and fiscal system and the fragmentation of the occupational structure converge in fostering the spread of informal work by pensioners. This is an important area for the informalization of work, alongside that fed by the inadequacies of national and social insurance schemes. It is not only or even mainly the low level of pensions that favours a complementary relationship with irregular forms of work, but above all the interweaving between institutional and fiscal restraints, on the one side, and the fragmentation of the labour market on the other. A growing number of old people who survive until the second stage may have to face the dramatic situation in which three factors coincide: the loss of a pension's purchasing power; a decreasing ability to undertake irregular work; and the increasing risk of illness and of long periods of almost total dependence on others. It is no accident that in many industrial societies, especially in the large cities, a growing proportion of the poor who become entrapped in serious social difficulties are isolated elderly individuals or couples.

I shall need to return to many of the problems associated with the social areas selected for welfare intervention in section 4. There, I consider the matter from the different angle of survival strategies and the working activities engaged in by the surplus population.

The limits to and contradictions in welfare-state provision of services

The recent trends towards the privatization and restructuring of the welfare state have been taking place mainly, though not exclusively, in the area of producing services essential for the quality of social repro-duction; in general, these are education, health, public transport and urban infrastructures, including housing. Since this is a huge field that throws up a vast array of controversial questions, I can do no more than discuss in schematic terms a small number of important issues.

It is difficult not to be attracted to the idea that the expansion of state involvement in the production of services has been determined by the need to transform the qualitative side of social reproduction in such a way as to favour the consolidation of increasingly productive labour processes. On the other hand, a too strongly deterministic connection reveals serious defects. It is sufficient to mention the controversy sur-rounding the 'functional utility' of high or growing levels of school attendance. The existing employment structure is unable to utilize adequately either those generations made up almost entirely of school-certificate holders or an ever increasing number of graduates and post-graduates. From this perspective, the high and growing school attendance index clearly represents a waste of human resources, given the continually low and often decreasing demand for qualified workers within the existing job structure. The level of this index is, however, also important from another angle, and increasingly so. Often, the resources provided by education are not only useful for work but also for life in general. Beyond the narrow horizons of job specialization, school prepares young people for the discipline of organized work and imparts to them the mental flexibility indispensable in difficult situations. Moreover, given the recent high occupational mobility and growing flexibility in production, the complex resources obtained through higher levels of education can be used either to find new employment quickly or gradually to advance a working career. All of this has been widely confirmed by studies into social mobility and stratification,[12] which show that the level of education continues to act as an important discriminating factor.

This digression has not only served to criticize the limits of deterministic approaches and to introduce the question of reproductive services as part of citizenship rights; it also provides some hints for shedding light on one of the most contradictory areas in welfare provision. From the ideological viewpoint of Beveridge and Marshall, the welfare state is seen as a system of citizens' rights which are universal and aim to counterbalance those disadvantages that continue to arise in the area of market relationships. This ideology comes up against the evidence that the most disadvantaged cannot avoid cumulating handicaps and that, as a general rule, even the most enlightened models of welfare provision unintentionally benefit middle- or middle-to-low-income groups, including large numbers of stable local working-class families, to the detriment of a persistent and substantial group of marginalized individuals, ethnic minorities, immigrants and unskilled workers.

It must be underlined that welfare services have developed within a twofold and contradictory reference system. On the one hand, they have been promoted for the purpose of supporting a qualitative transformation in the patterns of social reproduction in line with the growth in the productivity of labour. On the other hand, they have been the main field in which citizens' rights have progressed, but to a large extent they have no real connection with the world of work. Consequently, important contradictions have arisen on both fronts. Furthermore, the trends towards privatization and de-universalization or the limitations inherent in state welfare services have had a wide-ranging and decisive effect on the socio-occupational structure; this transformation is contributing extensively to the spread of irregular and heterogeneous forms of work.

I have already mentioned the first important limitation characterizing the advanced capitalist model of welfare provision: although it encourages the employment of women, they are persistently subjected to discrimination in this field, and this is increasingly in contradiction with the universalistic impetus arising out of the development of welfare systems. There is a variety of evidence to show that this is the case: the rise in female employment; the concentration of the latter in welfare services, whether private or public, and in relatively poorly paid jobs (moreover, in the private sector irregular, occasional, part-time and temporary employment is on the increase); and increasing equality of access for men and women to welfare services, in particular the system of mass education, including university. This limitation remained latent as long as the dominant model of social reproduction continued to function as such; in other words, as long as the number of jobs for men in manufacturing industry paying a family wage and in highly professional careers in services continued to rise. However, growing tensions accumulated and exploded with de-industrialization and the fiscal crisis of the state. The emergence at the end of the 1960s and subsequent growth of the contemporary feminist movement should be viewed in relation to the build-up of the above-mentioned contradiction.

The second limitation is the high and increasing cost of providing welfare services on a universalistic basis; in this respect, the important role played by demands that the quality of services be maintained and even improved must also be remembered. Since this question is dealt with in the next section, only a few introductory remarks will be made here.

As a general rule, the state's role is not only to extend access to welfare services to social strata that would never be able to procure them in the market; it also has the objective of controlling the quality of services. This is something that cannot be left solely to the unequal relation between user and market in what is a crucial social area. Yet quality control is so costly that the state has often found it more convenient to provide the services directly rather than set up a complicated system of state control over private provision. Examples of this are the history of the National Health Service in Britain; the original motives behind the setting up of a state health service in Italy at the very time when the welfare state was beginning to be dismantled elsewhere; and the fact that, in the Western world, the strongly dualistic American health service is the most expensive kind for the state to run, while being among the least efficient in terms of the number of citizens covered.[13] It is, however, true that the private sector is in a better position than the state to adopt flexible and irregular forms of using labour and thereby save on running costs; but it remains to be seen how much of the saving obtained in this way benefits the user in terms of reduced costs or taxes and how much goes towards boosting the profits of private companies. Several categories of workers in this sector are paid relatively low wages by the state; but generally this is compensated for by the guarantee of stable employment, as the state is unable to make direct use of the increasing forms of irregular employment – multiple jobholders, casual workers and immigrants.[14] The complete privatization and the contracting out of state welfare services means that the possibility of using irregular labour is being increasingly considered as a serious option. Thus, whether services are provided publicly or privately, the question of cost has two sides to it: first, the growing difficulty in controlling the quality of services, which is a serious matter since what is at stake is not a car or an electrical household appliance but medical care or education or nursery provision; and second, the possible spread of highly impoverished forms of employment, and this problem is also crucial if one takes into account that services in general form the most important sector for the growth in irregular jobs, though not the only one.

Mention has already been made of the third important limitation. This consists in the fact that even where there is greater emphasis on the universalistic nature of services and on the granting of citizens' rights, the system of state welfare services has been unable to eliminate discrimination in terms of access, which often compounds the inequalities created by the market. The development of school education and public health have at best extended the possibility of access to middle- and middle-to-low-income groups, but to the detriment of low-income groups who have thus found themselves subjected to a twofold discrimination. This is playing an increasingly significant role in social systems in which the access to high-quality services is becoming an essential factor in avoiding social marginalization. An important dispute has arisen around this limitation over the possibility of reducing the universalistic character of welfare services in order to direct them principally at more disadvantaged groups; such a policy, however, would also involve renouncing important democratic ideals and intensify the social stigmatization attached to these services.

This last limitation should also be viewed in conjunction with developments in the cost of services and their overloading due to massive demand. In many respects, the system is potentially infinite in its need to grow: once a demand has been satisfied, the cost of which is continually rising, another important one emerges, or else new ways of improving the quality of intervention. Health provides a clear example. The services in this area face increasing problems from all directions: new illnesses like AIDS; the extension of new techniques of treatment, in some cases very costly, to all those who need them; the increase in certain groups of the population subject to a higher risk of illness, particularly with reference to the overall ageing of the population; the emergence of more advanced and sophisticated issues such as demands for the development of preventive medicine and the widespread adoption of artifical insemination; and so on.

The picture of overloading outlined above is independent of the particular balance between private and public (see also Klein and O'Higgins,

1985). A highly privatized system is by definition more selective; but this does not mean that it can automatically solve problems of cost, efficiency, quality, extension of services and, lastly, overloading. On the whole, the critical problems re-emerge at different levels. The slimming down of the state welfare apparatus can bring about financial savings by reducing bureaucracy, but this does not automatically solve the above-mentioned problems. In this sense, it is important to consider actual examples of the complex balance between the social costs involved in privatization – such as giving up control over the quality of services and employment, renunciation of the political belief underlying the univer-salistic approach, the danger of being unable to intervene if further increases in costs are imposed on the users whom the state wishes to continue protecting – and the benefits from reducing the welfare state apparatus.

Summarizing, there are three areas of internal friction: first, the mal-functioning of an extensive bureaucracy whose uncontrollable tendency to expand is not related to any increase or improvement in the services provided; second, the crucial political role within the state apparatus assumed by several key professions in the welfare services; and third, the vitiating of state intervention as a result of the incompatibility between the efficiency of state services and their exploitation by political parties in terms of favouritism to boost electoral support. These areas of friction have been widely discussed in the socio-political literature and in specific studies of complex organizations and bureaucracies (see Cousins, 1987). The first and the third represent real extra costs to the public purse when placed alongside more restricted private organizations operating in the market. The second is more controversial and also affects privatized modes of provision. It cannot be dealt with here, apart from one obser-vation that directly concerns the spread of irregular forms of employment. It seems plausible to assert that the more state control over the welfare services and over their efficiency is weakened, the more those higher up on the occupational scale in these services also work informally in the private sector. This tendency is the greater where there is a more highly developed, complex and uncontrolled interweaving between the public and private sectors, as can be seen in the case of Italy in chapter 6.

The thesis according to which large bureaucracies cross the threshold at which functional efficiency is kept under control is entirely credible. In the case of welfare services, one possibility would be to replace oversized state bureaucracy with decentralized forms of local and sectoral autonomy and control. Recent political trends are highly debatable in this respect. The Thatcher governments in Britain, in particular, have married trends towards privatization with vigorous centralization, which may saddle the welfare state with a double burden: lack of control over the private sector and the rigidity and ungovernable nature of an overcentralized state apparatus (see Bean et al., 1985; Harris and Seldon, 1987). However, this transformation is still at too early a stage for any precise evaluation. In general, it may be stated that crossing the size threshold at which a system is manageable leads to both a decrease in efficiency and the adoption of alternative solutions. The diffusion of informal practices and employment in private services can be put down in part to this critical factor in the state welfare system, especially where the latter has for historical reasons taken on a concentrated and rigid form and is not subject to effective local and sectoral control.

It is also true that the increase in jobs in a state bureaucracy does not obey the rules of market competition. In simple terms, the entire bureaucratic hierarchy is in general favourable to hiring more staff, especially at the lower levels. The motive is to increase the power of those at the top and allow everyone else to take one more step up the career ladder, mainly based on years of service. Since it is difficult, impossible or impracticable to control efficiency and productivity, this motive becomes a permanent one. Furthermore, this is an area in which the interests of the bureaucracy may overlap with those of the political class, intent on exploiting welfare services to gain political support through favouritism. No politico-bureaucratic system can be considered as totally immune to this twin pressure, while some are strongly conditioned by it, as is shown below in the case of Southern Italy. Obviously, such a process leads to a crisis of efficiency in services, above all when it is in the hands of politicians who use it for dispensing patronage. Moreover, this is a process which has a high potential for expansion both from the bureaucratic and the political angles, in the sense that the most powerful and already oversized bureaucratic sectors have great power inside the system, which they use to expand even further, and that a political class oriented to consensus based on patronage and unable to offer efficient services has to continue recruitment on the basis of favouritism in order to stay in power. The specific analysis of Southern Italy shows that this process also leads towards the informalization of work.

In conclusion, what has been called the post-welfare age of privatized services and a much reduced public sector is characterized by very strong tendencies towards the fragmentation of the social fabric and the occupational structure. The very social policies of some governments, rather than bolstering the mainstream economy or directing more effective attention towards doubly penalized sectors of the population, are fostering informalization and the spread of irregular kinds of work in various ways. As specific contemporary cases show, these originate almost exclusively with the reorganization of services in terms of both the way labour is employed and the way in which services are provided (see also Johnson, 1987; Brown, 1988).

3 THE TERTIARIZATION CYCLE: SELF-PROVISIONING AND THE INFORMALIZATION OF SERVICE EMPLOYMENT

Critical remarks on the interpretation of tertiarization in terms of an emergent self-service society

The processes of tertiarization have much greater impact on the transformation of socio-occupational systems than the processes of industrial restructuring. Furthermore, the different ways in which services are provided and used has a strong impact on the quality of life for various social groups in diverse social settings. These are two reasons why it is important to take as a starting-point an interpretation which makes it possible to understand the meaning of contemporary trends in tertiarization. For the sake of clarity, the problems related to the reshaping of the welfare state discussed above will be ignored for the time being.

The interpretational model I have chosen is the one formulated by Gershuny to explain the 'self-service society' (Gershuny, 1978; 1983; Gershuny and Miles, 1983). It is founded on two assumptions: that Ernst Engel's law of the hierarchy of consumption applies, and that there exists a technological gap between different economic sectors in terms of increasing labour productivity. According to Engel's law, industrial development brings about an upward shift in demand along a scale with, at the bottom, subsistence goods for satisfying the basic needs of food, clothing and shelter and, at the top, increasingly refined non-essential services. By causing average incomes to rise, industrial development is seen to promote a more than proportional growth in the demand for services. This process is believed to provide the main explanation for the trend towards tertiarization in advanced capitalist societies.

The second assumption is that the different branches of the economy vary in their capacity to increase labour productivity through the introduction of technological innovations. Most of the sectors producing services are, for technical reasons, particularly unreceptive to such change. The technological gap is evident and has been documented in several activities like bars, restaurants, hotels, personal services and maintenance. In other cases, the situation is more complex and contradictory, as is shown below. The technological gap gives rise to an important problem in those sectors with a low capacity for increasing labour productivity: the rise in the cost of living brought about by increases in productivity in the rest of the economy leads to higher costs and prices in these sectors. Furthermore, the fast rate of tertiarization when measured by the number of employees is explained by the persistent labour-intensive nature of services.

What is original in Gershuny's thesis is the assertion that the simultaneous twin pressure on the service sector of expansion and the impossibility of directly increasing labour productivity tends to transform consumption patterns in the direction of self-service. There are two different sides to this change. In some cases consumption patterns are not modified, in the sense that a final service is still the object of consumption but the work process is transformed: the paid labour of employees is replaced by the unpaid labour of consumers. Examples are self-service in stores, restaurants, petrol stations and automatic cash dispensers. For Gershuny, however, the crucial change is that which entirely revolutionizes the act of consumption and provision, where the consumer no longer acquires a ready service but rather a product made by industry which he uses to provide the service himself. He maintains that the most important instances of this are the motor car and television, which heralded a revolution in transport and recreational services. Instead of purchasing a final service in the form of a train or bus ride or going to the theatre or cinema, consumers acquire automobiles for self-transportation or television sets to provide amusement in their own homes. To bolster the interpretational force of his thesis, he adds that in the age of microcomputers and audio-visual media, the tendency for change in the direction of self-service has the potential to penetrate the two most important areas in the service sector: education and health. Here, the spread of small, easy-to-use and inexpensive computers and video-recording equipment could make it possible for people to educate and cure themselves, obviously within certain limits. The success of the Open University in England in terms of both the quality of education and the number of enrolments, achieved with the sole aid of audio-visual media before more sophisticated instruments for conveying information became available, is put forward as a confirmation of this hypothesis (see Gershuny and Miles, 1983, pp. 85–7).

I will endeavour to show that Gershuny's main assumptions as expounded here are debatable and that the identification of the trend towards a self-service society as the sole important outcome of the tertiarization process is too simplistic. A useful starting-point can be found in some critical observations concerning the two basic assumptions in Gershuny's model. Taken in isolation, Engel's law is inadequate for understanding the process of tertiarization for at least two reasons, which drastically curtail its power to explain. First, it totally ignores one of the most important areas for the expansion of the tertiary sector: that of services to firms. Here, growth can be explained in terms of changes in the division of labour and in the organizational scale of highly industrialized societies (see also Walker, 1985). It is the industrial system itself which encompasses within its own forms of growth the expansion of pre-existing services (banks and other financial institutions), the separation and specialization of services previously incorporated in manufacturing industry (consultancy, maintenance, transport, research) or the demand for new kinds of services (advertising and marketing, market research). With regard to the expansion of final services, Engel's law leaves much to be explained. There are few final services which are of the luxury kind with an elastic consumption pattern and to which the law could be applied, such as, for example, recreational or free time services. For most final services, more complex explanations are required to account for the growth in their demand; the rise in incomes and changes in their distribution represent only a contributory factor. It is the social transformations of the industrial age which cause the emergence of mass services, such as transporting people over ever greater distances or acess to higher levels of education, and the break-up of traditional service areas. Despite this criticism, the essential point that Gershuny derives mainly from Engel's law is still plausible: industrialization is bringing about an irresistible expansion in service activities, whether they result from market demand or from needs that both lie outside the market and cannot be satisfied within traditional reciprocal networks.

As for the second assumption, a serious critical consideration would entail analysing in detail the relationship between types of work and the possibilities of real increases in labour productivity in widely differing areas, from banks to transport, from the retail trade to education and health. Here, it is only possible to make a few observations. To start with, it is insufficient to formulate the explanation of the technological gap exclusively in technical terms, that is, the non-availability of techniques for directly increasing labour productivity. In the use and consumption of many services, quality plays a role of fundamental importance and is what helps to maintain the intensive use of labour at high levels; standardization would end up by cancelling the use content of services. Also in the manufacturing sector, the handmade product of a craftsman, a unique object, is much more expensive and of a different quality than the mass-produced good. Nevertheless, the latter has its uses and the vast majority of consumers willingly accept standardized products. In theory, a doctor could use a sophisticated piece of technical equipment to reduce the time of an examination to a few minutes, thereby increasing his productivity. Most patients, however, would not be happy with a two-minute medical check-up in place of a reassuringly accurate examination lasting more than half an hour, even though the same individuals could not afford hand-decorated clothes. Naturally, the role assumed by the quality factor varies greatly in a sector as heterogeneous as services.

There is a further pre-technological consideration regarding services which is just as important. It concerns the bonds that tie the labour process to a particular locality and the impossibility of achieving accentuated forms of centralization and concentration. This does not apply equally to all branches either and, furthermore, renders the question of innovation problematical: many technological innovations can only be applied to labour processes in the service sector when they achieve a combination of low cost, high flexibility and simplicity of operation that allows them to be used in limited, decentralized local areas.

The above considerations help to account for the existence of two concurrent, but opposed, trends: on the one hand, standardization and reduced production costs and, on the other, higher quality and greater production costs. In the USA in the 1970s, for example, the proliferation of fast-food establishments occurred alongside a considerable growth in sophisticated expensive restaurants offering top-quality service. As is shown below, analogous processes are also taking place in other branches of this sector.

The conditions of and limits to self-service trends

The reasoning behind Gershuny's model can only be considered sound if it is subjected to further elaboration. At this stage, it is clearly necessary for the core of the model to be given a more complex structure, since it is that part which sees in the emergence of self-service activities the only response in terms of social change to the problems created by the expansion of services and their persistently labour-intensive nature. Careful consideration of the process of tertiarization reveals at least two other potential responses to the pressure caused by these factors: first, intervention by the state to supply free of charge or at a 'political' price services for which a mass 'need' arises, because it is impossible for such needs to be generally satisfied at market prices/costs; and second, a relative squeeze on the wages or incomes of workers and a deterioration of the working conditions in these activities, including the diffusion of various forms of irregular employment.

The identification of these three main responses needs to be completed by two further observations. In many aspects and phases of the tertiariz-

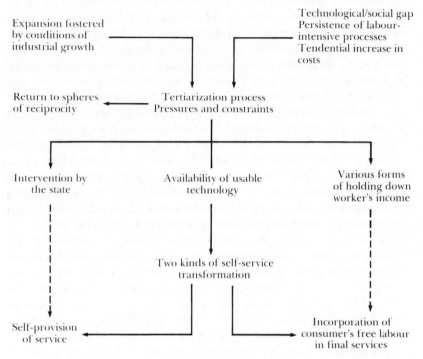

Figure 4.1 The service cycle

ation process, these three responses overlap in complex combinations. In some cases, it cannot be excluded that a service may return to the undergrowth of reciprocal relations from whence it arose, even though its social and technological conditions have changed. In this area, examples present many difficulties of interpretation; none the less, it is worth dwelling briefly on the most obvious one, housework done for third parties or, in other words, the employing of helpers in the home. For this type of service, intervention by the state is effective to a very limited extent, being feasible only in the case of activities that can be separated out from their domestic environment (canteens or kindergartens, hospitalization of the sick, etc.) or in the case of relatively limited strata of the population in particularly difficult situations (like lonely old people assisted at home by social services). Until now, the effect of technological innovation has been to modify the quality of services, but not to curtail drastically the time needed for domestic work (Vanek, 1974; Gershuny and Thomas, 1984). Thus, the more or less widespread phenomenon of a stock of standard household applicances which have no bearing at all on the question of who performs the housework: full- or part-time wage-workers, full- or part-time housewives, various divisions of tasks among the members of a household, or a mixture of the above. Until advanced all-purpose robots become available at a low price, the problem should be seen as lying within the unstable balance between complex and varying requirements and the availability of potential labour at accept-able conditions inside the household and on the labour market. The possibility of squeezing the relative incomes of workers plays a crucial role. If it becomes impossible, the service tends to fall back under changed conditions on the sphere of reciprocal relations; if, on the other hand, this possibility continues to exist, there is a further expansion in the use of paid labour. This line of argument is, of course, too simplistic; nevertheless it is able to explain why, with other conditions being equal, the number of home helpers shows a tendency to rise when and where there are workers ready to accept wages pegged at the same low levels and to fall if such a situation does not apply. In the USA, the figure tends to rise in those states with large concentrations of illegal immigrants and to fall in others where they find it more difficult to settle. This example has involved anticipating the question of the specific conditions that favour the prevalence of one trend over the other or particular combinations of the various solutions.

Gershuny discusses the socio-political conditions that make it possible for consumption patterns to move in the direction of those forms of self-service which interest him most. In these, instead of receiving a ready service consumers use a product manufactured by industry to provide the service themselves. As he puts it:

1 Investment in equipment (and purchase of necessary materials) typically by the individual or household seeking the service (e.g. cars, TV, petrol pumps);
2 collective investment in material ('hardware') infrastructure (e.g. roads, broadcasting networks);
3 provision of non-material activities ('software' activities, e.g. TV programmes), and other intermediate consumer services (such as maintenance of domestic equipment);
4 unpaid 'informal' labour using the first three elements to produce the final service functions (e.g. driving a private car)(Gershuny and Miles, 1983, pp. 84–5).

Apart from the third condition, where it can be assumed on the whole that the spread of the new mass forms of consuming services will provide more market opportunities to private operators, the social, economic and political significance of the other three is considerable.

The first involves a rise in income for wide sections of the population such that a sufficient number of households are able to afford their own basic equipment. It is not a coincidence, therefore, that the self-service transformation based on private vehicles and television sets occurred in a period of rapid economic growth. The second condition implies not only the capacity to undertake large-scale public investment, but also the political will to do this in one sector rather than another. Everyone is well aware of the important role played by the private vehicle lobbies in promoting the revolution in private mass transport. This case also serves to show the drastic and irreversible nature of the choices made in the attempt to render this transformation as profound as possible; they have led at a later stage to widespread difficulties. In the United States, for example, the urban public transit systems were largely neglected for thirty years with the consequence that their necessary reconstruction in the last fifteen years has been very costly. But even in the less radically altered European systems, private transport has in the long run brought with it an uncontrolled rising cost to the whole community, leading to the dilemma of whether to put up with a continual slowing down of increasingly chaotic traffic or to dedicate huge resources to building parking lots and multilevel road systems.

The examples that Gershuny puts forward are, however, controversial because in them the old patterns of consumption have not been totally abandoned in favour of the new; in fact, there is no doubt that they coexist in contemporary societies. This means that governments must increase investment in both directions. The new systems require a massive effort to be made, first in providing infrastructures and then in gradually adapting them. Precisely because they have been partly abandoned by the mass of the public, the old systems are less and less self-sustaining, with the result that, unless completely dismantled, they require increasing injections of public money. In short, the second condition entails the political will to act and the economic resources for increasing public intervention.

Finally, the fourth condition is particularly difficult to deal with since it concerns the allocation of consumers' time, so only a few remarks on this topic are possible here. Accurate knowledge is needed of how the time dedicated to a self-service activity is allocated compared to the previously existing allocation. In the case of television, the time devoted to self-service continues to have an effect on the ways in which free time is used, even though there is a considerable difference between playing cards with friends, going to the cinema or theatre or reading a book, and watching television at home. On the other hand, the driving of a motor car for relatively long periods is more problematical: it is radically different from snoozing or reading a newspaper on a commuter train. In general, the main beneficiaries in terms of time within the self-service transformation are those who are not forced into an unfavourable reallocation, because they dedicate to self-service either the time previously allocated to the same end or because they use free time released from other working activities.

From what has been said above there emerges a sociological profile both of the social groups which, under certain conditions, may help to bring about this kind of transformation and of the specific spatial and temporal factors that may facilitate it. It is evident that neither the pressures inherent in the tertiarization process nor technical innovations nor public sponsorship on their own are enough to promote such a transformation. There must also be a sufficiently wide layer of households to which it offers a rational way to invest money and allocate time. In other words, what is required is an extensive stratum of average- or above-average-income earners who expect to enjoy a stable rising income and have sufficient free time to be in a position to use self-service equipment rationally. Nevertheless, experience in the case of the private motor car and of the television set shows how, once this process is under way, consumers for whom this transformation is not fully rational become dragged into it. The dragging-in mechanism strongly affects both those who are short of time (they buy the tools but rarely use them) and those who do not have sufficient funds and are compelled to sacrifice primary consumption to the purchase of self-service items. This last situation leads to a marked distortion of 'models of consumption'; the well-known phenomenon of shanty dwellers who possess cars and television sets. At this level, the question of time/space is simple: the transformation only takes place when and where the preliminary conditions cumulate, although it does also spread elsewhere due to the dragging-in mechanism but with highly distorted results and effectiveness.

Gershuny does not dwell on the other form of self-service transformation, that is, the one involving no radical change in consumption patterns but simply the incorporation of a portion of the consumer's own unpaid labour into the act of consuming a ready service. Past experience shows that, in general, the consumer does not lose out in terms of time – on the contrary, self-service provides for greater rapidity in many cases – but rather meets with a considerable reduction in quality. What happens is that the service is subjected to increasing standardization. At a self-service petrol station it is not possible to have the oil changed or a faulty engine looked at. A department store will not stock minority sizes or highly sophisticated articles of clothing. And so on. It is not by chance that the process of standardization in self-service activities is accompanied by the spread of sophisticated forms of providing the service at a considerably higher and rising cost. Specific types of consumption are greatly disadvantaged by this organizational polarization. Take, for example, people who wear outsize clothes, those who have to follow special diets for reasons of health and anyone whose car breaks down at the weekend or in the evening and has to do without it because the only petrol stations open are of the self-service kind where there is no skilled mechanic to put right a simple fault.

From the point of view of changes in the labour process, this type of transformation often brings with it a radical de-skilling of the workers' tasks. The occupational skills affected by it are generally those at the higher levels, while jobs with little or no skill content may increase in number. A drastic example in this direction is the appearance of fast-food restaurants. Not only does the consumer supply free labour, but a saving is also made on waiters, head waiters, cooks and chefs, all jobs requiring a certain degree of skill, while there is a greater deployment of counter staff, dishwashers and cleaners, on tasks which require no apprenticeship or continuity of work, making it a simple matter to use temporary, often black market labour (immigrants, students or minors). In this sense, the spread of these types of self-service activities is entirely consistent with the other important change in the employment structure brought about by tertiarization, that is the squeezing of wages and/or incomes and the informalization of working conditions.

Again in the case of the diffusion of self-service activities characterized by the incorporation of consumers' free labour, there are several indicators which help us to build up a picture of the environment favourable to the spread of such a transformation. In the first place, it must have sufficient potential to absorb the various forms of service standardization and the accompanying process of polarization. It is essential that the consumption patterns are relatively concentrated within a particular area, since in small dispersed towns the market is not large enough for services to be developed along the two opposite poles of quality. A further requirement is a satisfactory level of cultural and economic acceptance of the standardization and polarization process. There are two sides to this. On the one hand, the potential consumers of the standardized service must be sufficient in number to render the operation profitable. For example, there must be a suitable number of customers willing to adopt the consumption patterns of hamburger restaurants from both a cultural as well as a monetary angle. If the potential customers are merely a handful of youngsters who can only afford to eat out once a month, the initiative will be a failure. This transformation reflects and heightens a trend towards social polarization already in existence for other reasons. This polarization acts as an input into both consumption patterns and the process whereby de-skilled jobs are made available for the reorganization of work in self-service establishments.

The complex picture of tertiarization and informalization

The question of state intervention has already been dealt with in the previous section. I will limit myself here to a few essential considerations in treating the problems raised by the present stage in the transformation of the tertiarization process. There is no doubting the fundamental role played by the state in furthering industrialization through the financing of infrastructures and the expansion of services. What are still today much more controversial issues are those connected with the logic and modes of intervention by the state, including the wide-ranging contemporary debate on the difficulties of the welfare state and how to move beyond it. For the specific purpose of formulating a model with which to interpret the tertiarization process, it is important to discuss several points concerning principally the resources required for tertiarization, independently of the specific ways in which they are allocated.

To begin with, it is evident that state intervention is costly and therefore presupposes an injection of resources into promoting forms of tertiarization. This occurs independently of the fact that such intervention is subsequently interpreted, in the final analysis, as a subsidy to maintain or expand the process of capital accumulation (critics on the left) or as wasteful and an obstacle to further growth (the 'neo-liberal' critics). In this sense, the availability of a growing stock of resources for investing in the process constitutes an essential prerequisite in this type of response to the pressures that mature within capitalist accumulation. I have already alluded to the fact that, as well as direct intervention by the state, this also involves fostering expensive ways to spread the first kind of self-service activities. The increasing public cost of private vehicles and radio and television broadcasting supports this interpretation. At the same time, Gershuny's hypothesis that the transformation of large areas of welfare in the direction of self-service, such as education and health, may instead lead to substantial savings in public money, is unconvincing.

Recent trends in the state provision of services, such as privatization, contracting out, selective de-universalization, etc., are not leading to a generalized expansion of self-provisioning; rather they are resulting in a complex mix of self-provisioning and a deterioration in working conditions, together with the holding down of wages in the services them-

selves. Consequently, the justifiable question arises of whether tertiarization may now begin to have a negative effect on industrial growth,
whatever the specific policies adopted by governments. That this concern
is in fact legitimate is confirmed by the generalized spread of difficulties
in the welfare state, though there are of course profound differences
between various individual cases. In this respect, Gershuny's one-way
model not only rests on a flimsy basis due to its failure to offer a practical
prospect for making savings in resources; it is also unrealistic in that it
boils down to a proposal to make big increases in additional investment
– and this in a period in which economic difficulties are having a negative
effect precisely in terms of the lack of additional resources that need to
be fed into the process to prevent problems arising. Here the example of
the Open University in Britain is significant. Although it was set up with
high standards in mind, which clearly entailed a notable injection of
resources by the state, it is not an alternative to maintaining and
developing the traditional university system. It is, instead, an additional
system which manages at a favourable cost-to-quality ratio to provide a
fairly large number of people with a university education who would
otherwise be unable to obtain one.

    The reformulation of Gershuny's model in more complex and struc-
tured terms leads to an approach in which particular emphasis is placed
on the reduction of incomes and the worsening of working conditions as
the main response to the internal pressures within the tertiarization
process. This line of reasoning is supported by a now sufficiently extensive
range of information and data. Already at the beginning of the 1970s,
Bravermann (1974) noted that in the United States jobs at very low or
inadequate rates of pay were concentrated in services and that this was
a progressively rising trend. Subsequent observers have pointed out that
in English-speaking countries there is a tendency for the lower end of
the retail trade to become the almost exclusive preserve of ethnic minorities. At the same time, studies of the informal sector and the kinds of
work involved have revealed that they are particularly widespread in
services. The further expansion of informalization indicates that the
squeezing of workers' wages in many branches of the service sector is
becoming increasingly incompatible with existing legal regulations
(Henry, 1981; *Inchiesta*, 1983; Redclift and Mingione, 1985; EEC,
1989b). It is not a chance occurrence that the vast majority of recent
immigrant workers from the Third World have been employed in the
service sector (see chapter 6 for data referring to Italy).

    All things considered, the hypothesis may be advanced that this type
of response to the internal pressures in the service sector is so strong that
it completely disrupts social stratification and the labour market. The

tendency to squeeze the wages and working conditions of an ever-increasing number of workers in the private tertiary sector reaches a lower limit below which, under normal circumstances, the local surplus population is unwilling to accept employment. It is at this point that, where possible, clandestine workers find an opening, since for various reasons they are able and willing to accept worse conditions; they include immigrants from underdeveloped countries, young people and women in temporary casual jobs, minors and moonlighters. This process contributes to a rapid acceleration in the trend towards a polarized social structure, which had been almost totally forgotten in the advanced capitalist countries during the twenty years of substantial economic growth following the Second World War. This trend is fully reflected in American data on the changes in social stratification in the 1970s (Sassen-Koob, 1983; 1984): social strata with low incomes grew considerably and those with high incomes very little, all to the detriment of middle-income strata, reduced by almost one half in a decade from just under 50 per cent to less than 30 per cent. Such a change cannot, of course, be put down entirely to the tertiary sector; it also follows from the consequences of the economic crisis and the forms assumed by the technological restructuring of manufacturing industry. The tertiary sector, however, plays a very important role in extending the overall trend. At the same time, it tends to generate the kinds of demand and supply of labour that characterize a process of social polarization. These will be looked at briefly. Stagnation restricts the possibility of releasing the tensions in the tertiarization process chiefly through transformations of the self-service type in conjunction with a radical change in consumption patterns (the main hypothesis in Gershuny's original model) and further massive state intervention. As a result, the tensions are released mainly through the standardization of public services and the squeezing of workers' incomes, unless the services are re-absorbed into the sphere of reciprocal relations. The consequent worsening of conditions at the lower end of the labour market in some branches of the service sector tends to boost even further the demand for services at a very low cost. The crisis in employment, generalized throughout society and increasingly linked to the international economy, provides a growing supply of labour for this type of response. At the other end, polarization towards the upper levels of employment generates a demand for highly personalized services in which the persistent supply of docile labour at low wages makes it possible to keep certain jobs in existence such as home helpers, shop delivery boys, sales staff in specialized boutiques and so on, which would otherwise die out due to the too high cost of labour. If what has been said above is true, the situation is quite different from the scenarios of the self-service society formulated by Gershuny.

Before moving on to my concluding remarks, I should like to mention again the question of the return of service activities into the area of reciprocal relations, self-provisioning within the household or kinship and local community networks. In this regard, the possibility has been discussed that the 'regression' of some service activities to reciprocal networks may be favoured by the availability of new technologies or by different social conditions (Burns, 1975; 1977; Gershuny, 1983). It seems to me that, given the present state of affairs, the problem must be viewed from the other end. Industrial development has stripped the traditional reciprocal networks of their capacity to resolve on their own many of the problems created by the need for certain services; this applies both to the structures of households and to that of kinship, friendship and communities. Here, the possible areas must be borne in mind in which the conditions for advantageous social relationships can be recovered without forgetting the existence of further disruptive pressures. Consider, for example, the increase in one-parent households and those made up of working women with dependent children or relations. The same applies to communities as a result of the more intense forms of social and geographical mobility corresponding to life-cycles with progressively longer periods of uncertainty and debilitation, as is the case with youth unemployment and the prolonging of the period of retirement and of old age. Under these circumstances, to rely on the mirage of a voluntary and solidarity-based 'third sector', in addition to the market and the state, may lead to considerable social discrimination and tension.

The improvement on Gershuny's model in the way proposed here permits a closer adherence to a reality that has a highly complex structure. At present the self-service option is not the only nor always the prevailing one, because it meets increasing obstacles: the polarization of the social structure; the relative decline of state investment; and the presence of conditions favouring the squeeze on incomes and the spread of various forms of irregular employment in the tertiary sector.

4 THE SURVIVAL STRATEGIES OF THE CONTEMPORARY SURPLUS POPULATION

The theoretical connections between the surplus population and informal activities

It is evident that the existence of widespread informal activities calls for some concept or other of surplus population. This term designates an excess part of the population that, either willingly or unwillingly and for different reasons, works and survives totally or partially outside formal labour channels, which are subjected to regulation in a wide sense by means of various legal, political and social mechanisms (Offe, 1985; Bagnasco, 1985; 1988).[15] Closer inspection, however, shows that any concept of surplus population is likely to suffer from theoretical inconsistency. It comes into being as a negative response to hegemonic explanatory models based on the roles played by political institutions and by a regulated and organized market. But the existence of surplus population, especially of the long-term kind, cannot be explained at all by referring to these models. In this sense, the Marxist theory of surplus population insists on its relative and transitory nature. As we saw above, according to Marx the growth and spread of capitalist relations of production continues to produce surplus population which is in excess relative to the economy's capacity to absorb the labour supply at the moment it is formed and acts as a reserve army for the subsequent waves of capitalist expansion. Neither Marx nor later Marxist writers are particularly interested in explaining in depth the 'mystery' of how surplus population survives. This is because its theoretical role is limited in Marx's theory of capital to its 'function' as a reserve army of labour and to its historically 'relative' nature.[16] I will return briefly below to the fact that, in reality, by putting forward a typology in which the reserve army is divided up Marx suggests its main conditions of survival. These are, however, increasingly less viable in contemporary societies.

Today, Marx's theory of relative surplus population is for the most part inadequate since the emphasis has necessarily been shifted on to the 'absolute' nature of the phenomenon (Paci, 1982; Ginatempo, 1983), its existence over a long period and, therefore, the ways in which it persists; the latter are difficult to locate in the socio-economic processes that may explain its origins. At the same time, however, it would at present be difficult to deny that the growth and spread of capitalism and the formation of surplus population are historically connected, given that one cannot fail to note the effects of labour-saving innovations, the increasingly rapid internationalization of capitalist competition, the penetration of modern market relations into the outermost reaches of the globe, and so on. It would perhaps be of more use to analyse in greater depth the relationship between specific patterns of industrial development and the creation of different forms of surplus population. In my view, it is possible to argue that chronically low labour productivity, the relative waste of resources and the scarcity of products in official markets, together with the expansion of the 'second economy' in socialist countries, represent another form in which the link between growth and surplus population is expressed, but I will come back to this issue in the next section. Correspondingly, the large increase in working married women may also reflect a tendency for a growing number of housewives to become part of the excess population.[17] If this is the case, future research will have to pay greater attention to the complex processes of development and, in particular, to those aspects connected with the formation of different types of surplus population.[18]

Before passing on to the informal sector and the very different types of activities it now encompasses, there is at least one other complex phenomenon that must be examined: the specific ways in which labour resources are 'formally' utilized when conditioned by the regulation of socio-occupational structures. It cannot be denied that there has been a tendency over a long period, at least in the advanced capitalist countries (and in very different ways in the socialist countries), for the socio-occupational structure to be subjected to an increasing number of regulations, which vary from country to country. This tendency clearly creates obstacles to inclusion in the socio-occupational structure and thereby prevents additional layers of surplus population from being absorbed under 'formal' conditions. The most obvious examples of such regulations are those intended to stop the use of child labour; those which exclude from certain professions people who have the ability but not the required educational or professional qualifications; and those which stifle the economic initiative of anyone who, at least when starting up an activity, does not have sufficient resources to register at the chamber of commerce, pay taxes or purchase a licence. As I argued in chapter 2, these regulations originated in a plurality of different interests and, in general, they are aimed at preventing the devastating impact on social life that could result from a totally unregulated and unlimited labour market (see also Offe, 1985). By taking into account this complex plurality of interests behind the tendency towards regulation, it is possible to understand better an entire aspect of the heterogeneous nature of informal activities.

A model for interpreting the link between the conditions of the surplus population and informal activities

I shall continue the analysis on the basis of figure 4.2. Starting from the processes by which surplus population is produced and labour resources are absorbed, it attempts to explain all the possible heterogeneous aspects of informal activities and to avoid functionalist short cuts. The model represented in the figure rests on the opening of a gap between the potential labour supply and the formal employment structure which persists over time, and on the plausible hypothesis that it is tending to widen even further. I have already briefly mentioned the arguments in favour of this hypothesis in terms of the creation of surplus population. Detailed research into the specific and local forms of economic growth

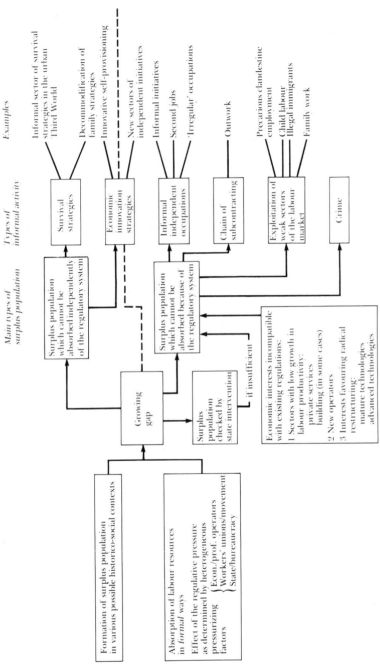

Figure 4.2 A model for interpreting the link between the conditions of the surplus population and informal activities (the broken line indicates the division between the two main types of surplus population)

could clarify what are the main ways in which surplus population is being generated in various contemporary economic and social contexts. Here, however, the general observation must suffice that despite the many different forms it assumes throughout the world, socio-economic development is still producing a high percentage of surplus population.

The hypothesis that the gap is tending to grow derives, above all, from what can be seen from the features and trends of the crisis in the Fordist-welfarist model of society. It could be argued that one of the most important and characteristic features of the contemporary process of irreversible social change is the potential, and in some areas already existing, decline in lifelong salaried employment in large and medium-sized firms in industry or the tertiary sector. It is essential to underline a further important point: the distinction that can be made between the variable extent to which this process has at present asserted itself and its even more radical potential consequences if it turns out to be irreversible. Lifelong jobs for blue- or white-collar workers do not vanish from one day to the next, and it may well be that a part of the surplus population will find work of this kind in the near future. The likelihood of decline in 'guaranteed' employment providing a family wage is having important consequences in all contexts, though in different terms. What is especially important for my analysis is the potential scope of the process and all the specific forms it may assume; these do not exclude the possibility that in some situations lifelong jobs of this kind will increase in number or that, in others, the increase will merely slow down.

A widening gap between the potential labour supply and the formal employment structure engenders two main types of surplus population: one which cannot be absorbed independently of the system for regulating working activities, and another which cannot be absorbed under the conditions established by the regulatory system. This distinction is important for interpreting the heterogeneous nature of informal activities, because the first type of surplus population is more likely to adopt survival strategies that are neutral with regard to the regulatory system. The second type, on the other hand, is more likely to adopt strategies that, in one way or another, run counter to this system. This line of argument must also be regarded with due caution, since a problematical methodological leap has been made in the transition from verifying the existence of surplus population to identifying the survival strategies adopted. Some examples may clarify what is meant by this methodological leap. A high degree of persistent youth unemployment is an indicator of surplus population. It tells us that a considerable number of young people fail to find work in the formal sector, yet do not die of starvation despite having no official source of income. Some of them do not undertake any kind of paid informal work and are maintained by their families while they seek employment. Some may engage in self-provisioning activities so as to help their families to maximize their resources; for example, it is not unusual for the young unemployed to help with domestic chores or temporarily in a family's economic activity where their contribution is not essential but useful as unpaid help, such as shopkeepers' children who make home deliveries, earning tips for themselves and new customers for the shop. Others, in contrast, undertake various types of temporary informal activities which may or may not conflict with the regulatory system. Lastly, a certain number end up in criminal circles.[19]

It still remains true, none the less, that if the results of research into the strategies of the young surplus population in Southern Italian towns (a surplus population conditioned by the regulatory system) is compared with the strategies adopted by young people in the shanty towns of Rio de Janeiro (a surplus population largely unconditioned by the regulatory system), a greater incidence of informal activities independent of the regulatory system, that is work which is not illicit, is found in the latter. Clearly, this depends on the fact that employment is much more highly regulated in the first than in the last case. For instance, in Southern Italy the employment of minors in building activities is illegal and the off-the-books temporary or casual employment of young unemployed persons in this or other sectors is illicit. In the *favelas* of Rio de Janeiro, it is perfectly legal for children or young adults to carry building material from the main road to the building sites for small cash payment (Valladares, 1986).

Another from among the many examples available serves equally well to illustrate the way in which the distinction between the two types of surplus population is hazy from the perspective of the strategies that can be adopted. Being in the surplus population may also be a partial condition; that is, there are workers in employment who for various reasons are willing to spend additional time in working activities to produce income or resources. This may find expression in self-provisioning strategies or in a second job, where the latter may involve evasion of the regulatory system.[20]

It is worth making a digression in this connection on the importance of the individual and social characteristics (household, environment, local culture, etc.) of surplus population both during its formation and in evaluating possible informal activity options or strategies. The formation of surplus population must be analysed in all its complexity. It is evident that if a growing supply of well-educated labour demanding long-term jobs for a family wage receives increasing offers of occasional and poorly paid unskilled jobs, a substantial layer of surplus population will be formed. It is quite acceptable to an eighteen-year-old student to work in a fast-food restaurant or pick fruit for low pay during the summer holidays. But he will not expect to do this kind of work after he has obtained his degree or diploma and is married with a family to support. The main reason for such an attitude is not the unwillingness of new generations to accept heavy or dirty work, or work with insufficient guarantees or professional content relative to 'sophisticated' expectations – but lies precisely in the fact that such work does not provide for survival in the specific socio-historical terms already established in different social contexts.[21]

It is worth while to state some considerations regarding the area of the model (figure 4.2) labelled 'economic interests incompatible with existing regulations'. These interests are incompatible with the regulatory system in specific ways and, as a result, vary widely in different places and historical periods; some general observations are, however, possible, which can then be incorporated into the interpretation of diverse forms of irregular activity. It may be assumed that the regulatory system is shaped by the pressure from those interests which are strongest and best represented within a given politico-institutional order. There exists the possibility, therefore, that weaker or newly formed interests are penalized by the regulatory system. From this a whole series of possible 'convergences' may arise between the surplus population whose absorption is prevented by the regulatory system and economic interests which are incompatible with the system. The most interesting and widespread example is represented by those branches of the economy with a high labour intensity and a low margin for increasing labour productivity. As seen in the previous section, they include many branches of the service sector and, in many countries, housing. In such cases, the cost of 'regulated' labour is a decisive factor and places a growing number of economic operators in difficulty. The partial or complete alternative to the disappearance or radical transformation of the economic activity in question, involving the spread of self-service or do-it-yourself building, or to very high price increases, which are not feasible in some branches, is often a growing informalization of work in violation of legal regulations or, in some cases, by exploiting family and/or ethnic resources.[22] It is therefore important to analyse the specific nature of the possible convergences between economic demands incompatible with the regulatory system and types of surplus population strategies, because this will make it possible to explain, in general, the presence of certain areas of informal activity.

The typology worked out by Marx suggested at least two important patterns of survival for the surplus population. The latent part of the reserve army underlined the persistent importance of rural subsistence economies. The stagnant part was understood as being able to survive on the very low incomes and under the relatively poor conditions of existence resulting from marginal urban activities. Both these patterns were viewed as becoming less and less viable due to the increasing competitive pressures generated by the expansion of 'proper' capitalist enterprises in agriculture and in the urban marginal economy. At the same time, Marx assumed that capitalist accumulation and expansion on a worldwide scale would continue to create new masses of latent surplus population in the periphery and that the commodification process would correspondingly renew the areas of stagnant urban surplus population or the possibility of their formation. As I have already extensively argued, both the historical picture and the contemporary scene are much more complicated, for at least two reasons. The first is the impact of the processes of regulation and limitation on the further extension of the labour market and of the employment structure. The second is the tendency for the positive developmental role of an industrial reserve army to die out in an age in which industrial employment is no longer increasing and in which, frequently, new investment and economic growth mean labour-saving strategies and that masses of new workers are no longer required. Neither of these trends interfere with or invalidate the assumption that capitalist development creates surplus population, but rather shift the emphasis away from the role of the surplus supply of labour in capitalist accumulation and development. We saw in chapter 2 that the main emphasis now falls on what happens to this oversupply, rather than on the fact that an oversupply is necessary to prevent wages from rising above historically set survival limits.

I pointed out in chapter 3 that regulatory processes have in theory been accompanied by socio-economic transformations, the aim of which is to provide sufficient resources to enable those who are excluded from access to the employment structure to survive. Generally, in advanced capitalist countries this has been achieved in part through the concurrent development of state subsidies, welfare provisions and the enforcement of a family wage system. In practice, this combination has never been sufficient to meet the full range of possible situations where individuals and households need additional survival income but are prevented from taking up opportunities to work either by institutional limitations or by an inadequate demand for labour. This has meant that not only has a part of the surplus population remained such, but also that in a regulated employment system the need to work in order to survive is increasingly finding expression in informal and, in some cases, illegal forms. This process relates in various ways to a number of different situations which involve both wage families and, to an even greater extent, the marginally productive self-employed and the patterns of survival of some groups among the surplus population. The cases of moonlighting and of irregular employment in traditional sectors have already been mentioned.

The dying out of the reserve army's proper function is a very controversial question. In order to demonstrate that this is happening, I propose to show that a wide range of situations characterized by a partial or total surplus in the supply of labour have become established and that in such situations people are able to survive even for an entire lifetime independently of their role as part of the reserve army of labour. These situations involve work providing an income which is well below the subsistence minimum historically linked to wage-work and/or under conditions of employment that are not officially authorized. However, the cumulation of various sources of income or the complement of 'favourable' reciprocal conditions allow these arrangements to persist even totally outside the normal competition for wage-work. From a certain perspective, this cannot but be taken as a kind of neo-dualist interpretation of contemporary socio-economic development; however, it is in the final analysis much more complicated. What appears as a dualist employment structure from a purely economistic point of view (besides informal activities, there is also the division between primary and secondary income jobs) becomes a complementary combination if seen from that of reproduction strategy. In the end, what has been said up to now points more in the direction of an increasingly fragmented and diversified employment structure, combined with an even more complex range of reproduction patterns, than to a clearly dualist structure and patterns. This is confirmed by the argument that the contemporary surplus population is performing the role of a reserve army to a limited extent. In fact, its existence is not irrelevant to the organization and restructuring of the official employment structure. Various examples could be given: the relocation of manufacturing plants in underdeveloped countries, which means an exploitation of low-paid workers made possible through a complementary relationship with the mode of survival of an extensive surplus population in the urban informal sector; the contracting out of services where the subcontractors use irregular workers; the unofficial hiring of moonlighting workers instead of new employees; and so on. But all this becomes highly problematical if it is assumed that it occurs to such an extent as to destroy the fragile social balances that allow survival of the contemporary surplus population as protected by various reproductive arrangements. A huge imbalance would simply lead to a progressive failure to limit the labour market and its devastating social impact: a return to Polanyi's nightmare of capitalism without society. It is not by chance that, although some neo-conservative governments in advanced capitalist countries have trumpeted their adherence to free market economics as loudly as possible, they have not dared to undermine this social equilibrium directly. Instead, they have tried to shift part of the support given to the surplus population away from the state and onto households, under the assumption that the latter have sufficient resources, which often is not the case. But still the most unstable kinds of balance are those typical of underdeveloped countries, particularly where state provision and household monetary income cannot compensate for the decreasing viability of traditional reciprocal support; that is, where it is being greatly undermined by strong competitive tensions produced by dependent industrialization based on very low wages.[23]

Figure 4.2 shows how and in what forms those making up the labour supply may end up in the surplus population, either partially or totally and either temporarily or indefinitely. The state of belonging to the surplus population is assumed to be complemented more or less satisfactorily by various social arrangements, state provisions, household income pooling and reciprocal support. The surplus population may increase without a serious social crisis breaking out if the complementary conditions remain more or less visible, as has been the case in advanced capitalist societies facing a dramatic rise in levels of youth unemployment. The figure illustrates the possible paths taken by the labour supply, and the predisposition of various kinds of potential workers to accept informal jobs, at least on a temporary or partial basis, because they do not have other or better opportunities and because the context of social arrangements in which they exist allows them to survive even if the income obtained is largely inadequate. It will be seen at the beginning of chapter 5 how various employer strategies and the patterns of development in some branches of the economy provides these workers with real job opportunities, found mainly in both new and traditional areas of the increasingly heterogeneous and fragmented service sector.

5 THE SOCIO-ECONOMIC BACKGROUND TO INFORMALIZATION IN SOCIALIST AND UNDERDEVELOPED COUNTRIES

Socialist industrial development and informalization

There is sufficient evidence to support the idea that in socialist countries second or black economy activities are expanding while in underdeveloped countries the urban informal sector has been growing in line with increasing urbanization. However, the general socio-economic transformations at the origin of the informalization processes in these different social contexts are not the same as the ones discussed for advanced capitalist countries. As will be seen more clearly in the next chapter, it is also the case that the range and typology of informal activities vary according to the different kinds of societies. Here I shall give a very general outline of the socio-economic background to informalization processes in socialist and underdeveloped countries.

Let us begin by looking briefly at the main features of industrial development in socialist countries during the various stages of recent history and at different times since the beginning of the socialist transformation. A periodization of socialist development is a controversial matter, if only because countries with different socio-economic backgrounds ranging from largely undeveloped agricultural to already advanced industrial societies, such as Czechoslovakia and East Germany, turned socialist at different times and under different historical conditions within a period stretching from 1917 to very recently. For my purposes, the periodization proposed by Murray and Szelenyi (1984) may be at least partially adopted. Following what they suggest, it is necessary to distinguish between three stages which, however, may differ in nature and length of time in the various cases: first, the stage of consolidating the revolution and pursuing immediate goals; second, that of achieving socialist industrialization; and third, that of more sophisticated industrial development in a wide range of sectors.

During the first stage, the goals of socialist industrialization are subject to various changes which in the second stage no longer exist. The conditions that are important initially are:

- the industrial and urban structure inherited from the pre-socialist society, including the level of industrialization and the role of the national economy within the international world system at a given stage of development (in this sense a certain degree of industrial development will have a different effect in 1917, in 1949 or in the 1970s, for example);
- the role played by the urgent priority given to guaranteeing the achievement of a minimum level of survival conditions in both urban and rural areas;
- whether revolutionary movements are centred more in the urban or in the rural classes (see Gugler, 1982);
- the possible existence or absence of foreign inputs and/or of the strong conditioning effect exerted by the world market on the newly constituted socialist order.

The necessity to achieve and maintain a minimum level of survival for every citizen is often an absolute priority for reasons of popular consensus

and may also run completely counter to the goal of socialist industrialization. In pragmatic terms, the existence of this kind of priority, and its
different combinations with the priorities of socialist industrialization,
contributes much to the understanding of different socio-economic policies at various times and in different situations. It is more likely that the
survival-level priority plays a role which is scarcely related to the goal
of industrialization during the initial stage and in less developed countries. In these cases, the redistribution of resources and short-term investment is oriented to renewing the capacity to survive for millions of
peasants and urban dwellers who previously existed below minimum
survival levels. Once renewal has reached an acceptable level, a substantial shift takes place towards socialist industrialization.

I believe that the interpretation of the first stage should be based
mainly on this priority of achieving the minimum level of survival possible
under the existing conditions of the national and international economies.
What is involved is not only a policy of redistribution in favour of
urban survival. If the existing urban resources are insufficient to achieve
survival, it becomes necessary to move some of the population from
urban areas to the countryside, where it is likely to be easier to achieve,
and to curb movement in the opposite direction by stopping migration
to large cities, where life is more expensive.[24]

The nature of the revolution may also be significant. The extreme
cases are an urban insurrection, on the one hand, and a national civil
or independence war fought mainly in the countryside and with a decisive
contribution by the peasants, on the other. In the first case priority is
given to renewing survival in the large cities, thereby making it impossible
to prevent a certain amount of migration to urban areas. The second
kind of revolution is generally hostile to cities and gives priority to
renewing survival in the countryside; as a consequence, it limits any
trend towards urbanization for a considerable period of time.

The second stage is closely associated with processes of socialist industrialization. The following approximate indications can be deduced from
the various experiences of socialist societies:

 - the redistribution of resources in support of forced industrial
   accumulation in specific sectors (heavy industry, means of production, energy, military and defence), to the detriment of certain
   areas of mass consumption;
 - a relative indifference to levels of productivity, which may vary
   enormously, with attention focused on absolute increases in production and attaining full employment;

– the possibility that the previous indifference to 'market' criteria is weakened by exposure to the world market.

There are also two interconnected tendencies that are quite different from those found in capitalist countries: the first is a tendency towards underproduction as the production of mass consumer goods expands slowly and a growing part of wages cannot be spent within the socialist sector of consumption; and the second is a tendency towards maintaining the monetary costs of reproducing the labour force at a low level. These tendencies are reflected in the social character of industrial development and assume an increasingly crucial importance in the transition from the second to the third stage, as I try to show below. But, first, it is necessary to return briefly to the first stage in order to discuss the importance that the 'original sin' of agrarian underdevelopment may assume within the course of socialist development.

Socialism emerged in countries that were still predominantly characterized by a large agricultural sector and by relatively undeveloped industry. This is particularly true in the case of the Soviet Union, China and most of the underdeveloped countries which joined the socialist bloc after the Second World War, but less so for the Eastern European countries. For this reason, the Eastern European countries need to be discussed separately and singly in order to take into account the different roles that the diverse inherited industrial bases played, both in the period of industrial reconstruction and consolidation throughout the 1950s and 1960s and in the more recent phase based on industrial diversification and the diffusion of mass consumption (see Murray and Szelenyi, 1984; Szelenyi, 1988). In the other cases, the most important goal has been to increase the surplus produced in agriculture and use it to promote industrial expansion. Increases in agricultural production through productivity gains have meant a decrease in agricultural employment and the transfer of labour to industrial production, specifically to those sectors given priority by state planning in the redistribution of available resources. As argued in the previous chapter, this has led to a radical change from situations characterized by the high levels of support based on traditional community/household reciprocity in rural villages to a persistently contradictory and inadequate mix of wages and state assistance in both urban (increasing and generally more costly for the state) and rural (decreasing) settings. The inadequacy of these reproduction arrangements becomes a dramatic distorting constraint on socialist development because it ends up by revitalizing forms of reciprocal support, leading to increasing inequality and other consequences that are incompatible with socialist ideology. This contradiction has assumed different forms at various times and in different countries. In general, it may be the case that during the first stage, the contradiction is more evident and explosive in the countryside, while at a more advanced stage the main focus shifts to industrial and service production and to the urban life-style.[25]

In most cases the original relocation of resources for accumulation has taken place under abnormal conditions: first, the initial substitution of agricultural commodities with goods and raw materials imported at falling prices – as happened in most late-industrializing capitalist countries (Mingione, 1981) – was not possible because of difficult international relations; second, incoming foreign investment and technology were very limited for the same reason; third, the transition took place when average industrial world production was already mature in many sectors, and this particularly affected those underdeveloped countries which joined the socialist club after the Second World War; and fourth, socialist societies had different pre-socialist industrial bases, but none was built upon the *tabula rasa* found by early industrial development in Britain.

To summarize, it can be said that different socialist regimes have had to face and manage difficult situations of transformation, including, to some extent, Eastern European countries during the industrial reconstruction period in the 1950s and 1960s. This difficulty derived from the fact that agricultural accumulation was at the same time both too fast and too slow to achieve the goal of rapid, balanced industrial development: too fast in creating a relative surplus population, which could not be immediately absorbed by industrial growth at a relatively high rate of productivity, and too slow to keep pace with a much more rapid industrialization process, in which even relatively backward technologies made possible appreciable gains in productivity. The centrally planned economies were able to keep this contradiction under control from the redistributive point of view, thereby avoiding increasing differentials in productivity, and, consequently, increasing gaps in income, profitability and life-chances, as well as uncontrollable migration and unemployment; but they could not avoid paying the social costs associated with the redistributive solutions they adopted. In general, these costs found constant expression in specific social phenomena and were strongly reflected in socialist life-styles, both in rural and urban settings. The rationalization of agriculture was slowed down by the protection given to unproductive work and the holding down of food prices, and/or through the toleration of a complex agricultural set-up aimed at preventing the formation of an excessively large surplus popu-

lation and which comprised, on the one side, large inefficient bureaucratized farms, and on the other, a vast area of small-scale petty commodity production. The result has been that few socialist countries are
food exporters, that many of them have food shortage problems from
time to time, and that the per capita average productivity of socialist
agriculture is well below that of advanced capitalist agriculture.

The impact of socialist industrial policies and priorities

Planned industrial accumulation has usually entailed preferential treatment for certain sectors such as heavy industry, machinery, means of
production, energy, primary subsistence goods and, increasingly in the
last few decades, military equipment, to the detriment of others, particularly durables for mass consumption. This strategy was initially successful
in accelerating industrial development, but it later created substantial
difficulties. In fact, the policy to hold back the production of mass-
consumer goods and the slow growth in productivity in the relevant
sectors was reflected in a limited expansion of the internal market,
accompanied in many cases by an increasing waste of the potential for
accumulative consumption. It is worth discussing briefly some of the
features and implications of this process in order to understand better
the trends characterizing socialist development, especially at times when
the industrial mix becomes more complex and consumer expectations
grow.

Planners give priority to the heavy industrial sectors of energy and
means of production in order to speed up the industrialization process
and, at the same time, to avoid tendencies towards underconsumption.
In the long run, this policy reveals dangerous limits for various reasons.
One of these is that technological progress has been confined to the
priority sectors and not sufficiently diffused throughout all of industry.
In general, technological progress is faster and less expensive in market
economies because it is based on a high degree of cross-fertilization
between sectors. For instance, innovations crucial to the military equipment industry are first discovered by a state-funded research laboratory
and then developed and improved by the durable goods sector industry,
which bears the costs and reaps the profits from operations of this kind.
Consequently, the military-industrial complex both stimulates technological advance in other areas and benefits from developments made elsewhere. The case of electronics technology is a very clear example of this
cross-fertilization process, which both speeds up progress and reduces
the level of investment financed directly by the state in order to achieve
progress in the top-priority sectors.

From another angle, socialist planners have consciously held back from increasing the production of individual mass-consumer durables, but have failed to encourage sufficiently the development of technologically advanced collective consumption which could satisfactorily substitute durables and other consumer products within the process of promoting a socialist life-style. In this respect, the various productive/reproductive arrangements in socialist countries have led to an increasingly dangerous void in such a very important area as the quality of life. As seen above, the basic socialist model is founded on a complementary balance between a theoretically egalitarian state provision of services and relatively low monetary incomes granted to a fully employed adult population for purchasing food and clothing of mass standardized quality, paying a low state-subsidised rent and, possibly, procuring other non-luxury consumer items. The model is oriented against the spread of mass consumerism, and as a result limits the growth of those branches of industry producing durables. Any improvements in life-style are accordingly almost wholly dependent on the development of the collective system of provision. But state provision remains chronically inadequate and expensive to develop, particularly in the areas of housing and sophisticated urban infrastructures, while all empirical experience has demonstrated that it is nearly impossible to cover completely the area of private consumption of durables by alternative collective provision. Cheap public transport has been unable to prevent the expansion of a demand/need for individual private vehicles. The same has happened with collective leisure services as an alternative to equipment for use by individuals (radios, television sets, hi-fi systems). The void or gap has been even more marked in the case of household appliances where the potential for collectivization has remained practically nil. In addition to this limit, socialist industrialization has found it particularly difficult to adapt production in the traditional branches of food processing, clothing and furniture to meet an increasingly sophisticated and diversified demand as the socialist economy has grown.

At a more advanced stage of socialist development, when further improvements in life-styles are conditioned by the access to mass-consumer durables, at least to a controlled extent, and by a more diversified and sophisticated range of consumer products, two fundamental limits that are particularly difficult to overcome have taken firm root. Average wages are generally too low to purchase durables, but, paradoxically, they have become too high for spending solely on food, standardized clothing and subsidised rent, at least at the controlled prices set by official distribution. But even more importantly, on the opposite front, the productivity gap has developed to such an extent that the quantity and quality of consumer goods produced is highly inadequate. The general result has been an increasingly perverse combination of, on the one hand, market pressures as a high, largely unsatisfied, demand has grown consequent on the fact that consumers often find ways to solve the problems created by the inadequacy of individual incomes through long-term saving and reciprocal strategies (for example, friends agree to share a car or a washing machine), and, on the other, a parallel distortion in redistribution depending on the low planning priority that keeps production at inadequate qualitative and quantitative levels. This is contrary to what happens in market systems where high demand, high prices and high profitability 'automatically' stimulate a rapid rise in production. The above combination helps to stimulate the growth of a black market and of a distorted mechanism of distributing goods. The latter becomes parasitically rooted in the political system, as it appears to be the least harmful way of allocating scarce goods and services to a restricted number of customers. The fact that this form of distribution is, at least in part, unofficial is in reality less detrimental to the egalitarian ideology of socialist regimes than would be the case with an officially enforced distributive strategy giving rise to substantial social inequalities. Clearly, the more the industrial base becomes developed and diversified but remains inadequate in the area of durables, the more such pressures destabilize the basic socialist equilibrium of production/reproduction. Taking this consideration into account, it is possible, despite the lack of accurate comparative studies, to put forward the hypothesis that these kinds of pressures are greater in the Soviet Union, where long-term unbalanced industrialization has penalized this area, than in East Germany, which inherited a relatively advanced industrial base, or in China, where the majority of the population still lives in the countryside.

The picture drawn above is still a very approximate one; none the less, it provides us with a first preliminary idea of the trends favouring the expansion of the second economy. Though still at a general level of discussion, it is useful to bring up some further questions. In the first place, it is important to underline that in order to raise sufficient money to buy durables or more sophisticated products, socialist consumers have to rely largely on reciprocal networks involving at least the household but often also kin, friends and others. Then, they are faced with the lack of goods of the required quality on the official socialist market, which means that since prices are fixed and imports controlled, three possible options are open to them. First, they wait a very long time until it is officially their turn to procure certain products. In the case of less expensive items distributed through official shops, this option consists in discovering which day the goods will be put on sale, queuing in front of the shop long before it opens and hoping to reach the counter before the desired item is sold out. Second, they obtain the desired product immediately or very quickly through the official distributive system because favoured by acquaintances in the system itself or recommendations from powerful figures, which also helps to consolidate informal networks. Third, if at all possible, the item is acquired straight away or after a very short while on the parallel black market. In this situation, a substantial and growing part of consumptive capacity is captured by the second economy, which is not under the direct control of the centrally planned economy, or by low accumulation sectors like internal tourism and restaurants. These last-named are also a vehicle for expansion of the second economy, but in a rather different way. As they are less concentrated and difficult for a centralized planning agency to keep under total supervision, their diffusion is at the same time both a symptom of the weakening of centralized control and an indicator that an increasing proportion of consumption lies outside the main official distributive system of the socialist economy. I shall return to this particular area of socialist informalization in the next chapter when discussing the specific contemporary model of change in socialist countries.

Finally, I will mention here another crucial question that will be properly discussed in the course of the next chapter, where I show why and how a number of official socialist enterprises contribute increasingly to informalization trends by sending a large part of their product to the black market instead of the official market. Moreover, this phenomenon is found to an increasing extent in the stage of complex industrialization, and it may be assumed that it reflects on the supply side the pressures that have just been discussed with regard to the demand side.

The impact of important recent trends in the transformation of social life in underdeveloped countries

As I have already stated on several occasions, a general discussion of the situations in underdeveloped countries will be inevitably approximate and superficial, given the highly heterogeneous conditions in which, excluding China, practically half the world's population lives. On the other hand, it is also true that underdevelopment is more or less everywhere a dead end, even though characterized by various forms of social change (Wallerstein, 1983). This question also fully involves the so-called newly industrializing countries (NICs), in particular large overpopulated ones like Brazil and Mexico. In this sense, it is important first to discuss some general trends that characterize contemporary underdevelopment and further the expansion of the informal urban sector. Then, in the conclusion to this section, I shall take a rapid look at the possibility that in some NICs social change may follow paths that are distinctly different from the closed circle of underdevelopment.

The most important macro-social processes that continue to characterize underdevelopment are, in general, the high rate of demographic growth; the persistence of large-scale urbanization, urban growth and large migratory movements also involving emigration; and the continual increase in accentuated forms of social polarization between a limited group with high incomes and the vast majority with very low incomes. The factors underlying the high birth rate have already been discussed in chapter 3. Here, other phenomena need to be looked at, starting with the impact of the global trends towards the growth and division of agricultural work in terms of the increasing pressures that are dismantling the various kinds of agricultural subsistence still found in the countryside.

The reproductive strategies of the agricultural population grow increasingly unstable due to demographic pressure, which continues to undermine the effectiveness of the complementary relationship between growing crops, self-provisioning activities and low wages. To this are generally added the negative effects of two large-scale global processes: the new forms of specialization and integration of agricultural production at a worldwide level, also including the changes brought about by technological innovations designed and applied in ways that are always very unequal (H. Friedmann, 1982; Friedmann and McMichael, 1989); and the surfacing of ever stronger and more effective agricultural protectionism in industrialized countries, against which less developed countries are unable to react with similar measures (see Hathaway, 1987; *Agriculture and Human Values*, 1989; Friedland et al., forthcoming). The first process is a complex matter and cannot be adequately gone into here. Roughly speaking, many countries have been heavily penalized by the new equilibria in world agriculture involving falling prices for several food products such as sugar, coffee, maize and exotic fruits. However, those countries specializing in products of growing importance, like soya, have not benefited from new periods of growth, except in exceptional and short-lived cases, because they are squeezed by the highly competitive, more advanced methods of production in the advanced parts of the world. Furthermore, biotechnology and the new techniques of glasshouse and test-tube cultivation tend to lessen the importance of climatic factors or large expanses of cultivable land, which in many cases are precisely the resources found in abundance in the less developed countries, and to place more emphasis on developing scientific research, in which the latter undoubtedly play a very weak and dependent role (see Goodman et al., 1987; Kloppenburg, 1988).

When to the effects of this first process are added those of the growing agricultural protectionism practised by advanced countries, one can more or less imagine the devastating impact from full exposure to the damping pressure of a market in which, moreover, protectionism serves the strong and not the weak. On top of all this, it is also the case that the growth of international debt continues to compel the governments of many underdeveloped countries to speed up the change-over from subsistence produce to commercial crops. Despite the worsening terms of exchange, the latter still represent one of the few resources with which to pay back part of a country's debt. This malign spiral has a disastrous effect on the rural arrangements for subsistence, as people in the countryside are increasingly deprived both of land and complementary sources of income. Such a situation suffices to explain the persistence and magnitude of urbanization and emigration.

We saw in the previous chapter that the patterns of reproduction in Third World cities end up being based on a combination of low incomes and a series of subsistence activities; at the same time, the latter account for the possibility of surviving under these conditions and reveal the true nature of the 'miraculous' informal sector. Persistent low incomes constitute a trap from which there is no escape for the majority of the urban population. Even when low wages attract a considerable amount of relocated industry or stimulate local initiatives to industrialize, the investment involved is insufficient to absorb a substantial part of the surplus population. Only exceptionally, where the pressure from the latter is markedly reduced for special reasons, does the consequent increase in incomes have an effect on the informal sector as well, favouring its horizontal contraction and the appearance of mechanisms of accumulation with the corresponding 'formalization' of several activities. In other contexts, the informal sector is totally unable to establish a model of conventional development and remains a complementary area of subsistence which is destined to expand horizontally as the low-income urban population rises.

In a certain sense, what is a state of chronic poverty for the majority of the population constitutes a favourable resource for improving the lifestyles and opportunities for enrichment of high-income groups. The most immediate example that comes to mind is the enormous reserve of service workers earning derisory wages: domestics, messenger boys, artisans, porters, babysitters and so on. Clearly, however, we could also look to the building sector, local manufacturing and the whole economy in general. The other side to urban growth accompanied by an ever-extending informal sector are the very high levels of social polarization. They reach almost unimaginable peaks in contexts where groups at the top end of the social scale are involved in international finance and, therefore, have at their disposal vast amounts of hard currency, which can be spent in countries where their relative value is considerably greater. As is to be expected, situations of this kind are accompanied by strong social tensions and by relative political instability or the presence of authoritarian regimes that hold on to power through fierce repression.

It is perhaps worth discussing whether it is in general possible to use the informal sector to promote economic growth (see also Friedmann and Salguero, 1988). The only possible brief answer to this complicated question is a straightforward no. Even the decade of the 'new economic order' (1970–9), the oil crisis and a certain redistribution of financial power in favour of countries producing raw materials failed to bring about self-generated industrial development for underdeveloped countries. The informal sector, therefore, may be seen as offering a last chance. Starting from some considerations relating to specific policies, also partially based on 'informal conditions', I will merely try to offer some suggestions which could be further developed. The idea behind them comes from housing policies. When, in the 1970s, it became evident that slum clearance was not a viable solution to the housing problem in Third World cities, international agencies and some governments became favourably disposed towards strategies of self-help building or renovation. Evaluating the success of these policies is still a controversial matter (see Bromley and Gerry, 1979; Safa, 1982; Gilbert and Gugler, 1982; Slater, 1985). It is even more difficult to draw from them any lesson concerning the potential of more general policies for promoting development on the basis of the informal sector. Nevertheless, these housing policies provide interesting examples of what happens when a strategy is applied which seeks to exploit informal conditions in order to solve a major problem. Generally speaking, self-help building programmes have encountered three difficulties: first, they require the allocation of a substantial amount of money; second, they easily escape any institutional supervision and lead to private speculation and control by local criminal gangs; and third, if they are successful they attract new migrants, which increases rather than diminishes the problem.

The same, and other even more intractable, problems have to be taken into account by any general policy to encourage economic growth based on the informal sector. The difficulties faced by self-help building will in this case be magnified. The cost of the programme is bound to rise rapidly to high levels. The amount of money and exploitation involved will attract a number of local and international speculators seeking to benefit from the expansion of the sponsored informal sector. Lastly, the creation of 'decent' jobs in the sector will draw new waves of migrants who will add to the pressure exerted by the urban surplus population, except in a few cases of countries without an overpopulated rural hinterland. But while self-help building is a self-provisioning activity and an operation strictly tied to a local market, other informal ventures are exposed to the laws of the market to a much greater extent. Informal activities are originally viable because they are based on labour-intensive working processes and on a very low cost of labour. This gives rise to further difficult problems.

I have already explained why, in my opinion, the experience of the large overpopulated countries classified among the newly industrializing nations, in particular Mexico and Brazil, differs little from that of others which have had much more limited industrial growth. The localization of new industrial initiatives has meant work for a number of workers which is not very large relative to the size of the local surplus population. Moreover, the wages they earn are only slightly higher than the general local rate and conditions of employment are relatively unstable, with very few guarantees. These new industrial workers still have to exist within a subsistence context in order to survive while they are in work and to have something on which they can rely totally when laid off. It is rather to South Korea (see Meyer and Kyonghee, 1988), Taiwan, Singapore and Hong Kong (see M. P. Smith, 1989; Henderson, 1989) that we must turn for different experiences. With regard to Singapore and Hong Kong, the effect of the tendency to subcontract and decentralize to small countries has been greater than in the larger nations. Thus, particularly in the case of Singapore, where the pressure of the local population was limited by the size of the city-state, the results of local transformation have been considerable. These cases appear unique, but they may teach us something about the conditions necessary to promote development starting from the informal sector. The same reasoning may also be applied to Korea and Taiwan, even though it is risky to use very generic data as a basis for comparisons. In both countries, industry has grown on a massive scale and this growth has coincided with vast waves of emigration. It may therefore be supposed that industrialization has been accompanied by a lessening rather than an increase in the pressure from the surplus population. The impact in terms of increasing wage levels has been partially reduced by highly authoritarian regimes. This process, together with a growing volume of remittances from emigrants, has presumably caused the real level of household incomes to rise while wages have been kept relatively low. In a certain sense, it would come as no surprise if accurate local studies were to indicate both a trend towards vertical accumulation starting also from the informal sector and a corresponding decrease in its horizontal extension in the form of less

casual work, less purely subsistence-based activities and less neighbourhood or street survival solidarity.

The surveys and studies on new towns in underdeveloped countries
are interesting for two reasons.[26] First, they usually confirm the hypothesis that the informal sector also develops in relatively small but rapidly
growing towns which are under pressure from a large surplus population
ready to migrate from the countryside or from other urban settlements.
Second, and of even greater importance, they illustrate the process of
expansion of the informal sector in particularly pure conditions, because
it is not mixed with the parallel transformation of already existing urban
traditions. Furthermore, it is also possible to gain an understanding of
the power of resistance of the informal sector, since it often has to
overcome obstacles deliberately imposed by national and local authorities
with the aim of keeping the new town as 'clean' as possible. The building
of a new town attracts to the site a large and growing population which
was not provided for in the original plan. The greatest town planners
and architects of our times who have worked in underdeveloped countries,
including Le Corbusier and his team at Chandigarh, have always neglected the fact that the realization of their projects would require a large
and increasing number of building workers and their families, who would
have to be housed and survive around the sites they work on. Moreover,
due to the large reserve of cheap labour, the housing sector in underdeveloped countries remains highly labour-intensive. Thousands of low-paid
unskilled labourers are employed instead of a few hundred specialized
workers. Even the most advanced and sophisticated architectural works
can be built using a highly labour-intensive organization of production
based on very low wage levels and large numbers of unskilled workers.
The members of Le Corbusier's team began to understand the problem
when they saw the 'miracle' of the Chandigarh plan being achieved
perfectly by ten or more times the number of workers they would have
used in France, while the overall cost of labour remained a fraction of
what it would have been in that country. By that time, however, it was
too late. The informal city had already started to grow up alongside the
planned city. Shanty towns, huts, encampments, street hawkers, informal
markets and other similar activities spread everywhere and survived
every attempt by the authorities to remove them (Sarin, 1984).

Yet although the problem of very low-paid building workers is the
'original sin' not only in a new town, where it is so evident, but also in
every growing town and city in an underdeveloped region, other factors
contribute to the extension and growth of the informal sector. To survive
on their persistently low and irregular wages, building workers need an
inexpensive informal consumption network. They cannot afford to live

in the planned residences, to buy their food from the stores, to travel by official transport and to buy clothing from shops in the formal sector. As a result, the new town draws a wave of service and craft workers who, in turn, have to survive on low and irregular incomes and are subjected to the unlimited competition of newcomers. Even a wide layer of employed workers at the bottom of the official employment hierarchy in the national and local administration or in manufacturing or mining cannot afford formal housing and consumption as they are paid low wages; they therefore end up by contributing to the growth of the informal sector. Later, when building activity slows down, the situation tends to worsen. Many of the building workers who have settled in the new town find themselves without employment. They have to survive by working in the informal sector, where competition increases and per capita income decreases.

This expansion of the informal sector shows no sign of leading to the forms of capital accumulation and development that characterized the growth of Western economies. Is it possible for it to be transformed and redirected? My tentative reply is that it cannot, unless there is a way of blocking the pressure from an incoming surplus population and, at the same time, of protecting local production against increasing imports.

NOTES

1 An influential interpretation of recent social change which focuses disproportionately on manufacturing is Piore and Sabel (1984). For the excessive
attention paid to the manufacturing side of informalization processes see,
for example, many of the contributions included in the collection edited by
Portes et al. (1989).

2 Among the many contributions made by economists, sociologists and geogra-
phers, see mainly Piore and Sabel (1984); Scott and Storper (1986); Lash
and Urry (1987); Tarling (1987); Storper and Walker (1988); Sayer (1989).

3 The decline in the number of jobs in the advanced capitalist countries began
in the early 1970s and was particularly sharp in Britain (Blackaby, 1978;
Massey and Meagan, 1982). During this same decade, a similar trend
became established in almost all other advanced capitalist countries, leading
to the loss of over twenty million jobs in the OECD countries by the
beginning of the 1980s (see Bluestone and Harrison, 1982; Colbjornsen,
1986; ILO, 1987; Gordon, 1988; EEC 1989a). The absolute decline in
manufacturing employment in the 1980s also affected countries which had
been spared in the previous decade, such as Italy (see chapter 6) and Japan
(*Nippon*, 1989).

4 For example, the labour processes used to produce more or less the same
Fiat vehicles in Turin and in Belo Horizonte are radically different, and the
gap is widening. Whereas, in Italy, Fiat has introduced computerized lines

of production and employment is highly specialized and tenured, in Brazil production remains characterized by the traditional assembly line system and employment by the prevalence of unskilled workers and a high turnover. For an important comparative analysis of the processes of change in the factory 'regimes' in advanced capitalist, socialist and underdeveloped countries, see Burawoy (1985). For a comparative analysis of production processes in advanced capitalist and in newly industrializing countries see, among others, the recent contribution by M. P. Smith (1989) and Henderson (1989).

5 The workers employed in these kinds of jobs are defined in the dual and segmented labour market literature as subordinate primary workers (Doeringer and Piore, 1971; Edwards, 1979; Gordon et al., 1982).

6 On international comparison of unemployment in advanced capitalist countries see, among others, the recent collections edited by Gunderson et al. (1987), by Fineman (1987) and by Lang and Leonard (1987), and the special issue of *Social Research* (1987) dedicated to unemployment (see in particular the contribution by Enrico Pugliese). See also the recent official reports on employment and unemployment by ILO (1987) and the EEC (1989a), and the particularly interesting interpretation of Therborn (1986).

7 Furthermore, although this still has to be verified by empirical research, it appears that a completely different structure of working careers in terms of the link between age and income has come into being, usually associated with the new profile of the so-called 'yuppie' (ie Young Urban Professional). This worker is held to achieve early success in his or her twenties, reach a peak in his or her thirties, and then be condemned in many cases to a dramatic decline in the very period of life when he or she may need increasing resources to support the rearing and educating of offspring.

8 As Paci (1989) argues in a recent essay, the Anglo-Scandinavian model is defined as 'institutional-universalistic' and the US model as 'residual', but 'almost all the other systems of state welfare provision in advanced capitalist countries, and in Continental Europe in particular, cannot be described directly in terms of this conceptual dichotomy'. (p. 32)

9 For a comparative discussion of the origin of welfare systems in advanced capitalist countries see mainly Marshall (1964); Titmuss (1966); Rimlinger (1971); Martin (1972); Wilenski (1975); Flora and Heidenheimer (1981).

10 The theoretical foundations for this 'golden age' of the welfare state were already laid in Keynesian economics. In the British case, which is certainly crucial for understanding this part of the history of the welfare state, the most important political contribution was made by Lord Beveridge while the outstanding contribution in the social sciences was that of T. H. Marshall (see mainly 1961, 1964, 1965).

11 For a comparative analysis of disablement policies in advanced capitalist countries see mainly Haveman et al. (1984) and Stone (1984). One of the important areas of welfare which is not taken into particular consideration here is housing. For a comparative look at this topic see mainly Ball et al. (1988).

12 See, for instance, the important contribution by Goldthorpe (1980) on the

British case, perhaps the most accurately studied. With regard to Italy, see the recent empirical study on social mobility in the Emilia Romagna region by Barbagli et al. (1988).

13 For the case of Britain see mainly Stevens (1966) and Abel-Smith (1972); for Italy see Ascoli (1984); Piperno (1984); Paci (1989); for the USA see Stevens (1971); Haller (1981).

14 For example, it is no accident that female Filipino workers in Europe are almost all domestics, whereas in the USA they are mainly nurses in private hospitals and have been a factor in the complete undermining of the profession.

15 Bagnasco (1985) starts from the idea that there are 'four main mechanisms for regulating economic activity' (p. 10): reciprocity, the market (the invisible hand), organization and political exchange. Socio-economic systems can be interpreted according to the particular mix of these four elements, taking into account the fact that over a long period industrial development has witnessed the growing importance of the last two as against the first two. In this perspective, what I have called the 'decline of the industrializing trend' could be seen as equivalent to an inversion of this trend during the last few decades. Bagnasco insists on the non-linearity of social development, on the locally diverse ways of combining the four mechanisms and on the specific discontinuities in the trade-off between the different mechanisms in various historical phases and in different contexts. Given the present state of highly accentuated heterogeneity and discontinuity of social change, Bagnasco holds that partial or medium-range theories must be worked out, starting from local conditions and defining the theoretical basis for comparative perspectives.

16 This is not the place to refer to Marx's theory of relative surplus population. None the less, it is worth underlining that the need to deal with the question arose in Marx as a polemical thrust against those who maintained that industrial growth would have soon absorbed all available labour and thereby caused high and irresitible wage increases in the long run. He started off a theoretical controversy in which he was not particularly interested for the very reason that, in his view, surplus population is an instrumental or 'functional' concept. How and why it persists, what the possible consequences are of a strong growth in surplus population on social stability and instability and of a concrete geographico-social separation between areas where surplus population is formed and areas where it is absorbed, are questions which Marx does not deal with adequately. He implicity assumes, therefore, that clear dividing lines (geographical, political, cultural and social) between the working class and the surplus population are never formed. Whereas most of his theory of the formation of a surplus population has stood the test of industrial history during the last century, the assumption of a definitive absence of dividing lines is questionable, to say the least, and not only with regard to the contemporary age.

17 Put in these terms, the question is undoubtedly economistic in nature. However, in its original terms at least, the whole problem of surplus popu-

lation cannot be viewed otherwise in as much as it is founded on comparing
current with possibly higher levels of labour productivity, taking into account
the real potential in each specific working activity. Moreover, it is clear that
the question of cultural factors and choices of alternative behaviour must
be looked at further; this applies not only to the supply of married women's
labour, but to all the other factors.

18   I wish to underline that almost all the approaches in the field of social and
economic policy assume an 'already formed surplus population' and do not
consider as a cost the creation or avoidance of a very high surplus population.
In this case also, we are faced with the influence of the paradigm of the
market, according to which the formation of surplus population is firstly
inevitable and secondly advantageous, that is, an essential feature of industrial development. In this regard, it would be possible to work out a
paradoxical 'Keynesian' principle: 'It is a good thing to create high surplus
population, it is a bad thing not to absorb it as quickly as possible.

19   It would be interesting to examine in more detail the relationship which is
formed between a high surplus population of young people and the spread
of various juvenile criminal activities (individual, in gangs, or at the service
of organized crime) (see Tomasello, 1986). Compared with other informal
strategies, criminal activities clearly have the 'advantage' of being more
profitable and the 'disadvantage' of greater risk (see Valladares, 1986).

20   In this regard, it is helpful to think of one possible progression from self-
provisioning to informal work and then, subsequently, to the formal sector.
Our hypothetical worker has an average income and adult children. In his
spare time he likes to make furniture, using all the latest do-it-yourself
equipment (self-provisioning). His friends and neighbours admire his inventiveness and ask him to make things for them, which they pay for in cash
(informal). He realizes that his network of connections could become very
profitable if he gave up his main job (early retirement) and opened a craft
workshop, possibly employing one of his sons who is out of work. After a
period of clandestine activity, business picks up and this neo-artisan decides
to formalize his activity by paying taxes and registering at the chamber of
commerce, so that he can count on having more customers and the protection
offered to officially registered operators.

The transition from the informal to the formal sector is not an occasional
phenomenon. As seen in chapters 5 and 6, many activities which at the
take-off stage need to rely on being clandestine are compelled later on to
assume a formal status, since the regulatory system safeguards their interests
more effectively. An example of this is the increased incorporation into the
formal sector of small and medium-sized firms in the Third Italy during the
1970s. In the preceding decade, these firms had become active participants
in rapid industrial growth by exploiting flexible and informal conditions
(Bagnasco, 1977).

21   The peddling of wares on the streets of Naples means something different
to a young Neopolitan than it does to a young Egyptian with a high school
or college certificate who is saving up a sum of money with which to return

to his native country, raise a family and open a shop in Cairo. If the first were to do the same, he would be unable to take part in a large number of public examinations in his search for a permanent job in the state and, consequently, he would not succeed in developing a life strategy.

22 The case of the retail trade and restaurants is especially interesting. It is no accident that in many advanced capitalist countries the retail food trade, for example, has come under the almost exclusive control of family businesses run by recent ethnic immigrants (Koreans in New York and Los Angeles, Afro-Indians and Chinese in Britain).

23 These situations come very close to the dangerous borderline of capitalism without society; the more so when traditional forms of social solidarity are greatly undermined, have not yet been revitalized in new locations and, consequently, present very little resistance to the devastating impact of competitive behaviour.

24 This explains most of the differences in the first stage and why Murray and Szelenyi (1984) find a number of options in the first phase of socialist development. 'Deurbanization is, of course, a relatively short stage in the first period of the transition to socialism. At later stages repeated "campaigns" of deurbanization may occur (the Cultural Revolution in China probably had elements of this) but normally one would expect that the urban population will stabilize soon after the initial deurbanization stage' (p. 75). According to these authors, in a subsequent phase 'two alternative routes are open to socialist countries: they could either follow the Soviet strategy of "primitive socialist accumulation"/extensive industrialization, or they could opt for the Maoist strategy which follows more organic growth patterns, with less emphasis on the division of labour between agriculture and industry. It appears that the two alternative routes of socialist economic development also represent two different patterns of urbanization' (ibid., p. 95).

25 In this regard, the case of the Soviet Union constitutes a unique radical experience since it is characterized by the mass suppression of family farmers or their banishment to the Asian republics implemented by Stalin in the 1930s (Wadekin, 1982; Atkinson, 1983; Shanin, 1986). Concerning the important debate on agrarian socialist strategies in the 1920s, see, among others, Chayanov (1925/1987) and Shanin (1972).

26 For information on Chandigarh see Sarin (1982); for Accra/Terra see Mitchell (1972; 1975); for Brasilia see Epstein (1976); and for Ciudad Guayana see MacDonald and MacDonald (1977).

5

Comparative analysis of informalization processes in different societies

1 INSTITUTIONAL REGULATORY SYSTEMS AND INFORMALIZATION

Introduction

One of the major interpretational difficulties posed by the present diffusion of informal activities arises from the multiform nature of the process and the wide range of phenomena included within it. The fact that roughly similar trends are at work in very different social contexts suggests something more than an extraordinary coincidence. There is a growing feeling among social scientists that by overcoming the difficulties posed by the heterogeneity of informalization, it may be possible to reach a better understanding of the contemporary socio-economic transition on a global scale. Consequently, it is important to discuss plausible interpretations which keep track of the various trends, without excluding the possibility that contemporary processes of social transformation have a common significance.

In this chapter, I follow two interconnected lines of interpretation, which form the crucial matrix for explaining the diversified diffusion of informal activities: first, the development of institutional regulatory systems, and second, the transformation of social factors and their impact in shaping industrial development in different contexts. The first section is devoted to a discussion of the patterns of development in Fordist-welfarist regulatory systems as a main source for the diffusion of informal activities in advanced capitalist societies. This is an obvious starting-point given that the term 'informal' only makes sense in relation to precise patterns of regulation. But, as will be seen, establishing this link is far from easy, and it is further complicated by the persistent idea among social scientists using different approaches that the 'hidden hand' of the market is *the* main regulator of social relations. Moreover, it is thought to be virtually independent of the institutional frameworks and the social constraints which have historically accompanied the process of industrial development. In this section I concentrate only on the specific forms of institutional regulations directly or indirectly enforced by the state. As already stated in chapter 1, within my approach these forms constitute the basic framework for the associative patterns of social organization.

In the second section, I return to the socio-economic areas where informalization tendencies find expression in terms of working opportunities. This analysis is intended to match what was said in chapters 3 and 4 with regard to the changing features of the labour supply, the persistence and formation of surplus population and the conditions and expectations dictated by different and changing social reproduction strategies. At the end of the section, all the findings will be synthesized in a comparative interpretation articulated into the five different models already referred to in chapter 1. These models are based on the different forms, degrees and scales of interaction between associative and reciprocal factors of social organization responding to market tensions as they have arisen historically in diverse types of society.

In the last four sections, I analyse the evidence of informalization and social change within each of these five models and discuss the impact of diverse social factors and conditions. Several examples deriving from the experience of the Three Italies (Bagnasco, 1977; 1981a) are anticipated in order to illustrate more clearly the phenomena characterizing three of the five models. The informalization tendencies in the Italian case are then described in greater detail in chapter 6.

The historical transformations of social factors and institutional patterns of regulation

Before following the first line of interpretation, it may be useful to recall my working hypothesis, introduced in chapter 1, on how institutional regulatory systems and diverse social factors interrelate within processes of industrialization. The crucial social transformation brought about by industrial development in various forms and at different times is the decline of traditional subsistence activities. Usually, the attention paid to the results of this process focuses on the formation of wage-work; but what has happened historically is in fact much more complicated. There are two sides to the outcome of this transformation: first, the diffusion of various forms of work in order to raise monetary income, involving not only wage and salary employment but also the growth of vast and persistent areas of self-employment and of various combinations in which households pool differing complementary forms of income; and second, the fact that subsistence activities do not disappear but for the most part change their nature. What is most remarkable about the latter is the emergence of modern homeworking as a separate field of activity. This area of social life remains predominantly organized in *reciprocal* networks, mainly households and communities. These are both active and passive factors in the transformation process: they both condition its development and are changed by it. On the other hand, the labour market and, more generally, the employment structure have to be regulated by social institutions for the obvious reason – emphatically pointed out by Polanyi (1944/1975) – that the hidden hand of the market is socially disruptive. Regulations are produced within the normative *redistributive* system and are entirely formal and visible, whereas reciprocal arrangements are not. The two processes of adapting and conditioning of reciprocal relations and institutional regulation maintain a degree of social cohesion, usually favoured by a reasonable rate of economic growth and widespread opportunities for social mobility. But there is also a persistent area of tension between the reciprocal and the associative systems, which is usually magnified by sudden changes, the absence of sufficient economic growth or its inadequate redistribution. In these cases, the socio-organizational patterns of the reciprocal kind extend their reach in various ways into areas where they are not normally assumed to be active. Such an extension may or may not be reflected in increased informal activity, and may or may not represent a direct challenge to the regulatory system. However, the growing breakdown in social cohesion and the diffusion of patterns of behaviour which are either unregulated or deviant with respect to the regulatory system are signs of a serious crisis in the institutional regulatory system itself. In other words, the increasing extension of market-competitive behaviour typical of industrial development does not alone produce patterns of social structuration. Instead, it leads to disorganizing tensions, which become absorbed in a contradictory fashion by two separate but necessarily interlinked organizational systems: the visible institutional system of redistribution and that based on reciprocal relations. The latter is largely invisible and unaccounted for in 'formal' economic terms, but equally crucial in shaping the different life-styles of different social groups at different times and in different social contexts. This is basically the reason for the importance attached to the history of regulatory systems in understanding informalization in advanced capitalist societies.

The approach is different in the case of socialist and underdeveloped countries. Socialist countries lay much more emphasis on the role of redistributive patterns of social organization than the most regulated capitalist societies. However, the interaction between the history of institutional regulation and the process of informalization is fundamentally different. Socialist countries start from already highly regulated conditions, which are not only difficult to adapt to changing reality but also accumulate increasing tensions in so far as they are unable to achieve the goal of industrial development in conjunction with limited social inequality. The diffusion of the second economy is a symptom of the fact that civil society outgrows a regulatory system that is basically stable, unchanging and prearranged to minimize social inequalities. In this sense, it is here less useful to look at developments in the regulatory system in order to understand the features of the second economy. The focus should rather be on the ways in which civil society outgrows its institutional shell, on how reciprocal factors become inconsistent with the redistributive system and on the unrestricted role of competitive tensions.

The same argument also applies to underdeveloped countries, but for almost opposite reasons. In general, the experience of these countries reveals a rather poor degree of regulation. Associative patterns of social organization remain fairly weak. Socio-political control is more often maintained and reproduced through repressive authoritarian regimes than through the development of a system of associative regulations. The urban informal sector reflects, as a whole, a subsistence strategy including a wide range of activities, few of which are illegal. Consequently, very little of the informal sector in Third World cities can be understood by starting from the institutional regulatory system. Here the connection between what is informal and what is regulated may be very tenuous: the informal sector is expanding within a persistently non-regulated social context.

The present stage of socio-economic development in advanced capitalist countries is characterized by the end of a long-term trend towards minimizing the non-cohesion between the two regulatory systems through the increasing resources produced by high growth. Generally speaking, this trend has been based on the combination of rising monetary incomes, welfare programmes to compensate for the decline in reciprocal resources brought about by urbanization and migration, and the consolidation of homeworking as a form of the division of labour and as the area of reciprocal arrangements most complementary to industrial development. This transformation lies at the root of the diversified diffusion of informal activities.

Irregular forms of employment are defined by the existing regulatory system. Black-market labour does not exist in a permissive context. However, the same kind of working arrangement may be perfectly regular according to the regulatory system in one country, but irregular according to the system in another. In this sense, the origins of what are now called 'irregular forms of employment' should be considered in connection with historical developments in regulatory systems at both the national and local level. I have already discussed in chapter 2 the interesting example of child labour in Western European societies. It is worth adding here that in underdeveloped countries the question of child labour is different, not only because the legal age at which employment is allowed is usually lower but also because any legal provision is difficult to enforce, particularly within the urban informal sector where children are involved in a wide range of activities (Valladares, 1986).

The historical matrix for irregular forms of activities is, therefore, connected with regulatory systems. It is possible to make approximate comparisons regarding the presence, diffusion or decline of irregular employment because regulatory systems have developed historically along similar lines, though still maintaining national and local differences which largely explain the present wide range of certain phenomena. By tracing the parallel history of regulatory systems, a set of socio-historical parameters can be established to help understand the origins and varying incidence of irregular forms of employment in different industrial contexts in the West.

1 With the only notable exception of Japan (see Dore, 1986; 1987; and section 5 below), advanced capitalist countries developed similar regulatory trends throughout a very long phase from about the 1880s to the late 1960s. During this time, an expanding network of regulations arose around the operational systems of the large Fordist factory, and increasingly offices and chain-stores, and of the welfare state (Lash and Urry 1987).

2 This roughly 'linear' process was interrupted at times by critical emergencies, when due to wars, persistent serious economic crisis or suchlike it was not possible to enforce compliance with the regulatory system, a situation reflected in a temporary sharp increase in irregular activities (black market, *travail au noir*, etc.). When these emergencies were over, not only was enforcement of the regulatory system restored but events themselves offered the opportunity to reshape, extend and tighten up such systems in order to be more effective in achieving the strategic goals of Fordist-welfarist societies.

3 The combination of the developing Fordist system, and the concurrent slow decline in traditional forms of work such as peasant farming, petty trade, persistently labour-intensive building or traditional local manufacturing, compelled these forms to become

progressively more 'irregular'. This was because full compliance with the developing regulatory system would have made it impossible for them to survive. By contrast, in some situations the regulatory patterns relative to pre-industrial craft corporations (mainly the very restrictive barriers against new entrants) were for the most part incorporated into the industrial regulatory system. The principal motive was to bring about the socio-political integration into industrial society of large sectors of the petty bourgeoisie. In the long term this also produced trends towards informalization, when the diffusion of skills and technical know-how enabled an increasingly large group of people to engage in craft activities without first obtaining the necessary legal authorization.

4 Beginning in the late 1960s, the Fordist-welfarist regulatory system has begun to show signs of crisis for different reasons that I will attempt to expound briefly later on. This has produced a new wave of irregular forms of employment different from that caused by the combination of the developing regulatory system and the persistent traditional forms of work.

I will not devote much attention to the temporary waves of irregular forms of employment caused by exceptional historical events (parameter 2), but will discuss the two historical processes outlined in parameters 3 and 4.[1]

Regulatory systems and informal work: the decline in traditional areas of employment

This is not the place in which to analyse the origins of the regulatory system and the ways in which it functions. These have in fact developed along different lines although, as a rule, a fairly similar system has arisen in almost all cases. It is based on the figure of the mass employee working in a large industrial or tertiary-sector enterprise, on formal job registration and complete state control over self-employed activities, on a very extensive and pervasive fiscal system and on the growth in comprehensive welfare services to complement increased consumer spending by the mass employee. What must be underlined, however, are the specific ways in which the development of the regulatory system together with the parallel survival of traditional working activities, highly labour-intensive and with a relatively low and stagnant labour productivity, has led to their being transformed into vast domains of irregular work. Furthermore, the general decline in such activities has often involved a decrease in these particular forms of irregular work and, in some cases, a growing irregularity in their organizational patterns.

There are two obvious general aspects to this combination of factors. First, traditional kinds of work are not subject to total control by the various regulatory systems. The reason is that they are not very concentrated and involve a high degree of unpaid family labour and various combinations of non-standard activities such as fixed-period or casual jobs, the exchange of work skills and the exchange of personal services between employer and employees. Second, traditional activities are unable to comply with the norms laid down by the regulatory system, like paying the minimum guaranteed wage, respecting trade union practices and government safety regulations and paying taxes, because they start off at low and inadequate levels of income. In fact, the more the regulatory system develops in line with increases in labour productivity in the highly concentrated industrial sectors and with the growing need for tax revenue to finance the welfare state, the more traditional activities – if they survive – are compelled to become even more irregular and/or seek complementary sources of income. The above-mentioned combination of factors is to be found especially in the agricultural activities of less developed regions, that is, those which are unable to develop modern forms of family farming which use advanced technology and exploit the family's work skills to the full.[2] However, in these regions the same can be said of the building industry, traditional local manufacturing, the retail trade and private services to individuals and families, such as bars, restaurants and hotels. This type of combination is characteristic of Southern Italy, Spain, Greece, Ireland and some areas of Southern France.

Speaking more generally, a combination of this kind characterizes several services to families and paid housework in particular. Full compliance with the growing regulation of work is not only difficult to enforce in a sector where the employers are households; it also causes the cost of labour to rise above what many potential employers can afford to pay. As a consequence, irregular employment persists as long as there is a supply of workers willing to do the work under the prevailing conditions. These workers are increasingly foreigners from poor underdeveloped countries or 'second-job' workers who look on such work as a way of supplementing their main income or obtaining a temporary income while awaiting other opportunities.

Regulatory systems and informal work: innovative post-Fordist developments

The other side to the historical picture is the absence of irregular forms of employment in some socio-economic areas. This is the case in those locations and branches of industry where up until the end of the 1960s labour productivity increased by more than the overall average, parallel financial and industrial concentration was relatively high and industrial production was financed or directly run by the state.

The immediate historical origins of almost all of the new forms of irregular work can be traced to several important socio-economic transformations which started at the end of the 1960s. The most notable symptoms of this process are two: first, what has been called flexible accumulation and, in particular, the search by manufacturing industry for less rigid and expensive forms of labour than full-time guaranteed jobs for blue- and white-collar workers, whom large industrial concerns find difficult to lay off; second, a phase of tertiarization which is no longer based on the expansion of the big public and private welfare bureaucracies and concentrated concerns but rather on the proliferation of highly diversified forms of employment, sometimes linked to one another and sometimes of a local, atomized and disparate kind. As a source of irregular forms of employment, the second phenomenon is the most significant, even though more attention has often been devoted to the first, and in particular to subcontracting, the re-emergence of industrial homeworking and the renewed importance of micro-firms based on non-standardized flexible working arrangements.

The two phenomena are interconnected: in the 'vertical disintegration' of large industrial concerns we find the hiving-off of office work and services supplied to firms, that is, the detaching and subcontracting of service activities ranging from consultancy to cleaning and maintenance. Furthermore, both phenomena may be linked to the crisis in the regulatory systems of Fordist-welfarist societies. In this sense, to interpret the contemporary phase as the 'end of organized capitalism' (Lash and Urry, 1987) or as that of 'disorganized capitalism' (Offe, 1985) is an obvious step. It is also obvious that in this phase working practices are spreading which are irregular but not traditional. Simplifying, it could be said that whereas the regulatory system is devised for a series of more or less standard jobs, both flexible industrialization and the new forms of tertiary activity open up an area of opportunities and demand for employment that may be described as 'fragments of work', more or less casual, part-time, for a fixed period, of differing intensity and providing variable incomes. In this perspective, no system for regulating working activities is able totally to contain the mounting pressures; thus figures everywhere show that forms of irregular work are on the increase once again. Regulatory systems which are on paper more tolerant towards unauthorized part-time jobs or homeworking, such as that in Britain or in a different way the one in the USA, or those which are more effective and better financed, as in Germany, are better able to resist the pressure for the spread and sharp increase of these forms of informal work; but this is true only in part. In some branches of services, it is difficult to contain this pressure as, for example, in domestic and mechanical repairs or personal services. Multiple jobholding and casual work in particular are on the increase in every advanced capitalist country (EEC, 1989b). As a rule, they are not easy to 'regularize' – or only at the risk of suffocating the new paths to economic growth being followed in industrialized countries or of increasing state bureaucracy beyond what is economically convenient.

What should also be underlined is the interconnection between, on the one side, the development of regulatory systems and the subsequent crises affecting them and, on the other, important social transformations within each specific local or national pattern. Urbanization and the emergence of a mode of consumption which is largely standardized and based on the spending of monetary income have been central factors in the development of existing patterns of regulation. The more or less radical decline in traditional forms of self-provisioning in rural settings has been the other side to this process of transformation. In contrast, an articulated mix of factors has contributed to the crisis of regulatory systems and to the diffusion of irregular forms of employment. These factors consist of the spread of a variety of suburban and small-town settlements, the increasing importance of new kinds of self-provisioning using modern means like computers, do-it-yourself equipment and light tractors for vegetable gardening, and new diverse forms of consumption.

From still another point of view, it should be noted that the specific historical patterns of institutional regulation have been largely promoted by or on behalf of powerful social groups as a way of safeguarding their sectional interests. This is evident where specific norms have been adopted for regulating the labour market and job entry in order to favour different segments of the workforce and categories of economic operators. We have already mentioned the restrictions aimed at protecting artisans in Central Europe, mainly based on corporative barriers and control of job entry, as one of the present sources of irregular employment. The same phenomenon occurs in a different way in the case of Italy where artisans have been protected rather through privileges and more flexible rules, involving in the main an advantageous fiscal and social security system which is radically different from the one adopted for industry. This has also contributed to the diffusion of irregular forms of employment in that an increasing number of economic operators, in no way definable as artisans, have opted for this particular system in order to benefit from its flexible conditions (Weiss, 1988).

A different but equally important set of examples emerges from the institutional regulations governing labour markets and working conditions with regard to workers who are not strictly Fordist in at least two different ways. The combination of relatively low wages and loose control over working hours and second-jobholding has contributed in some contries to widespread moonlighting by schoolteachers, civil servants, local government employees, bank clerks and others.

In other areas, at least in the case of Italian agricultural day-labourers and of Greek building workers, the historical strength of the workers in an abnormal labour market characterized by permanent alternation of employment and unemployment has been reflected in relatively higher but still largely inadequate unemployment benefit. In general, this has to be complemented during the year by a period of regular employment, necessary in order to qualify for unemployment benefit, and a period of continuous and/or occasional black-market work, sometimes even agreed on between worker and employer at the moment of hire (EEC, 1989b). By contrast, the Fordist workers who managed through their historical 'core' role within the trade union movement to gain reasonable cover against unemployment (not a recurrent but rather an 'exceptional' condition, at least during the Fordist age proper) through wage-comparable benefit (or in Italy the *'cassa integrazione'* system) are automatically excluded from access to informal activities when unemployed. An unexpected effect of the regulatory system has been that exclusion has hit the unemployed, who are presumably more in need of a complementary income, but not those already in employment. When discovered or denounced, the latter only risk having to give up their second job whereas the former lose their unemployment benefit, which represents a substantial part of the income in the household to which they belong.

To summarize, I will mention four specific processes that lead to this increase in a new type of irregular work:

1 The semi-privatization of welfare services and the need to decentralize welfare programmes and make them more differentiated;
2 the emergence of a highly disparate and atomized demand for 'personalized services' provided to families and individuals;
3 the growing interest on the part of industry and firms in reorganization into long lines of vertical disintegration and chains of subcontracting, in order to make production generally more flexible and to heighten the capacity for innovation and adaptability to specific situations and market fluctuations. This trend, moreover, is interrupting the traditional link between financial concentration and the concentration of production. Whereas financial operations are

continuing to be concentrated to an increasing extent, reaching the gigantic levels of multinational 'conglomerates', production is being deconcentrated along the various different lines mentioned in chapter 4;

4 the impact from the spread of light technology which provides new opportunities in certain kinds of jobs and opens up new areas to service activities – examples are do-it-yourself equipment, personal computers, video recorders, small electronic machine tools for making personalized products and so on.

When recent trends in social change are considered, the technological factor is often overestimated. Nevertheless, it plays an important complementary role in permitting labour processes to be reorganized. A movement is taking place away from the clear predominance of a rigid system of fixed jobs and towards the spread of flexible 'working fragments' both in manufacturing industry (consider the inexpensive electronic machines for producing knitwear in the home) and to an increasing extent in office work and tertiary activities (for instance, the opportunities for working at home using personal computers).

National and local differences in the types and presence of irregular work may be explained by starting from the specific interaction between the two above-mentioned historical processes concerning traditional informal activities and the new pressures towards irregular forms of labour arising from the crisis in the Fordist-welfarist regulatory system and from the new phase of tertiarization and flexible industrialization.

In general, it is important to underline that contemporary transformations in the comprehensive systems of social organization, whether or not they are reflected in substantial waves of informalization depending on the specific combination of institutional regulatory systems and socioeconomic features, lead to a substantial change in the balance between associative and reciprocal factors. From the strictly sociological perspective adopted here, this balance constitutes the core of the organizational patterns of societies and the key to understanding individual and household strategies as articulated by social groups with varied access to a wide range of resources. As Bagnasco (1985) has argued, after a long period of expansion and growing importance associative socio-organizational factors are now on the wane, while reciprocal factors are extending their influence, often along very innovative lines. How this changing balance is reflected in specific processes of informalization and social fragmentation within different social contexts is shown in the rest of this book.

2 OLD AND NEW AREAS OF INFORMAL ACTIVITIES IN DIFFERENT SOCIAL CONTEXTS

Introduction

I will first recapitulate the main economic areas where irregular forms of employment persist or become diffused and then discuss the main features of the interpretational models used to understand informalization and changing balances in social organization in different contemporary social contexts.

As already stated several times, irregular forms of employment display a great variety which depends on diverse socio-historical trends, local characteristics and legal, regulatory and political systems. Moreover, their presence or diffusion are not exclusively typical of only certain socio-economic sectors, nor do they reflect a single and unilateral historical transformation. On the demand side, three broad and complex socio-economic processes are generally associated with the presence or diffusion of irregular forms of employment: the ways in which traditional work processes decline; trends towards flexible arrangements in manufacturing; and trends towards tertiarization and expansion of services. Only the last of these accounts for any substantial part of irregular employment in advanced capitalist countries.

The impact of regulatory systems in socialist and underdeveloped societies is fundamentally different from that in capitalist societies. Furthermore, the difference between the first two is even greater. In socialist societies, the redistributive system has a very strong impact and is predisposed towards achieving pervasive social control. In underdeveloped countries, the associative system is poorly developed and, consequently, social control is generally based on political repression or co-option (clientelism). As a result of this difference the processes of informalization are bound to be different in these two contexts. However, the first and third above-mentioned processes are also important in socialist and underdeveloped societies. Flexible arrangements in manufacturing, on the other hand, are more difficult to compare on a global scale. For different reasons and under diverse conditions, both socialist and underdeveloped manufacturing set-ups are part of global restructuring and of new flexible arrangements, either directly or through subcontracting (see Frobel et al., 1980), often without promoting the diffusion of irregular forms of employment. Therefore, the phenomenon of informalization in manufacturing is indirectly related to the expansion of the second economy in socialist countries and of the urban informal sector in underdeveloped ones, at least in terms of the survival strategies of workers paid inadequate wages.

It is now worth recapitulating the argument concerning the varying extent to which productive units (enterprises) maintain and develop reciprocal organizational features both in general and in specific social settings, paying particular attention to the family business. Emphasis is placed on two questions already introduced in chapter 1 and touched on in chapters 2 and 3. The first question concerns the fact that large productive units are also based to extremely variable extents on reciprocal organizational principles both in their internal structure (loyalty and stability in the division and organization of the labour process) and in their relation to the external world (from the different angles of customers and suppliers). In this sense, all productive units can be classified on four different scales: the first concerns the internal organization of the labour process, the second and third the stability of customer or supplier networks respectively, and the fourth the degree of reciprocal organizational patterns. On this last scale, instances are likely to be found of polarized organizational patterns where at one end there are, for example, family shops with regular customers and suppliers, and at the other corporations struggling in the labour market to obtain the best workers at the lowest possible wage, even when this means a high turnover, and competing in the general market to continually capture new customers and new suppliers, which allows the business to be expanded and costs reduced.

The second question concerns the way in which highly developed reciprocal organizational patterns become sectionally or locally connected with the institutional organizational system that develops alongside the industrialization process. When and where economic activities characterized by strong reciprocal ties maintain a high degree of cohesion with the associative organizational system, usually because they keep the devastating effects of competition under control without suffocating economic growth, their persistence is not reflected in a trend towards informalization. Capitalist family farming (H. Friedmann, 1979) and the Japanese model of industrialization (Dore, 1986 and 1987) may be taken as examples of this kind of process. In section 5 below, I show what the specific social conditions are which allow a high degree of reciprocal social cohesion when following various paths to industrialization. In all other cases, the persistence of highly reciprocal productive units leads to increasing conflict with the institutional regulatory system brought forth by industrial development. Very often this is reflected in an increase of irregular forms of employment. This is not only a more sophisticated way of posing the problem of informalization in declining traditional activities, but also a way of raising the problem as far as innovative economic areas are concerned; the latter become established behind a high degree of reciprocal protection and include homeworking using advanced technology or new professions which take root within closed friendship networks based on solidarity.

The most obvious and important example of a productive unit that is highly characterized by reciprocal organizational patterns is the family business. Often, it is not only the case that the internal organization of labour is strongly affected by family rather than by associative or market interests, but also that the relations with suppliers and customers are particularly stable and community-oriented due to the local scale of activitites. In this sense, it must be kept in mind that the economic areas where family businesses are still numerous or expanding are likely to show a great deal of informalization, particularly where the reciprocal organizational patterns became increasingly inconsistent with the developing institutional regulatory system. This process will become clearer when specific examples are discussed in the rest of this chapter and in chapter 6.

Agriculture

Agriculture is a typical productive area where the family business remains persistently important, at least in some regions, in the two increasingly divergent forms of family farming and of peasant holdings. Where or when family farming units are able to produce enough income to promote a proper process of capital accumulation, the reciprocal organization of the family is adequate for coping with competitive market tensions (H. Friedmann, 1979; 1980) and maintaining a sufficient degree of cohesion with an increasingly associative-based institutional regulatory system. Furthermore, the role of subsistence activities and savings is progressively reduced, and underemployment and informalization are kept to relatively low levels. Where or when this is not the case, a process of intensive informalization may take place, since in order to survive on a decreasing farming income the family is obliged to adopt organizational strategies which are less and less coherent with the growing and extensive regulatory system, such as tax evasion, paying casual labour less than the minimum wage, employing children and family helpers, finding irregular part-time jobs, relying on community support and on informal exchanges of work, and so on.

Various forms of irregular employment in agriculture are found in some advanced capitalist countries for two contrasting reasons: the relatively high and growing level of underemployment of agricultural workers (both self-employed and wage-workers) in regions which have not developed adequate forms of capitalist family farming; and the very high peaks of temporary demand for cheap unskilled labour during the summer season. The peaks occur in these regions as a result of their economic weakness, which has prevented the diffusion of technological solutions, and of certain agronomic features: in particular, Mediterranean crops like citrus and other fruits, olives or some vegetables are more seasonal and labour-intensive than other products like grain, cow's milk and so on.

The picture of agriculture in the USA, on the other hand, is substantially different. The absence of pre-industrial peasant societies and the existence of large tracts of cultivable land have favoured the development of an agriculture based almost exclusively on family farming on the one side, and on corporate capitalist farming on the other, both of which are related to the growth of agribusiness. Irregular forms of employment play no role, for the most part, on the rather limited number of family farms which have survived despite their inability to accumulate adequately and which are mainly concentrated in the Appalachian region (Bonanno, 1987); rather, they are associated with the extensive and persistent use of predominantly Mexican migrants hired temporarily on an unofficial or semi-official basis in the border states, particularly California and Texas.[3]

Agriculture constitutes a breeding ground for communal forms of social organization which conflict, on a global scale, with the institutional regulatory system, bearing in mind that it is an important part of the second economy in socialist countries (for the case of Hungary see Szelenyi, 1988), and that subsistence agriculture faces increasing difficulties in many underdeveloped countries. In the last case, what we are dealing with is not informalization for the obvious reason that the regulatory system is vaguely defined and ineffective. Rather, the most important social change is due to the fact that as subsistence agricultural arrangements become less and less viable, pressures leading to migration and urbanization build up and set in motion the uncontrollable horizontal expansion of the urban informal sector as the only possible way to enable a growing section of the population to survive.

The relative decline in agricultural income in the less developed regions of advanced capitalist countries, only partially offset by increasing state intervention through subsidies and money transfers, has traditionally forced both small farmers and underemployed agricultural workers to defend their reciprocal arrangements and to look for other complementary part-time work which has often been of an irregular kind. Building, the retail trade and street trading, tourism and, in some cases, industrial homeworking and traditional manufacturing have been and are the economic basis for this kind of complementary mix. These forms of irregular work are declining in parallel with the decline in the rate of agricultural employment and, in some areas, with the introduction of female labour and the ageing of the agricultural workforce, as women and the elderly are less likely to complement low agricultural income with irregular working activities. In these regions, the presence of irregular employment and of part-time self-employment complemented by work outside agriculture remains essential for the survival of agricultural production, which otherwise would completely disappear under existing market conditions. Moreover, the other aspect of agriculturally induced irregular employment, temporary work during the peak season, is slowly declining; but it is worth mentioning that the working conditions associated with it are also deteriorating. For this reason, in general, a local labour supply is no longer available even in regions of high unemployment (Southern Italy, Spain and Greece), and foreign migrants may be irregularly employed in this kind of seasonal work (EEC, 1989b). As already mentioned, irregular employment of unofficial migrants during the agricultural season has characterized to a large extent and for a long period the organization of agriculture in many of the southern and western states in the USA.

Building

Building in the broad sense, that is including home repairs and restructuring, provides an important setting for irregular forms of work. It is worth distinguishing the complete construction of residential houses, where irregular forms of employment are widespread only under particular conditions, from repair and restructuring activities, where informalization including various forms of self-provisioning is a more or less general phenomenon. The second area is not worth discussing at length, apart from mentioning the fact that restructuring activities are becoming increasingly important in relative terms in densely built countries, particularly European ones, and that do-it-yourself equipment and technology contribute to the diffusion of broadly informal solutions (including self-provisioning and exchange of work with neighbours and friends), particularly where the cost of formal work is high and there are a limited number of small firms willing to do small jobs.

As far as concerns the first area, intended to include self-building and privately commissioned building of family houses, it is expanding especially where building has remained highly labour-intensive and is traditionally characterized by a high rate of irregular employment encouraged by a persistent local surplus in the supply of unskilled and semi-skilled labour. In some situations, the decline in black-market labour on large building sites following the slowdown both in urban development and in the rate of economic growth during the 1970s has been compensated for by a substantial wave of self-building, restructuring and the building of second holiday homes. Thus we have a transformation from organized black-market labour in the form of wage-work to more complex, temporary and irregular kinds of employment.[4]

In socialist countries, building activities are the breeding ground for the extensive presence of irregular forms of work, particularly in small towns, in outer suburbs and in the countryside. In these areas, the dominant type is not black-market jobs but rather various forms of work connected with self-building, and particularly exchanges of work (Sik, 1988). Mention has already been made of how self-building and related activities are crucial elements in community organization and in the economy of the informal sector in Third World cities.

Other traditional areas

Irregular employment is present in other traditional activities which may be declining or undergoing revitalization through recent transformations. Among the declining ones there are traditional local manufacturing activities which are either disappearing or being integrated into new subcontracting systems, depending on the specific branches involved. For instance, local agricultural processing industries tend to disappear or decline, while textiles, clothing and tailoring may become part of the flexible production process in a reorganized manufacturing system.

Petty trade and traditional services, particularly tourism, also provide opportunities for irregular employment in the same regions where traditional forms of agriculture survive. They may be declining (petty trade in particular) or expanding (tourist services) and the degree of regulation and irregularity may vary widely according to the local or national situation. The rapid expansion in Greek tourism offers an example of this increasing complexity: there is the parallel increase, on the one hand, in official formalized circuits (hotels, restaurants, etc.) and in authorized household and village hospitality and, on the other, in small unofficial family ventures and in irregular seasonal employment of migrants in general and young foreigners in particular (EEC, 1989b).

Flexible and hi-tech manufacturing

As already stated above, contrary to the expectations created by the great attention paid to restructuring and flexible employment in manufacturing, in industrialized countries irregular forms of work are not particularly concentrated in this sector, not even in those areas which have been called 'silicon valleys' after the first important hi-tech district in central California.[5] Neither is irregular manufacturing employment increasing at a noticeably rapid rate in any advanced industrial district. On the contrary, in some regions like North-Eastern and Central Italy (the so-called Third Italy model), where irregular employment in manufacturing was important in the late 1960s and early 1970s, these forms are now markedly declining.

In general, irregular forms of employment in manufacturing are almost entirely absent in countries where competitive restructuring trends have led to subcontracting outside the country, as in the case of Germany, Holland, the Scandinavian countries, Britain, Canada, Australia and Japan, and in some branches of industry also France and the USA. It is worth mentioning, as an example, that while the flexible transformation of the manufacturing sector in Spain takes place within the country, German capital is increasingly decentralizing manufacturing production to Hungary, Taiwan and other countries.

Although irregular work is not particularly concentrated in manufacturing, there are local cases of a large and persistent presence of irregular industrial employment: examples include the shoe industry in the Valencia region, the glove industry in downtown Naples and illegal garment and clothing ateliers using exclusively migrant labour in the Paris region or in New York City (Waldinger, 1986).

The fact that irregular forms of employment exist and that they are illicit depends not only on local historical factors in particular industries and on recent patterns in restructuring, but also on the regulatory and enforcement processes and on the extent to which capital is concentrated. Britain and the USA have less irregular forms of manufacturing employment partly because capital is more highly concentrated than in, say, Italy or Spain and also because the legislation regulating industrial homeworking and part-time employment is more flexible and 'tolerant' than in other countries. However, the concentration of capital has now become far less connected with the concentration of productive and labour processes due to various new organizational structures, the most famous of which is the Benetton model. This has developed to become a multinational industrial empire, although still based on a highly dispersed and diffuse productive organization, involving small and middle-sized subcontractors, homeworkers, etc., and on a corresponding system of dispersed distribution, with boutiques and shops oriented to local tastes throughout the world (Nardin, 1987). This is not inevitably reflected in a particularly high rate of employment, since these new forms of financial concentration with dispersal of production and distribution are better able to incorporate opportunities for official flexible employment than the traditional model of concentration in Fordist-style factories. One should also be wary of mechanistic interpretations in the case of subcontracting systems: they do not automatically lead to a high rate of irregular employment and they are likely to differ widely from place to place and branch to branch, even within the same country.

Contemporary organizational patterns in manufacturing are subject to formalization or informalization within relatively short periods of time. The take-off of 'made in Italy', which led to diffused industrialization in the NEC (North-East and Central) area in the late 1960s (see section 5 below and chapter 6), was characterized by high levels of irregular employment. However, after a time many forms of irregular work disappeared in the wake of the model's international success and the increasing severity of the Italian fiscal system.

In general, the organization of manufacturing is now oriented towards the development of complex and articulated systems of networks, which are more than just a consequence of relocation and subcontracting and declining employment in industrialized countries. These new organizational forms may or may not involve irregular employment, but in either case they reflect a break with the ever-increasing extension of standardized regulations and concentration of labour processes. These more complex organizational systems for production are based on a balance of reciprocal and associative patterns in which the former are becoming increasingly important.[6]

Tertiarization and irregular employment

As already stated, services are the economic area where irregular forms of employment are more widespread and in some cases expanding on a global scale, although variations are inevitable. There are three different processes which affect the diffusion of irregular forms of employment in services: first, industrial restructuring, especially reorganization involving vertical disintegration in which consultancy, accounting and marketing, legal and technical assistance, cleaning and other services are progressively hived off from the firm/factory; second, the expansion of a highly stratified and dispersed demand for personal and household services to which it is increasingly difficult to respond either through state or large-scale market-oriented economic units; and third, the fiscal and political-ideological problems faced by different welfare state systems, which lead to increasingly mixed and privatized solutions favouring further expansion in irregular employment.[7] Irregular forms of employment in the services are generally polarized between highly qualified jobs, like those in high technology, accountancy, professional consultancy under-taken as irregular second-jobholding, and low-skilled and badly paid jobs, like cleaning and other personal services to households.

Informal work in industrial and economic services is more diffused in Italy or in the USA, where the process of vertical disintegration is at an advanced stage as a result of the specific legal and fiscal context and where a modern universalistic welfare system has never been properly developed. In particular, the Italian system is extremely complicated and not very permissive in theory, but in practice it is very tolerant. Irregular forms of employment are less widespread both in a context of efficient regulation and enforcement, as in Germany, and in one which displays more tolerance towards flexible forms of employment, thus making them perfectly legal and formal, as in Britain. In the very dynamic and culturally diversified situation of the USA, business services are a breed-ing ground for a great range of short-lived innovative irregular activities which may become successful and regularized in the space of two to three years or just simply fold and disappear.

Another important source of various kinds of irregular employment are personal and household services, where the response to economic difficulties is usually a combination of more self-provisioning and an increase in informal work. In certain cases, the two responses may be connected: the development of self-provisioning skills in, say, household or car repairs also gives rise to the opportunity for irregular second-job activities for cash. Multiple jobholding is the type of irregular work which emerges in this context and this explains, perhaps, some of its recent increase in many advanced capitalist countries.[8] Personal and household services are also an area where traditional forms of irregular employment are likely to persist or die out very slowly: the best example is hourly-paid domestic help. The number of irregular jobs is here bound to increase inasmuch as the general cost of labour is increasing and oppor-tunities for employment of this kind are linked to the reciprocal advantage which both employer and employee derive from irregular conditions. This happens when the employer saves on social security payments, and in some cases also on wages, while the employee saves on social security contributions and income tax, yet may still be covered by the social insurance of his/her spouse or first job. In contrast, co-resident full-time maids have nearly disappeared in some countries, whereas in those where entry is relatively easy, for example Italy, Spain, Greece and some southern border states in the USA, this kind of irregular work is increas-ingly undertaken by migrants from underdeveloped countries (EEC, 1989b).

A further area of informal employment in the service sector is connected with the different history of welfare programmes in each country. Irregular forms of employment become more diffused in social contexts where the welfare state has developed in a less efficient and comprehensive form.

Irregular forms of employment and socio-economic innovation

Irregular forms of employment are in part connected with experiments in socio-economic innovation, with new professions and with the spread of new work tools and technologies. It should be noted that a period of innovation is usually short-lived: after a while the degree of irregularity tends to decrease as the experimental take-off phase leads to one of successful application. Often, there is a combination of success and formalization for some activities and failure and disappearance for others. Examples may be found in various contexts in the field of software consultancy and videoclip or film production and distribution. By contrast, it is much more difficult for the transformations produced by the diffusion of new light equipment and technologies in household repairs and homeworking activities to achieve regularization.

It has already been seen that in various social contexts, the demand or opportunities for irregular work depend on the available labour supply made up of individuals who are wholly or partly included among the surplus population. Their availability does not depend only on their being part of the surplus population, but also on the significance that irregular work may assume within diverse strategies of social reproduction. From this viewpoint, it is worth distinguishing between the opportunities open to workers to adopt irregular work strategies on a more or less voluntary basis. In advanced capitalist countries, the most significant examples of voluntary and convenient irregular work are generally second jobs, self-provisioning and work exchanges. In all these cases, such opportunities are usually supplementary to other work and end up by improving rather than worsening the standard of living of the families involved (Pahl, 1988b). The other forms of irregular labour, but especially the more badly-paid jobs done by young people, women or ethnic minorities, reflect a certain degree of involuntariness: there is no choice, given the lack of better opportunities. As a consequence, they often have a negative impact on living standards. This applies also to many of the irregular jobs done by women who used to be or still are housewives. It is true that, in this case, the argument concerning the supplementary rather than alternative nature of this kind of work is valid, above all when the irregular conditions are advantageous for the workers, such as flexible hours, working at home, evasion of income tax and so on. However, it is also true that 'involuntary' forms of irregular labour reproduce a state of dependence and subordination in which women are only able to engage in this type of activity if supported by their father's or husband's income. In the same perspective, several irregular jobs undertaken by temporary Third World immigrants in industrialized countries constitute a special case. If we exclude the Central Americans in the USA, temporary emigration is often a strategic option available to individuals with a high level of education and belonging to relatively well-off social strata. Several years of irregular work which is poorly paid by the standards of the host country but well paid by those of the native country, even though working conditions are very bad, make it possible for individuals to save up enough money to return home and set themselves up in a much more highly qualified activity. Not everyone adopts this strategic option with success. Nevertheless, it is worth while to point out that, in a successful case, irregular work in bad conditions can be associated with a strategy for social and economic self-advancement.

Comparative models based on differing connections between industrialization and socialization

At this point, it is important that what has been said so far on informalization should be reconsidered in the light of the theoretical approach outlined in chapter 1. It then becomes evident that the spread of irregular diversified forms of work, as well as the conditions and changes associated with survival strategies, should be seen as indicators of changes in the balance between diverse original factors of sociality, given that these forms, conditions and changes are reshaped through their interconnection with different modes of industrial growth in different periods and socio-cultural settings. The examples which have been given clearly illustrate that the interaction between social variables and the drive towards economic change arising out of market competition is a complex many-sided process.

My approach leads to a complex model of transformation. The probability that a relatively substantial growth in market resources will occur provokes an attack on the traditional social fabric, essentially based on strong reciprocal and weak associative links, undermining its effectiveness and transforming it so that it becomes more compatible with market competition. At the same time, new types of associative social relationships are formed which in turn act to limit and organize market competition. Furthermore, basic reciprocal social relationships also adapt in various ways in order to protect more adequately the social arrangements of survival and to become relatively cohesive with the newly developing associative relationships. This is a rather complicated cumulative process which has neither the character of a localized benign spiral (the progressive acceleration of modernization) nor that of a diffused and equalizing process (the progressive horizontal extension of modernization). Starting from this initial general model, it is possible to make some further observations.

First, the cumulative effect of transformations of this kind in the medium term and in an isolated social context gives rise to a more or less drastic reduction in the potential growth of market resources, increasingly obstructed by the reaction from new social relationships. In the advanced capitalist countries, economic growth either in combination with increasing associative limitations and regulations or with strong cohesive transformations of reciprocal relations has been possible because of the substantial input from the horizontal expansion of capitalism in underdeveloped countries, leading to the generation of competitive resources abroad.

Second, the presence of traditional social contexts which, for various reasons, are better equipped than others to adapt to specific forms of market competitivity constitute the basis for an alternative model of interaction between industrialization and sociality. Japan, the Third Italy and ethnic entrepreneurship fall into this category. In this model, reciprocal social relations adapt cohesively to specific patterns of consistent economic growth. To some extent, this possibility acts as a substitute for the expansion of associative social relations of the new kind. For example, a strong community-oriented system of industrial enterprises is combined with weak trade unions.

Third, this second transformational model also gives rise to cumulative forms of social conditions which hinder the maintenance of growth at high levels. A hypothesis can be made which states that it is possible to pass from the second type of industrial development to the first. Frequently, ethnic entrepreneurs end by transforming ethnic resources into resources suitable for market competition; their businesses therefore become 'normal' enterprises, and lose 'ethnic protection' once they have achieved take-off. It is almost impossible for the reverse to occur since involvement in transformational processes of the first type means the adapting of traditional social factors, thereby rendering them unsuitable for the second type. But, at this point, it is as well to remember that the potential for 'genetic regression' of these kinds of social factors makes it possible for them to continue to exist in a hidden form (Szelenyi, 1988).

Fourth, where, in a context of global industrial transformation, the potential for the growth of competitive resources is modest in underdeveloped countries and regions, traditional social factors become transformed so as to protect the local structure from external competition. The best example of this is the informal sector in Third World cities. It is only apparently a paradox that the defensive capacity of this kind of reaction is less effective when it is accompanied by sham or imitative forms of institutional associative organizations. For instance, in the informal sector the protective network of solidarity functions better if a modern strong trade union is not set up. If this is the case, it is probable that there are social contexts which are particularly problematical since they are exposed simultaneously to the weak pressure of the growth in competitive market resources, to the radical break-up of traditional reciprocal social relations and to the formation of the new associative relations in a merely imitative form.

Fifth, the experience of the socialist countries can be interpreted as a process in which the associative conditions for keeping industrialization under control are prearranged institutionally along rigid and codified lines. In these cases, when the two processes are unable to run side by side, the growth in market competitivity eventually slows down – this phenomenon has been called the tendency towards underproduction – and industrial development and economic growth become connected with social relations which provide an alternative to the institutional associative ones; the latter form the networks within which the so-called 'second economy' develops.

Sixth, the reasoning behind the first, second and fourth observations suggests some considerations on the long-term effects of the interaction between social factors and industrial development which may help us to understand better the contemporary situation. The persistence of a low-growth capacity on the part of competitive resources increasingly suffocated by associative organization and regulation means that various reciprocal resources grow in importance both as a surrogate, for example in the case of ethnic entrepreneurs, and as an alternative behavioural motivation, which often occurs in self-provisioning activities.

Taking into account that the interpretation of the principal macro-economic indicators suggests that in the last fifteen years there has been, generally speaking, a chronic and critical weakness in the potential for expanding resources arising out of market competitivity, it is possible to make the models of interaction more specific.

As illustrated in figure 5.1, five typical models may be constructed. Both types of advanced capitalist society (one more associative-oriented and the other more community-oriented) and industrial socialist society may be assumed to have reached a critical stage in the contradiction

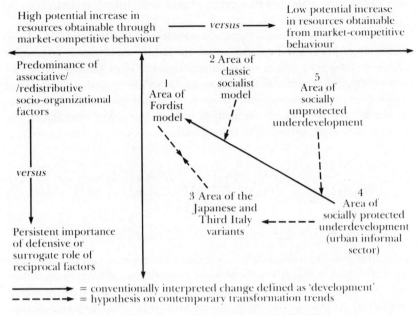

Figure 5.1 Models of industrial development based on different interactions between socialization mixes and the diffusion of individual and market competitive behaviour

between different forms of sociality and market competitivity, which points to changing balances in social organization. In general, contemporary trends in socio-economic change also mean that the first two models are becoming more similar. The crisis of the associative regulatory system and of economic concentration patterns promotes an increasing and new importance for reciprocal networks in the first model. In parallel, higher economic growth promotes a greater degree of networking and associative regulation in the second model. In this sense, I assume that they are converging towards a similar organizational model which is much more heterogeneous, complex and fragmented than the Fordist model but also less based on communal and solidarity networks than in the traditional pattern of Japanese 'flexible rigidities' or the diffused informal manufacturing in the Third Italy. The socialist model is also subject to increasing transformational tensions, the more the institutional associative set-up reveals its limitations and suffocates economic growth through persistent underproduction. The economic and institutional reforms of the Gorbachev age are 'officially' favouring combinations of competitive behaviour and reciprocal networks previously confined to the 'second economy' and are leading to a more heterogeneous and unbalanced model of social organization.

At the same time, both types of underdevelopment model (one more community-protected and the other relatively unprotected) express a chronic incapacity to generate alternative paths of development and are under highly destabilizing pressures from the outside. These are a consequence of advanced industrial society's obsessive need to obtain in underdeveloped countries the market resources necessary to substain the model of uneven global economic growth.

3 CHANGING SOCIAL RELATIONS AND INFORMALIZATION IN ADVANCED CAPITALIST SOCIETIES

The main transformations in the advanced capitalist model

The first macro-model of advanced capitalist societies assumes a social context which is highly conditioned by the diffusion of large manufacturing concerns and powerful financial groups and by a Fordist-welfarist regulatory system at the more or less critical stage in its development. Traditional subsistence activities have declined within a vast process of urbanization, and survival strategies have become almost entirely characterized by the combination of family and complementary incomes, domestic work and public welfare provision. Self-employment and small-scale activities have been greatly reduced by the extensive pressures resulting from industrial concentration. Household structure has become more and more based on the small nuclear family while high levels of social and geographical mobility have weakened kinship and community ties.

As we have already seen, the effectiveness of the mix of social organization predominantly based on the combination of strong associative factors and sustained by high rates of economic growth tended to diminish from the middle of the 1960s. Among the elements that have had repercussions on the organizational mix of society are to be found economic stagnation, the difficulties encountered by various kinds of welfare state, the reduction in employment in big manufacturing industry and the relatively smaller increase in the large bureaucracies of the tertiary sector, and a growing fragmentation, atomization and heterogeneity of the more dynamic occupational contexts in the private service sector. These elements have also favoured the emergence of a rather complicated and less linear picture, in which reciprocal factors take on an increasing importance, though in a context that remains essentially regulated along dominant associative lines. In the various forms in which it may be diffused, informalization constitutes one of the most important symptoms of this transformation. These forms are the underground economy, self-provisioning and income-producing work activities that are not entirely legal or impossible to record, which is a critical negative factor in regulatory contexts based on the assessment of all income produced in a money form.

The renewed importance of reciprocal factors of social organization generally occurs in two ways: on the one hand, contexts richer in reciprocal resources acquire advantages relative to other poorer contexts; on the other, organizational modes of reciprocity regain importance also in contexts that appear definitively oriented towards the sole combination of competition and associative organization. Take, for example, the growing importance of the networks set up between companies in the field of business.

Furthermore, the renewal of reciprocal factors can be differentiated according to the various ways in which they interrelate with the competitive market. In many cases, these factors function as 'surrogates' for a shortfall in market resources. Where this happens, combinations come about that are different from the normal economic combination of competition regulated by associative factors. They are often combinations that the economic establishment would define as 'unfair competition'. Ethnic entrepreneurship would be one example; but then we could also include a group of friends who are able to set up an enterprise without the necessary requisites because there exists a strong bond of loyalty between them and a protective link with the community in which they live, or innovative economic networks owing their success to informal and reciprocally advantageous agreements in conflict with existing legislation, or even the traditional ever-present productive households that only remain competitive due to the favourable, but increasingly 'irregular', effect of reciprocal resources.

This is not, however, the only socio-organizational sphere in which the importance of old and new modes of reciprocity is manifested. In many other cases, reciprocal resources are not directly used in economically competitive activities but rather in other areas of social life, that is, in individual or household strategies which are socially relevant but do not produce exchange-values. Self-provisioning is the most obvious, but not the only example. As shown below, the strong link with a context of reciprocity forms a possible motivation for alternative social behaviour in other cases. I return to the example of workers who prefer to remain in a job where the conditions are not fully satisfying, thus renouncing 'competitive' benefits, or who do not strike or join the union, thereby going against 'associative' principles, because, in a situation in which good jobs are increasingly scarce, the firm they work for guarantees jobs for their children or wives. In this case, I have defined the social factors of reciprocity as 'alternative' because they constitute a motivation leading to an alternative form of behaviour compared to other forms based on classic economic rationality.

The outcome of this transformation is not yet clear, but as can be seen in this and the following chapters, what we are dealing with is clearly social fragmentation. Social organization is more and more broken up along highly structured lines, not only in terms of strong horizontal aggregates such as social classes or interest groups but also of specific and localized segments where reciprocal resources and factors of sociality may or may not congregate. As was demonstrated in chapter 4, the principle problem facing contemporary societies is to reassemble these articulations both at the level of scientific analysis and that of political practice and mobilization.

Differences within the model: the presence or absence of surrogate reciprocal factors

Taking my cue from some recent sociological research, I shall now look at the significance of the changing balance between associative and reciprocal patterns of social organization. When carrying out a comparative analysis, it is useful to bear in mind that single cases included in any macro-models are highly diversified. In my approach, the most significant difference concerns the importance of the adaptation of reciprocal factors, including the degree of community orientation of the enterprise system, as opposed to the strengthening of associative factors. In the case of the macro-model of post-Fordist societies, a range of situations are found which lie between an upper and a lower limit. The first limit is constituted by the maximum weakening of reciprocal sociality compensated for by a marked corresponding strengthening of associative factors. The second consists of a more limited weakening and borders on the model in which industrialization has been accompanied by consistent and diffused innovative adaptation of reciprocal patterns. From a comparative international perspective, several cases can be identified which are closer to the upper limit, in particular Britain, Scandinavia, West Germany and Holland; other countries tend, for a variety of reasons, towards the lower limit. In the case of the USA, it is above all the importance of the multiracial impact which explains why this society is not, as a whole, near the upper limit. However, that segment of society which is made up of whites with Anglo-Saxon origins and of the descendants of European immigrants who are no longer identifiable with their ethnic origins is placed near the upper limit. In Italy, the strongest explanatory factor is provided by the differences between regions. Here, features typical of the upper limit have emerged in the north-west, the so-called 'industrial triangle'. In Spain, Greece and Portugal, the fact that advanced capitalist status has been attained only very recently has prevented them from undergoing sufficient transformation and moving closer to the upper limit.

In general, the range of local situations plays an important role with regard to contemporary tendencies of social change, since it is based on various patterns of reciprocal socio-organization, particularly those which I have called surrogate factors. The closer we get to the lower limit of this macro-model, the more we find, by definition, the types of surrogate social factors mentioned above. But in order to clarify what I mean, it is necessary to discuss a crucial argument concerning the use of an abstract model of the interaction between, on the one hand, associative and reciprocal factors and, on the other, competitive behaviour for interpreting complex and stratified societies where each individual has a diversified mix and amount of resources on the three levels of market competition, reciprocal and associative social relations.

Methodologically speaking, a model works when it is capable of explaining a variety of different cases. In this specific case, social stratification and wide-ranging inequalities are built into the model. It is in fact assumed that competitive behaviour is highly remunerative and continues to be so because fed by external resources, even when associative social factors limit the play of market forces. Unlike in the socialist model, limitative interaction does not aim to interrupt or even less to reverse the flow of advantages obtained through the use of abundant market competitive resources. Furthermore, the approach is generally based on the idea that associative and reciprocal factors fill alternative roles in which it is possible to verify the delicate balance in terms of complementarity and social cohesion at many different levels, such as different social classes or different racial or community groups, but also imbalance and lack of cohesion. This model is based on the assumption that certain associative factors constitute the fundamental cornerstones of social organization together with rather limited but still essential areas of reciprocity, chiefly the nuclear family and the kinship network; it is not by chance that these areas are explicitly acknowledged and regulated in law. Up to this point, it is possible to talk of a cohesive interplay of elements, even if it is characterized by the deep inequalities and social conflicts that are typical of organizations based on horizontal sociability such as classes, lobbies, political parties, trade unions, employers' associations or economic cartels. It has always been pointed out, however, that the organizational factors of reciprocity are at no time and in no sphere liable to take on solely limited and cohesive forms. The village, neighbourhood, ethnic group, friendship networks, school and work companions, and even the modern enterprise are spheres in which more or less strong organizational forms of reciprocity are consolidated; these forms interfere with the exclusive relationship between competitivity and association in diverse ways. This interference may be stronger or weaker and more or less critical either on the competitive side, inhibiting the growth of competitive resources, or on the associative side, curtailing the extension and effectiveness of associative organizational patterns.

Even before the end of the 1960s, the lack of cohesion between association and reciprocity existed everywhere and was more marked in contexts lying at the lower end of the macro-model range. However, this lack of cohesion always developed within social processes characterized by the growing domination of associative factors and their typical 'controlled capitalist' form of interaction with competitive behaviour. Subsequently, the renewed importance of reciprocal factors has everywhere modified socio-organizational mixes. The associative lines of division, such as social classes, trade unions and redistribution policies, have become less effective both in practice and in terms of a theoretical explanation. Other changes are more difficult to interpret in general for a series of reasons: in the first place, because the reversal in trend has not been a radical one and associative factors, although declining, continue to be very important; secondly, because the reciprocal modes have a different significance depending on whether they act as a surrogate of or alternative to market competition. Lastly, it is necessary to insist on the fact that reciprocal factors are numerous and difficult to classify in terms of all their possible meanings. In what follows, I attempt to point out some of the possible forms without any claim to dealing exhaustively with the subject. Besides, the actual presence or absence of reciprocal resources is often hidden. In a whole series of cases, potential reciprocity forms a historical memory that becomes weakened by the ways in which economic growth occurs, but it may reveal new vitality. This theme has been almost entirely neglected in recent sociological writing with the exception of the study by Szelenyi (1988) of agricultural family enterprises in Hungary, to which I shall return in the next section.

Taking the above clarifications into account, it is evident that the presence or absence of explicit factors of sociality able to play a surrogate role does not automatically mean a greater potential for economic growth; it is even less the case that it leads to ethical evaluations of what are the better or worse types of society. In other words, it is not possible to say that Swedish society is in decline compared to Spanish society because it is less rich in reciprocal sociality factors that can be used as surrogates. It is on the basis of this consideration, however, that one can begin to explain two socially important facts: first, in Swedish society associative criteria are still more effective and meaningful, even though they are tending to weaken; and second, in Spanish society there are more informal activities.

The increasing importance of reciprocal factors and informal work

There is a subcategory of reciprocal social factors playing a potential surrogate role which is untouched by the process of adaptation of the traditional social fabric and which has been influenced by other historical processes, in particular socio-political movements. These include the informal innovatory business ventures connected in one way or another with the youth movements of the 1960s and 1970s. In general, these initiatives were launched by activists who could rely on a tight social network, which grew up with the movement, and exploit the socio-cultural changes provoked either directly or indirectly by the movement. The link between the youth movement and the interest in macrobiotics, the production/consumption of certain types of audio-visual shows and other types of cultural innovations, is clearly apparent. Similar observations can be made with regard to the feminist and, more recently, the ecological movement.[9]

Furthermore, there is a type of surrogate social resource which can be considered partly independent of the adaptation processes operating in traditional social contexts. I am referring to residential stability and homogeneity, which favour the diffusion of activities like informal repair services. In this case, the type of activity is important since it is a field in which market competitivity regulated by institutional associative patterns is in a critical phase as a result of unfavourable costs, production and efficiency levels, and the income levels and social status of those operating in it. The existence of a stable and homogeneous network can promote the growth of second jobs or the exchange of services between neighbours or new kinds of communal arrangements. Still in the same field, the absence of stable homogeneous community networks tends, as seen below, to promote social resources which I define as alternative, and they are at the origin of the diffusion of innovative self-provisioning.

Overall, this trend towards the increasing importance of surrogate social factors of reciprocity is sufficiently evident in the continual increase in small-scale self-employment, second jobs and informal activities in those areas which are potentially rich in this type of social factor. A growing number of empirical studies appear to confirm the ways in which this occurs.[10] However, it is necessary to understand the socio-economic impact of this type of transformation above all in terms of the persistence of the initial conditions or of their reversibility. In this case, difficulties arise when attempting a macro-economic synthesis. The problem is to see how this uneven strengthening of various reciprocal patterns combines with economic restructuring in global terms. As a first approximation, this tendency produces changes which are not reversible and which are cumulative in terms of the interaction between socio-organizational patterns and competitive market behaviour, where various resources derived from reciprocal networks take on an increasing importance in order to compensate for the weakness of competitive market resources as suffocated by large institutional organizations and the persistence of stagnation.

This reasoning is more convincing if the second kind of socio-organizational pattern based on reciprocity is also taken into account, the importance of which is likewise on the increase. The most important factor in this respect is the spread of innovative self-provisioning activities, for which reference can be made to some studies of a more general nature (Gershuny, 1978; 1983; Gershuny and Miles, 1983) and to some more specific researches (Ferman and Berndt, 1981; Pahl, 1984; Ginatempo and Fera, 1985; Serpieri and Spanò, 1986). What has already been noted in chapter 4 is the widespread tendency to transform some forms of consumption by moving them away from the purchase of the end product or final service and towards the acquisition of the equipment required for self-provisioning. In the case of repairs in the home, the transformation accompanying the extraordinary success of do-it-yourself equipment is clear enough. In some cases, it may even involve building or restructuring a dwelling. A revival has also been noted in home-made foods and beverages and in clothing produced using modern equipment. Finally, emphasis is now being put on the fact that the use of the personal computer and new audio-visual equipment may make it possible for this trend to expand further into the increasingly sophisticated fields of communications, information, education and health.

Gershuny (1978; 1983) has given a wide-ranging economic interpretation of this trend. He argues that post-industrial society is being transformed into a 'self-service society', starting from the revolution introduced by the car and television set, which appeared before the spread of more recent forms of self-provisioning. However, it is mainly Pahl (1984), in his research on the inhabitants of Sheppey, who is responsible for bringing to the fore the relationship between social context and the inclination towards self-provisioning. The best-equipped households are those of homeowners favoured by geographical and social stability, with at least one adult employed full-time and without too great a burden of dependents such as a large number of children, handicapped or chronically sick persons, or disabled elderly. These households have the time and the resources to set in motion a process of family-based accumulation through self-provisioning which improves its members' standard of living, starting from social resources which are not used within the market economy. This also provides a buffer against the negative effects of inflation and the decline in full-time job opportunities. According to Pahl (1988b), these households enjoy a medium or medium-low standard of living which remains stable, and have no special problems in integrating into the local community. By means of self-provisioning, they enter into a benign spiral which permits them to become relatively well-off households, in part independently of the play of market forces.

Pahl's point about the importance of these kinds of household strategies in a specific context can be adopted within a different methodological perspective based on the motiviations underlying social behaviour. From this angle, the increasing importance of socio-organizational patterns of the reciprocity kind must be seen as redirecting human behaviour in different directions from those connected with maximizing the benefit from market competition or from institutional associative loyalties, the typical examples of economically or socially rational action. For instance, Pahl (1988b) holds that adults who work full-time and belong to families involved in self-provisioning have through their stable relationship with the world of work a greater possibility of finding jobs for their children who enter the job market or for their wives who wish to start working again. This is an advantage which is much appreciated, given the worsening situation of chronic mass unemployment. This idea acquires considerable importance if it is considered in terms of priorities with regard to socio-occupational behaviour. Stability and the possibility of offering jobs to household members are more attractive conditions than they were ten years ago and may be given priority by workers over higher income levels, greater career prospects or more prestigious jobs, or over enrolment and participation in trade unions and working-class parties if any of the latter hindered the achievement of their reciprocal goals.

This is just one among many possible examples, but it is perhaps more useful to discuss its significance than to list other possibilities. In the first place, one should note that this kind of behaviour may take on meanings that are more or less inconsistent with associative organizational forms. Diverse interactions can be assumed between the strengthening of these forms of behaviour and the strategy and effectiveness of trade union action. In some contexts, the trade union manages to include this objective among its demands, thereby reinforcing the loyalty of the workers involved. Where this does not happen, associative loyalty is weakened to the benefit of a closer bond between an enterprise and its workforce. In both cases, wide divisions are created both among the workers and among employers: in the first case, those who do not have a family are strongly influenced by competitive and associative interests; and in the second, those who cannot offer this benefit find themselves in an unfavourable condition that cannot be controlled at the level of economic rationality.[11]

Both in general and specifically with regard to the example chosen, the possible objection that behaviour directed towards reciprocal interests has always maintained a certain importance must be met. In the particular case of job allocation, the documentary evidence shows that strategies aimed at privileging family, friendship or community networks are also found in strongly associative/competitive contexts. Such strategies may equally characterize both enterprises and kinship groups (Grieco, 1987). This is certainly true, but it does not invalidate the reasoning behind the observation about the impact of recent social change. In a context of high socio-occupational mobility, these options had a relatively limited significance. This is confirmed by the experience of the productive households in which high priority was given to re-creating work environments for individuals within reciprocal networks; the logic of this re-creation clashed, however, with the fact that the jobs on offer were increasingly less attractive. As a consequence, the children of peasant families abandoned the countryside. Still in the same context, there were, on the other hand, few among the workers in the large Fordist concerns who wanted their children to follow in their footsteps; if they were to enter factories, then it should only be as white-collar workers or in management after some form of higher education. In this sense, the organizational modes of reciprocity have always existed but in terms that are increasingly subordinated to the logic of associative factors and of individualistic economic competition. In the contemporary world, by contrast, social change is bringing about, at least as a tendency, a reversal in the order of priorities, and it is this which is having an effect on the overall organization of those societies included in the after-Fordist macro-model.

The importance of social change as suggested by the example used here is illustrated by a further consideration. With regard to the family, it may be noted that Parsons started out from the opposite premise when developing his theory of the nuclear family. It can be seen that in some social contexts family ties may once more be important for the transmission of scarce occupational resources. This does not mean a return to patriarchal structures, but it does bring to the fore new and important forms of kinship which go beyond the weak and temporary bonds attributed to the family by theories based on the market paradigm.

Changes in socialization mixes and social fragmentation

There is another version of the interconnection between social relations and economic change which has recently dominated much sociological investigation into the role of women. The fact that the position of women lies at the heart of reciprocal social factors is so obvious that social scientists might well have continued to overlook it if feminist studies had not drawn attention to it.[12] The substantial increase in female employment and in the number of female heads of households has not, as is well known, diminished the central role of women in organizing the family. This role may be in part responsible for perpetuating discrimination in the job market, justifying relatively low incomes because women are supposed to earn only secondary or supplementary incomes, or the lack of career prospects, partly caused by a relative disinterest on the part of female workers themselves. However, it also gives rise to other complicated and far-reaching consequences, from the problem of job shift to that of flexitime or working hours which fit in with family commitments and to increasing pressure for a reduction in the number of working hours. Moreover, the female dimension in society goes well beyond the organizational role in the household and in the kinship system to include important areas such as consumption, the quality of social services, and more generally, the communal relations in everyday life. On the other hand, it is worth anticipating the fact that reciprocal patterns of social organization have been and remain highly unequal in ways that, by definition, are almost impossible to control or correct through institutional regulation. This is especially apparent in the case of women within various contemporary family structures. They are at the heart of reciprocal networks also because they are supposed to give more than they receive, at least regarding reciprocal resources, and in theory be compensated by access to market and redistributive resources through the family, an institutionally regulated practice embodied in family legislation in most advanced capitalist countries. As discussed below, it is not at all clear whether within the new socio-organizational patterns the condition of women is generally better or worse.

A difficult task is to pull together the threads of the new balances and mixes of different socio-organizational factors. They are connected above all with new 'borderlines' and 'differences' both in spatial terms, such as global cities, metropolitan areas, de-industrializing regions and silicon valleys, and in terms of social groups, such as yuppies, the new affluent middle class and new categories of the poor. Some of these issues are dealt with in chapter 7.

The kind of social transformation discussed in this section is neither transitory nor reversible; it is also unevenly distributed in various social contexts, geographical and otherwise, and constitutes one important factor in the division of society.

Generally speaking, the effects of social fragmentation result from a combination of the weakening of associative contexts and the highly discontinuous and unfairly distributed nature of emerging reciprocal resources. The phenomenon takes on greater importance since, unlike associative divisions and inequalities, the deficiencies and imbalances in reciprocal relations cannot easily be controlled through social policies. The consequence is that whereas, on the one hand, these associative bonds that favour the spread of welfare programmes or tight controls on the labour and commodities markets become weakened because a large portion of the population makes use of reciprocal resources to satisfy their needs, on the other, the social groups or individuals that do not have access to increasing reciprocal resources are completely abandoned and affected in a devastating way by the weakening of associative bonds. In other words, the state, political parties, trade unions and associations in general neither have the power nor are interested in intervening in situations arising out of the 'new poverty'. Pahl (1988b) has underlined this point with regard to what he defines as the 'malign spiral' within the new processes of social polarization, a theme dealt with in chapter 7.

The diffusion of various types of informal activities can be understood as a symptom of the crisis in institutional regulatory systems, but it is also related to the growing importance of organizational contexts based on reciprocity. Several of the more evident instances have already been mentioned, but the connection can easily be made in many other cases. The forms of irregular work that spread most rapidly in industrial societies are second jobs, casual work and self-employment. These activities are engaged in on a widespread scale only under when complemented by solid reciprocal contexts, above all those based on the family but often also on the community with its information and self-help networks. At first sight, casual work does not appear to depend on this condition. But poorly paid casual work permits survival only if it is complemented to a high degree by particular social conditions or the possibility of cumulating several work opportunities. In both cases, the family and various forms of community, neighbourhood, friendship and kinship networks are crucial. Outside of the protective sphere of reciprocity, casual workers are for the most part truly poor. In this sense, the growth of opportunities for casual work leads to both the reinforcement of reciprocal contexts and the opening up of wide social rifts between individuals doing the same kind of work. The new poor are socially unprotected; those trying out new forms of employment are socially protected. Take, as the most positive example, those young people going through a phase of casual jobs, but sheltered by their families and by the likely prospect of ending up in a good stable job.

While it is probable that in all the different local types of advanced capitalist society, there is to be found both a relative weakening of the effectiveness of associative social organization and a corresponding, often innovative, vitality of reciprocal relations, this is not manifested in all specific contexts in a substantial and widespread process of informalization. As seen above, this last phenomenon depends on the effectiveness and flexibility of institutional regulation. Informalization does not coincide with effective and flexible regulatory systems; instead it is extensively found in contexts characterized by ineffective and rigid regulatory systems, as the following example taken from Italy illustrates.

An example of recent transformations in the advanced capitalist model: North-Western Italy

Within this general picture, the industrial triangle[13] in Italy presents some interesting specific features. First of all, it is important to point out that Fordist-welfarist elements have been established relatively recently in a rapidly evolving but contradictory process: manufacturing has become hyper-concentrated both in its regional and internal organizational patterns, involving the construction of gigantic plants and the formation of huge working-class suburbs; from the 1960s tripartite agreements between trade unions, industrialists and the government have assumed great political importance. This has led to difficulties in the Fordist-welfarist regulatory system earlier than in other countries. These difficulties surfaced at a time when a modern welfare state had been set up only to a very limited extent: for example, the public health service was not set up until the late 1970s while plans for full-time eduction and public nurseries have never been properly implemented. Moreover, self-employment and small-scale activities have resisted to a much greater degree than in other cases included in the first macro-model and, as a consequence, a variety of non-Fordist-welfarist social arrangements have remained important, such as grown-up children living with parents, communal ties in more homogeneous and stable areas and the persistent relevance of kinship networks. In contrast, the regulatory system governing the labour market developed around very rigid patterns set by the trade unions and the large industrial concerns, particularly intolerant towards non-standard working activities like part-time work, temporary employment and industrial homeworking. This rigidity combined with the easy entry, persistence and informal protection of self-employment, small-scale activities and, to an even greater extent, small handicraft businesses led to a strongly dualistic socio-economic fabric. This dualism acted as an in-built basis for the diffusion of informal solutions as soon as the Fordist-welfarist system entered into its critical phase. In the industrial triangle several social factors which became revitalized, also in terms of economic resources, during the crisis of the Fordist-welfarist system have been preserved in a highly contradictory form. The spread of informal activities unrelated to traditional sectors has taken place at a greater rate than elsewhere due to the combination of rigidity in the official labour market and the presence of alternative social factors.[14]

The data on variations in the employment structure during the last fifteen years show the following trends: a marked decrease in wage employment in medium-sized and large manufacturing industry; a slight increase in employment in small manufacturing concerns; a substantial increase in self-employment and in employment in medium-sized and small concerns in the service sector. Unemployment, involving mainly young people, has risen considerably from the relatively low levels of the early 1970s. Specific surveys show that the large majority of the young unemployed in the North-West remain such for only a relatively short time, three to six months (IReR, 1988). This means that the increase in the rate of unemployment is mainly a sign of increasing labour mobility, affecting principally the initial stages of people's working lives. The rate of working activity for women is also increasing; it is much higher than the average level for Italy as a whole and varies appreciably from the peak reached in the city of Milan, where a vast range of employment opportunities are concentrated, to relatively low rates in medium-sized and small towns (IReR, 1983). Specific estimates for categories of irregular employment reveal a marked increase, chiefly in the large cities, in moonlighting (involving 20 percent or more of the working population), in Third World migrants and in casual and temporary jobs. Both vertical industrial disintegration and the new pace of tertiarization are producing substantial transformations in the employment structure and, in particular, an increasing differentiation in working conditions, a persistent diffusion of irregular forms of employment and a certain degree of casualization of work. Unlike in other advanced capitalist settings, these transformations have not been paralleled up until now by an extensive dismantling or reshaping of public welfare provision, for the very reason that here they have remained relatively undeveloped and inefficient.

The social impact of transformations in the employment structure is a problematical question. If we exclude the conditions in which Third World migrants exist and those applying to a relatively limited minority of unskilled young individuals from very poor educational and social backgrounds and socially isolated and disadvantaged households (no male adult, many dependents, pensioners without children in large cities, etc.), these transformations are not bringing about a vast social polarization in North-Western Italy. The fragmentation of the social fabric produced by casualization and informalization is counterbalanced by the compactness of the household structure and kinship system. The life/work-cycle and gender discrimination both affect and are affected by these transformations. In simple terms, young people remain for a relatively long time in a phase of high job instability and go through spells of both unemployment and informal work or, at least, work which is untenured and precarious. But they are sheltered to a greater extent by the household income, which is boosted by the moonlighting of the father and the part-time work of the mother. At the same time, women, particularly wives, are willing to accept irregular or untenured low-paid work in so far as it complements an above-average income from adult males and conditions are flexible with respect to time or place. All these arrangements are made relatively more convenient and more irregular by the nature of the Italian fiscal system: very strict on paper, but largely unable to control self-employment, moonlighting, casual and black-market work.

For these reasons, in a limited economic sense, this combination of de-industrialization and informalization has led to the creation of a great deal of wealth. However, underneath this appearance of prosperity lie mounting social and cultural tensions. There are three controversial questions worth discussing briefly here: the medium-term impact of the changing demographic structure; the fact that potentially weak forms of households are increasing rapidly; and whether an employment structure involving permanent gender discrimination is tenable.

On the labour supply side, the casualization of the employment structure has led to the absorption of, in the main, four groups: moonlighters; women; Third World migrants willing to accept long-term 'dirty' jobs unacceptable to local youth and women; and young individuals, the children of a baby boom period, who put up with a phase of provisional work instability before ending up in the still sizeable Fordist-welfarist structure or in the expanding sector of professional or service-related self-employment and small-scale activities. If the informalization process continues at the same pace it will have to confront a problem arising out of the demographic structure: a decreasing number of young people due to the fall in the birth rate in the 1970s and even more in the 1980s. As an increased use of the other three groups presents serious problems, the more likely perspective is that the phase of work instability for young people will become progressively longer and for a growing number of them will never come to an end. The consequences deriving from this situation are not of the kind that can be absorbed within the houehold structure either in economic or social terms. It will mean a marked increase in poverty and socio-political conflict between generations. At the same time, at the other end of the life-cycle the substantial increase in the number of old people who cannot survive without the economic and moral support of their relatives will also create growing social tension.

Contemporary trends of change in the household structure seem to be moving away from the marked presence of those social factors which now serve to compensate for the negative impact of informalization. These trends are very pronounced and quick to take effect in large metropolitan areas where the casualization and fragmentation of employment is also more radical. The result is that a rapidly growing number of individuals find themselves unable to compensate for the inadequacy of their working activities within the existing social context. Consequently what is today a small minority may tomorrow become a majority.

Finally, this is the same social context in which the pressures to reduce and abolish gender discrimination are stronger and gradually achieving some success. But every step in this direction is totally inconsistent with the informalization process and is bound to shift the tensions arising from irregular employment onto other groups. This will lead to more social fragmentation and to a reduced possibility of renewing social cohesion within the customary household setting.

4 SOCIALIST INDUSTRIAL DEVELOPMENT, SOCIAL FACTORS AND INFORMALIZATION

Socialist industrial development and the socialization model: an introduction

As has been seen throughout this book, in studying the processes of industrial development the social sciences have concentrated almost exclusively on the 'typical' interactions between the build-up of pressures on social organization cauded by the spread of competitive market behaviour and the consequent reactions of an associative kind. In this sense, the model of industrial society now adopted almost always coincides with the Fordist picture of industrial society. As a consequence, the approaches used in the social sciences are not effective for understanding societies that diverge from this model. Generally speaking, this divergence takes three different directions. First, there are the socialist societies where, as a result of important historical events, market pressures are subjected to the control of a pre-arranged associative-redistributive system. Its task is to keep to a minimum the growth of social inequalities caused by economic competition. Second, in Japan and in other sectoral or regional cases industrial growth has been accompanied by highly persistent forms of communal sociality and by a relatively weak or 'different' development of horizontal forms of sociality. Third, underdeveloped societies present a picture in which the pressure of economic competition ends, on the whole, by siphoning off their resources, understood in a general social sense and not just in narrow economic-monetary terms. This activates forms of social reorganization of a different kind from those found in the Fordist type of industrial development.

The four models above are, according to the approach adopted in this book, to be viewed as historical variants of industrial development and it is necessary to interpret them on the basis of a global approach (Chase-Dunn, 1989). In fact, the development of the advanced capitalist countries cannot be understood without taking into account the interconnection with areas that, through their impoverishment, provide resources for solving the problems created by the progressive weakening of the competitive impulse, stifled by growing associative control. But the other two models as well, and the particular historical realities behind them, can be understood on the basis of the idea that industrial development gives rise to diverse ways of organizing society, beginning with the devastating impact produced by the spread of competitive behaviour and by the reactions to it in terms of different combinations of associative sociality and of varying levels of reciprocal networks.

As I have already pointed out in chapter 1, my aim is not the impossible one of analysing all the possible kinds of societies in the industrial age. The attention and competence that I am able to dedicate to the other models of industrial development are limited. The goal I have set myself is to trace a global picture that is theoretically consistent and to fill in some of the analytical detail. The latter is concerned almost solely with societies that can be classified under the first model. Here, it is easier to be more detailed not only because I have personally carried out empirical research, but even more so because of the wealth of material provided by the social sciences. The other models have also been considered, but this is not taken very far nor backed up by wide-ranging documentation.

The build-up of contradictions between sociality and competition and, consequently, the specific forms of the tendency for social factors to adapt and change follow a different path in socialist countries; nevertheless, the basic terms remain the same. According to my approach, it is wrong to classify socialist societies as contexts based exclusively on redistribution as against capitalist societies based predominantly on the organizational principles of market competition. There are two reasons for this: first, market competition is not an organizational principle, and second, institutional redistribution takes place in every kind of society and not only in socialist ones. The latter are defined by the fact that the political class which comes to power believes that the 'normal' interaction between market pressures and organizational reactions of the associative and reciprocal kind is deficient, since it does not prevent ever-widening social inequality. Market pressures are subjected to the prearranged tight control of associative-redistributive norms formulated for the purpose of combining economic growth with a limited degree of inequality. This means that socialist societies are exposed to market pressures not only because or whenever they are not isolated within a global economy but also and fundamentally because they aim at industrial growth and preserve a relatively important and expanding sector of monetary exchange. In this sense, it is likely that the admiration Lenin expressed for Taylorist industrial organization was not just a personal inclination; neither can the recurrent adoption of Stakhanovite policies be simply put down to political aberrations. On the contrary, they both reflect the anxiety to increase productivity and to promote industrial growth using incentives other than monetary reward: in the first case, a supposedly 'scientific' organization of the labour process, and in the second, the substitution of monetary incentives by social prestige, given that Stakhanovite workers are officially recognized as socialist heroes.

Applying the approach adopted here, it is possible to summarize the macro-model of socialist industrial societies as being made up of the following three main features, together with two in-built defects:

1 Industrial growth in socialist societies is based on redistributive allocation of resources to a set of priority goals and industries which have been established by the ruling class;

2 strictly codified associative/redistributive patterns of social organization are institutionally established and enforced in order to promote industrial development with the minimum amount of social inequality possible, which, put differently, means a tight control over anti-social tensions caused by the diffusion of market-competitive behaviour;

3 all reciprocal patterns of social organization are dismantled, penalized or, at the very least, curbed by strict controls as it is thought

that they disturb the redistributive process and may be combined with market tensions in arrangements (the main example being family entrepreneurship) which invariably reproduce forms of social inequality;

4 the first in-built defect is due to the fact that growth is slowed down by underproduction, which is a structural consequence of economic development being under tight associative control;

5 the second is almost an automatic result from the first. It is a particular form of adaptation of various reciprocal networks which by absorbing and relaunching market tensions create a popular response to underproduction. These arrangements combining reciprocal sociality and market competition may be strictly illegal, not officially permitted or perfectly legal, but they are incompatible with the ideological model of socialist societies as expressed in the third feature mentioned above.

It can be immediately deduced from these five elements that an extensive form of 'second economy' is structurally embedded in socialist industrial development and that a very wide definition of the 'second economy' is perfectly consistent with any theory of socialism centred on the dominance, but not the exclusive existence, of associative/redistributive patterns of social organization. This kind of definition has been called 'the Hungarian definition' (Wiles, 1987) and one of its versions (see also Deszeny-Guellette, 1981; Sampson, 1987) is the following: 'The second economy includes all of the nonregulated (legal and illegal) aspects of economic activities in state and cooperative organizations, *plus* all unreported activities, *plus* all forms of private (legal, semi-legal and illegal) economic activity' (Marrese, 1981, p. 51).

As I have already stated, this is not the place to discuss in depth the workings of the socialist economy. However, some fundamental elements have to be mentioned in order to understand the varying significance of the second economy in the socio-organizational systems of contemporary socialist societies. These elements regard three interconnected problems which are difficult to discuss separately: the impossibility of matching production with needs and consumptive capacity; the independent role of the political class in the redistribution process; and the tensions created by the modes of adaptation of reciprocal networks. The second problem has already come up in chapter 2 and is dealt with again from a political angle in chapter 7. Towards the end of this section I return to it in order to make some observations on the impact that informalization tendencies may have on the role and nature of political elites in socialist countries. Various matters related to the first and third problems have already been looked at in chapters 3 and 4. To avoid repetition, I shall take what has already been said as a starting-point and concentrate on further aspects which are important for a sociological understanding of the socialist model of industrialization.

Contradictions in socialization at different stages of socialist development

The problem of the increasing difficulty in balancing production of goods for monetary consumption with the consumption strategies of the population arises at a stage of industrial development when socialist societies are no longer affected by severe scarcity, which poses other kinds of problems. Incidentally, some Eastern European countries turned socialist at a stage when their industrial productive capacities had already reached a relatively high level and, consequently, did not meet with any of the problems arising in the first stage. This applies to East Germany and Czechoslovakia in particular.

The need to increase agricultural productivity and to squeeze out of the countryside enough food and raw materials to feed and dress the population and enough resources to promote capital accumulation in industry is the main imperative at a primitive stage of socialist industrialization. When put into effect, it sets in motion three trends that are particularly difficult to keep under control: increasing urbanization and migration from the countryside resulting from the creation of a rural surplus population; a fall in agricultural prices, which has to be curbed to a sufficient extent; and polarization in the agricultural class structure. On the basis of their divergent experience of primitive industrialization, the Soviet Union and China formulated quite different strategies, which then took root as different modes of structuring societies in terms of balances between associative and reciprocal patterns of social organization. The Soviet experience has been more oriented towards associative patterns and has resulted in more concentrated large-scale collective forms of farming, since family, communal and individual entrepreneurship were reduced to a minimum by repression. The experience of the Chinese commune has also entailed the minimizing of family and individual entrepreneurship, but in a much more decentralized way where local community initiatives have maintained a relatively high degree of autonomy from central state directives. It is important to underline that, although in highly diversified forms, the experience of other Eastern European countries has differed widely from what has occurred in the Soviet Union, and they have been more tolerant towards community and family initiatives.[15]

Turning to the contemporary situation, it is important to stress that real socialism has nowhere gone beyond proclaiming the abstract ideal of building a non-monetary exchange society (for the theoretical debate, see Nove, 1986). On the contrary, socialist industrial development has also involved a considerable increase in monetary income and transactions, even though it has at the same time brought with it increasing provision of welfare services either free of charge (education and health) or at prices kept low for political reasons (housing and public transport). I have already discussed in chapter 3 the persistent difficulties connected with providing these services at a level sufficient to improve the quality of life and to complement effectively and equitably low levels of monetary income. Housing in large cities and urban facilities in general are the areas in which such difficulties have remained particularly evident. Here the problems do not lie so much in forecasting the needs of the population, but rather in investing enough resources as these are monopolized by other sectors given higher priority in socialist industrial development. The more this occurs, the more socialist societies become trapped within a mechanism of accumulating shortcomings reflected in 'underurbanization', a housing shortage and overcrowding, and dualistic and uneven housing distribution (for the case of Hungary, see Szelenyi, 1983). The shortcomings and inequality in the housing sector lead to the increasingly important role of reciprocal networks, expressed in various forms which are all inconsistent with the egalitarian philosophy of socialist regimes: self-help building and exchange of labour (Sik, 1988); multi-family cohabitation and subletting; informal lending of money between friends or relatives; an increasingly influential system of personal recommendation for obtaining priority in the allocation of a co-operative or state flat; and so on. Sik (1988; Galasi and Sik, 1988) suggests that a similar process of increasing self-provisioning through the use of kinship and personal recommendation networks and of private resources is taking place in health care also, at least in Hungary, leading to 'the further spread of corruption and to the formation of an extensive black market within the health-care network' (Galasi and Sik, 1988, p. 169).

The monetary transaction area of the socialist system presents different problems which also lead to the increasing importance and transgressive nature of reciprocal networks. It is worth discussing these problems from both the production and consumption sides. It is important, however, to underline that the main source of these problems lies in the fact that the consumer market remains to a certain extent unpredictable in socialist societies too. For this reason, the socialist strategy for avoiding the social disruption connected with overproduction ends up by creating large-scale and rising underproduction. Even if prices and the quantities and quality of goods produced in the official economy for monetary consumption are under the control of centralized planning, the consumption strategies of individuals and households cannot be made entirely subject to prior planning by a central authority; this becomes even less possible, the higher wages rise and the more consumer tastes becomes sophisticated (Rev, 1985). In ways that differ from capitalist societies, socialist ones also have to face growing difficulties in balancing, on the one side, the changing problematical relation between the residual needs not satisfied by welfare provisions and monetary consumption capacity and, on the other, the quantitative and qualitative levels of production needed to match the monetary consumption capacity. This may be interpreted as a part of the socialist variant of the contradiction between individuality and socialization typical of all industrial societies.

The shortcomings and problems of the socialist productive process: the black market part of the second economy

Very little documentation and analysis exists on the malfunctioning of the socialist productive apparatus.[16] From the institutional point of view, central planning systems are more or less flexible and decentralized. The method and extent of negotiation between the central authorities and the local productive units vary greatly. It may be assumed that, as happens with institutional systems in capitalist countries, the more planning is inflexible and unable to incorporate new and local factors and, at the same time, incapable of implementing a reasonably efficient system of control, the more this leads to the diffusion of that part of the second economy which operates underground within the socialist enterprises themselves. There is now sufficient documentation on how this part of the second economy works in terms of both selling part of production on the underground market and of setting up underground sub-units within official enterprises (Wiles, 1987). In the case of the USSR, the pioneering work of Berliner (1952; 1957) shows that these phenomena were deeply rooted in the Soviet economy as early as the 1930s.

From a sociological perspective, the starting-point is not lack of commitment, immorality or the corruption of some factory managers. On the contrary, the kind of malfunctioning referred to here is, at least partially, structurally embedded in the centralized planning system itself. The local units have to fulfil goals set through negotiation with the central authorities during the preparative phase of the plan. If they do not achieve these goals, they are subject to some kind of political sanction; functionaries are removed from their posts, or at least not promoted; the factory is branded as being anti-socialist; and so on. As a consequence, during negotiations the majority of local units attempt to have goals set which are below their productive capacities and to be assigned inputs above the quantity strictly necessary to produce the agreed output. In normal years, all local units overshoot the quantity of products set by the plan and, whenever possible, they conceal a part of the surplus production in order to avoid the risk of targets being increased in the following years. The 'whenever possible' applies to the surplus production of goods that can be sold underground either to other units or directly to consumers or to official or unofficial shops and traders. This tactic is so well known to the central authorities that they prepare in advance a set of accurate controls. These same controls bear witness to the importance of underground production in that they only exist as an attempt to keep this tendency to the minimum possible. For instance, the extent to which road transport of goods is subject to control by the central authorities in the Soviet Union is well documented (Altman and Mars, 1987a, b; Mars and Altman, 1987). A reasonable assumption is that controls are decreasingly effective, the more the scale of production of monetary wage goods increases and diversifies, the more the scarcity of such goods make it convenient to expand underground production and bribe some of the inspectors (recent trials in the Soviet Union show that this is a widespread practice), and the more high costs discourage further expansion of controls. Moreover, underground production by socialist enterprises, or at least a certain part of it, reveals an internal logic of accumulation; consequently, it also involves a number of firms producing capital goods and it is larger in regions where it became established earlier and has remained relatively undisturbed for a number of years.

For all these motives, it would be reasonable to expect a very high extent of underground production by socialist enterprises in some parts of the Soviet Union (Georgia, Armenia, the metropolitan regions of Moscow and Leningrad) and a very low extent in East Germany, where official industrial production easily meets local demand and where controls are much easier due to the small size and the cultural homogeneity of the country. A fair amount of documentation on how the socialist system of underground production works is now beginning to appear (Altman and Mars, 1987a, b; Mars and Altman, 1987). These studies confirm the great importance of reciprocal networks within the process of underground production and consumption of goods. Wide strata of the population are tied into a strong and compact reciprocal network, which they extend with extreme caution and use as a privilege. They include industrial managers at all levels, corrupt policemen, customs officers, state employees and frequently top local party officials (see ibid.) intermediaries and/or consumers, and also a certain number of factory workers. The latter are kept to as restricted a circle as possible when goods produced underground are not sold directly to final consumers, in which case a higher number of trusted intermediaries between the factory and the consumers is needed. It is not by chance that in Georgia or in Armenia, where the presence of these underground networks is documented as being particularly widespread, the general standard of living is visibly better than in other regions where official wages may be higher but the second economy is relatively undeveloped, such as heavy industry and military enterprises in scarcely populated districts of Siberia.

The petty commodity part of the second economy

Both the socialist productive apparatus and the parallel system of toler-ated small private entrepreneurs grow faster than controls are supposed to allow; therefore, a part of officially produced goods, especially in light industry, moves towards hidden distribution and consumption while certain forms of production, above all of foodstuffs and services, escape control or are legally tolerated by the institutional social apparatus. This second part of production in the 'second economy' is worth a few observations. The range of small private activities constituting this sector is diverse and changing, depending on various cultural and historical backgrounds and on differences in the institutional regulatory systems (for the case of Hungary, see Szita, 1987). Some of these activities are perfectly legal. This is the case with self-provisioning in general and with vegetable growing for own consumption in particular, also a widely diffused, persistent or growing phenomenon among town-dwellers (Musil, 1987), who cultivate small family plots on the fringes of the major cities. The pressures of the late 1980s for economic reform in Eastern Europe and China have been basically oriented towards an increasing tolerance of at least a part of these activities. At the same time, the fostering of a more competitive style of socialist enterprise management may bring back to the surface at least some of underground production.

It may be that the main reason why these small activities are on the increase, mainly in services like restaurants, coffee-shops, small boarding houses, boutiques, repairs, professional consultancy, is the same phenom-enon that is producing similar effects in advanced capitalist countries: the changing requirements, life-style and occupational structure of societ-ies where productivity in manufacturing industry is high and employment decreasing, even though in socialist countries these tendencies are counterbalanced by underproduction, which keeps productivity relatively lower, and by extensive state provision of welfare services, which obstructs the diversification of the demand for these services.

In the case of small private activities, the role of reciprocal socio-organizational patterns is so obvious that there is no need at all to discuss the subject. But because of this very fact, it is important to underline that, independently of whether they are permitted or not, the spread of these activities is having effects that diverge substantially from the egalitarian ideology embedded in the associative system of institutional social regulation. This does not happen because capitalism is reinstated or great fortunes originate in these petty private activities, which is not actually the case, as Szelenyi (1988) rightly points out, but because an increasing amount of resources and opportunities are beyond the reach of the redistributive system; consequently, society becomes more diversified and inequitable and the principles of 'fairness' on which it is founded are weakened, leading to a growing breakdown in social cohesion.

The consumption process and trends towards fragmentation

A brief look at consumption shows that there are other complementary elements in the transformation process that promotes the increasing importance of the second economy as embedded in reciprocal socio-organizational networks. In consumption, networking is important for two different reasons: income-pooling and access to privileged forms of consumption. Reciprocal networks larger than the cohabiting family are necessary if enough money is to be raised to buy expensive durables and motor cars and to build a house, as has already been argued in chapter 4. But strong reciprocal networks are an even more important requirement for obtaining access to certain consumption practices, particularly the following three: consumption of goods produced underground and sold unofficially for cash to individuals by socialist firms; consumption of agricultural produce and petty commodities produced by the private part of the second economy, when they are scarce and in great demand or when they are illicit; and privileged access in the official distributive system. Where transactions are officially permitted, the network system may be loosely based and only informational in character; where they are illicit, and in particular continuous or repeated, it may be more tightly organized, possibly leading to the formation of powerful reciprocal interest groups.

The role of kinship and family relations in small-scale market-oriented agriculture and that of ethnic and regional communities and friendship networks in organizing access to the parallel economy in terms of income and consumption has been sufficiently documented. Using data on the

Soviet Union, Grossman (1986; Grossman and Treml, 1987) shows how access to the parallel economy differs according to precise social factors. For example, Armenians and Georgians seem to enjoy privileged access even when they emigrate to Leningrad. This suggests not only that in this case social networks have an importance which is analogous to that of informal networks in advanced capitalist countries and in the cities of underdeveloped countries, it also gives rise to the hypothesis that in socialist countries, as in the experience of many other countries (see, for instance, Reyneri, 1979; Light and Bonacich, 1988), there is a transfer of ethnic-regional networks from their place of origin as a result of migration. People in socialist countries often point out that social networks play an important role in unofficial consumption. Only those who are outside these networks make their main purchases in shops. An individual who has lived for many years in Leningrad and then moves to Moscow returns to the first city to buy, for example, a coat, a dress or household appliances through informal networks.

It seems to me that all the documentary evidence available on socialist countries indicates that competitive market relations are being partially reinstated through the increasing importance of new and old reciprocal factors. This widening of market competition under reciprocal organizational control occurs at three different levels of incompatibility with or violation of the socialist legal order. First, the off-the-books operations in the socialist sector are clearly underground and illegal. Second, part of the activities connected with small entrepreneurship in agriculture and services, including moonlighting, are not permitted or accounted for within the existing legal framework. However, it is likely that they will be increasingly permitted in the present wave of economic reforms (for the case of Hungary see Hegedus, 1987), and consequently, shifted onto the third level. Third, another part of these activities have always been or are now being permitted, and some even officially recorded, as in the case of agricultural production for own consumption. But their growing importance, and the unequal distribution of opportunities among different layers of the population, are having an increasingly disturbing impact on the social order. In fact, it is important to underline that independently of the degree of illegality, the diffusion of these combinations of market tensions embedded in reciprocal social arrangements are incompatible with the socio-organizational model based on the priority given to social relations pre-structured by state intervention or by institutional forms of co-operation and association. It is also the case in socialist countries that the effect of increasingly important reciprocal social factors differs according to region, social and ethnic group and economic sector. Consequently, their interaction with the process of socio-economic change is expressed both in new and irreversible tendencies, among them previously unheard-of inflation (Hegedus, 1987), and in marked inequalities of opportunity across various social groups.

Lastly, I want to put forward a few brief considerations on the independent role of the political elite within the socialist model of industrialization, discussed further in chapter 7. It is worth underlining once again that this role is in contradiction with the purely ideological model of socialism. It is only under exceptional circumstances, and then for a short time, that a situation is avoided in which a relatively large, hierarchically organized group of individuals in control of the redistribution of scarce resources obtains a greater share and first pick. In the long run, even the internal rationale of selecting the best individuals, rewarding them accordingly and putting them in a position to do their job efficiently means that they get a larger slice of the cake and this leads inevitably to the formation of a privileged stratum, whether or not it be a 'new class'.[17] The problem is that this unavoidable outcome deeply conflicts with the ideological model based on the greatest possible egalitarianism. Some political leaders, particularly Lenin, have been aware of this contradiction in theory, but they have overestimated the capacity of revolutionary political practice to keep it sufficiently in check and underestimated the length of time required to achieve a level of productive growth at which its impact on the social redistributive system will diminish. An adequate level is one where a highly advanced productive capacity is able to satisfy the requirements of society in a relatively short time and, consequently, in a position to eliminate not only the difference between the haves and the have-nots but also the inequality between the first-served and the last-served. The contradiction has become deeply embedded within the very structure of everyday socialist experience, and it has played a substantial role in promoting the growth of the underground part of the socialist productive apparatus and creating the rigidity in the planning process described above. In this sense, it is easy to assume that the entire socialist leadership, and the party, state and industrial bureaucracies, have strong mixed feelings about the growth of the second economy. It implies a lessening of the centralized authorities' capacity to control society, but it also constitutes one of the main instruments for achieving the cohesion and compactness, the internal solidarity, of the entire ruling class. It is likely that things are now changing due to the increasing share of petty private initiatives in economic activity and to the need to improve the efficiency of the socialist sector, which has become very deeply enmeshed in underproduction. This change may be one of the most important reasons for the astonishing rapidity and radical nature of the 'political revolution' in the Soviet Union and Eastern Europe.

This brief analysis confirms that Polanyi's axiom concerning the fundamental incongruity between sociality and industrialization also applies to kinds of development which use institutionalized social forms to guard against the anti-social effects of an unlimited increase in competitive behaviour. Here too, the build-up of contradictions eventually leads to the increasing importance of reciprocal social factors, which interact with economic change in an unpredictable and differentiated manner; hence the underlying contradictions re-emerge in the form of new problems. For instance, one can imagine the impact that the enrichment of private family agriculture would have on the hinterlands of large cities in China, the consequences in the USSR of increasing permissiveness towards socio-ethnic groups which are extremely active in the parallel economy, like the Armenians and the Georgians, or the effect of increasing social fragmentation and diversification arising out of the recent economic reforms in Hungary (Galasi and Sik, 1988).

5 INDUSTRIAL DEVELOPMENT BASED ON EXTENSIVE ADAPTATION OF RECIPROCAL SOCIAL FACTORS

Introduction

I am not able to dedicate to the third model the attention it deserves for several reasons. In the first place, I am not familiar enough with Japan, which is the most important country to which this model applies. It would also be wrong to build an interpretational model on a single case, particularly if one cannot abstract it from its specific local and cultural features, an operation which presupposes a deep knowledge of the case in question. Furthermore, the combination of industrialization and relevant ways of adapting reciprocal factors has been insufficiently studied, making it particularly difficult to formulate an adequate model. On the one hand, the combination of viable economic ventures with reciprocal patterns of social organization has been considered either a peculiar exception (both family farming and the case of Japan) or a transitory phase destined to be absorbed by 'normal' processes of development (both ethnic entrepreneurship and petty commodity production) or an irrelevant general condition of all industrial societies (in the case of evidence of strong and persistent economic networks). On the other hand, the fact that the contemporary phase of change in advanced capitalist societies is characterized by the growing importance of reciprocal networks in every case, with the possible exception of those included in this model – for obvious reasons mentioned below – makes it particularly difficult from the methodological point of view to distinguish between contemporary general tendencies and the features of the specific model that are based on the persistent importance of reciprocal factors. This difficulty is especially evident in the analysis of the contemporary economic phase in terms of the 'second industrial divide' (Piore and Sabel, 1984).

For these reasons, I will make only a few observations which fall short of providing a full picture of the third model but may serve to initiate a discussion on the prospects for contemporary societies, characterized by increasingly complicated socialization mixes in which reciprocal factors are taking on a more important role. This is particularly the case in those societies which look as if they will become increasingly dominated by associative patterns.

Family farming and industrial family businesses

The first point to be underlined concerns the fact that the variant of industrial organization based on reciprocity is not an exotic exception. In order to understand this, it is also relevant to mention the most important differences between these organizational forms and those predominantly based on associative factors, which are usually considered the only 'normal' forms. It is useful to start this preliminary discussion with the case of family farming and, more generally, family businesses. From a strictly economic point of view, it has been noted (H. Friedmann, 1979; 1980) that family farming is recurrently competitive with capitalist corporate concerns because not only can it do without making a profit, but it can also adopt organizational solutions based on savings and underpaid labour, provided that such family undertakings can survive in the long run. In this sense, family farming is relatively flexible and has a long-term outlook. Some of the conditions typical of it, like self-provisioning of produce, savings in the cost of housing and transport and the support of rural communities, are features peculiar to production and life-styles in agriculture at certain historical times. It is now increasingly clear that they are no longer essential elements in explaining the persistence of family farming. Even in cases where self-provisioning has considerably diminished, traditional rural communities have mostly broken up and the way farmers live does not differ substantially from that of town dwellers, family farming may still remain competitive and a viable economic mode of social organization. These considerations confirm a hypothesis which is supported by wide-ranging contemporary evidence: that the persistence of family businesses accompanied by a variety of different arrangements is not specific only to agriculture and rural social settings (see Berger and Piore, 1980; Granovetter, 1984; Weiss, 1988). From the sociological point of view, family business organization is interesting for many reasons apart from the absence of the need to make a profit. The economic operations of the business are subordinated to the family's reciprocal strategy. It is the changing form of reciprocal social organization which mediates with market competition and with emergent individual consciousness. Here, the evidence is of a problematical nature. Family businesses often have a more long-term outlook and greater interest in stability: rather than unlimited expansion and economic success, they tend to achieve survival under changing conditions of market competition and variations in the needs and working capacities of the members of the family. The labour processes involved are designed more to suit the size and capacities of the family itself than the conditions set by the labour market. This means that various different options are available: not only a more intensive and flexible use of labour, but also combinations of part-time external activities as a source of complementary income or of innovative investments, strategies based on educational achievements of some members to upgrade the business, and various other possibilities. The power structure in family businesses also varies widely. It can be extremely authoritarian and discriminatory, as shown by the fact that in many cases it is persistently characterized by strong patriarchical elements (the 'father-boss' model). But it may also be highly receptive to the different needs, capacities and creativity of individual members. This happens particularly in social contexts where the self-fulfilment and creativity of individual members of the household may become a positive asset for the family business, as widely documented in cases of both family farming and handicraft, industrial and service family businesses in the Third Italy (Bagnasco, 1977; Brusco, 1979; Paci, 1980). Whatever the case, in these kinds of economic ventures the gap between individual needs, requirements and creativity and the logic of management and decision-making is less pronounced than in large bureaucratized and conflict-oriented associative organizations. As has been happening in the last few decades, this crucial difference tends to increase if the transformations of the two different socio-organizational systems follow opposite paths, the associative one becoming more and more bureaucratized and the reciprocal one increasingly receptive to individuals. The polarization between reciprocal forms of organization still characterized by strong patriarchal authoritarianism and those more open to emergent individuality is not so much due to cultural factors –

originally, all families were patriarchical in one sense or another – but rather depends on the opportunities offered or constraints imposed by the more general social context in which the family business is embedded. In this sense, it is likely that reciprocal networks in underdeveloped countries or of persistently poverty-ridden social groups remain more authoritarian than those in advanced countries or of wealthier social groups where there is a wide range of opportunities for simultaneously achieving both the self-fulfilment of individual members and the survival and upgrading of the family business. It is also likely that in the third model the authoritarian and discriminatory patterns are more persistent, since they play a more important role in shaping the social order than in the first and second models. The Japanese experience described below confirms this, whereas it is more debatable in the case of the Third Italy.

An outline of the main new features in the Japanese case

These initial considerations on the persistence and adaptation of family businesses do not provide an adequate basis on which to build an alternative interpretational model of industrial development, despite the evidence that they are still significantly present. Such a basis is even less adequate if account is taken of the fact that in some innovative branches of the service sector family, small-scale and self-employed ventures are far more numerous than in the rest of the economy. This last phenomenon may serve as an indicator of the contemporary transformation of all societies in the direction of the increasing importance of reciprocal patterns, but not of one particular variant of industrialization. It is only the great interest aroused in the 1970s by the success stories of Japan and the Third Italy that has given a decisive contribution to the building of an alternative model, one whose features have largely remained hidden within sectors, localities and temporary experiences but which has also been overshadowed by the exclusive attention paid by social scientists to associative trends and by the difficulty in conceptualizing phenomena characterized by extreme cultural variation and great complexity. Both the cases of Japan and the Third Italy help us to form an explicit picture of this variant model because, in them, the sectoral or local organizational scale has given way to a vast and complex networking system, involving 'relational contracts', subcontracting, stable links between large and small concerns and among different branches of activities and various ideologies of co-operation between workers and management to achieve consensual reciprocal goals.

It is important to recall the basic elements of the Japanese case, even if only schematically and indirectly; this is done mainly by referring to two recent works by Dore (1986; 1987). One of the essential points to stress is that while specific cultural features are an important factor in explaining the particular form that the socialization mix assumes in Japan, they cannot be considered a *conditio sine qua non* for the coming into being of an advanced industrial system in which reciprocal factors are relatively important. The Confucian/Buddhist culture based on 'benevolence', a relatively high degree of cultural homogeneity, a workaholic ethos and loyalty towards the country and the Emperor are important in the Japanese case, but given their specificity, they cannot be included as elements of the third model. In this respect, a general comparison between Japan and the Third Italy is crucial for an understanding of the general shape of the model, mainly because the Third Italy is very unlike Japan from a cultural point of view. The Italian cultural background is not only greatly influenced by Catholicism, it is also highly diversified and heterogeneous; in the political sphere, for instance, the North-East is predominantly Christian Democrat while the Centre is Communist. Historically, loyalty to the country or to a particular regime has been weak. Dedication to work is high in self-employment and family and small businesses but rather low in the large and medium-sized concerns, unless the workers are involved in institutional forms of co-operation or partnership. This indicates that important forms of adaptation of reciprocal factors become historically rooted in ways that are culturally diverse and in which the essential elements are strong and stable networks of co-operation.

Abstracted from their cultural specificity, so far as this is possible, the basic elements of the Japanese socio-economic system are:

1 A 'Community model' enterprise (Dore, 1986, p.125ff.), where the distribution of profits to shareholders is less important than continuity, long-term development and stability of employment. In Japan this element, which is typical elsewhere of small or family concerns, is strongly rooted in medium to large corporations. The same situation is found in the Third Italy in another culturally different form: the wide diffusion of co-operatives and consortia.

2 The strength and stability of networks of different size and importance, from the dominant groups of *keiretsu* to much smaller morally binding bilateral or multilateral informal agreements, which pervade economic organizations and society in general.

3 A system of industrial relations informally based on life-long tenured employment, the responsibility of the management for the welfare of their employees, workers' reciprocation in terms of loyalty and dedication, and careers based on merit and age (Nishikawa, 1980).

It is easy to recognize that this kind of interrelationship is a large-scale replica of the typical situation in family businesses.

4 A consensual, but probably decreasingly viable, system of counter-acting discrimination based on gender, age and meritocracy within a strong family/local community network (see mainly Fukutake, 1982; van Wolferen, 1989).

5 A life-style based on relatively little spending (limited consumerism compared to other countries) but highly quality-conscious, and corresponding high savings counterbalanced by persistent opportunities to export the industrial surplus produced.

This model, too, is characterized by critical and cumulative tensions between, on the one side, individualism and global market relations and, on the other, the particular socialization mix. These tensions are expressed in the last two elements. The fifth element indicates the necessity that an international economic equilibrium be maintained which is able to guarantee a relatively high degree of extroversion, typical of a socialization model where the productive capacity is greatly in excess of a persistently low capacity for consumption due to the protection afforded by the innovative adaptation of reciprocal networks. This is less problematical in the case of sectoral or local phenomena such as family farming or ethnic entrepreneurship, since surplus production is transferred to other sectors or areas, either through unequal exchange or through shifts in investment. But it is more problematical at the truly national or regional level because the disequilibrium is either relatively cumulative and increasing or, where at a standstill or reversed, it undermines the foundations of the socialization model itself.

The fourth element is more difficult to deal with in general and should be discussed in depth case by case. All that can be done here is to put forward a few hypotheses for testing in empirical research. The social division of labour is based on strong and persistent discrimination which is not fully mediated and socialized within the class system (see Fukutake, 1982). The role of the family and of the local community is crucial both in compensating for asymmetrical situations and in reproducing them. Given these conditions, it is likely that the main expression of the above-mentioned tensions occurs in exactly the opposite way to that in the first two models: associative forms of socialization express emancipatory impulses which are non-cohesive and difficult for the dominating socialization mix to bear.

In the specific case of Japan, for example, a persistently high level of gender discrimination is not opposed within the reciprocal system but rather through the increasing involvement of women in politics, social movements and associative organizations. This is the main reason why I would suggest the hypothesis that cases included within this general typology constitute an exception to the general trend towards the diversified but increasing importance of reciprocal networks. However, for the same reason, the first three models may be seen to be converging, along different paths and preserving their cultural specificity, towards similar end results in terms of socialization mixes; that is, situations in which renewed reciprocal factors are more important and less cohesive with associative factors compared to their limited and hidden role during the Fordist age in the first model, and in socialist countries from Stalin to the early Brezhnev, a period characterized by tough redistributive policies, in the second. In the third model, the same increasing conflict and non-cohesion within the socialization mix is promoted rather by individualistic demands expressed through a strengthening associative system which starts from a relatively weaker and less developed (hypothetically, also less bureaucratized and concentrated) form of organization. In these cases, the fragmentation tendencies do not originate in the fact that the increasing importance of reciprocal factors is weakening the associative forms of organization. Instead, they arise from the fact that the emergence of individuality subordinated and repressed within the socialization mix, accompanied by the increasing importance of associatively organized interest groups, is causing the internal cohesion in this typical socialization system to diminish, a phenomenon which is also connected with new developments in the international division of labour.

In this last respect, a crucial question arises which cannot be answered within an economistic approach: for how long and to what extent will the global economic system be able to tolerate the existence of a number of highly extroverted societies, considering that to the cases described here at least some of the Asian NICs like South Korea, Singapore, Taiwan and Hong Kong should be added? As seen above, savings and surrogate adaptation of reciprocal factors with a traditional origin but changing rapidly in innovative ways can render a specific socio-economic setting competitive on the international market; but this proves incompatible with substantial and increasing internal consumption of the domestic product due to the protection afforded by the very nature of the socialization mix.

The main features of the model as derived from the Third Italy

I shall now look briefly at how the third model has developed in the case of North-Eastern and Central Italy (or NEC, to use its acronym). This area is also called the Third Italy, after the title of an important work by Bagnasco published in 1977, *Le tre Italie*, in which the advanced industrialized region of the North-West is designated the First Italy and the Mezzogiorno the Second Italy. At the end of the 1960s, the NEC (Bagnasco, 1977; Paci, 1980; Bagnasco and Trigilia, 1984a and b) was characterized by a notable take-off in industrial growth. A large group of small and medium-sized handicraft and industrial concerns drew considerable advantage from particular social conditions, namely, family businesses, a community-based economy, inter-sectoral complementarity, the extension to industry of the preference for reciprocal and collaborative strategies which originally developed in agriculture (agricultural unions and co-operatives) and so on. The entire system was rapidly transformed away from productive capacity suited to the local market towards specialization in exported goods both in the traditional manufacturing sector, like clothing and footwear, and in the modern sector, for example household appliances, tractors and machine tools.[18]

The NEC, which covers a vast part of Italy including seven regions, remained relatively undeveloped industrially speaking in the immediate post-war period; none the less, in social and economic terms it was very stable. It was not affected by chaotic urbanization or waves of selective emigration or immigration; and specialized local industries or crafts mainly oriented to local markets resisted the pressure of international competition. Agriculture was characterized by the predominance of family farming involving sharecroppers or tenants, who showed an increasing vocation for small entrepreneurship and the ability to remain competitive and innovative, setting up a very strong co-operative movement as an alternative to capitalist concentration. A long-established network of cities and towns playing a role complementary to the economy of the surrounding countryside completes this approximate picture.

In schematic terms, as long as Fordist-welfarist industrial development continued, the Third Italy had enough social resources to resist economic decline but not to compete with standardized production in factories outside the setting of socially protected local markets. When in the second half of the 1960s these conditions changed, the process of diffused industrial expansion began. At first, it seemed that the change was mainly due to decentralization, subcontracting and the channelling of financial resources to the area by Fordist concerns in the industrial triangle. But later it became clear that these factors alone could not explain the phenomenon of diffused industrialization. A large number of small concerns in the area self-financed their growth, remained independent and were competitive with big industry. For instance, the small shoe-producers in one of the regions of Central Italy, Le Marche, organized themselves into various kinds of consortia. They concentrated on quality, product diversification and fashion and managed to oust the standardized production of the Milan district from the export market for Italian footwear. Also, a consortium of small and medium-sized engineering firms in Emilia became the main domestic competitor of Fiat in the production of tractors and agricultural machinery.

Reciprocal social factors and informal work have been two main elements in this experience. The starting-point is a stable community network and the possibility of complementing various kinds of income and resources, including traditional and innovative self-provisioning, within a solid household structure. From the point of view of the household and of survival strategies, these conditions entail a decisive propensity to save and limit consumption, the pooling of a mix of incomes and, consequently, the possibility of being able to accept more flexible work patterns and a less unequal redistribution of benefits generated by high rates of economic growth. In fact, these conditions lead to increasing work opportunities for all, but diversified and distributed into more or less tenured, formal or informal, permanent or part-time jobs. On the other hand, firms enjoy the bonus of a less expensive and more flexible labour force, on condition that they do not concentrate production or expand vertically beyond a certain point. As a result, expansion takes place predominantly in a horizontal direction through an increase in the number of small and medium-sized units and the development and reinforcement of co-operative concerns specializing in consultancy, accounting, marketing, product styling, export, innovation in production and advanced technology.

During the initial stage, the presence of irregular employment is quite marked. Unpaid family work, off-the-books employment and overtime, and black-market work are essential to the NEC experience for as long as a large portion of the revenue produced within the sphere of small enterprises remains hidden from the tax authorities. Evidence of this phenomenon is the discrepancy between the official statistics for employment in the early 1970s and the real figures resulting from local surveys: the offical rate was 35 per cent as opposed to the actual rate of around 55 per cent. A high rate of informal activities in the Third Italy during an initial stage, as compared with a low rate in Japan and with a substantial decrease in the following stage, also throws light on the importance of the specific comprehensive regulatory system. Informal activities are not *per se* a sign of the great or increasing importance of reciprocal factors, but rather of their non-cohesive role within the socialization mix as dominated by associative institutional regulations.

In a second stage, when the economic success and export vocation of these enterprises has become consolidated, their strategy is to formalize the conditions of employment as far as possible in order to close the gap between hidden costs and declared revenues and thereby avoid high rates of taxation on profits. In so far as they are able to preserve the advantageous conditions of small size, co-operation, better industrial relations than in large factories and flexible employment, the move towards formalization does not endanger their economic effectiveness. This is verified by the increase in official rates of employment in the 1970s and by the shrinking of the discrepancy between official and real rates.[19]

The original reciprocal factors have been partially weakened through the process of development but, for the most part, they have adapted in such a way as to prevent marked tendencies towards industrial concentration, unconditional competition between economic operators and the loss of the benefits from protection in the sphere of consumption. Besides typical associative factors, like trade unions, industrial and professional associations and government regulations, which were all strengthened during the 1970s, certain characteristic social forms like integrated company systems, consortia for export and marketing, networks of technical consultancy and service associations were also reinforced. At the same time, family economic involvement remained considerable as did that of kinship networks, complementarity between different activities, socioeconomic compatibility between many types of part-time jobs and so on. In this way, the standard of living increased more than the cost of labour and the propensity to consume.

The great importance of reciprocal social factors is here, as in Japan, conditioned by the opportunity that exists of feeding an increase in the flow of exports. The system is therefore extremely exposed to the global market and to the state of the international economy. Once again, the social context proves to be a double-edged weapon relative to market competitivity. Internal reciprocally-based limits on consumerism entail high dependence on foreign markets, and this gives rise to either growth or crisis according to the state of the global economy. The contemporary phase presents problems which are difficult to interpret. It might well be possible to identify contexts in which reciprocal factors could develop further without conflicting with global market equilibria and with the associative regulatory system – for example, the development of increasingly sophisticated community services – but in the long run that would increase the difficulties connected with the outward-looking nature of the model.

Contrary to what is generally thought, the case of the Third Italy is not based on a path of informalization but rather the opposite. It is likely that even the general trends of casualization of work in the service sector have been relatively contained by a combination of a strong and stable social background and the advantages arising from horizontal development. Moreover, it is not by chance that already in the 1970s Bagnasco (1977) noted that in this part of the country the Italian welfare state was less inefficient and that this was even more true of the provision of services depending on local government, whether in areas dominated by the Communists or by the Christian Democrats (Trigilia, 1986). The social structure is decidedly less polarized and more cohesive than in the other models. Community and family networks are more effective in counteracting the increasing heterogeneity of working conditions. Some forms of casualized work which are not socially acceptable have been diverted towards migrant workers from underdeveloped countries, who are present in large numbers in this area, chiefly in cities and tourist resorts.

The main problem in the NEC is that the more balanced social situation is guaranteed by high rates of economic growth promoted by industrial exports, in combination with an internal situation oriented towards preserving the social structure; again the parallel with Japan is evident. This outward-looking economy depends to a very large extent on two combined conditions: that local production remains competitive with that in other areas and that the international demand for goods typically produced in the area continues to increase at a sufficient rate. Alterations in these conditions are likely to produce marked tensions within the local balance of society. If one considers that advantageous but different flexible conditions of production are spreading in various areas of the world and that the number of consumers of high-quality and high-cost goods is no longer increasing at a fast rate, it is easy to imagine how unstable the social equilibrium on which this model is based may become. Long-term trends towards re-informalization and casualization of work are likely to reduce the capacity of family and community networks to provide social compensation. If and when this happens, gender and age discrimination is likely to give rise rapidly to a much more unstable, inequitable and tense social situation. This prospect parallels the different prospect in Japan, which is determined by the destabilizing impact on the socialization mix of emergent individuality, above all in the form of women's movements, organized through associative factors.

6 INDUSTRIALIZATION AND UNDERDEVELOPMENT: TWO MODELS OF INTERACTION BETWEEN MARKET EXPOSURE AND SOCIAL FACTORS

Introduction

At an abstract level, it is possible to deal with both these models together because they encompass a wide range of situations lying between two ideal extremes. At one end, there is the maximum protective adaptation of reciprocal social factors. These are opened up and transformed in order to accommodate the partial influence of the global market and individualistic behaviour but, at the same time, restructured so as to permit survival on extremely low levels of monetary income and render the local context relatively impervious to the antisocial effects of the market. At the other end, there is the state of practically complete vulnerability in the face of the same antisocial effects; it results from the weakening and dismantling of traditional reciprocal factors being combined with the feeble development of associative ones.

It is difficult to find situations that have been subjected to adequate longitudinal study and that have remained close to either of the ideal extremes for long enough to make it possible to fully understand how the two models function. For this reason, my remarks are approximate and preliminary in nature and open to verification by future research. The ordering of cases between the two extremes depends on the way social contexts react to detrimental trends towards the extension of competitive behaviour and the consequent onset of weak and badly functioning associative networks. In this sense, my interpretation cannot be limited to only industrial and market parameters. But it is worth stressing that where protection provided by adapted reciprocal factors is greater, an interpretation in terms of development parameters is more likely to describe such a situation as poor and backward. On the other hand, situations which are considered to be characterized by a high degree of social disintegration are treated as being relatively more advanced economically. By analogy, I believe that conventional industrial development policies, above all those which are successful, shift the local type more towards the extreme of social disintegration. Still speaking in general and approximate terms, there are some convincing indicators to back up this interpretation, mostly from recent rapid economic growth in NICs. These range from the transformation of underemployment protected by reciprocal networks and household livelihood strategies into socially isolated unemployment to the social disgregation syndromes in Brazil and the indomitable nature of many important social problems in countries which in the 1970s benefited financially from the oil price increases, for example some Arab countries, Mexico, Venezuela and Indonesia (see also Chase-Dunn, 1989).

The adaptation of social contexts based on reciprocal protection or, on the other hand, their forced break-up to make way for weak associative networks with limited protection, display characteristics which vary according to the locality and must be studied in each individual case. In general, it is important to reaffirm the incompatibility 'by definition' between protective adaptation of reciprocal factors and the conventional values associated with industrial development, intended as a combination of high economic growth accompanied by the diffusion of strong associative relations. From this perspective, the different transformations of the socialization mixes typical of underdevelopment appear to be inexorable spirals. The local constitution of individualistic interest groups is endemically feeble because the dynamic of capital is dependent on foreign markets and socialization arrangements predominantly based on wage-work, those which underlie what is meant by working class in the strict sense, remain extremely limited phenomena. The fact that associative factors remain endemically weak means, in turn, that the defence of existing socialization patterns against the devastating impact of competitive behaviour takes place almost exclusively within the adaptive processes of reciprocal factors. For this reason, it is easy to argue that where these processes are also unable to react sufficiently, social disintegration will become typical of the socialization mix. Moreover, it is worth underlining that in almost all situations where economic growth is not substantial, reciprocal social factors do not turn into potential surrogate resources for alternative patterns of industrial development, as happens in cases included in the third model. In the reality of underdeveloped countries this is obvious, and even more so if social change is interpreted from the non-economistic angle of the transformation of socialization mixes.[20]

General considerations

A few general considerations serve to introduce the theoretical foundations of the two ideal models of socialization typical of underdevelopment. The presence and expansion of the informal sector in Third World cities is taken as an example of adaptation of reciprocal socialization with a potential to provide protection against the disruptive impact of dependent penetration by the market. The case of Southern Italy is introduced as an example of the fifth model, the one characterized by high levels of social disintegration.

The first consideration concerns the original transformation of socialization patterns when these are subjected to industrial underdevelopment. Mention has already been made several times of the fact that preindustrial socialization mixes based on various kinds of collectivist and reciprocity-dominated arrangements have to be violently undermined so that they will succumb even partially to the influence of kinds of behaviour based on individual exchange and wage employment. There is general agreement on this side of the transformation; but this does not tell us much about how the socialization mixes become transformed in practice, that is the specific historical forms they assume in different underdeveloped countries and regions at different times. At this level, the question requires a huge effort in comparative investigation and understanding. For this reason, the general ideas advanced here are of a hypothetical nature.

In particular, it must be stressed once again that, by definition, underdevelopment does not lead to a substantial progressive diffusion of occupational systems based on the prevalence of wage labour, complemented only to a diminishing degree by domestic and subsistence economies, and accompanied by the overwhelming emergence of forms of associative socialization in defence of class or group interests. It is precisely for this reason that traditional systems of socialization are forcibly opened up to accommodate very limited opportunities for monetary exchange and wage labour, but subsequently transformed and adapted so as to complement, at the level of survival strategies, the persistently high inadequacy of these same opportunities in terms of guaranteeing material social reproduction for the great majority of the population. In this sense, I agree with Bettelheim (1972) when he asserts that in these countries pre-capitalist forms of socialization are not dissolved when subjected to market tensions but are largely preserved and adapted. This process of preservation should be interpreted as one of change because, once the socialization mix has been opened up to accommodate partially individualistic-competitive behaviour, it can no longer remain the same as before.

What we have, therefore, is a dual process of change that is particularly diversified and complex in its historical forms. This is true both in relation to the breaking down of the imperviousness of pre-capitalist systems towards individualistic behaviour and to the adaptation of reciprocal socio-organizational factors so that they become subsistence strategies for complementing persistently limited opportunities for wage-work and monetary exchange. The great majority of the population is forced to change social reproduction strategies in a context of transition from modes of agricultural-communal production to colonial or semi-colonial single-crop systems of farming based on plantations and the use of low-paid day-labourers and poor peasants. This historical transition is significant but not the only one possible, and it takes on numerous specific forms which are all unstable and characterized by growing contradictions and tensions, which cannot possibly be dwelt on here.

The general conditions of the contradictory process of transformation affecting the socialization mixes typically found in underdeveloped areas change in industrial history mainly as the result of two factors: the quantitative and qualitative penetration of the industrial system all over the globe, and the development of more marked productive systems with a high intensity of capital in both agriculture and manufacturing. According to Kahn, 'an important shift in the world-forms of capitalist accumulation took place starting in the 1930s' (1980, p. 11). This 'shift' has helped to push a large part of the rural population in underdeveloped countries much further into a state of surplus population and to bring about their urbanization at a progressively accelerating rate. The question of socialization is thus posed increasingly in the following terms: individuals become more and more socially isolated 'through the dissolution of communal tenure arrangements, and from any "traditional" elite; they now enter the economy as proletarians on the one hand, but in a situation where there is no employment on the other' (ibid., p. 12). The result is the growing importance of forms of petty commodity production, above all in urban services and in handicrafts and to a more limited extent in agriculture and industry. This question is essential for understanding changes in socialization mixes and relates to a complex set of problems that have not yet been sufficiently investigated and clarified.

The first thing to be taken into account is that 'households frequently evolve livelihood strategies which involve members participating in both capitalist and petty forms of production and only by a *combination* of these varied kinds of economic activity do households reproduce their labour-power' (Rogerson, 1985, p. 33). The problem is, however, even more complicated because the survival strategies encompass not only forms of wage labour and of petty commodity production but also old and new forms of self-provisioning and of various kinds of reciprocal relations that go beyond the household organization to include local, ethnic and kinship networks. At all events, the combination of wage employment and petty commodity production must not be interpreted, as often happens, in functionalist terms, that is, as being only determined by and useful for worldwide capital accumulation. It is true that this combination benefits capital by providing persistent low-wage labour and an area in which the economic cycle is flexible. But it is also true that the diffusion, persistence and adaptation of socialization systems based on self-employment and family labour and on the prevalence of reciprocal factors constitute a limit to the level of accumulation and an obstacle to the growing vulnerability of underdeveloped contexts in the face of the global market forces precisely because it allows survival where the capacity for monetary consumption is very limited. It is for these reasons that the transformations in the socialization mixes typical of underdevelopment or, economically speaking, the emergence of a vast area of petty commodity production, subsequently defined as the 'informal sector', should not be understood either as solutions fostered by capital so as to maintain a low-wage reserve surplus population or even as strategies for alternative industrial growth as against the persistent dependence on global equilibria. Rather, it is a matter of tension between, on the one side, the typical form of individual and competitive behaviour emerging in underdeveloped regions and, on the other, the overall historical transformation of the socialization system.

How far these sociality mixes are able in their growing rural and urban varities to accommodate profitably forms of development and emancipation of the individual is still a very open question. Under the conditions existing in underdeveloped countries, individual self-fulfilment cannot be accomplished within their too weak or distorted associative contexts. I have also put forward the hypothesis that reciprocal contexts remain more permeated by forms of authoritarianism and less receptive to individual values in situations characterized by scarce opportunities and by the constant struggle for mere survival. In fact, studies of the informal sector reveal the presence of a widespread creativity and high degree of inventiveness, at least in terms of the types of activities described. But, at the present state of knowledge, it is not possible to say what this description may signify as regards relations of socialization, the overcoming of traditional power hierarchies inside reciprocal networks and individual self-fulfilment.

There are two phenomena that should at least be pointed out because they may play a very important role in structuring different lines of transformation of socialization mixes and, consequently, of processes of development/underdevelopment. The first is the impact of the greater presence and persistence of small family farms in some underdeveloped countries than in others. Particularly in many Asian countries, the same degree of opposition has not occurred historically between the system of extensive plantations and the marginal subsistence economies complemented by low-paid wage-work on plantations that has been found in nearly all the countries of Latin America, the Caribbean and sub-Saharan

Africa (Sachs, 1989). The assumption may be made that in these Asian countries reciprocal factors also develop potential surrogate resources as an alternative to those of the market and, therefore, form starting-points for the development of family entrepreneurship outside agriculture as well, when global market conditions allow this to happen. This assumption is backed up by the recent cases of South Korea and Taiwan mentioned in chapter 4 (see also M.P. Smith, 1989; Douglass, 1988).

The second phenomenon is the different extent to which the formation and mobilization of strata in the relative surplus population may occur in different regional and national situations, above all in terms of migration from the countryside to the cities but also of rates of population growth and demographic strategies. In my approach, the question of surplus population, and especially its uncontrollable growth as a result of the demographic and migratory strategies mentioned in chapter 3, constitutes a crucial element in explaining the models of socialization typical of underdevelopment and the malign spiral that characterizes them. As already discussed in chapter 4, it is easy to assume that particular conditions which are liable to attenuate, limit or interrupt the pressure exerted by the surplus population can modify considerably the structuring of socialization mixes and the paths to development.

The urban informal sector

At this point, I propose to look briefly at the two cases that have been chosen to exemplify the two models of socialization typical of underdevelopment: the informal sector in Third World cities and the Italian Mezzogiorno. On the whole and from the viewpoint of socialization patterns, the informal sector furnishes an example of how, in underdeveloped areas, the social setting is adapted to safeguard survival against the devastating impact of behaviour associated with pure competition in underdeveloped areas. Other interpretations which insist that there are functional links between informal activity and large manufacturing industry, especially through subcontracting, or that the informal sector acts as a breeding ground for industrialization, tend to overestimate the proportion of manufacturing activity which is dependent on the international market and to underestimate the importance of the reciprocal socialization arrangements which are characteristic of informal activity.[21] Compared to those relying on local markets, above all in services and building, the proportion of informal activites which engage in manufacturing is everywhere very limited. Extensive research is now being undertaken into a wide range of situations in African, Latin American and Asian cities that fully documents both the predominantly tertiary and local orientation of the informal sector and the fact that its social background is mainly based on reciprocity.

Even though most of the now numerous studies on the informal sector have ignored the socialization question and have focused instead on describing a great variety of economic activities and on their interlinking with and significance in relation to the global economy and the prospects for development (Gerry, 1987), the only common and essential feature to have surfaced in every situation is connected with a typical socialization mix (see the crucial contribution of Lomnitz, 1977). The necessary condition for the existence of an informal sector is the formation of a socialization mix based predominantly on strong and integrated reciprocal networks which are made up of the family, the local community, occupational groups and, possibly, on ethnic-tribal solidarity transplanted relatively intact from a rural to an urban environment, as is shown by the first case study devoted specifically to the subject (Hart, 1973). Rickshaw operators, street artisans and traders, people who run small mobile canteens, self-help builders, outworkers or workers in small workshops subcontracted to firms in the formal sector and, frequently, thieves and dealers in stolen goods all take part in a community network which is self-complementing and self-protecting. The compatibility between informal sociality and competitive behaviour which is exposed to the international market tends to be limited to a few unskilled, as in building, or semi-independent jobs, as with subcontracting for large industry; or else it is linked to local markets, such as services and craft products for tourists, which can operate at low costs and with low incomes since they are protected by reciprocal social arrangements. Manufacturing entrepreneurial activities, on the other hand, have difficulty in keeping a foot in both camps. There are few enterprises which begin in the informal sphere and then manage to develop sufficient autonomy and competitivity to be able to do without the protection afforded by this specific socialization mix. However, the protective conditions of the socialization mix remain incompatible with conventional patterns of concentration and development. The informal sector expands horizontally by involving an increasing number of people in persistently labour-intensive operations in a growing number of economic activities, predominantly services, which continue to be organized in micro-units subjected to the pressure of a huge surplus population and essentially conditioned by the defensive patterns of socialization, particularly self-provisioning and kinship, ethnic and community solidarity.

The informal sector is essentially a subsystem of socialization permitting survival under conditions of extremely low individual monetary income raised mainly through petty commodity production but also through wage-work both within and outside the informal sector itself. This consideration suggests that two aspects should be emphasized which are often overlooked by studies on the subject: the strict internal interdependence of the various activities and the external interdependence of each activity and the specific socialization mix; and the continuous state of non-cohesion between the informal sector and the official economy in terms of wage, consumption and competition levels. It follows from the first aspect that it is not possible to consider each single branch of informal activities separately. One example is the fact that the work and survival strategies of street vendors and artisans are supported within the community by the existence of thieves and dealers in stolen goods and vice versa. This complementarity does not exist within a highly developed social setting where it is a simple matter to finance the former and put the latter in jail without causing profound social contradictions; it is found, rather, within a reciprocal micro-system of networks where what happens to the thieves and dealers in stolen goods immediately and directly affects the work and lives of the street-vendors and artisans. Here, the former are not only among the many customers of street artisans, they are often the providers of raw materials and always related to them by neighbourhood or kinship links when not actually members of the same household. Under these conditions, their support is essential for maintaining the viability of comprehensive strategies in the informal sector. This is an exaggerated picture but it illustrates the point. It is true that a large part of the population in the *favelas* of Rio de Janeiro opposes the increasing power and influence of gangs dealing in drugs and does not always object to police raids, but it is also true that this opposition decreases the more income from dealing in drugs becomes an essential asset of the community and the more effectively the drug dealers are integrated into it.

The second aspect, the continuity between the official economy and the informal sector, is a particularly complicated question. I therefore confine myself to a few brief observations on method. It is necessary to stress the contradictory nature of this continuity in order to avoid an unrealistic functionalistic approach. As argued in the quotation below, the origin and expansion of the urban informal sector depends on the global trends of industrial development but cannot be viewed as a direct strategy of capital; it is rather a popular response to difficult economic conditions and, as such, one of the essential elements in that increasing resistance to further capitalist penetration which Arrighi (1986) assumes to be a feature of the contemporary global crisis.

It was transparent by 1970 that the activities of the modern sector had not expanded fast enough to absorb the enormous stream of people who had migrated into the cities of Latin America, Asia and

Africa. The mass of the urban populations of the Third World were not sitting idly by, rather they had been compelled to find means of generating incomes which fell 'outside' the bounds of recognized forms of wage labour. (Rogerson, 1985, p. 5)

If it is clearly recognized that the existence and expansion of the urban informal sector is a contradiction of and limit to industrial accumulation or, more particularly, the most important sign of the tension between the diffusion of individualistic behaviour and the specific conditions of socialization, then the auxiliary 'functions' of the informal sector in relation to the operations of the official economy can be better understood. First, there is the direct and indirect function of reproducing relatively low-paid wage labour. This obviously occurs when workers employed in the internationalized official economy continue to live in an informal sector and, for this very reason, survive on a low wage. It also applies when they do not live in an area characterized by the prevalence of informal activities but benefit from the low costs of urban services generated by the informal sector. Second, informal sector workers are sometimes employed for very low pay and/or under black-market conditions by the middle and upper classes. This is the case of domestic helpers and repair and building workers, among others. Finally, there is subcontracting, although in my opinion its importance should not be overemphasized since in general it appears to be rather limited.

The second area of continuity arises from the fact that, both in terms of final consumers and of work processes, those involved in the informal sector are to a growing extent customers of goods and services produced by the official economy. Their consumption capacity is limited by their low levels of monetary income, complemented by the savings made possible through the specific protection patterns of the socialization arrangements, but it is much higher than that of the rural surplus population and even more so than that of social strata which are literally starving to death.

Lastly, there is an interesting question worth mentioning but to which it is still impossible to give a clear answer. This is whether, in the particular situations in which defensive mixes of social factors dominated by reciprocal arrangements are established, the possibility does or does not exist for the informal sector to grow while, at the same time, maintaining its protective social features and specializing in more sophisticated activities, such as education, health, welfare, less basic forms of building, some types of technologically advanced manufacturing for local consumption and so on, until eventually an alternative model of development takes shape. In this respect, the recent attention paid by governments and international agencies towards the informal sector is misleading as it is based on conventional parameters deriving from the development paradigm. The problem becomes a different one if we focus on socialization processes and on the alternative role they could play in creating a totally different economic perspective.

The Mezzogiorno as an example of the social disintegration syndrome

To end with, it is interesting to look at the Italian Mezzogiorno as an example of the extreme case in which there is a high degree of social disintegration. It can be used as a basis for suggesting what impact contemporary changes may have in societies of this kind. Social disintegration results from the cumulative impact of the interaction between a decreasingly effective reciprocal system and dependent industrialization accompanied by the insufficient formation of associative factors. Reciprocal factors are weakened and adapt without exhibiting strong resistance or the capacity to act as surrogates. In the case of the Mezzogiorno, the most important historical causes of this process are the almost total absence of family-based small farms in an agrarian situation dominated by the conflict between large absentee landowners and landless labourers, intense waves of selective migration and chaotic urbanization. On the other hand, the 'modern' associative patterns of socialization have become established in fragile forms which are ineffective since the growth in competitive market behaviour is insufficient and, therefore, does not support the constitution of viable organizations representing the interests of both local capitalist, professional and economic activities and the local working class. What has taken place in the Mezzogiorno is that nationally based associative factors have been formally extended to the region, but in practice have operated either in a completely different way or in a distorted fashion or not at all. Consequently, both associative and reciprocal social factors are rarefied and ineffectual, especially when their possible interaction with both protective and progressive economic change is considered.

Up to a point this model appears to be an outward-looking one, the reverse of the third model in which industrialization is accompanied by the strong adaptation of reciprocal patterns. The socialization mix and the economic prospects depend to a large extent on the resources produced externally. Internally, a high degree of competitivity is unleashed to maximize external resources which are used for the purpose of survival. From this point of view, this model is based on outward-looking consumption while the third model is based on outward-looking production.

As will be seen more clearly in the next chapter, the specific form assumed in the Mezzogiorno by the fundamental process of distributing and competing for external resources which are decisive in structuring opportunities and life-styles is patronage. It must be stressed, however, that this phenomenon is so important and pervasive in this area that it goes far beyond what is usually meant by this concept.[22] Interpreted on the basis of an approach that concentrates on socio-organizational factors and socialization systems, patronage in contemporary societies is usually believed to result from a distortion of associative processes of redistribution according to divergent criteria fixed by reciprocal relations. In the Mezzogiorno, the question is rendered difficult by the fact that the traditional system of reciprocity has been weakened while the local associative system has only taken shape as a regulatory extension of the national system, that is, more on a formal than a substantial level. In this sense, the assumption may be made that modern patronage in the Mezzogiorno has widely redefined *its* reciprocity networks to a degree that is partly independent of families, kinship groups and local communities (Graziano, 1974; Mingione, 1989). This redefinition plays an important role in complicating a socialization system in which, alongside the weak role of associative factors and the declining one of the traditional reciprocal system, there is also the different role played by the patronage networks. The latter siphon off state resources in opposition to both associative factors, that is the defence of common interests, and to the logic of market competition whether mediated by predominant associative sociality or by relations of 'traditional' reciprocity. Only comparative research into specific cases of societies coming under this fifth model would make it possible to clarify whether the emergence of a separate system of patronage-based reciprocity constitutes a local variant existing solely in the Mezzogiorno or a typical feature of the model. Personally, I tend towards the second assumption but at the present state of research it is impossible to be more definite.

In chapter 6, the discussion is centred on the modes assumed by different types of informal activities within contemporary strategies of urban living adopted by low-income families in the Mezzogiorno. To avoid repetition, only a few observations are made here for the purpose of understanding more clearly the socialization model. A large part of the informal activities that are now found in the Mezzogiorno are forms of black-market wage employment. The persistence of this kind of irregular labour can be explained in terms of the socialization system as follows. The Mezzorgiorno is an area characterized by the absence of industrial growth and the consequent limited number of stable jobs in industry, and by the distorting effects of patronage-based reciprocity on the distribution of state resources. This distortion leads to inefficient public services, the proliferation of subsidies and individual benefits and, in general, the scant importance attached to the link between work and professional responsibility. The imposition of the national regulatory system in such an area has ensured that a vast sphere of opportunities for persistently low-paid 'black' work continues to exist in both traditional sectors like agriculture and building and, to a growing extent, in private services. Unlike in the past, these conditions of precarious employment providing insufficient income are less and less complemented and protected by the 'traditional' system of reciprocity. Only the household is still able to interact with conditions of this kind. This is reflected in the corresponding persistence and extension of family strategies for self-provisioning and self-help, which are, however, always rather weak and not very innovative because the families lack the resources needed to be able to choose from among various options. The system of socialization does not permit the emergence of initiatives involving self-employment or family entrepreneurship either of the informal sector type or that characteristic of the third model, or in Italy of the NEC. The efforts to survive of vast strata of the relative surplus population are complemented by patronage-based redistribution of resources through subsidies, pensions, favours, a more frequent access to temporary jobs or the opportunity to engage in several working activities at the same time. Therefore, schematically speaking, for a considerable part of the Southern Italian population this model of survival and socialization has three aspects: irregular work; family practices of self-provisioning and self-help that are mainly traditional and based on long hours of domestic labour, a high number of full-time housewives and a correspondingly low rate of female employment; and the redistribution of patronage resources that bind even low-income groups to the existing political system.[23]

An interesting question is where the general trend towards the increasing importance of an innovative role for reciprocal social factors may lead to, in the context of a reduction in patronage resources. Above all, the reconstruction of social spheres within which the innovative tendencies of reciprocal networks can take effect is more difficult to achieve and a more uneven process than elsewhere. In fact, despite the traditional image of life in the Mezzogiorno being centred on the family and the community, both solid family networks and stable homogeneous local community contexts are rare. Families which have remained in close proximity and kept in contact could have a potential for innovative adaptation which is higher than in others on condition, however, that they renounce their preference for drawing on external resources. However that may be, the gap between the two ends on the scale of opportunities may be even greater than in the English case mentioned by Pahl (1988b) in terms of the difference between a benign and a malign spiral. Similarly, the increasing importance of sociality at a community level is more likely in settings which are more stable and homogeneous. But in this model, it is rarer than might seem the case at first sight because of the selective and chaotic nature of emigration and urbanization. It is only found in the urban centres of medium-sized towns which are not particularly affected by migration or in those very few areas where craft specialization has been kept alive. It is important to reiterate that in this case the innovative importance of reciprocal networks is strongly inhibited on two fronts: the impoverishment of the networks themselves and the strong competition for external patronage resources. Consequently, societies encompassed by this model risk being more heavily penalized by recent trends, and this becomes especially evident when they are not interpreted solely according to conventional macro-economic indicators and social factors and contexts are also taken into account.

NOTES

1   It is worth mentioning the fact that this outline does not take into account criminal organizations as an additional historical source of irregular forms of employment. In this regard, organizations which already existed in southern Italy or in the Marseilles area in France or within some ethnic minorities in the USA expanded dramatically when they became the focal points for international drug-trafficking. This is an area which is particularly difficult to estimate and to investigate.

The question of the borderline between crime and informal activities is discussed in Henry (1978). An estimation of the size and trends of illegal activities as part of the American underground economy is contained in Simon and Witte (1982). In principle, I agree with Bonanno (1989) that it would be wise to keep informal activities separate from criminal ones also because the latter, especially when part of organized crime, have different social characteristics than other informal activities. In reality, however, it is difficult to fix a precise borderline which allows a clearcut distinction to be made between the two kinds of activities.

2   See mainly Bonanno (1987), *Agriculture and Human Values* (1989), Hadjimichalis (1986).

3   See mainly Galarza (1977); Piore (1979b); Friedland (1980); Portes and Bach (1985); Sassen (1988).

4   In Spain, the recent transformation of a part of irregular building employment into self-employment is largely connected with the consolidation of the co-operative movement within the sector (EEC, 1989b). In Italy and even more so in Greece, building workers make a living by alternating periods

ANALYSIS OF INFORMALIZATION PROCESSES

336

of seasonal official employment, sufficient to obtain social insurance and unemployment benefit, and periods of unemployment in which they cumulate benefits and irregular working activities, sometimes occasional and sometimes continuing even on those sites where they were previously hired on an official basis (EEC, 1989b).

5 See, mainly, Gordon and Kimball (1985); Markusen et al. (1986); Boddy et al. (1986); Brotchie et al. (1987); Castells (1989).

6 Short-term contracts are becoming increasingly popular as a way of dealing with cyclical economic trends. The increasing importance of reciprocal arrangements may become visible within production reorganizational patterns, as in the case of subcontracting networks, but often it is only evident within household reproductive strategies, as in the case of temporary workers relying on other complementary incomes and on various reciprocal community arrangements in order to survive.

7 Examples are babysitters instead of public childcare; hospital cleaning contracted out to a private firm employing black-market labour, and so on.

8 Unfortunately, data on *irregular* multiple jobholding disaggregated for each branch of the economy do not exist, with the exception of Italy and partially the USA. The official ISTAT data on irregular moonlighting in Italy are reported in chapter 6. References to studies in Italy and the USA are reported below. Data on 'official' multiple jobholders in the EEC countries are reported in EUROSTAT (1982).

9 The presence of these kinds of innovative reciprocal networks leading to at least partially alternative life-styles underlies the interpretation of the informalization process as an alternative path of development (see for example Heinze and Olk, 1982; Szelenyi, 1981).

10 See mainly Weiss (1987); Portes and Sassen-Koob (1987); Portes et al. (1989).

11 In a certain sense, the diffusion of behaviour directed towards reciprocal interests renders these social contexts increasingly similar to those in which industrialization is characterized by substantial organizational factors of reciprocity. On the whole, however, an important difference persists that connects up with what was said above about the difficulty of reconverting an associative orientation into a reciprocal one. In the case of the first macro-model, contemporary changes are inducing a strong and increasing incompatibility between the two different modes of social organization, while in the second macro-model the interaction may turn out to be more balanced.

12 Among the vast literature on the condition of women in advanced capitalist societies, I shall note only the following contributions on women's employment and on domestic work: Fox (1980); West (1982); Fernandez-Kelly (1983); Porter (1983); Ruggie (1984); Oakley (1985); Fenstermaker Berk (1985); Walby (1986); Mies (1986); Bose et al. (1987); Brown and Pechman (1987); Beechey and Perkins (1987); Allen and Wolkowitz (1987); Hunt (1988); Rubery (1988).

13 It is so called because it includes the region in and around the triangle formed by the three most important industrial cities in Italy: Milan, Turin and Genoa.

14   It is worth making a few remarks about the internal structure of the industrial triangle. The two big conurbations of Milan and Turin have evolved in markedly different ways. Milan is probably the only city in Southern Europe to have developed features of what has been called a 'global city': a city with a high degree of financial concentration, a very complex advanced and non-specialized industrial mix, a dynamic leading role in both the national and international arena and wide-ranging innovative experimentation in every field. Turin (see Bagnasco, (1986a) is a gigantic single-industry city almost completely under the control of one corporation, Fiat, which in recent years has not only achieved a monopolistic control over Italian car production but has been transformed into a financial conglomerate with increasingly diversified interests. The case of Genoa is closer to that of Turin than of Milan, and is mainly negatively associated with heavy industries and harbour facilities, hit more severely than other sectors by the de-industrialization process (see Pichierri, 1989).

In the last fifteen years, both Milan and Turin have lost a substantial number of Fordist jobs in medium-sized and large manufacturing concerns and witnessed a vast casualization of work; but Milan seems to have been more capable than Turin of generating a wave of innovative self-employment and small-scale activities linked either to vertical disintegration or to the advanced service sector. While Milan is extending the range of its activities and increasing its hold over the economic life of the country, the destiny of Turin appears more and more tied to the economic strategy of Fiat.

Besides these two large metropolises and Genoa, there exists a vast background of advanced agricultural or specialized industrial towns and mountain districts. The former are often mono-industrial at the outset but, in the best of cases, increasingly drawn into a beneficial process of de-specialization; the latter are either isolated and subject to progressive depopulation or affected by the sudden economic benefits from the spread of mountain tourism.

15   The argument put forward here should not be given more importance than it deserves, the main message being *only* that agricultural policies have expressed a different balance between an associative and a reciprocal orientation and that this leads to important differences in the structuration of socialist societies also apart from the agricultural/rural context. It does not mean much in terms of empirical evaluation of the agricultural component of the second economy in various socialist countries.

'Private agriculture is a key component of the second economy in all socialist countries. The output of collective farmers' personal plots provides from 30 to 42 per cent of total agricultural output in the USSR, Hungary, Bulgaria and Romania. In Poland, where 77 per cent of all agricultural land is in private hands, the legal private sector occupied almost 32 per cent of the labor force in 1983' (Sampson, 1987, pp. 124–5). Grossman and Treml (1987) estimate that in the Soviet Union the agricultural component of the second economy is approximately five times greater than the reported official value of *kolkhoz* sales on urban markets, as shown in the following quotation:

338 ANALYSIS OF INFORMALIZATION PROCESSES

Soviet official sources report the value of sales on urban kolkhoz markets for 1977 as 7,300 million rubles, or 45 rubles per capita; our estimate on the basis of the emigré survey is 33,800 million rubles, or 210 rubles per capita. Soviet statistics are silent regarding off-market private sales or purchases, which we estimate at 3,200 million rubles for the urban population, or 20 rubles per capita per year. Total private purchases by the urban population by our reckoning are thus 37,000 million rubles, or 230 rubles per capita, for around 1977. The difference between the official sales figure and our estimate is therefore a remarkably high 29,700 million rubles. Most of it must represent hidden (gross) private income. (Grossman and Treml, 1987, p. 292)

16 From among the few recent, but pre-reform exceptions two are worth mentioning. The first is the so-called 'Novosibirsk document' signed by Zaslavskaja (1984), a collective analysis of the malfunctioning of the Soviet economy produced for internal discussion in the early 1980s and then smuggled to the West, where it was published in several languages. The second is a long paper written by a Hungarian social scientist, Istvan Rev (1985), during a study visit to the USA. To my knowledge, even now neither of them has been published in the original language.

17 On the class nature of the socialist state and party elite, see the short discussion of the debate and the references given in chapter 7, pp. 453–7.

18 The case of the Third Italy in the 1980s became the most popular among academics studying the new prospects for industrial development (Berger and Piore, 1980; Piore and Sabel, 1984; for a criticism of these works see Sayer, 1989), but was considered far less as an alternative variant of industrial development, the main Italian exception being the contribution by Bagnasco (1977; 1988).

19 It is important to underline that this vast area of the country is highly diversified internally. Typically, the most important distinguishing features are not large metropolitan districts or more or less mono-industrial towns and cities, but rather the presence of diverse kinds of 'industrial districts' (Becattini, 1987; Bagnasco, 1988). The region of Emilia is usually portrayed as an exemplary case (Capecchi, 1989) of economic and social success, based on the combination of a wealthy and advanced agriculture, highly diversified and innovative development in manufacturing, and an efficient local public and private tertiary sector. The picture is different in Tuscany and Le Marche where manufacturing is more specialized in traditional quality products for export (mainly the fashion business) and, consequently, more dependent on specific branches of the international market. The picture is different again in the North-East (the Three Venetias). This region is more affected by decentralization and subcontracting on the part of concerns in the industrial triangle and has a relatively more conservative and less innovative social background. However, in 1965, one of the main wonders of the new model of industrialization, the Benetton empire, originated in this very region (Nardin, 1987).

20 However, this is not yet clear to most international agencies, and to the
    ILO in particular when they interpret the diffusion of the informal sector
    in Third World cities as a potential alternative path for industrial develop-
    ment (see ILO, 1989).

21 See, for example, some of the essays included in the collection edited by
    Portes et al. (1989), and also the early interpretation of the phenomenon
    by Portes (1983).

22 A discussion of the concept of patronage and the particular case of Southern
    Italy, with references to the relevant literature, can be found in chapter 6,
    pp. 386–9.

23 It is interesting to point out that some traditional reciprocal social forms
    similar to those which are a feature of the informal sector in Third World
    cities and which were of some importance in towns in the Mezzogiorno
    approximately twenty years ago, such as the Neapolitan alley economy
    (Allum, 1973), have now alsmost disappeared. A convincing explanation of
    this phenomenon (Pinnarò and Pugliese, 1985) traces the causes to weak
    industrialization which imported both competitive forms of behaviour and
    the typical associative relations which react to them, in particular a working
    class, trade unions and the culture of mass consumption, and to the impo-
    sition from outside of an institutional regulatory system increasingly shaped
    according to Fordist-welfarist logic.

6

Informalization and socialization mixes in Italy

1 THE ITALIAN CASE IN A COMPARATIVE PERSPECTIVE

The regional question and the three Italies

The case of Italy is particularly interesting because it presents persistently high levels of irregular work. The explanation for the Italian syndrome can be summed up as follows. The growth of the Italian economy has given birth to a high level of polarization between, at one end, the concentrated industrial complex in the North-West and, at the other end, the slowly declining, though still surviving, traditional sectors in both the South and in the North-East and Centre, or NEC; but, as described below, polarization has affected the last two parts of the country in different ways. The strains caused by the conflict between the Fordist-welfarist regulatory system and a vast area of surviving traditional activities have been considerable, particularly in the period from 1955 to 1965. Furthermore, these strains have been increased by the extensive presence of traditional irregular work and the ineffectiveness of the regulatory system. It is also important to point to the hyper-concentration and growing rigidity of the highly concentrated industrial complex; the Fiat Mirafiori factory in Turin was a true monument to this trend with about 70,000 workers and administrative staff on a single factory site. The consequence was that in Italy the regulatory system was thrown into crisis almost a decade before other industrial countries, that is, in the second half of the 1960s instead of during the 1970s. Industrialization in the NEC with its strong trends towards vertical disintegration, subcontracting and co-ordination of small and medium-sized firms constitutes one aspect of the phenomenon. The other is the diffusion of precociously new informal activities in conjunction with the old vocation for work fragments and irregular employment expressed within the network of social, personal and family services, complemented by a welfare system undergoing increased modernization but subject to drastic reductions in efficiency at local and sectoral levels.

The case of Italy is also interesting because the above-mentioned three large areas into which the country is divided have remained different from one another. They do not, however, exist in isolation but are to a great extent complementary, which helps to explain the development of Italy's economy and institutional system. In order to study the difficult interconnection between social factors and economic and institutional patterns of development, the three Italies can be used as types exemplifying three out of the five macro-models described in chapter 5.

Before analysing the case of Italy in detail on the basis of the evidence for the presence of irregular forms of work and with a view to understanding their role in forming and modifying the social balance and life-styles in the diverse regional contexts, it is necessary to look at the regional structure of Italy. The divisions between the three Italys do not constitute a syndrome related to the 'question of regional imbalances' but rather an exceptional co-existence within a single country of different social formations have have not been amalgamated through industrial development. The origins of normal regional imbalances and their further development have been traced along and explained by two paths of interaction with industrial growth. First, there is the link between the centre and the periphery within a process of growth. In the long term and with the succession of different stages of industrial development, this kind of link ends up by assuming the form of a complex map in which the central metropolises, for example New York, and the depressed areas, for example the region of the Appalachians, are separated by great distances; however, the range of different situations is very wide and, moreover, characterized by differing dynamics in various historical periods. If an industrial country is observed from this perspective alone, then it is clear that it does not remain for very long split into two clearly distinct parts persistently characterized by divergent patterns of development. Second, there are those divisions that are rooted in diverse historical and cultural traditions, above all of the religious, nationalist and ethnic kind, which play a very important role in structuring social relations. The differences may be heightened by the cumulation of an economically peripheral condition with local situations containing a religious, ethnic or nationalist minority, or with traditions that are persistently hostile to economic competition. Even if these two explanations are combined, it is still difficult to find elsewhere socio-territorial divisions that are as clear-cut as those in Italy.[1]

What has been said above needs to be expanded further, but it is not possible to do this here. Nevertheless, it is important to dwell on several ideas that may derive from the assumption that regional imbalance in Italy is not only of the normal kind but also constitutes a fundamentally different type of socio-economic division. The long-standing tradition of studies dedicated to the Mezzogiorno question has, for the most part, taken this assumption as its manifest starting-point, at least up until the Second World War. In this approach, the Mezzogiorno has never been considered the usual kind of peripheral area, nor one discriminated against in terms of industrial growth, but rather an integral part of a particular model of development based on the complementary interaction between two socieities that remain different from one another. The more recent theory of the three Italys, in both its economic and sociological versions, has also put back into circulation the idea that regional imbalances in Italy do not represent a regional question in the strict sense.[2] In actual fact, this theory is founded on the assumption that the three Italies are three distinct formations which are integrated in different ways into a model of unified national growth.

In this sense, the large regional divisions in Italy are not only the expression of 'normal' imbalances between areas of the country that accompany the various models of industrial growth, nor simply the effect of a more unbalanced development than elsewhere. Rather, they are the outcome of a historical process in which deep differences at the level of socio-economic formation have remained chronically embedded. Then, within each large area imbalances have arisen, in different ways, that can be traced back to the regional question in the strict sense.

The diversity of the socialization mixes in the three Italies

The premise that the socialization mix in each of the three areas is different is indispensable for tackling the question of the role of regulatory systems and, consequently, the various processes whereby informal activities become widespread or previously irregular workers become formalized. In fact, the phenomena related to informal activities in the broad sense are heterogeneous, often hidden and may have a completely different significance (Gallino, 1983). In this respect, in order to avoid macroscopic errors, what is required is a sufficiently precise reference to the social context in terms of socio-economic formation, regulatory and organizational mechanisms and socio-historical background.[3]

In the context of an approach based on the clear distinction between diverse economic, political and social formations that maintain their separate identity within a process of unified industrial growth involving the various parts of the country in different ways, the North–South question has become so firmly consolidated and has been so thoroughly investigated that a special methodological or historical analysis is not worth while. What does require methodological and historical clarification, on the other hand, is the question of the distinction between the First and the Third Italy. There are two reasons for this. First, because this distinction was formulated as late as the 1970s and, as a consequence, its historical roots have only been partially reconstructed; and second, because the most recent data, both for the 1970s and even more so for the 1980s, continue to show a clear trend towards the convergence of the First and Third Italies (*Inchiesta*, 1990).

With regard to the historical origins of the Third Italy, the retrospective explanation furnished by Bagnasco (1977) and then taken up by other writers seems convincing in this specific case, but it has opened up a rather difficult theoretical dispute. In short, these writers identify and document the presence of a high number of peasant family farms, above all of the share-cropping kind, in the Third Italy from the end of the nineteenth century, whereas the agriculture of the north-western regions was already predominantly characterized by medium-large capitalist non-family farms and that of the South by the persistence of large landed estates with absentee landlords and a numerous landless peasantry. The explanation is convincing in this specific case because it allows us to understand three essential elements of diversity in the historical development of the Third Italy until very recent times: the original socio-economic differences; the reasons why these have remained practically invisible until the 1960s; and the main mechanisms that, starting in those years, have set off the process of diffused industrialization proper in these regions.

The theoretically fragile aspect of this thesis arises from the fact that the explanation is tailor-made to suit this specific case and is, therefore, difficult to apply to generalized or comparative contexts. Other regions of Europe are characterized by the large presence of peasant family farms in a proto-industrial phase, particularly in France and Germany; but in these regions this factor has combined differently with the process of industrial growth. They have not been especially disadvantaged in comparison with the growth of an industrial system increasingly founded on large-scale industry undergoing concentration. On the contrary, the development of capitalist agriculture has, in the main, promoted selected forms of family farms that are able to remain competitive with the large capitalist farm. Furthermore, these farms manage in various ways to exist side by side with the large factory system, with the concentration of production, finance and distribution in industry and in the service sector and, in particular, with the development of powerful agro-food

344   INFORMALIZATION AND SOCIALIZATION MIXES

groups at both ends of the agricultural production cycle (see H. Friedmann, 1979; 1980). In this sense, the persistent rupture between regions
of industrial concentration and agricultural regions characterized by
family farms is an accident of the Italian case.

These critical remarks lead in the direction of a suggestive hypothesis
already outlined in some of the literature on the Mezzogiorno. The
rupture between the First and Third Italies can be traced back to the
limits of an industrial growth conditioned by the persistence of the
'southern question'. The limited opening up of the internal market and
of the progressive potential in industrialization did not permit the large
factory system to spread throughout the entire Centre-North but forced
it to be hyper-concentrated in the industrial triangle with sporadic off-
shoots in the rest of the country. The Third Italy was not fully involved
in the process of 'Fordist' industrialization, not so much because mainly
characterized by family farming but rather because it was confined to an
industrial growth that necessarily remained stunted and geographically
limited. Family farming and a more stable socio-territorial context
characterized by a network of medium-sized historical towns and by
waves of migration that involved entire families and did not, therefore,
weaken residual family ties, favoured growth mainly oriented to the local
markets, which allowed craft and industrial specialization to be preserved
and adapted. Still according to this hypothesis, it is thought that very
early in the post-war period the threefold division of the country began
to be affected by a strong dynamic for change. The limits to the Italian
model of industrial growth had melted away, principally in the wake of
the new terms of integration into the expanding world economy, but also
because of the freeing of the South brought about by the transformation
of agriculture and the dismantling of the social order based on large
landed estates. The disappearance of these limits certainly benefited most
big industry concentrated in the industrial triangle, at least in a first
phase; but it also set in motion considerable socio-economic changes in
the Third Italy, and it is more than likely that the real take-off of diffused
industrialization occurred in the 1950s rather than in the following
decade.

This digression on a hypothesis regarding the origins of the division
between the First and Third Italies can serve as a useful introduction to
the question of the diverse, yet converging, paths that these two areas
have been following in recent years. The specific features of these paths
and the transformations involved have already been expounded in chapter
5 and are looked at further below. Here, however, it is worth dwelling
on some points that arise from the hypothesis.

In the first place, verification that the paths are converging would not imply homogeneity but rather the fact that territorial imbalances typical of an industrial set-up, like those between metropolitan areas of various sizes, more or less specialized urban peripheries and undeveloped remote or declining areas, are increasingly similar in the First and Third Italies and that the industrial amalgamation of the entire Centre-North is tending to intensify. Secondly, this hypothesis does not imply either that all the areas involved are following convergent paths in the same ways and at the same pace. In other words, not all of the economy in the First Italy is being restructured to an equal extent along the lines of decentralization of production, vertical disintegration, advanced tertiarization, territorial de-specialization and promotion of complex networks between firms of varying size and in different sectors. Correspondingly, not all the sub-regional areas of the Third Italy are moving to the same degree towards territorial de-specialization, the consolidation of networks and consortia and the strengthening and formalization of the system of small and medium-sized firms; one of the reasons for this is the desire to benefit over a growing range of activities from all the advantages offered by the new kinds of services and socio-economic innovation. To put it differently, the path of convergence is reshaping some of the central regions (in this specific case Lombardy and Emilia, with Piedmont and the three Venetias as the immediate hinterland) and several relatively peripheral regions (Liguria, Le Marche, Umbria and Tuscany) in line with the new prospects for industrial growth.

Taking these considerations as a starting-point, it may be the case that the secular model of Italian industrial growth with its threefold division is changing into a model with two distinct socio-economic formations, exactly as had been mistakenly assumed before the emergence of the Third Italy. The thesis of the convergence between the First and Third Italies is even more plausible in as much as it coincides with the general trends resulting from industrial restructuring and the new phase of tertiarization. Already extensively discussed in the preceding chapters, these trends reveal in general a convergence towards a model of complex economic organization that is relatively unstructured and decreasingly standardized, in which a very important role is taken on by small and medium-sized operators who are more or less dependent on subcontracting systems and networks of collaboration.

The Mezzogiorno question today

From the perspective of the convergence outlined above, the crucial problem is once again that of the South. In the interpretation based on distinct social formations, the Mezzogiorno is not viewed as a peripheral area of development nor as a 'normal' underdeveloped region. It is precisely for this reason that the Italian case is so interesting. The Mezzogiorno's internal social and economic equilibria are profoundly different, even though the underlying causes and the ways in which the area remains integrated in a composite national formation are to be found in the historical model of industrial development.

It is possible to raise two objections against the line of interpretation suggested above. The first concerns the reasons why the dismantling of the social order based on the large landed estates and the post-war economic miracle set in motion a growing convergence between the First and Third Italies and why they have not led to the disappearance of the southern question, despite having introduced radical changes in the South. The second regards differences within the South, in particular the dynamic nature of the regions on the Adriatic side. These differences suggest that it would be more exact to abandon the notion of a 'southern question' and adopt a perspective in which there are various different Souths (Catanzaro, 1989).

The first objection may be formulated on the basis that the dismantling of the social order characteristic of large landed estates and the processes it triggered off have undoubtedly entailed a different form of integration of the South within the model of development. These phenomena are, by and large, the abandoning of the countryside and large migratory movements, the decline of local markets and the growing integration of southern consumption into a model of standardized mass consumption, and the rise in employment in large manufacturing industry. The problem is that these transformations have not been sufficient to extend to the South a system of social structuration typical of industrial societies, one that is based on the spread of competitive market-oriented behaviour controlled by cohesive organizational forms of the associative (trade unions and industrial, artisanal and professional associations) and redistributive kind (universalistic welfare and taxation systems). As I have argued elsewhere (Mingione, 1989), the dismantling of social structuration 'based on large landed estates' and the impossibility of replacing it with a truly 'industrial' one have paved the way to a form of structuration that is essentially based on widespread political patronage. This fact has changed the face of the southern question, but has also prevented the Mezzogiorno from becoming progressively integrated into the model of growth in typically industrial terms. In this way, the separation of the South from the Centre-North has thereby been maintained. On the one side, the incidence of welfare payments, externally produced incomes and political patronage, and on the other particularism, the shortcomings and distortions in the system of citizens' rights and public welfare, and the chronic weakness of associative regulatory systems, are the two most important aspects of this different and separate social structuration.

The thesis outlined above also provides a basis for rejecting the second objection, according to which it would be more accurate to talk of various different Souths. In the Mezzogiorno, even the structuration based on the large landed estates was highly differentiated internally: take, for example, the big cities, like Naples and Palermo, and the small urban centres controlled by a restricted group of rural notables and professionals, but, above all, the diverse agricultural systems (Rossi Doria, 1956; Arrighi and Piselli, 1987). Moreover, the system of welfare payments and political patronage has become more deeply rooted in some areas of the South, in particular Campania, Calabria, Basilicata and Sicily, and less so in others; or else the latter display clear socio-economic variations. The point is that, leaving aside sporadic isolated cases, the alternative between the model of social structuration based on welfare payments and political patronage and that based on a capitalist market economy involves the whole of the South. The particular features of this part of the country form the specific subject of the last three sections of this chapter.

2 THE EMPLOYMENT STRUCTURE AND SOCIAL CHANGE IN POST-WAR ITALY

Changes in employment and irregular work

The socio-occupational structure of Italy has profoundly changed in the period following the Second World War with the accelerated development of a model of industrial growth integrated into the world economy and the concomitant rapid decline in agricultural employment. The most notable socio-occupational transformation has been the decline in agricultural employment: the more than eight million workers (42 per cent of the workforce) in 1951 dropped to little more than three million (17 per cent) in 1971. This decline was counterbalanced by substantial migration abroad and by the parallel growth in jobs both in industry and services. The increase in employment was similar in these last two sectors (just over two million in each), but whereas in the industrial sector almost three-quarters of the new jobs were created in the 1950s, in the service sector growth was greatest in the 1960s and continued at a faster pace in the following decade. These changes were accompanied not only by an intensive urbanization but also by large-scale internal migration, above all from the southern countryside to the industrial cities of the North-West. Moreover, in the 1960s, alongside these changes there occurred a large drop in the official rate of employment (from close to 40 per cent to just under 35 per cent), a phenomenon that was at the centre of the labour market debate in the following decade. Several of the elements that emerged from the debate are of direct interest for the questions dealt with here. First, it was noted that the decrease in employment affected above all the female workforce and the less developed areas of the country. The conclusion drawn was that de-ruralization had led to a situation in which many women, formerly employed in agriculture but now living in cities, and especially those in the less developed areas, stated that they were full-time housewives for two interconnected reasons: the lack of job opportunities and the heavy load of housework necessary to make up for the deficiencies in public and social services within an urban setting where arrangements based on kinship and community were less feasible. Second, specific surveys revealed that in many place the decline in the official employment rate reflected high increases in irregular activities, with the result that the real rate increasingly tended to be higher than the official one. This phenomenon affected in particular industry and services in the Third Italy, where many housewives, students and pensioners played a predominant role in the growth of small enterprises both as helpers in family businesses and as hidden temporary or part-time workers.

Late accelerated industrial growth has given rise to many opportunities for irregular work in Italy. In agriculture, the decreasing but still high number of peasant and day-labourer families have to face a growing need for complementary income, which they also obtain through black work, since the combination of pensions and subsidies and remittances from emigrated relatives is almost never sufficient to compensate for the gradual decline of income from agricultural work. This applies above all in the South, while in the Third Italy and in the less developed agricultural areas of the First Italy, complementary income from regular (there still exist numerous worker-peasants) or irregular work is becoming practically the only kind. One aspect of irregular forms of work is that they increasingly deviate from the norms of the regulatory system which is gradually being developed and in which, for example, the exchange of work between non-family members is prohibited, the conditions of work and safety on building sites are regulated, commercial, industrial and handicraft enterprises are subjected to special restrictions, and so on. In other words, the modes of industrial growth impose on a declining number of agricultural families, in increasing difficulty, strategies based on complementary work, which the parallel development of the regulatory system increasingly drives underground.

In building, black work is such a widespread phenomenon that it has even been identified in official statistics.[4] The number of employees in the sector according to the 1961 population census was almost three times higher than that recorded by the industrial census of the same year. The gap had closed but was still substantial by the time of the 1971 census (more than double). Trigilia (1978) estimated the number of precariously employed building workers at almost one and a half million in 1961 (7.4 per cent of the total workforce) and more than one million in 1971 (5.4 per cent). Whereas in 1951 most precariously employed building workers were found in the Centre-North, already in 1961 the South accounted for the largest share and the concentration of this category of worker in this part of the country continued at a high rate during the following years until it reached more than 80 per cent in the 1980s.

The persistently informal nature of building labour is a complex phenomenon and one that is subject to change, sometimes on a large scale. I must limit myself here to a few brief general indications. The requirements arising from reconstruction and from the modernization of large-scale infrastructures through public works and an increasingly intense process of urbanization initiated a long phase of dynamic expansion in this sector, which lasted from the immediate post-war years until the middle of the 1960s. A strong tendency towards speculation, a relatively low concentration of capital and the persistent presence of a plentiful supply of low-skilled and poorly educated labour willing to work irregularly, at least for a temporary spell, further characterize a sector that remains highly labour-intensive with a weak propensity towards technological and productive innovation. The patterns of industrial development tend to attenuate these features in the Centre-North and, in general, to increase the control, effectiveness and severity of the regulatory system alongside the concentration of capital and the strengthening of trade union and associative organizations. This process does not extend, however, to the South, where residential housing is firmly entrenched as the dominant branch of industry both in terms of investment and employment.

As for manufacturing industry and services, a detailed analysis is beyond the scope of this analysis, since it must necessarily be long and complex. In general, the highly fragmented nature of Italian society has been reflected both in a dual regulatory system and in a jungle of particular regulations; but this has not sufficed to prevent the spread of various forms of irregular work. On the contrary, it may well be the case that it is precisely the complex entanglement of regulations which rewards and fosters irregular employment. However, as is seen below, this is less and less true of manufacturing industry but increasingly the case in the various branches of the private service sector.

Regarding the latter, two important elements must be underlined with respect to the growing trends towards informalization now present in almost all other industrial countries. The first concerns the persistent fragmentation and relatively low level of concentration in private services in Italy compared to elsewhere. Self-employed workers and family enterprises continue to account for a high proportion of such services and to be protected by a favourable organization of production and an advantageous tax system that is also tolerant of tax evasion not only in the retail trade, the most glaring case, but also in more modern and innovative branches such as professional activities, advanced services to firms, private education and health or in strongly expanding traditional activities like restaurants, hotels, etc.

The second element is that of the expansion of welfare services in Italy, with their long-established deficiencies, special features and serious imbalances on both social and territorial levels.[5] Since this sector presents a very complex set of problems, my brief summarizing remarks provide a very sketchy picture. The persistent deficiencies in the Italian welfare system stimulate the spread of irregular work along two distinct and important paths: an anomalous symbiosis between public and private that anticipated in the worst possible way the trend towards privatization by at least two decades; and a persistent overburdening of families and kinship and reciprocal networks with welfare functions that in other countries are assumed to a greater extent by the state or the official market, or by cohesive combinations of the two. Examples of these typically 'Italian arrangements' can be found in almost all spheres of the social services system. I take as a general example the education system. State schools are persistently characterized by a limited number of teaching hours, a high degree of selectivity and lack of efficiency, and a poorly paid teaching staff that works for a small number of hours and is subject to very little supervision. This situation is complemented not so much by elitist private schools as by a high degree of delegated responsibility for education to families and by the growing practice of private tuition and after-school study and recreation run by volunteer and community organizations. Private lessons form an area of irregular employment and, generally speaking, serve to complement the income of many teachers who are unable to survive solely on their school salaries. In this case too, the social and economic differences between regions are not irrelevant and end by generating differences in the extent of informalization and irregular working practices. Finally, the latter have expanded in recent times with the ripening of the fiscal crisis of the state and the related need for more efficient, advanced and differentiated welfare services.

Changes in employment since 1970

Starting from the 1970s, the lines along which society has changed have been transformed in many ways and are still difficult to summarize in a general picture of complex trends and events. The demographic pattern has undergone a considerable modification. The birth rate, especially in the North, has declined gradually down to levels among the lowest in the world. A large part of the country is now characterized by negative demographic trends and by a marked ageing of the population. At the same time, the migratory balance has become positive again after being negative for many years. Officially, this phenomenon is not due to the arrival of foreign immigrants, which has been greatly underestimated as most of them enter the country illegally, but to the excess of repatriated emigrants over the outflow of new emigrants. There has also been a notable reduction in internal migration, caused not so much by the convergence of conditions of existence and those of the labour market in the Centre-North and the South as by the combination of the cost and difficulty of settling in the North, and the growth of a labour demand that is increasingly centred on occupations in the tertiary sector, which is very unlikely to draw on the internal surplus population. There has been, therefore, a clear reversal of the difference between the North and the South. The former is now characterized by negative ratios, above all births to deaths, only partially counterbalanced by more selective internal migration and immigrants from underdeveloped countries, whereas the latter continues to record positive birth to death ratios due to the higher birth rate and a positive migratory balance based on both the return of former emigrants and a certain number of foreign immigrants.

The central element in the transformation of the official socio-occupational structure is the growth of the service sector, especially of private marketable services. In the 1970s, the rise in the number of jobs exceeded two and a half million; between 1981 and 1987, the figure increased by a further 1.6 million, to which more than one million irregular jobs can be added, over 70 per cent of which are second jobs and 20 per cent working activities undertaken by non-resident workers.

In the years between the 1971 and 1981 censuses, the number of jobs in agriculture experienced an appreciable reduction (by 900,000), which tended to level out as the more marginal farms gradually disappeared; the decline in building jobs was relatively large (by 350,000 or just under one-fifth of total employment in the branch); while the drop in manufacturing industry was still limited (only 90,000). This last figure, however, requires further elucidation. First of all, it must be pointed out that up until 1980 employment in industry increased; the loss of 200,000 workers occurred only between 1980 and 1981. The capacity to preserve jobs completely collapsed during the 1980s. Between 1981 and 1987, regular employment in manufacturing industry fell by 756, 000. The decrease also involved self-employed workers, though to a less pronounced extent (a drop of 54,000 or 10 per cent). The end of the job-preserving capacity of manufacturing industry combined with the continuing decline in employment in agriculture (a loss of 430,000 jobs between 1981 and 1987) and in building (184,000) led to a considerable reduction in the increase in aggregate employment, from almost 120,000 additional jobs a year in the 1970s to less than 50,000 between 1981 and 1987. In the 1970s, the number of first-job seekers rose sharply, despite the striking growth in employment in the service sector and the maintenance of jobs in industry. In the 1971 census, they were less than one million or 5 per cent of the working population, while in that of 1981 they had increased to almost 2.3 million or more than 10 per cent, mostly young people and concentrated in the South. The matching of a substantial wave of increasingly more educated young workers with the growth of employment in the service sector is highly problematical. The reason is that this growth has been polarized between a relatively limited number of highly qualified stable professional jobs and a large number of precarious low-paid jobs. The question becomes even more complicated if regional imbalances are also taken into account. In the advanced areas of the country, the richer industrial fabric leads to them having a greater share of new stable jobs with a middle to high professional content, above all in services to firms and in the advanced tertiary sector, while at least a part of the less interesting jobs become a means of gaining 'work experience' or simply a transitional stage for young first-job seekers. In the less developed areas, by contrast, a malign spiral has developed through the lack of decent job opportunities and the growing pressure of the labour supply, which is also invading possible domains of work experience, making them less suitable for transitional stages of employment. I shall return to this theme when considering irregular work undertaken by young people in the South.

Data on recent trends in irregular forms of employment

As far as regards irregular work in particular, a distinction must be made between the 1970s and the following period. The 1970s were characterized by a sharp decline in irregular kinds of work, not only in the traditional sectors of building and agriculture but also, and above all, in the more dynamic small and medium-sized industrial sector; this applied to both the Third Italy and the First Italy, where economic success led to the surfacing of many previously hidden activities. In the 1980s, the informalization of an increasingly extensive service sector intensified concurrently with renewed, though limited, growth in irregular work in all branches of the economy.

On the whole, the data in table 6.1 indicate that work has been decisively affected by a process of informalization, given that in the period 1981–7 the recorded increase in irregular jobs is much higher than that in regular ones (870,000 as against 351,000).[6] This increase was due in large part to the rapid growth in second jobs and in the number of foreign workers. Casual labour experienced a sharp decline, almost all of which can be attributed to the drop in agricultural employment. Irregular work in the strict sense, which includes a large number of underemployed agricultural workers and all non-casual precarious workers, decreased slightly on aggregate, with falls in agriculture and in building and rises in manufacturing industry and marketable services. All the large sectors of employment were affected by trends towards informalization in two basic ways: in agriculture, building and manufacturing industry the decline in irregular labour was less (and in manufacturing it increased, though only slightly) than that of regular labour; and in marketable services irregular employment grew even more than the already substantial rise in regular employment (32 per cent as against 21 per cent on aggregate, but with second jobs increasing by almost 40 per cent and the number of foreign workers more than doubling in seven years). The same occurred in non-marketable services, where regular jobs increased at rates below 10 per cent whereas the rates for irregular ones exceeded 20 per cent.

From a different perspective, three questions already touched upon need underlining further. The above-mentioned data confirm that, at least in the Italy of the 1980s, irregular work in manufacturing industry represented a very limited share both of all irregular work and of total manufacturing employment. The forms of irregular work typical of the traditional sectors of agriculture and building tended to decline, but this was a slow process offset by the increase in new forms, above all in the tertiary sector. Finally, in Italy too, it is precisely in the tertiary sector that the key lies to an understanding of the processes of informalization, because it is in these activities that the new kinds of irregular work are being concentrated.

It is obvious that underlying these data is a qualitatively complex reality that I cannot even attempt to explore here; all that is possible is

Table 6.1 ISTAT estimates of employees in the principal economic sectors, divided into self-employed and wage-earners and regular or irregular workers (the data, in thousands, refer to 1987 and the variations to the period 1980–7)

	Regular 87	Regular Var 81/87	Irregular 87	Irregular Var 81/87	Casual 87	Casual Var 81/87	Foreign 87	Foreign Var 81/87	Multiple jobs 87	Multiple jobs Var 81/87
Agriculture	899.5	−351	1019	−79	210	−109	61	20		
Self-employed	787.5	−253.5	385	11	167	−105				
Wage-worker	112	−97.5	634	−90	43	−4				
Manufacturing + energy										
Industry	4670	−756	380.5	31	61	−8	12	3	237	−17
Self-employed	544	−54	114	0	28	−1				
Wage-worker	4126	−702	266	31	33	−7				
Building	1017	−159	466	−25	67	−5	43	15	102	4
Self-employed	376	19	103	−15	12	1.5				
Wage-worker	641	−178	363	−10	55	−6.5				
Services for sale	7369	1304	719	66	281.5	15	221	127	2602	722
Self-employed	3045	596	443	32	132.5	5				
Wage-worker	4324	708	275	34	149	10				
Services not for sale	3793	312	2	—	20	−11	223	75	246	46
Total	17749	351	2587	−7	640	−118	560	240	3187	755
Self-employed	4753	308	1047	28	340	−98.5				
Wage-worker	12996	42.5	1540	−35	300	−19.5				

Source: My elaboration of ISTAT data contained in Mamberti Pedullà et al., 1987

to outline some significant examples. Several of the phenomena relating to irregular work in agriculture can be identified more clearly by following the indications suggested in the recent literature on the subject.[7] Agricultural underemployment is an increasingly unreliable indicator of irregular labour for two different reasons. In the rich regions of the Centre-North, part-time agriculture, and especially that of employed workers, is increasingly carried out within a structured multiple-activity context. These partial work activities need not necessarily be irregular and are in fact increasingly less so, the more they constitute costs for firms whose income is mostly visible and, therefore, has to be declared in order to avoid an excessive taxation of profits. In the poor agricultural regions of the South, agricultural underemployment involves to a limited and diminishing extent adult male heads of families, who traditionally form the category of workers forced to look for complementary irregular work. Underemployment, both of self-employed workers and day-labourers, encompasses to a large extent pensioners, adult females who complement their condition of housewife with a limited number of days working in the fields, and young women seeking another job or waiting to get married and become full-time housewives. Since there exists a special national insurance scheme applied to agricultural work, underemployment also includes a number of 'false' workers.

Still in the field of agriculture, casual labour as recorded by ISTAT (the Italian Government Statistical Office) statistics is declining to an irreducible core of summer work by students and other town-dwellers for reasons that apply more or less to all agricultural areas. On the one hand, the transformation of agricultural labour processes tends to reduce the demand for casual labour, and on the other in most cases casual labourers cannot stand the competition from foreign workers and from those who are already underemployed in agriculture. It is probable that in the Centre-North the first trend is the stronger, while in the South it is the second which is more predominant.

With regard to irregular work in manufacturing industry, besides what is said above and below, it is worth while to refer to the specific question of the illicit production of fake designer clothes. This activity has not been subjected to regularization. There are at least two reasons for this: first, sales are wholly or partially hidden, and therefore firms do not come under pressure to officialize expenses in order to justify high profits to the tax authorities; and second, due to their clandestine nature these activities operate at a low intensity of capital and aim for low labour costs that are almost impossible to achieve with regular workers. For this latter reason, the great majority of the clandestine workshops are concentrated in the South where it is easier to find irregular female labour willing to work for very low rates of pay. According to ISTAT figures, over one-third of irregular workers in manufacturing industry are concentrated in textiles and clothing, which also has the highest rate of irregular labour (almost 20 per cent against an average of less than 10 per cent). The ISTAT estimates do not reveal the presence of foreign workers in this branch, which suggests the consolidation of an uncommon cycle of production and distribution. On the production side, the irregular workers are predominantly southern women, while distribution is almost exclusively carried out by African immigrants who sell the wares mainly through hawking in the large cities.

I do not think it is even possible to attempt a classification of the kinds of irregular jobs in the various branches of the service sector over the whole country, since they are extremely widespread, heterogeneous and diversified at a local level. Instead, some of the more significant regional trends and profiles will be outlined in the following sections. It is important, none the less, to underline that the informalization of the serive sector is taking place both in traditional forms of work and branches of the economy and in those that are relatively innovative. ISTAT estimates that irregular forms of work are a massive phenomenon in all kinds of trade, about one-quarter of all jobs in 1987, which in Italy has remained characterized by a high proportion of family businesses. The incidence of irregular jobs is even higher and close to one-half of all occupations both in the area of repairs and in hotels, cafés, restaurants, etc. It is also extremely high in the branch that is considered to be, in theory, the most advanced of all: services supplied to firms. They account for more than one-third of all jobs. In this last case, we are dealing mainly with second jobs and it can therefore be assumed that these are, to a large extent, activities involving consultancy and other white-collar skills engaged in by professionals and government and private-sector employees outside of their first job. Irregular forms of work are also to be found, however, in traditional branches of the service sector: for example, tax consultancy to small traders or computerized accounting by bank or public-sector staff outside normal working hours. In more or less similar terms, the errand-boys used for home delivery services are not only present on a massive scale as irregular workers in the retail trade but also in the most advanced and innovative branches.

3 QUANTITATIVE ESTIMATES OF THE PRESENCE AND TRENDS OF DIFFERENT KINDS OF IRREGULAR EMPLOYMENT

The Italian underground economy in the broad sense includes a variety of phenomena. If self-provisioning and other activities which are difficult to quantify in monetary terms, like barter and the exchange of work skills, are excluded in principle, three main areas are left which each have a different significance for my analysis: criminal activity; tax evasion by regular workers; and irregular work in the strict sense. These three areas partially overlap; they are by definition difficult to estimate and delimit; and they have in common the fact that they defraud the tax system. Furthermore, they are not entirely visible activities and as a result do not appear in any statistics or in national accounts.

As well as violating the penal code, criminal activity also contravenes laws governing work, taxation and national insurance contributions. CENSIS (the largest Italian social research centre, almost entirely state-supported) issued a report in 1985, related to the beginning of the 1980s, in which estimates were given for the number of workers and the total business involved in eleven areas of crime (see table 6.2). According to this report, the yearly volume of business amounted to roughly 100–150,000 billion lire. Some critics object that this estimate is too high; according to a recent new estimate by ISTAT, the volume in 1984 represented between 14 and 20 per cent of GDP – the two figures are not, however, comparable. Given that it is difficult to assess the estimate, I have adopted a cautious approach and take into consideration only the minimum CENSIS value. According to CENSIS, there may be between a half a million and one million people involved in criminal activities, that is, between 2.5 and 5 per cent of the working population. Similarly, the estimates of workers in the criminal sector are not comparable with employment statistics as it is not known how many of the former are recorded as workers in the latter.

Pure tax evasion occurs where work is fully regular. It involves, above all, the evasion of direct taxes by self-employed workers, particularly traders and shopkeepers, artisans, professionals and others employed in the service sector, but also the evasion of company taxes and VAT. In the commercial sector alone, a recent estimate by the Confcommercio (General Federation of Italian Traders and Shopkeepers) indicates that the total turnover of clandestine commercial firms lies above 40,000 billion lire. The total, conservative, figure for income which evaded

Table 6.2 *Estimate of the dimensions of illegal activity in Italy*

Items	Value of illegal activity in billions (lire)	Number of workers
1 Production and sale of drugs	25,000–35,000	20,000–30,000
2 Production and clandestine sale of arms	4,000–5,000	50,000
3 Production and clandestine traffic of works of art	1,000–2,000	5,000–10,000
4 Gain from prostitution	5,000	50,000
5 Clandestine gambling	3,000–7,000	10,000
6 Blackmail and distortion	15,000–20,000	75,000–150,000
7 Theft, robbery and receipt of stolen goods	20,000	400,000
Small-time theft	1,000–2,000	250,000–300,000
8 Contraband	(2,000–3,000)	25,000–50,000)
9 Illegal trade in currency	5,000–10,000	—
10 Illegal payment for services	8,000–12,500	50,000–100,000
11 Various other illegal activities (forgery, swindling, fraud, exploitation of incapacitated persons, etc.)	12,500–17,500	100,000–150,000

Source: CENSIS, *Illegal Activities Dossier*, 1985, Year XXI, No. 4, p. 29

taxation in the mid-1980s is estimated at over 150,000 billion lire per year. The new 1982 calculation of GNP at market prices elaborated by ISTAT attempted to give a conservative estimate of at least a part of the income produced in hidden forms. The resultant figure of more than 70,000 billion was more than 15 per cent above the previous estimate. For the years after 1982, the difference between the old estimate and the new ones continued to show an increase up to 17.7 per cent in 1985. In 1984, the year to which the CENSIS estimate of criminal activity refers, the difference is 17.2 per cent and amounts to around 120,000 billion lire at current prices. These differences may be considered to be an approximate indicator of some minimum thresholds for the income which evades taxation, given that the ISTAT calculation of GNP also takes into account non-taxable income, a percentage of taxable income which has evaded taxation and other variable items which cannot be classified under taxes and contributions.

The evasion of taxes and national insurance contributions may well involve up to three million regular workers, a large number of enterprises and the income produced by various categories of irregular work. Taking the ISTAT estimates for 1984 and re-elaborating them according to the criteria in table 6.3, it can be seen that there were nearly seven million irregular workers (including only the categories of workers that are assumed to produce hidden income) producing a substantial hidden income. It is possible to work out approximate percentages for all the types of irregular work mentioned relative to the total amount of business involved in tax evasion. This total comes to around 40,000 billion lire (see table 6.3). It may therefore be concluded that although irregular work involves a large number of workers, it represents less than 20 per cent of the total income produced by criminal and hidden activities, estimated at around 250,000 billion lire in 1984. This figure cannot be compared with GNP because it does not refer solely to produced income but also to transfers from clearing transactions and because it is difficult to say how much of this figure should be added to GNP, how much is already included and how much cannot be taken into consideration.

As stated in the opening remarks about the area of irregular work in Italy, it is clear that this type of work is particularly differentiated and heterogeneous. In order to estimate the different kinds of irregular employment, I mainly refer to the recent ISTAT recalculations of the Italian GNP, which also account for a part of the Italian underground economy. There are at least three good reasons for doing so: the ISTAT estimates are official, accurate (every possible institutional source is considered) and relative to the whole country, and they may be broken down by economic sector and by a certain number of branches. On the

Table 6.3 *ISTAT estimates for 1984 of irregular workers and author's estimates of gross hidden income produced by each category*

	(000)	Hidden income estimated as category product (billion lire)
Underemployed agricultural workers	1006	
Non-agricultural irregular workers	1484	15,000[a]
Undeclared hourly workers (ISTAT annual adjustment)	774	
My estimate of casual work including turnover of majority (multiplied by 2.5 out of a max. 4)	1935	6,000[b]
Non-resident foreigners	515	5,000[c]
Non-agricultural second job	2873	14,350[d]
Agricultural second job	3992	
Total		40,350

Source: Mamberti Pedullà, et al. 1987
[a] For all categories I have taken income produced in a year as 1984 millions to make it roughly comparable to other data. In this case the multiplicator is 10 million.
[b] The multiplicator is just above 2 million.
[c] The multiplicator is just short of 10 million.
[d] The multiplicator is 5 million.

other hand, they cannot be broken down by region, gender and age group. Moreover, it should be underlined at the outset that the new ISTAT series have been constructed for the purpose of estimating anew the national accounts system, using only institutional data. Consequently, they inevitably leave out some categories that may be of interest for a complete survey of irregular employment.

ISTAT data identify five types of irregular employment which are of immediate interest plus a sixth which is not taken into consideration here; it relates to second or multiple jobholding in agriculture by non-agricultural workers. While these agricultural activities produce a 'shadow' income that has to be added to GNP, I have decided to exclude them from irregular work in the strict sense as they are bound to be predominantly self-provisioning. But, in this regard, it is worth mentioning that the numbers of such workers persist at about four million while agricultural workers as a whole are declining fast, and that this may indicate that self-provisioning of food is not declining and possibly even increasing, taking into consideration the possibility that the introduction of light technology is leading to an increase in the productivity of both land and labour.

The five types of irregular employment which are of immediate interest here are the following:

- *Multiple jobholding outside agriculture.* This refers only to undeclared and irregular working activities. For this reason, the data are different from the estimate of multiple jobholding elaborated by ISTAT for the EUROSTAT series; here only regular cases are included, where there is cumulation of part-time jobs or a limited amount of officially declared work on top of full-time employment – to give an idea of the difference, the ISTAT estimate for 1986 is over three million while the ISTAT/EUROSTAT figure is under 130,000.[8]
- *Underemployed workers in agriculture.* Here both wage-workers and the self-employed working for less than 180 days per year are included. This is not *per se* a form of irregular employment but an indicator of a fully declared official form of employment which produces inadequate income and consequently could signify that it is supplemented by other income from work that is strictly irregular, because off-the-books and undeclared.
- *Irregular employment outside agriculture.* This is the crucial category of non-occasional irregular employment involving resident workers. It is usually identified through a comparison of the population census data with the trade and industry census data or with other data (see n. 4).
- *Occasional undeclared workers.* For this category, there is a set of data deriving from the official survey of the labour force, in which, starting in 1977, those defining themselves as non-employed (adult students, housewives, pensioners) are regularly asked whether they have worked occasionally during the last week.[9]
- *Non-resident foreign workers.* A category which is self-explanatory and which ISTAT estimates mainly from reports on their presence in every Italian district compiled by the Police and the Ministry for Home Affairs.

In addition to these types for which it is possible to produce reasonable estimates on the basis of recent ISTAT calculations, I will mention briefly the possible presence of other kinds of irregular employment which have not been taken into consideration by ISTAT for various reasons; but mainly because either they are irrelevant in terms of recalculating GNP or they cannot be estimated on the basis of the official sources from which ISTAT derived the new calculation. Consequently, it is not possible to produce viable quantitative estimates of these forms. They may be divided approximately into the following five types:

- *Occasional multiple jobholding.*
- *Occasional work by the unemployed.* The sample survey of the labour force does not question the unemployed about occasional work.
- *Undeclared occasional work by housewives, pensioners and students.*
- *Irregular work by those under the minimum legal age* (less than fourteen years old). Both local surveys and legal cases show that this form of irregular employment is widespread. In the South, it is still related to a relatively high rate of school-leavers who have not completed compulsory education (still about 10 per cent of young people) while, in the North, it is more diffused as a form of family help in after-school hours.
- *Irregular work in criminal areas* (see CENSIS estimates in table 6.2).

The following observations are put forward with the new ISTAT series for 1980–7 (table 6.4) in mind, integrated with other qualitative information derived from local surveys when available.

Multiple jobholding

Without doubt, the largest group of irregular workers is that of workers who for various reasons are available for additional jobs. As stated above, second jobs in agriculture – generally, workers in non-agricultural sectors who also cultivate small plots of land, either their own or rented for self-provisioning or to obtain modest amounts of extra income – should be distinguished from non-agricultural multiple jobholding. In most cases, second jobs are self-employed, non-temporary and are complementary to the first job. According to the ISTAT estimates, non-agricultural multiple jobholding in Italy has tended to increase regularly in the 1980s by approximately 100,000 additional jobs per year. Second jobs are particularly concentrated in marketable services. More than 80 per cent of second jobs are found in this sector, approximately one-half in trade and repairs, more than one-quarter in transport and the remaining less than one-quarter in teaching, research and economic services to firms.

The traditional profile of the multiple jobholder is that of a male employee in a relatively large standard-type firm who is the breadwinner

Table 6.4 *ISTAT estimates of employment in various sectors and branches divided by formal and informal types in 1980 and 1987, with variations in number and percentage, 1980–87 (totals do not include second jobholders)*

Sectors and branches	1980 (000)	1987 (000)	1980–87 (000)	1980–87 %
AGRICULTURE				
Total workforce	3430.1	2504.1	−926	−27.0
Employees:				
Regular wage-workers	229.2	112	−117.2	−51.1
Underemployed workers	774.8	633.9	−141	−18.2
Casual workers	148.5	106.7	−41.7	−28.1
Non-resident foreign workers	39.1	61.1	22	56.3
Self-employed:				
Regular self-employed	1108.7	787.5	−321.2	−29.0
Underemployed	389.1	385.5	−3.6	−0.9
Casual workers	740.7	417.5	−323.2	−43.6
Multiple jobholders	4007.9	3978.1	−29.8	−0.7
MANUFACTURING AND ENERGY INDUSTRIES				
Total workforce	6185.7	5215.4	−970.3	−15.7
Employees:				
Regular wage-workers	5033.7	4126	−907.7	−18.0
Irregular workers	244.3	266.3	22	9.0
Casual workers	108.2	82.5	−25.7	−23.8
Non-resident foreign workers	8.7	12.2	3.5	40.2
Self-employed:				
Regular self-employed	590.4	544.2	−46.2	−7.8
Irregular self-employed	117.9	114.2	−3.7	−3.1
Casual workers	82.5	70	−12.5	−15.2
Multiple jobholders	251.8	237.2	−14.6	−5.8
of which:				
Heavy industry				
Total workforce	1764.2	1538.5	−225.6	−12.8
Employees:				
Regular wage-workers	1544.5	1292.9	−251.6	−16.3
Irregular workers	60.9	70	9.1	14.9
Casual workers	23.2	29.5	6.2	26.9
Non-resident foreign workers	7.6	11.4	3.8	50.0

Table 6.4 *(Continued)*

Sectors and branches	1980 (000)	1987 (000)	1980–87 (000)	1980–87 %
Self-employed:				
Regular self-employed	103.6	110.1	6.5	6.3
Irregular self-employed	17.1	18.4	1.3	7.6
Casual workers	7.2	6.2	−1	−13.8
Multiple jobholders	49.9	48.8	−1.1	−2.2
Light modern industry				
Total workforce	1797	1434.2	−362.7	−20.2
Employees:				
Regular wage-workers	1634.6	1288.3	−346.3	−21.2
Irregular workers	44.9	41.5	−3.4	−7.6
Casual workers	13	12.2	−0.7	−5.8
Non-resident foreign workers	0.3	0.2	−0.1	−33.3
Self-employed:				
Regular self-employed	82.1	79.6	−2.5	−3.0
Irregular self-employed	10.1	11.4	1.3	12.9
Casual workers	12	1	−11	−91.7
Multiple jobholders	66	60.7	−5.3	−8.0
Traditional industries				
Total workforce	2624.5	2232.8	−391.7	−14.9
Employees:				
Regular wage-workers	1854.6	1544.8	−309.8	−16.7
Irregular workers	138.5	154.9	16.3	11.8
Casual workers	72	40.7	−31.2	−43.4
Non-resident foreign workers	0.8	0.6	−0.2	−25.0
Self-employed				
Regular self-employed	404.7	354.5	−50.2	−12.4
Irregular self-employed	90.7	84.4	−6.3	−6.9
Casual workers	63.2	53	−10.2	−16.2
Multiple jobholders	135.9	127.7	−8.2	−6.0
BUILDING INDUSTRY				
Total workforce	1850.5	1694.4	−156.1	−8.4
Employees:				
Regular wage-workers	815.5	640.9	−174.6	−21.4
Irregular workers	365.5	362.9	−2.6	−0.7
Casual workers	160	137.2	−22.7	−14.2
Non-resident foreign workers	26.4	43.1	16.7	63.3

Table 6.4 *(Continued)*

Sectors and branches	1980 (000)	1987 (000)	1980–87 (000)	1980–87 %
Self-employed:				
Regular self-employed	343.4	376.4	33	9.6
Irregular self-employed	113.5	103.4	−10.1	−8.9
Casual workers	26.2	30.5	4.2	16.2
Multiple jobholders	98	102.3	4.3	4.4
MARKETABLE SERVICES				
Total workforce	7317.2	9012.3	1695.1	23.2
Employees:				
Regular wage-workers	3546.9	4323.7	776.8	21.9
Irregular workers	244.5	275.4	30.9	12.6
Casual workers	362.2	372.7	10.5	2.9
Non-resident foreign workers	87.8	221.1	133.3	151.8
Self-employed:				
Regular self-employed	2309	3045	736	31.9
Irregular self-employed	403.3	443.4	40.1	9.9
Casual workers	363.5	331	−32.5	−8.9
Multiple jobholders	1780.9	2601.8	820.9	46.1
Trade and repairs				
Total workforce	3969.5	4739.4	769.9	19.4
Employees:				
Regular wage-workers	1392.9	1611.3	218.4	15.7
Irregular workers	143.1	151.7	8.6	6.0
Casual workers	108.7	106	−2.7	−2.5
Non-resident foreign workers	60.2	183.7	123.5	205.1
Self-employed:				
Regular self-employed	1727.2	2179.7	452.5	26.2
Irregular self-employed	282.9	287.8	4.9	1.7
Casual workers	254.5	219.3	−35.2	−13.9
Multiple jobholders	1138	1193.8	55.8	4.9
Transport				
Total workforce	907.7	844.7	−63	−6.9
Employees:				
Regular wage-workers	637.6	561.9	−75.7	−11.9
Irregular workers	54.1	53.2	−0.9	−1.7
Casual workers	18	15.7	−2.3	−12.5

Table 6.4 *(Continued)*

Sectors and branches	1980 (000)	1987 (000)	1980–87 (000)	1980–87 %
Non-resident foreign workers	25.6	35.3	9.7	37.9
Self-employed				
Regular self-employed	143	151.5	8.5	5.9
Irregular self-employed	20.9	19.6	−1.3	−6.2
Casual workers	8.5	7.5	−1	−11.8
Multiple jobholders	291.1	702.1	411	141.2
Services to industry, private health, education and entertainment				
Total workforce	1837.2	2727.9	890.7	48.5
Employees:				
Regular wage-workers	919	1455.8	536.8	58.4
Irregular workers	44.1	67.3	23.2	52.6
Casual workers	234	249.5	15.5	6.6
Non-resident foreign workers	2	2.1	0.1	5.0
Self-employed:				
Regular self-employed	438.2	713.2	275	62.8
Irregular self-employed	99.4	135.8	36.4	36.6
Casual workers	100.5	104.2	3.7	3.7
Multiple jobholders	345.8	699.9	354.1	102.4
NON-MARKETABLE SERVICES				
Total workforce	3619.8	4068.5	448.7	12.4
Employees:				
Regular wage-workers	3429.1	3793.4	364.3	10.6
Irregular workers	1.2	1.7	0.5	41.7
Casual workers	77.5	51	−26.5	−34.2
Non-resident foreign workers	112	222.4	110.4	98.6
Self-employed:				
Regular self-employed	–	–	–	–
Irregular self-employed	–	–	–	–
Casual workers	–	–	–	–
Multiple jobholders	200.8	246.2	45.4	22.6

Source: Mamberti Pedullà, et al., 1987

in a family with above-average needs due to size or special problems. This picture is being gradually altered by the fact that the fragmentation of work and the disappearance of some home repair services increase opportunities for multiple jobs. As these jobs are without tenure, provide an insufficient income and last for widely varying periods, they are much more suitable for the multiple jobholder than other kinds of workers. The advantages to both the multiple jobholder and his clients or employers are at a peak when there is a high degree of overlap between the occupational skill involved in the first job and that in the second or further activities: for instance, a skilled car worker in industry who repairs his neighbours' cars or who works for a few hours per week in a small car-repair shop, or a bank clerk offering after-work advice on banking operations, and so on. Such possibilities may arise over a large range of both intellectual and manual occupational skills. It is worth mentioning that the overlap between the first job and other activities may even involve the position of power associated with the first job. Examples are the school-teacher who gives home tuition to his weak pupils for a cash payment; the bank official responsible for the loan department who prepares the applications for some customers privately; the income tax officer who fills out the tax declarations for some of the taxpayers in his district. In these cases, the borderline between informal multiple jobholding and corruption becomes blurred. Furthermore, the diffusion of do-it-yourself and its related equipment has enormously increased these kinds of opportunities; even without any specific skill or qualification, anybody who becomes experienced in undertaking certain repair or manufacturing jobs for his family can also do so for paying customers.

While occasional multiple activities are in any case likely to be informal, whether non-temporary ones become informal depends greatly on the existing fiscal system. The Italian fiscal system gives rise to a very high degree of informality for three reasons: first, tax is levied at a highly progressive rate on employees' declared personal income, and consequently, the level of taxation for additional income is high; second, it is not particularly efficient in tracing income from self-employment or irregular work; third, tax allowances for family needs are low, with the result that an unmarried worker and the breadwinner of a large family earnining the same gross income end up with a similar net income. As a result, all three categories of multiple jobholders (traditional, new non-temporary and occasional) are likely to keep their further activities hidden to more or less the same extent. This also explains why the official data for multiple jobholding greatly underestimate the phenomenon.

Irregular workers

A second type of substantial irregular employment is constituted by non-temporary irregular workers, approximately 1.5 million according to ISTAT estimates for the 1980s. They are predominantly 'vulnerable' workers in that they have little education or few qualifications, are young or old or women and reside in areas with high rates of surplus population. They are forced to accept irregular conditions of work either for certain periods in their lives or permanently.

Nearly one-third of non-agricultural irregular workers are concentrated in the building industry. It is also known from other sources that 80 per cent are concentrated in the southern regions. They comprise male workers who throughout the year are regularly employed on officially registered building sites for relatively short spells, an average of ten to fourteen weeks, unemployed – and doing other small restructuring or repair jobs – for some time and employed off-the-books during other periods.

Another kind of irregular worker is persistently employed in trade, cafés, restaurants and repair activities. Unlike in building, where irregular workers are predominantly wage workers, in this case the large majority are irregular self-employed workers and family helpers. This kind of worker is also more concentrated in the southern regions; and it is also likely that there is a much wider spectrum of types with regard to age groups, gender, levels of income and professional qualifications. They range from the totally unskilled young male who works as a delivery boy for bars and shops to the adult male working as an irregular self-employed street-vendor or as an irregular plumber and to the married female who engages in an irregular activity by running a greengrocer's in place of her husband.

The economic areas where irregular workers have increased rapidly in the 1980s are marketable services to firms, and health, education and entertainment services. Here, irregular workers rose from less than 150,000 in 1980 to nearly 300,000 in 1987. On the other hand, irregular workers are decreasing in manufacturing industry and, in particular, in the older branches where they have been traditionally concentrated – from nearly 230,000 in the early 1980s to approximately 170,000 in 1987. It is worth mentioning that irregular self-employed workers in traditional manufacturing, including family helpers and industrial home-workers in decentralized and subcontracting industries, are declining at a slower rate than irregular wage workers (see table 6.4).

Agricultural workers who are officially underemployed (those working less than 180 days per year) can be added to this category. More than one million workers were underemployed in this sense at the beginning of the 1980s. Underemployed agricultural workers underwent a decline in the 1980s, from over 1.1 million in 1980 to approximately 900,000 in 1987; but they have been declining at a slower rate than other occupational groups and, as a result, account for an increasing percentage of agricultural employment, from one-third to slightly less than 40 per cent, particularly underemployed self-employed workers who declined by only a few thousand in the same period.

Occasional workers

The third category of irregular workers comprises young people, pensioners, students and housewives who undertake irregular employment on a more or less occasional basis. They are estimated at two million and to have been declining at a discontinuous rate in the 1980s. This trend was mainly the result of the reduction in the number of casual agricultural workers, who formed more than 40 per cent of the total at the beginning of the 1980s and less than one-third by 1987, dropping from nearly 900,000 to approximately half a million.

On the other hand, occasional workers are becoming increasingly concentrated in the marketable services sector, and particularly in services to firms, private education, health and entertainment, where they increased from 330,000 in 1980 to approximately 400,000 in 1987. High figures for occasional workers are recorded by ISTAT also in trade and repairs, more than 300,000 – though gradually declining; in traditional manufacturing, declining from 135,000 to less than 100,000 in the last few years; in the building industry, where the figure was more than 180,000 in the early 1980s, with only a slight decline affecting exclusively young or old males; and finally in non-marketable services, mainly services to households such as hourly-paid domestic work, where the decline has been very substantial: from nearly 80,000 to less than 50,000.

As has been said above, these data reflect the source from which they have been elaborated, which is the sample quarterly survey of the national workforce and, more precisely, the questionnaire on occasional work addressed to housewives, students and pensioners. Most of the respondents to this questionnaire are women, and in fact this is the only type of irregular employment where females are predominant. However, this set of data does not take into consideration occasional work done by those under fourteen and by the unemployed. Neither is it possible to consider the occasional activities undertaken by the respondents to this questionnaire but not reported for at least two different reasons: either because the fragment of work is too occasional and/or too small to be reported or because the respondents want to keep quiet about it.

Work done by non-resident foreigners

Lastly, there is the category of non-resident foreigners. The figures which interest us here regard people from underdeveloped countries who take on irregular jobs. Estimates from various different sources of the numbers involved vary widely, from 300,000 to one million.[10] Generally speaking, they are young people of both sexes with relatively high levels of education who emigrate without their families for periods of between two and five years. Included here are seasonal/migrant workers from North African countries.

The new ISTAT series estimates that this category of irregular employment increased dramatically in the 1980s from less than 300,000 to more than 600,000 workers. According to ISTAT, in recent years non-resident foreigners have become particularly concentrated in the following sectors: non-marketable services, where they account for nearly 50 per cent and are predominantly domestic helpers; trade, repairs and transport, where they make up more than 30 per cent and are particularly concentrated in irregular street trade; building and agriculture, where they comprise slightly less than 10 per cent in both sectors. Very few non-resident foreigners are employed in manufacturing and those that are all work in heavy industry.

4 THE STRUCTURE OF THE DEMAND/OPPORTUNITIES FOR IRREGULAR EMPLOYMENT

Opportunities for undertaking irregular work are of a diverse kind. In general, the following areas of demand/opportunity can be identified:

1 Modern services and areas particularly subject to transformation and innovation where irregular work is used experimentally or reflects a phase in which the introduction of work mobility is still incomplete (software, subcontracting in the reorganization of office work, marketing and advertising surveys, and so on);

2 agriculture, local traditional industry, building, services in the home and services to the public where the seasonal nature of the work and/or high labour costs in relatively labour-intensive processes encourage irregular employment;

3 export-oriented manufacturing industry where strong competition and the relatively high cost of regular work encourage the consider-

able use of informal labour; this is much less extensive than the first two.

A common cliché regarding irregular employment in Italy is the idea that its widespread use in export-oriented manufacturing concerns explains their international competitiveness. According to recent ISTAT estimates, irregular jobs are not highly concentrated in manufacturing industry. Strictly irregular workers in manufacturing made up 13.7 per cent of the total for all sectors in 1980, rising to 14.7 per cent in 1987 (an increase from 362,000 to 380,000); they accounted for 5.8 per cent of manufacturing employment as a whole in 1980 and for 7.3 per cent in 1987. Casual workers in manufacturing formed 9.2 per cent of the total in 1980, increasing to 9.5 per cent in 1987; but their numbers declined by nearly 40,000; they fell as a percentage of aggregate manufacturing employment from 3 to 2.9 per cent. Foreign workers comprised 3.2 per cent of the total in 1980, falling to 2.2 per cent in 1987; they formed a negligible percentage of manufacturing employment (0.2 in 1987). Total irregular employment as a percentage of manufacturing employment increased from 8.8 per cent in 1980 to 10.4 per cent in 1987 due to the sharp decrease in regular employees, but fell in absolute terms. The percentage of non-agricultural second jobholding in manufacturing was not particularly relevant either and was on the decline (10.8 per cent in 1980 and 7.4 per cent in 1987). Irregular jobs are concentrated, on the other hand, in agriculture and building (though declining), and in marketable services and personal services (increasing rapidly). Therefore, in order to explain the competitiveness of Italian manufacturing industry, one should look in a different direction, one of the most probable being the high rates of tax evasion by the self-employed and by small firms and even by large corporations.

The connection between the informal economy and self-employment and small-scale employment is very controversial and needs clarification.[11] First, there is no automatic correlation between the informal economy and self-employment or employment in small-scale firms. Second, the problem of irregular employment should be dealt with separately and starting from the problem of tax evasion by the self-employed. As already stated, in Italy tax evasion accounts for a very large share of unrecorded income; but, at the same time, it includes evasion by officially registered workers and corporations in various sectors. As far as the first point is concerned, the following aspects should be stressed: first, only a part of irregular employment is related to small-scale activities and self-employment, the magnitude of this part varying according to country, sector and period; second, the reverse is also true, with only a part of

372   INFORMALIZATION AND SOCIALIZATION MIXES

self-employment and small-scale employment revealing various degrees of irregularity; and third, there are, as a consequence, important trends in which the spread of self-employment and small-scale activities is not accompanied by a corresponding increase in informal employment, while the spread of irregular forms of employment may not be accompanied by a parallel rise in self-employment and small-scale activities. Examples of the first trend are the building industry in the last fifteen years and the consolidation of manufacturing in North-Eastern and Central Italy between 1975 and the early 1980s. The second can be seen in the development of a vigorous subcontracting outwork system where the real employers are large firms and the informal workers are fully clandestine, and also in the diffusion of areas of precarious employment such as casual employees in large private standardized service enterprises, like fast-food establishments.

The main areas for which it is important to discuss the relation between informal work and self-employment or small-scale employment are the following: family and flexible employment in small-scale systems of firms; socio-economic innovation and informal self-employment; casual self-employment activities of the unemployed and the inactive population; and second informal self-employed jobholding by regular workers.

Family and irregular flexible employment has been variously linked to the development of a system of small firms in North-Eastern and Central Italy. In some sectors, the development has been accompanied by an increase in subcontracting, but in others it has only reflected the high competitiveness resulting from a different organization of the labour process than that found in large and rigid economic enterprises.

Socio-economic innovation is variously connected with both self-employment and informal working conditions, mainly in the service industries. This connection applies both when there is a new area of activity, in some cases dependent on technological innovation, like software consultants or small-scale video producers, and where there is not, as with new food or leisure fashions, or a new way of organizing the labour process in an already existing area: for example, the possibility of subcontracting jobs previously done in large integrated firms. In a first phase, these innovations are small-scale, use little capital, show great organizational imagination, rely on social networks and, at the same time, are subjected rather inadequately to regulation. Then, in a subsequent phase, there is a tendency for the scale of activities to increase and for the degree of informality to decrease; but these two trends do not always run parallel. Some areas may tend to concentrate activities and remain tied to high levels of irregular employment, for instance, several so-called 'Pony Express' enterprises supplying a rapid mail-delivery service. Others may remain relatively small in size but eventually regularize their working activities, like some of the software consultant co-operatives.

An age of mass unemployment with a declining number of regular tenured jobs has opened up a vast area of casual self-employment, which does not fill the employment gap adequately and meets only partially the unsatisfied need for work of large social groups that are particularly weak in the labour market due to age, gender or social origin. Babysitters, home typists, occasional irregular street vendors and many other old and new occupations are typical examples of this kind of situation.

Casual work for the unemployed eventually comes up against irresistible competition from the very large number of multiple jobholders, who are in a much stronger position to engage in irregular part-time self-employment since they are protected by the income and the national insurance contributions of their first job. The ISTAT estimates are impressive in this respect: self-employed second jobs (almost always irregular) were estimated at less than one and a half million in 1980, increasing to over two million in 1987.

To summarize, it may be said that, in the Italian case, it is particularly evident that the present stage of industrial development is promoting a concomitant increase in both informal activities and self-employment and small-scale activities. But these two trends are not mechanically related.

5 FACTORS DETERMINING THE EXTENT OF IRREGULAR WORK

In general, it is possible to detect three main, often interrelated, factors which explain the presence and extent of irregular work in Italy. The first lies in the forms of transformation typical of traditional labour-intensive activities. In agriculture, this tendency is further accentuated by the persistence of seasonal work, especially that related to some Mediterranean crops grown on small plots of land; moreover, income from work is very low and falling relative to the cost of survival. Building, agriculture and some traditional services in particular function in such a way as to encourage both the frequency of fragmented working activity (part-time work, seasonal work, etc.) which is often irregular and for a below-subsistence-level income, making it necessary to find other forms of income, and the related deterioration in working conditions (hours of work, job stability, etc.) compared to standard official work, which is subject to taxation and legal regulations.

The second factor favouring irregular work is the relatively high cost of labour due also to taxation and social insurance costs but, above all, to the rigidity of the institutionally established conditions of employment. This factor makes irregular work convenient, especially in the most competitive sectors of the economy. In this light, the convenience of a second job both for workers and employers is evident.

The third factor is the fact that general economic transformations increase the types of jobs which are fragmentary and/or provisional, above all in the sector of private marketable services. I have in mind the reorganization of some services to firms, like advertising and market research, and the restructuring of some office jobs, using home subcontracting, and also of the technologically most advanced fields with high rates of obsolescence, from software consultancy to image creation.

All these factors share a formidable common denominator which combines the advantages of irregular work: the evasion of taxes and social insurance costs. The collection of the latter is rigorous and effective for formal activities, especially standard wage work, but particularly lax and ineffective in the case of self-employment and hidden work.

It is worth while to mention that, as a general economic and political trend, the Italian model, based on an inflexible and complicated fiscal structure whose regulations have never been properly enforced, has not only worked in favour of a *de facto* protection of self-employment and small-scale activities, but has also obstructed, at least to some extent, 'normal' capitalist concentration. Small ventures both in manufacturing and in services have always found it more convenient to expand horizontally rather than vertically. In other words, a small successful entrepreneur in Italy finds it more convenient to start another small venture rather than enlarge the first and grow to a size where it becomes more difficult to evade taxes or ignore trade union and safety regulations. This situation is even more clearly reflected in the different criteria for taxing 'artisanal' concerns compared to other kinds of enterprise. The considerable advantages of being an 'artisan' have meant that a large number of artisanal concerns have persisted and that many define themselves as such without possessing the minimum requisites that are officially required in other countries. For the same reason, trade in the general sense has remained much less concentrated than in other countries and small shopkeepers have survived to a much greater extent than elsewhere. It could be said that the Italian institutional system has been a forerunner in favouring the trend towards extensive 'vertical disintegration' and that the Italian economy has developed in a very polarized fashion with, at one end, an extremely concentrated formal manufacturing system in financial and operational terms, at least until the 1970s, and, at the other, highly dispersed and fragmented economic enterprises.

The specific local features of the various possible kinds of informal working activities depend, in general, on a variety of patterns: the degree of survival or adaptation of traditional ways of organizing work; the territorial structure – inner cities, peripheries, small cities, the country-side; and the degree of social and geographical stability versus mobility. In addition to these general characteristics, the problem can be considered from the point of view of the different socio-economic histories of large regions.

I shall now briefly recapitulate what has already been stated in chapter 5 and in the second section of this chapter on the local impact of irregular forms of employment in the three Italies. In the North-West (major industry and advanced sectors), the types of informal activities which are particularly widespread are innovative ones, both personal services to customers and high-tech, organizational and informal services to economic units, with a high concentration of new services for large manufacturing and informational activities.

In the North-East and Centre, the spread of informal activities has been connected with the trend towards diffused industrialization based on small and medium-sized manufacturing industry. This has involved a substantial increase in irregular working activities, mainly in manufacturing but also complementary to agriculture and services during the initial stage of the boom in diffused industrialization (1965–75); an accentuated trend towards formalization during the following period due to the consolidation of the system, its redirection away from the local market and towards exports, and the consequent necessity for economic enterprises to be fully above board (1975–83); and a third, more contradictory, contemporary phase in which informalization tendencies are typical of the service sector, exactly as in the North-West, and of some traditional manufacturing branches (shoes, clothing, etc.) where increasing competition is stimulating a new wave of submerged activities motivated by the desire to save on production costs, mainly, but not only, the cost of labour.

In the South, two general types of situation can be distinguished. In areas where agriculture prevails, the irregularity of work is largely conditioned by labour processes in agriculture which leave a large proportion of the workers idle for long periods of time. As a result, these workers are available for other irregular work in non-agricultural sectors, above all in building but also in trade, basic services and traditional sectors. Moreover, this situation produces a large increase in the demand for work in the brief harvest season.

By contrast, in the large and medium-sized southern cities irregular work has always been concentrated in building and is tending to spread in the service sector, but with a less innovative and experimental character compared to the forms found in cities in the Centre-North. It largely consists of street pedlars, boys working in bars and shops, waiters and waitresses, seasonal workers in the tourist industry, multiple jobholders in services, etc. Particularly in the South, but also in the rest of the country, irregular forms of employment are widespread and on the increase in the service sector partly as a consequence of the relative lack, imbalance or inefficiency of public welfare programmes (IRES Campania, 1987).

In general, I would stress that the most interesting cases for comparison at an international level are, first, the highly unstable and heterogeneous inner cities. They show a negative vocation for certain kinds of informal activities due to social instability and heterogeneity, but also a much more powerful positive one due to a wide range of advantages from other points of view: proximity to services, trade and research centres, seats of multinational companies and high-income residential areas with an increasing need for personalized services in the home (delivery of goods, babysitting, cleaning and cooking, occasional secretarial help, etc.). Then there are the various types of stable 'peripheries' (small and medium-sized towns, metropolitan peripheries, the urbanized countryside) where the degree of local complementarity between formal and irregular activities is high and growing. From this perspective, it is important to stress that in Northern and Central Italy worker-peasants have been a crucial element in every sector of manufacturing employment in the relatively recent past (Villa, 1986). They are the immediate historical precursor to, and are not so different from, the highly 'self-provisioning' households in contemporary Britain described by Pahl (1984). A stable local community, home (and land) ownership and sufficient opportunities for modern full-time jobs, at least for adult males, are in both cases the essential elements which reinforce both traditional and modern forms of self-provisioning and informal activities, often also multiple jobholding, manufacturing work in the home and various forms of subcontracting.

In addition to what has already been said in terms of factors which facilitate the presence of irregular forms of employment, it is useful to underline once again the processes which are active in the service sector in Italy. The persistence of inefficient public services and the relative poverty of many consumers aggravate the tendencies which encourage irregular work. Here I have in mind innovations in the work process which reflect more the abuse of cheap irregular labour than an increase in the productivity of regular labour. Furthermore, many services carried out in the home, repairs for example, tend to become too costly and sporadic if they are organized formally, and so they are transformed into areas of self-provisioning and/or irregular work: second jobs or jobs for undeclared cash payments. It is also worth underlining that the numbers engaged in paid household work, both full-time co-resident maids and workers paid by the hour, is persistently higher than in other advanced capitalist countries. In this case, too, the degree of irregularity is high and difficult to control both where the work is done by non-resident foreigners and where it is done by indigenous maids, all the more so if the latter are the wives of regularly employed workers, and consequently uninterested in social and health insurance and keen to avoid relatively high rates of marginal taxation.

As regards the public sector, there are numerous examples in every possible branch of the welfare services. The lack of public nurseries and the high cost of private ones has given rise to several alternatives based on irregular work. They involve a range of activities from daytime babysitters to full-time domestic helpers, increasing numbers of whom come from the Third World. Some private nurseries have emerged which use irregular workers. The inefficiency of the state education system has led to the widespread practice of private lessons and private after-school training. Another example is the 'Pony Express' rapid mail delivery service in the metropolitan areas, employing young men with their own means of transport, usually mopeds or motor-bikes, which fills in for the inefficient and unreliable public postal service.

The cultural and socio-political impact of informalization is a vast and complex problem, which makes it possible to mention only those aspects relating to the family, gender and age, focusing mainly on the last. With regard to the family, Pahl (1984; 1988) is right when he stresses that it makes a great social difference whether irregular low-income activities are undertaken for breadwinning or for a supplementary income, as in the case of multiple jobholding and activities done by previously non-employed members of a household with one or more full-time regular workers. In the first case, the spread of irregular activities can upgrade some middle- to low-income families in economic terms and multiply their opportunities. In the second case, they may be the first step towards social marginalization and poverty. An important example of the latter case in Italy are the irregularly employed unskilled building workers in the South. Their families have become trapped in a state of poverty and marginalization. Children are forced to leave school even before completing compulsory education in order to work (males in building, females as hourly-paid maids). As a consequence, the same social conditions are reproduced in the following generation: semi-illiterate, totally unskilled workers obliged to accept the lowest kinds of black-market work.

The gender question is controversial. There is no evidence that a majority or a large and increasing proportion of irregular poorly paid activities are done by adult females. In the advanced capitalist countries, gender discrimination is in many cases simple to operate and 'legal' within the official employment structure: part-time workers are largely females and low-paid jobs are reserved for women while high-income jobs remain the prerogative of men. It is likely that the two most important aspects of irregular employment in terms of gender concern young females and domestic helpers.

An incorrect assumption about irregular forms of employment in Italy is that it mainly involves female workers (Weiss, 1987). It is true that ISTAT estimates are not broken down by gender, age and region, but this assumption is easily disproved by other data and the results of research. Females make up a sizeable majority of occasional workers, according to data contained in the quarterly survey of the labour force and based on a questionnaire to the non-employed, the largest subgroup of which by far consists of housewives. A large proportion of underemployed workers in agriculture in the South are females; but they are less likely to supplement their insufficient income through complementary casual work outside agriculture than adult males, who traditionally combine official underemployment in agriculture with unofficial temporary work in building and street trade. Females are a minority of irregular workers outside agriculture and a tiny minority of informal multiple jobholders.[12] But even official data for multiple jobholders produced by ISTAT for EUROSTAT give a male : female ratio of 85 : 15 for 1986.

The question of irregular work should be linked in diverse ways to that of the condition of women. Above all, the extension in Italy of irregular work into private services also reflects the deficiencies of the state welfare system, which is normally a crucial element in determining the contemporary condition of women in society. In short, these deficiencies are reflected both in the proliferation of irregular jobs in private services (full-time foreign domestics, babysitters, private tuition, home delivery errand-boys, and so on) and in the persistence of an army of full-time housewives compelled by necessity to fill the gaps in social reproduction resulting from the failure to develop public services, particularly in the cities of the South but also in those of the Centre-North, as well as in the inadequate growth in regular job opportunities for women, including married ones, typical of modern services in mature welfare systems. Within this general picture, it is also the case that several forms of innovative irregular work have arisen out of the particular situation of women, ranging from home typists to irregular part-time office workers and many other occupations. The basis for this diffusion is the strong competition in the labour supply and the willingness to accept irregular conditions, provided they are compensated for by flexible working hours compatible with onerous domestic chores.

The unemployed also appear to be largely excluded from irregular jobs, with the exception of a limited number of occasional temporary activities. Recent empirical research in Southern Italy, where the large majority of the unemployed are concentrated, fully confirms this hypothesis and shows that unemployed females are even less involved in casual irregular forms of employment than unemployed males (*IRES-materiali*, 1989a).

The area of paid domestic services to households in the Italian case is giving rise to an important socio-cultural transformation: the supply of indigenous workers ready to accept the poor conditions of employment and the low status attached to working as a domestic helper is decreasing everywhere. These jobs are filled to a growing extent by immigrants from underdeveloped countries; however, a relatively high proportion (50 to 60 per cent) are legal and the work they do is, therefore, not irregular. This has important social consequences: the increasing multi-ethnic nature of Italian society and, at the same time, the appearance and spread of racial discrimination, partly because certain migrant ethnic minorities are concentrated in 'dirty' and poorly paid irregular jobs.

There is evidence of a relatively high concentration of irregular work, with the exclusion of multiple jobholding, among young people. Instability and irregular working conditions for young workers are nothing new. There is, however, a new aspect which may have an important negative social impact: evidence suggests that such a condition may persist over a long period, and continue throughout the working lives of some, and become increasingly incompatible with life projects. This last point is important and has not been given sufficient consideration. To be a poorly paid temporary part-time worker employed in a restaurant or in a coffee bar is a different matter for a university student (compatible with his life project and a free choice to earn some pocket money during a limited period) than for a young semi-skilled unemployed person who is ideally looking for a good permanent job and will never find one (incompatible with his life project). In Italy, this emerges very clearly from interviews with young irregular workers, such as 'Pony Express' delivery boys, in the North (compatible) and with young workers in a similar condition, like coffee bar delivery boys, in the South (incompatible). The former only undertake irregular work during a limited temporary period of their lives; the latter are confined to this kind of work either for a very long period, possibly even over ten years, or for life. Moreover, in the second case they reproduce and possibly aggravate an already vast area of poverty and social marginalization, given that in the South there is a youth unemployment rate of over 40 per cent with peaks of over 70 per cent for females in certain districts. In the case of young people, the additional impact of the gender question should be taken into account. Young Italian males and females show an inverse relation between levels of education and the average length of involvement in irregular or occasional activities. Most males have a low level of education and occupational training. Young females with high school diplomas, on the other hand, form the relative majority of the unemployed and a large part of the women involved in irregular activities and for longer periods. This does not mean that poorly educated females easily find a regular job but that, on the contrary, a large proportion of them 'officially' become full-time housewives, even before marriage, and end up doing work that is even more occasional, irregular and low-paid and is also difficult to identify.

6 THE CASE OF SOUTHERN ITALY IN A COMPARATIVE PERSPECTIVE

Extensive surplus population, unemployment and poverty

From the very end of the Second World War, Southern Italy has provided an example of an area in which there is a wide gap between the formation of surplus population and the local absorption of labour resources, as argued when discussing the connection between surplus population and informal activities in chapter 4. For a certain time, surplus population remained to a great extent a phenomenon characterized by high levels of social mobility. As waves of young labourers precariously employed in building and clandestine workers in industry emigrated to find permanent jobs, they were replaced by a new generation; then the same cycle was repeated. In the last fifteen years, the reduction in the rate of increase of formal jobs, both in the South and in the regions of immigration in Northern Italy and in Europe, has led to a considerable qualitative change, even though the widening of the gap has been contained by a massive injection of public spending in the form of direct money transfers to families and of an expanding state bureaucracy. The development of specific types of informal activities can be explained, at least as a first approximation, by tracing the interconnections between the characteristics of the surplus population and local economic interests incompatible with existing regulations. In the 1950s and 1960s most informal jobs were to be found in building and traditional industries, whereas they are now increasing in the private service sector.

Innovative strategies have played no role owing to the chronic weakness of the economic fabric, mummified by the growing intervention of the state. A submerged world has come into being, difficult to grasp in its entirety, in which the domestic strategies of families are little influenced by the market; in other words, isolated nuclear families have had to get by without modern services and strong kinship and community networks. This process has undoubtedly overburdened the role of the full-time housewife.

The informal sector in the South or Mezzogiorno is becoming an ever-expanding and fragmented kaleidoscope of working activities, which rests on its much discussed complementarity with family and state resources. This function works in such a way, however, that it produces immediate solutions but no prospects of reducing the social unease caused by the jobs crisis. Moreover, it must be said that the qualitative features of the contemporary surplus population in Southern Italy, mainly composed of young people with a moderate or high level of education and with particular job expectations, render the picture of the local informal sector even more complicated. A series of jobs can no longer be filled from a potentially large local workforce, precisely because of the above-mentioned tendency towards the creation of increasingly informal working conditions. In this respect, the role played by the waves of foreign immigrants, especially from North Africa, is also relevant in Southern Italy.

A superficial analysis might lead to the serious mistake of thinking that the three phenomena of surplus population (and informal work strategies), unemployment and poverty completely overlap. Although there is some overlapping, it must not be overestimated. In the Mezzogiorno, the figure of the unemployed and that of the informal worker coincide in two cases, building labourers and young people; here there exists real overlapping. With regard to the former, it is generally assumed that in every case the job is for a limited time, which almost always compels these workers to alternate periods of formal employment with periods on low unemployment benefit; during such periods it is essential for survival that they undertake a good deal of informal activity or clandestine work in building. Young people and women seeking their first job, on the other hand, are either not generally entitled to unemployment benefit or receive paltry sums. Consequently, if their families are not able to support them, they engage in informal work whenever and wherever possible.

Similarly, the informal strategies of those making up the surplus population cannot necessarily be viewed as a response to poverty. Although there is in the Mezzogiorno an important link between informal work and poverty, it does not account for the whole of the story. In this area, urban poverty is a problem of young males who, in the 1960s, were entrapped in the world of precarious employment in the building industry. Often, their wives worked as hourly-paid domestics before the birth of their first child. Later, these women became full-time housewives, sometimes able to earn some extra income through work done at home: sewing and mending, laundering, etc. Their children probably left school as soon as possible in order to work: the females in domestic service or farm labouring, or helping their mothers with household chores; the males in building or as low-paid helpers in workshops, cafés and restaurants. In this way, the cycle of precarious work, semi-illiteracy and poverty is often passed on from one generation to the next. Informal activities in Southern Italy, however, extend well beyond this slice of social reality. They include multiple jobholding; the practice of self-provisioning by a very large number of families; the informal micro-firms for specialized building, self-help building and renovation; the activities of young people with a high level of education from middle-income families; and possibly, though rarely, innovative activities which in an informal phase invent new or strengthen old economic undertakings and may at a later stage be formalized.

Southern Italy is still, perhaps, the most populous large underdeveloped region in an industrialized country. To say this does not mean to deny that a series of profound social transformations have taken place in the area since the end of the Second World War. In the immediate post-war period, the term 'underdeveloped' was used especially to refer to the high incidence of very poor agricultural activities and the concomitant absence or sporadic nature of modern industry in this part of the country. In 1981, the rate of agricultural employment in the Mezzogiorno[13] went down to 17.3 per cent, and the greater part of the population now lives in urban areas with one-third in towns of over 100,000 inhabitants.

The thirty years from 1950 to 1980 were characterized by large-scale emigration from the area, the almost total depopulation of the poorer agricultural regions, a very profound change in agricultural systems, at least two much debated phases of industrialization[14] and the drastic effects of the social and economic policies adopted by governments with a Christian Democrat majority. These governments promoted employment through patronage in the public tertiary sector and transfers of money to families in the form of pensions and allowances (Boccella, 1982; Mingione, 1989), which led to the modernization and unification of consumption patterns at the expense of an ever-increasing dependence by the South on resources produced outside the area. Today, 'underdevelopment' means above all weak industrialization relying on investment from outside, the parallel concentration within the area of unemployment and underemployment in all economic sectors (see table 6.5, p. 391) and a relative lack of or inefficiency in public welfare services. The latter have been greatly penalized by the priority given to monetary transfers to families over the modernization of such services.[15]

The differences between informalization in the South and in other parts of the country

The approximate picture that can be drawn from socio-occupational data is useful for verifying the presence and estimating the extent of informal activities in the South. Almost one-quarter of the active population is made up of people seeking employment, and a further 20 per cent is accounted for by precariously employed workers in industry and the tertiary sector and farm labourers hired on a daily basis. The remaining 56 per cent includes a very substantial number of self-employed workers and workers without job security employed by small or very small firms in all three sectors of the economy. For these workers, income from work is usually low and irregular. In short, only just over one-third of the active population in southern Italy enjoys a stable average or above-average income. In this area, there is a conspicuous number of civil servants and employees in the modern private tertiary sector (banking and insurance), while those working in large and medium-sized industrial firms form less than 10 per cent of the active population.

What is said below may be clearer if I first explain some of the ways in which the picture of the urban Mezzogiorno based on the assumed presence of informal work fails to correspond with the types of informal work described in the literature on the subject. In particular, there are four areas in which I define precisely the general non-correspondence of the present informal sector in the cities of Southern Italy with the established models: the 'traditional' type of 'street-corner' economy; the informal sector characteristic of the large metropolitan areas in under-developed countries; the informalization found in diffused industrialization, namely the type based on small and medium-sized specialized manufacturing firms; and lastly, the innovative and alternative informal type in both the German/Californian version of alternative youth life-styles and the 'technological/self-service' version identified by Gershuny (1978; 1983; Gershuny and Miles, 1983).

The first type is important because it was formulated as a direct result of the kind of phenomena witnessed twenty years ago in the large cities of Southern Italy and, above all, in Naples (Allum, 1973). The 'street-corner' economy was a poor community system of economic organization at the very margins of legality and with a strongly hierarchical set-up. The inhabitants of an alley combined their resources and submitted to a set of regulations, alternative to those of the market and the state, in order to organize their survival. The principal 'ingredients' in this informal community organization were hawking, traditional handicrafts and services, contraband, prostitution, petty theft and receiving stolen goods; but reciprocal relations based on a group-specific code also played a considerable role. In general, I agree with those who maintain that current informal activity in the urban Mezzogiorno is not an offshoot of the 'street-corner' economy (Pinnarò and Pugliese, 1985; Pugliese, 1983). In the course of the last twenty years this economy has, for the most part, been swept away by intensified modernization of the social structure and of consumption and behaviour patterns. Even those activities in the 'street-corner' economy which have survived in present-day informal occupations, for example hawking and illicit activities, are now organized on very different bases and the 'street-corner' community is dying out.

The problem of comparing informal activities in the Mezzogiorno with those in Third World cities requires detailed analysis. It is important, however, to make a few observations, since superficial comparisons between Southern Italy and underdeveloped countries are made all too frequently. The specific features of the informal sector in Third World cities and, above all, the processes of social transformation underlying this sector are in reality very different from those that characterize the Mezzogiorno. Illicit street markets and trading, handicrafts in the home, informal urban transport, semi-independent occupations linked to multinationals, the rearing of domestic animals in overcrowded huts, and the thousand different ways of squeezing a little money out of an increasing number of tourists do not play a very important part in the economy of Southern Italy. In this respect, it is worth emphasizing that here the informal sector is principally made up of black-market wage-work, while in Third World cities informal self-employment with very low earnings is almost always predominant. There is another important basic fact that makes the informal sector in Southern Italy different from that in underdeveloped countries. In the former, the consolidation of the informal sector took place mostly after urbanization, which is already slowing down, and was accompanied by persistent economic stagnation rather than by economic growth as is occurring in the latter, although based on dependency and indebtedness.

The informal sector in the Mezzogiorno does not have much in common either with the knock-on effect of diffused industrialization, such as that in the NEC and in other similar experiences. In the NEC, small firms and specialized workshops make use of outwork, the 'flexible' utilization of all members of the family and the complementary relationship between a relatively rich part-time agriculture and the modernization of those specialized handicraft and manufacturing activities which have not been swept away by the international integration of markets during the last few decades. In Southern Italy, by contrast, these informal systems of small manufacturing enterprises, revitalized by the industrial restructuring of the last fifteen years, are only found sporadically and are not particularly significant. The traditional specialization of leatherware production (gloves, shoes and clothing) in small workshops in the city of Naples may be considered to be in a phase of decline. The decentralization of small industry from the NEC to the Adriatic side of the Mezzogiorno assumes a local importance only in the region of Abruzzi; in Apulia it is already failing to deal with the persistent employment crisis and absorb a significant number of young people.

Finally, the ever-pressing and chronic restraints of 'a life with no options', a relatively poor local market demand increasingly dependent on income transfers from outside, and a social fabric which is segmented yet homogeneous in its expectations (the desperate search for secure employment, preferably in public administration), end by suffocating the type of potential source of alternative creativity which is said to exist in the new informal activities as practised by young people in California or Germany or in the technological innovation of the revolution in personal computers and informatics.

In the case of Southern Italy, the informal sector is characterized by two main areas which, even though they do not account for the whole of the phenomenon, certainly go a long way towards explaining part of it. First, there is the question of informal wage employment, mainly of male workers, which in the past was more accurately called '*lavoro nero*', that is black-market labour. Then there is the area of predominantly female labour consisting of housework and other family-based self-provisioning activities. Here both the persistently high number of full-time housewives and the pressure from recent social transformations must be included. Manifested in the destruction of traditional forms of community and family solidarity, in the need for modern services and in the concomitant inefficiency of public services, they have led to the opening-up of an ever-widening gap which is difficult to bridge, between demands and needs and the resources to satisfy them. Both in the true domestic sphere and in the service sector, a process of informalization is making headway since it is the only possible short-term answer in the absence of other solutions.

*Southern Italy as a society predominantly structured by party-
political patronage*

The above-mentioned differences between the social phenomena found
in the South and those found in other contemporary societies recall a set
of problems already mentioned in the first section of this chapter. Before
analysing the various areas of informal work in the South in general and
the results of a specific survey of family strategies in several southern
towns, it is worth going back to the more general questions of what kind
of society the South is and why it is how it is.

My previous remarks provide some negative indications but no true
idea of what southern society is really like. In the Mezzogiorno, social
relations that are based on reciprocal networks typical of so-called traditional societies – 'street-corner' economies in towns and stable village
economies in the countryside – have been dismantled. This process has
not been accompanied by a vigorous and dominant industrial transformation in line with either the main model of associative industrialization
based on medium to large industry, progressive concentration and the
development of a universal welfare system or with the variation in
industrialization that is strongly tinged by reciprocal relations, or with
mixed or intermediary kinds between these two paths. Industrialization
in the South has been a latecomer, weak and dependent, and it has never
been sufficiently vigorous to be able to 'structure' southern society. This
does not mean, however, that the South can be mechanically described
as resembling underdeveloped countries. It is not only the different social
characteristics of irregular work that lead to this conclusion, but also
many other socio-economic indicators. The Mezzogiorno is closest to the
model of an 'underdeveloped' society, in the sense that the impact of
market tensions has always been negative, where the reciprocal social
relations have been much weakened or distorted by industrial integration
and where, at the same time, the redistributive-associative social relations
develop in a distorted manner and end up as ineffective copies of social
relations accompanying industrial development elsewhere.

The key to understanding the nature of contemporary southern society
is the hypothesis that relationships based on patronage acquired the force
to structure social life in the South in the post-war years. This occurred
when the social order based on the large landed estates vanished for ever
and was not replaced to a sufficient extent by an industrial structuration
of society based on competitive market behaviour controlled by the
growth of associative and redistributive social relations. An interesting
way to approach the question is to look at the history of how the

contemporary patronage system emerged. To begin with, it is useful to outline briefly the concept of patronage relations.[16] By patronage I mean a system of stable social relations which are often passed on from generation to generation. Within these relations certain types of exchange are given priority. Compared with the economic concept of 'clientele', referring to a market-oriented system, the type of exchange involved here is wider, going beyond the exchange of goods for money, and the rules regulating it are not those of market competition. It has now been verified that various types of patronage relations are widespread in industrial society and operate in addition to market relations as a general regulatory device and to control the exchange of resources which do not have a market value. This is particularly the case with political favouritism. As far as the Mezzogiorno is concerned, the post-war situation is rather different: 'widespread party patronage' as against 'traditional patronage' is a new development (Graziano, 1974). The most convincing hypothesis is that the mechanisms of party-political patronage and the resources which are distributed through them have become the most important factor in the social structure of the Mezzogiorno. The extent to which this is the case can be seen from the fact that alternative regulatory mechanisms, especially market competition and universal welfare services, are subordinated to the logic of these mechanisms, distorted by them and even at times totally eclipsed.

The first phase in the transformation of processes of social structuration was drastic and partly hidden, since many members of the dominant class or those involved in the process of mediation were not ousted by the transformation. Most of the large landowners became agricultural capitalists or building and financial speculators. The middlemen and professionals went over to the political parties and the public sphere where they became involved in urbanization, agrarian reform and the development of public-sector infrastructures. The key to understanding the new form of social structuration lies in the fact that a drastic change took place in the direction in which the main resources for social structuration flow and in the criteria for their distribution. These resources come from outside the region. They are, above all, the result of central state policy and their distribution takes place through political parties, largely on the basis of patronage. The structure of the mass political parties, especially the Christian Democratic Party, was created in tandem with the system of social control; the result was that the state and party apparatuses became intertwined with and structured by patronage. This is one of the principle characteristics of the Mezzogiorno. The shaping of a social structure based on clientelism and financed by public bodies with resources distributed through the system of patronage was consolidated through agrarian reform, the speculative boom in residential housing and a spate of public works.

In the 1960s, the system of party patronage definitively established its function as an instrument of social control, taking advantage of the growth of the modern Italian welfare state. The complete interdependence which exists between government intervention, the welfare state and the practice of patronage is one of the most significant developments to have emerged in a Western industrial country. Yet it has been taking place behind the great waves of migration, building and financial speculation, and the controversy surrounding the industrial policy in favour of the *Cassa per il Mezzogiorno* (Southern Italy Development Fund) and of the 'poles of industrial development'.[17] A welfare state and patronage relations are a contradiction in terms. In this sense, it can be said that there is no real welfare state system in the Mezzogiorno, even if it exists on paper. The task of creating a modern system of private and public services has been permeated by patronage relations in a variety of ways. Widening public intervention has provided the means for strengthening the party patronage system in a number of sectors including central government services, the railways, the Post Office, electricity, education, health and the relationship between the private and the public sectors. Evidence for the existence of this process is massive and relates to the absence of services or their malfunctioning, recruitment of personnel – from top management to the local authority dustmen in Naples – and the individualistic basis on which services are provided.

The main lines of the consolidation of the party patronage system as one of social control are not difficult to trace. What is difficult, on the other hand, is to fully understand its, so far, irreversible consequences. The 'natural' expansion of the state bureaucracy and the public services apparatus has made an increasing quantity of resources available which the party patronage system has used to strengthen its position as a central element within an uncommon social structure. The resources have been of two types. The most sought-after resource is a good job, especially in the private and public tertiary sector, and it has been used to bolster the consensus of the middle classes. The result has been the formation of a middle class which is apparently definable in terms of its professional function, but which, in reality, is strictly tied up with the patronage system. Clearly, this state of affairs has irreversibly compromised the regular functioning of the sector. The second type of resource, which is less valued, is constituted by direct welfare payments, pensions, subsidies, supplementary earnings and a certain number of manual jobs. These resources have been used to ward off social unrest in the vast area affected by precarious work and among the semi-proletariat in the Mezzogiorno by attracting large numbers into the patronage system. In this way, social struggles have been channelled into growing competition for resources controlled by the powerful political party apparatuses on the basis of patronage.

The last fifteen years have seen a further dramatic spread of the patronage system which has given rise to great social tension. Concerted efforts in other parts of the country to reform and modernize the welfare state have been distorted in the South by clientelistic influence. At this point, a considerable difference between the two parts of the country is emerging once again. However, the fiscal crisis of the state has provoked a crisis in the patronage system of welfare payments; competition for even scarcer resources is fiercer. The patronage system has become fragile and unstable and at the same time organized crime, especially the Mafia and the Camorra, has become stronger.

The success of the party patronage system of social control is difficult to measure quantitatively since it is not a visible phenomenon, particularly in the occupational structure of the tertiary sector. Employment in the various branches of the public and private sectors shows no significant quantitative variation in the South with respect to the national average. Instead, the perverse nature of the system has had profound consequences of a qualitative kind. Recruitment based on patronage leads to inefficiency, given the failure to adopt proper professional criteria. The effects are wide-ranging since a large number of occupations are involved, as noted above. The public bureaucracy is worst affected because it is full of people who do not respond to the notion of professional responsibility but rather to loyalty based on patronage. But the system has also invaded the private sectors of the economy, ranging from manufacturing ventures dependent on political favours (Catanzaro, 1979) to the even tighter links between professional and service activities and state/party control.

7 THE FEATURES OF INFORMAL LABOUR IN DIFFERENT SECTORS

The building industry

In the last few decades, events in the building industry have constituted a very important factor in terms of the social structure underlying the question of the Mezzogiorno. In the immediate post-war period the massive financial resources of landowners, freed by sales and expropriations, were to a great extent poured into this sector. Concomitantly, the economic policy of the 'moderate' governments in the 1950s was directed towards large-scale public works in infrastructure; in addition, there was a progressive increase in the demand for houses on the part of the urban middle and upper classes, strengthened economically by public intervention, bureaucratic expansion, the abandonment of rural areas and the corresponding growth of bureaucratic urban centres. High profits were made in the building sector and the interweaving of public affairs and private business was permeated by corruption and misappropriation of public money. The result was that the large criminal organizations in the South were soon able to corner a major part of these activities. However, what is really of interest here are the characteristic ways in which labour is employed in this sector. The presence of a large and growing surplus population prepared to accept precarious underpaid jobs led to the spread of the use of black-market labour.

Speculative building, based on black-market labour on the 'big' construction sites, reached its peak in the 1960s. In this decade, precariously employed labourers in the building industry alone represented 45 per cent of all the wage-workers employed in industry in the South. Then, in the following decades, this type of building fell into decline, as can be seen in table 6.6, owing mainly to the saturation of the market. None the less, even in the 1980s, precariously employed labourers in the building industry constituted the greater part of all non-agricultural irregular workers and more than one-fifth of all industrial employees in the Mezzogiorno. Moreover, as shown below, it can be assumed that there has been a tendency in the last ten years for this estimate no longer to include an entire group of even more precariously employed labourers who work intermittently on 'small building jobs'. It must be emphasized that even that part of the small army of black-market building labourers which has been accounted for is equivalent to almost 60 per cent of wage-workers employed in large and medium-sized manufacturing firms, who are considered to form the backbone of the working-class movement. In other words, for every ten 'central' workers (see table 6.5) in manufacturing industry potentially belonging to a trade union, there are six black-market workers in the building sector.

It is interesting to re-examine the period 1971–86 for possible changes in the condition of these black-market workers following the radical transformation that took place in the house-building industry. The big construction sites suffered a drastic decline and the 'official' housing industry almost entirely vanished. It is with some surprise, therefore, that we learn of the enormous volume of residential building which took place in the 1970s, as recorded by census data for 1981; 70–80 per cent involved three main kinds of unauthorized building: self-help building,

Table 6.5 *The employment structure in Southern Italy at the 1971 and 1981 censuses (including Lazio)*

	1971 no. (000)	%[a]	1981 no. (000)	%[a]	Change 1971–81 %
Resident population	23,564	43.5	24,801	44.3	+5.2
Active population	7,843	39.6	8,975	40.3	+14.4
First-job seekers	594	60.9	1,547	67.7	+160.3
Unemployed			624	62.0	
Employed plus unemployed	7,249	38.5	7,428	37.2	+2.5
Employed: agriculture	1,850	57.05	1,289	57.6	−30.3
industry	2,495	29.9	2,237	28.1	−10.3
services	2,905	40.2	3,902	39.8	+34.3
Precariously employed workers in industry	1,173	63.8	667	81.6	−43.1
Precariously employed workers in services	84	68.7	288	63.2	+244.8
Workers in small firms (fewer than 10 employees)	158	20.7	209	21.6	+32.4
Self-employed and family workers in agriculture	831	44.1	445	41.0	−46.4
Agricultural workers and (mainly) day-labourers	999	76.1	818	75.8	−18.2
Central[b] workers in large and medium-sized firms (more than 10 'regular' employees)	590	16.4	830	21.8	+40.7

[a]Percentage of the national data.
[b]The term *central* is used to refer to workers in large and medium-sized industry who have job security and regular contracts, and in most cases belong to a trade union.
Source: The figures are elaborated from the data of the ISTAT censuses (industry and commerce 1971, 1981; population 1971; provisional and final results of population 1981) by Dr Marina La Rocca in her doctoral thesis 'Changes in the Italian social structure in the 1970s' (Faculty of Political Science, University of Messina, June 1984).

holiday homes, and renovation and extension work (see Ginatempo and Fera, 1985).

In the period 1971–81 the number of black-market workers in the building industry decreased considerably, even though the decline was less accentuated than the reduction in the number of such workers in all of industry (see table 6.6). In the case of the building industry, this decrease was the combined result of trends that at first sight are difficult

Table 6.6 *The employment structure in the building industry in Southern Italy at the 1971 and 1981 censuses (including Lazio)*

	1971 no. (000)	%	1981 no. (000)	%	Change 1971–1981 %
Total self-employed and employees	1002		872		−13.0
% of employment in industry		40.2		39.0	
Of which males aged 14–24	242		183		−24.4
% of employment in building		24.15		21.0	
Total wage-workers	884		726		−17.8
% of employment in building		88.2		83.3	
Precarious wage-workers	726	82.2	481	66.2	−33.7
Wage-workers in small firms	39	4.4	90	12.3	+127.5
'Central' wage-workers	119	13.4	156	21.5	+31.2
Precarious wage-workers in building as % of:					
workers in building		72.45		55.2	
workers in industry		29.1		21.5	
precarious workers in industry		61.9		72.1	
All precarious workers (except agriculture)		57.8		50.4	

Source: My elaborations of ISTAT data in the 1971 and 1981 censuses of population and industry and commerce

to understand. The census of industry and commerce shows that a substantial increase in employment in fact occurred in this sector, especially as regards small firms (with fewer than ten employees). At the same time, according to the population census the overall number of employees declined. Consequently, the hypothesis may be put forward that between 1971 and 1981, a period which witnessed an extraordinary growth in unauthorized building, the activity of a vast array of small firms was consolidated and formalized. This apparent paradox can easily be explained by taking into consideration the type of activity that was becoming widespread and the concomitant modifications in fiscal and economic legislation which, in some cases, made it worth while to put an activity on a legal footing. As a consequence, a certain number of workers in the building industry were taken out of black-market employment. However, there is a legitimate doubt as to whether there really has been such a large drop in black-market employment in building.

There is good reason to believe that a high number of young men apparently seeking their first job are actually precariously employed in the building industry (*Inchiesta*, 1986; *IRES-materiali*, 1989b). However, whereas ten or twenty years previously their fathers and elder brothers declared themselves to be workers because employed at fairly regular intervals on big construction sites, the younger generation 'rightly' describe themselves as looking for work since the casual labouring jobs they do in building are more temporary and precarious. Although their number is still high, black-market building labourers are on the decline. Despite this decline, it cannot be taken for granted that informal building activity is also effectively diminishing. On the contrary, small and medium-sized enterprises in the field of renovation, self-help building and the construction and repair of unauthorized dwellings operate outside the law. Small-scale building still remains one of the main areas of tax evasion and non-compliance with legal regulations.

Using quantitative data and qualitative information, it is possible to build up a picture of black-market workers employed in the building industry. They are almost exclusively males and either illiterate or with a very low level of education. A large number of them begin working when minors and, as a result, figure among the young age groups over a long period. During the large-scale emigration of the 1950s and 1960s, one of the possible first stages of mobility was black-market employment in the building trade. Today, it increasingly represents a dead end with no long-term prospects or opportunities for social mobility. It is, therefore, an important factor in the creation of poverty, which is also transmitted from one generation to the next.

Agricultural labour and self-provisioning by town dwellers

My qualitative research on the low-income urban strata in the South (see the final section of this chapter) identified few cases of cultivation for personal consumption and few families who regularly receive non-marketed agricultural products from relations or friends. A previous investigation of the workers in the chemical centre of Siracusa-Augusta and those in the steel centre of Taranto showed that this kind of resource represented a minimal factor, even in families of peasant origin with near relations still engaged in agriculture (Mingione, 1977). This is confirmed by more recent research on consumption patterns in Naples (Serpieri and Spanò, 1986). Agricultural resources for personal consumption are of little relevance for either workers or the poorer and more marginal strata in Southern Italian towns. Exceptions are households which include agricultural pensioners and suburban areas where there is still an appreciable amount of cultivation on 'small plots' for personal consumption (Randazzo, 1986). It can be estimated, therefore, that agricultural production for personal consumption involves directly or indirectly less than 5 per cent of the low-income urban population.

It is difficult to estimate how many members of low-income families living in towns work intermittently as farm labourers by the day, especially at harvest times. In 1982, more than 650,000 agricultural day-labourers were recorded in southern Italy; of these a good 80 per cent worked fewer than 100 days in the year (Pugliese, 1983). Moreover, this army of part-time agricultural day-labourers is concentrated in several agricultural regions, and so an obvious supposition is that it includes a number of town-dwellers. Given the fact that it is in the interest of both labourers and employers to formalize or register this agricultural work, it is plausible to assume that such seasonal farm labourers also engage in unregistered informal activities in the towns where they live. It is interesting to note that this category comprises a considerable number of young women, those aged fourteen to twenty-four. In fact, the rate of female youth employment in agriculture in the Mezzogiorno is extremely variable and reaches its peak in the same areas where the army of seasonal day-labourers is most concentrated.[18]

The growth of precarious employment in the service sector

Table 6.5 shows that workers precariously employed in the tertiary sector represent the category which increased most in the 1970s. In general terms, this confirms the hypothesis that the growth of the tertiary sector in a relatively poor economic setting is accompanied by a notable expansion in black-market employment and in the informalization of working conditions. In this case, however, I must comment on the estimated figure. The fact that precariously employed workers are still 7.4 per cent of all those working in this sector should be put in perspective for two important reasons: first, black-market workers in the tertiary sector are concentrated in only some branches, whereas they are almost completely absent in others, such as public administration and credit and insurance companies; and second, a large part of the black-market labour known to exist in these branches is excluded from the estimated figure.

In commerce, especially in the retail trade, in services to the public (bars, restaurants, garages) and in services to families (domestic help and services rendered in the home), the incidence of black-market labour is not only growing rapidly but is also quite high compared with the number of people in regular employment (more than one-third). In particular, the estimate in table 6.5 excludes a number of cases that are found in this area to a relevant extent: minors; the unemployed; housewives who work occasionally; young people looking for their first job; foreign workers from underdeveloped countries; and black-market workers who gain by declaring that they do not work, like undeclared domestic helpers paid by the hour. What we are dealing with, therefore, is a vast and growing area of informal labour, but one which also covers very disparate kinds of work. It includes occasional activities, the small jobs done by young people during long periods of unemployment, and others which are true informal life-long occupations, such as undeclared waiters and unauthorized hawkers. Much of the work is of a self-employed or semi-independent kind: for example, the immigrants who sell goods on street corners in Naples often operate under the control of a local entrepreneur; and there are several types of outwork in rapid expansion, like commissioned typewriting. However, there also exists a large number of black-market wage workers.

A similarly heterogeneous picture presents itself when the profile of the informal worker is outlined. All categories of workers are in supply, especially the weak categories: minors and young people looking for their first job, women who wish to re-enter the labour market, elderly people (pensioners and non-pensioners) and immigrants from underdeveloped countries. However, where the labour is in an extremely weak position in the market, it is plausible to assume the presence of a substantial number of males in the central age groups who have heavy family responsibilities, no educational or professional qualifications and are condemned to particularly difficult lives by erratic employment. They give up compulsory education in order to earn a bit of money and help their families. For four or five years they work for very low wages as helpers in bars or as shop boys. Later, they do undeclared work as manual labourers in the wholesale trade or in engineering plants. They spend their entire lives in this way, changing jobs and working in many different fields (Cammarota, 1977).

The service sector is permeated by kinds of informalization which do not conform to official job categories and are typical of the economic poverty, the lack of a modern system of welfare and the pervasiveness of patronage and corruption in public office that exist in the South. What we are dealing with, first of all, is the extension of housework to cover all those assistance and service activities that are not covered either by the social services or by a 'modern' branch of low-cost private services. Secondly, there are forms of family and community solidarity which compensate for the shortcomings of the state and the market. These resources, however, are used in very questionable ways and distributed unfairly because they have largely fallen into disuse as a result of the 'modernization' and geographic mobility of the population.

Lastly, a whole area of informal activity must be considered which originates from personal dependency and patronage in the public welfare system. By this I mean not only corruption and the exchange of political favours but also all those services supplied against cash payments by public employees in and outside their normal working hours, such as nurses and doctors who offer their services privately and do not declare the income earned (Jedlowski, 1986; forthcoming).

Black-market labour in manufacturing industry

It can be seen from the data in table 6.5 that in 1971 the number of black-market workers employed in manufacturing industry in the South was almost 450,000 and that this had fallen to 186,000 in 1981: a sharp reduction of nearly 60 per cent.[19] During the same period, employment in small and very small firms remained stable, unlike in the North where it increased substantially. This second figure is the result of aggregating decreases and increases in different branches. An appreciable fall occurred in the numbers of independent craftsmen and of small family firms in the branches hardest hit by the crisis of the 1970s. Against this, employment went up as a result of industrial decentralization in some branches in which Italian industry typically specializes: electromechanics, clothing and knitwear.

The decrease in irregular workers in manufacturing reflects the persistent crisis in traditional local industry. Furthermore, this has not been compensated for by a diffusion of the model of industrialization based on small firms which is characteristic of the NEC. From this, it can be assumed that the types of informal manufacturing labour connected with this model, that is work done in the home, undeclared overtime, subcontracting, long hours of family labour, are not very common in the South. It is not surprising, therefore, that my research into the towns of Sicily and Calabria revealed few cases of this kind (see section 8 below).

The situation of black-market labour in manufacturing in the city of Naples needs to be looked at separately. Here there has always existed a widespread industrial and handicraft production in small workshops, often located in the home, which specializes in leatherworking but also comprises other branches of the clothing industry. This is, for the most part, a highly fragmented industry which makes abundant use of black-market labour and long working hours by family members, often greatly exploited by those who market such products. Always in great difficulty in terms of economic survival and already in decline owing to competition from larger enterprises and from producers in new developing countries, it was particularly hard hit by the 1981 earthquake and the way in which reconstruction was carried out; there was no longer any space for the small home workshops (IRES CGIL, 1981; Giannola, 1983). However, the results from a recent examination of the records relative to the settlement of disputes arising from the termination of black-market work relationships (Fortunato et al., 1986) show that the footwear and clothing industry is especially characterized by the presence of black-market workers. While this branch of industry accounts for just over 20 per cent of manufacturing employment in Naples, black-market labour disputes make up 55.9 per cent of the total. The authors of this research maintain that 'footwear is apparently the branch which employs black-market labour most "integrally", in all the various kinds of enterprises and productive units. There is a high concentration of women workers in both branches. As a matter of fact, nearly all the workers are women' (ibid., p. 85).

Multiple jobholding

It is worth referring briefly to the question of multiple jobholding or 'moonlighting', since the results are now available of at least three investigations in areas that include important towns in Southern Italy: Caserta (Ragone, 1983); Catania (Reyneri, 1984); and Bari (Chiarello, 1985).

These three surveys did not take into account multiple jobholding by individuals having a first occupation with no job security. This means they are unable to supply data for the figure of the 'black-market multiple jobholder' fairly common among low-income groups in the Mezzogiorno (Cammarota, 1977). The surveys report a fairly high number of multiple jobholders: 15.7 per cent for the district of Caserta; 21.7 per cent for the conurbation of Catania; and 22.8 per cent in the sample taken in Bari. The second jobs are mainly self-employed activities which are continuous, of long duration and clearly informal in the sense that they evade taxation and are not officially registered. In the Catania and Caserta surveys, half of the cases concern non-manual workers with relatively above-average incomes. In the case of Bari, the figure for this kind of 'moonlighter' is much lower (21 per cent of the total).

Multiple jobholding in medium- to low-income groups, comprising semi-skilled manual workers or those with only basic qualifications, accounts for 54 per cent of the cases in Bari, 38 per cent in Catania and 34 per cent in Caserta. These workers are part of a traditional family structure in which the wife/mother is a housewife, the children have great difficulty in finding work and the husband/father manages to make ends meet by also taking up a second and, if need be, a third activity. In these circumstances, economic motives play a more important role in starting another activity than in other cases. This situation fully reflects the highly rigid and segmented state of the labour market, since those already working are able to find a second job whereas it is almost impossible for women or young people to find a first job. The surveys show that in the majority of cases the first job constitutes an important social resource, making a second activity possible both for direct reasons of social connections, professional qualifications etc., and for indirect reasons – such workers can face the economic uncertainty of the second occupation because they have a first job to fall back on. As Reyneri rightly points out (1984, pp. 253–73), the combination of a high incidence of multiple jobholding with concomitant high levels of unemployment is a feature of Southern Italy that is extremely difficult to eliminate. The reason for this is that in the majority of cases second jobs are not jobs taken away from the unemployed but rather activities invented within the interstices of the economic and institutional system.

Self-provisioning activities

I am unable to make any significant observations on the historical development of this kind of work, because no research material is available which documents to what extent and in what way activities like production in the home of preserved footstuffs, clothing or furniture have changed in the last few decades. The self-provisioning activity which appears to be most widespread and which expanded greatly in the 1970s is self-help building. This category comprises not only renovation, extension work, finishing or maintenance but also the complete construction of dwellings by urban families with the aid of informal labour offered for a similar favour in return or for payment in cash (Ginatempo and Fera, 1985). The presence of this kind of activity is not surprising if three elements typical of the specific situation in the Mezzogiorno are brought together: the high incidence of experienced workers specialized in building; the crisis of large building sites specializing in houses for above-average income groups, a crisis which has left a substantial number of potential labourers 'unemployed'; and the chronic underproduction of dwellings for low-income groups by state-financed bodies, co-operatives or private builders. Nor is it surprising that self-help builders belong predominantly to lower- and middle-income families. Unlike the case of England (Pahl, 1984), in Southern Italy it is more convenient for families with above-average incomes to use informal workers for this kind of work. However, it is the case here, too, that very low-income groups do not engage in self-help building because they do not have the necessary resources, above all, money for materials.

What has been said above also applies to other types of self-provisioning, such as those identified by a recent investigation into consumption patterns in Naples (Serpieri and Spanò, 1986). The numerous group of low- to middle-income earners are very active in self-provisioning, especially in those activities carried out by women but also in typically male activities. Although largely inspired by local culture (for example, traditional use of home-made tomato sauce and pasta), it can be readily assumed that such activities are now mostly carried out using modern do-it-yourself equipment. In middle-income families, the housewife has more time available, both because she does not have to face problems of real poverty and because she is often helped by relatives, as well as more monetary resources for investing in self-provisioning activities. This is reflected in the fact that the production of foodstuffs in the home is very widespread, as is also dress-making. These families almost always possess a sewing machine and often a small knitting machine as well.

Apart from self-help building, the question of male self-provisioning activities, such as carpentry, electrical repairs and plumbing, furniture-making, decorating, constructing door and window frames, agricultural cultivation for own use, repairing vehicles, is ambiguous. As Serpieri and Spanò (1986) rightly point out, this type of work is widespread and is correlated mainly with need and ability. Unlike those in a state of poverty, the large majority of families enjoy a social status which brings with it many additional needs. Normally, they have sufficient monetary resources to be able to turn to the market, preferably the informal market. This occurs when their own technical skills are inadequate to do the job by themselves or if they possess no particular skill which they can exchange for the help of neighbours and friends. This is the case, above all, with electrical repairs, plumbing and carpentry, which are less common than self-help building repairs and painting jobs. However, more than one-third of families are self-sufficient for all repairs in the home, a further 10 per cent resolve all their problems except for one particular repair job, and only a small minority turn to the market in all cases. The number of families which do their own repairs to motor vehicles is about 30 per cent.

It is worth mentioning the importance of two areas that have not been considered so far: crime and housework. Criminal activities, especially those organized by the Mafia and the Camorra, deal with huge sums of money, pervade people's daily lives, involve a not insignificant part of the population and range from drug-trafficking to theft, contraband, prostitution, protection rackets and receiving stolen goods (Catanzaro,

1987; 1989). It is difficult, if not impossible, to carry out specific research
in this field and so I am reluctant to put forward general estimates on
the amount of money and the number of people involved. It does seem,
however, that the recent judicial investigations in Naples and Palermo
have revealed an extensive and complex network in which a small number
of bosses at the head of a military-style hierarchy extend their control
over the illegal activities of several thousand people, more or less aware
of their involvement in a criminal organization.[20]

With regard to housework in the urban South, it must be said that
few married women go out to work and most of them are full-time
housewives: in 1981, 36 per cent of the total number of women were
full-time housewives and the official rate of female employment was low,
at 22 per cent. If only the towns are considered, the proportion of
housewives is still higher and the rate of female employment lower since
in the countryside the latter is especially high in agriculture. If only the
urban strata with relatively low incomes is taken into account, the
proportion of housewives is still higher and the rate of employment drops
to very low figures. My own research also shows that those in or seeking
employment are almost exclusively made up of young women and a few
older unmarried women. The qualitative research shows that housework
is an unavoidable necessity for less prosperous urban families, involving
long hours of work for at least one woman per family (Randazzo, 1986).
Under these conditions, because of the failure of both the public and the
private sector to develop them, there are no modern services to offset the
social imbalance brought about by the weakening of traditional forms of
kinship and community solidarity, which represent the customary ways
of satisfying the need for services. This dual process has had the effect
of extending the tasks involved in housework so that it covers any gaps
that open up and any new needs that emerge.

In conclusion, it can be said that the extended form of housework is
to be found in almost all low-income families, and that the housewife
who also engages in self-provisioning and service activities is the most
common type of informal worker in the urban South. Next, there are a
large number of informal workers, in the sense that they are precariously
employed under black-market conditions. Most of them are males and
the most substantial and homogeneous group, though on the decline, is
concentrated in the building industry; similar types of workers, however,
are also found in manufacturing industry and increasingly in the service
sector. Apart from these, there is a large area of fragmented informal
work (small jobs) of two kinds: multiple jobholding, and very precarious
and/or intermittent informal activities carried out from time to time by
the 'non-active' population (students, housewives, pensioners) and by

young people and women in search of work, and on a more regular basis, but for very low pay, by minors.

If I limit my calculations to the part of the population with low and lower-middle incomes, it can be estimated that just under 10 per cent of urban families are involved in multiple jobholding. But it is very difficult to estimate the extent of the second category: fragmented informal labour. All I can do is to state my conviction that it is almost impossible to find low- or middle-income households where at least one member has not engaged, at least once in his or her life, in informal labour in this sense. It has also been seen that self-provisioning is very widespread. Self-help building, in particular, increased dramatically in the 1970s in both small and medium-sized towns and in the suburban peripheries of large cities. Except for the building industry, it has proved difficult to put forward a hypothesis about contemporary trends in self-provisioning. I can do no more than make the observation that this kind of activity will probably increase considerably as, on the one hand, the surplus population rises and, on the other, the use of cheaper do-it-yourself equipment, for example pasta-making machines, microwave ovens and electronic home knitting machines, becomes more widespread.

8 INFORMAL ACTIVITIES AND URBAN SURVIVAL STRATEGIES IN SOUTHERN ITALIAN CITIES

The combination of informal activities, subsidized incomes and remittances from emigrants explains the survival of a large stratum of marginalized urban population. The internal stratification of this stratum is very marked, ranging from the new middle classes to a substratum condemned to reproduce aberrant forms of poverty from generation to generation. As seen above, the fundamental matrices of this social environment are the specific forms of industrial accumulation and the distorted ways in which the welfare state functions.

The activities of the state and of specific public bodies are particularly important in determining the nature of the informal sector in the South. Let us look at the two fundamental fields in which the welfare state operates: monetary subsidies to needy families and the direct or indirect production of services. In the absence of a programme of subsidies for the poor, the state has granted a disproportionately high number of disablement pensions. When given to poor people who are not disabled, they have the advantage of creating and perpetuating political support. Throughout the South, the number of disablement pensions is much greater than that of old age pensions and in some districts they are given to about 50 per cent of the adult population (Boccella, 1982). If the part played by old age pensions and unemployment allowances are also taken into account, it is possible to get an idea of the contribution made by the state towards maintaining a very large part of the surplus population. Nevertheless, the income derived from state subsidies is never enough to ensure the survival of a family. The result has been the development of a complementary relationship between state-assistance policies and the spread of the informal sector in the South. An important aspect of this complementary relationship is the lack or inefficiency of welfare services in every field from public housing, education, transport and health to assistance for the elderly and children under school age (Graziani, 1987; IRES Campania, 1987). Whereas families with a middle or high income can make up for these shortcomings by turning to private services or to public services outside the local area, the less well-off have to resort to the informal sector, to 'making do' or to 'do-it-yourself'. Thus, in the South, instead of an active public housing sector there has been a spread of self-built dwellings; instead of kindergartens a variety of parental arrangements for the care of pre-school children, invariably of an informal and non-professional nature; and so on. In the cities taken into consideration, the informal sector is particularly active in building, the retail trade and domestic and personal services. It is not very evident in manufacturing, though this is probably not true of certain areas on the Adriatic side of the country and in the Naples area (Collidà 1979; Pinnarò and Pugliese 1985; Liguori and Veneziano 1986).

In my own investigation, I sought above all to identify the possible forms of informal activity and to understand the part that they play in the survival strategies adopted by the various strata of the surplus population.[21] Five urban localities with different characteristics were chosen in Sicily and Calabria where, in view of their poor and marginal character and the lack of employment in the local formal industries, it was assumed that there would be a large number of informal activities. A detailed questionnaire was distributed to a sample of the resident population,[22] which included a section relating to the family and a 'budget-time' form for each adult with an income. Since the sample was non-representative, the findings are of descriptive interest only and cannot be used to measure the presence of informal activities or to define precise chains of causality.

The localities selected have the following main features. Before being demolished, Messina 1 was a municipal residential hotel and it was inhabited by relatively young and highly marginalized families, mostly made up of occasional and unskilled workers in the building trade.

Messina 2 (Santa Lucia sopra Contesse) is a zone of low-cost public housing on the outskirts of Messina to which a number of low-income families have been transferred from run-down housing. The Reggio Calabria locality (Reggio Calabria is the largest city in Calabria) is likewise a zone of mainly cheap public housing located in the city's outskirts. In Milazzo and Barcellona, after Messina the two largest towns in the province, the surveys were carried out in the old town centres, in which there is a great mixture of different social fabrics, the prevalence of marginality being reflected in the serious state of decay of the dwellings. Milazzo and Barcellona were chosen because of the very wide differences between them. Milazzo is an old trading and fishing port with a troubled industrial history. A large refinery was installed nearby in the 1960s, but recently it has been going through a serious crisis and has started laying off large numbers of employees. Numerous interviews were carried out in Milazzo in order to throw light on the complexity of a pronounced industrial crisis in a typical medium-sized town in the Mezzogiorno. Barcellona, on the other hand, is a large agricultural market town in which various attempts, with dubious results, have been made to set up small and medium-sized industrial enterprises using mainly local state capital.

The general analysis of the findings from the survey confirms the hypothesis that informal activities play an important role in the household survival strategies of the southern urban population with low or medium-low incomes, but that they differ according to the specific characteristics of the localities (tables 6.7 and 6.8). However, it should immediately be made clear that no more than a slight and sporadic presence was found of systematically informal activities associated with the restructuring of manufacturing industry.[23]

In these localities, the informal sector is mostly concentrated in the building trade. A large number of occasional workers manage to survive on a small amount of 'undeclared' work involving alterations to private houses, maintenance and an increasing amount of irregular self-help construction. A smaller number of specialized craftsmen, nearly always engaging in undeclared work, manage to achieve relatively high incomes.

The most evident difference between the five localities is that between Messina 1, with its very homogeneous and marginalized social fabric, and the other four, where the social fabric is more mixed and complex. The inhabitants of Messina 1 are nearly all couples with children, the ages of the parents ranging from twenty to forty, and the males are employed on an occasional and informal basis in the building trade as labourers. The wives are nearly all full-time housewives obliged to remain in the home because of the need to save on subsistence activities, in view

Table 6.7 *Income earners over fourteen in five localities in the Mezzogiorno*

Variable	Messina 1	Messina 2	Reggio Calabria	Barcellona	Milazzo	Total
Individual cases (N)	17	44	58	49	131	299
	%	%	%	%	%	%
Individuals per household	1.2	2.75	2.1	1.8	2.1	2.0
Cases of informal work	82.3	22.7	29.3	30.6	29.0	31.4
Formal white/blue-collar workers	11.8	36.3	50.0	53.1	34.35	39.5
Individuals who do no informal work	17.6	77.2	75.9	57.1	71.0	67.5
Individuals who do no domestic work	64.7	81. 8	13.8	51.0	38.9	43.8
Individuals with pensions and allowances	64.7	20.4	36.2	26.5	37.4	34.4
Females with income	17.6	47.7	37.9	38.8	38.2	38.5
Under 25-year-olds with income	29.4	47.7	32.7	20.4	30.5	31.8
Over 65-year-olds with income	0.0	6.8	15.5	6.1	12.2	10.4
Illiterate or without any school-leaving certificate	23.5	25.0	15.5	22.4	37.4	28.1

Table 6.8 Results from the survey of householders in five localities in the Mezzogiorno

Variable	Messina 1	Messina 2	Reggio Calabria	Barcellona	Milazzo	Total
Households (N)	14	16	28	27	63	148
	%	%	%	%	%	%
Without help from non-cohabitant relatives	85.7	68.7	32.1	33.3	52.4	50.0
Internal making of clothes	28.6	37.5	7.1	51.8	30.1	30.4
Internal mending and repair of clothes	92.8	62.5	50.0	70.4	87.3	87.4
Informal or household activities:						
plumbing	78.6	31.2	50.0	33.3	49.2	47.3
masonry	92.8	56.2	67.8	37.0	49.2	55.4
painting	100.0	37.5	96.4	37.0	63.5	65.5
carpentry	85.7	25.0	42.8	29.6	44.4	43.2
electrical repairs	85.7	37.5	82.1	59.2	47.6	58.8
Solidarity relations with neighbours	64.3	25.0	32.1	37.0	63.5	35.1
Females doing 100% of domestic activities within the home	92.8	100.0	42.8	88.9	88.9	81.7
Couples with children	71.4	87.5	64.3	85.2	66.7	72.3
Extended families	21.4	12.5	28.6	7.4	19.0	18.2
Less than 0.5 rooms per capita	92.8	18.7	32.1	25.9	36.5	37.2

of the sporadic and low earnings of their husbands, and to look after a large number of children of pre-school age, there being no public nurseries in the area. The few working women do undeclared work as maids paid by the hour and rely on domestic help from their daughters aged over ten.

In this specific case of a high degree of informalization, linked to casual and unofficial work in building and to very low and irregular earnings, some interesting features can be pointed out: the very low level of female employment; a high proportion of complementary state-assisted incomes (pensions and allowances); a greater degree of isolation from the help and solidarity of relatives living elsewhere; and a large amount of self-provisioning and informal consumption in house repairs and the mending, but not making, of clothes. Even though it is impossible to generalize, certain hypothetical conclusions can be drawn concerning the more markedly marginal aspects of the social fabric in southern urban areas, a fabric which tends to coincide with urban poverty. The very low incomes deriving from occasional and/or informal activities find an indispensable complement in state allowances and pensions. This confirms that the spread of informal activities providing a low level of income is not an alternative to state assistance, but instead necessitates the persistence of state assistance as an indispensable complement to the survival of poor families. On the other hand, the level of these contributions can be kept low because they constitute complementary sources of income rather than being the only income of these families. It is important to remember, however, that whereas initially this complementarity was a provisional survival strategy, pending emigration or the finding of formal employment at an adequate wage, this form of survival is now tending to endure. The result is that the social stratum involved becomes larger because the new poor – young families and recent immigrants from the countryside – are being added to, rather than replacing, the old poor. This poses serious questions as to the capacity of the state, already undergoing a serious fiscal crisis, to undertake new commitments and of a narrowly based informal sector to provide complementary incomes for an increasing proportion of the population.

The connection between the low level of female activity, whether formal or informal, is related to both the situation of the labour market and the specific subsistence strategies found in the South. In a situation of low income and a difficult labour market, women are deterred from looking for a job and confined to carrying out extremely laborious housework. This is confirmed by the findings of the investigation as a whole, in which the desire for the creation of new jobs for women always ranks very low among the measures of economic policy that this stratum of the population would like to see enacted. Unlike the situation in underdeveloped countries (Portes and Walton, 1981), the survival strategy here does not involve additional income earned by women in informal activities, such as a few hours a week as domestic helpers, undeclared work in petty trade, laundering and mending clothes in the home, and in the direct production of subsistence goods through rearing animals and cultivating small urban vegetable allotments. In the South, women are engaged full-time in trying to reduce monetary consumption in various ways: careful spending; searching for the cheapest prices and shopkeepers who will give credit; resorting to do-it-yourself when the cost of a service is too high; and other solutions which take up considerable time, such as looking after children in turn, and which make it impossible to undertake a paid activity.

The other localities present more difficulties since their social fabric is less homogeneous. Messina 2 and Reggio Calabria are fairly similar in that both are localities with cheap public housing and a large proportion of blue- and white-collar workers employed full-time in formal jobs. This has the effect of reducing to below the average the proportion of informal activities which are engaged in only occasionally and for short periods of time. This further confirms the hypothesis that regular workers in the South, with the exception of those employed by government, local authorities or in modern economic services, rarely have two jobs and that the combined formal and informal worker is not found very frequently in low-income families. This worker is more common in Reggio Calabria than in Messina 2 and is less likely to be the wife of the head of the family than one of the other adult male members; this is also reflected in the above-average incidence of large households with more than two income earners. Furthermore, Reggio Calabria differs from all the other localities by virtue of its divergent, and for the South unusual, distribution of domestic work. The percentage of income earners who do not participate in domestic work is very low (13.8 per cent as against an average of 43.8 per cent) and the proportion of households in which domestic work is not all carried out by the wife/mother or by other women is accordingly high (57.2 per cent as against an average of 18.3 per cent). This difference is difficult to explain, because it is not accompanied by a higher level of female activity outside the home or by the presence of a high proportion of young people. Neither can the difference be explained by the high proportion of formal employees, since in Barcellona this is associated with a typically uneven distribution of domestic work, carried out almost exclusively by women. The explanation probably lies in a number of factors: the higher proportion of non-nuclear households; the lower proportion of couples with small children; and, above all, the higher proportion of all-male households (bachelors and separated and divorced men). In this sense, Messina 2 is at the opposite end of the scale; there is a rigid distinction between domestic work and income-earning work. An interesting fact here is that a fairly high proportion (13 out of 21) of women working outside the home do no domestic work. This, too, is difficult to explain because it is extremely unusual and such a situation is found only in this locality: of the 115 females with an income in the sample, 43 did over twenty hours of domestic work per week, and three-quarters of the 21 cases where no domestic work was done were in Messina 2. The only possible explanation is that this situation is linked to the presence in the area of a high proportion of young people with an income, including married working daughters who do not help their mothers with domestic chores.

It is worth considering the role played by the various types of informal consumption and activities within the social reproduction of these complex situations. Messina 2 has a relatively low proportion of informal activities and, in general, a lower level of self-provisioning. There are only ten people engaged in informal work, five males and five females. The males work in the building sector and one of them is an irregular craftsman who works more than forty hours per week and earns a fairly high income. The women work as domestic helpers paid by the hour or as irregular shop assistants. Self-provisioning and the consumption of informal services are well below the average, with the exceptions of building work and, in particular, of home-made clothing. The first exception can be explained by the fact that a large proportion of the local inhabitants have worked in the building trade and the second by the fact that the clear-cut allocation of domestic work and the relatively higher household income leaves a large number of full-time housewives sufficient time and resources for this activity. They are less occupied with other reproductive activities and, at the same time, not as hindered by the lack of a regular money income as the housewives of Messina 1. As in Messina 1, but to a smaller degree, the households of Messina 2 are mostly detached from relationships of solidarity and help from relatives; but in this case the absence of family solidarity is not compensated for by more extensive solidarity in the local community.

As stated above, in Reggio Calabria a greater mingling of regular and irregular work within the household is found, though not in the form of having two jobs, which is uncommon. Informal activities are equally distributed between men and women and are of the same kind as in Messina 2. In Reggio Calabria, the isolation from relationships of family solidarity is less marked than in the other localities. This could be due to earlier urbanization than in Messina or to a more compact urban

structure facilitating contact between family members, as also in Barcellona and, to a lesser extent, in Milazzo. The access to self-provisioning
and to certain informal services is generally problematical. The relatively
small presence of full-time housewives is reflected in the fact that households making their own clothes are almost non-existent and very little of
the mending work is done directly by a member of the household. Other
forms of self-provisioning and informal consumption play an important
part in maintenance work on dwellings, above all where electrical repairs
and redecorating are concerned. Here again, it is probable that this is
largely due to the existence of an informal building trade, which for
many years has specialized in self-help construction and renovation.

The case of Barcellona is interesting because, besides a large contingent
of formal workers (both blue-collar and low-paid white-collar), over 30
per cent of the workforce are informal workers. Here, one finds not only
multiple jobholding but also many households with both formal and
informal workers. The informal workers are mostly women (12, as against
7 men) who work as domestic helpers or do irregular work in trade; two
others are farm labourers and another two work at home for a decentralized wig-making enterprise. The men are all occasional building labourers. Self-provisioning and informal consumption are in general below the
average, except with regard to the making of clothes, which here reaches
a high of 51.8 per cent. The only possible explanation for this picture is
that Barcellona is still mainly based on agriculture and the practices
typical of rural families have been retained. It can also be said that in
Barcellona, despite its close links with the countryside, there is a very
high number of couples with children and the lowest proportion of non-
nuclear households. This could be due to the relatively less serious
housing shortage and to the possibility of maintaining links with relatives
living in the country and of continuing to receive help from them.

Particular attention has been paid to one neighbourhood in Milazzo,
the Borgo Antico, in order to throw light on a situation in which the
traditional informal sector is combined with a serious and persistent
crisis in industry and employment. Despite the Borgo Antico being
close to industrial locations, the proportion of its inhabitants in formal
employment is relatively low, a little over one-third. On the other hand,
the number of informal workers is not high either. As in Barcellona, the
informal jobs are mainly undertaken by women; the men work in the
building trade and as costermongers. There is, however, no multiple
jobholding and the division between formal and informal activities is
clear-cut.

The social fabric in Milazzo is highly complex. Apart from some middle-
income households, which are few compared with the other localities,

apart from Messina 1, there exists a wide variety of households with low or very low incomes. The relatively high proportion of persons receiving state benefits (37.4 per cent) reflects the less distinctly defined borderline of poverty. Furthermore, there are also a large number of adults who lack any kind of educational qualification. Informal services and self-provisioning are distributed evenly and are at a high level, as is to be expected in the run-down city centre of a town in the midst of an industrial crisis. The great extent of solidarity between neighbouring families is worth noting and, in this particular case, reflects the age and stability of the city centre; this is typical of the Mediterranean region and the reverse of what has been happening for a long time in American cities, where the inner city is characterized by a high turnover of population (Gans, 1968).

The analysis confirms the view that informal strategies are unable to provide those sectors of society hardest hit by the employment crisis with easy alternative means of survival. This assumption seems even more plausible with regard to the South, where the informal sector has a limited economic base. The only area of expansion has been self-help building. From a strictly economic point of view, it is reasonable to doubt that the subsector of self-building and undeclared construction work will be able to go on expanding. The main reasons for this are the large volume of building in the recent past and the increasingly limited geographical mobility of the population, together with a declining birth rate.

The other aspect of the informal sector in the South is even more closely linked to a cycle of recession. It relates to irregular trade and personal services, above all those provided to the middle classes, such as domestic help paid by the hour, services in the home, repairs and maintenance, dressmaking. Inflation and economic recession have a contradictory effect on the demand for informal services from intermediate income groups. A deterioration in the standard of living causes a considerable reduction in the highly elastic demand for non-essential services. This occurs especially when the price of the service cannot be further reduced through competition between workers, because the resultant wage rates would be too low for the work involved. The clearest example of this play of supply and demand is found in the job market for domestic helpers. Apart from the unfavourable social connotation of this type of work, if the income it provides falls below a certain amount it is more advantageous for women in the South to stay at home because, in this way, they can 'earn' more in the form of subsistence savings. Thus, even in the South, the paradoxical situation exists in which a not inconsiderable number of domestic helpers are immigrants from underdeveloped countries, despite the existence of a large local surplus population.

With regard to goods and services for which the demand is stable, the question is whether the informal sector is able to supply acceptable alternatives to what is offered by the formal market, thereby permitting the same standard of living to be maintained and, at the same time, a certain amount of money to be saved. This is a difficult problem. It seems to me, however, that in the South the informal sector has already been stretched to the limit in providing an alternative supply to meet the demand for goods and services on a local scale. The possibility of further expansion could depend on industrial decentralization of the type carried out by small manufacturing concerns in the NEC, along the Adriatic strip and in the Naples area. However, the high degree of marginalization of the social fabric and the relatively high costs of subsistence constitute serious obstacles. It is indicative that, up until now, industrial decentralization has steered clear of these areas in the South in favour of other localities, such as Taiwan, Singapore or North Africa, where subsistence costs are appreciably lower.

Finally, some general assumptions are possible concerning the social consequences of the nature of the informal sector in the South and its progressive transformation from acting as a transitory phase in which a surplus population awaits absorption into a process of industrialization to representing a definitive survival strategy for a growing surplus population. Just to mention one, it should be borne in mind that although the existence of a large informal sector involves a lower degree of commodification relative to the more advanced areas, the high level of state subsidies to individuals permits a relative over-commodification in the consumption of certain durable goods which have characterized industrial growth in Italy. In all five localities, over 90 per cent of families possess a radio, a refrigerator and a black-and-white or colour television set and over 60 per cent a car or a motorcycle and a washing machine. Other commonly owned objects are bicycles, cameras, record-players, tape recorders, electric mixers and sewing machines.

The findings of my investigation make it possible to assume that a number of contradictory social processes are at work. In part they are peculiar to the South, and in part they are also common to advanced capitalist areas and, more frequently, to the underdeveloped world. A first hypothesis relates to the social role of women. In this regard, there are two problem areas that are both connected with the poor prospects for employment in the formal sector: a marked tendency to being confined to domestic work, which increases in line with the poverty of the household, and a parallel tendency to being limited to work in the informal sector. The first assumes the form of a particularly perverse cycle, which has its origins in the social pressures on poor families in the South. The lack of public assistance and the need to make considerable subsistence savings combined with bad conditions in the labour market, consequent poor employment prospects and low wage levels, forces married women to shoulder a very heavy burden of domestic work. Many girls leave school early in order to carry out dressmaking or laundering in the home or to take over from their mothers so that they can work as hourly-paid domestic helpers. The cycle reproduces a social environment based on a low level of extra-family female employment and occasional male work providing low incomes. On the other hand, where informal work by women exists, it is notable that a large supply of labour, with consequent low wages, is accompanied by a demand which has a very narrow structural base. It has little to do with the decentralization of production in manufacturing industry and depends almost exclusively on domestic service, household services for private citizens, the retail trade and seasonal agricultural work; it is also because women play no part in the largest organized branch of the informal sector in the South, which is the building trade.

These marginal urban families in the South belong to a more general type of 'proletarian' family that can be classified as a 'family with multiple inadequate incomes'. In general, these families are characterized by a high level of working activity and a high birth rate. The families in the investigation show, for the above-mentioned reasons, a very high rate of male working activity, which is in the main counterbalanced by a relatively low rate of female working activity. The propensity towards a high birth rate represents a strategy that is clearly rational for families that survive by means of the large number of working members rather than adequate levels of individual income. The 'family with multiple inadequte incomes' is, in one of its variants, the most widespread form of proletarian family in capitalist society prior to the advent and diffusion of family wages. The English industrial towns of the last century contained the best examples of this variant due, above all, to the scarcity of worker-peasants and other forms of mixing wage-earning families and productive households. The most common contemporary variant is the multiple wage-earning family in the informal sector of Third World cities.

The first variant was very weak in terms of reciprocal networks;[24] but it was accompanied by the development of a strong associative system (trade unions and socialist parties), which was something that could not be taken for granted given the high rate of turnover, very high mobility of labour and short timespan of a worker's 'career'. The second variant, on the contrary, expresses and underlies strong and protective networks of household, kinship and community reciprocity. It is these which make possible the organizing and combining of various types of formal and informal work, self-consumption, solidarity and illegal activity. In contrast, the loyalty towards associative organizations is weak or at least problematical.

The cases found in the contemporary urban Mezzogiorno reveal different characteristics. The transference to towns of a type of farm-labouring family with multiple inadequate incomes, characterized by an uncommon associative strength rooted in communal resources (Mottura and Mingione, 1989; Mingione, 1989), was a highly problematical process. The majority of male breadwinners became building labourers, and even though they had a relatively higher income than before, the standard of living of these workers and their families came under more pressure due to a series of factors: the higher cost of living; the impossibility of making economies and subsistence savings; geographical instability; and a high level of competition, unregulated by any community-based control, for black-market work brought about by a dynamic demand – but one which lacks the local and seasonal regularity of agricultural employment. Furthermore, the influence of the patronage system has been greater in this sector. In areas where organized crime is rife, it has become the main employer of building labour; in many other areas the large real-estate companies have been almost exclusively run in terms of patronage and political corruption. Other proletarian families with multiple inadequate incomes who also find themselves in a diverse and fragile condition are those working mainly in the service sector. For them, the possibility of protection through associative networks is almost non-existent, and neither is the shield of reciprocal relations very effective: very little remains of the 'street-corner economy' that still played an important role in the 1950s.

The second hypothesis concerns children and young people. Here two opposite, but equally perverse, cycles operate. The first involves child labour. Children leave school or neglect their schooling in order to contribute to the survival of their families, by means either of unpaid family work or of badly paid work. By doing so, they remain illiterate or semi-literate and do not learn a trade. This leads to the reproduction of a generation of poor, unskilled and semi-literate casual workers. There is a large number of semi-literates in the sample of adults with an income; this is due not so much to the high proportion of old people as to the low level of education of the intermediate age groups and of the young.

The other aspect of the youth question concerns those young people who, at the cost of great effort on the part of their families, complete their schooling but do not succeed in finding jobs conforming to their expectations and educational qualifications. Only the state and para-state organizations offer acceptable employment prospects. However, young people who have grown up in these marginalized social environments find it difficult to compete for state employment against members of the middle and upper classes who have access to the system of 'recommendations' and political favouritism which governs the allocation of these jobs. This creates a notable tendency towards informal employment which tends, at least in a large number of cases, to be transformed into a permanent condition.

The informal sector, therefore, is one which tends to reproduce and to extend itself but which has limitations that prevent it from ensuring the survival of even the existing surplus population. This necessitates a high level of monetary assistance from the state to needy families, which plays an indispensable role in the social reproduction of these urban social strata (Boccella, 1982). The complementary relationship between the informal sector and state assistance assures social reproduction in terms of low commodification but with a monetary consumption potential which is relatively high and oriented towards certain durable goods. These are usually produced outside the local area and are typical of the model of industrial development found in Italy and Western Europe.

The existence of a large informal sector does not lead automatically to a reduction in the cost of formal work because of the obstacle constituted by the unified nature of the national employment structure. It does, however, affect the standard of living both of the tenured 'central' workers and of the middle classes in the South. The former are less inclined to have a second job or to favour the employment of other members of the household. The latter benefit from certain informal services at low cost, for example domestic services, made-to-measure clothing and house maintenance services, which are difficult to obtain in the North.

Even in the contemporary situation, the effect of the informal sector in the South, in the sense of an unfair economic redistribution in favour of the middle and upper classes, is evident. However, the most serious political question relates to the prospect, which the informal sector does not seem to offer, of ensuring a permanent basis of subsistence for a growing surplus population. In this respect, Southern Italy appears to be at a dead end with no future. The state cannot afford to increase its public assistance. The manufacturing and service industries do not offer employment possibilities sufficient to absorb the generation resulting from a baby boom which continued in the South up to the mid-1970s. Moreover, the informal sector appears to be incapable of expansion even in the contemporary context of industrial decentralization, since the restructuring of Italian manufacturing industry is also oriented towards relocalization in NICs, which offer considerably more advantageous conditions. This picture of the increasing disgregation of the social fabric provides the framework for my concluding remarks in the final chapter.

415

NOTES

1 Italy can be compared in this respect to Northern Ireland and Yugoslavia. In the first case, the division between Catholics and Protestants does not follow a clear territorial line of demarcation, and this is one of the reasons why it is difficult to control. In the second, regional differences are marked and often run along economic, ethnic and religious lines but within a structure in which both the most advanced regions, Slovenia and Croatia, and the most undeveloped, Kossovo and Montenegro, are relatively peripheral with respect to the political and numerical predominance of Serbia. In this case too, a map of persistent advantages and disadvantages can be drawn, but one which does not represent a clear division into two or three relatively homogeneous parts.

2 For a critical review of the literature on the southern question see Nocifora (1978). Both the classic 'Meridionalismo' and the different versions developed in the last fifty years interpret the South as a persistently different social formation. Important contributions range from the classic analyses of Fortunato, Nitti, Salvemini and Dorso (see the collections edited by R. Villari, 1966, and B. Caizzi, 1970) to the writings of Gramsci (1966), the 'colonialist' interpretation of Capecelatro and Carlo (1972), and the crucial works of Rossi Doria (1956; 1959), P. Saraceno (1959; 1974) and Graziani (1978). As far as the Three Italies interpretation is concerned, see mainly Bagnasco (1977); Paci (1980); Garofoli (1978); Goglio (1982); Fuà and Zacchia (1983); Becattini (1987; 1989).

3 Those who are interested in the 'informal economy' will immediately think of the apparent opposition between Pahl's thesis (1984; 1985; 1988b) and that of many writers who have studied the problem of the informal sector in Southern Italy (Pinnarò and Pugliese, 1985; *Inchiesta*, 1986). The former holds that informal activities are above all a resource available to the middle classes, to work-rich families, while according to the latter they are predominantly one element in the survival strategies of the poor and often a sign of a degraded condition of life, but never an additional resource on which to build stability and affluence. The difference depends on the different social contexts in which the spread of informal activities takes place and not on a theoretical opposition.

4 Beginning with an important article by Sylos-Labini (1964), Italian economists and sociologists have begun using the discrepancies between the number of workers recorded in the population census and the much lower figures in the industrial census to account for precariously employed workers. Their argument is a simple one: since the data in the population census come from forms filled out by individuals while those in the industrial census are compiled from questionnaires given to economic units and employers, it is reasonable to assume that at least a part of the precarious workers will define themselves as workers in a particular branch of the economy in the population census but not appear in the industrial census, because managers or employers declare only regular employees. This method of estimation was further developed in the debate on social classes in Italy (see mainly Sylos-Labini, 1976; Braghin et al., 1978; Trigilia, 1978; Bagnasco, 1978).

5 See mainly Ascoli (1984); Ferrera (1984); Mingione (1988a); Paci (1989).

6 All the data quoted here on trends in regular and irregular employment in the 1980s have been collected and elaborated officially by the team of the Italian Statistical Office (ISTAT), given the task by the Craxi government in 1986 of making a new calculation of the Gross National Income including reasonable estimates for the impact of the underground economy on employment and income. One work group estimated the employment figures for all the sectors and branches of the economy divided into wage and self-employed regular and irregular categories of employment (ISTAT, Mamberti Pedullà et al., 1987). Irregular workers are divided into four different sub-categories: strictly irregular workers, precarious workers employed on a non-temporary or casual basis; casual workers; non-resident foreign workers including both clandestine and legal immigrants from underdeveloped countries; multiple jobholders.

7 See Brusco, 1979; Pugliese, 1985; Bonanno, 1987; Mottura and Mingione, 1989.

8 The ISTAT estimates for second non-agricultural jobs are in part based on the number of employees registered as paying VAT. This means that they inevitably underestimate the number of multiple irregular jobs held by self-employed workers and, above all, by multiple jobholders who also evade VAT. The numbers involved may be high. Six recent local surveys on irregular multiple jobholding, co-ordinated at a national level by Luciano Gallino, confirm that the ISTAT estimates are approximately correct (see Barsotti and Podestà, 1982; Gallino, 1982; 1985; Reyneri, 1982; Ragone, 1983; Chiarello, 1985; Paci, 1985).

9 The ISTAT estimate for this category may be considered conservative since it is seasonally adjusted. In reality, the seasonal adjustment is not suitable for my purposes, but ISTAT officials had to apply it in order to assess correctly the real figures for GNP. Since we are here dealing with casual work, it is very probable that a large majority of the workers who are included in the statistics in one season are no longer working in the next. They will have been replaced by other workers. It seems to me that in order to obtain a realistic figure for the number of people involved in irregular work throughout the year, the ISTAT figure should be multiplied by 2.5.

10 See mainly two recent issues of *Studi Emigrazione* (nos. 82–3, 1986; 91–2, 1988) including various articles on the subject; Barsotti (1988); Melotti et al., (1985); Calvanese and Pugliese (1988).

11 Pahl (1989a) correctly criticizes Portes and Sassen-Koob (1987) for using data on employment in very small establishments 'as a proxy for the growth of the informal economy' (p. 97). The arguments underlying Pahl's criticism is the same as those adopted here to stress the difference in the Italian case.

12 In Italy, this category is correctly calculated on top of full-time jobs to avoid the inclusion of official multiple jobholders, like domestic helpers employed by the hour in a number of different families.

13 Southern Italy is usually understood to include the following regions: Abruzzi, Molise, Campania, Apulia, Basilicata, Calabria, Sicily and Sardinia. Bagnasco (1977) also includes the region of Lazio. In my opinion, the best definition includes Lazio but excludes the province of Rome. Most of the data given here, elaborated by Marina La Rocca and myself, comply with Bagnasco's

definition, while the data taken from other authors exclude Lazio.

14 In approximate terms, it can be said that there have been two phases of industrial decentralization towards Southern Italy. The first began in the 1950s and, after peaking at the beginning of the 1960s, declined throughout the following decade apart from a few upsurges prior to the oil crisis in 1973. The leading protagonists in this phase were predominantly state-owned firms in heavy industry, iron and steel and petrochemicals. The second phase got under way at the start of the 1960s and, through a series of ups and downs, is still in progress (the automated Fiat factory at Termoli in Molise was inaugurated in 1984). In this phase, the leading role has been played by light industry, above all metallurgical, engineering and electromechanical firms; these are mainly located in the private sector and are experiencing a period of radical restructuring. Both phases have led, on the whole, to the creation of fewer jobs than the numbers lost in the same periods in traditional local industries (Graziani and Pugliese, 1979; Nocifora, 1978; Martinelli, 1985).

15 There exists a vast amount of data on the scarcity and inefficiency of public services in Southern Italy: from overcrowding of hospitals to pupils attending schools in two or three shifts; from average train speeds at 40–50 per cent less than in Central and Northern Italy to the almost total absence of day nurseries, homes for the aged and specialist centres for the handicapped; from the sporadic and insufficient nature of state-financed housing to the fact that twice the normal time is needed to carry out public works.

16 Among other contributions, see mainly Graziano (1974 and 1980); Gellner and Waterbury (1977); Eisenstadt and Lemarchand (1981); Eisenstadt and Roniger (1984).

17 For the debate on 'industrialization' in the South and the 'poles of industrial development', see the critical reviews of the literature by Nocifora (1978) and by Martinelli (1985).

18 In 1981, the rate was still over 60 per cent in the provinces of Reggio Calabria and Brindisi, while it was about 50 per cent in the provinces of Taranto, Catanzaro, Messina and Benevento, and over 40 per cent in those of Cosenza, Salerno and Potenza.

19 The decrease in black-market labour is in part due to a manipulation of the statistics, since a large group of these workers in repair workshops were transferred from the secondary to the tertiary sector during the decade in question, 1971–81. This fact also puts the exceptional expansion of the tertiary sector into perspective.

20 A survey carried out on young deviants in Messina (Tomasello, 1986) shows that patterns of deviant behaviour are closely intertwined and lead these young people into the hands of those who control drug-trafficking, even if they are at first far from being involved in such activity – like petty thieves who, paid in heroin by receivers, become drug addicts and pushers. It is obvious that a youth unemployment rate of about 50 per cent, with ever-lengthening periods in search of work, constitutes a very useful 'reserve army' of labour for organized crime.

21 The purpose of the investigation was to identify a sufficient number of survival solutions based on a combination of informal work, public assistance and extensive domestic work. A strictly qualitative methodology (a few detailed descriptions of family life) was not adopted because it would not have provided

the survey with an adequate horizontal extension. On the other hand, defining a representative sample for a quantitative survey presented great difficulties. Therefore, an ambiguous solution was chosen, midway between the two methodologies, which involved distributing a structured questionnaire to a fairly large sample of families and individuals living in particular urban areas in the South. Naturally, the sample is not representative of overpopulation in general (impossible to define with certainty). The findings are indicative of and illustrate the existence of different and complex survival solutions. As such, they permit the formulation of hypotheses for verification by subsequent quantitative and qualitative research, but they cannot be generalized to provide a definitive interpretation of the situation and role of informal activities in the towns of Southern Italy.

22 The questionnaire is divided into two sections. The first concerns the household: number of members, structure of the family nucleus, number of rooms in the dwelling, whether it is rented or owned, the type and quality of the dwelling and the approximate specification of the subdivision in terms of percentage of the domestic work between the members of the family. Further questions are: Does the family own or cultivate a piece of land? Does the family include minors under fourteen years old who perform paid work? How are relationships with neighbours? How are repairs and maintenance of the dwelling carried out? How does the family obtain and mend clothes? What durable goods does the family possess? Does the family have solidarity relationships with relatives who are not members of the household? Does the family have working relationships with friends or relatives engaged in agricultural activities and does it receive agricultural produce from them? Finally, the respondents were asked to which of various measures to improve their standard of living they would give priority.

The second section relates to information concerning all adults (over fourteen years old) with an income deriving from work, a pension, a state allowance or other. In particular, the following questions were put: Does the individual work? Is he/she in search of work because he/she is unemployed, or will it be his/her first job? Is he/she a pensioner? Does he/she receive a pension or a state allowance and, if so, of what type? What are the average number of weekly hours dedicated to different types of work (formal, informal, occasional, unpaid non-domestic, domestic work or errands), looking for work, leisure activities and study and cultural activities? Information is requested concerning the type of employment from the employed, the type of work sought by job-seekers, the last type of work done by pensioners and everyone else, and whether they are or have been multiple jobholders and have or have had a part-time, occasional or seasonal job.

23 In the course of the survey, only two cases of this kind were found: a network for the home-production of wigs, organized on the basis of a relationship between semi-independent craftsmen and a large commercial company, and female embroiderers working at home for a large textile firm based in the North.

24 The reciprocal relations were so weak that, with this historical experience in mind, Engels (1969) believed that the 'proletarian' family organization was about to disappear.

7

Polarization, social classes and power in fragmented societies

1 SOCIAL STRATIFICATION AND POWER

Introduction

In this book I have tried to understand the significance of current transformations in the increasingly heterogeneous world of work, devoting particular attention to informalization processes in advanced capitalist countries but also referring to similar processes in socialist and under-developed countries. From the theoretical point of view, much emphasis has been placed on the transformation of social factors and of socialization mixes. It has been argued that contemporary societies can be defined as 'fragmented' because the impact of individualism is being increasingly reflected in non-cohesive ways in both reciprocal and associative factors. The analysis of the Italian case has been useful for understanding how these transformations are working themselves out in different social contexts, given that, as I have maintained, Italy is a particularly diversified country which includes regions belonging to three different models of industrialization. In this concluding chapter, I undertake the difficult task of extending the analysis to encompass the significance in terms of social stratification and power relationships of what has been said above concerning the heterogeneity of work, informalization and changes in socialization mixes.

As the previous chapters show, social situations and change on a global scale present a complex picture that is particularly difficult to interpret using the intellectual tools developed by the social sciences during the industrial age. Furthermore, it is not sufficient merely to look at topical aspects of contemporary socio-economic change in advanced capitalist countries: industrial and urban restructuring, flexible accumulation and diffused industrialization, the numerical decline of the working class employed as wage-workers in large concerns, the increasing heterogeneity of work patterns and the growing casualization of labour, the failure and reshaping of welfare programmes and the new trend towards privatization. In order to achieve a coherent understanding of what is really happening, the relevant data must be cogently set within a well-founded theoretical framework. An approach that is too empiricist is now inadequate for at least two reasons. First, local and sectoral phenomena are not independent of complex global relationships. In this sense, a theoretical framework is required that also makes it possible to handle problems and trends relating to socialist and underdeveloped societies, even if in an approximate manner. Second, the interpretation of the impact of socio-economic transformations in terms of power balances and socio-political relations must not be mechanical nor follow patterns established once and for all by the founding fathers of the social sciences. It is, rather, an intricate process which needs to be reformulated taking both new data and the critical revision of interpretational concepts as its starting-point.

In this final chapter, I mainly focus on the concept and reality of 'class', not so much as a passive organizational context but more as an important active 'force' within the political system in shaping the alternative prospects for, and options open to, contemporary societies. My general interpretational hypothesis centred on the emergence of 'fragmented societies' suggests at once that the importance of purely class-based political interaction is decreasing and that the contest for power is becoming more complicated. But this idea remains vague if it is left undiscussed and not compared with various other phenomena and interpretations. In this first section, I will start by briefly raising three problems: the meaning of urbanization and the current relevance of the urban/rural dichotomy; the debate on class structure and on the interpretation based on the class consciousness–collective action link; the growing shortcomings of the nation-state as an appropriate basis for defining societies and autonomous political systems.

The urban/rural dichotomy in the contemporary context

From an interpretational angle, the ubanization question is strategically relevant beyond its technical and numerical aspects, that is, the variation in the proportion of the population living in cities relative to that living in villages or dispersed in the countryside. Sociologically speaking, urbanization is an important question in as much as it is assumed to signify a radical social transformation in people's life-styles and socialization mixes. It involves the transition from a socialization mix where community, traditions, subsistence activities and intergenerational stability have a pre-eminent role to one in which mobility, impersonal relationships, monetary income (mainly wages) and the nuclear family form the dominant elements in social life. In this perspective, it is important to underline that data on urbanization trends should be considered only as approximate indicators of such a process of change and verified against different social realities.

Starting from this assumption, contemporary demographical evidence on urban decline, the growth of small towns and dispersed residential locations in advanced capitalist countries does not automatically belie the strategical presupposition that these societies are becoming almost totally characterized by a uniform urban life-style. Neither does it directly entail that a new rural and dispersed way of life is emerging and that socio-economic locational priorities are disappearing. The question of a uniform urban life-style in radical opposition to a rural one has been challenged by critics for at least two decades (Gans, 1968), and the trends towards de-urbanization and urban decline and restructuring have shed new light on the matter and reinforced such criticism.[1] Moreover, the question should be considered on a global scale, that is, by also encompassing the diverse experience of socialist and underdeveloped countries. The latter, in particular, are still characterized by strong urbanization tendencies and by the growth of gigantic conurbations such as Mexico City, Rio de Janeiro, Calcutta and Cairo, where the phenomenon is accompanied by the extraordinary expansion of the urban informal sector in which a not fully proletarianized population survives through various forms of subsistence strategies. Furthermore, an almost wholly exclusive attention to demographic data and trends has lead to serious mistakes in interpretation. Cities like New York and Paris which appeared irreversibly condemned to sharp demographical decline have shown signs of reversing this trend. But, even more importantly, the urban metropolitan systems of various countries are undergoing important changes but show no signs of losing their socio-economic hegemony and predominance. The most obvious and topical example is the case of Los Angeles (Soja, 1989; Scott, 1988), but other experiences show that same logic of gigantic regional urban integration exists in many advanced capitalist countries.[2] For these reasons, it is much more profitable to read the 'urbanization question' solely in terms of the qualitative transformation of socialization mixes and life-styles. This also implies that any simplified version of the urban/rural dichotomy must be abandoned (Mingione and Pugliese, 1988).

The decline of traditional subsistence activities, life-styles and socialization mixes predominantly based on rural community arrangements should be viewed as a long-term strategical process of change. However, this trend is less radical than has been thought; it is not necessarily accompanied by urbanization or geographic mobility, and furthermore, 'new' subsistence activities and social relations also become established in widely differing kinds of urban locations. Peasant workers, suburban vegetable gardening and 'urban villagers', to name only a few extreme examples, have accompanied the process of urbanization in its different historical experiences. These patterns are even more differentiated if the experience of socialist (Konrad and Szelenyi, 1977) and underdeveloped countries is also taken into account. De-urbanization, urban decline, flexible and diffused industrialization, but *above all* the pace of tertiarization based on the decline of standard and centralized services and on increasingly differentiated forms of provision further contribute to the critical dismantling of the simplified paradigm of a 'standardized urban life-style', based predominantly on monetary consumption, anonymous individualist competition and associative organizations for defending common interests.

What matters is not so much the pace of urbanization or the size of cities, towns or villages but the crucial heterogeneity of socialization mixes and survival strategies which are adopted by different social groups in diverse locations. The idea that advanced capitalist societies have become fully urbanized is acceptable, as is also the assumption that informational and transport technologies dramatically reduce differences due exclusively to size and geographical location. However, this does not mean that the socialization mix is becoming more homogeneous, stratified only along standard class and associative patterns. On the contrary, employment opportunities are persistently and increasingly diversified, particularly when looking at the patterns of development in the numerically predominant service sector, and at the same time, family and local community reciprocal strategies are growing in importance and are still very diverse in different localities and social groups. These strategies may be more or less cohesive with the associative patterns of social organization within different socialization mixes but can no longer be defined as simply 'traditional', for at least one reason which is very significant when considering power relations and the political sphere. They appear to be more and more receptive to individual needs, creativity and expectations, even if the tension between individuality and reciprocal socialization persists to a varying extent. In this sense, they bear an innovative message and show a continuing capacity to adapt, absorb and give expression to market competition and the complex requirements of emergent individuality.

A similar reasoning applies to the socialist model of industrialization. The 'under-urbanization' syndrome (Konrad and Szelenyi, 1977;

Szelenyi, 1983) can be seen as a political response to the difficulty of fully proletarianizing large masses of the population and, consequently, devoting huge resources to expensive urban services; but it inevitably gives rise to the persistent importance of various kinds of reciprocal networks, that is ethnic, village, family, kinship and friendship arrangements. A similar phenomenon of adaptation/change (Szeleny, 1988) takes place in agriculture in conjunction with the failure of the project to fully collectivize production and with the modernization of family farming and individual plots. These reciprocal strategies inevitably survive the phase of 'under-urbanization' and agricultural collectivization and become increasingly important in a stage characterized by more extensive urbanization, the further expansion of services and economic reforms. They are even less cohesive than in advanced capitalist countries because they conflict with rigid pre-structured associative patterns of socialization, and this is reflected in the crucial extent to which the 'second economy' expands. In this case, too, the urban/rural dichotomy is decreasingly reliable as a main indicator of radical differences in the socialization mixes; the differences, however, do not disappear but re-emerge in new and increasingly important ways in different localities and social groups. Moreover, due to the strong hegemonic collectivist ideology of institutional redistributive patterns the reciprocal arrangements and strategies take on even more explicitly the role of guardian of the individual's identity and needs. I shall return to this question below when discussing class structure and social stratification. None the less, I am fully aware that given the present state of sociological research on socialist countries, it remains extremely difficult to achieve an adequate comparative understanding of contemporary changes in their socialization mixes.

The question of urbanization and the urban–rural dichotomy is still important in underdeveloped countries. At a global level the dichotomy can, in certain respects, be seen as the watershed between development and underdevelopment. But from the point of view adopted here, which focuses on the systems of socialization and their interaction with individualism and competitive behaviour, the question is losing its significance as a touchstone of the radical differences between socialization mixes in underdeveloped countries as well. It has been seen that the informal sector constitutes a variant, though considerably transformed, of the sociality mixes typically found in rural subsistence economies. The degree of monetary consumption is much higher in relative terms, given that in urban contexts there are serious limits to transplanting traditional forms of saving and the consumption of own produce typical of rural contexts. But this fact does not contradict the fundamental importance of family, kinship, ethnic, friendship, neighbourhood and community solidarity in permitting survival at very inadequate levels of individual monetary income. The crucial problem is that rural socialization mixes are more vulnerable and unstable than those transplanted to the big cities. This widening gap is reflected in and confirmed by various phenomena and, in particular, by excessive urban growth, the difficulty of halting the influx of people into the cities and the fact that famines and food shortages have severe consequences almost exclusively in the countryside. Therefore, what is interesting from a sociological perspective in the processes of urbanization in underdeveloped countries is not the move from forms of socialization where reciprocal strategies are predominant to forms where associative strategies have the upper hand; it is, rather, the persistent gap between the two conditions of life which not only continues to foster the rural exodus but also remains an essential aspect of the solutions and strategies typical of survival in the informal urban sector. In other words, the constant heavy pressure of the rural surplus population is one of the main elements for understanding both the formation and expansion of the informal sector in Third World cities, as well as its dominant features. In this case, too, I return briefly to this question when dealing with classes and social stratification.

Notes on the theoretical debate on the concept of class

The theoretical debate on social classes is complex and impossible to summarize in a few lines. For this reason, I raise here only the few points that are indispensable for introducing the next section dedicated to current interpretations of changes in social stratification and consider this debate in the light of the approach adopted in this book with its focus on socialization mixes and social factors.

The analysis of stratification and social inequalities is still the key operation within macro-sociology, especially in the two fundamental currents of the European school inspired by Marx and Weber. In both cases, the meaning of social stratification is not given by a passive classification of individuals according to their position in more or less simple or complex scales based on available resources and opportunities. Instead, it is derived from the social relationships of property and work, which are seen to be particularly significant. 'Social class . . . could not be measured in the same way as status or "prestige"; rather it represented, and was necessarily a structure of, social *relationships* which were not simply embodied in individual or family characteristics' (Crompton and Mann, 1986b, p. 2). In this sense, using my terminology, social class may be considered as the most important associative kind of socio-organizational setting typically found in industrial societies. Thus, both

Marxists and Weberians anchor the concept of social class in employment and the distribution of property, understood as typical social relationships that generate diverse and important interests, thereby implying opportunities, prospects and the probability of different forms of behaviour. At this point the Weberian and Marxist lines diverge. The first is satisfied with pointing to social class as a highly important associative aggregate that makes it possible to identify uniformities in behaviour, opportunities and life-chances. The second singles out class as the most important collective historical actor, that is, the promoter of social change. I return below to the Marxist approach in order to show both its limits for and positive contribution towards interpreting contemporary societies. Here, I consider in schematic terms the basis of these two approaches compared to the one I have adopted.

In the first place, it is worth confirming the obvious fact that the identification of the social classes that arise in industrial societies as the main associative settings is highly consistent with both a Marxist and a Weberian approach.[3] Where my approach is least compatible with them is, above all, in the use of the concept of social class as a collective actor or as an aggregate of homogeneous behaviour. Social class as the fundamental associative socio-organizational factor diverges from the Weberian concept of class in two respects. First, it is not only an aggregate of similar interests, individual behaviour and life-chances but also a sphere of collective action, precisely because it is defined as a socio-organizational factor. In this regard, the Weberian approach ends up by attributing an excessive flexibility to the concept of class (see Pahl, 1989b). This is the reverse of the Marxist approach in which the concept is too rigid. Weber, in fact, does not exclude that the aggregation of similar important interests can constitute the matrix for collective action to defend these same interests; but the almost exclusive methodological emphasis on individual action leaves the problem in such a theoretically undeveloped state as to allow the concept to be applied in a variety of ways. Thus, the formation of classes and the defining of their limits and, above all, the goals of collective action, are seen in too changing and flexible a fashion to achieve a sufficiently rigorous theory.

Secondly, the analysis of class action is erroneously linked to the associative context only, viewed as an autonomous area for organization based on similar interests. Instead, it needs to be compared with the entire system of socialization, understood as a variable and not fully cohesive complex mix of associative and reciprocal relationships with their diverse distributions of power and of receptiveness towards and mediation of individual interests and aspirations. In this sense, the macro-sociology constructed solely on the basis of class inequalities according to a Weberian interpretation of social stratification (see Lockwood, 1988, and Goldthorpe, 1980) is limited. Moreover, these limitations become even more apparent in fragmented societies, which are characterized by the increasingly complicated interweaving of associative and reciprocal factors. For this reason, analyses of social stratification and mobility generally draw a restricted and distorted picture, even when they are centred on areas and periods in which the role of associative factors is decisively predominant and, especially, when the interweaving of the latter with reciprocal factors of persistent or mounting importance imposes the need to formulate correctives to the socio-occupational hierarchy of the heads of families. Although women and ethnic groups are not social classes, it is none the less the case that an accurate analysis of social stratification cannot disregard either questions of gender (see for this aspect Crompton and Mann, 1986) and race or the impact of the various different reciprocal networks in which individuals are inserted; these problems must be considered in terms of both the prospects and options that such networks offer and the diverse hierarchies and distributions of power in various areas, groups and classes in different periods. In other words, the behaviour, expectations and life-chances of individuals belonging to the same social class are conditioned by the different ways they are inserted into different areas of reciprocity. Although it may be assumed that such conditioning was sufficiently homogeneous and limited in the case of the Fordist working class earning a family wage in the advanced capitalist countries (see, for example, Goldthorpe et al., 1968a; 1968b; 1969) this assumption cannot be extended to contemporary social situations. These are characterized by widely varying conditions of employment, and by the growing importance of complex and diversified strategies of reciprocity. The same also applies to the significance of the studies of social mobility centred on changes in male employment, where the predominant 'transformation' is the passing of poor peasants and agricultural day-labourers into the ranks of the Fordist working class (see, for example, Goldthorpe, 1980). In comparison, the multiple contemporary 'transformations' are increasingly difficult to interpret precisely because underpinned by widely differing conditions of socialization, which not even the most accurate and detailed socio-occupational classification is able to take into account.

Roughly speaking, there are two crucial questions concerning the class analysis of contemporary societies: the changing shape of class divisions along many different lines; and the basic methodological problem of relating objective conditions (the social structure) to individual and collective consciousness of the immediate and strategical interests emerging from these conditions and to socio-political collective action in defence of these supposedly common interests as mediated by historically established or spontaneous political organizations. As for the advanced capitalist countries, the central question with regard to the contemporary transformation in the structure of class stratification is the impact of the decline in the number of wage-workers in life-long jobs providing a family income employed in large manufacturing industry. This group has been realistically interpreted as a kind of 'core' within the modern working class: concentrated in both factories and cities, extensively unionized, increasingly able to control its section of the labour market, made up almost exclusively of male 'breadwinners' with dependent families, characterized by relatively homogeneous conditions of employment and life-styles and involving that part of the population which relies predominantly on its wage income in struggles to further its own interests. Although the specific histories of working-class movements do not always conform strictly to this picture, in which key roles are played by building workers, agricultural labourers, miners or others, it is difficult to deny that this tendency for a 'core' to arise within the working class is a basic assumption underlying the interpretation of stratification in Fordist industrial systems. Consequently, the numerical decline of this group poses increasingly serious problems.

The simultaneous increase in white-collar and in service workers, a marked phenomenon for at least the last fifty years, has not created an alternative pole but contributed to the growing complexity of the employment structure due to the heterogenous composition of this group. Recent trends have led to a third factor being added to the strong polarization between skilled professional and poorly qualified menial white-collar occupations: an expanding range of casual, temporary or part-time jobs. White-collar jobs, broadly interpreted to include this latter segment, are extremely and increasingly diversified in terms of pay and conditions of work. This heterogeneity is also reflected in different socialization arrangements depending on the fact that the casual, part-time, temporary or badly paid job is done by a married woman or a pensioner to complement an inadequate household income, by a young man or woman in a transitory phase or by a 'breadwinner' in life-long poverty and emargination from the mainstream of the labour market. Think, for instance, of the wide gap separating what are apparently the same associative interests of two badly paid part-time waiters employed in a fast-food establishment or coffee shop in an American city when one is a white college student and the other is an adult black 'breadwinner'.

Self-employment and small-scale activities, on the other hand, are now much more persistent than was held to be the case by the classical interpretations of industrial development. And it is not only a matter of their persisting in some sections of the economy such as retail trade, craft production or agriculture, but also of new developments connected with recent trends in the vertical disintegration of productive processes and even more with the expansion in the need for services, the privatization of welfare services and the establishment of diverse ways of providing services.

In brief, casualization, heterogeneity and a slowly increasing number of various self-employed activities are consistently undermining the idea of a society largely founded on tenured wage-work or salaried jobs for life. This situation is also reflected in the distribution of different jobs among the various sections of the total available labour force. The most striking aspect has been the increasing proportion of married women in employment, but the strong connection between life-cycles and differing access to work opportunities is also important, with the age factor being added to those of gender, race, education, social and geographical origin in an increasingly complex interplay of discrimination and privilege.

The declining role of the family income is matched by the increasing importance of the household which pools income from various activities as a crucial factor in social stratification.The simple approach in which social classes are mainly classified according to the job held by the adult male 'breadwinner' is becoming to a large extent inadequate and imprecise. The cumulation of several opportunities (including moonlighting) by each adult member in some households and the negative discrimination against all adult members in others is an increasingly important element in shaping contemporary trends in social stratification (Pahl 1986; 1988b).[4] As shown in the following sections, this combination of actors is crucial for evaluating change in social stratification in different social contexts. Furthermore, this operation is rendered increasingly difficult by the fact that the creation of job opportunities depends not only on big industrial and financial capital and on the state but also on a set of widely diversified local conditions of socialization, where different reciprocal networks play an increasingly important role, whether cohesive or non-cohesive with associative factors.

The interpretation of the main changes in the social base of socialist and underdeveloped countries presents even more difficult problems, starting above all from two considerations. First, a theoretical foundation does not exist which is sufficiently consolidated to allow a clear unequivocal meaning to be attributed even to the principal associative aggregations of class. On the other hand, a mechanical application of the theoretical basis used for the advanced capitalist countries leads to serious errors of evaluation, though this is often undertaken particularly for underdeveloped countries. Second, a sufficient number of longitudinal studies on modifications in socio-occupational structure are not available, let alone studies that reveal the main conditions of socialization with diverse and changing, underlying occupational situations. For these reasons, the few preliminary and hypothetical considerations possible have been incorporated in the discussion in the next section of interpretations of the changes in job structure and of power relations in contemporary societies.

Notes on the class 'structure-consciousness-action chain'

The theoretical debate on social structure as a basis for the formation of social consciousness and, consequently, for collective action by social class has for some time provided the arena for a critical confrontation between neo-Weberian flexible (see mainly Parkin, 1979; D. Rose, 1988; Pahl, 1989b) and neo-Marxist rigid approaches (see mainly Poulantzas, 1979; Wright, 1985). This is particularly true for interpretations of the contemporary working-class movement in advanced capitalist countries. It is worth mentioning some methodological points which are relevant to a related and intricate question that is still unresolved: the relationship between, on the one side, social stratification and the class base and, on the other, social movements, political action and social change.

The logic behind collective action remains the most difficult area to interpret in the social sciences both for those who believe in it (mainly Marxists) and for those who deny any possibility of a general explanation (mainly neo-Weberians). While it is generally accepted that common positions and interests influence socio-political behaviour, the real difficulties arise when one attempts to explain the goals and strategies of collective action in terms of consciousness. In this perspective, while the weak link in the various Marxist approaches is the explanation of working-class behaviour on the basis of a necessary 'revolutionary and socialist rationale' (Lockwood, 1988), the alternative neo-Weberian approaches are also controversial with their diverse interpretations of the 'capitalist rationale' in a historical perspective and their too flexible interpretations of class strategies in general. It is not by chance that practically every position in the debate can be criticized for being 'ahistorical' and 'aspatial', and on the basis of the approach followed in this book it can be added that they are unable to incorporate into class analysis the contradictory impact of the existence of different reciprocal arrangements both within particular societies and within particular socio-political organizations.

Here is one example with which I am more familiar. In urban and regional studies the methodological debate on this specific question has

always been characterized by a controversial problem which has anticipated current difficulties in interpreting class structure and action
(Pickvance, 1977). Urban and regional movements have been variously
assumed to be 'anti-capitalist' but not strictly or mechanically 'working-
class' (Castells, 1985). Nowadays, the question has been brought into
sharp focus by the increasing importance of environmental movements
and by their, at times, conflict-ridden relationship with institutionalized
working-class political and trade union organizations. The conjunction
of these two separate rationales – which nevertheless in theory converge,
since working-class strategy is considered as necessarily anti-capitalist,
at least by Marxists – gave rise to difficulties in interpretation in the
past when the 'working-class' rationale in advanced capitalist countries
was considered to be less controversial than is the case today. The
present problem is that we have to assume, on the one hand, the further
development of a spatially articulated and fragmented social base and,
on the other, a concurrently increasing diversification of the social
fabric.

Spatial proximity, common geographical and cultural origins, concentration and segregation are obviously the basis on which common interests are constituted, as well as being a possible starting-point for organization and mobilization. But they are not necessarily so and, furthermore,
do not tell us much about the socio-political rationale which may be
generated by a localized mobilization. In other words, history shows that
a relatively high spatial concentration of very poor conditions of existence
together with a considerable feeling of dissatisfaction (marginalized social
groups) does not necessarily lead to collective mobilization and organization. And the question becomes even more problematical when it is
assumed that the social fabric is increasingly fragmented both in spatial
and social terms. As has already been stated several times above, the
real formation of consciousness and the mobilization of collective action
take place under conditions dependent on the socialization mix, where
the reciprocal system may play a cohesive, as in the case of the Fordist
working class, or non-cohesive role, as in the case of a dispersed minority
working class widely protected by communal and household arrangements. Then, the appeal, effectiveness and capacity to mobilize of class
actions depend on their internal power distribution, discrimination and
dispersion. Also at this level, the mix between associative and reciprocal
factors is of decisive importance, as in the example of the unavoidable
tensions between shopfloor and leadership interests.

In order to proceed with the analysis of the goals and rationale of
class action, in particular concerning the working-class movement, I will
briefly outline in advance the reason why Marxist interpretations of class

action have been criticized for being rigid or weak. The crucial question raised by Weberian critics is the supposed immense logical distance between what are assumed to be the immediate interests of the working class, presumably reflected in terms of consciousness and directing the 'everyday' collective action of the class, and the final goal of the working-class movement, which is the establishment of a socialist society through revolution. In the words of Lockwood, 'Marx did expect that workers would be able to come close to such an understanding [revolutionary consciousness], and mainly as a result of their own experience and powers of ratiocination. Indeed, this revolutionary consciousness of the proletariat would be a necessary condition of the success of genuine revolution' (1988, p. 61).

In reality, the matter is more complicated and the logical gap between 'everyday' and 'revolutionary' consciousness and action is closed by arguments that I will now discuss. According to Marx, this apparently enormous gap is filled by a long, historical, conflict-ridden experience where the mediating element is not so much the 'power of ratiocination' but rather the growing accumulation of evidence that the interests of the proletariat, including their everyday immediate ones, are increasingly incompatible with the capitalist social order. As will be seen again in the next section, if there is a weak link in Marx's theorization of working-class action, it is not the supposed logical gap between 'everyday' and 'socialist' interests but his underestimation of the capacity of the capitalist social order to adapt and absorb tensions through global accumulation, development and penetration into the underdeveloped countries, and increasingly to use resources to undertake the institutional incorporation of the demands put forward by the working class. It is reasonable to assume that this not only enlarges the capacity of capitalism to reproduce itself but also substantially changes the historical perspectives of the working-class movement in its national and local components from what Marx had envisaged, by shifting to the periphery the most incompatible, anti-capitalist and revolutionary kinds of consciousness and action. This brief and schematic observation has been made here solely in order to raise the question of class actions which become, but only under given conditions, compatible with a given social order, even though they raise the level of tensions and non-cohesion in the socialization mix. In other words, political democracy and high wages for a small minority of workers have become compatible with capitalism, contrary to Marx's expectations, but only in few advanced capitalist countries and on condition that unequal market relations are extended on a global scale.

Also for this reason, an even greater crucial difficulty lies in identifying 'capitalist' and 'anti-capitalist' rationales of collective action or, at any rate, the rationale of collective action relative to the dominant social order. Local social mobilizations for more or better jobs, conflicts over safety and environmental protection, struggles to obtain improved public services may be complementary or alternative. They may all have a disruptive anti-capitalist potential, at least in the short run, but they cannot be viewed as part of a coherent strategy to build an alternative society; furthermore, they have a highly contradictory impact on social stratification and social structure. In this sense, there is an increasingly urgent need to construct a consistent social typology starting from local and historical diversities in the socialization mixes, that is, by taking into account both associative and reciprocal factors and their conflict-ridden interconnections, in which the passage from structure to consciousness and action under different organizational and ideological conditions provides a suitable basis for understanding contemporary trends towards fragmentation.

The political arena and the decline of the nation-state

Several questions were introduced in the first chapter that have only been developed in part during the course of this book. They concern the relationships of power, the nation-state as a typical delimiting form of society and the political struggle, the growing problems that the nation-state could pose given the possible decline in its significance and the relation between redistributive processes and sociality factors. At the very least, a schematic look at these questions is indispensable.

It is important to underline the point made at the theoretical level that socio-organizational networks are on the one hand systems of power, in as much as they are based on an internal division of tasks, opportunities and resources, and on the other collective entities competing in terms of general relationships of power for the redistribution of resources and opportunities at the level of the total social context. The first pattern is more clearly visible in the reciprocal factors, in particular in those contexts directly involved in economic activity, like productive households. The second, by contrast, is very evident in associative contexts which take on meaning from an economic point of view only if they are understood as being formed to defend similar interests in the political contest centred on the overall redistribution of resources which, for the most part, are no longer generated in local, communal or tribal micro-organizations but in large industrial societies. However, power relationships and redistributive processes always involve the entire socialization mix in its growing complexity. For this reason, they are easier to interpret in Fordist-type industrial societies or in socialist ones of the Stalin-

Brehznev period, given that one could correctly presuppose a clear prevalence of some key types of associative factors correlated with partially cohesive, and in any case relatively weak, systems of reciprocity. For this reason, too, in these societies both the Weberian and Marxist use of the concept of social class to interpret the political contest was simpler and more effective. This greater effectiveness also applied to the sociological reading of the political system in terms of electoral behaviour, the political strategies of mass parties and the social legitimation of different kinds of local and national government. Social fragmentation does not signify so much disorganization or that political systems are necessarily less governable, but that the key associative aggregations are less predominant and break up into divergent and non-cohesive areas of interest both in terms of associative fragmentation and in the wake of the more complicated impact of reciprocal networks. To give just one example of the former, there is the often documented mounting complexity of the socio-occupational structure; for the latter, see the example given in chapter 5 of workers who express solidarity towards their firms because they offer the possibility of jobs for family members in a period of mass unemployment. Therefore, it is not a question of abandoning the concept of class when interpreting socio-political relationships, and adopting parameters that are not only questionable but also not very significant and difficult to theorize, like issue groups or value-oriented politics; rather, the concept of class and that of associative factors should be used with greater caution, incorporating at least the most significant forms of division that are emerging in the diverse socialization mixes.

The question of power relationships and political systems is further complicated by two problems which here can only be mentioned in passing. The first has already been indicated in the first chapter and concerns the impression, though one supported by various contemporary phenomena and studies, that the nation-state is progresssively losing its central significance as a typical area of delimitation for social contexts and the political contest which it had acquired during the industrial age. As Lash and Urry (1987) maintain, recent history confirms the existence of two processes that undermine the centrality and significance of the nation-state. On one side, there is the internationalization of economic and socio-cultural operations, the consolidation of large multinational conglomerates, the globalization of the financial sector and the formation of supra-national bodies such as the UN, the EEC, the FAO, the World Bank and so on, which restrict the ability of nation-states to control and regulate social life in an independent and different way. On the opposite side, the mounting complexity of local socialization mixes, which is reflected in the relative failure of the grand national and universalistic welfare programmes, is putting back on the agenda the importance of decentralization, self-government and local solutions. In the countries of the European Community, this highly contradictory process of the dismemberment of nation-states and the move towards supra-national and local aggregation is already very apparent. It is hazardous to assume that these are trends that will not redraw the map of social and power relationships on a global scale in the medium to long term. This is even truer following the recent rapid and dramatic changes in Eastern Europe.

The second problem is interwoven with the first, and also with the entire syndrome of the growing complexity of power relations in less simple and internally cohesive systems of socialization, and concerns the 'viscosity' of political-institutional systems, that is, their resistance to adapting to new conditions. Overcoming the central role of the nation-state is already presenting notable difficulties, to which can be added the declining effectiveness and legitimation of traditional mass parties and of the relationship between political leaders and the individual voter or political activist. Modern politico-institutional systems were established under social conditions that differed greatly from those existing today and are very difficult to transform, even and above all in the case of parliamentary democracies, where majority forces assiduously defend their own methods of obtaining electoral consensus (see also Chase-Dunn, 1989).

Recent political history shows how rapid and radical the transformation of political systems can be in socialist countries, although it is a traumatic process and the prospects are difficult to predict in the medium term. Similarly, however, the systems in advanced capitalist countries continue to find it extremely difficult to adapt, even when the politico-electoral mechanisms show serious and persistent signs of sclerosis and crisis, as is the case in Britain, Italy and the United States. It is worth pointing out, moreover, that the pressure towards the transformation of existing political systems does not depend only on the less central role of associative factors and on the greater complexity of socialization mixes, but also on what O'Connor (1984) defines as the emergence of new dimensions to individuality. By this he means citizens with high levels of education, a greater capacity to be informed and participate, a complex and structured political sensibility, though at the same time open to being 'fascinated' and 'frustrated' by the new horizons of politics as a 'television spectacular' introduced into age-old electoral systems.

Finally, I must mention the debate on welfare programmes and systems since it plays a key role in interpreting the differences in life-styles. In brief, there are two interconnected sides to the problem: the conflict-ridden crisis in public welfare programmes and the growing diversification of needs and of ways of providing welfare services. In general, the crisis of the welfare state constitutes a dramatic issue, especially for industrialized democracies; it represents the failure of the dream to partially compensate for the persistent inequalities generated through the economic system by making resources available to all citizens. Of little relevance is the fact that welfare projects have been diverse in nature, more or less successful and effective, have involved working-class organizations to a greater or lesser degree and have been implemented by governments to varying extents. Nor can much significance be attached to the fact that critics in the progressive camp have for a long time noted the different impact of welfare programmes in terms of being favourable to middle-income groups and detrimental to the poor or, as Cloward and Piven (1971) put it, keeping them under control but also confining them to poverty from one generation to the next. The new pace at which welfare policies are being introduced, whether implemented by different governments through more privatization or through less universalistic and more *ad hoc* programmes, is an explicit confession that the inequalities rooted in the economic system cannot be compensated for by a parallel universal system of minimum acceptable living standards and of access to opportunities which is at the same time independent of 'market' discrimination.

This situation is further aggravated by the increasing complexity of the interconnection between welfare needs, resources and the provisions for satisfying such needs. Both privatization and de-universalization of welfare systems tend to increase the importance of reciprocal networks and factors. Furthermore, these appear extremely diversified in different localities, for different social groups, and even for differently structured households. Thus, it becomes extremely difficult to reconstruct the impact on social stratification of new, less universalistic, social welfare policies. Residential stability, the access to a wide number of good jobs and to complementary working opportunities, the degree of resistance and efficiency of at least some public welfare programmes are certainly indicators of better welfare opportunities. On the other hand, late-comers, especially when they settle in mixed or discriminatory neighbourhoods, social or ethnic groups with poor access to working opportunities, and disadvantaged households such as those with single parents or with many dependent children or adults, are also penalized in terms of their welfare needs being satisfied. This happens on the two fronts of their own resources and access to a mix of ways of providing the services (self-provision, various forms of social solidarity, formal and informal market provision) and of the declining efficiency and comprehensiveness of the public system. However, this roughly drawn picture of polarization is largely insufficient for understanding the increasingly fragmented social stratification found in different social settings.

This brief reference to some issues in the theoretical debate provides a first glimpse of how difficult and diversified the situation is with regard to the fragmentation and recomposition of the social structure in industrial societies. The question to be tackled in the next section of this chapter is whether it is possible to construct typologies that are sufficiently meaningful at a general level, rather than merely restricting analysis to the local impact of contemporary economic and socio-political change on social stratification, the patterns of collective action and the political struggle, to shape the prospects for existing societies.

2 POLARIZATION AND FRAGMENTATION AS TOOLS FOR INTERPRETING CONTEMPORARY TENDENCIES IN SOCIAL STRATIFICATION

Introduction

Although contemporary trends in social stratification are interpreted in different ways, two terms are frequently used: polarization and fragmentation. At first sight, it does not appear that they can be easily combined to form a single consistent picture. Polarization evokes the image of a limited number of social conditions, possibly only two, which increasingly diverge from one another and/or encompass a growing percentage of the total population. Fragmentation, on the other hand, basically entails an increasing number of different social conditions. The combining of polarization and fragmentation is possible according to one complex line of interpretation: that contemporary social structures are indeed becoming more and more diversified but that the micro-typologies tend to concentrate around two major poles, or macro-typologies, which differ greatly in terms of conditions of existence, life-chances, and the quantity and quality of available social resources. The idea of a fragmented polarization has been little explored or theorized. It presents great difficulties, also of an analytical nature, which become a tremendous obstacle when we move into the area of social and political behaviour. However weak and controversial their methodological underpinnings, the simple theories of social polarization have been powerful tools in explaining social action and conflict. This is not the case with fragmented polarization.[5] Here, the idea of fragmentation is based on the assumption that roughly similar conditions of existence at one of the poles do not imply the same social and cultural background, common interests and similar patterns of social action. This possibility has to be studied and discussed focusing on specific cases and attempting to construct intermediate typologies and to isolate a set of crucial conditions.

I shall now briefly compare some interpretations of the main contemporary transformations of the social structure in different types of social context, starting with an up-to-date, critical version of the classical Marxist theory which is less rigid than orthodox versions. This provides a further opportunity to discuss the theoretical difficulties of the 'structure-consciousness-action chain' in social conditions that differ from those encountered by the classic social polarization theories. I shall then mention four different, but not incompatible interpretations of important changes affecting the social structure of advanced capitalist countries and what can be interpreted as the main phenomena characterizing contemporary changes in the social structure of underdeveloped and socialist countries. In this discussion, the most important *de facto* elements in the contemporary social transformation are also mentioned. In the last section, I rearrange these elements in an attempt to put forward a preliminary typological framework for understanding contemporary social change in terms of social stratification and political action in fragmented societies.

Critical comments on the classical Marxist theory of social polarization

The Marxist theory of capitalist accumulation is the classical source for interpretations of the social structure in terms of polarization. In this respect, it is worth considering some of its elements which do not lead to a simple and radical opposition between capital and the proletariat but rather to a better understanding of the complex structures that are currently assuming greater importance. This means going beyond the linear approach based exclusively on the concentration and centralization of capital and on the consequent generalized opposition between, on the one side, a powerful and bureaucratized capitalist class with its social allies and, on the other, an increasingly uniform, impoverished and urbanized working class totally dependent on monetary/wage resources for survival.

There are at least three important questions deeply rooted in the Marxist theorization of capital accumulation and of capitalist societies which modify the rigid orthodox assumption of simple polarization in the direction of a more articulated and problematical conception.

First, capital accumulation brings about not only a continuous process in which an exploitable labour force is immediately and directly recreated, but also a permanent army of surplus population that survives in various ways, both historically and geographically speaking. Because it survives in a different social situation, this social stratum is by definition separate and distinct from the regularly employed working class. It is also worth mentioning the obvious and historically verified hypothesis that the progressive decline of its rural/latent component is compensated for by the increase in its diversified and changing urban/stagnant component.

Second, the history of accumulation, and in particular starting from the specific socio-organizational effects of class struggle, is necessarily reflected in the conquest by different fractions of the working class of diverse socio-political opportunities, cumulated through different levels of organizational strength and bargaining power.[6] The history of working-class trade union and political movements in different industrialized countries shows that this process has been heterogeneous, discontinuous and complex. Often, the strictly economistic reasoning is not fully confirmed which assumes that some sections of the working class, starting from positions of relative bargaining strength in the labour market, are able to reinforce their political organization and through it obtain an improvement in employment conditions and life-chances. It is, however, interesting to underline the fact that even if one remains within a limited economistic framework, one necessarily ends up by accepting the idea of a historical process of differentiation within the working class and its trade union and political organizations.

The movement of capital away from sectors and areas where the workers have become better organized and stronger attenuates, but does not stop, the trend towards the diversification of capital and of the working class. This transformation is perfectly comprehensible as the main outcome of higher productivity and of capital-intensive investment, which is the first and simpler reaction of capital to the relative strengthening of the specific working-class component prior to any complicated restructuring of production, as Marx noted in the first volume of *Das Kapital*. But while investment aimed at increasing labour productivity curbs the labour-market power of workers, at the same time it consolidates the gains and positions of those workers who remain employed in the more dynamic and advanced sectors. This process has contributed greatly to the formation of the so-called 'internal labour markets'. Thus, it is possible to formulate the hypothesis of an increasingly diversified working class in terms that are consistent with Marx's approach. This would involve carrying out a much more difficult and detailed socio-political and historical analysis of the different effects accumulated through the historical consolidation of the trade union movement and through access to direct or indirect forms of power for social-democratic, socialist and generally progressive political parties.

Third, the Marxist concept of capital accumulation as a long-term process of capital mobility is intrinsically problematical. This is because it assumes the parallel presence of factors working in favour of equalization and those which work in the opposite direction and end up by magnifying inequalities both among workers and fractions of capital; the first factors are the movement of labour from less developed sectors and areas characterized by labour-intensive production towards sectors and areas of the opposite kind which, consequently, offer higher wages, and the movement of capital in the reverse direction in search of opportunities for relatively higher profits; the second are imperialism, unequal exchange and the growing gap between development and underdevelopment. In other words, accumulation is by definition 'flexible' and capitalist strategies for achieving reasonable conditions of accumulation are neither linear nor evolutionary, and they move neither in a vertical (automatic concentration) nor a horizontal (progressive diffusion of equal conditions) direction.

If these three theoretical aspects are taken together, a picture results which is very far from the idea of simple homogeneous social polarization. Both the capitalist class and the working class in the broad sense appear highly diversified. There are, however, two sides to this picture. If accurate, it also provides a much more realistic analytical framework in which to understand contemporary tendencies in social stratification in advanced capitalist countries. Within this framework, no trace is left of what may be defined as the most abnormal and historically least credible theoretical result of Marxist analysis (see in this connection various essays included in D. Rose, 1988): the idea of a uniformly impoverished working class increasingly conscious, organized and moving towards a revolutionary socialist strategy. On the other hand, it is also true that, given these conditions, it becomes much more difficult to work out a theory of collective action which can be applied in the same way to the entire class and is capable of covering very diverse strata and areas.

As already mentioned in the previous section, the consciousness/action part of the Marxist theorization of class is not mechanically linked with a radically polarized class structure (this is certainly an insufficient condition and it could be questioned whether it is a necessary one) but, rather, with a discontinuous conflict-ridden historical process fundamentally based on the 'limits' of the capitalist social order. Revolutionary consciousness and action does not originate in poverty and marginalization but is reached through the long-term historical experience that the capitalist order is incompatible with 'decent' incomes and life-styles and with the progressive extension of individual social and political rights and expectations. Marxists also assume that the maturation of this 'negative' consciousness is accompanied by the development of a 'positive' side in terms of an organizational capacity capable of creating alternative perspectives.

On the basis of this theoretical framework, a crucial question can be raised that may serve as a starting-point for contemporary neo-Marxist reflection. Industrial development and unequal capital accumulation on a global scale have rendered the 'limits' of the capitalist order more flexible and partially diverse in nature; but such limits have not at all disappeared (Hirsch, 1976). There is nothing to indicate the possibility within any contemporary capitalist order of both improving the conditions of life for the large majority of the population in underdeveloped countries and at the same time consolidating and expanding the rights of individuals and the conditions for their self-fulfilment, including the emancipation of subordinated individualities (based on gender, race or age). Neither the fragmentation of the social base nor the failure of contemporary socialist attempts to provide a better life-style and alternative conditions for emancipation and political participation stand, from a historical perspective, in a logical contradiction to the 'limits' of the capitalist social order; they are, rather, signs of the tremendous complexity that the question of 'limits' assumes from a socio-political point of view.

For this reason, what may be a crucial point in the contemporary debate is not so much the composition of the working class (Poulantzas, 1979; Wright, 1978) or multiple class loyalties (Wright, 1985). One should look, instead, to the changing complex balance between segments of the 'core' working class, declining numerically and more difficult to mobilize and organize, and an extremely diverse area of peripheral working class, which overlaps and competes with a sizeable and renewed surplus population worldwide. The urgent question is whether or not (and why and under what conditions) this large and fragmented social area can be considered a 'pole' for collective action, that is, can give expression to the unifying logic of a socio-political strategy rather than to a wide range of divergent immediate interests or even to a passive resignation born of despair in the face of poor or worsening conditions of existence.

Polarization and marginalization interpreted as the disappearance of middle-income groups

This interpretation of social polarization in advanced capitalist countries has been mainly built on evidence of recent change in the economy in the USA, but it can be extended to other post-Fordist countries. Essentially, the reasoning behind it is as follows:

> As the economy shifts away from its traditional manufacturing base to high-technology and service industries, the share of jobs providing a middle-class standard of living is shrinking. An industrial economy employs large numbers of relatively well-paid production workers. A service economy, however, employs legions of keypunchers, salesclerks, waiters, secretaries, and cashiers, and the wages for these jobs tend to be comparatively low. (Kuttner, 1983, p. 60)

On the one side, there is the decline in wage-work and salaried jobs offering average or above-average incomes and usually reserved for adult male breadwinners; this decline is brought about by de-industrialization, industrial restructuring and the reorganization of welfare programmes. On the other, there is the highly polarized employment structure typical of both the new private services and the expanding sectors of manufacturing. These are characterized by a number of high-income professional and managerial jobs at the top and a vast mass of low-income casual, informal, temporary and part-time forms of employment at the bottom. In some industrial regions, *vertical disintegration* and the spread of several kinds of subcontracting systems into traditional manufacturing industry is further extending this polarization trend.[7]

The polarization trend is basically interpreted as a consequence of a structural socio-economic transformation. The neo-conservative policies of Thatcher and Reagan have helped to accelerate and amplify it through privatization, the cancellation of welfare programmes, anti-union policies and the support given to rampant entrepreneurial activity, involving the abuse of every possible form of unprotected labour. On the opposite front, strong trade unions defending middle-income jobs and, where possible, working to achieve some protection for new less stable forms of employment, a high degree of social support for public welfare programmes and increasing state intervention in the employment system have limited the effects of polarization. Neither of the opposed political strategies is, according to this interpretation, capable by itself of generating or neutralizing this structural trend.

The polarization in employment is greatly accentuated by the general increase in unemployment, especially among young people. Two questions need to be underlined at once regarding this way of posing the problem of social stratification. First, it should be noted that simply recording changes in the employment structure is inadequate for building up a picture of social stratification, which is also significant for my approach based on socialization mixes and social factors. It is important to indicate which actors do which kinds of work in the context of a changing socio-demographic structure. Casual, temporary and poorly paid jobs lead to differentiated stratification if they are filled by the following groups: a growing army of women interested in work as a means of providing a complementary or even supplementary income; young people looking for a transitory period of work experience before settling in permanent tenured jobs; pensioners who are still relatively young and need to complement an inadequate income; and heads of families of both sexes who require a sufficient income to maintain numerous children or family members unable to work. Furthermore, an important role is played by the socio-economic conditions, including the geographical area, in which the transformations take place. The effects of de-industrialization are by their very nature most deeply felt in the old industrial districts, whereas the substantial growth of the new polarized employment systems in services and in high-technology industry is more evenly distributed, but highly concentrated in several large metropolises (the *global cities* which will be dealt with below) and in some types of industrial district (the various Silicon Valleys). In the latter, the cost of living and, above all, the cost of housing also rises disproportionately, especially in the absence of costly large-scale public investment in residential building. The widespread paradoxical situation is, therefore, now apparent in which a large part of the growing army of casual or low-income or part-time workers cannot afford to live in the areas where job opportunities of this kind are most concentrated. The result is growing tensions on the labour market, concurrent rises in employment and unemployment, an increase in commuting, more illegal or semi-illegal immigration into areas of high unemployment and so on. In this sense, it is important to keep in mind that this interpretation may be only a starting-point, requiring more detailed analysis along the lines indicated here, as well as along other lines, before it can be used to explain change in terms of social structure and stratification.

Secondly, it is worth pointing out that though limited and preliminary, this approach points to some of the potential results of fragmented polarization. The army of new workers is not only polarized but also highly diversified internally, unlike the relatively uniform conditions of employment that characterize the apparatus of the large Fordist-welfarist industrial or service-sector firms. Obviously, fragmentation, as well as polarization, needs to be verified beyond the pure and simple conditions of employment found in the concrete social typologies in which it occurs and is structured.

Social polarization as opposition between an affluent 'middle' class and an impoverished marginalized group

Although at first sight this interpretation appears the reverse of the previous one, it is in part based on the same kind of evidence and can serve to complement it. The basic argument, as put directly by Pahl (1988a), is the following:

> certain households are becoming increasingly more fortunate, whereas others are becoming increasingly more deprived. Thus, to put it positively, some – but certainly not all – households with 'core' workers and other members of the household also in employ- ment (either full or part-time) are able to achieve and to maintain high household incomes and substantial affluence, despite the indi- vidually weak labour market position of some of their members. (Pahl, 1988a, p. 251)

Pahl's argument rests on the assumption that a substantial number of complementary working opportunities, in addition to self-provisioning abilities[8] and the positive effects of household investement in durables and property, become concentrated in certain households, mainly those headed by a male 'core' worker with a secure blue- or white-collar job. These are work-rich households. At the opposite end of the scale, there are households which become increasingly work-poor in the sense that they have little and decreasing access not only to job and self-provisioning opportunities and to the new advantages offered by investment in prop- erty and household technology, but also to complementary activities.

Pahl's interpretation is strongly supported by evidence from Britain where flexible legislation in favour of part-time employment, an above- average rate of home-ownership even in large cities, and restrictions on the cumulation of working opportunities in households receiving unemployment benefit further contribute to the spread of this form of polarization (Pahl, 1988b; Harris and Morris, 1986; Morris, 1988). In general, there are clearly two pieces of evidence which back up his hypothesis: the increase in multiple jobholding, often undeclared so as to evade taxation, on top of tenured 'core' jobs by both professionals and skilled and non-skilled workers and office personnel in the public and private tertiary sector (EEC, 1989b); and the diffusion of self-provisioning and informal work, most probably engaged in by members of households with at least one adult in secure employment. In this case, too, the process of polarization is evidently furthered by the dismantling of comprehensive welfare programmes. The latter takes place entirely to the disadvantage of deprived households, which do not have sufficient resources to turn to the private sector or adopt self-provisioning substitutes, and consequently remain dependent on a deteriorating public sector, when not abandoned to their fate altogether.

Even more than the preceding one, this interpretation of social polarization implies radical consequences in terms of socio-political collective action. The opposed spirals of affluence and deprivation largely involve the traditional working class and divide it into two branches with supposedly different interests and patterns of action. Relatively well-off families defend their jobs, the possibility of passing on job opportunities to their children, their property and household investments, the consequent possibilities of self-provisioning and the advantageous cumulation of various incomes. A consequence of this last factor is that such families are in favour of lowering the marginal rate of taxation for above-average incomes, even at the cost of cuts in welfare expenditure, as they have the resources to substitute public welfare services with privatized ones or through self-provisioning. Deprived households grow increasingly marginalized and politically isolated. They have no 'voice'; they are dispersed, internally diversified, compete with one another for decreasing resources and are also abandoned by the political parties on the left. They are pushed into apathy or individualistic action and end up becoming merely a problem of 'legal order', at least when social deprivation and marginalization is not highly concentrated in spatial and social terms. Only then, as in the case of ethnic minorities or generational groups in some areas of large cities, does their action take on a socio-political relevance and become a real problem for the political system.

It is important to mention a possible variant of the thesis on the polarization between benign upward spirals and malign downward spirals that concerns the working careers of young people in a period of growing occupational instability, the spread of precarious and heterogeneous forms of work and high rates of youth unemployment. These changes in the socio-occupational structure have different consequences for different groups of young people. It depends on whether they open up an area where employment conditions can be tested, which permits greater flexibility and the possibility of trying various activities and 'carving out' a better self-employed or salaried occupation; or whether, in contrast, they reflect a persistent lack of decent work opportunities which compels young people to accept poor jobs as they have no alternative. Such a situation is destined to last for many years or even for entire lifetimes.

In diverse social contexts and typologies, the number of young people within the benign spiral of work experience as part of upward careers and those in the malign spiral of persistent employment difficulties depends on the number of both self-employed and salaried occupations (new or replacement) with a stable average income that are available relative to the generational groups making up the labour supply. A high insufficiency of this type of occupation has a twofold effect: it lengthens the period of work experiments in the benign spiral, thus making it more difficult and problematical, and increases the number of young people condemned to the malign spiral. Moreover, the fact must be taken into account that everywhere the competition for a limited number of positive employment opportunities is intensifying due to the growing participation of young women, who are justifiably demanding on the basis of equality access to working careers with acceptable conditions and stable incomes.

The underclass

Another set of observations on the social structure of advanced capitalist countries which are compatible with and complementary to both polarization theses involve the emergence of a new persistent area of urban poverty; the term 'underclass' has been used to refer to those groups who display some of the features typical of this conditon (see Auletta, 1982, and the recent review of literature on the subject by Ricketts, 1987). The idea of an underclass increasingly present in large capitalist cities has not yet been sufficiently explored and defined. For instance, it is difficult to say how much the concept and the reality it expresses differ from the classical Marxist concept of 'lumpenproletariat'. At first sight, the difference seems to be greatest in terms of collective action and political roles. This difference is essentially rooted in the different mixes of socialization underlying the two concepts. Marx's lumpenproletariat was a social stratum strongly characterized by illegal activities or on the borderline of legality and by its mobilization, or more exactly, instrumentalization in the conflict between classes. It could be mobilized politically because it was characterized by strong associative and reciprocal ties at a time when individualistic behaviour was not as developed as today. In other words, it was concentrated in particular districts of cities, protected by a strong household and community structure, and possibly connected in horizontal associative organizations. Parallels in the contemporary world are both large organized crime, like the Mafia, and, partially, the informal sector in the large cities of underdeveloped countries. The underclass, on the other hand, is defined by its chronic and irreversible poverty, by behaviour that is deviant but not necessarily illegal and, above all, by a resigned attitude and the lack of mobilization in terms of political and social action. This is mainly due to the weakness of its typical socialization mixes characterized by high degrees of social isolation and marginalization.

The distinction between those in the underclass and those in a condition of poverty is not sufficiently clear either in conceptual or numerical terms. Poverty is defined and calculated according to different standards. The problem is even more complex if the starting-point is that of social scientists, for whom poverty means a condition specifically characterized by resources that are insufficient to meet needs and, thus, a social condition. Given, however, that it is not possible to measure the matching of resources to needs within large aggregates of population, one is constrained to use standardized statistical indicators of official per capita monetary income or consumption levels; such as operation leads to notable discrepancies when the results are compared with the original concept of social condition. For instance, many relatively self-reliant and socially integrated old people end up by being included among the poor because they earn and consume little, even if, in reality, they not only meet their own needs but in some cases also manage to save. By contrast, not included among the poor are groups with substantial needs due to illness, old age and dependency on others, mental or physical handicaps or other negative social conditions. They are unable to satisfy these needs not only because they have a relatively modest income (though above the poverty line) but also because they are socially isolated both in terms of associative and reciprocal networks. The above-mentioned problems also apply to the ways in which the underclass is measured, in so far as the latter has generally been understood as a (statistically estimated) chronic and long-term component of the poor, that is, not in a temporarily difficult situation that will be overcome in a relatively short time.

Nevertheless, the existence of an underclass is becoming a much discussed and increasingly important part of contemporary theories on social polarization. At least a part of those who are permanently disadvantaged and with no hope of ever having a decent job or access to public services finish up by adopting deviant survival strategies. These may or may not involve criminal activity, but, whatever the case, they represent a move away from the standards of behaviour accepted by the majority of the population (Auletta, 1982, pp. 27–8). Indirect indications, such as the existence of the homeless, vagrants, mentally confused or abandoned individuals and families affected by chronic and intergenerational poverty, show that this group of people is growing. Furthermore, this growth is taking place above all in the big cities where the means of social control, public assistance and state repression are less efficient, and where the resources essential for guaranteeing a normal standard of living are substantial, but out of reach for an increasing number of families and individuals that are socially isolated and have access only to intermittent opportunities for poorly paid casual and informal work. The evidence that both the number of long-term unemployed and discouraged workers and the number of casual badly paid jobs are increasing suggests that the underclass may also grow to become a not insignificant proportion of the urban population. In fact, hard-core unemployability and life-long permanence in casual badly paid jobs both reflect and reinforce conditions of social isolation and, most of the time, foster what is defined as deviant behaviour.

It is worth mentioning that the combination of persistently low and insufficient monetary income and social isolation is what makes the poverty of the underclass appear a visibly more dramatic problem than urban poverty in underdeveloped countries, where monetary income is much lower but complemented by highly protective reciprocal arrangements. This is also reflected at a political level since the poor in the informal sector express a clear interest in defending and upgrading their communities while vagrants, the homeless, and mentally disturbed and marginalized members of the underclass are left with nothing to defend and with no political issue of interest to them.

Flexible economic units and the emergence of a new self-employed middle class

It is worth while considering briefly the evidence for and interpretation of changes in the socio-economic structure which do not lead to polarization. These are the social transformations underlined in the so-called 'Third Italy model' or, even better, in the Emilia model, and extensively discussed, among others, by Piore and Sabel (1984) in *The Second Industrial Divide*. Different, though not very dissimiliar, conditions of social stratification apply in the case of Japan and in other cases characterized by a model of industrialization built on the persistent and significant adaptation of reciprocal factors.[9]

Industrial restructuring and decentralization and the increase in relatively small flexible enterprises in both private services and manufacturing constitute the major factors used to support both the previous polarization interpretations. The fundamental difference between these and the interpretation based on the increasing importance of a new self-employed middle class is that the processes involved are not viewed as accompanying de-industrialization and the decline of state intervention; instead, they are seen as elements in a model of industrial growth that has developed outside the system of large factories and is accompanied by greater local state attention to the changing and differentiated social and political requirements of developing integrated micro-firms and by the persistent adaptation and importance of reciprocal networks. Under these conditions, the social structure does not become more polarized in either direction but rather brings forth trends towards a better redistribution of income and opportunities, at least in areas where the rate of growth has remained persistently high. This happens in two ways. First, there is a consistent increase in the number of small-scale and self-employed activities which do not express strong tendencies towards concentration and selection but rather towards increasingly sophisticated forms of networks based on co-operation. This not only minimizes any polarizing tendencies but also widens access to innovation and high technology to small operators and newcomers. Second, there is evidence, mentioned in chapters 5 and 6, that during the successful expansion of 'diffused industrialization', what are originally convenient conditions of informal employment become increasingly formalized.

In this model, the advantages of economic growth are partially redistributed also to those at the bottom end of the work hierarchy, both directly (the possibility of cumulating two or more part-time jobs) and via a high degree of complementarity promoted by stable and efficient household and community networks. Or, to make a comparison with the second polarization model, the favourable conditions of work-rich households are more widespread and do not rest on at least one secure job in major industry being held by the adult breadwinner, since they are based on a favourable situation due to regional economic growth.

It is worth underlining, however, a very important caveat with regard to the Emilian model in the narrow sense (see Capecchi, 1989). As seen in detail in chapters 5 and 6, the latter has been a unique experience based on the presence of specific original social factors, set in motion spontaneously at a particular time in recent industrial history. This explains why the model cannot be adopted as a universal political strategy and why under different conditions of flexible industry, vertical disintegration and the spread of homeworking and subcontracting systems, these transformations end up by generating a large number of precarious low-skilled and low-income jobs, the result of which is polarization and marginalization rather than family and community-based recomposition of stratification and heterogeneity of work opportunities.

Radical polarization, protective reciprocal networks and socio-political struggles in underdeveloped countries

In practically all underdeveloped countries, social stratification is persistently characterized by the radical social polarization between a relatively restricted group of very high-income families, rarely covering more than 10 per cent and often less than 5 per cent of the population, and a very large stratum, almost always over 50 per cent, with very low monetary incomes complemented by complex and variable forms of both urban (increasing) and rural (declining) subsistence strategies. On the basis of this general affirmation and several themes touched upon above, it is possible to put forward some interpretational hypotheses, at least at a preliminary level.

The assumption that underdeveloped societies are very heterogeneous is fully confirmed by the physiognomy of social stratification. Even at the superficial level of measuring the difference between the monetary incomes of the privileged minority and of the poor majority, an immensely wide gap is seen to exist in many Latin American countries whereas in several Asian countries it is much less wide, even though still within a range typical of underdevelopment rather than development. This difference may largely depend on its origin in agricultural systems almost solely based on extensive plantations and large landed property, as against those involving more intensive farming, which have made it possible for a large number of family farms to adapt.[10]

Returning to the question of interpreting social stratification in underdeveloped countries in general, it is worth underlining again that heterogeneity of the qualitative aspects of survival strategies and life-styles is very accentuated, particularly among both the urban and rural poor. Therefore, typological generalization is much more difficult than in the case of other contemporary societies. In fact, my approach focusing on the role of the transformation of socio-organizational factors has shown that the modes of industrial *development*, accompanied by a strong growth in associative factors and the concomitant weakening of traditional reciprocal networks, have led to relatively homogeneous patterns with regard to the profile of the mass Fordist worker, the formation and development of the welfare state, economic and organizational concentration, similar forms of standardized monetary consumption and the crucial role in politics of large associative aggregations of interest groups. This process of homogenization does not occur when reciprocal factors adapt to act as a surrogate for *industrial growth* (the difference between Japan and the Third Italy is much greater than that between two Fordist societies), or when they adapt to play a defensive role against *underdevelopment*. Indeed, the wide-ranging historico-cultural variability of reciprocal strategies persists, at least partially, in the adaptative transformation. This variability is inherent in the very concept of socio-organizational factors of reciprocity, understood as collective micro-organizations with a high degree of internal interaction and exclusion of outsiders. The heterogeneity does not appear to be very marked if only households and kinship groups in advanced capitalist and socialist countries with a strong prevalence of associative factors are considered. But it is particularly manifest when attention is focused on ethnic groups and on communities both where reciprocal factors play a surrogate role and where they a play a defensive one. Different householding strategies and kinship systems, diverse alimentary and agricultural traditions, different micro-divisions of work and handicraft skills and many other historico-cultural diversities in reciprocal systems are elements that make up the process of adaptation of sociality mixes.

Already a serious obstacle to analysing the transformation of life-styles and strategies and grasping the particular meaning assumed by urban and rural subsistence systems, such diversity is an even greater impediment to general reflection on social stratification and politics. With this kept in mind, it is none the less possible to undertake a preliminary discussion of some themes; the most important thing to remember is that caution must be exercised when applying to underdeveloped countries the conceptual tools used to interpret the social question in advanced capitalist countries.

In the first place, it is obvious that dramatic social polarization between rich and poor in underdeveloped countries is not a simple variant of the relationship between capitalists and the working class. The extremely rich are often connected in some way to international financial circles, but given the weakness of native capitalism their great wealth depends more on landed property, import/export and control of the state apparatus. In the vast majority of countries in Latin America and in some other countries beset in recent decades by a growing foreign debt and astronomical inflation rates, the very rich have tended to widen the gap between themselves and a fragile layer of professional middle classes and medium-sized local producers. This is due to the fact that the wealth of the former predominantly takes the form of real estate and financial investments in foreign currencies, whereas the latter depend on incomes in local currencies. The situation is different but not necessarily more compact in those NICs that are characterized by a smaller pressure from the surplus population and a relatively stronger growth in employment in manufacturing industry. Here, the more or less repressive regimes do not protect so much the interests of big landowners but, rather, those of industrialists by holding back the rise in wages in situations where the labour market is partially saturated. In this case, too, however, though for different reasons, a separation takes place between the dominant industrial interests and those of the new middle classes, above all technicians and service workers who are penalized by wage freezes.

Workers employed in medium to large manufacturing concerns, almost always foreign multinationals, are everywhere a limited part of the population and take on political significance only in areas with a high industrial concentration, like the metropolitan district of São Paulo in Brazil or of Seoul in South Korea. In these cases too, however, the serious problem arises of non-cohesiveness between associative and reciprocal interests. The first take the form of the defence and improvement of wage levels, working conditions and job stability and the second the defence and improvement of conditions in the informal sector for complementing inadequate wages. The associative interests are persistently frustrated by strong competition on the labour market, which is reflected both in the low wage level and in the state of working conditions and job stability. The reciprocal interests are often strong but difficult to manage politically due to their varied, fragmented and local nature.

The most important and frequently studied political struggle in which the reciprocal strategies of underdevelopment have stood in opposition to global capitalist interests is that involving land ownership and tenancy.[11] Even though the picture of this struggle, which in some places has continued for more than a century, is a varied one, ranging from the defence of rights, traditions and customs to the demand for agrarian reform and land redistribution, its content, strategies, forms and the motives for mobilization are clear enough. In passing, I want to underline the fact that agrarian struggles have almost always been about possession of the land and the possibility of using it, the nub of rural reciprocal strategies, and practically never about the level of agricultural wages, which, if they were to rise, would modify the socialization mix in the direction of more clearly associative outcomes.

The urban front in the political struggle, that is the informal sector and the immense shanty towns, is of mounting importance but also difficult to interpret. In this case, too, the struggle for land and space has been explicit, in particular in the 1960s when many regimes decided on the forceful implementation of a policy of slum clearance. Today, it appears that the battle for a minimum amount of urban survival space in the informal sector has been won by the shanty-dwellers, at least in many countries. Clearly, the matter may be reopened at any moment by a change in government or due to strong economic-speculative interest in areas on which the poor are squatting. It is significant that even those regimes most tolerant towards informal sector settlements are almost always reluctant to concede property rights or land possession to squatters or to grant for long periods official permission to undertake working activities typical of the informal sector.

The most important political issues and the prospects for informal sector inhabitants are probably linked to the upgrading of their conditions of existence, in particular those relating to modern services, health, welfare and education. The informal sector as a whole cannot, by definition, be reduced to a single social class, given the importance of reciprocal relations in defining the typical socialization mix. As a consequence, the power relationships between the informal sector, the urban middle classes, the upper bourgeoisie together with the national ruling class and international capital are varied and particularly intricate; furthermore, they cannot be reduced to a constant clash of interests or to forms of domination free of serious contradictions. In this sense, an improved standard of living in the informal sector has become an important political objective, above all for the populist parties and movements in Latin America, a region where the urban informal sector is very large. Their aim is to unite the interests of the urban populace with those of the professional, administrative and intellectual middle classes.[12] At first sight, this strategy of recomposition does not appear to clash head-on with the political interests of big international capital or of the local financial and landowning bourgeoisie. The problem is that this strategy can be put into effect only under two conditions, if it is to have any hope of success. The first condition, manifestly explosive in the existing political context, is that a concurrent radical agrarian policy succeeds in increasing strategic opportunities for wide sectors of the rural masses and in defending them against the attacks of international capital and the big landowners. Without this complementary political strategy, the inexorable pressure from new waves of urbanization ends up by vitiating any real attempt at upgrading introduced into the urban informal sector. The second condition consists of the difficulty in sharing out equitably the considerable social and economic cost of strategies of this kind, the aim being to avoid throwing into crisis the fragile balance between reciprocal strategies and monetary resources and public expenditure. Seen from the perspective of my interpretation of social factors, a balanced sharing out of the costs is an immensely difficult operation; it has resulted in all the progressive or populist political programmes that have been tried out in Latin America in recent decades being overwhelmed by problems, from those associated with Perón and Allende to that being undertaken by reborn Brazilian democracy. Clearly, the political difficulties in tackling the first condition in a radical manner also play an important role in the contemporary world, though less decisive than, for instance, in the Mexican revolution at the beginning of the century.

Lastly, it is important to point out that, from an economistic point of view, these political strategies are largely based on financial policies involving the granting of big wage increases in tandem with large-scale public investment. In this sense, the inter-class recomposition comes up against the interests of international capital and the big commercial and financial bourgeoisie and also finds it difficult to win over the middle classes, who in the long run end up being hit by uncontrollable waves of inflation and astronomically high taxation. I am fully aware that I have gone no further than presenting a schematic and partial picture here; but this was precisely the limited goal I had set myself.

The impact of social fragmentation, liberalization and economic reforms in socialist countries

The recent political and economic changes in socialist countries have attracted a lot of interest in this model of society. There are at least two reasons why these cases are difficult to interpret. The first is the oft-mentioned theoretical difficulty. This applies in full to the understanding of social stratification, classes and relationships between classes, as I underline below. Furthermore, given the theoretical doubts that have not been cleared up by the interpretation of the social structure, the social basis of the political struggle is practically impossible to understand. It is no accident that the radical nature of the socio-political changes in these countries has taken all the political pundits and social scientists completely by surprise. It could in fact be said that we are running behind events that are considered impossible shortly before they occur.

The second reason for which it is objectively difficult to interpret situations in these countries and the prospects for the models of real socialism is the almost total lack of detailed accurate research on the ways in which the system of social stratification works and changes. This is the case even in terms of the socio-occupational structure alone, not to mention a more accurate picture which takes into account the interplay of reciprocal factors and the complexity of socialization mixes. For both these reasons I confine myself to recapitulating a certain number of hypotheses already expressed throughout this book and to reinterpreting them in terms of social stratification; I shall also refer to some aspects of the debate on the class nature of socialist societies.

Basically, two questions raised during my exposition take on particular importance in the discussion of social stratification, class nature and the socio-political struggle in socialist societies. The first concerns the definition of the socialist model of industrialization as a society in which associative/redistributive factors are preset institutionally to keep under control the tensions created by the market and individual competition; the second relates to the discrepancy between the political-ideological model, oriented to minimizing or eliminating reciprocal factors, and a social reality in which these factors have survived to play an important role in rendering the sociality mixes more complex. With regard to social stratification, the first question links up with the problem of polarization and with the debate on the specific class nature of socialist societies; the second, on the other hand, hints at a specific problem of social fragmentation.

The definition of socialist societies I have adopted means little from the point of view of classes and social stratification. It is presupposed that the divisions typical of capitalist societies cannot be applied mechanically in these cases because forms of sociality prearranged in line with redistributive control limit in advance the play of market forces. In this sense, the processes of industrial growth are not characterized by the clash of interests between the owners of the means of production and the direct producers. This does not, however, automatically entail the assertion that socialist societies are not characterized by social classes and inequalities. As Nove (1986, pp. 51–62) correctly notes, the classical Marxist theory of the class nature of socialism is strongly characterized by utopian elements and by conditions that have not come about in reality: in particular, the emergence of the 'new Man and Woman, who will need no incentives and will do the right thing for the benefit of all' (ibid., p. 52) and the rapid overcoming of a situation of scarce resources and the great simplification of the processes of control and redistribution, which would allow an increasing participation in the holding of power and constant turnover of those in positions of power.[13] Under such conditions, social inequalities and classes are considered to exist but to be dying out since there exist diverse, but not opposed, interests. The fact that these conditions have been impossible to achieve in the now long experience of socialist societies forces one to interpret the relationship between the vast proletarianized masses and a relatively restricted group controlling the processes of redistribution as a relationship between classes, and not one dying out but marked by persistently diverse and, therefore, often opposed interests. Furthermore, the above-mentioned processes are growing more and more complex rather than simpler and their control is not characterized by a growing participation and turnover but by a long-lasting monopoly, the advantages of which are sometimes passed on in the same family. A heated theoretical debate on this question has been under way since the 1920s and is far from being concluded. The central issue is the class nature of the elite of cadres that has taken over permanent control of the redistributive processes; this elite has been variously defined as a bureaucracy, 'new class' (Djilas, 1966), 'intellectuals' (Konrad and Szelenyi, 1979), *nomenklatura*, 'official class' and so on (see Nove, 1986, pp. 220–38). This is not the place to go any further into this debate, which it was none the less important to mention, not merely because it confirms that a gulf has been opened up between the controlling apparatus and the various categories of workers and citizens, but also because it points to the nub and major theoretical difficulty of the question. In order to be able to interpret the social structure and class nature of these societies being subjected to rapid change, at least in their socio-political order, the complex logic behind their class relationships must be more clearly defined on the basis of more detailed research; it is necessary to go beyond the stereotyped notions of the preservation of power for the sake of power, of privileges in terms of priority access to scarce resources or even of political-adminis-trative immorality and corruption. The most recent events appear to falsify these stereotypes, which no social scientist worth his salt should have taken as a basis for reasoned analysis.

The analysis of the associative-redistributive part of socialist socializ-ation mixes, therefore, poses the difficult problem of verifying how the relationship between the interests of a composite apparatus of cadres and those of diverse sectors of workers differing in age, sex, education and skills, who thus develop different abilities, expectations and shades of individuality, is historically structured and how it changes. As long as the theoretical rationale behind the relationship has not been clarified, which also implies the need for more detailed historico-social research, it is an error to presuppose both that diversity can never mean divergence, as Stalinist doctrine declared, and that it is always a matter of a critical and irremediable divergence, as many Western observers suggested up to a few years ago. And what is even more important is that it is still not possible to explain what the social conditions are which promote reconciliation of the differences as against those that ossify the divergence.

Though quite manifest in terms of life-styles and life-chances, the division between cadres and proletariat is not comparable with the social division existing in advanced capitalist countries, nor can it be interpreted by the theories of polarization applied to the latter. The privileged condition of the cadres is, at least in the medium to long term, dependent on their capacity to guarantee an accceptable standard of living without systematic discrimination against any specific group of citizens. The tendencies of underaccumulation and economic inefficiency make the relationship between classes problematical without adding any process of polarization; if anything, growing social polarization occurs because of the increasingly important role of the second economy. This is probably one of the reasons why the cadres themselves are interested in re-establishing conditions of acceptable economic efficiency and better cohesion between the institutional associative system and reciprocal systems, before class relationships deteriorate any further.[14]

In all cases, the crux of the question turns on the problem of the specific contradictions in this model of industrialization and to what extent a political-institutional system strongly rooted in the model is able or unable to adapt to different conditions. It is not a matter of how much space can be conceded to relatively limited and controlled market initiatives, but rather of the degree of local and sectoral autonomy, of how this autonomy is to be managed and co-ordinated so as to avoid a high level of economic anarchy, strong centrifugal impulses in the political sphere and social re-stratification leading to intolerable forms of inequality and social polarization.

This set of problems, though very complicated, is still not a sufficient one on which to base an interpretation of the socialist countries since it is necessary to introduce the role of reciprocal factors into the socialization mixes and processes of social stratification. This discussion should be extended, even only on a preliminary basis, to the entire range of social life; but given that this is complicated even at a purely hypothetical level, I confine myself to recapitulating the recent contribution by Szelenyi (1988), discussed above, on the role in Hungary of small farming enterprises in complicating and fragmenting the processes of social stratification.

Leaving aside altogether the role that reciprocal factors may play in promoting small-scale economic initiatives in the market, social stratification and class mobility typical of socialist societies are limited to two processes: the formation of cadres and proletarianization. These processes lead to the formation of two divided and more or less internally differentiated social strata, that is a kind of polarization, though different from that found in capitalism. The possibility that a petty bourgeois class may be formed and consolidated through small entrepreneurial activities, whether officially permitted or taking place in the second economy, considerably complicates the picture of social stratification and the complex interplay of interests. Moreover, by widening the area in which such initiatives are permitted, economic reforms in socialist countries are giving a certain degree of official recognition to this third line of social stratification. I believe that in this case, too, what we have is a process of social fragmentation, the outcome of which is impossible to predict at present.

In conclusion, I think it worth pointing out that I fully agree with Szelenyi on two points. First, that the persistence of this form of reciprocity does not point to a possible return to capitalism, not even in that phase in which economic reforms lay the conditions for an expansion of family farming and the diffusion of small market entreprises in services and craft activities. Second, that this kind of status takes on a significance different from that assumed in capitalist and, in particular, underdeveloped countries. This last observation is an obvious one following our discussion of reciprocal factors and small family ventures in the informal urban sector. I disagree with Szelenyi, however, when he describes these mixed socialist economies as representing a 'Third Road' between the capitalist and socialist models, first of all because it is mistaken to compare two ideal models with a real specific case. Though in a variety of different forms, all the real specific capitalist and socialist societies can be classified as belonging to this Third Road. The reason for this is that, on the one hand, a society organized around an unregulated market is historically implausible and, on the other, a society based on the total centralized redistribution of resources according to criteria of equality is likewise a historical absurdity, at least as long as resources remain scarce. Moreover, Szelenyi's idea of the Third Road is built on the assumption that this is possible only in countries such as Hungary and Poland where petty market activities were widespread before the socialist revolution and have managed to survive a relatively short period of disfavour; consequently, he ends up by ignoring the case of the Soviet Union where the above-mentioned phenomena are widespread and active, as well as others relating to the 'second economy'. Furthermore, the reforms of the Gorbachev era are no less exemplary as a consequence of the gap between the ideal model of socialism and the reality of Soviet society. On the other hand, if the Soviet Union is included in the Third Road debate, there is no longer a specific case on which to base the model of a Soviet-type society, as it is constructed by Szelenyi.

3 CONCLUSIONS: IDEAS ON THE POLITICAL ASPECTS OF FRAGMENTED SOCIETIES

Introduction

In advanced capitalist countries the trends giving rise to the above-mentioned interpretations have been documented as discrete phenomena, but in reality they operate in conjunction in various mixes. Not even the Japanese and Third Italy cases, in which industrialization characterized by reciprocity is still a particularly important phenomenon, are by themselves sufficient for formulating a well-defined typology of clear transformations in social stratification and political struggle. In the case of the Third Italy, it is chiefly the quality and quantity of the new self-employed and wage or subcontracting service jobs which lead to a relatively balanced and less polarized social stratification reflecting a productive structure sufficiently modern and innovative and highly resistant to the pull of concentration. In the Japanese case, on the contrary, a characterization in terms of reciprocity does not apply so much because of the persistent importance of small and medium-sized firms and stable and local communites based on solidarity; rather, it covers the entire socio-economic system, from the big concerns to the role of the family and the importance of 'loyalty' in all economic-social relationships. The outcome in terms of social stratification is not much different: a relatively higher social fragmentation is largely, though not fully, reintegrated through reciprocal social factors. These eventually weaken the importance of the large horizontal divisions between workers and employers, between those with a stable well-paid occupation and those who are unemployed or in a precarious low-paid job and so on. The great political issues are, therefore, not only the associative conflicts but also, and to a very important extent, those concerning the ways to achieve integration and, above all, their capacity to adapt to changing and diverse social conditions. In Japan, for example, three fronts come to mind on which the system of social integration could be overwhelmed: discrimination against women in the face of emergent female identity and individuality; the customary retirement age of 55 within an ageing population; and the rigidly hierarchical and selective educational system with a strong bias towards engineering and technical-scientific subjects in a situation where post-industrial transformations are promoting services and leisure activities. The various combinations of contemporary trends give a general picture of an increasingly fragmented social structure, clearly different from the largely uniform picture resulting from the two classical predictions concerning the future prospects for industrial societies: the politically positive one of the welfarist-social-democratic dream of widespread well-being among a tenured and stable white- and blue-collar middle class, and the politically negative one based on the generalized mechanistic application of the theory of proletarian impoverishment.

In underdeveloped and socialist countries too, the complex interface between social polarization and fragmentation complicates the reality and the interpretation of the political struggle and the immediate prospects for socio-economic change. In the underdeveloped countries, the persistent extreme polarization between the very rich and the very poor involves less and less directly the crucial and transparent question of land ownership and agrarian reform. This remains a difficult and conflict-causing precondition for the feasibility and effectiveness of populist or progressive policies; then, however, there is the urban informal sector which poses other economic and social questions, particularly fragmented and localized and not immediately and easily linked to the global confrontation between multinational capitalist interests and local export-oriented activities able to contain and repay foreign debt. In the socialist countries, the fragmentation tendencies are becoming extremely visible in terms of both a widening space for small-scale market initiatives and a rising demand for local and sectoral independence. These pressures interact with the centralized socio-economic system, which is conflict-ridden, highly inefficient and very rigid. What still needs to be answered is how this fragmentation can be reintegrated politically; how to co-ordinate this more flexible and decentralized economy in order to achieve the desperately needed increase in efficiency; and how the political redistributive system should avoid suffocating the newly born greater degree of autonomy, while at the same time preventing the consolidation of progressively widening social and regional inequalities.

The idea of social fragmentation opens up difficult questions in the area of collective behaviour and political action. None the less, it helps to throw light on the persistent or renewed importance of certain social factors, *above all* that of households and local communities in managing the integration of increasingly unequal working opportunities. In this regard, I want to make some final observations which should be taken only as initial suggestions aimed at stimulating research and discussion.

Polarization and fragmentation within a socio-political typology of social situations

In the advanced capitalist countries, a possible typology of social situations from the point of view of social stratification could be established by starting from the impact, both at a social and a spatial level, of trends in de-industrialization and the dismantling of the welfare state. This could then be combined with the possibility of pooling a structured mix of survival resources, the cost of living and the presence or absence of social factors that play an important role in the fragmentation and diversity of work, such as well-off and stable family and community networks, a local economy favourable to the development of innovative service activities and disadvantaged or discriminatory social backgrounds.

The global cities

In addition to the combinations created within this range of possibilities, it is increasingly important to take into separate consideration the specific physiognomy of what have been called the 'global cities'. Here the trends towards polarization and fragmentation are both magnified at the same time and to such an extent that they often give rise to one of the great paradoxes of the contemporary world: the concomitant substantial increase in both employment and unemployment. The growing casualization of work attracts migrant workers who are the target of discrimination and who are more willing than the local supply of labour to accept permanent casual low-income jobs. At the same time, it forces into unemployment or emigration other components of the local population: those that have been socialized and are available for family wage jobs typical of the Fordist-welfarist system. On the other hand, a much higher than average increase in the number of new self-employment opportunities, sometimes short-lived or particularly precarious, provides relatively well-off groups and households, which also possess sufficient economic or ethnic-cultural resources and an adequate academic or technical education, with a good chance of starting up their own businesses. These opportunities also attract minorities with strong community or ethnic solidarity networks, small amounts of capital and a sufficient level of eduation. The most manifest example of this last trend is the Korean conquest of the retail food trade in New York and Los Angeles (Light and Bonacich, 1988).

A further factor is the cost of living in the global cities, which is particularly high and increasingly beyond the means of socially isolated individuals and households earning income from casual, low-skilled and intermittent work. In particular, the cost of housing is growing out of all proportion to the income of many households. The competition between manufacturing, financial and local and national headquarters, and general service-sector districts and residential zones for the new technical-professional middle-upper classes causes prices to rise even where there is a sharp decline in population; it ends up by also pushing out groups earning stable middle incomes, especially young people at the start of their working careers and in search of a new house but without a particularly well-off family background. For all these reaons, and others, the socio-occupational structure of 'global cities' is in a stage of constant rapid change, which it is impossible to control and which produces a high degree of conflict (see Soja, 1989; Scott, 1988; Sassen, forthcoming).

A reasonable hypothesis is that several phenomena and features typical of 'global cities' are also spreading to some metropolitan districts in the underdeveloped and socialist countries. In the case of the former, some megalopolises like Mexico City, São Paulo, Rio de Janeiro, Bombay or Jakarta are not only subject to unrestrainable population growth accompanied by increasingly radical and transparent forms of social polarization: they are also the scene of chaotic economic development which is highly complex, partly tied to global interests but, above all, reflects the demographic situation and the heterogeneity and polarization of the need and effective demand for services. All of this also presents a picture of growing social fragmentation reflected in countless diverse work opportunities, more or less traditional or innovative and immaginative, which are always insufficient to absorb the constant pressure from the surplus population; none the less, they still serve to split the vast mass of citizens on low incomes into groups that are more or less successful, inventive and enterprising. In this sense, it is possible to assume that the social fabric is more fragmented and political recomposition more problematical and unstable at the level of these megalopolises than at the overall national level. Strong social movements and large mass mobilization may play an important political role before becoming absorbed in the complex local interaction between reciprocity and the multiple division of interests (see Friedmann and Salguero, 1988). Thus, it is also possible to assume that the mounting importance of megalopolises, with their increasingly complex combinations of local solidarity and self-help and the fragmentation of the conditions of existence and life-chances, has the effect of making populist and progressive movements and their policies more ambiguous but also more receptive to local autonomy and grass-roots democracy.[15]

In the socialist countries, too, the assumption can be made that the large cities are characterized by a more accentuated syndrome of social fragmentation. This is not only the effect of the concentration of various different ethnic and national groups in localities other than their places of origin, but also the consequence of the extent to which tertiarization

and the demand for services has expanded, involving both the proliferation of small service activities in the second economy and the diversification of the ways in which state services are used.[16]

The intermediate de-industrialization typology

The other clear-cut types which I shall now mention follow naturally
from what was stated above, at least in their general outlines in advanced
capitalist countries. They are, at one end, the industrial cities and regions
worst hit by de-industrialization and the dismantling of the welfare state
(for example, Liverpool or Detroit) and, at the other, the regions favoured
by the so-called *second industrial divide* (for example, the region of Emilia
in the 1970s and early 1980s). It is also possible to include among this
last group regions where a substantial amount of high-tech industrial
and service industries have been set up, bringing with them a series of
advanced tertiary sector firms and research and development activities.
An example are those regions that have followed the example of Silicon
Valley in Central California and have become centres for the development
of the electronics industry. From the perspective of social stratification,
however, the latter group is more problematical than the models of the
Third Italy and of Japan. In this case, in fact, industrial growth occurs
where there is not a relatively stable and closed social background and
no fixed relations of reciprocity at the level of co-ordination between
enterprises or, above all, of household, kin and community networks
which tend to counteract the effects of polarization and fragmentation
inherent in the new job opportunities. The specific case of Silicon Valley
reveals some strong social tensions due both to the polarization and
fragmentation of employment and the great instability of the economic
environment and career prospects.[17] Consequently, this case resembles
the situation in the global cities more than the Japan or Emilia models.

Most cases lie between the two extremes mentioned above. Therefore,
it becomes important to inquire into the balance that has been established
in diverse localities between the following phenomena: de-industrialization, the growing casualization of work opportunities, the presence of
social factors and networks able to react positively to these tendencies
and the qualitative and quantitative level reached by new middle-class,
self-employed or small-scale activities; the cost of living and the impact
of local policies also have to be taken into account. The regions around
Boston, Turin, Lyons, Barcelona and Manchester are clearly among
the vast array of possible forms that these intermediate mixes may
assume.

For reasons of space, it is here impossible to discuss in greater detail the
current socio-political transformations typical of this vast and diversified

intermediate typology; nevertheless, one brief point needs to be mentioned. The process of de-industrialization does not give rise unequivocally to economic and social decline, with its consequent effect of transforming political confrontation.[18]

The combination of de-industrialization and a declining population with a certain amount of growth in new advanced tertiary activities has the potential to open up several, though problematical, possibilities of urban 'renaissance' rather than decline. Manufacturing industry is moving away from large areas leaving them free for 're-utilization' and a decreasing population, if not too polarized and impoverished, may benefit from improvements in living standards in terms of services, housing space and other socio-cultural initiatives after several decades of chaotic growth and the heavy congestion of social demand relative to the limited potential supply. In this case, too, we are dealing with a hypothesis to be subsequently verified in the different socio-political realities of various industrial social contexts but which, none the less, confirms the invalidity of mechanistically linking de-industrialization, de-urbanization and the qualitative decline in urban life.

The industrially undeveloped regions

There is another separate typology consisting of regions which have never been properly industrialized and do not offer favourable opportunities in terms of widespread and flexible industrialization. The case which comes particularly to mind is that of Southern Italy, to which a large part of chapter 6 is dedicated; but it applies to all the 'chronically' undeveloped regions of Europe, including large parts of Spain, Portugal, Greece, Ireland and perhaps some regions in France. Here the negative impact of the casualization of working opportunities is hardly compensated for by an increase in the number of good self-employed jobs, since the social fabric is particularly fragmented and impoverished, with the result that it is totally incapable of giving rise to these new forms of work. The well-off household mentioned by Pahl applies to only a relatively small group of civil servants, teachers and bank and insurance employees, and cannot be extended to the local working class. At the same time, long-term youth unemployment is having a widespread and lasting effect on an entire generation.

The politico-social syndrome found in the Mezzogiorno cannot be automatically applied to all areas of this kind. It is difficult to discover precise historical analogies with what happened in this region in the post-war period, from the breaking up of the traditional power structure based on the large landed estates and class of notables to the overwhelming and pervasive establishment of party-political patronage and the creation of the system based on the redistribution through patronage of local and central public resources in place of welfare services.[19] Proceeding very cautiously, the Mezzogiorno can, however, give us some essential hints on the socio-politial syndrome within abortive or weak industrial development. Systems of socialization characterized by the too weak formation of modern associative factors, above all a working class with solid trade union traditions, almost always develop political syndromes marked by local parochialism, a particular vulnerability to widespread corruption and the absence of strong stable organizations representing horizontal interests. The end result is practically always narrow-minded provincialism and patronage. The political balance remains precarious and tends to deteriorate with the fiscal crisis of the state and rampant mass unemployment and underemployment; yet this process is translated neither into the appearance of long-lived protest movements nor into a high degree of receptiveness towards radical or innovative political formations and other movements. Even solely at the electoral level, the depressed regions of Southern Europe with their characteristic lack of industrial growth show no propensity to vote for radicals, progressive forces or green parties, unlike the electorate in the areas of Central and Northern Europe most severely affected by de-industrialization.[20]

With regard to the political role of typical forms of socialization and weaker, less mobilized political practices, and to the interaction between them in relatively poorly industrialized regions, it is interesting to note that the problem may also arise in socialist countries. Even socialist industrial growth is characterized by marked economic imbalance between regions, though this often occurs in ways that differ from those under capitalism. Leaving aside the extreme case of Yugoslavia, since it cannot easily be assimilated to the experience of the other socialist countries, there are the Islamic regions of the USSR and many of the internal and mountainous regions of China. Here, the question is often complicated by the overlapping of strong ethnic-cultural and religious differences, which may in themselves form a strong factor in political mobilization. The case of Tibet is exemplary in this respect. On the basis of media reporting of the reawakening of national identities in the USSR, it could be asumed that such a situation is comparable with the political syndrome in the depressed regions of Southern Europe. Here, too, the less developed regions appear to be politically and socially more disgregated and less easy to mobilize by innovative movements; but, when cemented by strong cultural and religious feelings, they are mobilized by traditional separatist movements, as in the case of Azerbaijan.

The impact of demographic change and of multi-cultural systems

The whole typological range of situations needs to be seen against quantitative and qualitative population trends, such as rates of birth and mortality, age composition, questions relating to the life-cycle and migratory movements. These are complex matters to which only a few comments can be dedicated here.

In the first place, the fact must be emphasized that the decline in population, the fall in the birth rate and the tendency for the population to age are features that cannot be generalized to all social, and possibly ethnic, groups in the population. Furthermore, a form of household persists and is on the increase which involves high birth rates more as part of strategies for survival than because of ideological and religious convictions or traditional customs. It concerns those households that survive by cumulating a high number of incomes, all of which are insufficient when taken singly; thus more importance is given to the number rather than the level of incomes. This form of household now seems to be typical of the urban informal sector in underdeveloped countries; but it is also found to a variable extent in the urban contexts of advanced capitalist countries, and it may be assumed that the more the employment situation is fragmented, the more this particular form tends to spread. The largest presence of this social stratum with high birth rates is to be found in the industrially undeveloped regions. Here, the stratum is spreading on an already consolidated pre-existing basis of urban marginalization. In Southern Italy, as we saw in chapter 6, the clearest example is that of families in which the husband-father is a precarious building worker. In the global cities, too, this stratum is tending to expand considerably, above all when the growth in employment is very dynamic and heavily weighted in favour of work fragments and where the *de facto* situation permits increasing waves of new long-term or permanent immigration; the most significant examples can be seen in New York and Los Angeles.

As far as concerns multiracialism and migratory flows, although it is true that all advanced capitalist societies are or are becoming multiracial, it is also the case that the degree and nature of this situation differs from one society to another. Many socialist and underdeveloped countries are historically founded on multi-ethnicity and this question, which has never been an easy one to manage, particularly in the latter, is now assuming an increasing importance and leading to greater social conflict also in the former. As far as concerns the advanced capitalist societies, it is important to note that there are three different types of multiracialism:

the American, firmly established but continually subject to reshuffling due to inflows of new, potentially permanent immigrants and also to substantial unofficial cross-border immigration; the English and French, which applies in less clear-cut terms to all countries in Central and Northern Europe with an established and stable multiracialism; and that found in Southern Europe, where multiracialism is a recent phenomenon and mainly characterized by high turnover rates among immigrants. In this sense, the problems of young West Indians in London's Brixton are similar to those of their black American contemporaries in Watts or Harlem (disadvantaged but established ethnic minorities), but different from those of illegal young Mexican immigrants in Los Angeles or the Senegalese in Italian cities. The problems facing the waves of new immigrants also differ depending on whether they are either seasonal or long-term or potentially permanent. The first kind have less impact on local social stratification and on the consolidation of areas of marginalization, poverty and discrimination; it is for this reason neither a coincidence nor a sign of widespread racial tolerance that they do not meet with much racial prejudice from the local population. Another obvious reason is that 'guest-workers' are weaker and easier to exploit and blackmail, since they can be easily expelled.

Next, it is necessary to mention, at least, the persistent differences in the logic underlying the fact that low-income strata and disadvantaged ethnic groups, if the decreasingly important cases of certain poor agricultural regions are excluded, are located in cities, and in certain areas of cities. The traditional American model of central segregation seems, in theory, better equipped than the European model of peripheralization to tackle the paradoxical situation in which there is a progressive physical separation between low-income job opportunities and possible residential zones for workers. This situation is also due, as already stated, to the tendency of the cost of living to rise at a disproportionately higher rate in the old city centres. In the case of the USA, the effects of the phenomenon of gentrification in many central neighbourhoods and of the progressive decline in the attractiveness of suburbia must now be taken into account. In this sense, the socio-ecological models of American and European cities could become more alike and in both cases a serious problem might arise: the progressive separation between the localities where low-income job opportunities are concentrated and those in which the labour supply willing to accept them finds it reasonably less inconvenient to live.

Finally, it is also worth briefly touching on the question of age groups and the life-cycle, at least as far as regards old people; young people have already been mentioned in relation to previous topics, particularly unemployment and work strategies. The lengthening of the lifespan and the increase in the percentage of old and very old people undoubtedly pose important problems in terms of social stratification. In general, urbanized old people still tend to go on living in urban areas and to be concentrated in the old densely populated quarters. The rest home in the country, the oases for old people in Florida or Southern California and the various Mediterranean and English rivieras are luxury solutions that only a limited minority of the old population can afford. What perhaps poses the most serious problem is the transition from a phase of independence to one of dependence as a person grows older. The city, above all the big city and in particular its central districts with many opportunities for complementary work, constitutes an environment that is on the whole favourable to relatively young pensioners. It is especially the case that when old people are already well integrated and home-owners, they eventually become increasingly rooted in these favourable urban areas, even if they are isolated from family networks. However, the loss of independence with the advance of old age in areas where the cost of living is high, communication between people is difficult and large numbers live in isolation is becoming a serious problem, with which partially dismantled welfare systems are unable to cope.

Young occasional workers who travel long distances every day in the hope of finding a 'fragment' of work, and chronically sick, abandoned and impoverished old people, are two elements that will have to be increasingly taken into account in any attempt to predict the near future of Western cities and to interpret their complex systems of social stratification.

Conclusions: notes on the impact of social fragmentation on the political sphere

It is obvious that in advanced capitalist countries accelerated and unopposed de-industrialization and the dismantling of welfare programmes, or in the case of the United States the historical absence of a comprehensive welfare system, lead to a significant extent to the problems depicted in the first polarization theory. A sizeable decrease in the number of opportunities for breadwinners to find stable tenured employment and a concomitant substantial casualization of jobs providing a complementary income clearly limit the extent of compensation and recomposition carried out by stable households and communities, as suggested by Pahl. In this case, instead of forming a majority, the affluent blue- and white-collar middle class becomes a shrinking minority.

Alternatively, the problem is to understand how many new self-employed possibilities of work are created in different urban contexts and how appealing they are. The cases of Japan and the Third Italy are exceptional precisely because they have not been affected by de-industrialization and the decline in public welfare provision but by processes of a completely opposite kind. This means that, in general, an increase in relatively permanent and decently paid self-employed or small-scale activities does not compensate for the loss of tenured jobs in large manufacturing industry and in public and private welfare bureaucracies. Thus, serious doubt is thrown on the possibility that the benign spiral of polarization identified by Pahl can operate properly throughout a reasonable period of time. If actual trends do not change, work-rich households will be increasingly selected both by decreasing opportunities for tenured full-time jobs held by breadwinners and by the insufficient increase in highly rewarding self-employed or professional or small-scale activities.

Current evidence is controversial but suggests that the area of poor jobs and of households entirely dependent on them is expanding in many different areas. The unequal distribution of diversified work opportunities is, moreover, producing paradoxical levels of social fragmentation, particularly in large cities. Here are just two examples relating to the USA and Italy. The substantial increase in the demand for low-income casual work has attracted new waves of illegal Mexican migrants to Los Angeles. The same is happening in New York where Manhattan is once again showing a demographic upturn after two decades of decline; those attracted to the area are mainly Asian and Latin American migrants. In the case of Los Angeles, the increase in the number of jobs is greater than the increase in the officially recorded population (Soja, 1989). But the black areas of the city, in particular Watts, are persistently characterized by high rates of unemployment. The black communities are transformed irreversibly into areas where the presence of the 'underclass' is pervasive. Some of them are almost totally reliant on the 'generosity' of those engaged in drug-trafficking, which on the streets has largely fallen into black hands. The community reciprocates by protecting the drug 'business' from the periodical assaults of the police. For black workers the loss of employment opportunities produced by the decline in Fordist employment in the car and durables industries has still not been offset by new jobs, even though in the meantime the city's economy is experiencing an exceptional phase of growth.

In Southern Europe, the recent increase in the rate of youth unemployment has been accompanied by an increase in immigration from underdeveloped countries. The immigrants are employed mainly in casual service-sector jobs which are unacceptable to the local youth or merely viewed by them as a temporary stop-gap during periods of study or unemployment. This is also the case in Milan, for example, where a relatively low rate of youth unemployment, but much higher than that recorded at the beginning of the 1970s, may be considered principally as a sign of increasing work instability and where the effective resistance of Fordist-welfarist jobs is accompanied by a sizeable growth in new self-employment opportunities. Conversely, a large number of migrants from underdeveloped countries is settling in Naples, and in Southern Italy in general, and in other less industrialized regions of Southern Europe, where the social and economic context is one that has been stigmatized and impoverished by the lack of industrial growth and the dramatic absence of state welfare services. Here an entire generation of young people from fifteen to thirty is almost entirely unemployed, and good employment opportunities are few both in the Fordist branch of the local economy and in that based on small-scale and self-employed activities (see *IRES-materiali*, 1989a; Pugliese, 1987; 1989).

It is worth remembering that the most difficult question of interpretation concerns the mobilization of class interests and the patterns of collective action. Apart from the defence of the Fordist-welfarist system put up by the trade unions and working-class parties, in which, however, the social base that acts as the protagonist in such collective action is by definition neither marginalized nor impoverished, there is practically no evidence of mobilization arising from situations of deprivation. Some current forms of increasing deprivation are spatially concentrated while others are not. But even in the former case, it is difficult to imagine political programmes being successfully promoted that start from the current heterogeneous conditions of marginalization, pass through cohesive processes based on mobilization and political organization and develop as far as collective action backed by a political strategy. Although the black community in Watts has become even more deprived since the revolt of the 1960s, nothing of the kind has occurred since then. The riots by black youths in Brixton were met with political isolation and repression. While the problem of high rates of unemployment has not been tackled, discontent is still perceived and dealt with as a problem of legal order. The movement of the 'organized unemployed' in Naples lasted only for a short while and faded away with a further increase in the city's rate of youth unemployment.

The only important indication in the opposite direction may be that represented by the 'rainbow coalition' which was set up in the United States to support the Reverend Jesse Jackson's attempt to become the presidential candidate of the Democratic Party. In many respects, the strength of this coalition has suprised social scientists and politicians. It is difficult, however, to say to what extent this coalition constitutes a permanent change in the forms of political mobilization in the USA following the growth of fragmented polarization.

Social fragmentation in advanced capitalist countries is leading in many cases to increasing inequalities and to a large area of social deprivation, which is only partially offset by social resources and welfare programmes. This phenomenon is not as easy to control as the neo-conservative regimes imagined it would be in their heyday at the beginning of the 1980s, when they implemented their plans for privatization and 'radical' social change. But, at least up until now, the new forms of social marginalization have not revealed, either, any clear signs of coherent political mobilization capable of effectively opposing the powerful trends which are giving rise to the spread of large areas of social deprivation and marginalization even in the supposedly affluent societies. At the same time, however, social fragmentation and the impact of the development of individuality on many different fronts, from female emancipation to the long-term impact of mass education and the growing receptiveness towards preserving the ecological balance of nature and towards various particular socio-political demands, are having a debilitating effect on institutions and modes of political participation that have grown up under highly different social conditions but are particularly resistant and impervious to the pressures for change. The socio-political systems in the capitalist democracies are in a critical phase of 'dragging their feet', which is not leading to unmanageable crises, radical changes or the formulation of new alternative policies. In these cases, the political syndrome of fragmented societies is bound up with slow shock-absorbing change, a capacity to adapt which, however, is unable to find stable and lasting solutions to the problems encountered; instead, these problems are pulling them into increasingly difficult situations.

At the same time, socialist societies are putting up much less resistance to socio-political change; but it is impossible to say where the present trend towards 'controlled democratization' is leading. This trend reflects profound processes of social fragmentation and diversification and is unleashing individual and local demands, though I would exclude the simplistic and propagandistic idea of a return to capitalism. Even more than in advanced capitalist countries, the crucial problem does not lie only in the economic order and the political form of participation but, above all, in the difficulty of combining more and more complex, structured and internally conflictual processes of socialization with the demands for individuality and personal identity, which industrial development eventually ends up promoting. In this regard, the problem of harmonizing self-fulfilment and individual freedom with adequate forms of socialization expressed more than a century ago by Durkheim still surfaces today even in a type of society that has gone very close to achieving the ideals of 'associative order', the corporative institutions underlying the development of organic solidarity, put forward by the great French sociologist.

The global picture needs to be completed with a final brief comment on the political syndrome in underdeveloped countries and on its impact on the world economy. The growing importance of the informal sector and, more generally, of urban subsistence economies forms the most important among the limits to the further expansion of capitalism in underdeveloped countries, even though it would be a mistake to interpret this process automatically as an alternative model of industrial growth. The limits are set by the strongly defensive role played by reciprocal factors and by the fact that this defence is difficult to break down by political means, even when repressive and where there is no marked economic growth of the conventional kind. A confirmation comes from the recent experience of Chile, where the urban solidarity and subsistence economies blossomed in the very context of Pinochet's repressive regime (Razeto, 1984; 1985). Both during the course of history and still today, rural subsistence economies have displayed a much greater vulnerability. This seems a paradox of politics because, as I have already had occasion to note, the struggle over the tenancy of agricultural land has made possible clear political alignment and strong mobilization. Horizontal forms of both, on the other hand, are not very likely in contexts dominated by urban subsistence economies. What Friedman and Salguero say about the *barrios* in Latin America is probably true in general: 'Beyond question is the surge of new activities in the *barrios* of large Latin American cities: a growing capacity for self-organization, self-reliance and self-governance in a process of collective self-empowerment' (Friedmann and Salguero, 1988, p. 7). It is precisely this capacity for self-government that gives to urban subsistence economies their political imperviousness and their defence of social conditions that remain marked by low monetary incomes. The other side to this situation, however, is the inexorable fact that political organizations in the urban informal sector are locally isolated and play a weak, ambiguous and unstable role in national politics. So here, too, social fragmentation is opening up new political horizons, where the historical confrontation between populist and progressive governments and authoritarian regimes, backed by the big landowners and international imperialism, is diminishing more and more in importance; but the new terms of the political struggle are not clear, considering that these societies also remain radically polarized and constantly plagued by serious economic problems.

In conclusion, it would be wrong to use traditional labels and definitions for the transformations taking place in contemporary societies. The hypotheses put forward here on the impact of social fragmentation suggest the need to move beyond the simple impression that change makes capitalist societies less dominated by the iron laws of capitalism, socialist societies less subject to the monopoly of redistribution and centralized planning, and underdeveloped societies persistently 'poor' but less vulnerable to the unopposed laws of international capital.

NOTES

1   See, among many other contributions, Berry (1976); Perry et al. (1986); Mingione and Pugliese (1988).

2   See, mainly, Friedmann and Wolff (1982); Castells (1989); Sassen, forthcoming.

3   At this level, a divergence exists with the historico-philosophical approach of Marx; but it is of secondary importance for the scientific analysis of industrial societies. As associative contexts, classes can constitute an important social factor only on condition that individual interests are freed from the excessively suffocating control of dominant collective organizations of reciprocity. The slaves in ancient Rome or the serfs in the Middle Ages cannot be defined, in my view, as social classes in the same way as the bourgeoisie and the industrial proletariat; furthermore, it is not easy to interpret pre-industrial history in terms of class struggle, whereas this can be done for the industrial age.

4   Within a Weberian analysis, multiple class location does not create difficult theoretical problems; these arise, on the other hand, within a Marxist approach, as shown in the important contribution of Wright (1985). The same difficulties, however, crop up generally in international comparative studies on class structure, as Marshall, Rose, Newby and Vogler argue (1988).

5   An important element which complicates the fragmentation trend is the timescale, in the sense of the interconnection of life-cycles with different historical experiences. This element has not been discussed properly in this book. However, its importance may be considered a further argument in favour of a 'fragmented polarization' approach. See mainly Bryman et al. (1987); Belloni and Rampazi (1989).

6   For relatively recent contributions see mainly Hobsbawm (1984); Katznelson and Zolberg (1986).

7   For the case of New York and Los Angeles see, for example, Sassen-Koob, 1983; 1984; Sassen, forthcoming; Ross and Trachte, 1983; Soja, 1989; Scott, 1988.

8   These are understood here as the innovative capacity to produce by oneself, using do-it-yourself equipment and new electronic or mechanical devices,

goods and services for direct consumption by the family.

9 I put forward some hypotheses on the Japanese case in terms of social stratification in the next section and not here in order to simplify the discussion. The main economic and structural difference between the Third Italy and Japan is the fact that in the latter, reciprocal factors have been and still are also typical of large corporations while, in the former, they mainly reflect the persistent importance of small enterprises.

10 See mainly the recent comparative analysis of the recent wave of indebtedness in developing countries edited by Jeffrey Sachs (1989), and particularly the introduction by the editor. See also Lipietz (1987).

11 See, mainly, Barrington Moore (1969); Wolf (1969); Stavenhagen (1970); Lewis (1977); Zamosc (1986); Shanin (1987).

12 See especially the recent critical discussion and review of the problem by Friedmann and Salguero (1988). See also Castells (1983); Safa (1982); Razeto et al. (1983); Hirschman (1984); Slater (1985); Fagen et al. (1986); J. Friedmann (1987).

13 This is clearly Marx's position in his writings on the Paris Commune (*The Civil War in France*) which largely inspired the ideas on the socialist state expressed by Lenin in *State and Revolution*. See also Nove (1986); Gellner (1988); Paul et al. (1988).

14 These are the lines along which we should interpret recent events in Hungary, the Soviet Union, and subsequently East Germany, Bulgaria and Czechoslovakia, whereas the case of Poland and the emergence of an independent trade union and political movement like Solidarnosc prior to rather than following the reformist changes in the regime constitutes a further different phenomenon. At present, it can only be explained in specific historico-cultural terms that do not permit generalization. The case of Romania, on the other hand, also appears to differ from both the Hungarian/ Soviet and Polish developments.

15 I am thinking particularly of recent political events in Brazil with the electoral success of Brizola's neo-populist party in Rio de Janeiro and of the PT (an extreme left-wing Catholic and populist-oriented labour party) in São Paulo and other cities. In both cases, the success of the locally ruling party is connected with attention being paid to and policies formulated in favour of the *favelas* and of the new urban social movements.

16 Before anything further can be said on the political effects of these phenomena, detailed comparative research needs to be carried out. This has yet to be done. It is still worth noticing, however, that, with some exceptions, the core of the mass mobilization in favour of political change and socio-economic reforms is extremely concentrated in large cities like Budapest, Berlin, Leipzig, Prague, Sofia, Moscow and Leningrad. The highly metropolitan character of what is now called 'the second socialist revolution' (Zaslavskaja, 1990) will certainly be reflected in the outcome of these changes and increase further their 'coreness'.

17 I have dealt with this problem and the relative literature in chapter 5. For

a recent extensive evaluation of the problem see mainly Castells (1989).

18 Manchester and Liverpool are two geographically contiguous industrial cities with fairly similar social histories, but they have been hit in different ways. Moreover, in Britain local autonomy is relatively limited and Thatcher's policies of dismantling the welfare state have been spread evenly across the board. If anything, the local administration in Liverpool has demonstrated a greater readiness than the one in Manchester to put up resistance and intervene firmly in the economy. The difference probably lies in the fact that Manchester, from the very beginning, has had a more articulated and differentiated socio-economic structure and, as a consequence, it has been more receptive to the new transformations taking place in the tertiary sector.

19 A discussion of and references relating to the Mezzogiorno patronage syndrome can be found in chapter 6.

20 See, mainly, Giner (1985) and Keane (1988).

Bibliography

Abel-Smith A., 1972, 'The history of medical care', in Martin, 1972, 219–40.
Abercrombie N. and Urry J., 1983, *Capital, Labour and the Middle Class*, London, Allen and Unwin.
Abrams P., 1982, *Historical Sociology*, West Compton House, Somerset, Open Books Publishing.
Adair P., 1985, *L'Economie informelle*, Paris, Editions Anthropos.
Aglietta M., 1979, *A Theory of Capitalist Regulation. The US Experience*, London, Verso.
Agriculture and Human Values, 1989, special issue on 'The crisis in European agriculture', ed. A. Bonanno, 6, nos 1 and 2 (Winter–Spring).
Alessandrini S. and Dallago B. (eds), 1987, *The Unofficial Economy*, Aldershot, Gower.
Alford R. R. and Friedland R., 1985, *Powers of Theory: Capitalism, the State, and Democracy*, Cambridge, Cambridge University Press.
Allan G. and Crow G. (eds), 1989, *Home and Family: Creating the Domestic Sphere*, London, Macmillan.
Allen S., 1983, 'Production and reproduction: the lives of women homeworkers', *Sociological Review*, 31, no. 4., 649–65.
Allen S. and Wolkowitz C., 1987, *Homeworking: Myths and Realities*, London, Macmillan.
Allum P., 1973, *Politics and Society in Post-war Naples*, Cambridge, Cambridge University Press.
Altman Y. and Mars G., 1987a, 'Case studies in second economy production and transportation in Soviet Georgia', in Allessandrini and Dallago, 1987, 197–218.
Altman Y. and Mars G., 1987b, 'Case studies in second economy distribution in Soviet Georgia', in Alessandrini and Dallago, 1987, 219–46.
Amsden A., 1980, *The Economics of Women and Work*, Harmondsworth, Penguin.
Archambault E. and Greffe X. (eds), 1984, *Les Economies non officielles*, Paris, Editions La Découverte.
Arizpe L., 1982, 'Relay migration in the survival of the peasant household', in Safa, 1982, 19–46.

Arrighi G. (ed.), 1985, *Semiperipheral Development: The Politics of Southern Europe in the Twentieth Century*, London and Beverly Hills, SAGE Publications.

Arrighi G., 1986, *Custom and Innovation: Long Waves and Stages of Capitalist Development*, Duplicated paper, Fernand Braudel Center, State University of New York at Binghamton.

Arrighi G. and Piselli F., 1987, 'Capitalist development in hostile environments: feuds, class struggles and migrations in a peripheral region of southern Italy, *Review*, 10, no. 4, 649–751.

Ascoli U. (ed.), 1984, *Welfare State all'italiana*, Bari, Laterza.

Atkinson D., 1983, *The End of the Russian Land-Commune*, Stanford, Stanford University Press.

Auletta K., 1983, *The Underclass*, New York, Vintage Books.

Aziz S. (ed.), 1975, *Hunger, Politics and Markets: the Real Issues in the Food Crisis*, New York, New York University Press.

Bagnasco A., 1977, *Tre Italie: la problematica territoriale dello sviluppo italiano*, Bologna, Il Mulino.

Bagnasco A., 1978. 'Struttura di classe e articolazione di tre formazioni territoriali in Italia', in Paci, 1978, 351–60.

Bagnasco A., 1981a, 'Labour market, class structure and regional formations in Italy', *International Journal of urban and Regional Research*, 5 no. 1, 40–4.

Bagnasco A., 1981b, 'La questione dell'economia informale', *Stato e Mercato*, 1 no 1, 173–96.

Bagnasco, A., 1985, 'La costruzione sociale del mercato: strategie di impresa e esperimenti di scala in Italia', *Stato e Mercato*, 13, 9–45.

Bagnasco A., 1986a, *Torino, un profilo sociologico*, Turin, Einaudi.

Bagnasco A. (ed.), 1986b, *L'altra metà della economia*, Naples, Liguori.

Bagnasco A., 1988, *La costruzione sociale del mercato*, Bologna, Il Mulino.

Bagnasco A. and Trigilia C. (eds), 1984a, *Società e politica nelle aree di Piccola Impresa; il caso di Bassano*, Venice, Arsenale.

Bagnasco A. and Trigilia C. (eds), 1984b, *Società e politica nelle aree di Piccola Impresa; Il caso della Valdelsa*, Milan, Angeli.

Bahro R., 1978, *The Alternative in Eastern Europe*, London, New Left Books.

Bahro R., 1982, *Socialism and Survival: Articles, Essays and Talks, 1979–1982*, London, Herche Books.

Balbo L., 1976, *Stato di Famiglia*, Milan, Etas.

Balbo L., 1980, 'Riparliamo del Welfare State', *Inchiesta*, nos. 46–7, 1–20.

Ball M., Harloe M. and Maartens H., 1988, *Housing and Social Change in Europe and the USA*, London and New York, Routledge.

Bamford J., 1987 'The development of small firms, the traditional family and agrarian patterns in Italy', in Goffee and Scase, 1987, London, Croom Helm.

Barbagli M., Capecchi V. and Cobalti A., 1988, *La mobilità sociale in Emilia Romagna*, Bologna, Il Mulino.

Barnard A. and Good A., 1984, *Research Practices in the Study of Kinship*, London, Academic Press.

Barrett M., 1980, *Women's Oppression Today*, London, Verso.

Barsotti O., 1988, *La presenza straniera in Toscana*, Milan, Angeli.

Barsotti O. and Potestà L., (eds), 1982, *Segmentazione del mercato del lavoro e doppia occupazione*, Bologna, Il Mulino.

Bawly D., 1982, *The Subterranean Economy*, New York, McGraw Hill.

Bean P., Ferris J. and L. Whynes D. (eds), 1985, *In Defence of Welfare*, London and New York, Tavistock.

Becattini G. (ed.), 1987, *Mercato e forze locali: il distretto industriale*, Bologna, Il Mulino.

Becattini G. (ed.), 1989, *Modelli locali di sviluppo*, Bologna, Il Mulino.

Bechhofer F. and Elliot B. (eds), 1981, *The Petite Bourgeoisie. Comparative Studies of the Uneasy Stratum*, London and Basingstoke, Macmillan.

Beechey V., 1977, 'Some notes on female wage labour in capitalist production', *Capital and Class*, 3, 45–66.

Beechey V., 1978, 'Women and production: a critical analysis of some sociological theories of women's work', in Kuhn A. and Wolpe A. M. (eds), *Feminism and Materialism*, London, Routledge and Kegan Paul, 155–97.

Beechey V., 1979. 'On patriarchy', *Feminist Review*, 3, 66–82.

Beechey V., 1983, 'What's so special about women's employment? A review of some recent studies of women's paid work', *Feminist Review*, 15, 23–45.

Beechey V., 1987, *Unequal Work*, London, Verso.

Beechey V. and Perkins T., 1987, *A Matter of Hours; Women, Part-time Work and the Labour Market*, Oxford, Basil Blackwell.

Bell D., 1973, *The Coming of Post-Industrial Society*, London, Heinemann.

Belloni M. C. and Rampazi M. (eds), 1989, *Tempo Spazio Azione sociale. Tredici saggi per discuterne*, Milan, Angeli.

Bendix R., 1956, *Work and Authority in Industry*, New York, Wiley.

Bendix R., 1964, *Nation Building and Citizenship*, New York, Wiley.

Beneria L., 1979, 'Reproduction, production and the sexual division of labour', *Cambridge Journal of Economics*, 3, 203–25.

Beneria L. and Roldan M., 1987, *The Crossroads of Class and Gender*, Chicago, University of Chicago Press.

Berger B., and Berger P. L., 1983, *The War Over the Family*, London, Hutchinson.

Berger S. (ed.), 1981, *Organizing Interests in Western Europe. Pluralism, Corporatism and the Transformation of Politics*, Cambridge, Cambridge University Press.

Berger S. and Piore M. J., 1980, *Dualism and Discontinuity in Industrial Societies*, Cambridge, Cambridge University Press.

Berliner J., 1952, 'The informal organization of the Soviet firm', *Quarterly Journal of Economics*, 66, no. 3, 342–63.

Berliner J., 1957, *Factory and Manager in the USSR*, Cambridge, MA, Harvard University Press.

Berrett M. and McIntosh M., 1980, 'The "family wage": some problems for socialist and feminist', *Capital and Class*, 11, 51–72.

Berry B. J. L. (ed.), 1976, *Urbanisation and Counterurbanisation*, London, Arnold.

Bettelheim C., 1972, 'Theoretical Comments', in Emmanual A., *Unequal Exchange:*

A Study in the Imperialism of Trade, London, New Left Books.

Bilac E., 1978, *Familias de Trabalhadores: Estrategias de Sobrevivencia*, São Paulo, Simbolo.

Binns P. and Haynes M., 1980, 'New theories of Eastern European class societies', *International Socialism*, Ser. 2, no. 7.

Birkbeck C., 1980, *Theft, Robbery and Conning in Cali, Colombia: Some Implications for Policy*, Swansea, University College of Swansea, Centre for Development Studies, 8.

Birkbeck C., 1982, 'Property crime and the poor: some evidence from Cali, Colombia', in C. Sumner (ed.), *Crime, Justice and Underdevelopment*, London, Heinemann, 162–91.

Blackaby F. (ed.), 1978, *De-industrialization*, London, Heinemann Educational.

Bluestone B. and Harrison B., 1982, *The Deindustrialization of America*, New York, Basic Books.

Boccella N., 1982, *Il mezzogiorno sussidiato*, Milan, Angeli.

Boddy M., Lovering J. and Basset K., 1986, *Sunbelt City? A Study of Economic Change in Britain's M4 Growth Corridor*, Oxford, Clarendon Press.

Boer L., forthcoming, '(In)-formalization: the forces beyond', *International Journal of Urban and Regional Research*.

Bonacich E., 1973, 'A Theory of Middleman Minorities', *American Sociological Review*, 38, 583–94.

Bonacich E., 1975, 'Small business and Japanese American ethnic solidarity', *Amerasia Journal*, 3, 969–112.

Bonacich E., 1981, *The Economic Basis of Ethnic Solidarity: A Study of Japanese Americans*, Berkeley, Los Angeles and London, University of California Press.

Bonacich E. and Modell J., 1981, *The Economic Basis of Ethnic Solidarity: A Study of Japanese Americans*, Berkeley, Los Angeles and London, University of California Press.

Bonanno A., 1987, *Small Farms: Persistence with Legitimation*, Boulder, CO, Westview Press.

Bonanno A., 1988, 'Economia informale e contesto sociale', *Economia e Lavoro*, 22, no. 3, 103–12.

Boris E. and Daniels C. (eds), 1988, *An Anthology on Homework*, Champaign, IL, University of Illinois Press.

Bose C., Feldberg R. and Sokoloff N. (eds), 1987, *Hidden Aspects of Women's Work*, New York, Westport and London, Praeger.

Bott E., 1971, *Family and Social Network*, London, Tavistock.

Boudon R., 1986, *Theories of Social Change*, Cambridge, Polity Press.

Boulding K. E., 1972, 'The household as Achilles' heel', *Journal of Consumer Affairs*, 2.

Boulding K. E., 1978, 'Réciprocité et échange: l'individu et la famille dans la société', in Michel, 1978, 21–37.

Bourdieu P. and Passeron H., 1964, *Les Héritiers*, Paris, Editions de Minuit.

Bourdieu P. and Passeron H., 1970, *La Reproduction*, Paris, Editions de Minuit.

Bourgeois F., Brener J., Chaubaud D., Cot A., Fougeyrolles D., Haicault M. and

Kartchevsky-Bulport A., 1978, 'Travial domestique et famille du capitalisme', *Critiques de l'Economie Politique*, 3, 3–23.

Braghin P., Mingione E. and Trivellato P., 1978, 'Per un' analisi della struttura di classe dell'Italia contemporanea', in M. Paci (ed.), *Capitalismo e classi sociali in Italia*, Bologna, Il Mulino, 257–304.

Brannen J. and Wilson G. (eds), 1987, *Give and Take in Families. Studies in Resource Distribution*, London, Allen and Unwin.

Braverman H., 1974, *Labour and Monopoly Capital*, New York, Monthly Review Press.

Bremen J. A., 1976, 'A dualistic labour system? A critique of the informal sector concept', *Economic and Political Weekly*, 2, 48–50.

Bromley R., 1978, 'The urban informal sector: why is it worth discussing?, *World Development*, 6, Nos. 9/10, 1033–9.

Bromley R., 1981, 'Begging in Cali: image, reality and policy', *International Social Work*, 24, no. 2, 22–40.

Bromley R. and Gerry C., 1979 (eds), *Casual Work and Poverty in Third World Cities*, New York, Wiley.

Brotchie J., Hall P. and Newton J. (eds), 1987, *The Spatial Impact of Technological Change*, London, Croom Helm.

Brown C. and Pechman J. A. (eds), 1987, *Gender in the Workplace*, Washington, DC, The Brookings Institution.

Brown M. K. (ed.), 1988, *Remaking the Welfare State. Retrenchment and Social Policy in America and Europe*, Philadelphia, Temple University Press.

Bruno S., 1979, 'The industrial reserve army: segmentation and the Italian labour market, *Cambridge Journal of Economics*, 3, 131–51.

Brusco S., 1979, *Agricoltura ricca e classi sociali*, Milan, Feltrinelli.

Brusco S. and Sabel C., 1982, 'Artisan production and economich growth'. In Wilkinson F. (ed.), *The Dynamics of Labor Market Segmentation*, London, Academic Press.

Brusco S. and Capecchi V. (eds), 1980, *Sindacato e piccola impresa in Italia*, Bari, De Donato.

Bryman A., Bytheway B., Allat P. and Keil T. (eds), 1987, *Rethinking the Life Cycle*, Basingstoke and London, Macmillan.

Burawoy M., 1979, *Manufacturing Consent. Changes in the Labor Process under Monopoly Capitalism*, Chicago and London, The University of Chicago Press.

Burawoy M., 1985, *The Politics of Reproduction*, London, Verso.

Burns S., 1975, *Home Inc.: The Hidden Wealth and Power of the American Household*, Garden City, NY, Doubleday.

Burns S., 1977, *The Household Economy*, Boston, Beacon Press.

Business Week, 1978, 'The fast growth of the underground economy', 13 March, 73–7.

Business Week, 1982, 'The underground economy's hidden force', 5 April, 64–70.

Caizzi B., 1970 (ed.), *Nuova antologia della questione meridionale*, Milan, Feltrinelli.

Calvanese F. and Pugliese E., 1988, 'Emigration and immigration in Italy', *Labor*, 3, 181–99.

Cammarota, A., 1977, *Proletariato marginale e classe operaia*, Rome, Savelli.

Capecchi V., 1989, 'The informal economy and the development of flexible specialization in Emilia-Romagna', In Portes et al., 1989, 189–215.

Capecelatro E. M. and Carlo A., 1972, *Contro la questione meridionale*, Rome, Savelli.

Casey J., 1989, *The History of the Family*, Oxford, Basil Blackwell.

Castells M., 1983, *The City and the Grassroots*, London, Arnold.

Castells M., 1984, 'New technologies and spatial structure in the United States', unpublished paper given at the International Workshop, *Cities and their Environment*, Bratsk-Irkutsk, USSR.

Castells M., 1985, 'High technology, economic restructuring, and the urban-regional process in the United States', in M. Castells (ed.), *High Technology, Space, and Society*, Beverly Hills and London, SAGE Publications, 11–40.

Castells M., 1989, *The Informational City*, Oxford, Basil Blackwell.

Castles S., Booth H. and Wallace T., 1984, *Here for Good*, London, Pluto Press.

Castronovo V., 1975, 'La storia economica', in *Storia d'Italia*, vol. IV. I, Turin, Einaudi.

Catanzaro R. (ed.), 1979, *L'imprenditore assistito*, Bologna, Il Mulino.

Catanzaro R., 1987, 'Imprenditori della violenza e mediatori sociali. Un'ipotesi di interpretazione della mafia', *Polis*, 2.

Catanzaro R. (ed.), (1989), *Società, politica e cultura nel Mezzogiorno*, Milan, Angeli.

CENSIS, ISFOL and CNEL, 1976, *L'occupazione occulta*, Rome, CENSIS.

Cetro R., 1978, 'Lavoro a domicilio a Pomigliano d'Arco', *Inchiesta*, 33, 57–65.

Chase-Dunn C., 1989, *Global Formation. Structures of the World-Economy*, Oxford, Basil Blackwell.

Chayanov A. V., 1925/1987, *The Theory of Peasant Economy*, new edn, Madison, Wisconsin University Press.

Cheal D., 1988, *The Gift Economy*, London and New York, Routledge.

Chiarello F. (ed.), 1985, *Sistema economico, bisogni sociali e occupazione, il doppio lavoro nell'area barese*, Bologna, Il Mulino.

Choate P., 1986, *The High-Flex Society*, New York, Knopf.

Clawson D., 1980, *Bureaucracy and the Labour Process*, New York, Monthly Review Press.

Clegg S., Boreham P. and Dow G., 1986, *Class, Politics and the Economy*, London, Routledge and Kegan Paul.

Close P. and Collins R. (eds), 1985, *Family and Economy in Modern Society*, London, Macmillan.

Cloward R. and Piven F., 1971, *Regulating the Poor*, New York, Pantheon.

Clutterbuck D., 1979, 'Moonlighting comes out of the shadows', *International Management*, (June), 27–31.

Cohen J. L., 1982, *Class and Civil Society. The Limits of Marxian Critical Theory*, Amherst, University of Massachusetts Press.

Colbjornsen T., 1986, *Dividers in the Labor Market*, Oslo, Norwegian University Press.

Collidà A. 1979. 'Città Meridionale e sovraurbanizzazione', in Accornero A. and

Adriani S. (eds), *Gli anni '70 nel Mezzogiorno*, Bari, De Donato, 168–221.

Cornuel D., 1980, '*Propositions pour une theorie duale de l'economie informelle*', unpublished paper, University of Lille.

Cousins C., 1987, *Controlling Social Welfare*, Brighton, Wheatsheaf.

Coward R., 1983, *Patriarchal Precedents*, London, Routledge and Kegan Paul.

Coxon A. P. M. and Davies P. M. with Jones C. L., 1986, *Images of Social Stratification. Occupational Structures and Class*, London, Beverly Hills, Newbury Park and New Delhi, SAGE Publications.

Crompton R. and Mann M. (eds), 1986a, *Gender and Stratification*, Cambridge, Polity Press.

Crompton R. and Mann M., 1986b, 'Introduction', in Crompton and Mann (eds), 1986a, 1–10.

Crow G., 1989, 'The use of the concept of 'strategy' in recent sociological literature', *Sociology*, 23, no. 1, 1–24.

Cummings S., 1980, *Self-help in America: Patterns of Minority Economic Development*, Port Washington, NY, Kennikat Press.

Dale Tussing A., 1975, *Poverty in a Dual Economy*, New York, St Martin's Press.

Davis H. and Scase R., 1985, *Western Capitalism and State Socialism*, Oxford, Basil Blackwell.

Davis J., 1972, 'Gifts and the UK economy', *Man*, 7, no. 3, 408–29.

De Marco C. and Talamo M., 1976, *Lavoro nero*, Milan, Mazzotta.

Deakin N., 1987, *The Politics of Welfare*, London, Methuen.

Deem R. and Salaman G. (eds), 1985, *Work, Culture and Society*, Milton Keynes and Philadelphia, Open University Press.

Dezsenyi-Gueullette A., 1981, 'The parallel economy in the East: the Hungarian case', *Revue d'Etudes Comparatives Est-Ouest* (June), 25–39.

Dickinson J. and Russell B., 1986, *Family, Economy and State*, Toronto, Garamond Press.

Djilas M., 1966, *The New Class: An Analysis of the Communist System*, London, Allen and Unwin.

Doeringer P. and Piore M. J., 1971, *Internal Labour Markets and Manpower Analysis*, Lexington, MA, D. C. Heath.

Dore R., 1986, *Flexible Rigidities. Industrial Policy and Structural Adjustment in the Japanese Economy 1970–80*, London, The Athlone Press.

Dore R., 1987, *Taking Japan Seriously. A Confucian Perspective on Leading Economic Issues*, London, The Athlone Press.

Douglass M., 1988, 'Transnational capital and urbanization on the Pacific Rim: an introduction', *International Journal of Urban and Regional Research*, 12, no. 3, 343–55.

Drewnowski J. (ed.), 1982, *Crisis in the East European Economy: the Spread of the Polish Disease*, London, Croom Helm.

Durkheim E., 1984, *The Division of Labour in Society*, London, Macmillan.

Edwards R. C., 1979, *Contested Terrain*, New York, Basic Books.

Edwards R. C., Reich M. and Gordon D. M. (eds), 1975, *Labour Market Segmentation*, Lexington, MA, D. C. Heath.

EEC, 1989a, *Employment in Europe*, Luxembourg, EEC.

EEC, 1989b, *Underground Economy and Irregular Forms of Employment: Synthesis Report and Country Monographies*, Brussels, ECC duplicated.

Eisenstadt S. N. and Lemarchand R. (eds), 1981, *Political Clientelism: Patronage and Development*, London, SAGE Publications.

Eisenstadt S. N. and Roniger L., 1984, *Patrons, Clients and Friends. Interpersonal Relations and the Structure of Trust in Society*, Cambridge, Cambridge University Press.

Eisenstadt S. N., Roniger L. and Seligman L., 1987, *Centre Formation, Protest Movements and Class Structure in Europe and the United States*, London, Frances Pinter.

Elson D., 1988, 'Market socialism or socialization of the market?', *New Left Review*, 172, 3–44.

Engels F., 1969, *The Condition of the Working Class in England*, London, Panther.

Epstein D. G., 1976, *Brasilia, Plan and Reality*, Berkeley, University of California Press.

Esping Andersen G., 1990, *The Three Worlds of Welfare Capitalism*, Cambridge, Polity Press.

EUROSTAT (Statistical office of the European Communities), 1982, *Multiple Job Holders*, official publication of the European Community, Luxembourg.

Evers H. D. et al., 1984, 'Subsistence reproduction: a framework for analysis', in Smith et al., 1984, 23–36.

Fagen R. R., Deere C. D. and Corragio J. L. (eds), 1986, *Transition and Development: Problems of Third World Socialism*, New York, Monthly Review Press.

Fagin L. and Little M., 1984, *The Forsaken Families*, Harmondsworth, Penguin.

Farber B., 1971, *Kinship and Class*, New York and London, Basic Books.

Feige E. L., 1979, 'How big is the irregular economy', *Challenge*, 5/13.

Feige E. L. (ed.), 1989, *The Underground Economies. Tax Evasion and Information Distortion*, Cambridge, Cambridge University Press.

Fenstermaker Berk S., 1985, *The Gender Factory. The Apportionment of Work in American Households*, New York and London, Plenum Press.

Ferman L. A. and Berndt L., 1981, 'The irregular economy', in Henry, 1981, 26–42.

Ferman L. A., Berndt L. and Selo E., 1978, 'Analysis of the irregular economy: cash flow in the informal sector', unpublished report to the Bureau of Employment and Training, Michigan Department of Labor and Industrial Relations, Wayne State University, Ann Arbor, Michigan.

Ferman L. A. and Ferman P. R., 1973, 'The structural underpinnings of irregular economy', *Poverty and Human Resources Abstracts* 9, (March), 13–17.

Ferman L. A., Henry S. and Hoyman E., 1987, *The Informal Economy. The Annals of the American Academy of Political and Social Science*, 493, London and Beverly Hills, SAGE Publications.

Fernandez-Kelly M. P., 1983, *For We Are Sold, I and My People. Women and Industry in Mexico's Frontier*, Albany, NY, State University of New York Press.

Ferrera M., 1984, *Il Welfare State in Italia*, Bologna, Il Mulino.

Fineman S. (ed.), 1987, *Unemployment: Personal and Social Consequences*, London, Tavistock.

Flora P. and Heidenheimer A. J., 1981 (eds), *The Development of Welfare States in Europe and America*, New Brunswick and London, Transaction Books.

Fluitman F. (ed.), 1989, *Training for Work in the Informal Sector*, Geneva, International Labour Office

Fortunato R., Liguori, M. and Veneziano, S., 1986, 'Il lavoro irregolare del sommerso alle istituzioni: le vertenze di lavoro nell'area napoletana', *Quaderni IRES CGIL-Campania*, no. 2, 57–92.

Foudi R., Stankiewicz F. and Vaneecloo N., 1982, 'Chomeurs et économie informelle', in *Travail noir, productions domestiques et entr'aide. Observation du changement social*, Lille, Action Thématique Programme du Conseil National Recherches Sociales, Lille.

Fox B. (ed.), 1980, *Hidden in the Household. Women's Domestic Labour Under Capitalism*, Toronto, Women's Educational Press.

Fox Piven F. and Cloward R. A., 1979, *Poor People's Movements. Why They Succeed, How They Fail*, New York, Vintage Books.

Fox Piven F. and Cloward R. A., 1982, *The New Class War: Reagan's Attack on the Welfare State and its Consequences*, New York, Pantheon.

Friedland W., 1980, *Manufacturing Green Gold*, Berkeley, University of California Press.

Friedland W., Buttel F., Busch L. and Rudy A. (eds), forthcoming, *The New Political Economy of Advanced Capitalist Agriculture*, Boulder, COLO, Westview Publishers.

Friedman K., 1984, 'Households as income-pooling units', in Smith et al., 1984, 37–55.

Friedmann H., 1979, 'World market, state, and family farm: social bases of household production in the era of wage labour', *Comparative Studies in Society and History*, 20, 545–86.

Friedmann H., 1980, 'Household production and the national economy: concepts for the analysis of agrarian formation', *The Journal of Peasant Studies*, 7, no. 2, 158–84.

Friedmann H., 1982, 'The political economy of food: the rise and fall of the postwar international food order', *American Journal of Sociology*, 88, Supplement, 248–86.

Friedmann H. and McMichael P., 1988, *The World-Historical Development of Agriculture: Western Agriculture in Comparative Perspective*, London, Research Committee on the Sociology of Agriculture, Working Paper Series, University College London.

Friedmann J., 1987, *Planning in the Public Domain: From Knowledge to Action*, Princeton, NJ, Princeton University Press.

Friedmann J. and Salguero M., 1988, 'The barrio economy and collective self-empowerment in Latin America: a framework and agenda for research', in Smith M. P., 1988, 3–37.

Friedmann J. and Wolff G., 1982, *World City Formation*, Los Angeles, UCLA, Comparative Urbanization Studies.

Frobel H., Heinrichs J. and Kreye O., 1980, *The New International Division of Labour*, Cambridge, Cambridge University Press.

Fuà G. and Zacchia C. (eds), 1983, *Industrializzazione senza fratture*, Bologna, Il Mulino.

Fuchs R., 1968, *The Service Economy*, New York, National Bureau of Economic Research.

Fukutake T., 1982, *The Japanese Social Structure. Its Evolution in the Modern Century*, Tokyo, University of Tokyo Press.

Gaertner W. and Wenig A., 1985, *The Economics of the Shadow Economy*, New York and Heidelberg, Springer.

Galarza E., 1977, *Farm Workers and Agri-business in California, 1947–60*, Notre Dame, Ind., Notre Dame University Press.

Galasi P. and Sik E., 1988, 'Invisible incomes in Hungary', *Social Justice*, 15, nos. 3–4, 160–78.

Galasi P. and Sziraczki G. (eds), 1985, *Labour Market and Second Economy in Hungary*, Frankfurt and New York, Campus Verlag.

Gallie D. (ed), 1988, *Employment in Britain*, Oxford, Basil Blackwell.

Gallino, L. (ed.) 1982, *Occupati e bioccupati, il doppio lavoro nell'area torinese*, Bologna, Il Mulino.

Gallino L., 1983, 'Ripensare l'economia', *Inchiesta*, nos. 59–60 (January-June), 1–25.

Gallino, L. (ed.), 1985, *Il lavoro e il suo doppio: seconda occupazione e politiche del lavoro in Italia*, Bologna, Il Mulino.

Gans H., 1968, 'Urbanism and suburbanism as ways of life', in Pahl R. E., *Readings in Urban Sociology*, London, Pergamon.

Gappert G. and Rose H. (eds), 1975, *The Social Economy of Cities*, Beverly Hills and London, SAGE Publications.

Gardiner J., 1976, 'Political economy of domestic labour in capitalist society', in Barker D. L. and Allen S. (eds), *Dependence and Exploitation in Work and Marriage*, London, Longman, 109–20.

Garnsey E., Rubery J. and Williamson F., 1985, 'Labour market structure and work-force divisions', in Deem and Salaman, 1985, 40–76.

Garofoli G. (ed.), 1978, *Ristrutturazione industriale e territorio*, Milano, Angeli.

Gaughan J. P. and Ferman L. A., 1987, 'Toward an understanding of informal economy', in Ferman et al., 1987. 15–25.

Geiger T., 1949, *Die Klassengesellschaft im Schmelztiegel*, Cologne, Kiepenheuer and Witsch Verlag.

Gellner E., 1973/1987, *The Concept of Kinship*, Oxford, Basil Blackwell.

Gellner E., 1988, *State and Society in Soviet Thought*, Oxford, Basil Blackwell.

Gellner E. and Waterbury J. (eds), 1977, *Patrons and Clients in Mediterranean Societies*, London, Duckworth.

George S., 1976, *How the Other Half Dies: The Real Reasons for World Hunger*, Harmondsworth, Penguin.

Gerry C., 1974, *Petty Producers and the Urban Economy: A Case Study of Dakar*, Geneva, World Employment Working Paper, International Labour Office.

Gerry C., 1987, 'Developing economies and the informal sector in historical perspective', in Ferman et al., 1987, 100–19.

Gershuny J. I., 1977, 'Post-industrial society: the myth of the service sector', *Futures*, 9 (April), 103–14.

Gershuny J. I., 1978, *After Industrial Society: The Emerging Self-service Economy*, London, Macmillan.

Gershuny J. I., 1979, 'The informal economy: its role in industrial society', *Futures*, 11 (February), 3–15.

Gershuny J. I., 1983, *Social Innovation and the Division of Labour*, Oxford, Oxford University Press.

Gershuny, J. I., 1988, 'Time, technology and the informal economy', in Pahl, 1988a, 579–97.

Gershuny J. and Miles I., 1983, *The New Service Economy*, London, Frances Pinter.

Gershuny J. I. and Pahl R. E., 1979, 'Work outside employment: some preliminary speculations', *New Universities Quarterly*, 34, no. 1, Winter, 120–35.

Gershuny J. I. and Pahl R. E., 1981, 'Work outside employment', in Henry, 1981, 73–88.

Gershuny J. I. and Thomas G. S., 1984, *Changing Times: Activity Patterns in the U.K., 1937–1975*, Oxford, Oxford University Press.

Gerstel N. and Engel Gross H., 1987 (eds), *Families and Work*, Philadephia, Temple University Press.

Giannola A., 1983, 'Delocalizzazione e deindustrializzazione nella città di Napoli', *Quaderni IRES CGIL-Campania*, 1, 57–65.

Giddens A., 1982, *Sociology. A Brief but Critical Introduction*, London, Macmillan.

Giddens A., 1984, *The Condition of Society: Outline of the Theory of Structuration*, Cambridge, Polity Press.

Gilbert A. and Gugler J., 1982, *Cities, Poverty and Development*, Oxford, Oxford University Press.

Gill C., 1985, *Work, Employment and the New Technology*, Cambridge, Polity Press.

Ginatempo, N., 1976, *La città del Sud*, Milan, Mazzotta.

Ginatempo, N., 1983, *Marginalità e riproduzione sociale*, Milan, Giuffrè.

Ginatempo, N. and Fera, G., 1985, *L'autocostruzione spontanea nel Mezzogiorno*, Milan, Angeli.

Giner S., 1985, 'Political economy, legitimation and the state in southern Europe', in Hudson R. and Lewis J. (eds), *Uneven Development in Southern Europe*, London, Methuen.

Glatzer W. and Berger R., 1988, 'Household composition, social network and household production in Germany', in Pahl, 1988a, 513–26.

Goddard V., 1981, 'The leather trade in the Bassi of Naples', *Institute of Development Studies Bulletin*, 12, no. 3, 30–6.

Godelier M., 1980, 'Work and its representations: a research proposal', *History Workshop Journal*, 10, 164–74.

Goffee R. and Scase R., 1987, *Entrepreneurship in Europe*, London, Croom Helm.
Goglio S. (ed), 1982, *Italia: centri e periferie. Analisi regionale e politiche d'intervento*, Milan, Angeli.
Goldthorpe J. H., 1980. *Social Mobility and Class Structure in Modern Britain*, Oxford, Clarendon Press.
Goldthorpe J. E., 1984, *Order and Conflict in Contemporary Capitalism*, Oxford, Oxford University Press.
Goldthorpe J. E., 1987, *Family Life in Western Societies*, Cambridge, Cambridge University Press.
Goldthorpe J. H., Lockwood D., Bechofer F. and Platt J., 1968a, *The Affluent Worker: Industrial Attitudes and Behaviour*, Cambridge, Cambridge University Press.
Goldthorpe J. H., Lockwood D., Bechofer F. and Platt J., 1968b, *The Affluent Worker: Political Attitudes and Behaviour*, Cambridge, Cambridge University Press.
Goldthorpe J. H., Lockwood D., Bechhofer F. and Platt J., 1969, *The Affluent Worker in the Class Structure*, Cambridge, Cambridge University Press.
Goode W., 1963, *World Revolution and Family Patterns*, New York, The Free Press.
Goodman D. and Reddcliff M. R., 1981, *From Peasant to Proletarian: Capitalist Development and Agrarian Transitions*, Oxford, Basil Blackwell.
Goodman D., Sorj B. and Wilkinson J., 1987, *From Farming to Biotechnology. A Theory of Agro-Industrial Development*, Oxford, Basil Blackwell.
Goody J., 1976, *Production and Reproduction. A Comparative Study of the Domestic Domain*, Cambridge, Cambridge University Press.
Goody J., 1983, *The Development of the Family and Marriage in Europe*, Cambridge, Cambridge University Press.
Gordon A., 1988, *The Crisis of Unemployment*, London, Christopher Helm.
Gordon D. M., 1972, *Theories of Poverty and Underemployment*, Lexington, Lexington Books.
Gordon D. M., Edwards R. and Reich M., 1982, *Segmented Work, Divided Workers*, Cambridge, Cambridge University Press.
Gordon R. and Kimball L. M., 1985, *High Technology, Employment, and the Challenges to Education*, Silicon Valley Research Group Monograph, Santa Cruz, University of California.
Gorz A., 1982, *Farewell to the Working Class: An Essay in Post-industrial Socialism*, London, Pluto Press.
Gorz A., 1988, *Critique of Economic Reason*, London and New York, Verso.
Gough, I., 1979, *The Political Economy of the Welfare State*, London, Macmillan.
Gramsci A., 1966, *La Questione meridionale*, Rome, Editori Riuniti.
Granovetter M., 1984, 'Small is bountiful: labour and establishment size', *American Sociological Review*, 49 (June), 323–34.
Granovetter M., 1985, 'Economic action and social structure: the problem of embeddedness', *American Journal of Sociology*, 91, no. 3, 481–510.
Graziani A., 1978, 'The Mezzogiorno in the Italian economy', *Cambridge Journal of Economics*, 2, 355–72.
Graziani A., 1987, 'Mezzogiorno oggi', *Meridiana*, 1, 201–19.

Graziani, A. and Pugliese, E. (eds), 1979, *Investimenti e disoccupazione nel Mezzogiorno*, Bologna, Il Mulino.

Graziano L. (ed.), 1974, *Clientelismo e mutamento politico*, Milan, Angeli.

Graziano L., 1980, *Clientelismo e sistema politico*, Milan, Angeli.

Grieco M., 1987, *Keeping it in the Family. Social Networks and Employment Chance*, London and New York, Tavistock.

Grossman, G. 1977, 'The "second economy" of the USSR', *Problems of Communism*, 26, no. 5, 25–40.

Grossman G. (ed.), 1988, *Studies in the Second Economy of Communist Countries*, Berkeley, University of California Press.

Grossman G. and Treml V. G., 1987, 'Measuring hidden personal incomes in the USSR', in Alessandrini and Dallago, 1987, 285–96.

Gulger J., 1982, 'The urban character of contemporary revolutions', *Studies in Comparative International Development*, 17, no. 2, 60–73.

Gunderson M., Meltz N. M. and Ostry S. (eds), 1987, *Unemployment: International Perspectives*, Toronto, University of Toronto Press.

Gutmann A. (ed.), 1988, *Democracy and the Welfare State*, Princeton, NJ, Princeton University Press.

Gutmann P., 1977, 'The subterranean economy', *Financial Analysis Journal* (November/December), 26, 27 and 34.

Gutmann P., 1978a, 'Are the unemployed, unemployed?', *Financial Analysis Journal* (September/October), 26–9.

Gutmann P., 1987b, 'Professor Gutmann replies', *Financial Analysis Journal* (November/December), 67–9.

Gutmann P., 1979a, 'The subterranean economy', *Taxing and Spending* (April), 4–8.

Gutmann P., 1979b, 'Statistical illusions, mistaken policies, *Challenge* (November/December), 14–17.

Gutmann P., 1980, 'Latest notes from the subterranean economy', *Business and Society Review* (Summer), 25–30.

Habermas J., 1975, *Legitimation Crisis*, Boston, Beacon Press.

Habermas J., 1984, *The Theory of Communicative Action*, vol. I: *Reason and the Rationalization of Society*, Boston, Beacon Press.

Habermas J., 1987, *The Theory of Communicative Action*, vol. II: *Lifeworld and Systems: A Critique of Functionalist Reason*, Boston, Beacon Press.

Hadjimichalis C., 1986, *Uneven Development and Regionalism: State, Territory and Class in Southern Europe*, Beckenham, Croom Helm.

Haller J. S., 1981, *American Medicine in Transition 1840–1910*, Chicago, University of Illinois Press.

Hann C., 1987, 'Worker-peasants in the three worlds', in Shanin, 1987, 114–19.

Harding P. and Jenkins R., 1989, *The Myth of the Hidden Economy*, Milton Keynes and Philadelphia, Open University Press.

Harris C. C., 1983, *The Family and Industrial Society*, London, Allen and Unwin.

Harris C. C. (ed.), 1987, *Redundancy and Recession*, Oxford, Basil Blackwell.

Harris C. and Morris L., 1986, 'Households, labour markets and the position of women', in Crompton and Mann, 1986, 86–96.

Harris O., 1981, 'Households as natural units', in Young K., Walkowitz C. and McCullagh R. (eds), *Of Marriage and the Market: Women's Subordination in International Perspective*, London, CSE Books, 136–55.

Harris R. and Seldon A., 1987, *Welfare without the State: A Quarter-Century of Suppressed Public Choice*, London, The Institute of Economic Affairs.

Harrison J., 1973, 'The political economy of housework', *Bulletin of the Conference of Socialist Economists*, Winter 1973.

Hart K., 1973, 'Informal income opportunities and urban employment in Ghana', *Journal of Modern African Studies*, 11, 61–89.

Hasluck C., 1987, *Urban Unemployment*, Harlow and New York, Longman.

Hathaway D. A., 1987, *Agriculture and the GATT: Rewriting the Rules*, Washington, Institute for International Economics.

Haveman R., Halberstadt V. and Burkhauser R. V., 1984, *Public Policy Toward Disabled Workers: Cross National Analyses of Economic Impacts*, Ithaca, Cornell University Press.

Heertje A. and Barthelemy P., 1984, *L'Economie souterraine*, Paris, Economica.

Heertje A., Allen M. and Cohen H., 1982, *The Black Economy*, London, Pan Books.

Hegedus J., 1987, 'Reconsidering the roles of the state and the market in socialist housing systems', *International Journal of Urban and Regional Research*, 11, no. 1, 79–97.

Hegedus J. and Tosics I., 1983, 'Housing classes and housing policy: some changes in the Budapest housing market', *International Journal of Urban and Regional Research*, 7, no. 4, 467–95.

Heinze R. G., and Olk, T., 1987, 'Development of the informal economy: a strategy for resolving the crisis of the welfare state', *Futures*, June, 189–204.

Henderson J., 1989, *The Globalisation of High Technology Production*, London and New York, Routledge.

Henderson J. and Castells M., 1987 (eds), *Global Restructuring and Territorial Development*, London, SAGE Publications.

Henry S., 1978, *The Hidden Economy: The Context and Control of Borderline Crime*, Oxford, Martin Robertson.

Henry S. (ed), 1981, *Can I Have it in Cash?*, London, Astragel Books.

Heyzer N., 1981, 'Towards a framework of analysis: women and the informal sector', *Institute of Development Studies Bulletin*, 12, no. 3, 3–7.

Himmelweit S. and Mohun S., 1977, 'Domestic labour and capital', *Cambridge Journal of Economics*, 1, 15–31.

Hirsch F., 1976, *Social Limits to Growth*, Cambridge MA, Harvard University Press.

Hirschman A. O., 1970, *Exit, Voice, and Loyalty: Responses to Decline in Firms, Organizations, and States*, Cambridge, MA, Harvard University Press.

Hirschman A. O., 1977, *The Passions and the Interests*, Princeton, NJ, Princeton University Press.

Hirschman A. O., 1982a, 'Rival interpretations of market society: civilizing, destructive or feeble?', *Journal of Economic Literature*, 20, no. 4, 1463–84.

Hirschman A. O., 1982b, *Shifting Involvements: Private Interests and Public Action*, Oxford, Martin Robertson.

Hirschman A. O., 1984, *Getting Ahead Collectively: Grassroots Experiences in Latin America*, New York, Pergamon Press.

Hobsbawm E. J., 1984, *Worlds of Labour, Further Studies in the History of Labour*, London, Weidenfeld and Nicolson.

Hodgson G. M., 1988, *Economics and Institutions*, Cambridge, Polity Press.

Hudson J., 1988, *Unemployment After Keynes*, Hemel Hempstead and New York, Harvester.

Hugon P., 1980, 'Le secteur 'non structure' ou 'informel' des économies des pays du Tiers Monde', *Revue Tiers Monde* (April-June), 3–9.

Humphries J., 1977, 'Class struggle and the persistence of the working-class family', *Cambridge Journal of Economics*, 1, 241–58.

Humphries J., 1977, 'The working class family, women's liberation and class struggle: the case of nineteenth century British history', *Review of Radical Political Economics*, 9, no. 3 (Autumn), 25–41.

Hunt A., 1988, *Women and Paid Work*, London, Macmillan Press.

Illich I., 1981, *Shadow Work*, London, Marion Boyars.

ILO (International Labour Office), 1987a, *World Labour Report*, vols 1–2, Oxford, Oxford University Press.

ILO (International Labour Office), 1987b, *World Labour Report*, vol. 3, Oxford, Oxford University Press.

ILO (International Labour Office), 1989, *Training for Work in the Informal Sector*, ed. Fred Fluitman, Geneva, ILO.

Inchiesta, 1983, Special Issue on Informal Economy, Year XIII, nos. 59–60, January-June.

Inchiesta, 1986, special symposium, *Economia informale, strategie familiari e Mezzogiorno*, 74 (October-December).

Inchiesta, 1990, special monograph issue on regional inequalities in Italy, 88–9.

Ingrosso M., 1979, *Produzione sociale e lavoro domestico*, Milan, Angeli.

IReR (Istituto Regionale di Ricerca della Lombardia), 1983, *L'offerta di lavoro delle donne sposate*, Milan, IReR.

IReR (Istituto Regionale di Ricerca della Lombardia), 1988, *La segmentazione degli iscritti alle liste di disoccupazione in Lombardia: caratteristiche individuali e offerta giovanile*, Milan, Regione Lombardia.

IRES (Istituto Ricerche Economiche e Sociali) Campania, 1987, *Welfate State e Mezzogiorno. Dall'assistenza allo stato sociale*, Naples, Liguori.

IRES CGIL (Istituto ricerche Economiche e Sociali – Confederazione Generale Italiana dei Lavoratori), 1981, *L'evoluzione delle strutture economiche e sociali dell'organizzazione del territorio a Napoli*, Naples, DAEST (Dipartimento Architettura Economia e Studi Territoriali).

IRES (Istituto Ricerche Economiche e Sociali)-*materiali*, 1989a, *La disoccupazione in Italia*, 1, Rome, IRES.

IRES (Istituto Ricerche Economiche e Sociali)-*materiali*, 1989b, *Il collocamento senza lavoro*, 5, Rome, IRES.

Jagannathan N. V., 1987, *Informal Markets in Developing Countries*, New York and Oxford, Oxford University Press.

Jallade J. P. (ed.), 1981, *Employment and Unemployment in Europe*, Stoke-on-Trent, Staffs, Trentham Books.

Jedlowski P., 1986, 'Il servizio informale', in *Inchiesta*, 73–82.

Jedlowski P., forthcoming, 'Professionalism and clientelism: the new middle class in southern Italy', in P. Berger, *The New Class*, New York, Basic Books.

Jelin E., 1974, 'La Bahiana en la fuerza de trabajo: actividad domestica, produccion simple y trabajo asalariado en Salvador, Brazil', *Demografía y Economia*, 7 no. 3.

Jewell K. S., 1988, *Survival of the Black Family*, New York, Westport and London, Praeger.

Johnson N., 1987, *The Welfare State in Transition*, Brighton, Wheatsheaf.

Joyce P. (ed.), 1987, *The Historical Meanings of Work*, Cambridge, Cambridge University Press.

Kahn J. S., 1980, 'Small-scale enterprise and petty commodity production on the periphery: a discussion paper', University College, London, unpublished.

Kahn J. S. and Llobera J. (eds), 1981, *The Anthropology of Pre-capitalist Societies*, London, Macmillan.

Karlechevsky-Bulport A., 1978, 'Travail domestique et famille du capitalisme', *Critque de l'Economie Politique*, 3 (April, June), 3–23.

Katznelson I. and Zolberg A. R. (eds), 1986, *Working-Class Formation. Nineteenth-Century Patterns in Western Europe and the United States*, Princeton, NJ, Princeton University Press.

Keane J. (ed.), 1988, *Civil Society and the State*, London and New York, Verso.

Kerr C., 1950, 'Labour markets: their character and consequences', *American Economic Review, Papers and Proceedings*, 40, no. 2 (May), 278–91.

Kerr C., 1954, 'The balkanization of labor markets', in Bakke E. W. and Hauser P. M. (eds), *Labor Mobility and Economic Opportunity*, London, MIT Press, 92–110.

Kerr C., Dunlop T., Harbison F. and Myers C., 1960, *Industrialism and the Industrial Man*, Cambridge, MA, Harvard University Press.

Keynes M., Coleman D. A. and Didsdale N. H. (eds), 1988, *The Political Economy of Health and Welfare*, Basingstoke and London, Macmillan Press.

Klein R. and O'Higgins M. (eds), 1985, *The Future of Welfare*, Oxford, Basil Blackwell.

Kloppenburg J. R. Jr., 1988, *The First Seed: The Political Economy of Plant Biotechnology*, New York, Cambridge University Press.

Kohn M. L. (ed.), 1989, *Cross-National Research in Sociology*, London, SAGE Publications.

Konrad G. and Szelenyi I., 1977, 'Social conflicts of under-urbanization', in Harloe M. (ed.), *Captive Cities*, New York, Wiley, 157–74.

Konrad G. and Szelenyi, I., 1979, *Intellectuals on the Road to Class Power*, Brighton, Harvester.

Korpi W., 1980, 'Social policies, strategies and distributional conflict in capitalist democracies', *West European Politics*, 3, 296–316.

Kuhn A. and Wolpe A. M. (eds), 1978, *Feminism and Materialism: Women and Modes of Production*, London, Routledge and Kegan Paul.

Kuttner B., 1983, 'The declining middle', *The Atlantic Monthly* (July), 60–72.

Lane, D., 1985, *Soviet Economy and Society*, Oxford, Basil Blackwell.

Lane, D. (ed.), 1988, *Elites and Political Power in The USSR*, London, Allen and Unwin.

Lane J. E. (ed.), 1985, *State and Market. The Politics of the Public and the Private*, London, SAGE Publications

Lang K. and Leonard J. S. (eds), 1987, *Unemployment and the Structure of Labor Markets*, Oxford, Basil Blackwell.

Lange P. and Regini M., 1987, *Stato e regolazione sociale*, Bologna, Il Mulino.

Lash S. and Urry J., 1987, *The End of Organized Capitalism*, Cambridge, Polity Press.

Lee P. and Raban C., 1988, *Welfare Theory and Social Policy. Reform or Revolution?*, London and New Delhi, SAGE Publications.

Levine D., 1977, *Family Formation in an Age of Nascent Capitalism*, New York, Academic Press.

Lewis J. (ed.), 1977, *Peasant Revolution and Communist Revolution in Asia*, Stanford, Stanford University Press.

Light I., 1972, *Ethnic Enterprise in America*, Berkeley, Los Angeles and London, University of California Press.

Light I., 1979, 'Disadvantaged minorities in self-employment', *International Journal of Comparative Sociology*, 20, 31–45.

Light I., 1983, *Cities in World Perspective*, New York, Macmillan.

Light I., 1984, 'Immigrant and ethnic enterprise in North America', *Ethnic and Racial Studies*, 7, 195–216.

Light I. and Bonacich E., 1988, *Immigrant Entrepreneurs: Koreans in Los Angeles 1965–1982*, Berkeley, Los Angeles and London, University of California Press.

Liguori M. and Veneziano S., 1982, *Disoccupati a Napoli*, Rome, ESI.

Liguori M. and Veneziano S., 1986, 'Dal sommerso al . . . sommerso attraverso le istituzioni', in *Inchiesta*, 1986, 93–103.

Lindblom C. E., 1977, *Politics and Markets*, New York, Basic Books.

Lipietz A., 1987, *Mirages and Miracles. The Crises of Global Fordism*, London, Verso.

Lipietz A., 1989, 'The Debt Problem, European integration and the new phase of world crisis', *New Left Review*, 178, 37–50.

Litwak E., 1960, 'Occupational mobility and extended family cohesion', *American Sociological Review*, 25, no.1, 9–21.

Lockwood D., 1988, 'The weakest link in the chain? Some comments on the Marxist theory of action', in Rose D., 1988, 57–97.

Lomnitz L., 1977, *Networks and Marginality: Life in a Mexican Shantytown*, New York, Academic Press.

Lowenthal M. D., 1975, 'The social economy in urban working class communities', in Gappert and Rose, 1975, 447–69.

Lowenthal M. D., 1981, 'Non-market transactions in an urban community', in Henry 1981, 90–104.

Luhmann N., 1979, *Trust and Power*, New York, Wiley.

Luhmann N., 1982, *The Differentation of Society*, New York, Columbia University Press.

Lyon L., 1987, *The Community in Urban Society*, Chicago, The Dorsey Press.

MacDonald L. and MacDonald J. S., 1977, *People of the Plan: Ciudad Guayana 1965 and 1975*, London, Centre for Environmental Studies.

Malinvaud E., 1984, *Mass Unemployment*, Oxford, Basil Blackwell.

Mamberti Pedullà C., Pascarella C. and Abbate C., 1987, 'New estimates of the employed population in the National Accounts. Methodological concepts and results', run off by ISTAT (Italian Government Statistical Office).

Manchin R. and Szelenyi I., 1987, 'Social policy under state socialism: market redistribution and social inequalities in East European socialist societies', in Rein et al., 1987, 102–39.

Mann C., 1987, 'Worker-peasants in the Three Worlds', in Shanin, 1987, 114–20.

Markusen A., Hall P. and Glasmeier A., 1986, *High Tech America: The What, How, Where and Why of the Sunrise Industries*, Boston and London, Allen and Unwin.

Marrese M., 1981, 'The evolution of wage regulation in Hungary; in Hare P., Radice H. K. and Swain N. (eds), *Hungary: A Decade of Reform*, London, Allen and Unwin.

Mars G. and Altman Y., 1987, *Private Enterprise in the USSR: The Case of Soviet Georgia*, Aldershot, Gower.

Marsden D., 1986, *The End of Economic Man? Custom and Competition in Labour Markets*, Brighton, Wheatsheaf.

Marshall G., Rose D., Newby H. and Vogler C., 1988, *Social Class in Modern Britain*, London, Boston, Sydney and Wellington, Unwin Hyman.

Marshall T. H., 1961, 'The Welfare State: a sociological interpretation', *Archives of European Sociology*, 2, 284–300.

Marshall T. H., 1963, *Sociology at the Crossroad*, London, Heinemann.

Marshall T. H., 1964, *Class, Citizenship and Social Development*, New York, Doubleday.

Marshall T. H., 1965, *Social Policy*, London, Hutchinson.

Martin G. W. and Beittel M., 1987, 'The hidden abode of reproduction: conceptualizing households in Southern Africa', *Development and Change*, 18, 215–34.

Martin W. (ed.), 1972, *Comparative Development in Social Welfare*, London, Allen and Unwin.

Martinelli F., 1985, 'Public policy and industrial development in southern Italy: anatomy of a dependent industry', *International Journal of Urban and Regional Research*, 9, no. 1, 47–81.

Marx K., 1972, *Grundrisse*, Harmondsworth and London, Penguin/New Left Books.

Marx K., 1973, 'The eighteenth Brumaire of Louis Bonaparte', in *Surveys from Exile*, Political Writings, vol. II, London, Penguin.

Marx K., 1976, *Capital*, vol. I. 2, Harmondsworth and London, Penguin/New Left Books.

Massey D., 1984, *Spatial Division of Labour*, London, Macmillan.

Massey D. and Meegan R., 1982, *The Anatomy of Job Loss: The How, Why and Where of Employment Decline*, London, Methuen.

Mattera P., 1985, *Off the Books*, New York, St Martin's Press.

Meier U., 1989, 'Equality without limits? Women's work in the socialist society of the German Democratic Republic, *International Sociology*, 4, no. 1, 37–50.

Meillassoux C., 1981, *Maidens, Meal and Money*, Cambridge, Cambridge University Press.

Mellor J. W. and Desai, G. M. (eds), 1985, *Agricultural Change and Rural Poverty*, Baltimore and London, Johns Hopkins University Press.

Melotti U., Aimi A. and Ziglio L., 1985, *La nuova immigrazione a Milano*, Milan, Mazzotta.

Menefee Singh A. and Kelles-Viitanen A., 1987, *Invisible Hands*, New Delhi, Newbury and London, SAGE Publications.

Merton R. K., 1957, *Social Theory and Social Structure*, Glencoe, IL, The Free Press.

Meyer D. R. and Kyonghee M., 1988, 'Concentration and specialization of manufacturing core and peripheral cities during rapid industrialization: Korea, 1960–1970', in Smith, M. P., 1988, 38–61.

Michel A., 1978, *Les Femmes dans la société marchande*, Paris, PUF.

Michelotti K., 1975, 'Multiple jobholders in May 1975', *Monthly Labour Review* (November), 56–61.

Michels R., 1915/1962, *Political Parties*, New York, The Free Press.

Mies M., 1986, *Patriarchy and Accumulation on a World Scale: Women in the International Division of Labour*, London, Zed Books.

Milardo R. M. (ed.), 1988, *Families and Social Networks*, London, SAGE Publications.

Miliband R., 1989, *Divided Societies: Class Struggle in Contemporary Capitalism*, Oxford, Oxford University Press.

Miller G. H., 1972, *Multiple Jobholding in Wichita*, Wichita, Kansas, Western State University.

Mills C. W., 1951, *White Collars: The American Middle Class*, New York, Oxford University Press.

Mingione E., 1977b, *Relazione finale della ricerca sui poli di sviluppo industriale nel Meridione*, Rome, Centro per la Formazione nel Mezzogiorno.

Mingione E. (ed.), 1977a, *Ricerca sociologica sui poli di sviluppo industriale nel Meridione*, 6 vols, duplicated, Rome, Centro per la Formazione nel Mezzogiorno.

Mingione E. (ed.), 1981, *Classi sociali e agricoltura meridionale: contraddizioni e prospettive*, Milan, Giuffrè.

Mingione E., 1985, 'Social reproduction of the surplus labour force: the case of southern Italy', in Redclift and Mingione, 1985, 14–54.

Mingione E., 1986, 'Ristrutturazione del welfare e politiche sociali nel Mezzogiorno', Politica ed Economia, 6, 65–9.

Mingione E., 1987, 'The urban question in socialist developing countries', in Forbes D. and Thrift N. (eds), The Socialist Third World, Oxford, Basil Blackwell, 27–52.

Mingione E., 1988a, 'Problems and prospects of the welfare state in Italy', in Brown, 1988, 211–31.

Mingione E., 1988b, 'Work and informal activities in urban southern Italy', in Pahl, 548–78.

Mingione E., 1989, 'Note per un'analisi delle classi sociali', in Catanzaro, 1989, 43–77.

Mingione E. and Pugliese E., 1988, 'La questione urbana e rurale: tra superamento teorico e problemi di confini incerti', La Critica Sociologica, 85, 27–50.

Missiakoulis S., Pahl R. E. and Taylor-Gooby P., 1986, 'Households, work and politics: some implications of the divisions of labour in formal and informal production', International Journal of Sociology and Social Policy, 6, no. 3, 28–40.

Mitchell M., 1972, The Growth of Terra, London, Architectural Association.

Mitchell M., 1975, Shanty Cash, London, Architectural Association.

Mizruchi E. H., 1987, Regulating Society: Beguines, Bohemians, and Other Marginals, Chicago and London, The University of Chicago Press.

Molyneux M., 1979, 'Beyond the domestic labour debate', New Left Review, 116, 3–27.

Moore B., 1969, Social Origins of Dictatorship and Democracy, London, Penguin.

Morris L., 1988, 'Employment, the household and social networks', in Gallie, 1988, 376–405.

Morris L. D., 1987, 'The household in the labour market', in Harris, 1987, 127–40.

Moser C., 1978, 'Informal sector or petty commodity production? Dualism or dependence in urban development?', World Development, 6, nos. 9/10, 1041–64.

Moser C., 1981, 'Surviving in the suburbs', Women and the Informal Sector: Institute of Development Studies Bulletin, 12, no. 3 (July), 19–29.

Moser C. and Young K., 1981, 'Women of the working poor', Women and the Informal Sector: Institute of Development Studies Bulletin, no. 12, 3 (July), 54–62.

Mottura G., 1989, 'La "persistenza" secolare. Appunti su agricoltura contadina ed agricoltura familiare nelle società industriali', Materiali di discussione, 38, Modena, Università degli Studi.

Mottura G. and Mingione E., 1989, 'Agriculture and society: remarks on transformations and new social profiles in the case of Italy', Agriculture and Human Values, 47–58.

Murray P. and Szelenyi I., 1984, 'The city in the transition to socialism', International Journal of Urban and Regional Research, 8, no. 1, 90–107.

Musil J., 1987, 'Housing policy and the sociospatial structure of cities in a socialist country – the example of Prague', *International Journal of Urban and Regional Research*, 11, no. 1, 27–36.

Nardin G. (ed.), 1987, *La Benetton: strategia e struttura di un'impresa di successo*, Rome, Edizioni Lavoro.

Nash J. and Fernandez Kelly M. P. (eds), 1983, *Women, Men, and the International Division of Labor*, Albany, State University of New York Press.

Netting R., Wilk R. R. and Arnould E. J. (eds), 1984, *Households: Comparative and Historical Studies of the Domestic Group*, Berkeley, Los Angeles and London, University of California Press.

Nippon, 1989, *A Charted Survey of Japan, 1989/90*, Tokyo, Kokusei-sha Corporation.

Nishikawa S. (ed.), 1980, *The Labor Market in Japan*, Tokyo, University of Tokyo Press.

Nocifora E., 1978, 'Poles of development and the Southern Question', *International Journal of Urban and Regional Research*, 2, no. 2, 361–87.

Norton A. J., 1983, 'Keeping up with households', *American Demographics*, 5 (February), 17–21.

Nove A., 1978, *Political Economy and Soviet Socialism*, London, Allen and Unwin.

Nove A., 1986, *Socialism, Economics and Development*, London, Boston and Sydney, Allen and Unwin.

Oakely A., 1985, *The Sociology of Housework*, Oxford, Basil Blackwell.

O'Connor J., 1973, *The Fiscal Crisis of the State*, New York, St Martin's Press.

O'Connor J., 1974, *The Corporation and the State*, New York, Harper.

O'Connor J., 1984, *Accumulation Crisis*, New York and Oxford, Basil Blackwell.

O'Connor J., 1987, *The Meaning of Crisis: A Theoretical Introduction*, New York and Oxford, Basil Blackwell.

OECD (Organization for Economic Co-operation and Development), 1986, *Flexibility in the Labour Market: The Current Debate*, Paris, OECD.

Offe C., 1984, *Contradictions of the Welfare State* (ed. by Michael Keane), London, Hutchinson.

Offe C., 1985, *Disorganized Capitalism: Contemporary Transformations of Work and Politics*, Cambridge, Polity Press.

O'Higgins M., 1980, *Measuring the Hidden Economy: A Review of Evidence and Methodologies*, London, Outer Circle Policy Unit.

Paci M. (ed.), 1978, *Capitalismo e classi sociali in Italia*, Bologna, Il Mulino.

Paci M. (ed.), 1980, *Famiglia e mercato del lavoro in una economia periferica*, Milan, Angeli.

Paci M., 1982, *La struttura sociale italiana*, Bologna, Il Mulino.

Paci M. (ed.), 1985, *Stato, mercato, occupazione*, Bologna, Il Mulino.

Paci M., 1989, *Pubblico e privato nei moderni sistemi di Welfare*, Naples, Liguori.

Pahl J., 1989, *Money and Marriage*, London, Macmillan.

Pahl R. E., 1980, 'Employment, work and the domestic division of labour', *International Journal of Urban and Regional Research*, 4, no. 1, 1–20.

Pahl R. E., 1984, *Division of Labour*, Oxford and New York, Basil Blackwell.

Pahl R. E., 1985, 'The politics of work', *Political Quarterly*, 13 (Autumn), 331–45.

496 BIBLIOGRAPHY

Pahl, R. E., 1986, 'Social polarization and the economic crisis', Mimeo, Canterbury, University of Kent.

Pahl R. E., 1987, 'Does jobless mean workless? Unemployment and informal work', in Ferman et al., 1987, 34–46.

Pahl R. E. (ed.), 1988a, *On Work: Historical, Comparative and Theoretical Approaches*, Oxford and New York, Basil Blackwell.

Pahl R. E., 1988b, 'Some remarks on informal work, social polarisation and the social structure', *International Journal of Urban and Regional Research*, 12, no. 2, 247–67.

Pahl R. E., 1989a, 'From "informal economy" to "forms of work": cross national patterns and trends', in Scase, 1989, 90–119.

Pahl R. E., 1989b, 'Is the emperor naked? Some questions on the adequacy of sociological theory in urban and regional research', *International Journal of Urban and Regional Research*, 13, no. 4, 709–20.

Pahl R. E. and Wallace C., 1985, 'Household work strategies in economic recession', in Redclift and Mingione, 1985, 189–227.

Pahl R. E. and Wallace C., 1988, 'Neither angels in marble nor rebels in red: privatisation and working-class consciousness', in Rose D., 1988, 127–49.

Pampel F. C. and Williamson J. B., 1989, *Age, Class, Politics and the Welfare State*, Cambridge, Cambridge University Press.

Papola T. S., 1981, *Urban Informal Sector in a Developing Economy*, New Delhi, Vikas.

Parkin F., 1979, *Marxism and Class Theory*, London, Tavistock.

Parsons T., 1949, *The Structure of Social Action*, Glencoe, IL, The Free Press.

Parsons T., 1951, *The Social System*, Glencoe, IL, The Free Press.

Parsons T. and Bales R. F., 1955, *Family Socialization and Interaction Process*, New York, The Free Press.

Paul E. F., Miller F. D. Jr., Paul J. and Greenberg D., 1988, *Socialism*, Oxford, Basil Blackwell.

Peet R. (ed.), 1987, *International Capitalism and Industrial Restructuring*, Boston, Allen and Unwin.

Perry R., Dean K. and Brown B., 1986, *Counterurbanisation*, Norwich, Geo Books.

Pichierri A., 1989, *Strategie contro il declino*, Turin, Rosenberg and Sellier.

Pickvance C. G., 1977, 'From "social base" to "social force": some analytical issues in the study of urban protest', in Harloe M. (ed.), *Captive Cities*, London and New York, Wiley.

Pinnarò G. and Pugliese E., 1985, 'Informalization and social resistance: the case of Naples', in Redclift and Mingione, 1985, 228–47.

Piore M. J. (ed), 1979a, *Inflation and Unemployment: Institutionalist and Structuralist Views*, White Plains, NY, M. E. Sharpe.

Piore M. J., 1979b, *Birds of Passage*, New York and Cambridge, Cambridge University Press.

Piore M. J. and Sabel C. F., 1984, *The Second Industrial Divide: Possibilities for Prosperity*, New York, Basic Books.

Piperno A., 1984, 'La politica sanitaria', in Ascoli, 1984, 153–84.

Pitrou A., 1978, *Vivre sans famille? Les Solidarités familiales dans le monde d'aujourd'hui*, Toulouse, privately printed.

Poggi G., 1983, *Calvinism and the Capitalism Spirit: Max Weber's Protestant Ethic*, London, Macmillan.

Polanyi, K., 1944/1975, *The Great Transformation*, Boston, Beacon Press.

Polanyi K., 1957, 'The economy as instituted process', in Polanyi K., Arensberg C. and Pearson H. (eds), *Trade and Market in the Early Empires*, Glencoe, IL, The Free Press.

Polanyi K., 1977, *The Livelihood of Man*, New York, Academic Press.

Porter M., 1983, *Home, Work and Class Consciousness*, Manchester, Manchester University Press.

Portes A., 1978, 'The informal sector and the world economy: notes on the structure of subsidised labour', *Institute of Development Studies Bulletin*, 9, no. 4, June, 35–40.

Portes A., 1983, 'The informal sector: definition, controversy, and relation to national development', *Review*, 7, no. 1, 151–74.

Portes A. and Bach R., 1985, *Latin Journey: Cuban and Mexican Immigrants in the United States*, Berkeley, Los Angeles and London, University of California Press.

Portes A., Castells M. and Benton L. A., 1989, *The Informal Economy: Studies in Advanced and Less Developed Countries*, Baltimore and London, The Johns Hopkins University Press.

Portes A. and Sassen-Koob S., 1987, 'Making it underground: comparative material on the informal sector in Western market economies', *American Journal of Sociology*, 93, no. 1, 30–61.

Portes A. and Walton J., 1981, *Labor, Class and the International System*, New York, Academic Press.

Poulantzas N., 1979, *Classes in Contemporary Capitalism*, London, Verso.

Pugliese E., 1983a, *I braccianti agricoli in Italia*, Milan, Angeli.

Pugliese E., 1983b, 'Aspetti dell'economia informale a Napoli', *Inchiesta*, 13 (59–60) (January-June), 89–97.

Pugliese, E., 1985, 'Stratificazione sociale e part-time', *La Questione Agraria*, 18, 27–45.

Pugliese E., 1987, 'The three forms of unemployment', *Social Research*, 54, no. 2, (Summer), 303–17.

Pugliese E., 1989, 'Strutture e comportamenti dell'offerta di lavoro nel Mezzogiorno', in *Disoccupazione e mercato del lavoro nel Mezzogiorno*, Atti IV Convegno Nazionale di Economia del Lavoro, Bari, Associazione Italiana. Economisti del Lavoro (AIEL), 605–28.

Purcell K., Wood S., Waton A. and Allen S. (eds), 1986, *The Changing Experience of Employment*, London, Macmillan.

Ragone G. (ed.), 1983, *Economia in trasformazione e doppio lavoro, il doppio lavoro nell'area casertana*, Bologna, Il Mulino.

Randazzo R., 1986, 'Strategie familiari, ruolo e identità femminile in trasformazione nell'Italia meridionale', *Atti del convegno: strategie familiari, stili di vita e attività informali*, Università di Messina, 30–31 May.

Razeto L, 1984, *Economia de solidaridad y mercado democratico*, vol. I, Santiago, Academia de Cristianismo Humano.

Razeto L, 1985, *Las empresas alternativas*, Santiago, Academia de Cristianismo Humano.

Razeto L. et al., 1983, *Las organizaciones economicas populares*, Santiago, Academia de Cristianismo Humano.

Redclift N. and Mingione E. (eds), 1985, *Beyond Employment*, Oxford and New York, Basil Blackwell.

Rein M., Esping-Andersen G. and Rainwater L. (eds), 1987, *Stagnation and Renewal in Social Policy*, Armonk, NY, and London, M. E. Sharpe.

Renooy P. H., 1984, *Twilight Economy: A Survey of the Informal Economy in the Netherlands*, Amsterdam, Faculty of Economic Sciences, University of Amsterdam.

Rev I., 1985, *The Advantages of Being Atomized*, duplicated paper, Princeton, Princeton University.

Reyneri E., 1979, *La catena migratoria*, Bologna, Il Mulino.

Reyneri E., (ed.), 1984, *Doppio lavoro e città meridionale, il doppio lavoro nell'area catanese*, Bologna, Il Mulino.

Ricketts E., 1987, 'Issues in the underclass debate', Duplicated paper, Washington D. C.

Rimlinger G. V., 1971, *Welfare Policy and Industrialization in Europe, America and Russia*, New York, Wiley.

Roberts B. Finnegan, R. and Gallie D. (eds), 1985, *New Approaches to Economic Life*, Manchester, Manchester University Press.

Robertson Elliot F., 1986, *The Family: Change or Continuity*, London, Macmillan.

Robertson J., 1985, *Future Work: Jobs, Self-employment, and Leisure after the Industrial Age*, Aldershot, Gower.

Rogerson C. M., 1985, 'The first decade of informal sector studies: review and synthesis', *Environmental Studies*, Occasional Paper, 25, Johannesburg, Witwatersrand University.

Rose D. (ed.), 1988, *Social Stratification and Economic Change*, London, Melbourne, Auckland and Johannesburg, Hutchinson.

Rose R., 1985, 'Getting by the Three Economies: the resources of the Official, Unofficial and Domestic Economies', in Lane, 1985, 103–41.

Rosenberg A., 1980, *Sociobiology and the Preemption of Social Science*, Oxford, Basil Blackwell.

Ross D. P. and Usher P. J., 1986, *From the Roots Up*, Toronto, James Lorimer.

Ross R. and Trachte K., 1983, 'Global cities and global classes: the peripheralization of labor in New York City', *Review*, 6, no. 3, 393–431.

Rossi Doria M., 1956, *Riforma agraria ed azione meridionalista*, Bologna, Il Mulino.

Rossi Doria M. (ed.), 1959, *Aspetti e problemi sociali dello sviluppo economico in Italia*, Bari, Laterza.

Rostow W., 1960, *The Stages of Economic Growth*, Cambridge, Cambridge University Press.

Roustang G., 1982, *Le Travail autrement. Travail et mode de vie*, Paris, Dunod.

Rubery J. (ed.), 1988, *Women and Recession*, London and New York, Routledge and Kegan Paul.

Ruggie M., 1984, *The State and Working Women*, Princeton, NJ, Princeton University Press.

Ruiz Perez S., 1979, 'Begging as an occupation in San Cristobal las Casas, Mexico', in Bromley and Gerry, 1979, 251–66.

Saba A., 1980, *L'industria sommersa*, Padua, Marsilio.

Sabel C. F., 1982, *Work and Politics*, Cambridge, Cambridge University Press.

Sachs J. D., 1989, *Developing Country Debt and the World Economy*, Chicago and London, The University of Chicago Press.

Safa H. (ed.), 1982, *Towards a Political Economy of Urbanization in Third World Countries*, Delhi, Oxford University Press.

Sahlins M., 1972, *Stone Age Economics*, Chicago, Aldine; repr. 1988, London and New York, Routledge.

Sahlins M., 1976, *The Use and Abuse of Biology: An Anthropological Critique of Sociobiology*, Ann Arbor, The University of Michigan Press.

Salaman G., 1986, *Working*, London, Tavistock.

Sampson S. G., 1987, 'The second economy of the Soviet Union and Eastern Europe', in Ferman et al., 1987, 120–36.

Saraceno C. (ed.), 1980, *Il lavoro mal diviso*, Bari, De Donato.

Saraceno C., 1986, *Età e corso della vita*, Bologna, Il Mulino.

Saraceno C., 1988, *Sociologia della famiglia*, Bologna, Il Mulino.

Saraceno P., 1959, *Iniziativa privata e azione pubblica nei piani di sviluppo economico*, Milan, Edizioni di Comunità.

Saraceno P., 1974, *Il meridionalismo dopo la ricostruzione*, Milan, Edizioni di Comunità.

Sarin M., 1982, *Urban Planning in the Third World*, London, Mansell.

Sassen S., 1988, *The Mobility of Labor and Capital*, Cambridge, Cambridge University Press.

Sassen S., forthcoming, *The Global City*, Princeton, NJ, Princeton University Press.

Sassen-Koob S., 1983, 'Capital mobility and labour migration: their expression in core cities', in Timberlake, F. (ed.), *Urbanization in the World Economy*, New York, Academic Press.

Sassen-Koob S., 1984, 'The new labour demand in global cities' in Smith M. P. (ed.), *Cities in Transformation*, London, SAGE Publications, 139–71.

Sauvy A., 1984, *Le Travail noir et l'économie de demain*, Paris, Calmann-Lévy.

Sayer A., 1989, 'Postfordism in question', *International Journal of Urban and Regional Research*, 13, no. 4, 666–95.

Scase R. (ed.), 1989, *Industrial Societies: Crisis and Division in Western Capitalism and State Socialism*, London, Unwin Hyman.

Schneider D. M., 1968/1980, *American Kinship*, Chicago, The University of Chicago Press.

Schneider D. M., 1984, *A Critique of the Study of Kinship*, Ann Arbor, The University of Michigan Press.

Schumacher F., 1973, *Small is Beautiful*, New York, Harper and Row.

Schwartz Cowan R., 1983, *More Work for Mother*, New York, Basic Books.

Scott A. J. and Storper M. (eds), 1986, *Production, Work, Territory: The Geographical Anatomy of Industrial Capitalism*, Boston, London and Sydney, Allen and Unwin.

Scott J., 1988, *Metropolis: From the Division of Labor to Urban Form*, Berkeley, Los Angeles and London, University of California Press.

Sen A. L., 1981, *Poverty and Famines: An Essay on Entitlement and Deprivation*, Oxford, Clarendon Press.

Serpieri R. and Spanò A., 1986, 'Scelte informali nell'agire di consumo', *Inchiesta*, 1986, no. 74, 32–51.

Shanin T., 1972, *The Awkward Class: Political Sociology of Peasantry in a Developing Society: Russia, 1910–1925*, Oxford, Clarendon Press.

Shanin T., 1986, *Russia 1905–07: Revolution as a Moment of Truth*, London, Macmillan.

Shanin T. (ed.), 1987, *Peasants and Peasant Societies*, Oxford, Basil Blackwell.

Shlapentokh V., 1989, *Public and Private Life of the Soviet People*, New York, Oxford University Press.

Shorter E., 1976, *The Making of the Modern Family*, Glasgow, Fontana.

Sik E., 1988, 'Reciprocal exchange of labour in Hungary', in Pahl, 1988a, ch. 24.

Simon C. P. and Witte A. D., 1982, *Beating the System: The Underground Economy*, Boston, MA, Auburn House.

Slater D. (ed.), 1985, *New Social Movements and the State in Latin America*, Amsterdam, Centre for Economic Development of Latin America.

Smith J., 1984, 'Nonwage labor and subsistance' in Smith J. et al., 1984, 64–89.

Smith J., Wallerstein I. and Evers H. D. (eds), 1984, *Households and the World-Economy*, London and Beverly Hills, SAGE Publications.

Smith M. P. (ed.), 1988, *Power, Community and the City*, New Brunswick, NJ, and Oxford, Transaction Books.

Smith M. P. (ed.), 1989, *Pacific Rim Cities in the World Economy*, New Brunswick, NJ, and Oxford, Transaction Books.

Smith S., 1986, *Britain's Shadow Economy*, Oxford, Clarendon Press.

Smithies E., 1984, *The Black Economy in England since 1914*, Dublin, Gill and Macmillan, Humanities Press.

Social Research, 1987, special issue on Unemployment, ed. A. Keisser, 54, no. 2, Summer.

Soja E. W., 1989, *Postmodern Geographies: The Reassertion of Space in Critical Social Theory*, London and New York, Verso.

Sreeramamurty K., 1986, *Urban Labour in the Informal Sector*, Delhi, B. R. Publishing Corporation.

Stack C. B., 1974, *All Our Kin: Strategies for Survival in a Black Community*, New York, Harper and Row.

Stanback, T. M. Jr., Bearse P. J., Noyelle T. J. and Karasek R. A., 1983, *Services: The New Economy*, Totowa, NJ, Rowman and Littlefield.

Stavenhagan R. (ed.), 1970, *Agrarian Problems and Peasant Movements in Latin America*, New York, Doubleday.

Steinmetz G. and Wright E. O., 1989, 'The fall and rise of the petty bourgeoisie: changing patterns of self-employment in the postwar United States', *American Journal of Sociology*, 94, no. 5, 973–1018.

Stevens R., 1966, *Medical Practice in Modern England: The Impact of Specialization and State Medicine*, New Haven, Yale University Press.

Stevens R., 1971, *American Medicine and Public Interest*, New Haven, Yale University Press.

Stone D. A., 1984, *The Disabled State*, Philadelphia, Temple University Press.

Stone D. A., 1989, 'At risk in the Welfare State', *Social Research*, 56, no. 3 (Autumn), 591–633.

Storper M. and Walker R. A., 1988, *The Capitalist Imperative: Territory, Technology and Industrial Growth*, Oxford, Basil Blackwell.

Sweezy P., and Bettelheim C., 1971, *On the Transition to Socialism*, New York and London, Monthly Review Press.

Sylos-Labini P., 1964, 'Precarious employment in Sicily', *International Labour Review* (March), 268–85.

Sylos-Labini P., 1976, *Saggio sulle classi sociali*, Bari, Laterza.

Szelenyi I., 1978, 'Social inequalities in state socialist redistributive economies', *International Journal of Comparative Sociology*, 1–2, 63–87.

Szelenyi I., 1981, 'Structural changes and alternatives to capitalist development in the contemporary urban and regional system', *International Journal of Urban and Regional Research*, 5, no. 1, 1–14.

Szelenyi I., 1983, *Urban Inequalities under State Socialism*, Oxford, Oxford University Press.

Szelenyi I., 1988, *Socialist Entrepreneurs: Embourgeoisement in Rural Hungary*, Cambridge, Polity Press.

Szita E., 1987, 'New types of entrepreneurial and organizational forms in the Hungarian economy', in Alessandrini and Dallago, 1987, 181–96.

Tanzi V., 1982, *The Underground Economy in the United States and Abroad*, Lexington, Lexington Books.

Tarling R. (ed.), 1987, *Flexibility in Labour Markets*, London, Academic Press.

Therborn G., 1986, *Why Some Peoples are More Unemployed than Others*, London, Verso.

Tievant S., 1982, 'Vivre autrement: échanges et sociabilité en ville nouvelle', *Cahiers de l'Observation du Changement Social*, 6, 61–121.

Tilly C. (ed.), 1975, *The Formation of the Nation-State in Western Europe*, Princeton, NJ, Princeton University Press.

Tilly C., 1984, *Big Structures, Large Processes, Huge Comparisons*, New York, Russel Sage.

Tilly L. A. and Scott J. W., 1987, *Women, Work, and Family*, New York and London, Methuen.

Titmuss R. M., 1966, *Essays on the 'Welfare States'*, London, Allen and Unwin.

Tomasello S., 1986, 'Devianza giovanile: strategie e tipologie familiari a Messina',

Atti del Convegno: strategie familiari, stili di vita e attività informali, Università di Messina, 30–31 May.

Tönnies F., 1887, *Gemeinschaft und Gesellschaft*, Leipzig, O. R. Reislad.

Touraine A., 1971, *The Post-Industrial Society*, New York, Random House.

Trigilia C., 1978, 'Sviluppo, sottosviluppo e classi sociali in Italia', in Paci, 1978, 305–50.

Trigilia C., 1986, *Grandi partiti e piccole imprese*, Bologna, Il Mulino.

Urry J., 1986, 'Capitalist production, scientific management and the service class', in Scott and Storper, 1986, 43–66.

Valladares L., 1986, 'Growing up in the favela', paper presented at XIth World Congress of Sociology, New Delhi, India.

Vanek J., 1974, 'Time spent in housework', *Scientific American*, 231, 116–20.

Villa P., 1986, *The Structuring of Labour Markets*, Oxford, Clarendon Press.

Villari R. (ed.), 1966, *Il Sud nella storia d'Italia*, Bari, Laterza.

Van Wolferen K., 1989, *The Enigma of Japanese Power*, London, Macmillan.

Walby S., 1986, *Patriarchy at Work*, Cambridge, Polity Press.

Waldinger R. D., 1986, *Through the Eye of the Needle: Immigrant and Enterprise in New York's Garment Trades*, New York and London, New York University Press.

Walker R., 1985, 'Is there a service economy? The changing capitalistic division of labor', *Science and Society*, 49, 42–83.

Wallace C. and Pahl R. E., 1986, 'Polarisation, unemployment and all forms of work', in Allen S., Waton A., Purcell K. and Wood S. (eds), *The Experience of Unemployment*, London, Macmillan.

Wallerstein I., 1979, *The Capitalist World-Economy*, Cambridge, Cambridge University Press.

Wallerstein I., 1983, *Historical Capitalism*, London, Verso.

Wallerstein I., 1984, Household structures and labor-force formation in the capitalist world-economy', in Smith et al., 1984, 17–22.

Wallman S., 1984, *Eight London Households*, London and New York, Tavistock.

Weber M., 1947, *The Theory of Social and Economic Organization*, New York, The Free Press.

Weiss L., 1987, 'Explaining the underground economy: state and social structure', *British Journal of Sociology*, 38, no. 2, 216–34.

Weiss L., 1988, *Creating Capitalism: The State and Small Business since 1945*, Oxford, Basil Blackwell.

Wellman B. and Berkowitz S. D., 1988, *Social Structures: A Network Approach*, Cambridge, Cambridge University Press.

West J. (ed.), 1982, *Work, Women and the Labour Market*, London, Boston and Henley, Routledge and Kegan Paul.

Wilenski H. L., 1975, *The Welfare State and Equality: Structural and Ideological Roots of Public Expenditures*, Berkeley, University of Calfornia Press.

Wiles P., 1987, 'The second economy, definitional problems', in Alessandrini and Dallago, 1987, 21–33.

Wilkinson F. (ed.), 1981, *The Dynamics of Labour Market Segmentation*, London, Academic Press.

Wilson E. O., 1975, *Sociobiology: The New Synthesis*, Cambridge, MA, Belknap Press of Harvard University Press.

Wilson E. O., 1978, *On Human Nature*, Cambridge, MA, and London, Harvard University Press.

Wilson W. J., 1987, *The Truly Disadvantaged: The Inner City, the Underclass, and Public Policy*, Chicago, University of Chicago Press.

Wolf E. R., 1969, *Peasant Wars of the Twentieth Century*, New York, Harper and Row.

Wood S. (ed.), 1982, *The Degradation of Work? Skill, Deskilling and the Labour Process*, London, Hutchinson.

Wright E. O., 1978, *Class, Crisis and the State*, London, New Left Books.

Wright E. O., 1985, *Classes*, London, Verso.

Wrong D., 1961, 'The oversocialized conception of man in modern sociology', *American Sociological Review*, 26, no. 2, 183–93.

Zamosc L., 1986, *The Agrarian Question and the Peasant Movement in Colombia: Struggles of the National Peasant Association*, Cambridge, Cambridge University Press.

Zaslavskaja T. 1984, 'The Novosibirsk Report', *Survey: A Journal of East and West Studies*, 28, no. 1, 83–108.

Zaslavskaja T., 1990, *The Second Socialist Revolution*, London, Taunus.

Index